Tiomchai Lertratanakul

W9-CVZ-208

Automotive Principles

VOLUME I
Theory and Fundamentals

Don Knowles

PRENTICE HALL
Englewood Cliffs, New Jersey 07632

Library of Congress Cataloging-in-Publication Data

Knowles, Don.
   Automotive principles.

   Includes index.
   Contents: v. 1. Theory and fundamentals.
   1. Automobiles. 2. Automobiles—Maintenance and
repair. I. Title.
TL146.K619   1988   629.2   87-14469
ISBN 0-13-054545-7 (v. 1)

Editorial/production supervision: Evalyn Schoppet
Cover design: Karen Stephens
Manufacturing buyer: Rhett Conklin
Page layout: Richard Dombrowski and Gail Collins

© 1988 by Prentice Hall
A Division of Simon & Schuster
Englewood Cliffs, New Jersey 07632

All rights reserved. No part of this book may be
reproduced in any form or by any means, without
permission in writing from the publisher.

Cover photograph courtesy of
Cincinnati Milacron, Industrial Robot Division.

Printed in the United States of America

10   9   8   7   6   5   4   3   2   1

ISBN 0-13-054545-7   025

Prentice-Hall International (UK) Limited, *London*
Prentice-Hall of Australia Pty. Limited, *Sydney*
Prentice-Hall Canada Inc., *Toronto*
Prentice-Hall Hispanoamericana, S.A., *Mexico*
Prentice-Hall of India Private Limited, *New Delhi*
Prentice-Hall of Japan, Inc., *Tokyo*
Simon & Schuster Asia Pte. Ltd., *Singapore*
Editora Prentice-Hall do Brasil, Ltda., *Rio de Janeiro*

Contents

6

Exhaust Systems, Turbochargers, and Intake Systems   80

7

Computer-Controlled Diesel Injection and Emission Systems   97

8

Fuel Economy and Emission Control   109

9

Electricity and Electronics   132

10

Lead-Acid Batteries   155

11

Charging Systems   164

25
Brake Systems   485

26
Heating and Air Conditioning Systems   509

Preface

More new technology has been introduced in the automotive industry during the 1980s than in any other decade in automotive history. Domestic car manufacturers have made a vast change from building large cars with high fuel consumption to smaller, lighter, more fuel-efficient vehicles. The introduction of corporate average fuel economy (CAFE) standards in the United States and increased competition from import car manufacturers were two of the main factors creating this change in domestic car manufacturing.

Another extensive change by the automotive industry in the 1980s has been the manufacture of front-wheel-drive cars in place of rear-wheel-drive vehicles. This has introduced much new technology in the areas of engine design, transaxles, drive axles, suspension systems, and steering components.

The greatest technological change in the current decade has been in the area of electronics. Sophisticated on-board computer systems now control such functions as air-fuel ratio, spark advance, emission equipment, turbocharger boost pressure, air conditioning, cruise control, instrumentation, lighting, and transaxle shifting. Many cars have several computers interconnected by data links.

This book was written as a comprehensive text to explain much of this new technology. Basic principles are clearly explained so that the new technology is easily understood. Some of the new technology explained in the book includes:

1. Engine design and service.
2. Turbochargers.
3. Electronic diesel injection and emission control.
4. Exhaust emission standards and systems.
5. Methods of meeting CAFE standards.

6. Automatic and manual transaxles.
7. Front-wheel-drive suspension systems.
8. Brake systems for front-wheel-drive cars.
9. Air conditioning systems, including lightweight computer-controlled compressors.

The new electronics technology covered in the book includes:

1. Computer basics.
2. Computer-controlled carburetor systems.
3. Electronic fuel injection (EFI) systems.
4. Electronic and computer-controlled ignition systems.
5. Computer-controlled cruise controls.
6. Electronic instrumentation and voice-alert systems.
7. Anti-lock brake systems.
8. Computer-controlled air conditioning.
9. Computer-controlled four-wheel-drive shifting.
10. Computer systems with several computers and data links.

The text includes information on front-wheel-drive and rear-wheel-drive vehicles. This text is designed to be used with Automotive Principles, Repair and Service, Volume II, which provides comprehensive service information. These two books combined meet Automotive Service Excellence (ASE) requirements in all eight areas.

I would like to thank all the companies who granted us permission to use their diagrams in the book. Special thanks to the Prentice Hall publishing staff for another excellent production.

1

Engine Principles and Ratings

Chapter Completion Objectives

1. Check the valve timing on a four-cycle engine.
2. Calculate the engine displacement.
3. Calculate engine brake horsepower (BHP).
4. Calculate engine indicated horsepower (IHP).
5. Understand methods of increasing volumetric efficiency.
6. Calculate engine torque.

Engine Fundamentals

Four-Stroke Cycle Principle

When the piston is at bottom dead center (BDC), it is at its lowest point of travel in the cylinder. The highest point of piston travel in the cylinder is referred to as top dead center (TDC). A piston stroke occurs when the piston moves from TDC to BDC, or from BDC to TDC, as shown in Figure 1-1.

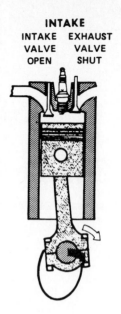

Figure 1-2.   Intake Stroke. (*Courtesy of Sun Electric Corporation*)

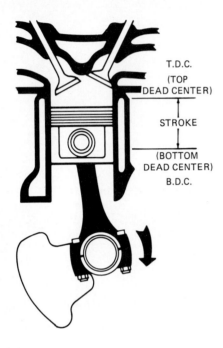

Figure 1-1.   Piston Stroke. (*Courtesy of Sun Electric Corporation*)

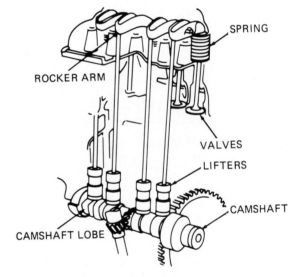

Figure 1-3.   Camshaft and Valve Operation. (*Courtesy of Sun Electric Corporation*)

The intake stroke is the first stroke in the four-stroke cycle. During this stroke the piston is moving downward and the intake valve is open, as indicated in Figure 1-2.

When the piston moves down in the intake stroke, a vacuum, or low pressure, is created in the cylinder. Atmospheric pressure is present outside the air cleaner on top of the carburetor. The pressure difference between atmospheric pressure and vacuum in the cylinder causes the air-fuel mixture to move through the carburetor and intake manifold into the cylinder. The valves are opened by the lobes on the camshaft. When the camshaft is mounted in the engine block, the lobes push the valve lifters and pushrods upward, which causes the rocker arms to open the valves as illustrated in Figure 1-3.

In some engines the camshaft is located in the cylinder head and the lobes are in direct contact with the rocker arms. This type of engine is referred to as an overhead-cam engine, as shown in Figure 1-4.

When the piston moves past BDC on the intake stroke, the camshaft lobe rotates so the intake valve will be closed by the valve spring.

During the compression stroke the piston is moving upward with the intake and exhaust valves closed, and the air-fuel mixture is being compressed in the cylinder, as shown in Figure 1-5.

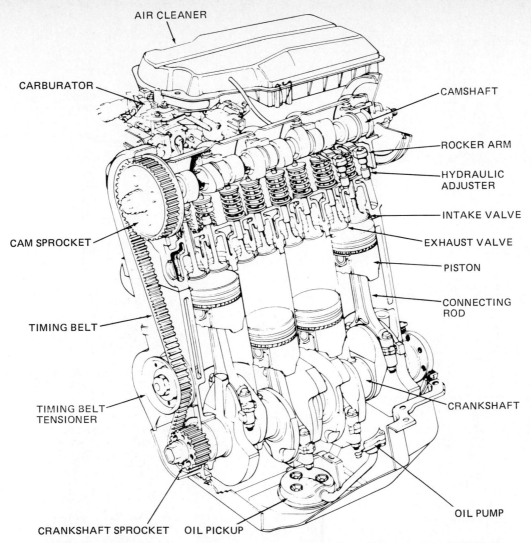

AIR CLEANER

CARBURATOR

CAMSHAFT

ROCKER ARM

HYDRAULIC
ADJUSTER

CAM SPROCKET

INTAKE VALVE

EXHAUST VALVE

PISTON

CONNECTING
ROD

TIMING BELT

TIMING BELT
TENSIONER

CRANKSHAFT

CRANKSHAFT SPROCKET   OIL PICKUP

OIL PUMP

Figure 1-4. Overhead-Cam Engine. (Reference taken from SAE paper No. 810007. *Reprinted with permission of Society of Automotive Engineers,* © 1981)

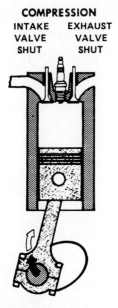

COMPRESSION

INTAKE   EXHAUST
VALVE   VALVE
SHUT   SHUT

Figure 1-5. Compression Stroke. (*Courtesy of Sun Electric Corporation*)

The sealing capabilities of the piston rings and valves are extremely important so that the air-fuel mixture will be highly compressed, as illustrated in Figure 1-6.

When the piston approaches the TDC of the compression stroke, the ignition system causes a spark to occur at the spark plug electrodes, which ignites the air-fuel mixture. The burning air-fuel mixture creates a very strong expanding force in the cylinder that drives the piston downward in the power stroke. The downward thrust on the piston and connecting rod causes the crankshaft to rotate, and this circular action is transmitted through the drive train of vehicle to the drive wheels to drive the vehicle.

During the power stroke the sealing qualities of the piston rings and valves are very important to prevent the loss of air-fuel mixture from the cylinder, which would result in a reduced thrust on the piston. The intake and exhaust valves remain closed during the power stroke, as shown in Figure 1-7.

3

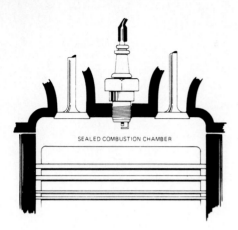

Figure 1-6.   Sealed Combustion Chamber.

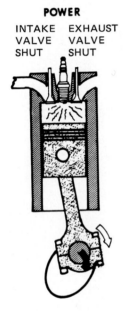

Figure 1-7.   Power Stroke. (*Courtesy of Sun Electric Corporation*).

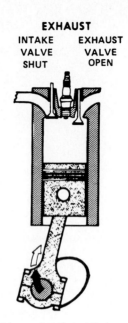

Figure 1-8.   Exhaust Stroke. (*Courtesy of Sun Electric Corporation*)

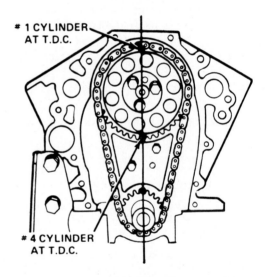

Figure 1-9.   Timing Gear and Chain Installation. (*Courtesy of Chevrolet Motor Division, General Motors Corporation*)

When the piston is near bottom dead center on the power stroke, the exhaust valve is opened by the camshaft lobe. The piston moves upward on the exhaust stroke and the exhaust gases are forced out through the open exhaust valve and the exhaust system. The camshaft lobe opens the intake valve when the piston is a few degrees before top dead center (BTDC) on the exhaust stroke, and the exhaust valve is closed when the piston is a few degrees after top dead center (ATDC) of the exhaust stroke. The exhaust stroke is shown in Figure 1-8.

Valve Timing

In many engines the timing gear on the camshaft is driven by a chain from the crankshaft gear. When the camshaft gear and chain are installed, the timing marks on the gears must be positioned as illustrated in Figure 1-9.

If the camshaft gear is correctly installed, the valves will open and close at the right time in relation to crankshaft rotation. A complete valve timing chart for the four-stroke cycle is shown in Figure 1-10.

The term valve overlap refers to the brief period of crankshaft rotation when the piston is at TDC of the exhaust stroke and both valves are open. Two

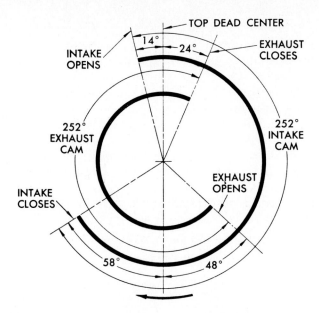

Figure 1-10. Valve Timing Chart. (*Courtesy of Pontiac Motor Division, General Motors Corporation*)

revolutions of the crankshaft are necessary to complete the four-stroke cycle. The camshaft completes one revolution and opens each valve once in the four-stroke cycle. Therefore, the crankshaft turns twice as fast as the camshaft in a four-cycle engine.

As illustrated in Figure 1-10, the intake valve opens at 14° before top dead center (BTDC) and closes 58° after bottom dead center (ABDC). When the intake valve is left open ABDC, additional air-fuel mixture will still rush into the cylinder because of intake manifold velocity. The exhaust valve opens at 48° before bottom dead center (BBDC) on the power stroke. Cylinder pressure near the end of the power stroke helps to force exhaust gases from the cylinder. The exhaust valve closes at 24° ATDC on the exhaust stroke. When both valves are open for a brief period of crankshaft rotation near TDC on the exhaust stroke, the incoming air-fuel mixture helps to purge any exhaust gases from the cylinder.

Multi-cylinder Engines

If the cylinders are arranged on a straight line, the engine is referred to as an in-line engine. These engines usually have four or six cylinders. The crankshaft must rotate for two revolutions, or 720 degrees, to complete the four-stroke cycle for each piston. On an in-line four-cylinder engine, there must be a power stroke every 180 degrees of crankshaft rotation, because there are four power strokes in 720 degrees of crankshaft rotation. The crankshaft from an in-line four-cylinder engine will have

the crankpins spaced 180 degrees apart, as shown in Figure 1-11.

The order in which the power strokes are delivered in an engine is referred to as the firing order. A common firing order for an in-line four-cylinder engine is 1, 3, 4, 2.

An in-line six-cylinder engine delivers six power strokes in 720 degrees of crankshaft rotation. Therefore, a power stroke must occur every 120 degrees of crankshaft rotation and the crankpins are spaced 120 degrees apart, as indicated in Figure 1-12.

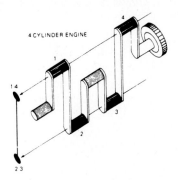

Figure 1-11. Four-Cylinder Crankshaft.

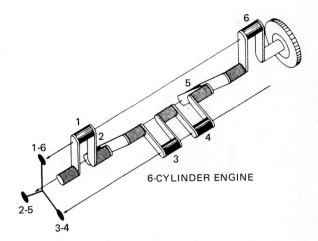

Figure 1-12. In-line Six-Cylinder Crankshaft.

The most common firing order for an in-line six-cylinder engine is 1, 5, 3, 6, 2, 4. In an in-line engine, number one cylinder is located at the front of the engine and the other cylinders are numbered in numerical order from the front to the rear of the engine.

The cylinders in V-type engines are arranged in two equal banks that are inclined from each other at an angle of 60 degrees or 90 degrees. Most V-type engines have six or eight cylinders. An eight-cylinder V-type (V8) engine block is shown in Figure 1-13.

Some V8 engines have cylinders 1, 2, 3, and 4 in the right bank and cylinders 5, 6, 7, and 8 in the left

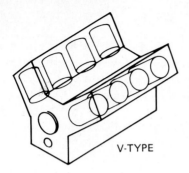

Figure 1-13. V8 Engine Block. (*Courtesy of Sun Electric Corporation*)

bank. In other V8 engines, cylinders 1, 3, 5, 7 are in the left bank and cylinders 2, 4, 6, and 8 are in the right bank, as illustrated in Figure 1-14.

A V8 engine delivers eight power strokes in 720 degrees of crankshaft rotation. Therefore, the crankpins are spaced 90 degrees apart, as shown in Figure 1-15, and the power strokes are delivered at 90-degree intervals.

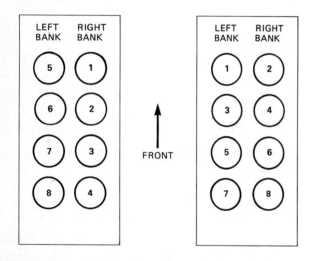

Figure 1-14. Cylinder Location in V8 Engines. (*Courtesy of Sun Electric Corporation*)

Figure 1-15. Crankshaft from a V8 Engine.

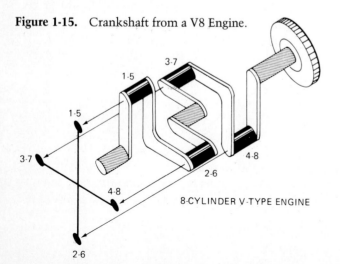

In a V8 engine, two connecting rods are mounted on each crankpin. A common firing order for a V8 engine is 1, 8, 4, 3, 6, 5, 7, 2. In a V-type engine, if the angle between the cylinder banks is equal to the angle between the crankpins, the power strokes occur at even intervals.

Six-cylinder V-type (V6) engines have the crankpins spaced at 120-degree intervals, and many V6 engines have a 90-degree angle between the cylinder banks. In this type of engine the crankpins are offset 30 degrees where each pair of connecting rods is mounted, as illustrated in Figure 1-16. The offset crankpins cause the power strokes to occur at even intervals of 120 degrees, as shown in Figure 1-17.

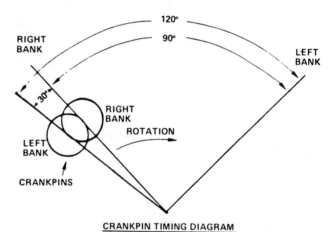

Figure 1-16. Crankshaft with Offset Crankpins for a V6 Engine. (*Courtesy of Buick Motor Division, General Motors Corporation*)

Figure 1-17. Power Stroke Intervals in a V6 Engine. (*Courtesy of Buick Motor Division, General Motors Corporation*)

On some V6 engines used in rear-wheel-drive cars, number 1 cylinder is located at the left front of the engine and the other cylinders are numbered as pictured in Figure 1-18. Other V6 engines in rear-wheel-drive cars have the cylinders numbered as illustrated in Figure 1-19.

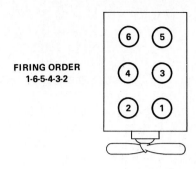

Figure 1-18.   Cylinder Numbering for General Motors 231 CID (3.8L) V6 Engine. (*Courtesy of Sun Electric Corporation*)

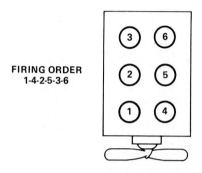

Figure 1-19.   Cylinder Numbering for Ford 231 CID (3.8L) V6 Engine. (*Courtesy of Sun Electric Corporation*)

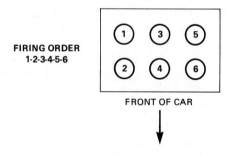

Figure 1-20.   Cylinder Numbering for General Motors 173 CID (2.8L) Transversely Mounted V6 Engine. (*Courtesy of Sun Electric Corporation*)

In most front-wheel-drive cars the engine is mounted transversely. A General Motors 173 CID (2.8L) transversely mounted V6 engine has the cylinders numbered as shown in Figure 1-20.

Diagnosis of Valve Timing

The camshaft gear and chain may become so badly worn that the chain jumps some of the teeth on the camshaft gear, which results in the valves opening at the wrong time in relation to crankshaft rotation.

The automotive technician can use the following procedure to check the valve timing.

1. Remove the spark plug from number 1 cylinder.
2. While the engine is being cranked, place a finger in number 1 spark plug hole.
3. When compression is felt at number 1 spark plug hole, stop cranking the engine.
4. Rotate the crankshaft until the timing mark on the crankshaft pulley is lined up with the zero position on the timing indicator. Number 1 piston will be at TDC on the compression stroke.
5. Rotate the crankshaft one revolution until the timing mark is lined up with the zero position on the timing indicator. Number 1 piston will be at TDC on the exhaust stroke.
6. Remove the rocker arm cover and observe the valve action. The exhaust valve should be closing and the intake valve should be opening in the overlap position. The crankshaft may be turned back and forth a few degrees to check the valve position. If the valves are not in the overlap position, the valve timing is incorrect and the timing chain and gears should be replaced.

Two-Stroke Cycle

Basic Principles

The two-stroke cycle is used in some one-cylinder gasoline engines such as lawn mower engines, and in some heavy-duty diesel engines. Since the two-stroke cycle is not widely used in the automotive industry, we will simply compare it briefly to the four-stroke cycle. The two-stroke cycle, heavy-duty diesel engine has an intake port just above BDC in the cylinder, and two exhaust valves in the cylinder head. A blower, or supercharger, is used to force air into the cylinder when the piston is near BDC, as shown in Figure 1-21.

When the piston is at BDC, the exhaust valves are open and the incoming air forces exhaust gases from the cylinder. Upward piston movement covers the intake ports and the piston continues its upward travel on the compression stroke. The exhaust valves close when the piston covers the intake ports, as indicated on the compression stroke shown in Figure 1-22.

When the piston is near TDC on the compression stroke, the injector injects diesel fuel into the cylinder. Since the diesel engine has a very high compression ratio, the air temperature in the cylinder is hot enough to ignite the fuel. The expansion

---

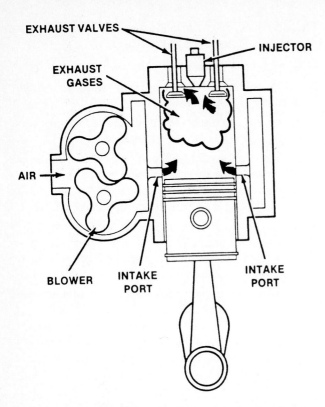

Figure 1-21. Two-Stroke Cycle with Piston at BDC. (*Courtesy of Ford Motor Co.*)

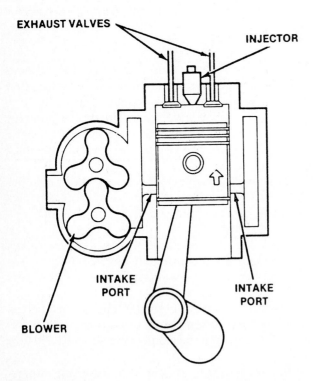

Figure 1-22. Two-Stroke Cycle Compression Stroke. (*Courtesy of Ford Motor Co.*)

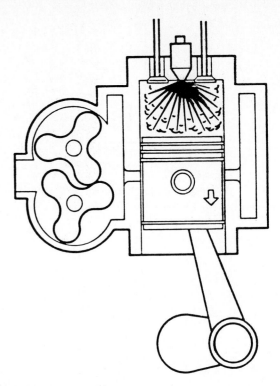

Figure 1-23. Two-Stroke Cycle Power Stroke. (*Courtesy of Ford Motor Co.*)

force created by the combustion of the air-fuel mixture drives the piston down on the power stroke, as shown in Figure 1-23.

In the two-stroke cycle, each upward piston stroke is a compression stroke and each downward stroke is a power stroke. The two-stroke cycle is completed in one crankshaft revolution, whereas two crankshaft revolutions are required to complete the four-stroke cycle. A two-stroke cycle engine usually has a higher horsepower rating than a four-stroke cycle engine of the same size, because each downward piston stroke is a power stroke in the two-stroke cycle.

In small, two-cycle gasoline engines, the exhaust valves are eliminated and exhaust ports are located near BDC in the cylinder. In this type of engine the air-fuel mixture is moved into the crankcase when the piston is on the compression stroke. The air-fuel mixture moves from the crankcase through the intake port into the cyclinder when the piston is near the bottom of the power stroke. In this type of two-cycle engine, the lubricating oil is mixed with the fuel, so an oil supply is not required in the crankcase.

A small two-cycle engine with an exhaust port is illustrated in Figure 1-24.

(Refer to Chapter 7 for diesel engine principles.)

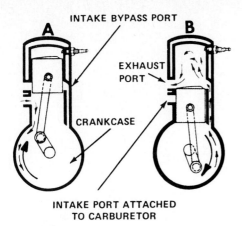

INTAKE BYPASS PORT

EXHAUST PORT

CRANKCASE

INTAKE PORT ATTACHED TO CARBURETOR

Figure 1-24. Small Two-Cycle Engine with Exhaust Port. (*Courtesy of Sun Electric Corporation*)

Engine Measurements

Cylinder Bore

The diameter of the cylinder is referred to as cylinder bore, which is measured in inches or millimeters. When the cylinder bore is increased, the engine displacement is also increased.

Piston Stroke

A piston stroke takes place when the piston moves from bottom dead center (BDC) to top dead center (TDC) in the cylinder (see Figure 2-1). Engine displacement may be increased by designing the crankshaft to provide a longer stroke. The crankthrow is the distance from the center line of the crankshaft to the center of the connecting rod journals. A piston stroke is twice as long as the crankthrow.

Displacement

The total amount of air displaced by all the pistons when they move from TDC to BDC is referred to as engine displacement. Displacement may be calculated by finding the piston displacement volume in one cylinder and then multiplying this displacement volume by the number of cylinders. A General Motors 151 cubic inch displacement (CID) four-cylinder engine has a 4.0 in. bore and a 3.0 in. stroke.

Piston displacement volume = $\Pi R^2 \times$ stroke.

radius (R) = $\frac{1}{2}$ diameter

$R^2 = R \times R$

The displacement in one cylinder of the 151 CID engine is:

$22/7 \times 2 \times 2 \times 3 = 37.7$ CID cubic inches.

Hence, the total displacement of the 151 CID engine is:

$37.7 \times 4 = 150.8$ cubic inches.

In the metric system, 151 CID is equal to 2.5 liters (L), so

4.0 in. = 101.6 mm, and 3.0 in. = 76.2 mm.

Piston displacment volume = $R^2 \times$ stroke.

The displacement in one cylinder of the 2.5L engine is:

$22/7 \times 50.8 \times 50.8 \times 76.2$.

Since 10 mm = 1 cm, therefore,

50.8 mm = 5.08 cm

76.2 mm = 7.62 cm

$22/7 \times 50.8 \times 50.8 \times 76.2$

$= 22/7 \times 5.08 \times 5.08 \times 7.62$

$= 618$ cm^3 = .618 liters (L).

Therefore, the total displacement of the 2.5L engine is:

$.618 \times 4 = 2.472$ L.

Engine displacement may be increased by increasing the cylinder bore, lengthening the piston stroke, or increasing the number of cylinders. When engine displacement is increased, engine power is usually increased because more total volume of air-fuel mixture can be taken into the cylinders.

Compression Ratio

The compression ratio of an engine is a comparison between the total volume of the cylinder when the piston is at BDC and the combustion chamber volume when the piston is at TDC. Compression ratio is calculated by dividing the combustion chamber volume into the total cylinder volume. If the total cylinder volume is 42 cu in. and the combustion chamber volume is 4.941, the compression ratio would be:

$42 \div 4.941 = 8.5 : 1.$

In the metric system, 1 cu in. equals 16.387 cubic centimeters (cm^3), so:

42 cu in. = 688.254 cm^3

4.941 cu in. = 80.968 cm^3

Therefore, the compression ratio is:

$688.254 \div 80.968 = 8.5 : 1.$

A General Motors 151 CID (2.5L) four-cylinder engine has a compression ratio of 8.2:1. This engine has a specified compression pressure of 140 psi (965 kPa). The compression ratio may be increased by reducing the combustion chamber volume and maintaining the same cylinder volume. When the combustion chamber volume is left unchanged and the cylinder volume is increased by a change in bore or stroke, the compression ratio is increased. A reduction in compression ratio occurs if the combustion chamber volume is increased and the cylinder volume remains the same. The compression ratio may be reduced by decreasing the cylinder volume with a change in bore or stroke, while maintaining the same combustion chamber volume.

When the compression ratio is increased, higher pressure is created in the cylinder on the compression and power strokes. This increases engine power. However, high compression ratios and cylinder pressures also create higher cylinder temperatures, which cause detonation during the combustion process. Detonation results in a loss of power and possible engine damage. (Refer to Chapter 16 for a complete explanation of detonation.)

Some pre-catalytic-converter vehicles had an engine compression ratio of 10.5:1. Leaded premium gasoline with an octane rating of 98 was available to prevent detonation in these engines. Since catalytic converters will not operate on leaded gasoline, lower octane unleaded fuel must be used in vehicles equipped with catalytic converters; therefore, the compression ratios had to be lowered in these vehicles.

Unleaded gasoline will have an octane rating of 87 to 89, whereas premium unleaded fuel has a 90 to 92 octane rating. Engine compression ratios used with these fuels vary from 8.2:1 to 9.5:1. (An explanation of octane ratings is provided in Chapter 16, and a description of catalytic converters is given in Chapter 6.)

Factors Affecting Engine Power

Atmospheric Pressure

Atmospheric pressure at sea level is 14.7 psi (101.3 kPa). At 10,000 ft (3,048 m) above sea level, the atmospheric pressure is 12.2 psi (84.1 kPa). This decrease in atmospheric pressure indicates that the density of the atmosphere decreases as the altitude increases above sea level. The atmospheric density and pressure increases as the humidity of the air increases.

Since atmospheric pressure and engine vacuum cause the air-fuel mixture to flow into the engine cylinders, engine power is affected by atmospheric pressure. Higher atmospheric pressure will increase the air flow into the engine, which causes an increase in power. Therefore, engine power increases slightly when the engine is operated at lower altitudes, and reduces when the engine is operated at high altitudes.

Friction

Friction may be defined as the resistance to motion when one object is moved over another object. For example, a certain amount of power is required to move a metal bar across the top of a metal bench. If the weight of the bar is increased, the power required to move the bar is also increased; thus, friction increases with load. Lubricating oil reduces friction in the engine. (A description of friction and engine oil purposes is included in Chapter 4.)

Engine friction reduces engine power. For example, a certain amount of engine power is required to overcome the friction of the piston rings on the cylinder walls. If engine friction can be reduced, increased engine power will result. Some engines are now equipped with roller-type valve lifters which reduce friction between the lifters and the camshaft. Synthetic lubricating oil reduces engine friction and provides a slight increase in power. (Lubricating oils are explained in Chapter 4.)

Inertia and Wind Resistance

An object in motion tends to stay in motion, and an object at rest tends to remain at rest. This principle is referred to as inertia. Kinetic inertia refers to the tendency of objects in motion to remain mobile, while static inertia describes the tendency of an object at rest to remain at rest. The static inertia of a parked car must be overcome by engine power in order to put the car in motion. As the vehicle weight is increased, more engine power is required to overcome the static inertia.

Each vehicle offers a specific amount of wind resistance, or aerodynamic drag (Cd). At 45 MPH (25 KPH), half of the engine power is used to overcome the aerodynamic drag of some vehicles. When Cd is increased or vehicle speed is increased, more engine power is required to overcome Cd.

An engine will have the same power regardless of the vehicle weight or Cd, but as the vehicle weight and Cd are reduced, more engine power is available to drive the car and less engine power is wasted in overcoming these forces. (Refer to Chapter 8 for methods of reducing vehicle weight and drag coefficient (Cd) to improve fuel economy and power.)

Engine Ratings and Related Factors

Force

Any push, pull, or twist that acts on an object may be defined as a force. A force always attempts to change an object's state of motion. Force is used in many automotive applications. The force of expanding gases during the power stroke drives the piston down in the cylinder and results in crankshaft rotation. Force is measured in pounds force (lb f) in the English system or newtons (N) in the metric system, and 1 lb f is equal to 4.44 N.

The twisting force applied by the crankshaft to the drive train is called torque. This force is measured in pound feet (lb ft) in the English system and newton meters (Nm) in the metric system.

Pressure

A force applied over a certain area is referred to as pressure. In the English system, pressure is expressed in pounds per square inch (psi), whereas the metric measurement for pressure is kilopascals (kPa). The psi rating is calculated by dividing the lb f by the area to which the force is applied. For example, if 700 lb f is applied to a 3 in. piston, the psi applied to the piston equals 700 divided by the piston area. Hence, the piston area is

$$\pi R^2 = 22/7 \times 1.5 \times 1.5 = 9.4 \text{ sq in.}$$

The pressure applied to each square inch of the piston is:

$$700 \div 9.4 = 74.7 \text{ psi}$$

In the metric system, 1 psi is equal to 6.895 kilopascals (kPa). The prefix kilo represents 1,000 and 1,000 pascals = 1 kPa. A pascal is equal to the force of 1 newton applied to an area of 1 square meter (1 Nm^2)

Torque

Torque is a twisting force which may be calculated by multiplying force (F) and radius (R). Therefore,

$$\text{torque} = F \times R$$

The force is applied to the end of a lever, and the radius is distance from the center of the lever to the point where the force is applied. If the force moved through a complete revolution, R is the radius of the circle through which the force would be applied.

When engine torque is measured, a friction clutch is connected to the engine flywheel. An arm is connected from the friction clutch to a scale which has a meter that reads the pounds of force applied by the friction clutch through the arm. A basic friction clutch and scale are illustrated in Figure 1-25.

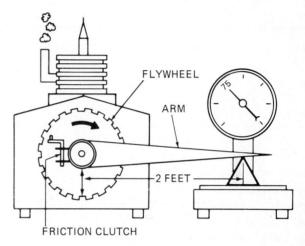

Figure 1-25. Friction Clutch Measuring Engine Torque.

If a 2 ft arm is connected between the brake and the scale, and the highest reading on the scale is 75 lbs with the engine running and the clutch engaged, and the engine torque is:

$$F \times R = 75 \times 2 = 150 \text{ lb ft}$$

In the metric system, 1 lb ft is equal to 1.3358 Nm.

Torque indicates the amount of force an engine can exert, but does not measure how much work the engine can do in a specific length of time.

Maximum engine torque is produced when the highest pressure is available in the cylinders. The highest cylinder pressure occurs when there is maximum air-fuel mixture flow into the cylinders. Torque decreases at high speeds, because the air-fuel mixture has less time to flow into the cylinders on the intake strokes and hence the air-fuel mixture is reduced. If the air-fuel mixture flow into the cylinders can be increased by improving intake manifold design or with the use of a turbocharger, engine torque will be higher.

A turbocharger on the Chrysler 2.2L engine provides a 35 percent increase in torque. (Refer to Chapter 6 for a description of this turbocharger.) The Ford 231 CID (3.8L) V6 engine has a Society of Automo-

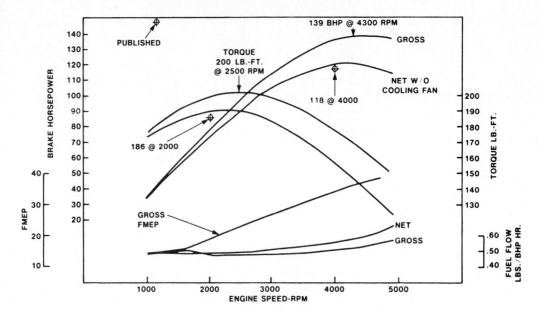

Figure 1-26. Torque and Horsepower Rating, Ford 231 CID (3.8L) V6 Engine. (Reference taken from SAE paper No. 820112. *Reprinted with Permission of Society of Automotive Engineers,* © 1982)

tive Engineers (SAE) gross torque of 200 lb ft (271.16 Nm) and an SAE net torque of 186 lb ft at 2,000 rpm, as indicated in Figure 1-26.

The SAE gross torque is calculated in a laboratory test procedure with engine accessories such as the air cleaner, cooling fan, radiator, and exhaust system removed. The engine is liquid-cooled by the laboratory equipment, and a less restrictive laboratory exhaust system is installed. Standard engine equipment is installed for the net torque rating tests, and this is the advertised rating.

Horsepower

An understanding of energy, work, and power is essential before horsepower is explained. Energy is the potential to do work. Gasoline in a fuel tank has potential energy. When the gasoline is mixed with air and the air-fuel mixture is ignited in the combustion chamber, the resulting explosion force drives the piston down on the power stroke. The potential energy is changed to kinetic energy when combustion takes place. Hence, potential energy does not result in motion or work, whereas kinetic energy is the ability to do work.

Work is accomplished when an applied force overcomes resistance and moves a specific distance. Work is equal to force (F) multiplied by distance (D). When five pounds are moved a distance of one foot, five pound feet of work have been done. In the English system, work is measured in pound feet, and

the metric measurement is newton meters (Nm). When a force of one newton moves an object for one meter, a Nm of work has been done. One Nm is equal to one joule in the metric system.

Power is the rate at which work is done. When power is produced, a certain amount of work is accomplished in a specific time. Horsepower (HP) is the measurement for power in the English system, whereas in the metric system power is measured in kilowatts (kW). The formula for calculating power (P) is:

$$P = F \times D \div T$$

where F = force, D = distance, and T = time.

Brake Horsepower For the friction clutch illustrated in Figure 1-25, to calculate the brake horsepower (BHP), we must know the circumference of the circle through which the arm would rotate on the friction clutch if this arm were allowed to turn. Circumference is:

$$2 \Pi R = 2 \times 22/7 \times 2 = 12.57 \text{ ft}$$

To calculate the work done by the engine, multiply the circumference of the circle by the 75 pound reading on the scale. Therefore, engine work is:

$$12.57 \times 75 = 942.75 \text{ lb ft}$$

However, we still do not know how fast the engine work is being done. To make this calculation, we must know the engine speed. If the engine is running at 2,000 rpm, the speed of the work is:

942.75 × 2,000 = 1,885,500 lb ft per minute

Many years ago when horses were used to work in coal mines, an engineer named James Watt calculated that the average horse could lift 33,000 lbs of coal a distance of 1 ft in 1 minute. Therefore, a standard calculation for 1 horsepower (HP) became:

33,000 lbs × 1 ft × 1 minute = 33,000 lb ft per minute

In our example, the engine is doing 1,885,500 lb ft of work per minute. Since 1 HP is equal to 33,000 lb ft per minute, HP for this engine is:

1,885,500 ÷ 33,000 = 57.136 HP

The formula for brake horsepower may be expressed as

$$BHP = \frac{torque \times 2\Pi \times rpm}{33,000}$$

This formula can be shortened to

$$BHP = \frac{torque \times rpm}{5,252}$$

The Society of Automotive Engineers (SAE) gross BHP is the BHP rating of an engine that is operated without accessories, such as the water pump, radiator, air cleaner, and exhaust system. The SAE net BHP is the BHP with these accessories installed on the engine. (Refer to the section on engine torque rating in this chapter.) The Ford 231 CID (3.8L) V6 engine has a gross BHP of 139 at 4,300 rpm and a net BHP of 118 at 4,000 rpm, as indicated in Figure 1-26.

Relationship Between Brake Horsepower and Torque Engine torque decreases when the engine speed reaches a point where the cylinders begin to take in less air. Brake horsepower will still increase beyond this speed because of the increasing number of power strokes per minute. A decrease in BHP occurs when the effect of the increasing number of power strokes per minute is offset by the reduced air intake to the cylinders.

In Figure 1-26, the Ford 231 CID (3.8L) V6 engine experienced a decrease in net torque at 2,000 rpm, but net BPH did not begin to decrease until 4,000 rpm. The BHP and torque are closely related to the volumetric efficiency of the engine, which will be discussed later in this chapter.

Indicated Horsepower When the indicated horsepower (IHP) is calculated, the following facts must be known:

P = mean effective cylinder pressure in pounds per square inch.

L = piston stroke length in feet.

A = area of the cylinder cross section in square inches.

N = number of power strokes per minute in one cylinder.

K = number of engine cylinders.

The mean effective pressure (MEP) is the average pressure during the power stroke minus the average pressure during the other three strokes. The MEP is the pressure that actually forces the piston down in the power stroke. To calculate the IHP, use this formula:

$$IHP = \frac{PLANK}{33,000}$$

The IHP is the actual power that is developed in the engine cylinders, and this rating is always higher than the BHP because of loss of power due to friction in the engine.

Friction Horsepower Friction horsepower (FHP) is the horsepower that is required to overcome the loss of power due to friction in an engine. Friction horsepower increases in relation to engine speed, and this horsepower is calculated by subtracting the BHP from the IHP. Therefore,

FHP = IHP − BHP

Horsepower in Metric System Horsepower can be calculated in the metric system. In the metric system, the equivalent rating to HP is kilowatts (kW) and 1 HP is equal to 0.746 kW, or 1 kW is equal to 1.305 HP.

Engine Efficiency

Thermal Efficiency

An engine converts the heat or thermal energy in the fuel to mechanical energy to drive the vehicle. Thermal efficiency refers to the relationship between the engine power output and the available heat energy in the fuel. This relationship is expressed as a percentage.

Much of the heat energy in the fuel is carried away by the cooling system and lubrication system as these systems cool the engine parts. The exhaust gases carry away part of the heat produced by combustion. Some of the heat energy in the fuel is used to overcome friction in the engine and power train. From the total thermal energy in the fuel, the following losses may occur:

35 percent loss to cooling and lubrication system.

35 percent loss to exhaust gas.

5 percent loss to engine friction.

10 percent loss to drive train friction.

Therefore, only 15 percent of the thermal energy in the fuel is actually left to drive the vehicle. Improvements have been made in engine design and in engine and drive train lubricants, but thermal efficiency is usually below 30 percent. At present, experimental work is being done with ceramic engine components which could operate at much higher temperatures and reduce thermal energy losses to the cooling and lubrication systems.

Mechanical Efficiency

Engine mechanical efficiency is the relationship between the power delivered (BHP) and the power that would be available if the engine operated without any power loss. Mechanical efficiency is the relationship between BHP and IHP, expressed as a percentage:

$$\text{Mechanical efficiency} = \frac{\text{BHP} \times 100}{\text{IHP}}$$

If an engine has 118 BHP and 146 IHP, the mechanical efficiency is:

$$\frac{118}{146} \times 100 = 80\%$$

Volumetric Efficiency

Volumetric efficiency refers to the amount of air that an engine is able to take into the cylinder on the intake stroke, compared to filling the cylinder completely with air at atmospheric temperature. This comparison is also expressed as a percentage. Assuming that a cylinder has a volume of 47 cu in. (770 cc) with the piston at BDC, 0.034 ounce (0.964 gram) of air would completely fill the cylinder at atmospheric pressure. When the engine is operating at 3,000 rpm, only 0.027 ounce (0.725 gram) can enter the cylinder on the intake stroke. Therefore the volumetric efficiency is:

$$\frac{0.027}{0.034} \times 100 = 79.4\%$$

Volumetric efficiency is determined by such factors as valve and port diameter, intake manifold design, exhaust system design, and valve timing. If the airflow into the cylinders is increased by installing larger valves, the volumetric efficiency could be increased. However, the exhaust system must be capable of expelling this additional air.

Exhaust emission equipment on modern engines may limit the volumetric efficiency. For example, the catalytic converter creates a significant exhaust backpressure. On some engines, a specific exhaust backpressure is necessary to force enough exhaust through the exhaust-gas recirculation (EGR) valve.

Dynamometers

A dynamometer is used to determine the horsepower and torque of the engine. Some engine dynamometers connect to the engine flywheel, as mentioned previously. Chassis dynamometers are used in the automotive service industry. This type of dynamometer contains a set of steel rolls upon which the vehicle drive wheels are positioned, and as the vehicle is operated the vehicle drive wheels turn the rolls on the dynamometer. A power absorption unit is connected to one of the dynamometer rolls. This unit contains rotating vanes, and oil directed against the vanes acts as a brake on the rolls. The dynamometer operator can control the oil flow against the vanes to increase or decrease the engine load.

Water cooling is necessary for the oil in the power absorption unit. An arm is connected from the power absorption unit to a torque bridge which converts a hydraulic signal to an electric signal to operate the dynamometer test meters. When the engine load is increased, the arm movement on the torque bridge increases, and the bridge signal to the meters reads the horsepower.

The dynamometer indicates the road horsepower that is available at the drive wheels. This rating is less than BHP because some power is lost in the drive train. A correction factor may be used to change road horsepower to actual BHP.

The dynamometer may also be used to operate the vehicle under normal road driving conditions to diagnose various operating problems.

Safety precautions must be followed when a dynamometer is used. The non-driving wheels of the vehicle must be blocked, and an air circulation fan must be positioned in front of the radiator to increase airflow and prevent engine overheating. The dynamometer must be operated as outlined by the manufacturer. Careless dynamometer operation can result in serious injury to the operator or to the vehicle.

Test Questions

1. In a four-cycle engine, the intake valve opens when the piston is:

   a) at top dead center (TDC) on the exhaust stroke.

   b) before top dead center (BTDC) on the exhaust stroke.

   c) after top dead center (ATDC) on the exhaust stroke.

2. The intake and the exhaust valve are open at the same time when the piston is at:

   a) bottom dead center (BDC) on the exhaust stroke.

   b) before bottom dead center (BBDC) on the exhaust stroke.

   c) top dead center (TDC) on the exhaust stroke.

3. In a six-cylinder engine, a power stroke takes place every:

   a) 90°

   b) 120°

   c) 180°

4. An even-firing crankshaft from a 90° six-cylinder engine will have the crankpins offset at:

   a) 15°

   b) 30°

   c) 45°

5. In a two-cycle engine, every downward piston stroke is a power stroke.   T F

6. The SAE net torque rating is higher than the SAE gross torque rating.   T F

7. Define brake horsepower BHP, gross BHP, and net BHP.

8. Define indicated horsepower (IHP).

9. The IHP is higher than the BHP.   T F

10. What is the formula for friction horsepower (FHP)?

11. List three engine modifications that could increase volumetric efficiency.

12. Calculate the displacement of V6 engine that has a 4.25 in. bore and 3.50 in. stroke.

13. The following facts are known about an engine:

    a) The engine is operating at 2,500 rpm.

    b) The reading on the clutch brake scale is 100 lb.

    c) The arm from the clutch brake to the scale is 2 ft in length.

    Calculate the brake horsepower for this engine.

14. A four-cylinder engine is running at 2,000 rpm. This engine has a 4.0 in. bore, a 3.0 in. stroke, and a mean effective pressure (MEP) of 300 psi. Calculate the indicated horsepower (IHP) on the engine.

15. A cylinder head with valves larger than those on the original head is installed on an engine. This should increase volumetric efficiency.   T F

16. When the piston is at top dead center (TDC) of the exhaust stroke, the intake valve should be just opening and the exhaust valve should be closed.   T F

2

Engine Components, Gaskets, and Seals

Chapter Completion Objectives

1. Identify all engine components and explain their purposes.
2. Recognize proper bearing crush and spread.
3. Select the correct type of engine bearings for specific operating conditions.
4. Recognize different types of piston rings and identify their proper applications.
5. Install oil seals correctly.
6. Diagnose excessive gasket wicking.
7. Install engine gaskets correctly.
8. Select the correct head gasket for specific applications, such as aluminum heads.
9. Apply room temperatures vulcanizing (RTV) and anaerobic sealers properly in their intended applications.

Cylinder Blocks

Design

Cylinder blocks are made of a cast iron alloy in many engines. Aluminum alloy blocks are also used in some engines. Some aluminum engine blocks have steel cylinder sleeves. A cast iron block is heavier and more rigid than an aluminum block. Aluminum blocks have better heat-conducting qualities than cast iron blocks, but they are also more subject to distortion.

When cylinder blocks are manufactured, molten metal is poured into a mold with a sand-based core. The mold and sand core are removed after the metal has cooled. Removal of the mold and core exposes the openings for the cylinders, bearing bores, and cooling jackets. Holes in the sides of the block through which the sand core was supported are machined and closed with dish-type or cup-type core plugs. Oil galleries may be cast in the block or drilled and plugged during the machining process.

On some engines, the cylinder block supports many of the other engine components, such as the crankshaft, pistons, valve lifters, water pump, oil pump, timing gear cover, cylinder heads, and the camshaft. A four-cylinder block and related components in the lower part of the engine are shown in Figure 2-1, and a parts list is provided in Table 2-1.

The upper components are illustrated in relation to the same four-cylinder block in Figure 2-2, and a parts list is provided in Table 2-2.

Cylinders and Cylinder Sleeves

In most cylinder blocks that are used in cars and light trucks, the cylinders are cast integrally with the block. Some heavy-duty engines have wet-type or dry-type replaceable cylinder sleeves. The outside of a wet-type sleeve is in contact with the engine coolant, whereas the dry-type sleeve exterior contacts the block casting. A wet-type sleeve must be sealed in the engine block.

Figure 2-3 illustrates a replaceable cylinder sleeve. Each cylinder must have a precision finish.

Main Bearing Bores

The main bearing bores and main bearings support the crankshaft. The crankshaft, main bearings, and engine block are subject to extreme explosion forces from the pistons and connecting rods. Therefore, the main bearing bores must be strong enough to withstand these forces without distorting or stretching. Larger engines have larger-diameter main bearing bores with four-bolt main bearing caps, whereas in smaller engines the bores are smaller with two-bolt caps.

The main bearing bores must be perfectly round and aligned with each other. An oil hole in the upper half of the main bearing bore supplies oil from the main oil gallery to the main bearings.

Camshaft Bearing Bores

Camshaft bearing bores with circular bearings support the camshaft if it is mounted in the block. These bearing bores and bearings must be strong enough to carry the value train load to which the camshaft is subjected. The camshaft bearing bores and bearings contain an oil hole that supplies oil from the main oil gallery to the camshaft bearings. To prevent oil leaks, a core plug is installed in the block opening from the rear camshaft bushing. Oil is often supplied from the front camshaft bearing to the timing chain and gears.

Lifter Bores

The value lifters are supported in the lifter bores directly above the camshaft. Oil is supplied directly to each lifter bore from the main oil gallery. (Refer to Chapter 4 for a complete description of the lubrication system.)

Water Jackets

To cool the pistons, rings, and cylinder walls, engine coolant is circulated through the water jackets which surround each cylinder. A threaded coolant drain plug is located near the bottom of the water jacket. (The cooling system is discussed in Chapter 3.)

Crankshafts

Design

Crankshafts may be manufactured from cast iron alloy or forged steel. Forged steel crankshafts provide greater strength, but cast iron crankshafts are quite satisfactory in car and light truck engines.

The main bearing and connecting rod bearing journals are machined to a highly polished finish. All the main bearing journals must be in line with

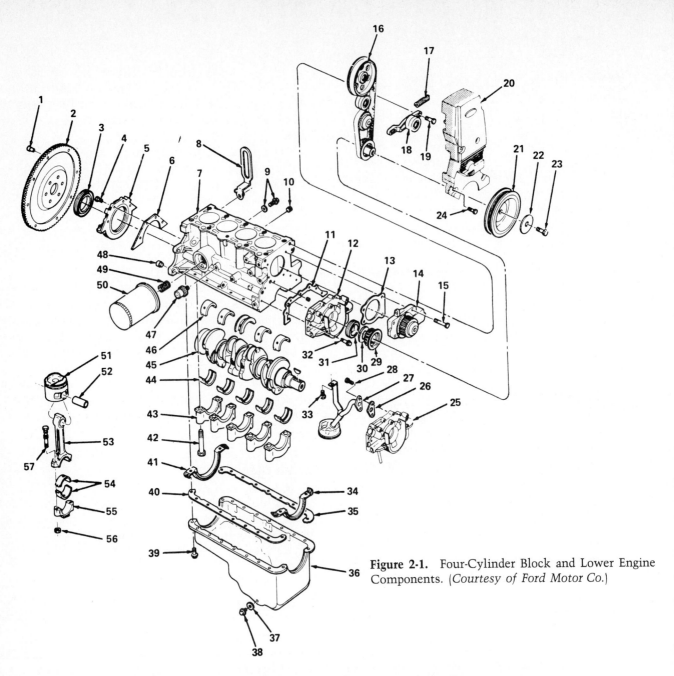

Figure 2-1. Four-Cylinder Block and Lower Engine Components. (*Courtesy of Ford Motor Co.*)

TABLE 2-1. Parts List for Four-Cylinder Block and Lower Engine Components.
(*Courtesy of Ford Motor Co.*)

1. DOWEL, PRESSURE PLATE ALIGNMENT
2. FLYWHEEL
3. SEAL, CRANKSHAFT REAR
4. BOLT, RETAINER ATTACHING (6)
5. SEAL RETAINER
6. GASKET, RETAINER
7. CYLINDER BLOCK
8. ENGINE LIFTING EYE
9. PLUG AND GASKET, MONOLITHIC TIMING
10. PLUG, COOLANT DRAIN
11. GASKET, PUMP (OIL)
12. OIL PUMP
13. GASKET, PUMP (WATER)
14. WATER PUMP
15. BOLT, PUMP (WATER) ATTACHING (4)
16. TIMING BELT – INSTALLED VIEW
17. SPRING, TENSIONER
18. BRACKET AND IDLER, TENSIONER
19. BOLT, TENSIONER ATTACHING (2)

20. TIMING BELT COVER
21. CRANKSHAFT PULLEY
22. WASHER, PULLEY BOLT (1)
23. BOLT, PULLEY ATTACHING (1)
24. BOLT, COVER ATTACHING (4)
25. OIL PUMP
26. GASKET, PICK UP TUBE
27. PICK UP AND TUBE ASSEMBLY
28. BOLT, PICK UP ATTACHING (2)
29. GEAR, CRANKSHAFT
30. GUIDE, TIMING BELT
31. SEAL, CRANKSHAFT FRONT
32. BOLT, PUMP (OIL) ATTACHING (6)
33. BOLT, BRACE ATTACHING (1)
34. SEAL, PAN FRONT
35. GASKET, PAN SIDE
36. OIL PAN
37. SEAL, DRAIN PLUG
38. PLUG, OIL PAN DRAIN

39. BOLT, PAN ATTACHING (18)
40. GASKET, PAN SIDE
41. SEAL, PAN REAR
42. BOLT, CAP ATTACHING (10)
43. MAIN BEARING CAPS
44. MAIN BEARING INSERTS, LOWER
45. CRANKSHAFT
46. MAIN BEARING INSERTS, UPPER
47. OIL PRESSURE SENDING UNIT
48. DOWEL, TRANSMISSION ALIGNMENT
49. ADAPTER, OIL FILTER
50. OIL FILTER
51. PISTON
52. PISTON PIN
53. CONNECTING ROD
54. CONNECTING ROD BEARINGS
55. CONNECTING ROD CAP
56. NUT, CAP ATTACHING
57. BOLT, CAP ATTACHING

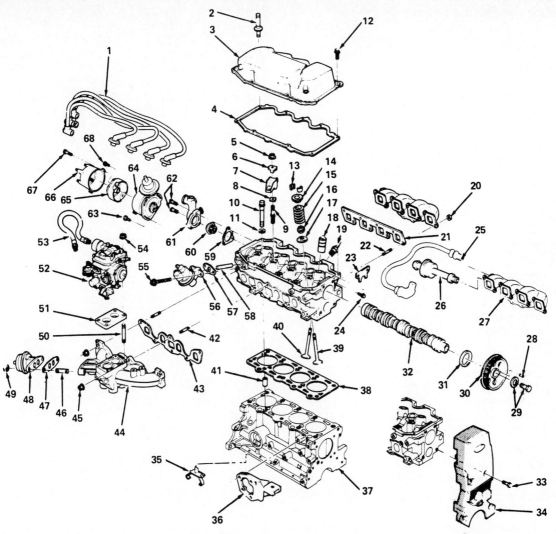

Figure 2-2. Four-Cylinder Block and Upper Engine Components. (*Courtesy of Ford Motor Co.*)

TABLE 2-2. Parts List for Four-Cylinder Upper Engine Components. (*Courtesy of Ford Motor Co.*)

1. SPARK PLUG CABLE SET
2. BOLT/STUD, COVER ATTACHING (2)
3. ROCKER ARM COVER
4. GASKET, ROCKER ARM COVER
5. NUT, FULCRUM ATTACHING (8)
6. FULCRUM, ROCKER ARM
7. ROCKER ARM
8. WASHER, FULCRUM (8)
9. STUD, FULCRUM ATTACHING (8)
10. BOLT, CYLINDER HEAD ATTACHING (10)
11. WASHER, CYLINDER HEAD BOLT (10)
12. SCREW, COVER ATTACHING (7)
13. KEEPERS, VALVE SPRINGS
14. RETAINER, VALVE SPRING
15. VALVE SPRING
16. SEAL, VALVE STEM
17. WASHER, VALVE SPRING
18. VALVE LIFTER
19. SPARK PLUG
20. NUT, MANIFOLD ATTACHING (8)
21. GASKET, EXHAUST MANIFOLD
22. STUD, MANIFOLD ATTACHING (8)
23. PLATE, CAMSHAFT THRUST

24. BOLT, THRUST PLATE ATTACHING (2)
25. EGR TUBE
26. CHECK VALVE, AIR INJECTION
27. EXHAUST MANIFOLD
28. SHAFT KEY, CAM SPROCKET
29. BOLT/WASHER SPROCKET ATTACHING (1)
30. CAMSHAFT SPROCKET
31. SEAL, CAMSHAFT
32. CAMSHAFT
33. BOLTS (2) & NUTS (2), COVER ATTACHING (2)
34. TIMING BELT COVER
35. CRANKCASE VENTILATION BAFFLE
36. ENGINE MOUNT
37. CYLINDER BLOCK
38. GASKET, CYLINDER HEAD
39. EXHAUST VALVE
40. INTAKE VALVE
41. DOWEL; CYLINDER HEAD ALIGNMENT (2)
42. STUD, MANIFOLD ATTACHING (6)
43. GASKET, INTAKE MANIFOLD
44. INTAKE MANIFOLD
45. NUT, MANIFOLD ATTACHING (6)
46. STUD, VALVE ATTACHING (2)

47. GASKET, EGR VALVE
48. EGR VALVE
49. NUT, VALVE ATTACHING (2)
50. STUD, CARBURETOR ATTACHING (4)
51. GASKET, CARBURETOR MOUNTING
52. CARBURETOR
53. FUEL LINE
54. NUT, CARBURETOR ATTACHING (4)
55. BOLT, PUMP ATTACHING (2)
56. FUEL PUMP
57. GASKET, FUEL PUMP
58. PUSH ROD, FUEL PUMP
59. GASKET, HOUSING
60. THERMOSTAT
61. THERMOSTAT HOUSING
62. BOLT, HOUSING ATTACHING (2)
63. BOLT, DISTRIBUTOR ATTACHING (3)
64. DISTRIBUTOR
65. ROTOR
66. DISTRIBUTOR CAP
67. SCREW, CAP ATTACHING (2).
68. SCREW, ROTOR ATTACHING (2)

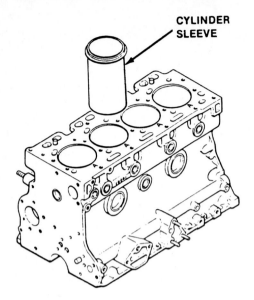

Figure 2-3. Replaceable Cylinder Sleeve. (*Courtesy of Ford Motor Co.*)

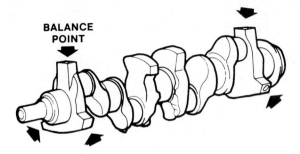

Figure 2-4. Four-Cylinder Crankshaft with Counterweights. (Reference taken from SAE paper No. 820111. *Reprinted with Permission of Society of Automotive Engineers,* © 1982)

Figure 2-5. Crankshaft Oil Passages. (Reference taken from SAE paper No. 810007. *Reprinted with Permission of Society of Automotive Engineers,* © 1981)

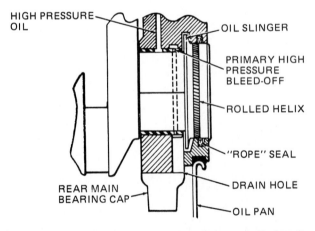

Figure 2-6. Rear Main Bearing Oil Slinger, Rolled Helix, and Rope Seal. (Reference taken from SAE paper No. 820111. *Reprinted from Permission of Society of Automotive Engineers,* © 1982)

each other, while the connecting rod journals are offset from the crankshaft center. This causes the connecting rod journals to orbit around the main bearing journals. The distance from the center line of the main bearings to the center line of the connecting rod journal is equal to $\frac{1}{2}$ of the piston stroke.

Counterweights are an integral part of the crankshaft. A drill is used to remove some metal from the counterweights so that the crankshaft is balanced during the manufacturing process. The balance points on the crankshaft counterweights are illustrated in Figure 2-4.

Oil is supplied through drilled passages from the main bearing journals to the connecting rod journals, as pictured in Figure 2-5.

An oil slinger is located behind the rear main bearing journal. This slinger helps to direct excess oil from the rear main bearing to the oil pan to prevent seal leakage. A rolled helix is positioned on some crankshafts between the oil slinger and the seal to move oil away from the seal. A rope-type seal is used at some rear main bearings, with half the seal in the upper bearing bore and the other half in the bearing cap.

The oil slinger, roller helix, and rope seal are shown in Figure 2-6.

The flexplate or flywheel is bolted to the back of the crankshaft. (Refer to Figure 2-1.) The reciprocating movement of the pistons is converted to rotary motion by the crankshaft. This rotary motion is transmitted through the vehicle drive train to the drive wheels. Some energy is absorbed by the flywheel, or torque converter, during each piston power stroke, and then this energy is released during the other three strokes. The action helps to smooth out the engine power pulses and provide a smoother running engine.

A crankshaft sprocket and a vibration damper are mounted on the front of the crankshaft. (See Figures 2-1 and 2-2.) Keys mounted in slots in the crankshaft and corresponding slots in the sprocket and damper prevent these components from slipping on the shaft. The crankshaft sprocket drives the camshaft sprocket via the timing chain. Torsional vibrations in the crankshaft are dampened by the vibration damper.

When each cylinder fires, that crankpin attempts to speed up, but the rest of the crankshaft tends to lag behind. This results in a twisting action on the crankshaft, which could result in engine vibration. The vibration damper reduces the effect of these twisting, or torsional, vibrations. Split-type main bearings are used on each main bearing jour-

nal, as pictured in Figure 2-7.

The second main bearing from the rear of the engine has lip flanges that fit against the crankshaft journal sides and control crankshaft endplay. The correct procedure for installing the lip-type rear main bearing seal is provided in Figure 2-7.

Main Bearings and Connecting Rod Bearings

Bearing Requirements

Connecting rod and main bearings must have excellent fatigue strength to withstand the explosion impacts when the engine is operating under heavy load. Bearings must have satisfactory conformability to allow the bearing material to creep slightly and compensate for any misalignment between the bearing

Figure 2-7. Crankshaft and Main Bearings, V6 Engine. *(Courtesy of Ford Motor Co.)*

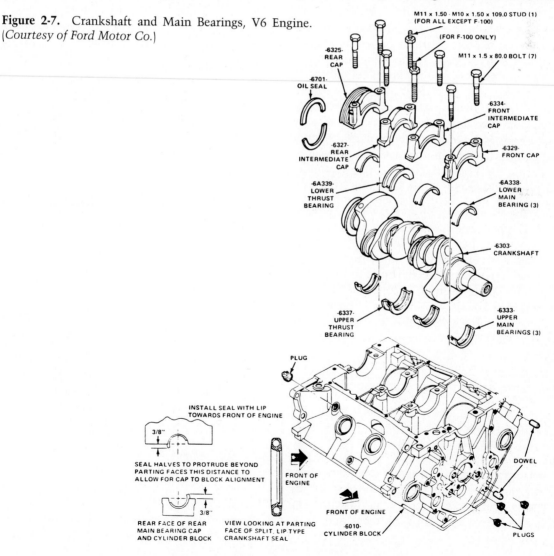

and the crankshaft journal. Bearings must also have embedability in order to absorb foreign particles that would otherwise scratch the crankshaft journal surface.

Bearings must provide good surface action to prevent seizure if the bearing makes momentary contact with the crankshaft journal. Bearings also require corrosion resistance to resist acids that form in the oil. In addition, bearings must provide excellent temperature strength so they will not flow out of shape or break under high temperatures and heavy engine loads.

Thermal conductivity is another important requirement so that bearings will conduct heat from the bearing surface to the bearing bore.

Bearing Materials

Babbitt Babbitt bearings have a steel back with a babbitt lining which may contain a lead or tin base. Tin-base babbitt contains approximately 89 percent tin, 7.5 percent antimony, and 3.5 percent copper, whereas lead-base babbitt contains 83 percent lead, 15 percent antimony, 1 percent arsenic, and 1 percent tin. Lead- and tin-base babbitt are excellent bearing materials when they are used in moderate-load conditions. Tin-base babbitt offers more resistance to corrosion than lead-base babbitt.

Babbitt bearings have good conformability and embedability, but their fatigue strength is not as high as other bearing materials. Babbitt bearings may be identified by the letters SB, SI, or SA, as indicated in Figure 2-8.

Overplated Copper-Lead Bearing The overplated copper-lead bearing has a five-layer construction which provides high fatigue strength by limiting the amount of lead in the copper-lead lining to less than 30 percent. A five-layer overplated copper-lead lining is shown in Figure 2-9.

The copper-lead lining contains 24 percent lead, 1 percent tin, and 75 percent copper. This type of bearing is used in heavy-duty applications because it provides good conformability and embedability, plus excellent fatigue strength, corrosion resistance, and thermal conductivity.

Non-Overplated Copper-Lead Bearing The copper-lead lining in this type of bearing contains 65 percent copper and 35 percent lead. This composition is softer than the material in the overplated copper-lead bearing, and therefore fatigue strength is reduced. A non-overplated copper-lead bearing, as illustrated in Figure 2-10, may be classified as a medium-duty bearing.

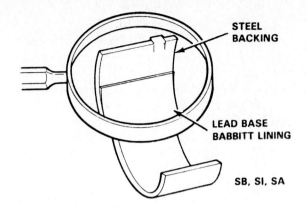

Figure 2-8. Babbitt Bearing. (*Courtesy of Federal-Mogul Corporation,* © *1982*)

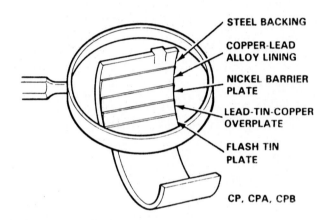

Figure 2-9. Overplated Copper-Lead Bearing. (*Courtesy of Federal-Mogul Corporation,* © *1982*)

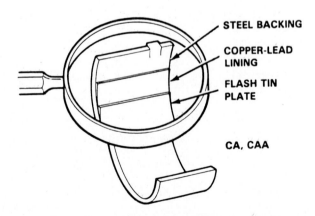

Figure 2-10. Non-Overplated Copper-Lead Bearing. (*Courtesy of Federal-Mogul Corporation,* © *1982*)

Non-Overplated Aluminum Bearings Aluminum-type bearings have excellent load-carrying capabilities, but the aluminum must be alloyed with other metals, such as lead or tin, to make it compatible with the crankshaft journal surfaces. The aluminum alloy in some bearings contains 79 percent aluminum, 20 percent tin, and 1 percent copper, whereas other aluminum alloys have 89.5 percent aluminum, 6 percent lead, 4 percent silicon, and 0.5 percent tin. Both types of aluminum alloys provide good fatigue strength, high thermal conductivity, and excellent corrosion resistance.

A non-overplated aluminum bearing is shown in Figure 2-11.

Overplated Aluminum-Cadmium Bearings This type of bearing has a four-layer construction, as indicated in Figure 2-12. The aluminum alloy lining contains 95 percent aluminum, 3 percent cadmium, 1 percent nickel, and 1 percent copper. This type of bearing may be used in heavy-duty and extra-heavy-duty applications because it has excellent qualities in all bearing requirements.

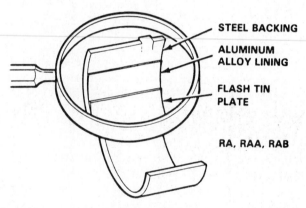

Figure 2-11. Non-Overplated Aluminum Bearing. (*Courtesy of Federal-Mogul Corporation, © 1982*)

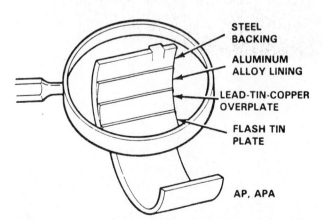

Figure 2-12. Overplated Aluminum-Cadmium Bearing. (*Courtesy of Federal-Mogul Corporation, © 1982*)

Bearing Spread and Crush

Before connecting rod bearings are installed, the curvature of the bearing insert is larger than the rod bore curvature. This bearing condition is referred to as spread. When the bearing is installed in the rod bore or cap, it will snap into place and conform exactly to the rod bore.

Bearing spread is illustrated in Figure 2-13.

Bearing inserts are manufactured so that they are slightly longer than the circumference of the rod bore and cap. This additional length is called bearing crush. When the rod cap bolts are tightened, the bearing crush forces the inserts to make complete contact with the rod bore. This provides good heat dissipation and prevents the bearings from turning in the rod bore.

Bearing crush is shown in Figure 2-14.

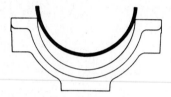

Figure 2-13. Bearing Spread. (*Courtesy of Sunnen Products Company*)

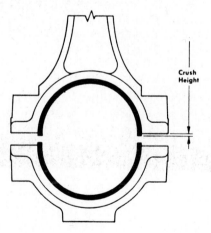

Figure 2-14. Bearing Crush. (*Courtesy of Sunnen Products Company*)

Locking tabs in each half of the bearing fit into slots in the cap and rod to help prevent the bearings from turning in the rod bore, as pictured in Figure 2-15.

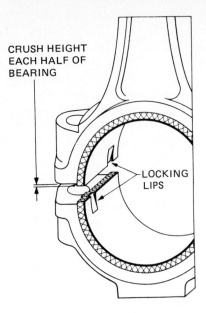

CRUSH HEIGHT
EACH HALF OF
BEARING

LOCKING
LIPS

Figure 2-15. Bearing Locking Pins. *(Courtesy of Sunnen Products Company)*

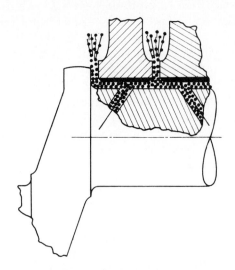

Figure 2-16. Bearing Oil Film. *(Courtesy of Sunnen Products Company)*

A thin film of oil must be maintained between the bearings and the crankshaft journals at all times to transmit the load from the connecting rod to the crankshaft. It also prevents direct contact between the bearings and the crankshaft journals by completely filling the bearing clearance space, as illustrated in Figure 2-16.

Since the load area on a connecting rod bearing is in the upper part of the connecting rod, no oil can be fed into the bearing when the crankshaft oil hole is sweeping the top of the rod bearing. In this position the oil fed into the bearing previously is sustaining the load. New oil must be fed into the bearing when the crankshaft oil hole is sweeping the no-load section of the bearings. Sufficient clearances at the bearing parting line are absolutely essential to ensure an adequate oil supply, as shown in Figure 2-17.

Correct bearing clearance is necessary to ensure proper lubrication. Excessive bearing crush will buckle the bearing in the parting line area, which could starve the bearing for oil. Excess oil from the connecting rod bearings is thrown off at the sides of the rod to lubricate the pistons and cylinder walls, as indicated in Figure 2-18.

Excessive bearing clearances result in too much oil being supplied to the cylinder walls, resulting in high oil consumption, whereas insufficient bearing clearances reduce the cylinder wall oil supply, which can damage the pistons, rings, and cylinder walls.

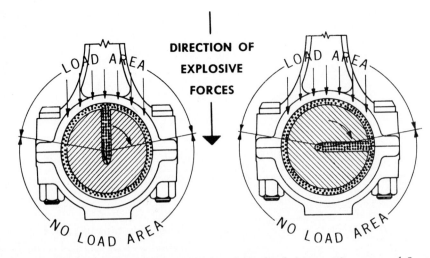

DIRECTION OF EXPLOSIVE FORCES

LOAD AREA

NO LOAD AREA

LOAD AREA

NO LOAD AREA

Figure 2-17. Bearing Lubrication in Load and No-load Areas. *(Courtesy of Sunnen Products Company)*

24

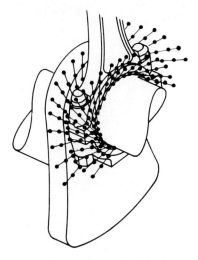

Figure 2-18. Oil Thrown from Connecting Rod Bearing to Lubricate Cylinder Walls. (*Courtesy of Sunnen Products Co.*)

Connecting Rods

Design

Connecting rods are usually a tapered I-beam design made from steel forgings. The eye of the connecting rod is connected to the piston pin and the rod bore is mounted over a crankshaft journal, so that the connecting rod transmits the load from the piston to the crankshaft.

If a full-floating piston pin is used, the connecting rod may have an oil passage to supply oil from the rod bearing to the piston pin bushing. Some connecting rods have a spray hole in the side of the rod bore which sprays oil on the piston and cylinder walls. When oil holes are present in the rod bore, the rod bearing must have matching holes.

A connecting rod from an automotive engine is shown in Figure 2-19.

Pistons

Design and Cam Action

Aluminum alloy pistons are used in most gasoline engines. Ring grooves are cut near the top of the piston. The material between the ring grooves is called a ring land. The piston skirt is the area from the lowest ring land to the bottom of the piston, opposite the pin hole bosses. The piston skirt is slightly larger in diameter at the bottom than directly below the ring land.

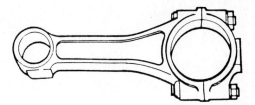

Figure 2-19. Automotive Connecting Rod. (*Courtesy of Ford Motor Co.*)

An aluminum alloy piston is pictured in Figure 2-20.

When the piston is being forced upward on the compression stroke, the cylinder pressure forces the piston against the cylinder wall. The side of the piston that is thrust against the cylinder wall under this condition is referred to as the minor thrust side. As the piston is driven down on the power stroke, the high cylinder pressure drives the major thrust side of the piston against the cylinder wall, as illustrated in Figure 2-21.

Figure 2-20. Aluminum Alloy Piston. (*Courtesy of Ford Motor Co.*)

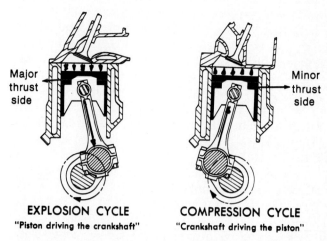

EXPLOSION CYCLE
"Piston driving the crankshaft"

COMPRESSION CYCLE
"Crankshaft driving the piston"

Major thrust side

Minor thrust side

Figure 2-21. Minor and Major Thrust Sides of the Piston. (*Courtesy of Sunnen Products Company*)

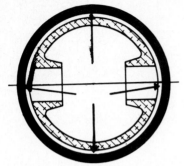 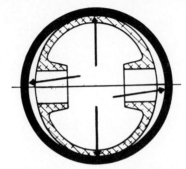 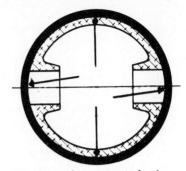

Diagram of round piston in cylinder before heat causes it to expand. Note that piston has clearance all the way around.

Diagram of cam-ground piston in cold engine — "full-cam" position. Note that piston has cylinder-wall contact in the direction of thrust, and clearance along the axis of the pin bosses.

Diagram of cam-ground piston at engine operating temperature — "expanded cam" position. The piston has expanded till it is now practically round in the cylinder. Note that pin bosses are now further apart than when the piston was cold.

Figure 2-22. Piston Cam Action. (*Courtesy of Sunnen Products Company*)

In many pistons the pin is offset from the center of the piston. For example, in Figure 2-21 the pin would be offset to the right, which causes the tip of the skirt to contact the cylinder wall first as the piston moves past top dead center (TDC) and the pressure changes from the minor to the major thrust side. This action prevents the piston from slapping against the cylinder wall.

Pistons must always be installed in the cylinder in the right direction because of the offset pin and thrust faces. Many piston tops have a notch that must face toward the front of the engine.

If a perfectly round piston had 0.012 in. (0.254 mm) clearance between the piston and the cylinder wall, the piston would slap against the cylinder wall when cold and cause undesirable noise. This same piston would seize in the cylinder at normal operating temperatures. To avoid slapping and seizure, pistons are cam-ground so that there is a very small clearance between the piston skirt and the cylinder wall, but a larger clearance at the pin boss sides of the piston. This forces the piston to expand in the direction of the pin bosses as it is heated. When the piston cools, it shrinks inward in the pin boss area. Therefore the pin bosses actually move in and out on the pin as the piston is cooled and heated.

Piston cam action is very important to maintain piston clearances in the cylinder and prevent piston slapping. Piston cam action is illustrated in Figure 2-22.

Pistons may have various top designs to match the combustion chamber design in the cylinder head. Two different piston top designs are shown in Figure 2-23.

Some pistons used in diesel engines have struts mounted inside the piston to provide extra strength, as indicated in Figure 2-24.

VALVE CLEARANCE RELIEF

Figure 2-23. Piston Top Designs. (*Courtesy of Pontiac Motor Division, General Motors Corporation*)

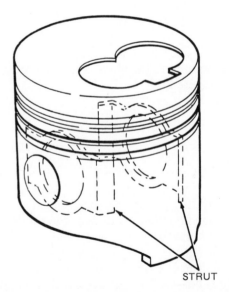

STRUT

Figure 2-24. Heavy-Duty Aluminum Piston with Struts. (*Courtesy of Ford Motor Co.*)

Other automotive diesel pistons have a Ni-Resist ring carrier that is cast into the top ring groove to provide improved ring groove wear. Some of these pistons also have an autothermic ring cast into the piston behind the skirt to provide precise expansion control and reduce piston noise.

A piston with a Ni-Resist top ring carrier and an autothermic ring is shown in Figure 2-25.

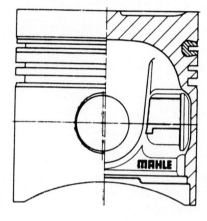

Figure 2-25. Automotive Diesel Piston with Ni-Resist Top Ring Carrier and Autothermic Ring. (Reference taken from SAE paper No. 770113. *Reprinted with Permission of Society of Automotive Engineers,* © *1977*)

Piston Pins

Types of Piston Pins

Piston pins are made from hard steel with a finely polished surface. The piston pin retains the piston to the connecting rod. Five different types of piston pins are illustrated in Figure 2-26.

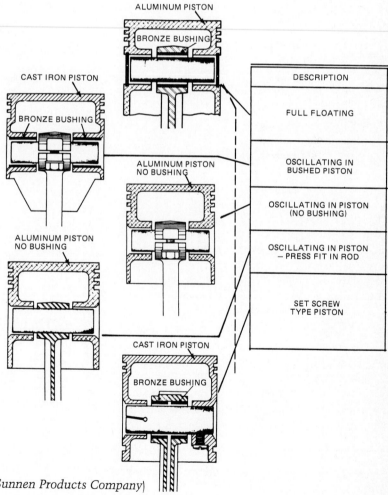

Figure 2-26. Types of Piston Pins. (*Courtesy of Sunnen Products Company*)

The fit of the piston pin within the pin bosses or connecting rod is extremely critical to provide long piston and pin life.

Piston Rings

Design

Piston rings may be manufactured from cast iron or nodular iron. Various types of piston rings are pictured in Figure 2-27.

Many pistons have two compression rings. The scraper-type ring is often used as the second compression ring and on diesel engines the keystone-type ring may be used as the top compression ring. Different types of ring joints are illustrated in Figure 2-28.

The butt joint is most commonly used in automotive engines. The oil ring usually has an expander and two side rings or rails, as indicated in Figure 2-29.

45° ANGLE JOINT

BUTT JOINT

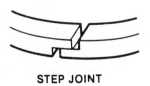

STEP JOINT

Figure 2-28. Piston Ring Joints. (*Courtesy of Ford Motor Co.*)

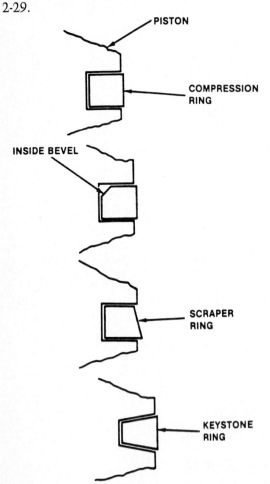

Figure 2-27. Types of Piston Rings. (*Courtesy of Ford Motor Co.*)

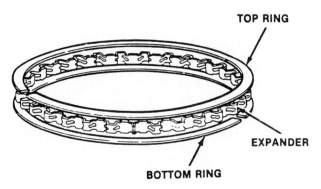

Figure 2-29. Oil Ring with Expander and Side Rails. (*Courtesy of Ford Motor Co.*)

Figure 2-30. One-piece Oil Ring with Expander. (*Courtesy of Ford Motor Co.*)

An oil ring cast in one piece with an expander behind the ring is shown in Figure 2-30.

Some compression rings and oil rings have a thin coating of chrome or molybdenum to improve ring life. On some oil ring side rails, the chrome coating is applied to the inside and outside surfaces. The piston rings must control the oil on the cylinder walls and minimize blow-by from the combustion chamber to the crankcase. The oil ring scrapes excess oil from the cylinder walls and returns this oil to the crankcase through the openings in the oil ring and piston oil ring groove. The rings must resist wear and sticking in their grooves. A scraper-type compression ring also helps to move oil down the cylinder walls.

Camshafts

Design and Purpose

Camshafts are made from a hardened cast iron alloy. There is a lobe on the camshaft for each valve in the engine. The camshaft changes rotary motion to the reciprocating motion of the valves. If the camshaft is mounted in the engine block, the cam lobes push the lifters and push rods upward. When the push rod end of the rocker arm moves upward, the other end is forced down to open the valve. The valve will be in the closed position when the lowest part of the cam lobe is under the lifter, as shown in Figure 2-31.

Some camshafts are mounted in the engine block. With this type of camshaft mounting, the camshaft journals are mounted in circular bearings in the block bores. A core plug is installed in the rear camshaft bore to prevent oil leakage. Many camshafts have a distributor drive gear in the camshaft casting.

A four-cylinder camshaft mounted in the engine block is illustrated in Figure 2-32.

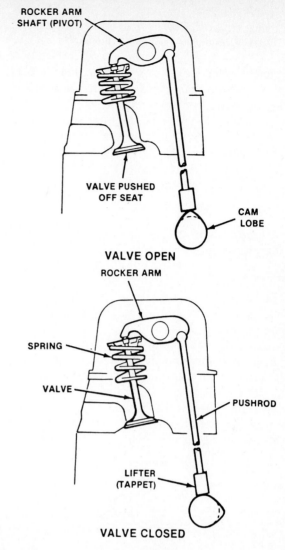

Figure 2-31. Camshaft and Valve Operation. (*Courtesy of Ford Motor Co.*)

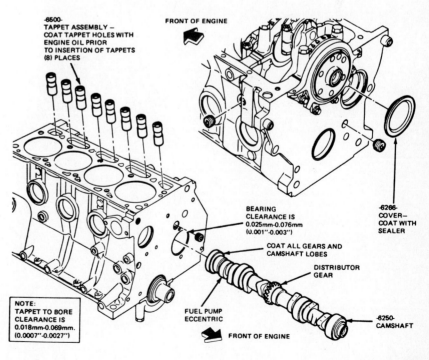

Figure 2-32. Four-Cylinder Block Mounted Camshaft. (*Courtesy of Ford Motor Co.*)

Many block-mounted camshafts are held in place by a thrust plate. A camshaft sprocket is bolted to the camshaft and a dowel pin in the camshaft fits in a slot in the sprocket to prevent rotation on the shaft. The camshaft sprocket may be made from a cast alloy, aluminum, or aluminum with plastic teeth. A matching sprocket is attached to the crankshaft with a key, and a steel timing chain surrounds the two sprockets. The crankshaft sprocket is usually made from a hardened cast alloy. In many engines the sprocket and chain are lubricated from the front camshaft bearing.

The sprockets, timing chain, and related components are pictured in Figure 2-33.

The camshaft and crankshaft sprockets must be installed with their timing marks positioned as illustrated in Figure 2-34.

A dial indicator should be used to make a camshaft endplay measurement as shown in Figure 2-34. Excessive endplay is usually caused by a worn thrust plate.

Some block-mounted camshafts have a direct drive between the crankshaft and camshaft sprockets. A fiber camshaft gear may be used in these applications, and the timing marks on the gears must be assembled in the specified location.

A direct-drive camshaft gear is pictured in Figure 2-35.

Block-mounted camshaft drives are surrounded by a metal or aluminum cover which is sealed to the block and the front of the oil pan with a gasket or sealer.

Some overhead-cam engines have the camshaft mounted in cylinder head bores and driven with a cogged belt. In the engine shown in Figure 2-36, the camshaft journals are supported directly on the cylinder head bores without the use of bearings.

In other overhead-cam engines, the camshaft is mounted above the rocker arms and the lobes make contact with the top of the rocker arms. A lash adjuster, similar to a valve lifter, is positioned under one end of the rocker arm, as illustrated in Figure 2-37.

Many overhead-cam four-cylinder engines, such as the ones shown in Figures 2-36 and 2-37, have been designed for front-wheel-drive cars. In the engine shown in Figure 2-37, the camshaft journals make direct contact with the cylinder head bores.

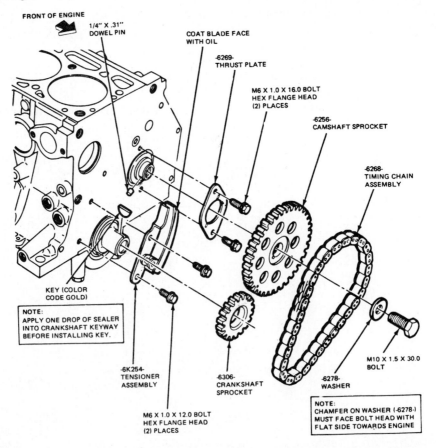

Figure 2-33.   Camshaft and Crankshaft Sprockets with Timing Chain. (*Courtesy of Ford Motor Co.*)

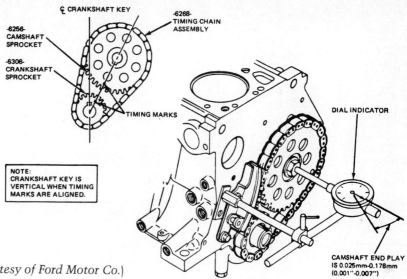

Figure 2-34. Timing Mark Alignment. *(Courtesy of Ford Motor Co.)*

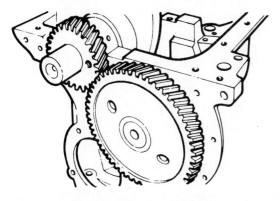

Figure 2-35. Direct-Drive Camshaft Gear. *(Courtesy of Chevrolet Motor Division, General Motors Corporation)*

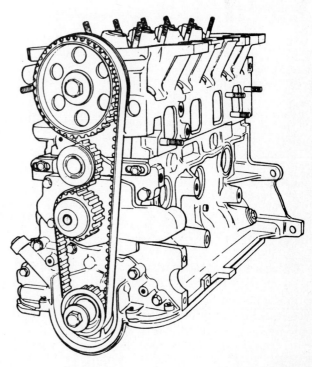

Figure 2-36. Overhead-Cam Engine with Camshaft Mounted in the Cylinder Head. *(Courtesy of Ford Motor Co.)*

Figure 2-37. Overhead-Cam Engine with Camshaft Mounted Above the Rocker Arms. (Reference taken from SAE paper No. 810007. *Reprinted with Permission of Society of Automotive Engineers,* © *1981*)

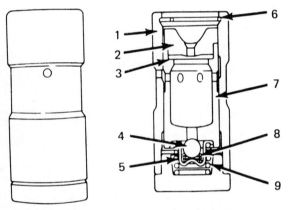

1. Lifter Body	6. Push Rod Seat
2. Push Rod Seat	Retainer
3. Metering Valve	7. Plunger
4. Check Ball	8. Check Ball Spring
5. Check Ball Retainer	9. Plunger Spring

Figure 2-38. Valve Lifter Design. (*Courtesy of Pontiac Motor Division, General Motors Corporation*)

Valve Lifters

Operation

Valve lifters contain a movable spring-loaded plunger inside the lifter body. A check ball valve is located in the bottom of the plunger. The bottom of the lifter body is slightly convex, which causes the lifter to rotate as it contacts the camshaft lobe.

Valve lifter components are illustrated in Figure 2-38.

When the valve is closed, oil is supplied from the lifter feed port in the block, or cylinder head, through the hole in the side of the lifter. From this point the oil flows through the lifter plunger past the check ball to the chamber under the plunger. Notice that oil can also flow from the side of the lifter through the lifter cup and hollow push rod to lubricate the rocker arm. (Refer to Chapter 4 for a complete explanation of the lubrication system.)

When the cam lobe begins to move the lifter body upward, the pressure increases in the chamber under the plunger and the check ball becomes seated. When this condition occurs, the oil is trapped under the plunger and the plunger is forced to move upward with the lifter body. This upward movement opens the valve to which the push rod and rocker arm are connected. The lifter maintains valve clearance at zero.

Free movement of the plunger without excessive oil leakage is essential for proper lifter operation.

Rocker Arms, Push Rods, and Valves

Rocker Arm and Push Rod Design

Rocker arms are made from a hardened iron alloy or stamped steel. Some engines with a block-mounted camshaft have individual rocker arms that are mounted on cylinder head studs. A pivot is located in the center of each rocker arm, and a self-locking nut holds the pivot and rocker arm in position, as shown in Figure 2-39.

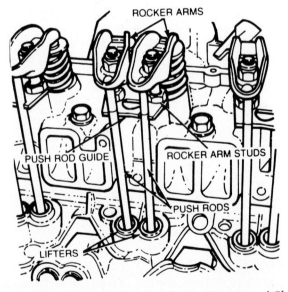

Figure 2-39. Individual Rocker Arms. (*Courtesy of Chevrolet Motor Division, General Motors Corporation*)

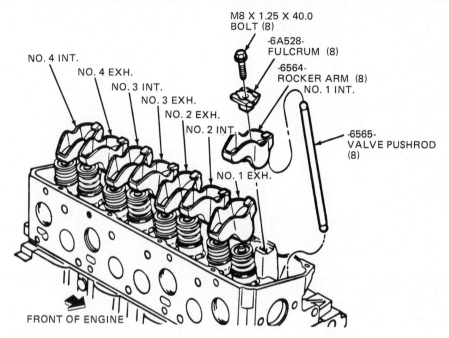

Figure 2-40. Nonadjustable Individual Rocker Arms. (*Courtesy of Ford Motor Co.*)

Individual rockers require adjusting. In some overhead-cam engines, the camshaft lobes are mounted directly above the rocker arms. These rocker arms (shown in Figure 2-37) are not adjustable. Some other individual rocker arms have a pivot that extends through the rocker arm. With this type of nonadjustable rocker arm, the pivot is bolted directly against the cylinder head, as illustrated in Figure 2-40.

Push rods are made from steel and have a round tip on each end. One end of the push rod fits into the valve lifter and the other end is located in the rocker arm. Push rods are usually hollow to allow oil to flow from the valve lifter to the rocker arm.

Rocker arms are mounted on a common shaft in some engines, as pictured in Figure 2-41. Shaft-mounted rocker arms are adjustable on some engines.

Valves

Valves are usually made from a steel alloy. For example, the Chrysler turbocharged 2.2L engine has exhaust valves made from a nickel alloy and intake valves made from a silicon alloy. (The features of this engine and the turbocharger are explained in Chapter 6.)

Valves must be designed to open and close many times per minute, and exhaust valves have to withstand temperatures up to 1,000°F (815°C). The incoming air-fuel mixture cools the intake valve;

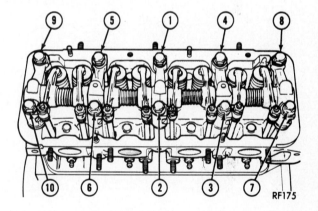

Figure 2-41. Rocker Arms on a Common Shaft. (*Courtesy of Chrysler Canada*)

therefore the intake valve does not encounter such high temperatures.

The valve faces must seat against the valve seats without leaking. If cylinder pressure leaks past the valves on the compression or power strokes, a decrease in engine power results. Most valve faces have an angle of 45° or 30°. Some valves used in heavy-duty applications have sodium-filled valve stems which dissipate heat faster than a conventional steel valve stem and provide longer valve life.

The main valve features are illustrated in Figure 2-42.

The valve guide must position the valve so that it is concentric with the valve seat. Most valve guides are made from hardened cast iron. Valve stem seals prevent excessive amounts of oil from leaking down the valve guide into the combustion chamber.

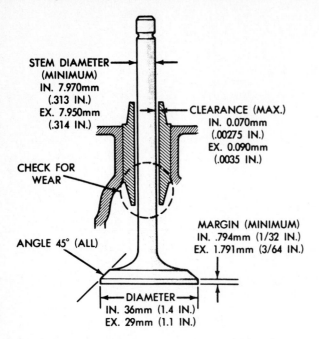

Figure 2-42. Valve Features. (*Courtesy of Chrysler Canada*)

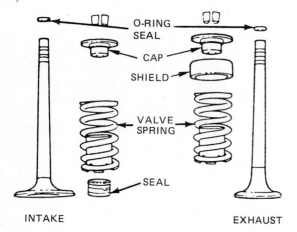

Figure 2-43. Complete Valve Assemblies. (*Courtesy of Chevrolet Motor Division, General Motors Corporation*)

Worn or broken seals result in high oil consumption. If the valve face is misaligned by a worn guide, the face will not seal properly on the seat and rapid valve burning is likely to result.

Two complete valve assemblies are pictured in Figure 2-43.

The tension of the steel valve springs is also important for proper valve seating. Valves and their related assemblies are designed to rotate as they are opened and closed. This rotation helps to prevent burning of the valve faces. Some valves have a small rotator cap on top of the stem to assist valve rotation. Aluminum cylinder heads usually have a steel valve spring seat to prevent the spring from scoring the head surface.

Cylinder Heads

Design

Some cylinder heads are made from cast iron, while many newer engines have lightweight aluminum cylinder heads. This type of cylinder head is used on many modern fuel-efficient engines because weight reduction is one of the most effective methods to improve fuel economy. The lower side of the cylinder head contains the combustion chambers.

An aluminum cylinder head with hemispherical-type combustion chambers is shown in Figure 2-44.

The hemispherical-type combustion chamber has a valve located on each side of the chamber. (Refer to Chapter 5 for other combustion chamber designs.) Threaded spark plug openings are also located in the combustion chambers.

The head surface that fits against the head gasket and engine block must be flat and smoothly machined. The cylinder head illustrated in Figure 2-44 also contains camshaft journal bores, valve lifter bores, and rocker-arm studs. Coolant passages in the head provide cooling for the valves, spark plugs, and

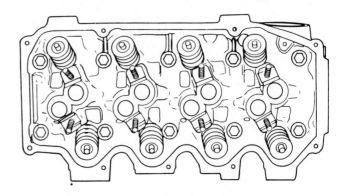

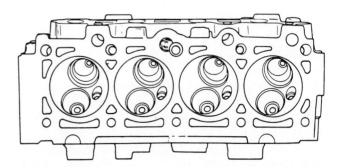

Figure 2-44. Aluminum Cylinder Head with Hemispherical-Type Combustion Chambers. (*Courtesy of Ford Motor Co.*)

combustion chambers. This aluminum head has sintered iron valve-seat inserts and hardened cast iron valve guides. Harder stellite valve seats may be used in some applications.

The exhaust manifold is bolted on one side of the head and the intake manifold is bolted on the other side. A rocker-arm cover seat and attaching bolt holes are located on top of the head, and a gasket seals this cover to the head. The cylinder head is installed on the engine with the rocker arms and valve lifters as shown in Figure 2-45. (Refer to Chapter 5 for valve timing on this engine, and Chapter 6 for intake and exhaust manifold design.)

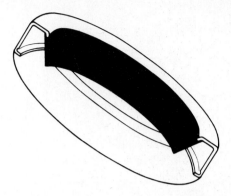

Figure 2-46. Springless Seal. (*Courtesy of Chrysler Canada*)

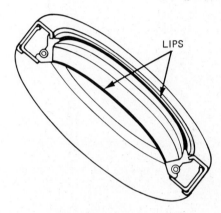

Figure 2-47. Spring-Loaded Seal. (*Courtesy of Chrysler Canada*)

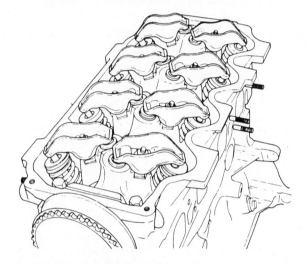

Figure 2-45. Cylinder Head Installed on the Engine. (*Courtesy of Ford Motor Co.*)

Seals

Types and Materials

A molded seal has a steel case on which the seals are built. This case has a surface coating which is rust resistant and acts as a bonding agent with the synthetic rubber seal. Seals have one or more lips to seal liquid in the housing and keep dirt or foreign particles out. The actual seal material is made from a variety of synthetic rubber compounds, such as nitrile, polyacrylate, silicon, and fluoroelastomers such as Viton. Seal material is determined by the application and by the liquids or dirt particles to which the seal will be subjected.

All seals may be divided into two categories: springless and spring-loaded. A spring-loaded seal has a small garter spring behind the lips. A springless seal is shown in Figure 2-46 and a spring-loaded seal is shown in Figure 2-47.

Springless seals are used in front wheel hubs where they seal a heavy-bodied lubricant. In a spring-loaded seal, the garter spring provides additional lip-sealing force and compensates for lip wear, shaft runout, or bore eccentricity.

When a seal must direct oil back into a housing, flutes on the seal provide a pumping action to redirect the oil, as indicated in Figure 2-48.

Some seals, such as transaxle front pump seals, have a sealer painted on the outside diameter to provide sealing between the case and the bore. When a seal is installed, the garter spring must always face toward the fluid flow. Split-rubber seals or rope-type seals may be used in rear main bearings, as pictured in Figure 2-49.

Before a seal is installed, the seal bore in the case and the sealing area of the shaft should be checked for scratches, roughness, or burrs. Minor flaws can be polished out with an oil stone. Always polish the affected area with a motion that is at a right angle to the shaft. A polishing motion that is parallel to the shaft can result in fine parallel scratches that can cause oil to leak past the seal.

If a seal does not have a sealer painted on the case, a small amount of anaerobic sealer such as stud

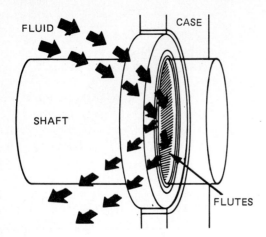

Figure 2-48. Fluted Seal Action. (*Courtesy of Chrysler Canada*)

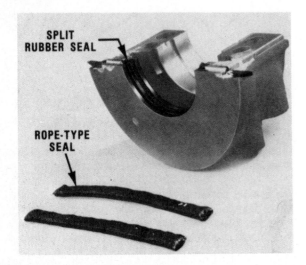

Figure 2-49. Split-Rubber and Rope-Type Seals. (*Courtesy of Chrysler Canada*)

and bearing mount, should be placed on the outside of the seal case. Seal lips should be lubricated before installation and the seal should be installed according to the manufacturer's recommendations.

Gaskets

Types

Gaskets are used to seal minor variations between the flat surfaces. Oil pan gaskets or rocker-arm cover gaskets are usually made from cork, rubber, or a combination of cork and rubber, as shown in Figure 2-50.

Paper gaskets may be used when operating temperatures are relatively low, such as in a timing gear cover. Fibrous gaskets are used where higher heat

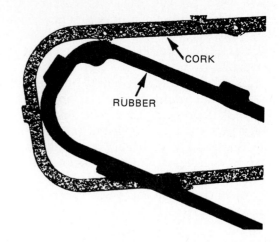

Figure 2-50. Rubber and Cork Gaskets for Oil Pans or Rocker Arm Covers. (*Courtesy of Chrysler Canada*)

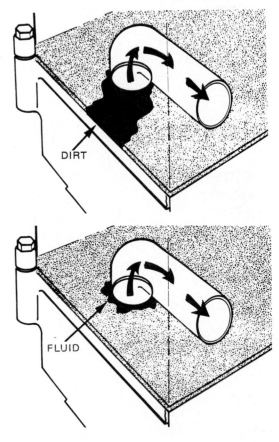

Figure 2-51. Gasket Wicking. (*Courtesy of Chrysler Canada*)

and pressure are present, for example in a thermostat gasket. Gasket wicking occurs when a liquid enters an inside edge of the gasket and travels through the gasket to the outside edge, as illustrated in Figure 2-51.

The moisture on the outside edge of the gasket will collect dirt, but this does not indicate that gasket replacement is necessary; however, if drops of fluid escape, the gasket must be replaced.

Cylinder head gaskets must seal the extreme heat and pressure of the combustion chamber and also seal oil and coolant passages at all temperatures. These gaskets are usually made from fibrous materials sandwiched between metal plating, such as copper or tinplate, as pictured in Figure 2-52.

Some head gaskets do not require retorquing after the engine has been run because the gasket is precompressed during the manufacturing process. A low-friction coating on other head gaskets allows for the expansion of the cylinder head while the engine is warming up. This type of gasket is essential with aluminum cylinder heads.

A compressed asbestos nitrile elastomer facing is glued to both sides of a steel core of some head gaskets. In this type of gasket, a stainless steel flange surrounds each combustion chamber opening, as illustrated in Figure 2-53.

Sealers

Room-Temperature Vulcanizing Sealer

Room-temperature vulcanizing (RTV) sealer dries in the presence of air by absorbing moisture from the air. This type of sealer may be used on oil pans or rocker arm covers in place of a conventional gasket. Before the sealer is installed, all the old material must be removed from the surface area. A chlorinated solvent must be used to clean the surface area where the RTV will be applied. Oil-based solvents leave an oily residue that prevents the RTV from adhering.

The mating surface areas must be straight to provide tight sealing. Apply a bead of RTV that is $\frac{1}{8}$ in. (3.175 mm) in diameter along the center of the surface to be sealed. The RTV must also surround bolt holes, as indicated in Figure 2-54.

Apply the RTV to one mating surface only and assemble the components within five minutes, or the RTV will cure. Never apply excessive amounts of RTV.

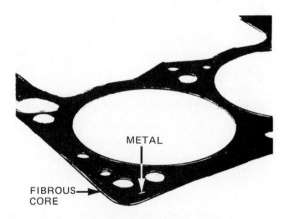

Figure 2-52. Head Gasket with Fibrous Materials and Metal Plating. (*Courtesy of Chrysler Canada*)

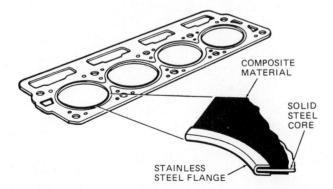

Figure 2-53. Head Gasket with Nitrile Elastomer Facing and Steel Core. (Reference taken from SAE paper No. 820111. *Reprinted with Permission of Society of Automotive Engineers,* © *1982*)

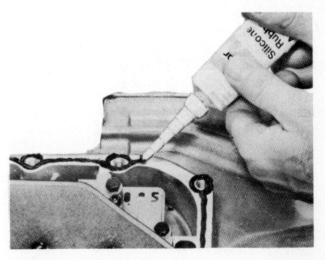

Figure 2-54. Room-Temperature Vulcanizing (RTV) Applications. (*Courtesy of Chrysler Canada*)

Anaerobic Sealer

Rigid machined surfaces with very small clearances between them may be sealed with anaerobic sealer. This type of sealer dries in the absence of air and adds strength to some assemblies because it eliminates movement between parts. The same cleaning procedure is used for both RTV and anaerobic sealers. Apply the anaerobic sealer as shown in Figure 2-55.

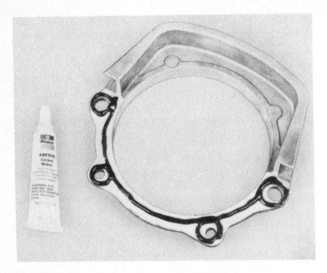

Figure 2-55. Anaerobic Sealer. (*Courtesy of Chrysler Canada*)

The anaerobic sealer should be applied to one mating surface only. Because anaerobic sealer dries in the absence of air, components sealed with this type of sealer do not have to be assembled within a certain time period.

Thread-Locking Compounds

Thread-locking compounds seal threads as well as lock them in place. This type of compound can be used whenever a bolt screw or stud is exposed to a liquid. The threads should be clean before the compound is applied, but oil residue does not need to be removed. Apply just enough locking compound to cover the first half of the threads. After a locking compound has been used, bolts may be removed without thread damage.

(Refer to Chapter 2 in *Automotive Principles: Repair and Service*, Volume II, for engine service.)

Test Questions

1. The vibration damper on the front of the camshaft smooths out _____ vibrations.

2. An overplated copper-lead connecting rod bearing has a higher fatigue strength than a babbitt bearing.   T F

3. The curvature of a connecting rod bearing should be slightly larger than the curvature of the connecting rod or cap.   T F

4. A connecting rod bearing should be slightly shorter than the circumference of the rod or cap bore.   T F

5. Oil is fed into the connecting rod bearing when the crankshaft oil feed hole is sweeping the highest load area in the bearing.   T F

6. Most piston pins are located in the center of the piston.   T F

7. When a cam-ground piston is heated, the pin bosses move outward on the piston pin.   T F

8. In some rear main bearings a _____ _____ is located between the oil slinger and the seal.

9. Embedability refers to the ability of a bearing to absorb _____   _____.

10. The highest load area is in the upper half of a connecting rod bearing.   T F

11. Excessive connecting rod bearing clearance can result in high oil consumption.   T F

12. The second compression ring is often a _____ type ring.

13. Worn or broken valve stem seals may cause excessive oil comsumption.   T F

14. When room-temperature vulcanizing (RTV) sealer is applied, the sealer bead should be $\frac{1}{4}$ in. (6.35 mm) wide.   T F

15. Components sealed with RTV sealer should be assembled within a maximum of:

    a) 5 minutes.

    b) 10 minutes.

    c) 15 minutes.

3

Cooling Systems

Chapter Completion Objectives

1. Identify different types of radiator cores.
2. Understand the effect of a pressure increase on the coolant boiling point.
3. Know the difference between the boiling point of water and the boiling point of a 50 percent ethylene glycol and water solution.
4. Explain the purpose of each cooling system component, such as the thermostat, radiator cap, water pump, radiator, and cooling fan.
5. Describe the advantage of thermal fan clutches and electrically driven cooling fans in relation to belt-driven fans that turn continuously.
6. Explain the operation of a thermal fan clutch.

Radiators

Core Types

The engine coolant flows through the tubes in the radiator core and the cooling fan moves air through the fins surrounding the tubes, which dissipates heat from the engine coolant. Air is also forced through the radiator by the forward motion of the vehicle.

Several different types of radiator cores are used, including the tube type with plate fins, or serpentine fins, and the cellular type as shown in Figure 3-1.

Some automotive radiators have vertical tubes with an inlet tank soldered to the top of the radiator tubes and an outlet tank soldered to the bottom of the tubes, as illustrated in Figure 3-2.

The tubes, fins, and tanks in many radiators are made of a copper and brass compound. Many vehicles have cross-flow radiators in which the tubes are positioned horizontally, as indicated in Figure 3-3.

Some later model radiators have aluminum tubes and fins with plastic tanks. A sealing washer is positioned between the core plates and the tanks,

and the plates are crimped over the edge of the tanks to provide complete sealing, as shown in Figure 3-4.

An adequate cooling system is extremely important to protect the engine components. The size of the radiator is matched to the cubic inch displacement (CID) of the engine so that the radiator will have adequate cooling capacity for the engine. An air conditioned vehicle will usually have a larger radiator because of the extra load on the engine from the air conditioning compressor.

Complete Cooling System

Coolant Flow

Engine coolant is forced from the water pump into the engine block. The coolant flows around the outside of the cylinders to cool the cylinder walls. Coolant continues to flow from the engine block through passages in the head gaskets into the cylinder head. The coolant flow through the cylinder head provides cooling for the valves, combustion chambers, and spark plugs.

Figure 3-1. Types of Radiator Cores. (*Reprinted with Permission of Society of Automotive Engineers,* © *1983*)

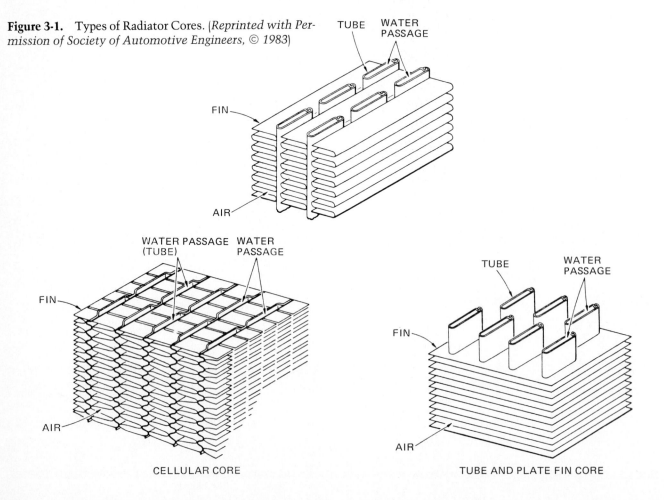

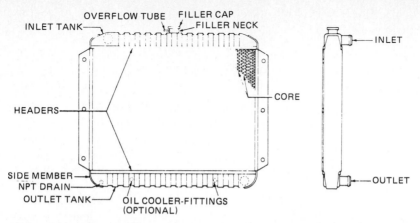

Figure 3-2. Down-Flow Radiator. (*Reprinted with Permission of Society of Automotive Engineers, © 1983*)

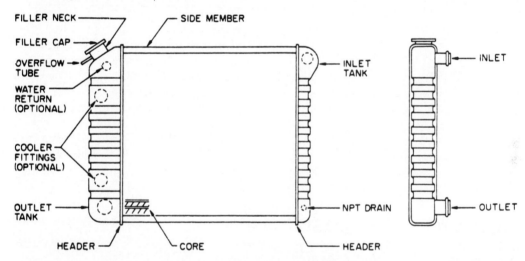

Figure 3-3. Cross-Flow Radiator. (*Reprinted with Permission of Society of Automotive Engineers, © 1983*)

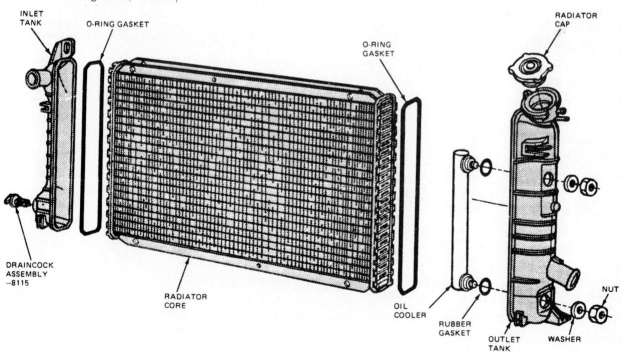

Figure 3-4. Aluminum Radiator Core with Plastic Tanks. (*Courtesy of Ford Motor Co.*)

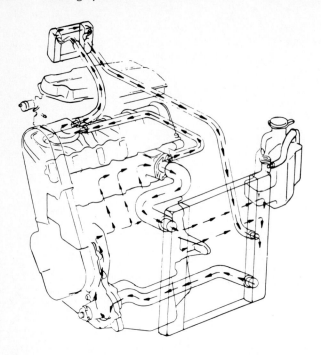

Figure 3-5.   Coolant Flow Chrysler 2.2L Engine. (Reference taken from SAE paper No. 810007. *Reprinted with Permission of Society of Automotive Engineers,* © *1981)*

After flowing through the cylinder head, the coolant flows through the thermostat housing and top radiator hose to the right-hand radiator tank. (Right- or left-hand sides of the car are determined from the driver's seat.) As the coolant flows through the radiator, heat is transferred to the air flowing through the radiator. Coolant returns from the left radiator tank and lower hose to the water pump, as shown in Figure 3-5. A cross-flow radiator is used in this type of cooling system.

When the coolant is cold, the thermostat is closed and the coolant flows through the intake manifold and heater core. Under this condition there is no coolant flow through the radiator. Once the engine reaches normal operating temperature, the thermostat opens and coolant begins to flow through the radiator. When the thermostat is open, coolant continues to flow through the intake manifold passage and the heater core.

Coolant flow at different engine temperatures is illustrated in Figure 3-6.

The coolant flow through the intake manifold provides improved fuel vaporization. The cooling system shown in the previous two diagrams is used

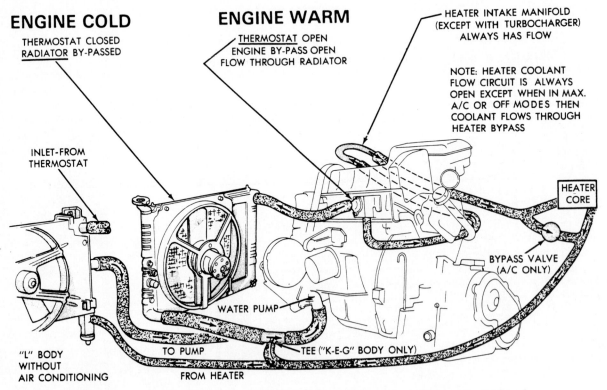

Figure 3-6.   Coolant Flow at Cold or Hot Engine Temperatures. (*Courtesy of Chrysler Canada*)

with a transversely mounted four-cylinder engine in a front-wheel-drive car. (The importance of fuel vaporization is discussed in Chapter 16.)

Pressure Cap and Coolant Recovery Bottle

The pressure cap fits over the radiator filler tube and seals tightly around the edges. A vacuum valve and a pressure, or blowoff, valve are located in the pressure cap, as illustrated in Figure 3-7.

Various pressure ratings are used in radiator caps, but the average cap is designed to maintain 15 psi (103 kPa) in the radiator. For every 1 psi that the radiator pressure is increased, the boiling point of the coolant is raised approximately 3°F (1.6°C). Water boils at 212°F (100°C) at atmospheric pressure and sea level. At higher altitudes, water boils at a lower temperature.

When coolant is pressurized to 15 psi (103 kPa), the pressure valve is forced open against the spring pressure and coolant flows out of the overflow pipe. In most cooling systems this pipe is connected to a coolant recovery bottle into which any coolant escaping from the radiator will flow. (A coolant recovery bottle is shown in Figure 3-5.) On this type of cooling system the radiator is filled completely with coolant and the coolant recovery bottle is filled to the "cold level" indicator line. Coolant should always be added to the coolant recovery bottle if the coolant level is low.

After the engine is shut off, the coolant temperature and pressure gradually decrease. When the cooling system pressure decreases below atmospheric pressure, the vacuum created in the radiator opens the vacuum valve and allows coolant to flow from the coolant recovery bottle into the radiator.

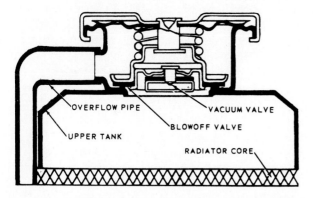

Figure 3-7. Pressure Cap. (*Courtesy of Pontiac Motor Division, General Motors Corporation*)

The pressurized cooling system allows the engine to operate at higher temperatures without boiling the coolant. The amount of heat transfer from the cooling system to the atmosphere depends on the difference between coolant temperature and atmospheric temperature. Therefore, if the engine coolant temperature is higher, the cooling system transfers additional heat to the atmosphere.

Never loosen a pressure radiator cap when the engine is warm. If the coolant pressure is suddenly decreased, severe coolant boiling will occur, which could scald anyone standing near the vehicle. A replacement radiator cap must have the same pressure rating that is stamped on the original cap.

Coolant

A mixture of 50 percent ethylene glycol and water is used in many coolant solutions. Since this mixture freezes at −34°F (−36°C), it provides adequate antifreeze protection in most areas of North America. A lower or higher percentage of ethylene glycol may be used in the coolant depending on the lowest atmospheric temperatures at which the vehicle will be operating.

Ethylene glycol has a higher boiling point than water. A coolant solution of 50 percent ethylene glycol and water boils at 229°F (109°C). With a 15 psi (103 kPa) radiator cap and a coolant solution of 50 percent ethylene glycol the boiling point of the coolant is 274°F (135°C).

Most antifreeze manufacturers supply rust and corrosion inhibitors in the ethylene glycol to help prevent corrosion in the cooling system. When the antifreeze is being replaced in an aluminum radiator, the ethylene glycol antifreeze used must be compatible with aluminum.

Thermostat

The thermostat is located in the engine coolant outlet housing, as shown in Figure 3-8. Some thermostat housings have a special cap. The thermostat may be pulled from the housing once the cap is removed, as illustrated in Figure 3-9.

Most thermostats have a wax-filled pellet connected to the thermostat valve. This pellet must face toward the engine block when the thermostat is installed. When the engine coolant is cold, the thermostat valve is closed. Under this condition a small amount of coolant circulates through the intake

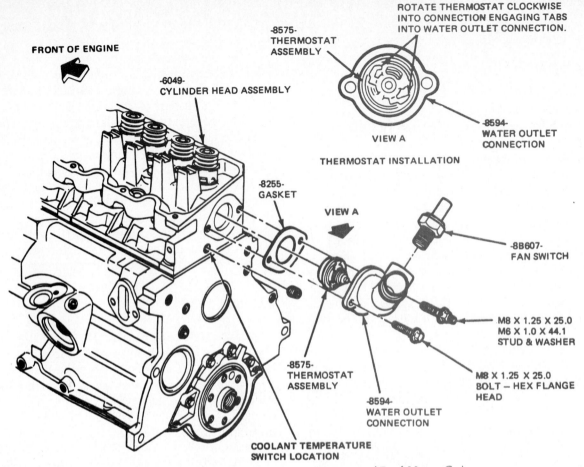

ROTATE THERMOSTAT CLOCKWISE
INTO CONNECTION ENGAGING TABS
INTO WATER OUTLET CONNECTION.

-8575-
THERMOSTAT
ASSEMBLY

VIEW A

THERMOSTAT INSTALLATION

-8594-
WATER OUTLET
CONNECTION

FRONT OF ENGINE

-6049-
CYLINDER HEAD ASSEMBLY

-8255-
GASKET

VIEW A

-8B607-
FAN SWITCH

M8 X 1.25 X 25.0
M6 X 1.0 X 44.1
STUD & WASHER

M8 X 1.25 X 25.0
BOLT – HEX FLANGE
HEAD

-8575-
THERMOSTAT
ASSEMBLY

-8594-
WATER OUTLET
CONNECTION

COOLANT TEMPERATURE
SWITCH LOCATION

Figure 3-8. Thermostat Location. (*Courtesy of Ford Motor Co.*)

1 THERMOSTAT HOUSING CAP

2 THERMOSTAT

3 THERMOSTAT HOUSING ASM.

4 CYLINDER HEAD

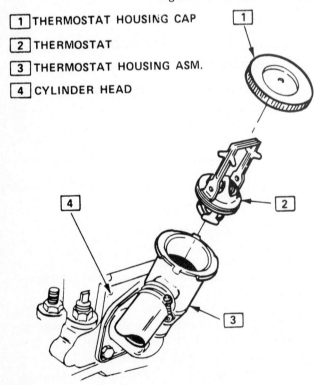

Figure 3-9. Thermostat Housing with Removable Cap. (*Courtesy of Chevrolet Motor Division, General Motors Corporation*)

manifold and heater core to the engine block, as indicated in Figure 3-5. When the thermostat valve is closed, the coolant temperature increases rapidly. Most thermostats are rated to open at 180°F (82°C) or 195°F (90.5°C).

When the coolant temperature reaches the rating of the thermostat, the wax pellet expands and begins to open the valve, which allows coolant to flow through the top radiator hose to the radiator. The thermostat maintains the coolant temperature near the rated temperature of the thermostat. If the engine coolant temperature increases slightly because a heavy load is placed on the engine, the wax pellet provides increased valve opening, and therefore more coolant flows through the radiator to decrease the coolant temperature. If coolant temperature decreases because colder air begins flowing through the radiator, the thermostat closes partially to maintain the coolant temperature.

A thermostat is illustrated in Figure 3-10.

Water Pump

A vaned impeller is pressed on the inner end of the water pump shaft, and a hub is pressed on the outer end of the shaft. The pulley and fan blade assembly is bolted to the water pump hub on many cooling systems. A bearing is mounted between the shaft and the housing, and a seal on the shaft behind the impeller prevents coolant from entering the bearing, as shown in Figure 3-11.

The water pump shaft is driven by a belt which surrounds the crankshaft and water pump pulleys. The rotating impeller vanes create water pressure at the pump outlet, which forces the coolant through the cooling system.

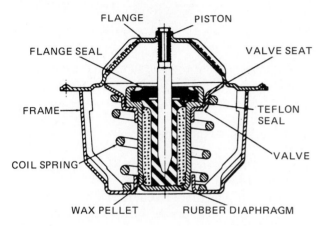

Figure 3-10. Thermostat. (*Courtesy of Chevrolet Motor Division, General Motors Corporation*)

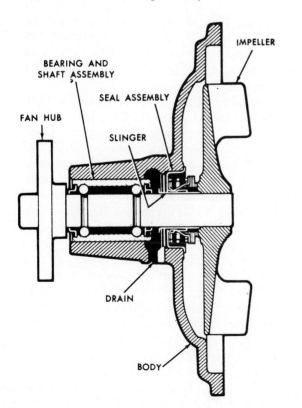

Figure 3-11. Water Pump. (*Courtesy of Pontiac Motor Division, General Motors Corporation*)

Cooling Fans

Belt-Driven Fans

Some fan blades are bolted directly to the water pump hub with the pulley, as indicated in Figure 3-12. The fan blades are curved so that they pull air through the radiator as they rotate. This type of fan is rotated continuously, regardless of engine cooling requirements.

While the engine is warming up, the cooling fan is not required to move air through the radiator. If the vehicle is operating at normal cruising speed on a cool day, the forward motion of the vehicle provides enough airflow through the radiator to provide adequate cooling without the action of the cooling fan. Since a certain amount of engine power is required to turn the fan, some energy is wasted by rotating the fan when it is not required.

Some fan assemblies have flexible blades that straighten out as engine speed increases. This type of fan provides adequate cooling at low speeds and reduces the power required to rotate the fan at higher speeds.

Each fan blade makes a certain amount of noise as it cuts through the air. Most fan assemblies have unequally spaced blades so that the sound of the blades does not accumulate to an excessive noise level.

Thermal-Control Fan Drive

Many vehicles are equipped with a thermal-control fan drive which is bolted between the fan blades and

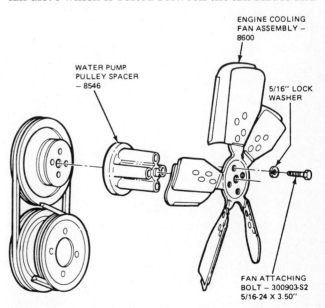

Figure 3-12. Cooling Fan. (*Courtesy of Ford Motor Co.*)

the water pump hub. The thermal control increases the fan speed and provides additional airflow through the radiator when cooling requirements are high, such as during prolonged idle and low-speed conditions or when the engine is operating under heavy load.

A thermal-control fan drive is shown in Figure 3-13.

The thermal control contains a silicon oil. When additional airflow through the radiator is required to provide adequate cooling, the bimetallic coil unwinds because of the increased underhood temperature. The movement of the bimetallic spring moves a control piston outward, which forces more oil into the fluid coupling and therefore drives the clutch plate against the surface of the thermal control housing. When this occurs the hub and the thermal control housing must rotate together. Since the thermal control hub is bolted to the water pump hub and the fan assembly is bolted to the thermal control housing, the water pump hub now rotates the fan blades.

When engine cooling requirements are low, the bimetallic spring winds up because of reduced underhood temperature. Under this condition the control piston moves upward and some oil flows out of the fluid coupling into the reservoir. This action allows the clutch plate to move away from the thermal control housing. Since the hub of the thermal control unit is not connected directly to the thermal control housing, the fan blade speed decreases.

The thermal-control fan drive saves engine power because it only rotates the fan blades at high speed when cooling requirements are high. The internal design of the thermal control is illustrated in Figure 3-14.

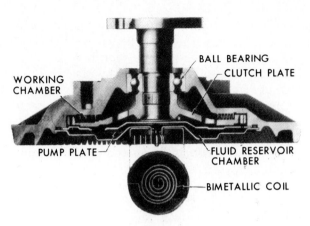

Figure 3-14. Internal Design of Thermal-Control Fan Drive. (*Courtesy of Buick Motor Division, General Motors Corporation*)

Electrically Driven Cooling Fan

Many vehicles have cooling fans which are driven by an electric motor, as shown in Figure 3-15.

Many electrically driven fans have unequally spaced fan blades to provide quieter operation, as illustrated in Figure 3-16.

On some vehicles a shroud is placed around the fan blades, which allows the fan to move additional air through the radiator. Voltage is supplied to the fan motor through a set of relay contacts, and the relay winding is grounded through a temperature switch in the cooling system, as indicated in Figure 3-17.

When the engine coolant reaches 220°F (104°C), the coolant switch contacts close and complete the circuit from the relay winding to ground. Under this condition the relay coil magnetism closes the relay contacts and supplies voltage to the fan motor. The condenser switch also grounds the relay winding if the pressure in the air conditioner system exceeds 270 psi (1,863 kPa). This causes the relay contacts to supply voltage to the fan motor when the coolant temperature is below 220°F (104°C).

The electrically driven fan only runs when additional cooling is required. Therefore, this type of fan uses less engine power than a belt-driven fan that rotates continuously. Since less engine power is used to drive the cooling fan, fuel economy and performance is improved. Many fuel-efficient front-wheel-drive cars have electric cooling fans.

Some electric cooling fan circuits are designed to supply voltage to the fan motor for a short time after a hot engine is shut off. In this circuit a solid-state timer is built into the fan relay, as shown in Figure 3-18.

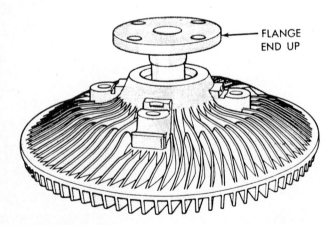

Figure 3-13. Thermal-Control Fan Drive. (*Courtesy of Chrysler Canada*)

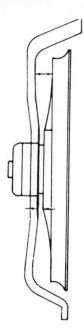

Figure 3-15. Electrically Driven Cooling Fan. (Reference taken from SAE paper No. 790722. *Reprinted with Permission of Society of Automotive Engineers,* © *1979)*

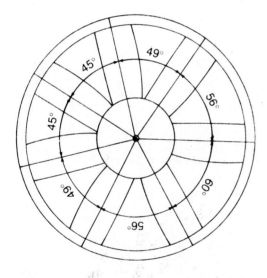

Figure 3-16. Fan Blade Electrically Driven Fan. (Reference taken from SAE paper No. 790722. *Reprinted with Permission of Society of Automotive Engineers,* © *1979)*

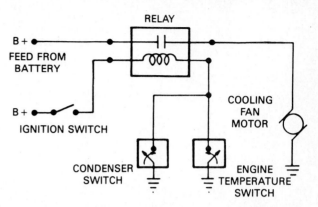

Figure 3-17. Electric Cooling Fan Circuit. (Reference taken from SAE paper No. 790722. *Reprinted with Permission of Society of Automotive Engineers,* © *1979)*

This system has a radiator fan switch mounted in one of the radiator tanks, and a radiator air sensor mounted near the fan motor. If the engine coolant becomes hot while the engine is running, the radiator fan switch closes and current flows through the switch and timer relay winding to ground. When this occurs, the coil magnetism closes the timer relay contacts and current flows from the alternator battery terminal through the relay contacts and fan mo-

tor to ground. The fan motor continues to run until the coolant temperature decreases and the radiator fan switch opens.

If the radiator fan switch is open, the timer relay is energized by the circuit from the air conditioning clutch thermal switch if the air conditioner is operating. The two diodes in the timer relay prevent any flow of current between the radiator fan switch circuit and the air conditioning clutch thermal switch circuit.

If the air temperature surrounding the radiator air sensor becomes hot, the air sensor contacts close. When the engine is running, the radiator air sensor and the timer are ineffective because the air sensor circuit is connected to the alternator diode trio terminal. This terminal and the alternator battery terminal supply equal voltage to both sides of the timer while the engine is running, which makes the timer ineffective.

When the engine is stopped and the air sensor contacts are open, battery voltage is supplied from the alternator battery terminal to the timer and the relay winding. Under this condition the timer also supplies battery voltage to the other end of the relay winding, which prevents any current flow through the winding.

If the engine is stopped and the air temperature around the fan motor is hot, the air sensor contacts close and the timer is grounded through the air sensor contacts and the alternator field circuit. This signals the timer to remove the battery voltage from the other end of the relay winding, so that current flows from the alternator battery terminal through the timer relay winding to ground. When this occurs the relay contacts close and supply current to the fan motor.

When the air temperature around the fan motor decreases, the air sensor contacts open and the timer

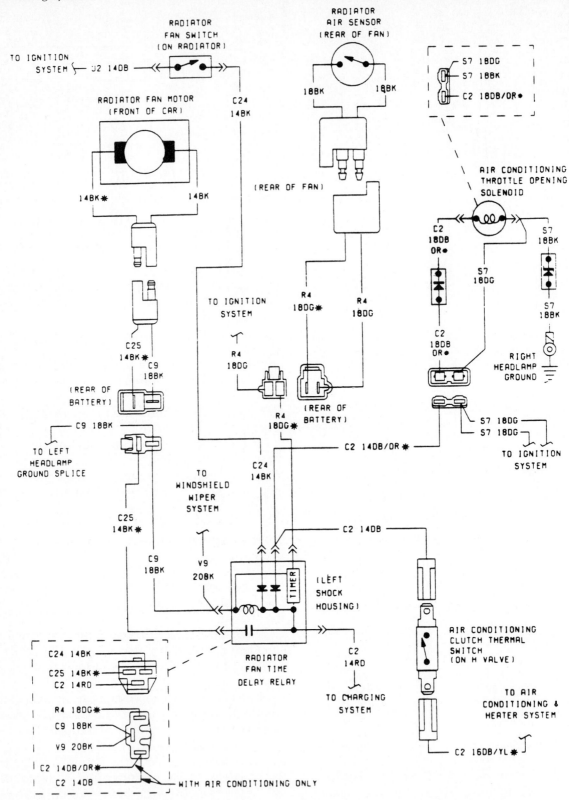

Figure 3-18. Electric Cooling Fan Circuit with Timer. (*Courtesy of Chrysler Canada*)

supplies battery voltage to the other end of the relay winding. This stops the current flow through the relay winding, so that the relay contacts open and shut off the fan motor. If the air sensor contacts are still closed after five to ten minutes of cooling fan operation with the engine not running, the timer shuts off the fan motor to prevent the battery from becoming discharged.

If the cooling fan does not run immediately when the engine is shut off, the air temperature around the fan motor may increase and close the air sensor contacts, which causes the cooling fan motor to start running. Therefore, the cooling fan may start unexpectedly on this type of circuit, so the service technician must always keep his or her fingers away from the fan blades when working under the hood.

On many late-model vehicles the electric cooling fan is operated by the computer. This type of electric cooling fan circuit is described with the complete computer systems in Chapter 17 and 18.

Transmission Coolers

On vehicles equipped with automatic transmissions, a transmission oil cooler is located in the outlet radiator tank. The transmission fluid is circulated through the oil cooler, and heat is dissipated from the fluid as the engine coolant circulates around the cooler. A transmission oil cooler located in the radiator is shown in Figure 3-19.

On vehicles equipped for heavy-duty service, such as trailer hauling, an external transmission oil cooler may be used to provide additional cooling. In most installations the external cooler is connected

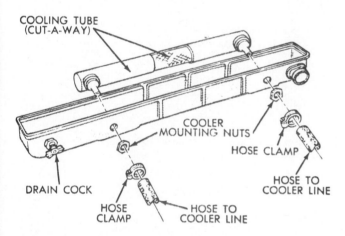

Figure 3-19. Transmission Oil Cooler Located in the Radiator. (*Courtesy of Chrysler Canada*)

in series with the transmission oil cooler in the radiator. The external transmission cooler and related tubing are illustrated in Figure 3-20.

Engine-Temperature Warning Light

Operation

Some engine-temperature warning lights are connected to the oil pressure switch and the water temperature switch, as shown in Figure 3-21.

When the ignition switch is turned on, current flows through the warning light and the oil-pressure switch contacts to ground. If the engine is started, the oil pressure opens the switch contacts and the warning light goes out. When the engine coolant temperature reaches approximately 235°F (113°C), the bimetallic strip in the water temperature switch moves over and completes the circuit from the "H" terminal in the switch to ground. This illuminates the engine warning light to inform the driver that the coolant temperature is approaching the boiling point.

(Refer to Chapter 3 in *Automotive Principles: Repair and Service*, Volume II, for lubrication system and cooling system service.)

Test Questions

1. When the radiator pressure is increased 1 psi (6.9 kPa), the boiling point of the coolant is raised _____ degrees F.

2. A mixture of 50 percent ethylene glycol and water has a higher boiling point than pure water.   T F

3. The thermal-control fan drive increases fan speed when the air temperature around the thermal control reaches _____ degrees.

4. The electrically driven cooling fan operates when the coolant temperature is 150°F and the air conditioner is off.   T F

5. Unequally spaced blades provide _____ operation.

6. On an electrically driven fan circuit with a timer relay, the fan motor may start a few minutes after the engine is shut off.   T F

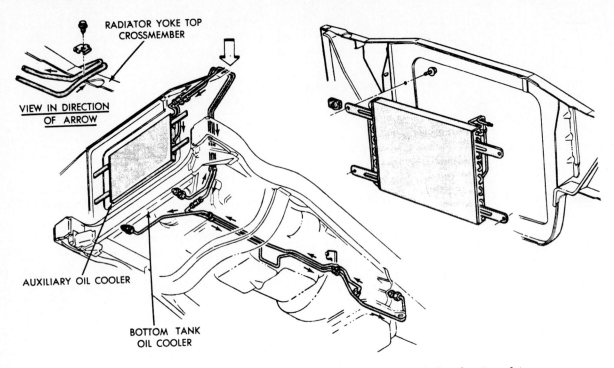

Figure 3-20.   External Transmission Oil Cooler. (*Courtesy of Chrysler Canada*)

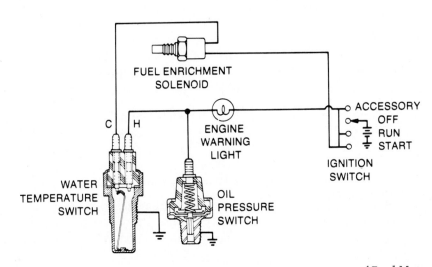

Figure 3-21.   Engine-Temperature Warning Light Circuit. (*Courtesy of Ford Motor Co.*)

4

Engine Lubrication Systems

Chapter Completion Objectives

1. Explain the purposes of engine oil.
2. Describe the functions of seven oil additives.
3. Demonstrate an understanding of oil ratings.
4. List the oil classifications for gasoline and diesel engines and the type of engine service that is suitable for each.
5. Explain the advantages of synthetic oil.
6. Describe how the engine oil flows through the lubrication system to each of the following engine components:

a) Main bearings.
b) Connecting-rod bearings.
c) Cylinder walls and pistons.
d) Camshaft bearings.
e) Rocker arms.
f) Camshaft lobes.
g) Valve lifters.
h) Timing chain and gears.

Engine Oil Purposes

Lubrication

A very important purpose of engine oil is to lubricate engine parts to reduce friction and wear. Friction may be defined as the resistance to movement of two bodies in contact with each other. For example, a certain amount of energy is required to pull a steel bar across the top of a metal bench because of the friction between the two components caused by surface irregularities catching against each other. If the steel bar and the top of the metal bench are machined to extreme smoothness, the friction is reduced. When a second steel bar is placed on top of the original bar, the additional weight increases the friction.

As the steel bar is pulled across the metal bench and the surface irregularities catch on each other, metal particles are torn off, and the surfaces in contact with each other soon will be pitted and scratched. Considerable amounts of heat could also build up between the two surfaces and cause momentary melting and welding of the two metal components, which further increases the friction. As the relative movement continues to occur, the welded spots break and pull large pieces of metal out of the steel bar or bench surface, which causes a further increase in friction.

If a film of oil is placed between the steel bar and the bench surface, a wedge-shaped oil film will form between the two surfaces as the bar is pulled across the bench. This oil film will be thicker at the leading edge of the steel bar, as illustrated in Figure 4-1.

The wedge-shaped oil film that occurs between two moving surfaces is referred to as hydrodynamic lubrication. Hydro refers to liquids, as in hydraulics, and dynamic refers to motion. For any specific bar weight and speed of motion, there is an oil thickness which requires the least amount of effort to move the bar. The force required to pull the bar divided by the bar weight is known as the coefficient of friction. If the oil film becomes too thin, surface high points touch and increase the coefficient of friction; this is called boundary lubrication. If a thicker oil is used, the coefficient of friction is also increased. Therefore, the thickness of an engine oil is extremely important to prevent boundary lubrication and provide a low coefficient of friction.

The thickness of an oil is referred to as its viscosity. Another definition for viscosity is the tendency of an oil to resist flowing. As the steel bar is pulled across the metal bench on a film of oil, a certain amount of friction, or resistance to movement,

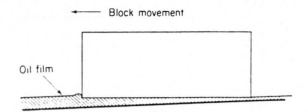

Figure 4-1. Hydrodynamic Oil Film.

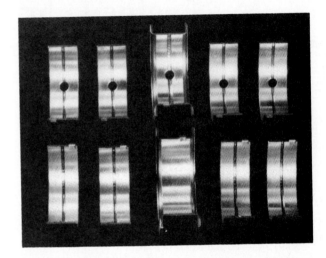

Figure 4-2. Main Bearing Shells. (Reference taken from SAE paper No. 810007. *Reprinted with Permission of Society of Automotive Engineers,* © 1981)

occurs between the layers of oil. This is referred to as viscous friction. As an oil becomes colder, its viscosity increases which creates more viscous friction.

Some examples of flat-surface lubrication in a gasoline engine would be thrust bearings, valve tips, and valve-lifter bases. The same hydrodynamic lubrication principles apply to the curved bearing surfaces in an engine, such as a crankshaft main bearing. A set of main bearing shells is illustrated in Figure 4-2.

Oil is supplied from the engine oil system through the hole in the upper half of the bearing shell. A groove in the bearing shell retains some oil in the bearing when the engine is stopped. The groove also assists in spreading a film of oil across the bearing surface when the engine is running. A locking lip on each half of the bearing shell prevents rotation of the shells. When the crankshaft is not turning, the load is straight down and the oil is squeezed out from between the shaft and the bearing, as shown in Figure 4-3.

When the crankshaft begins to rotate and oil is supplied to the bearing, oil layers wedge between the shaft and the bearing, which lifts the shaft off the bearing. The crankshaft tries to "climb" the right

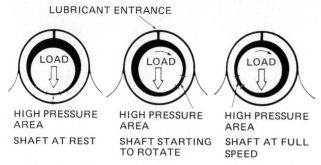

LUBRICANT ENTRANCE

HIGH PRESSURE AREA
SHAFT AT REST

HIGH PRESSURE AREA
SHAFT STARTING TO ROTATE

HIGH PRESSURE AREA
SHAFT AT FULL SPEED

Figure 4-3. Main Bearing Lubrication.

side of the bearing because of the frictional effect of the oil layers. If the crankshaft speed increases, the wedging action of the oil also increases, which transfers the maximum pressure around the bearing to the left, as indicated in Figure 4-3.

Some oil will leak from the sides of the bearing, which flushes out contaminants and helps cool the bearing. Oil is also fed from the main bearings to the connecting-rod bearings. (The complete lubrication system will be discussed later in the chapter.)

The lubrication system must supply a continuous flow of oil to all the engine bearings and lubricated surfaces to maintain the hydrodynamic oil film of each component and minimize wear. The correct oil viscosity is also essential to reduce friction.

Cooling

The oil carries heat away from each bearing or component that is lubricated. When the oil is returned to the oil pan, some of the heat is dissipated from the oil by air surrounding the crankcase. Engines that are designed for heavy-duty applications, such as those in trucks, usually have oil pans that hold a larger supply of oil to provide more heat dissipation. Some diesel engines use external oil coolers to assist in oil cooling.

Cylinder walls, pistons, and piston rings may operate at temperatures of several hundred degrees Fahrenheit. The engine oil in contact with these surfaces may break down or burn to some extent and produce carbon. It is important that the oil temperature be kept below the flash point of the oil, which is the temperature at which the oil will ignite and burn. An engine oil must have a high heat-resistance so that carbon formation is kept to a minimum.

Cleaning

The engine oil has a cleaning effect on all the engine components that it contacts. Carbon formations are cleaned from the pistons and rings by engine oil. Ex-

cessive carbon deposits can cause the piston rings to seize in their grooves, which results in excessive leakage of gases past the rings on the compression and power strokes. This excessive leakage in an engine is called blow-by. When blow-by becomes extreme, engine performance and fuel economy are reduced.

The engine oil also cleans other engine components, such as valve stems, valve lifters, rocker arms, and camshafts. Additives in the engine oil help the oil to perform its cleaning operation. (Oil additives will be explained later in the chapter.) Carbon particles will be removed from the oil by the oil filter.

Sealing

The engine oil helps the piston rings to form a tight seal between the rings and cylinder walls. Microscopic irregularities in the piston rings or cylinder walls are filled by the oil film, which prevents the escape of combustion chamber gases. The engine oil clings to the metal surfaces and resists the tendency of combustion chamber gases to blow by the piston rings. The oil film also provides lubrication between the rings and the piston ring grooves to allow free movement of the rings and therefore continuous contact between the rings and cylinder walls.

Oil Additives

Pour-point Depressants

The pour point of an oil is the lowest temperature at which the oil will pour or remain fluid. At extremely low temperatures, some oils become so thick that they will not pour at all. When this happens, excessive wear will occur on bearings, piston rings and cylinders during initial operation after the engine is started in cold weather.

Certain additives are used in many engine oils to depress or lower the pour point. These additives tend to reduce engine wear in cold-weather operation.

Oxidation Inhibitors

A considerable amount of oil agitation occurs in the oil pan because of the rotation of the crankshaft and connecting rods. When high-temperature oil is agitated, oxygen in the air combines with the oil and oxidizes some of the oil into a sticky, tarlike substance and other corrosive compounds. The tarlike substance can clog oil passages, which may cause some components to operate without proper lubrication.

Bearings may be eroded prematurely by the corrosive compounds. Therefore, oil oxidation is undesirable. Oxidation inhibitors are added to engine oils to assist the oil in resisting oxidation.

Corrosion and Rust Inhibitors

Moisture may form on engine parts because of the extreme temperature changes encountered in colder climates. Rust inhibitors are added to the oil to disperse the water from the metal surfaces and allow an oil film to form on the surfaces.

Small amounts of acid formed from the combustion process can cause corrosion of engine bearings. For example, sulphuric acid may be formed in very small quantities because of the sulphur content in gasoline. Corrosion inhibitors help to neutralize acids that get past the piston rings and collect in the oil.

Extreme Pressure Resistance

The oil pump delivers oil to the engine lubrication system at 30 to 60 psi (207 to 414 kPa) in many engines. However, the wedge-shaped oil film in engine bearings may be subjected to pressures up to 1,000 psi (6,900 kPa) when the engine is operating under heavy load. Extreme pressure additives prevent the oil from being squeezed out of the bearing surfaces when high pressures are encountered.

Detergents and Dispersants

Since carbon is a byproduct of the combustion process, carbon formation occurs in the combustion chamber and around the piston ring grooves. Oxidation of the oil may result in thick, tarlike deposits in the oil or on engine parts. Detergents in the oil slow down the formation of these deposits. The detergent loosens the deposits of carbon or tarlike material and carries them to the crankcase. Smaller particles are removed from the oil by the oil filter. Heavier particles drop to the bottom of the crankcase and are removed when the oil is changed.

A dispersant added to the oil keeps the carbon particles in the oil separated. Without the dispersant, carbon particles would clot together in the oil and form large particles, which could plug the oil filter and reduce its effectiveness. These large parti-

cles could also restrict oil passages, which could damage engine components due to insufficient lubrication.

Anti-foaming Additives

The rotating action of the crankshaft and connecting rods may cause the oil in the crankcase to foam. Excessive foaming of the oil destroys the normal hydrodynamic oil film on bearing surfaces and other engine parts. Oil foaming can also cause noisy valve lifters. Engine parts wear prematurely when oil foaming causes inadequate lubrication of the bearing surfaces and other components. Anti-foaming additives prevent excessive oil foaming.

Oil foaming can result from overfilling the oil pan. Therefore, it is very important that the oil level be at the specified mark on the dipstick.

Friction Modifiers

Some refiners add friction modifiers to their engine oil to reduce the friction between the layers of oil in the hydrodynamic oil film on bearings or other surfaces. Oil manufacturers claim that fuel economy is improved when friction modifiers are used in the engine oil.

Oil Ratings

Viscosity Rating

For many years, organizations such as the Society of Automotive Engineers (SAE), the American Petroleum Institute (API), and the American Society for Testing and Materials (ASTM) have worked together on standardizing oil ratings and oil classifications. The first oil classifications were developed by SAE in 1911. Since engines, fuels, and engine load conditions are changing continually, the work of these organizations in rating and classifying engine oils is ongoing.

It is extremely important to have an oil with the correct viscosity for the engine in which it is used. The atmospheric temperature in which the engine will be operating also changes the oil viscosity requirements. Engine oils with low viscosities are thinner and flow easily, while high-viscosity oils are thicker and do not flow as easily. The engine oil must have a viscosity that is low enough to allow the oil to flow into the small clearances between the engine bearings and the crankshaft journals, even in extremely cold temperatures.

If the oil viscosity is too high, the bearings could be damaged by lack of lubrication immediately after a cold engine is started. When heavy engine loads and high temperatures are encountered, a low-viscosity oil may be squeezed out of the engine bearings until the oil film becomes too thin. This could allow the metal surfaces of the bearings and crankshaft journals to contact each other, which could cause severe damage to the bearing and crankshaft. Therefore, a standard method of rating and classifying engine oils is absolutely essential so that engine manufacturers can recommend the right type of oil for their engines in relation to atmospheric temperatures.

Engine oils are rated by SAE as winter oils or as oils designed for use in other conditions. Pumpability and crankability are the two most important considerations in low-temperature oil performance. Pumpability refers to the ease with which an oil can be pumped through the lubrication system. Crankability is related to the friction that the oil creates, which increases the power required to crank the engine.

A cold-cranking simulator (CCS) is used in the standard test procedures for cold oil performance. These tests are conducted at 0°F (−18°C). The power required to turn the CCS is reported in centipoise or poise. A mini-rotary viscometer may also be used to test cold oil performance.

Prior to 1980, SAE established the J300 performance tests, which included the viscosity ratings of 5W, 10W, 15W, 20W oil. The "W" designates a winter oil. Since September of 1980, SAE has established new W ratings for engine oils, as shown in Table 4-1.

In the new rating system, each grade of oil has a slightly higher viscosity compared to the oils in the previous rating system. This was done to overcome some concerns about engine wear and oil-consumption problems with 5W oil. This rating system establishes uniform standards of cold oil performance, so that any oil with the same "W" rating will have the same pumpability and crankability.

A viscometer is used to test oils that are rated for other-than-winter conditions. These tests are conducted at 212°F (100°C). Several types of viscometers have been used for these tests, including the Saybolt viscometer and the kinematic viscometer. When a viscometer is used, the time is measured for a given amount of oil to flow through a specific size of orifice. These tests indicate the viscosity of an oil at normal operating engine temperature. The oil ratings in this group are SAE 20, SAE 30, and SAE 40. Prior to 1980, an SAE 50 rating was also included in this group. An oil with an SAE 20 rating will have a lower viscosity than an oil with an SAE 30 designation.

All the oils we have mentioned are single-grade oils; however, most oils now have a multiple viscosity rating, such as SAE 10W30. This type of oil would have the same viscosity as an SAE 10W oil at low temperature, and the same viscosity of an SAE 30 oil at high temperature.

Viscosity Index

When oil temperature decreases, oil viscosity increases. Some oils show a large change in viscosity in relation to temperature, while other oils experience a smaller viscosity change as a result of variations in temperature.

A viscosity index (VI) scale has been developed to provide an accurate indication of an oil's viscosity change in relation to temperature variations. If an

TABLE 4-1. Winter Oil Viscosity Ratings. *(Reprinted with permission of Society of Automotive Engineers, © 1981)*

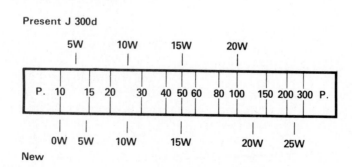

Engine cranking

Max. CCS viscosity at −18°C, poise

oil has a high VI rating, it has less tendency to change viscosity in relation to temperature variations. For example, an oil with a VI rating of 200 would not change viscosity as much in relation to temperature changes as an oil with a VI rating of 55. Multiple-viscosity oils have higher VI ratings than single-grade oils.

Oil Classifications

Gasoline Engines

The American Petroleum Institute (API) has been largely responsible for the classification of engine oils in relation to engine service requirements. A great deal of testing has been done to arrive at the various oil classifications. Some of the tests used in classifying engine oils are as follows:

1. Low-temperature rust test.
2. Low-temperature engine deposits.
3. High-temperature oxidation resistance.
4. High-temperature deposits and sludge.
5. Engine scuffing and wear.
6. Engine cleanliness.
7. Bearing corrosion.

The classifications for engine oils that are primarily intended for gasoline engines are listed in Table 4-2. The oil classifications in Table 4-3 are primarily for diesel engines.

TABLE 4-2. **Oil Classifications Gasoline Engines.**

Letter Designation	Service Description	Oil Description
SA	Utility service	Straight mineral oil
SB	Minimum-duty service	Inhibited oil
SC	1964 engine warranty service	1964 motor severe (MS) automobile manufacturer's warranty requirements
SD	1968 engine warranty service	1968 motor severe (MS) automobile manufacturer's warranty requirements
SE	1972 engine warranty service	Improved oxidation inhibitors
SF	1980 engine warranty service	Improved oxidation resistance and anti-wear properties

TABLE 4-3. **Oil Classifications Diesel Engines.**

Letter Designation	Service Description	Oil Description
CA	Light-duty diesel engine service	Meets U.S. military specifications MIL-L-210-4A
CB	Moderate-duty diesel engine service	Meets U.S. military specifications MIL-L-210A Supplement 1
CC	Moderate-duty diesel and gasoline engine service	Meets U.S. military specifications MIL-210-4B
CD	Severe-duty diesel engine service	Meets U.S. specifications MIL-L-45199 and series 3 Caterpillar Tractor specifications

The classification and viscosity of oil recommended by the engine manufacturer must always be used. A typical oil viscosity chart for a moderate-duty diesel engine is shown in Table 4-4.

TABLE 4-4. **Oil Classification Chart.** (*Courtesy of General Motors Corporation*)

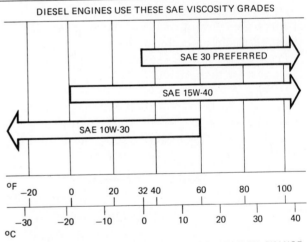

Synthetic Oil

Most synthetic oils are made from a petroleum or crude-oil base stock. The content of the crude-oil base stock in synthetic oils may vary from 10 to 100 percent.

The differences between most conventional oils and synthetic oils are in the refining process and the additives that are used. When conventional oils are refined, the molecular structure of the crude oil is not changed. However, in the synthetic oil refining process, smaller molecules from the crude oil are combined with molecules from other sources to make the large molecules of the synthetic oil. Oil additives are then blended with a synthetic stock, and the synthetic oils usually have more additives than conventional oils.

Classifications for synthetic oils have not been developed at the present time. Additional energy is used in the preparation of synthetic oils; therefore these oils are much more expensive. Some of the advantages claimed by synthetic oil manufacturers are as follows:

1. Increased oil change intervals of up to 50,000 miles (80,000 km).
2. Reduced wear on engine parts.
3. Increased fuel economy because synthetic oil has less friction.
4. Improved high-temperature protection of engine parts.
5. Easier cold-weather starting because of reduced friction.

Most car manufacturers have not accepted the performance claims of synthetic oil manufacturers. Some car manufacturers allow the use of synthetic oils in their engines, but they demand that the synthetic oil be changed at the same intervals recommended for conventional oils.

Rerefined Oil

Rerefined oil is used engine oil that has been recycled. Engine oils made from recycled base stock can be equivalent in performance to those made from virgin petroleum base stock, provided proper quality control is given to the used oil's base stock and the processing procedure. The use of rerefined oil reduces pollution from the careless disposal of used oil.

Oil for Alternate Fuels

Some oil refiners produce an oil that is specially formulated for propane or natural-gas fueled engines. These oils have a reduced detergent and dispersant additive content because propane and natural gas have less carbon content than gasoline. When these fuels are used, the carbon deposits on pistons and piston rings are reduced and an oil with less detergent and dispersant additives can be used. If other alternate fuels, such as methanol or hydrogen, are used in a large number of cars, oils will have to be developed that will be more compatible with these fuels.

Oil Requirements of the Future

As new engines and engine materials are developed and alternate fuels are used, engine oil requirements will continue to change. Some of the oil requirements and developments foreseen for the future are as follows:

1. Energy conservation properties for both gasoline and diesel engine oils through friction modifiers or other additives.
2. Lower phosphorus content to protect the exhaust emission catalyst.
3. The use of new 5W oils for improved cold starting and energy conservation.
4. Extended oil drain performance.
5. Light-duty diesel performance.
6. New high-temperature viscosity evaluation methods.
7. The use of rerefined and synthetic oils.
8. Compatibility with engine seal materials and other new materials used in engine parts.
9. Compatibility with alternate fuels.

Lubrication Systems

Lubrication System for Four-Cylinder Engine

The distributor gear is in mesh with a gear on the camshaft, and a short drive shaft is connected between the distributor shaft and the oil pump, as shown in Figure 4-4.

A pickup assembly is mounted near the bottom of the crankcase, where it is submerged in the oil supply at all times. The pickup assembly is connected to the inlet opening in the oil pump, and a screen in the pickup prevents coarse particles from entering the pump.

As the pump rotates, a vacuum is created at the inlet and a high pressure is created at the outlet. The vacuum at the pump inlet moves oil from the crankcase into the pump. Oil is forced from the pump outlet through the oil filter into the main oil gallery in the engine block, as illustrated in Figure 4-5.

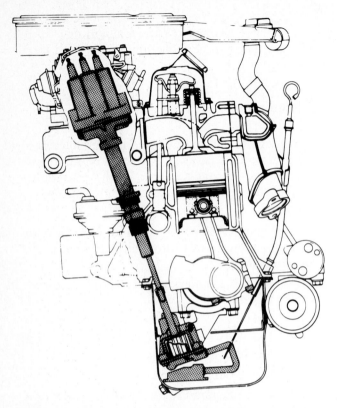

Figure 4-4. Distributor and Oil Pump Drive. (Reference taken from SAE paper No. 820111. *Reprinted with Permission of Society of Automotive Engineers*, © 1982)

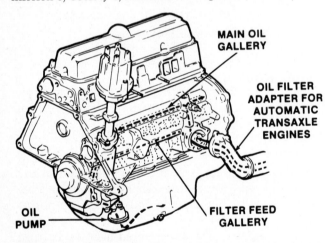

Figure 4-5. Main Oil Gallery. (Reference taken from SAE paper No. 820111. *Reprinted with Permission of Society of Automotive Engineers*, © 1982)

Oil is forced from the main oil gallery to each camshaft bearing and crankshaft main bearing. The valve lifters are also lubricated directly from the main oil gallery. A hole is drilled in the center of the cup located in the top of each valve lifter. Oil flows out of the hole in the valve-lifter cups and up through the hollow push rods to the rocker arms, as indicated in Figure 4-6.

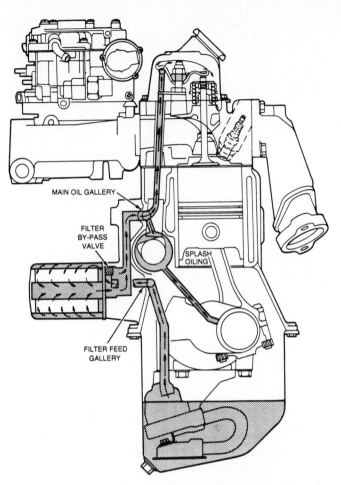

Figure 4-6. Lubrication System for 1.8L Engine. (*Courtesy of Chevrolet Motor Division, General Motors Corporation*)

A bypass valve in the oil filter allows oil to bypass the filter if the filter becomes plugged and the pressure drop across the filter increases to 12 psi (83 kPa). The rocker arms are lubricated by the oil coming out of the top of the push rods, and oil splash from the rocker arms lubricates the valve stems and guides. Openings in the cylinder head and engine block allow oil to drain from the top of the cylinder head into the crankcase.

Rocker arm and valve stem lubrication are illustrated in Figure 4-7.

Oil is forced through passages in the crankshaft from the main bearing journals to the connecting rod journals to provide oil for the connecting rod bearings. The oil passages in the crankshaft are shown in Figure 4-8.

Some connecting rods have an oil hole that sprays oil from the connecting rod bearing to the cylinder walls and pistons. In other engines the cylinder walls, pistons, and piston rings are lubricated by

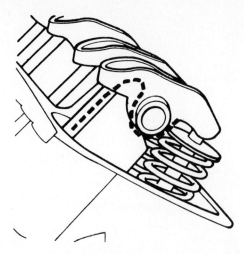

Figure 4-7. Rocker Arm and Valve Stem Lubrication. *(Courtesy of Chevrolet Motor Division, General Motors Corporation)*

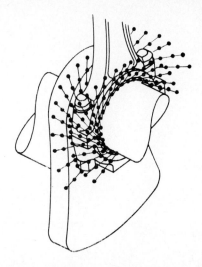

Figure 4-9. Piston and Cylinder Wall Lubrication. *(Courtesy of Sunnen Products Company)*

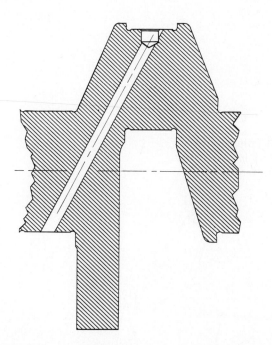

Figure 4-8. Crankshaft Oil Passages. (Reference taken from SAE paper No. 810007. *Reprinted with Permission of Society of Automotive Engineers,* © 1981)

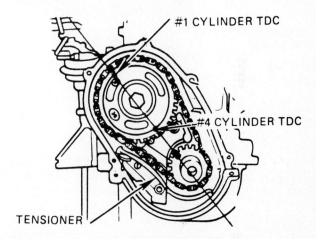

#1 CYLINDER TDC

#4 CYLINDER TDC

TENSIONER

Figure 4-10. Camshaft Gear and Timing Chain. *(Courtesy of Pontiac Motor Division, General Motors Corporation)*

Lubrication System for Four-Cylinder Overhead-Cam Engine

Many overhead-cam engines have a notched timing belt surrounding the crankshaft and camshaft gears as well as the accessory shaft gear, so that the timing belt drives both the camshaft and the accessory shaft. A belt tensioner applies the correct tension to the timing belt. The accessory shaft drives the distributor and the oil pump, as pictured in Figure 4-11.

Oil is forced through the oil filter to the main oil gallery by the oil pump pressure. The oil flows from the main oil gallery to the crankshaft main bearings and the accessory shaft bearings. A vertical passage in the block and cylinder head conducts oil to the valve lash adjusters and camshaft bearings, as illustrated in Figure 4-12.

oil splash from the sides of the connecting rod bearings, as illustrated in Figure 4-9.

Some engines have the camshaft mounted on bearings in the engine block. This type of engine usually has a camshaft gear driven by a steel timing chain from the crankshaft gear, as pictured in Figure 4-10. This type of timing chain and gear arrangement is usually lubricated by a small opening from the front camshaft bearing.

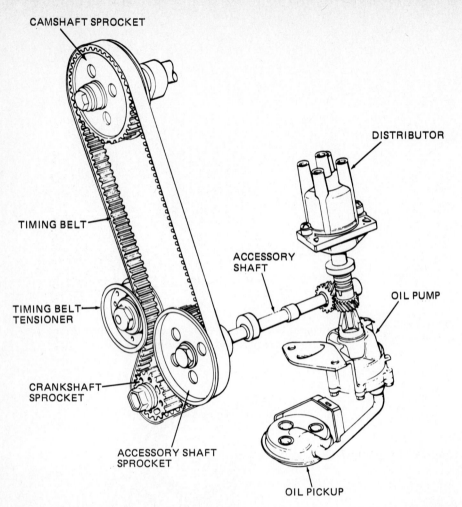

CAMSHAFT SPROCKET

TIMING BELT

TIMING BELT
TENSIONER

CRANKSHAFT
SPROCKET

ACCESSORY SHAFT
SPROCKET

ACCESSORY
SHAFT

DISTRIBUTOR

OIL PUMP

OIL PICKUP

Figure 4-11. Overhead-Cam Engine Camshaft, Distributor, and Oil Pump Drive for Chrysler 2.2L Engine. (Reference taken from SAE paper No. 810007. *Reprinted with Permission of Society of Automotive Engineers*, © 1981)

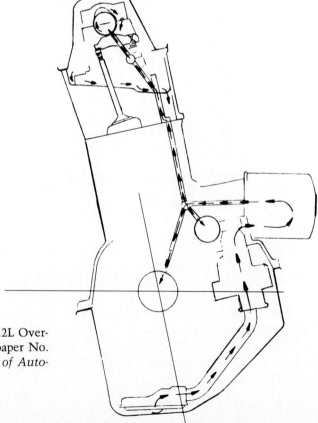

Figure 4-12. Lubrication System for Chrysler 2.2L Overhead-Cam Engine. (Reference taken from SAE paper No. 810007. *Reprinted with Permission of Society of Automotive Engineers*, © 1981)

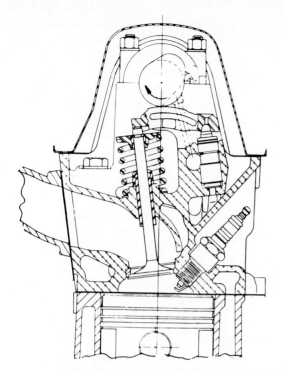

Figure 4-13. Overhead Cam Valve Mechanism for Chrysler 2.2L Engine. (Reference taken from SAE paper No. 810007. *Reprinted with Permission of Society of Automotive Engineers,* © 1981)

An enlarged view of the lash adjusters, rocker arms, valves, and camshaft is shown in Figure 4-13.

Oil is sprayed from a jet hole in both sides of each camshaft bearing cap to lubricate the cam lobes, rocker arms, and valve stems, as pictured in Figure 4-14.

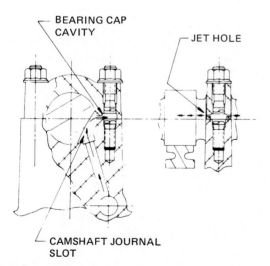

Figure 4-14. Cam Lobe, Rocker Arm, and Valve Stem Lubrication for Chrysler 2.2L Engine. (Reference taken from SAE paper No. 810007. *Reprinted with Permission of Society of Automotive Engineers,* © 1981)

On this type of engine, the timing belt does not require lubrication; therefore, oil is not supplied to the timing belt or gears at the front of the engine. The Chrysler 135 CID (2.2L) four-cylinder engine and the General Motors 110 CID (1.8L) four-cylinder engine are specifically designed for Chrysler and General Motors front-wheel-drive cars.

Lubrication System for Automotive Diesel Engine

The lubrication system in a diesel engine is very similar to the systems in gasoline engines. However, there are some significant differences between the two systems. An oil cooler is connected in series with the oil filter on some diesel engines. Engine coolant is circulated around the oil passages in the cooler to dissipate heat from the oil.

Oil is supplied from the passages in the engine block to curved discharge tubes at the bottom of each cylinder. The oil is sprayed from an orifice in the discharge tubes against the undercrown of the piston to provide additional piston cooling and more uniform piston temperature. This extra piston cooling allows tighter clearances between the piston rings and ring grooves. Figure 4-15 shows the oil-cooled piston feature.

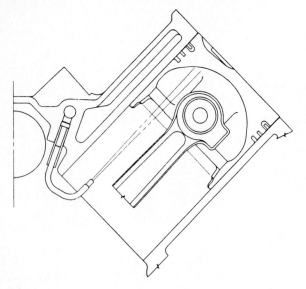

Figure 4-15. Oil-Cooled Pistons. (Reference taken from SAE paper No. 830381. *Reprinted with Permission of Society of Automotive Engineers,* © 1983)

Oil Pumps

Design and Operation

Many oil pumps are the rotor-type pump, as pictured in Figure 4-16. In this type of pump, the outer rotor is eccentric to the center of the drive shaft. This causes the spaces between the inner rotor and the outer rotor to vary in size as the drive shaft rotates both rotors.

The operation of the rotor-type oil pump is outlined in Figure 4-17.

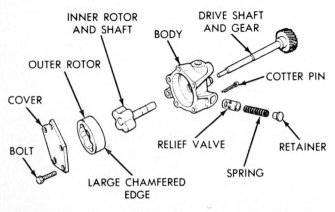

Figure 4-16. Rotor-type Oil Pump. (*Courtesy of Chrysler Canada*)

The pressure relief valve returns some of the oil flow from the pump outlet to the pump inlet when oil pressure reaches 55 to 60 psi (380 to 414 kPa), which limits the pump pressure.

A gear-type oil pump is used in some engines, as shown in Figure 4-18. To achieve proper balance of pump gears and pump drive, the timing marks on the oil pump gears must be aligned as indicated in Figure 4-18 when the oil pump is assembled. Most other gear-type pumps do not have timing marks on the gears.

Oil Filters

Design and Operation

Most oil filters are the spin-on, disposable type. Oil flows from the oil pump into the outside area of the filter between the filter case and paper element. When the oil flows through the paper element, carbon and metal particles, sludge, or other contaminants are filtered from the oil. The oil flows from the center of the paper element to the main oil gallery in the engine block, as illustrated in Figure 4-19.

A check valve in the top of the oil filter prevents oil from draining back out of the lubrication system through the filter into the crankcase when the engine is shut off. The oil filter mounting plate contains a bypass valve which allows unfiltered oil to flow from the oil pump directly to the lubrication system if the filter becomes plugged. The bypass valve opens when the pressure drop from the inlet to the outlet side of the filter exceeds 12 psi (83 kPa).

The oil filter bypass valve is shown in Figure 4-20.

When the filter is working normally, all the oil flow from the pump passes through the filter. Therefore, this type of filter is referred to as a full-flow filter.

Test Questions

1. The friction that occurs between the layers of oil in an oil film is referred to as _____ friction.

2. When an engine is operating under heavy load, the oil in the main bearings and connecting rod bearings could be subjected to pressures up to _____ psi (_____ kPa).

3. The dispersant additive in an oil prevents _____ particles from clotting together.

4. If the oil viscosity is too low in relation to engine load and temperature, the crankshaft bearings may be damaged.   T F

5. An oil with an SAE 30 rating would have a higher viscosity than an oil with an SAE 40 rating.   T F

6. An oil with a viscosity index rating (VI) of 300 would have less viscosity change in relation to temperature than an oil with VI rating of 125.   T F

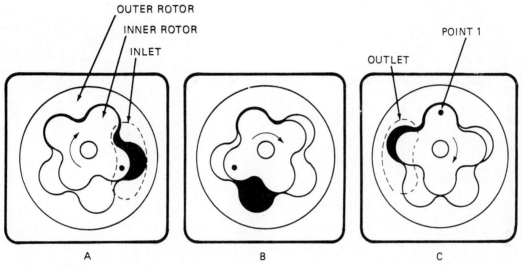

A. Oil is picked up in lobe of outer rotor.
B. Oil is moved in lobe of outer rotor to outlet.
C. Oil is forced out of outlet because the inner and outer rotors mesh too tightly at point 1 and the oil cannot pass through.

Figure 4-17.   Rotor-type Oil Pump Operation.

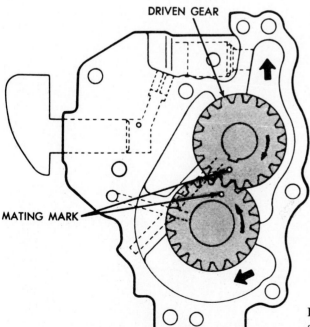

Figure 4-18.   Gear-type Oil Pump for Mitsubishi 2.6L Engine. (*Courtesy of Chrysler Canada*)

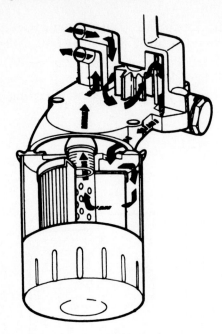

Figure 4-19.   Oil Filter. (*Courtesy of Chevrolet Motor Division, General Motors Corporation*)

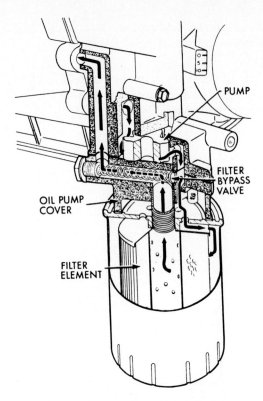

Figure 4-20.   Oil Filter Bypass Valve. (*Courtesy of Buick Motor Division, General Motors Corporation*)

5

Fuel-Efficient High-Performance Engine Design

Chapter Completion Objectives

1. Demonstrate an understanding of the advantages of an engine equipped with silent shafts.

2. Demonstrate an understanding of the methods used in various engines to reduce engine weight and improve fuel economy and performance.

3. Explain the operation of the high-swirl combustion (HSC) combustion chamber.

4. List the advantages of the high-swirl combustion (HSC) combustion chamber.

5. Demonstrate a knowledge of the durability features that may be designed into a modern engine in front-wheel-drive cars.

Chrysler 156 CID (2.6L) Engine

Design

The 156 CID (2.6L) Chrysler engine is manufactured by Mitsubishi, and is available in many front-wheel-drive vehicles.

The four-cylinder overhead-cam engine has a cast iron block with an aluminum cylinder head and a silent shaft system. Since there are more degrees of crankshaft rotation between the power strokes on a four-cylinder engine compared to a six-cylinder or eight-cylinder engine, the four-cylinder engine is subject to more vibration at idle and low speeds. The vibration problem is more pronounced when a four-cylinder engine and transaxle are mounted transversely in a small front-wheel-drive car because of the additional weight on the front chassis and suspension. This vibration may be unpleasant for the occupants of the car when it is transferred through the engine mounts to the steering column and the passenger compartment. The silent shafts are counterbalance shafts which reduce vibration and provide a very quiet, smooth-running engine for front-wheel-drive vehicles.

An engine block with the crankshaft and silent shafts is illustrated in Figure 5-1.

The inner ends of the silent shafts are supported by circular bearings in the engine block. A bearing in the thrust plate supports the outer end of the upper (left) silent shaft.

Inner silent shaft bearing removal and installation are shown in Figure 5-2, and the upper silent shaft and related components are pictured in Figure 5-3.

The outer end of the lower (right) silent shaft is connected to the driven gear in the oil pump. A sprocket is connected to the oil pump drive gear, as shown in Figure 5-4.

A key in the silent shaft is mounted in a slot in the oil pump driven gear. The marks on the oil pump

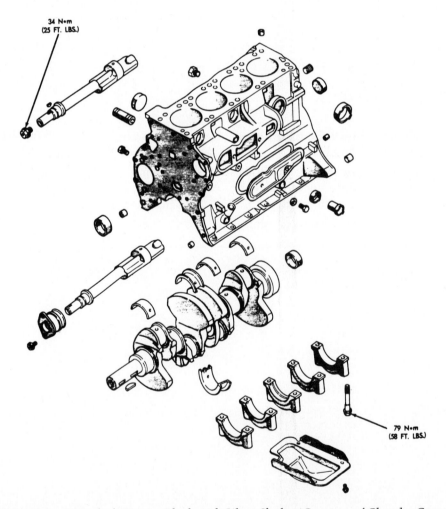

Figure 5-1.   Mitsubishi Engine Block with Silent Shafts. (*Courtesy of Chrysler Canada*)

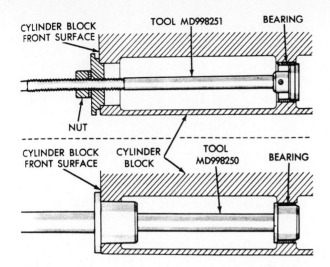

Figure 5-2. Inner Silent Shaft Bearing Removal and Installation, Upper or Lower Shaft. (*Courtesy of Chrysler Canada*)

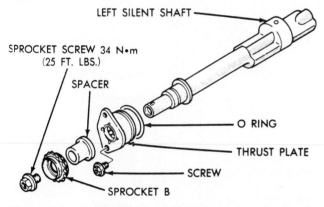

Figure 5-3. Upper Silent Shaft. (*Courtesy of Chrysler Canada*)

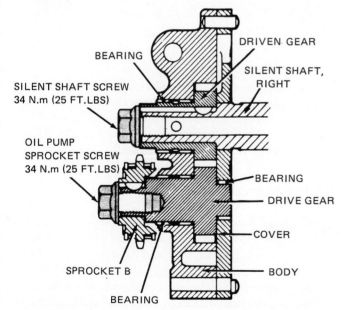

Figure 5-4. Lower Silent Shaft and Oil Pump. (*Courtesy of Chrysler Canada*)

gears must be aligned as outlined in Figure 5-5 to maintain proper silent shaft balance.

The exhaust valve is located on one side of the combustion chamber and the intake valve is positioned on the other side to form a hemispherical-type combustion chamber, as illustrated in Figure 5-6.

The camshaft is mounted in the cylinder head bearings and the rocker arms are connected directly between the camshaft lobes and the valve stems. Therefore, valve lifters are not required in this engine. Dual rocker-arm shafts are also mounted in the camshaft bearing caps. The rocker-arm shafts must be assembled in the front camshaft bearing cap as shown in Figure 5-7, and the rocker arms must be installed on the shafts as indicated in Figure 5-8.

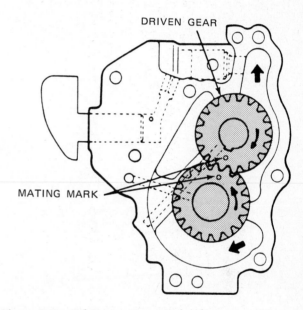

Figure 5-5. Oil Pump Gear Mark Alignment. (*Courtesy of Chrysler Canada*)

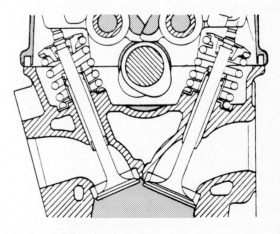

Figure 5-6. Hemispherical-Type Combustion Chamber. (*Courtesy of Chrysler Canada*)

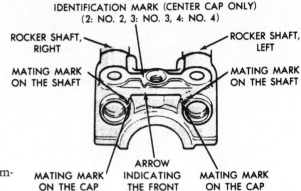

Figure 5-7. Rocker-Arm Shafts Installed in Front Camshaft Bearing Cap. (*Courtesy of Chrysler Canada*)

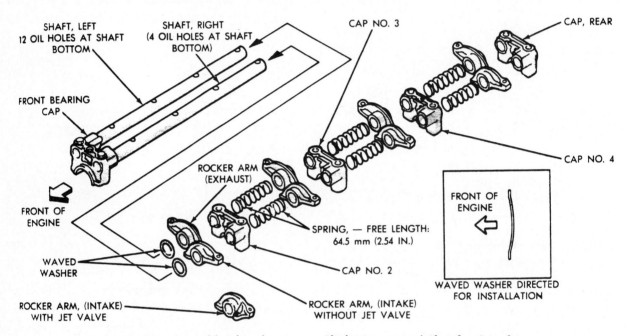

Figure 5-8. Assembly of Rocker Arm to Shaft (*Courtesy of Chrysler Canada*)

Chrysler 135 CID (2.2L) Engine

Design

The Chrysler 135 CID (2.2L) engine is a four-cylinder engine with an aluminum cylinder head and a cast iron block. This engine and the 156 CID (2.6L) engine are transversely mounted in front-wheel-drive Chrysler-built vehicles.

The compression ratio on the normally aspirated 135 CID (2.2L) engine is 9:1, while the turbocharged engine has "dished" pistons which provide a compression ratio of 8.6:1. The Shelby version of this engine has a compression ratio of 9.5:1.

The external features on the 135 CID (2.2L) engine are shown in Figure 5-9. (This engine is described extensively in other chapters of this book.

Refer to Figure 4-13 for camshaft and rocker-arm design. The cooling system is illustrated in Figures 3-5 and 3-6, and the lubrication system in Figures 4-11 and 4-12. Refer to Chapter 6 for an explanation of the turbocharged version of this engine.)

Design Objectives

This engine was designed to meet the objectives of low weight, compact size, excellent power output, fuel economy, durability, and serviceability. The transverse location of the engine in front-wheel-drive vehicles required that the engine be shortened as much as practical without compromising accessory equipment, serviceability, or basic displacement. A number of design features are used to accomplish this goal:

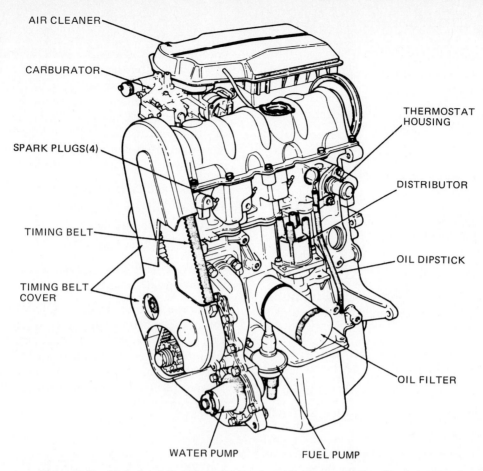

Figure 5-9. Chrysler 135 CID (2.2L) Engine. (*Courtesy of Chrysler Canada*)

1. Cylinder walls are joined directly in the area between the cylinders to provide a shorter engine block. This design is referred to as Siamesed cylinders.
2. The pulley on the end of the camshaft faces the transaxle and is used to drive the air pump, which provides a compact drive mechanism.
3. The intake and exhaust manifolds are located on the firewall side of the engine. This location provides easier accessibility to many components on the front side (radiator side) of the engine.

Serviceability The following components are located on the front side of the engine for easier accessibility:

1. Spark plugs.
2. Ignition distributor.
3. Fuel pump.
4. Fuel filter.
5. Oil filter.
6. Oil filler cap.
7. Water pump.
8. Alternator.
9. Air conditioning compressor.

Other design features which provide improved serviceability are the following:

1. Retorquing of head bolts after cylinder head replacement is not required.
2. Hydraulic valve lash adjusters eliminate the need for periodic valve lash adjustment. (Refer to Figure 2-37 for a diagram of these adjusters.)
3. The screw adjustment provided for alternator belt tension is readily accessible from the front of the vehicle.

Reduced Weight One of the most effective methods of improving fuel economy is to reduce the vehicle weight. (Other methods of improving fuel economy are explained in Chapter 8.) In the Chrysler 135 CID (2.2L) engine, the following components are manufactured from aluminum to reduce the engine weight:

1. Cylinder head.
2. Pistons.
3. Intake manifold.
4. Oil pump body.
5. Water pump body and housing.

6. Camshaft bearing caps.

7. Front and rear camshaft seal retainers.

8. Accessory shaft seal retainer.

9. Alternator, air pump, and air conditioning compressor mounting brackets.

10. Timing belt sprocket shield.

Plastic components which are used to reduce weight are the following:

1. Timing belt upper and lower covers.

2. Crankcase vent module.

3. Air cleaner body.

4. Air pump pulley guard.

Another method of weight reduction in this engine design was to minimize iron content in some of the parts:

1. A lighter engine block was designed with Siamesed cylinders and short skirt cylinders.

2. Nodular iron is used in the exhaust manifold.

The current base engine assembly weighs 216 lbs (98.2 kg).

Durability   Various features were used in the engine component design to increase durability:

1. Cast iron cylinder block with five main crankshaft bearings.

2. Nodular cast iron crankshaft with deep rolled fillets on the main and crankpin journals.

3. Hardened iron alloy camshaft with phosphate-treated lobes and five camshaft bearings.

4. Oil jet camshaft lobe lubrication. (Refer to Chapter 4 for this design.)

5. Molybdenum-filled nodular iron top piston ring.

6. Chrome-plated intake and exhaust valve stems.

7. Hardenable iron alloy exhaust valve guides.

8. Cobalt-iron exhaust valve seat inserts.

9. Heat-resistant synthetic rubber seals on the valve stems, crankshaft, camshaft, and accessory shaft.

10. Use of room-temperature vulcanizing (RTV) and anaerobic sealers to avoid leaks caused by gasket shrinkage.

11. Ceramic water pump shaft seal seat.

Power and Fuel Economy   In the design and development of this engine, the overhead cam allowed the optimization of intake and exhaust ports in the cylinder head. It was possible to place a spark plug in the center of each cylinder and provide generous cooling from the cooling system, because both the intake and exhaust ports are on the firewall side of the head. The intake and exhaust ports were optimized for performance and economy by conducting airflow tests with plastic cylinder head models. During this airflow testing, the following parameters were evaluated and optimized for performance and economy:

1. Intake and exhaust port shape and size.

2. Valve under head angle (valve configuration between stem and face).

3. Valve neck radius.

4. Port cutter angle.

5. Valve guide length.

These engine design features, combined with computer control of the fuel system and spark advance, improve economy and performance. (Computer-controlled carburetors and electronic fuel injection used on this engine are explained in Chapters 17 and 18, and electronic ignition systems are described in Chapter 13.)

Chrysler 152 CID (2.5L) Engine

Design

The Chrysler 152 CID (2.5L) engine is similar to the 135 CID (2.2L) engine. Both engines have a 3.44 in. (87.3 mm) bore. A 3.61 in. (91.8 mm) stroke is used in the 135 CID (2.2L) engine, whereas the 152 CID (2.5L) engine has a 4.09 in. (103.8 mm) stroke. The block height has been increased .47 in. (12 mm) in the 152 CID (2.5L) engine compared to the 135 CID (2.2L) engine.

Two silent shafts are located in the oil pan of the 152 CID (2.5L) engine. These shafts have interconnecting helical drive gears which are driven by a sprocket on the crankshaft. A short drive chain surrounds the crankshaft sprocket and the silent shaft drive gear. The silent shafts rotate in opposite directions at twice the speed of the crankshaft to cancel out vibration.

Two openings in the silent shaft housing allow oil to be pumped out of the housing by the unique silent shaft design. This action prevents oil aeration and power loss which would occur if the shafts were spinning in oil.

The basic design of the 152 CID (2.5L) engine is illustrated in Figure 5-10, and the silent shafts are shown in Figure 5-11.

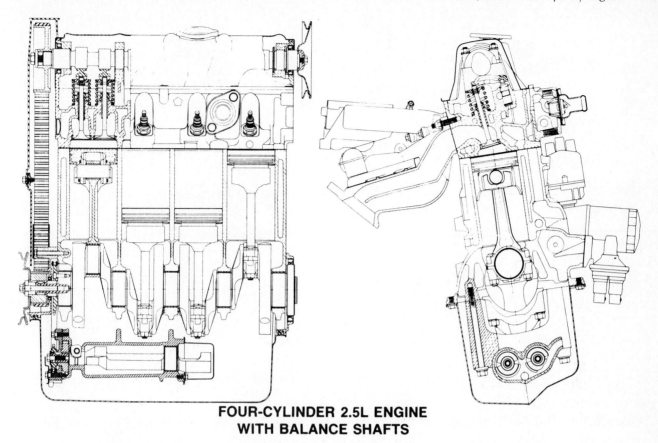

**FOUR-CYLINDER 2.5L ENGINE
WITH BALANCE SHAFTS**

Figure 5-10. Chrysler 152 CID (2.5L) Engine Design. (*Courtesy of Chrysler Canada*)

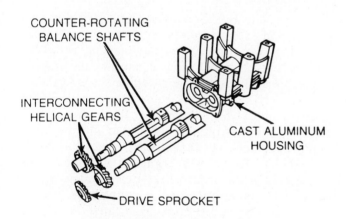

**BALANCE SHAFTS FOR
2.5L ENGINE**

Figure 5-11. Silent Shafts in Chrysler 152 CID 2.5L Engine. (*Courtesy of Chrysler Canada*)

Fast-burn cylinder heads are used on 1986 and later model Chrysler 135 CID (2.2L) and 152 CID (2.5L) engines, as pictured in Figure 5-12. The modifications and related components of the fast-burn cylinder head shown in Figure 5-12 are the following:

1. Intake valve.
2. Intake port filled to direct tangential airflow.
3. Intake port.
4. Intake valve shrouded to promote tangential airflow.
5. Piston.
6. Material removed from the combustion chamber to allow tangential airflow.

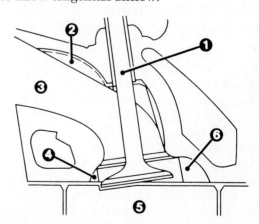

Figure 5-12. Fast-Burn Cylinder Head Design. (*Reprinted with Permission of Society of Automotive Engineers,* © 1985)

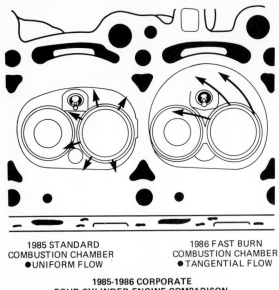

1985 STANDARD
COMBUSTION CHAMBER
● UNIFORM FLOW

1986 FAST BURN
COMBUSTION CHAMBER
● TANGENTIAL FLOW

1985-1986 CORPORATE
FOUR-CYLINDER ENGINE COMPARISON
COMBUSTION CHAMBER

Figure 5-13. Tangential Airflow Compared to Normal Air Flow. (*Courtesy of Chrysler Canada*)

The tangential airflow in the combustion chamber of a fast-burn cylinder head is compared to the normal airflow in a conventional cylinder head in Figure 5-13.

The tangential combustion chamber airflow creates greater cylinder turbulence, which provides improved air-fuel mixture. This reduces the tendency for detonation and gives smoother, more consistent engine operation. Fast-burn cylinder heads also allow increased compression ratios without increasing fuel octane requirements.

The 135 CID (2.2L) engine in 1986 and later models has a compression ratio of 9.5:1 and the 152 CID (2.5L) engine has a compression ratio of 9.0:1.

Ford 98 CID (1.6L) Engine

Design

The Ford 98 CID (1.6L) engine is a four-cylinder overhead-cam engine with an aluminum cylinder head and a cast iron block. This engine was described extensively in Chapter 2. (Refer to Figures 2-1, 2-2, 2-44, and 2-45.)

One of the unique features of this engine is the camshaft mounting and valve mechanisms. The camshaft is mounted in the cylinder head below the hydraulic valve lifters. Bearing surfaces for the camshaft are provided directly on the cylinder head surface without the use of insert bearings. Camshaft drive is accomplished by a cogged belt that surrounds the crankshaft and camshaft sprockets.

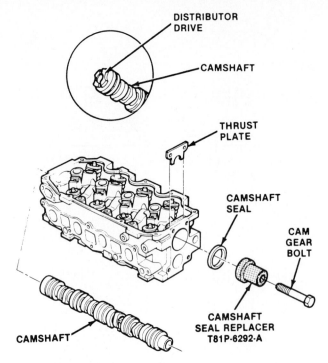

Figure 5-14. Camshaft and Cylinder Head. (*Courtesy of Ford Motor Co.*)

The camshaft and cylinder head are illustrated in Figure 5-14.

Hemispherical combustion chambers with centrally located spark plugs are designed in the cylinder head. This type of combustion chamber has the intake and exhaust valves on opposite sides of the chamber, which provides good engine breathing, volumetric efficiency, fuel economy, and low exhaust emissions. (Volumetric efficiency is explained in Chapter 1.) The intake and exhaust manifolds are located on opposite sides of the cylinder head. Other cylinder head features are illustrated with the hemispherical combustion chambers in Figure 5-15.

The 98 CID (1.6L) engine is mounted transversely in some front-wheel-drive Ford cars. Hydraulic lifters are mounted in cylinder head bores, and individual rocker arms are located on cylinder head studs, as pictured in Figure 5-16.

Ford 140 CID (2.3L) High-Swirl Combustion Engine

Design

The Ford 140 CID (2.3L) high-swirl combustion (HSC) engine and the 98 CID (1.6L) engine are both transversely mounted in front-wheel-drive vehicles.

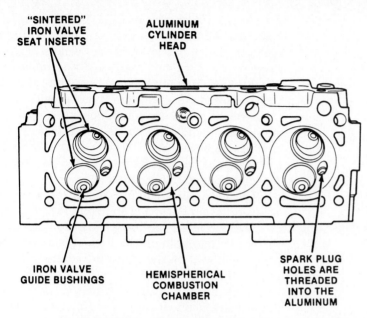

Figure 5-15.   Hemispherical Combustion Chambers. (*Courtesy of Ford Motor Co.*)

CYLINDER HEAD

- Cast aluminum on both 1.3L and the 1.6 L engines.
- Cross-flow design with the intake manifold on one side and the exhaust manifold on the other side.
- The camshaft does not use insert bearings...the cylinder head provides the bearing surfaces.
- The valves travel in iron valve guide bushings.
- The valve seats are "sintered" iron inserts.

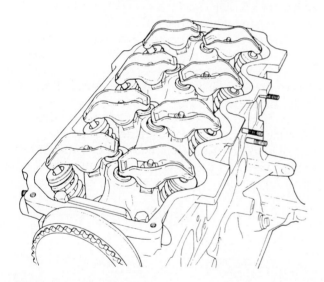

Figure 5-16. Rocker Arm and Valve Lifter Location. (*Courtesy of Ford Motor Co.*)

The 140 CID (2.3L) HSC engine is a four-cylinder engine with a cast iron block and an aluminum cylinder head. In this engine the camshaft is mounted on bearings in the engine block. The intake valve ports and the combustion chambers are designed to provide a swirling of the air-fuel mixture when it is drawn into the cylinders, as indicated in Figure 5-17.

The following features are included in the HSC engine:

1. The compact combustion chamber provides a minimum amount of surface area for a specific combustion chamber volume. This combustion chamber design combined with a flat-top piston results in a reduced flame front and a shorter period of combustion.

2. The masked intake port creates high swirl and turbulence of the air-fuel mixture, which provides better mixing of the air-fuel charge, faster burning, and more complete combustion.

3. The central spark plug location provides shorter flame travel and faster combustion. The flame front travels an equal distance from the spark plug to the outer edges of the combustion chamber.

4. A higher compression ratio results in an air-fuel mixture that is more densely compressed and more completely atomized. This also results in more complete combustion in a shorter time period.

The advantages gained in the HSC engine are the following:

1. Fuel economy is improved because a leaner air-fuel ratio can be used when the mixing and atomizing of the air-fuel mixture is improved.

2. Improved power output is available because the higher compression ratio and HSC design improve thermal efficiency.

3. Thermal efficiency is improved because the shorter combustion period provides a reduced time for heat loss to the cooling system.

4. A fast-burn engine can tolerate more exhaust-gas recirculation (EGR), which reduces oxides of nitrogen (NOx) emission levels.

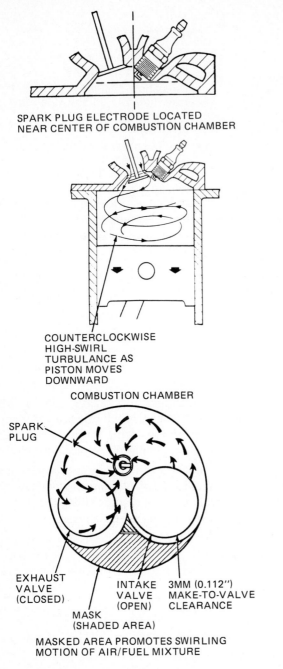

SPARK PLUG ELECTRODE LOCATED
NEAR CENTER OF COMBUSTION CHAMBER

COUNTERCLOCKWISE
HIGH-SWIRL
TURBULANCE AS
PISTON MOVES
DOWNWARD

COMBUSTION CHAMBER

SPARK
PLUG

EXHAUST
VALVE
(CLOSED)

MASK
(SHADED AREA)

INTAKE
VALVE
(OPEN)

3MM (0.112")
MAKE-TO-VALVE
CLEARANCE

MASKED AREA PROMOTES SWIRLING
MOTION OF AIR/FUEL MIXTURE

Figure 5-17. High-Swirl Combustion Chamber Design. *(Courtesy of Ford Motor Co.)*

General Motors 122 CID (2.0L) Engine

Design

The General Motors 122 CID (2.0L) four-cylinder engine has a cast iron cylinder head and block. In this engine the camshaft is mounted on bearings in the engine block. The engine is mounted transversely in front-wheel-drive vehicles.

During the design process, engine weight was kept to a minimum without sacrificing component strength. The block and cylinder head are cast with thinner 0.177 in. (4.5 mm) walls to reduce their weight. Special machining and handling techniques were devised to maintain component strength. Lightweight accessory components are used on this engine, as described previously in this chapter. The engine weighs 300 lbs (136 kg), which is identical to the weight of the smaller 98 CID (1.6L) General Motors engine used in Chevette cars.

The transverse engine mounting in a front-wheel-drive car chassis is shown in Figure 5-18.

The cylinder head has a cross-flow design with the intake manifold on the firewall side and the exhaust manifold on the front, or radiator, side. Bearings in the engine block support the camshaft. This camshaft-in-block design provides the largest cylinder displacement for a given engine length with cylinder bore sizes that allow the use of large valves and ports to provide optimum combustion chamber breathing and volumetric efficiency.

One of the main engine features is a fast-burn open combustion chamber, which increases air-fuel concentration around the spark plug and results in a rapid burn rate. This rapid rate makes a relatively high compression ratio of 9.0:1 possible. The end result of this combustion chamber design is improved economy and performance.

The combustion chamber is illustrated later in this chapter with the valve train components. The

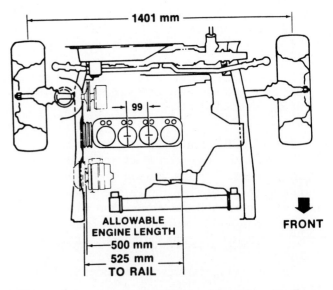

1401 mm

99

ALLOWABLE
ENGINE LENGTH

500 mm
525 mm
TO RAIL

FRONT

Figure 5-18. Transverse Engine Mounting in Front-Wheel-Drive Chassis. (Reference taken from SAE paper No. 820111. *Reprinted with Permission of Society of Automotive Engineers,* © 1982)

Figure 5-19. Complete Transversely Mounted Four-Cylinder Engine in Front-Wheel-Drive Car. (Reference taken from SAE paper No. 820111. *Reprinted with Permission of Society of Automotive Engineers*, © 1982)

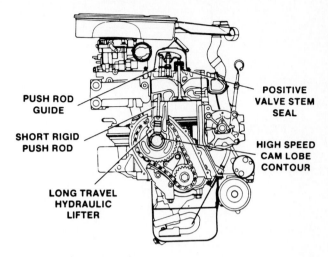

Figure 5-20. Valve Train of General Motors 122 CID (2.0L) Engine. (Reference taken from SAE paper No. 820111. *Reprinted with Permission of Society of Automotive Engineers*, © 1982)

complete engine installation in a front-wheel-drive car is pictured in Figure 5-19.

Design efforts were made to reduce the weight of the reciprocating parts on the valve side of the rocker arm. Valve stem size was reduced and a lightweight valve spring retainer was used. A net reciprocating weight reduction of 15 percent on these valve components allows a 600 rpm increase in maximum engine speed. Other valve train features include the following:

1. The camshaft is mounted high in the engine block to reduce push rod length.
2. Five camshaft bearings provide improved camshaft rigidity.
3. Push rod, rocker arm, and valve lifter offset are kept at a minimum.

The main features in the valve train are illustrated in Figure 5-20.

General Motors 173 CID (2.8L) V6 Engine

Design

The General Motors 173 CID (2.8L) V6 engine has a cast iron block with a 60° angle between the cylinder banks. This engine is equipped with cast iron cylinder heads. Since an engine with a 60° block is narrower than an engine with a 90° block, this type of engine is more suitable for transverse mounting in smaller front-wheel-drive cars, as indicated in Figure 5-21.

Since the engine is mounted transversely, cylinders 1, 3, and 5 are on the firewall side of the engine and cylinders 2, 4, and 6 face toward the front of the

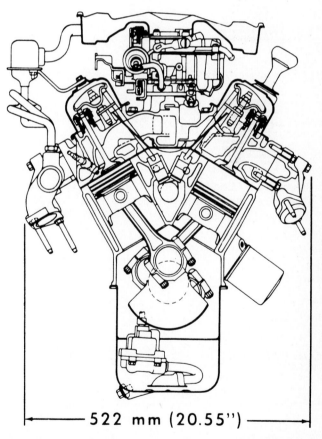

Figure 5-21. General Motors 173 CID (2.8L) 60° V6 Engine. (Reference taken from SAE paper No. 790697. *Reprinted with Permission of Society of Automotive Engineers*, © 1979)

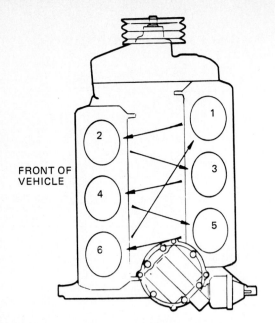

Figure 5-22. Cylinder Numbering and Firing Sequence, 173 CID (2.8L) Engine. (Reference taken from SAE paper No. 790697. *Reprinted with Permission of Society of Automotive Engineers,* © 1979)

(PARALLEL COOLANT FLOW THROUGH CYLINDER HEAD AND BLOCK)

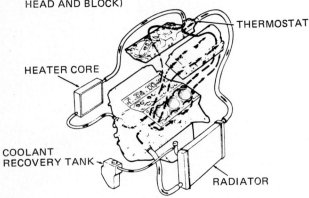

Figure 5-23. Cooling System, 173 CID (2.8L) Engine. (Reference taken from SAE paper No. 790697. *Reprinted with Permission of Society of Automotive Engineers,* © 1979)

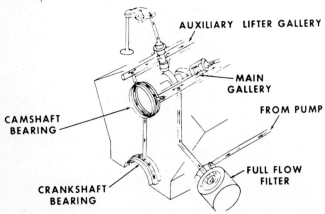

Figure 5-24. Lubrication System, 173 CID (2.8L) Engine. (Reference taken from SAE paper No. 790697. *Reprinted with Permission of Society of Automotive Engineers,* © 1979)

car. A firing order of 1, 2, 3, 4, 5, 6 is used on this engine, as indicated in Figure 5-22.

The 173 CID (2.8L) engine has a compression ratio of 8.5:1. Cooling system operation is shown in Figure 5-23, and oil flow through the lubrication system is pictured in Figure 5-24.

Toyota 80 CID (1.3L) and 89 CID (1.5L) Swirl-Port Engines

Design

The Toyota 80 CID (1.3L) and 89 CID (1.5L) swirl-port engines have four cylinders with aluminum cylinder heads and cast iron blocks. The 80 CID (1.3L) engine has a 3 in. (76 mm) bore and a 2.8 in. (71.4 mm) stroke, whereas the 89 CID (1.5L) engine has a 3.1 in. (77.5 mm) bore and a 3.03 in. (77 mm) stroke. Except for the difference in bore and stroke, the engines are basically the same.

These engines have a single overhead camshaft driven by a cogged belt. The in-line valves are positioned in a wedge-shaped combustion chamber. Five main bearings are used to suport the crankshaft, and the compression ratio on both engines is 9.3:1. A cutaway view of the engine is provided in Figure 5-25.

Figure 5-25. Toyota Swirl-Port Four-Cylinder Engine. (*Reprinted with Permission of Society of Automotive Engineers,* © 1983)

76

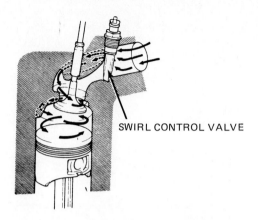

Figure 5-26.   Main Intake Passage Swirl Port Action. (*Reprinted with Permission of Society of Automotive Engineers*, © 1983)

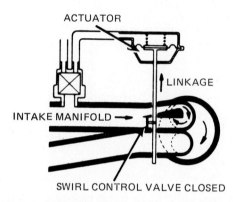

Figure 5-27.   Swirl Control Valve Actuator with Valve in the Closed Position. (*Reprinted with Permission of Society of Automotive Engineers*, © 1983)

The swirl-port engines are available in front-wheel-drive Toyota cars. Each intake port contains a main air passage and a bypass passage. An oar-like swirl control valve is located in each bypass passage. When the engine is operating under light load, moderate cruising-speed conditions, the swirl control valve closes the bypass passage and the air-fuel mixture is directed through the helically shaped main air passage to the intake valve. This helically shaped passage produces a strong swirling motion of the air-fuel mixture in the cylinder, as pictured in Figure 5-26.

The swirl control valves are operated by a vacuum actuator. In the light-load, moderate cruising-speed mode, vacuum is supplied to the actuator, which closes the swirl control valve as shown in Figure 5-27.

When the engine is operated at high speed or under heavy load, manifold vacuum applied to the swirl control valve actuator is shut off. Under this condition the actuator opens the swirl control valve and the air-fuel mixture then flows through bypass pas-

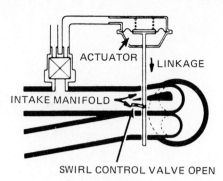

Figure 5-28.   Swirl Control Valve Actuator with Valve in the Open Position. (*Reprinted with Permission of Society of Automotive Engineers*, © 1983)

sage in addition to flowing through the main passage. The helically shaped main passage would provide excessive restriction of the air-fuel mixture at high speeds if the bypass passage was not opened.

The swirl control valve is shown in the open position in Figure 5-28.

When the swirl control valve is closed and the air-fuel mixture flows through the helically shaped main passage, the swirling motion in the combustion chamber provides improved burning of lean air-fuel mixtures that are heavily laden with exhaust gas from the exhaust-gas recirculation (EGR) valve.

Honda 110 CID (1.8L) Three-Valve Engine

Design

The Honda 110 CID (1.8L) three-valve engine is mounted transversely in the front-wheel-drive Honda Prelude. Each cylinder contains two intake valves and one exhaust valve. The valves are operated by a single overhead camshaft that is driven by a cogged belt, as pictured in Figure 5-29.

The intake valve that is positioned directly opposite to the exhaust valve opens 10° later than the other intake valve. This staggered timing of the intake valves produces a swirling motion in the incoming air-fuel mixture that promotes faster combustion. The different timing of the intake valves also prevents air-fuel mixture loss through the exhaust valves when the valves are in the overlap position.

Combustion chamber and valve design are pictured in Figure 5-30.

Since the three-valve combustion chamber increases volumetric efficiency, there is a trend toward this type of design in the automotive industry. A fourth valve is located in each combustion cham-

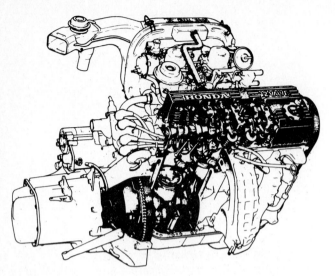

Figure 5-29. Honda 110 CID (1.8L) Three-Valve Engine. (*Reprinted with Permission of Society of Automotive Engineers,* © 1983)

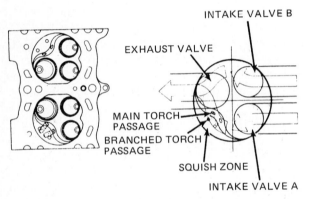

Figure 5-30. Combustion Chambers with Three Valves. (*Reprinted with Permission of Society of Automotive Engineers,* © 1983)

ber beside the exhaust valve. This valve is only 0.472 in. (12 mm) in diameter and is operated by a separate rocker arm, as indicated in Figure 5-31.

When this small intake valve is opened, the air-fuel mixture flows into a very small auxiliary combustion chamber. A small carburetor is used to provide a rich air-fuel mixture to the small intake valve and the auxiliary combustion chamber. Two side-draft variable venturi carburetors supply a very lean air-fuel mixture to the main combustion chamber. This two-in-one carburetor arrangement is shown in Figure 5-32.

Since the spark plug is located very close to the auxiliary combustion chamber, the rich air-fuel mixture ignites very easily. The burning air-fuel mixture

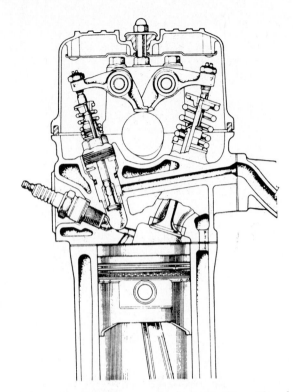

Figure 5-31. Small Intake Valve and Auxiliary Chamber. (*Reprinted with Permission of Society of Automotive Engineers,* © 1983)

blows through the main torch passages in the auxiliary combustion chamber into the main combustion chamber, which ignites the lean air-fuel mixture in this chamber. Some of the burning air-fuel mixture also blows through the branched torch passages into the squish area of the main combustion chamber. The torch passages are illustrated in Figure 5-30.

This type of combustion chamber arrangement provides very complete combustion of a lean air-fuel mixture. This type of engine may be referred to as a compound vortex combustion chamber (CVCC) engine.

Test Questions

1. The silent shafts in a Chrysler 156 CID (2.6L) engine prevent _____ and _____.
2. The silent shafts in a Chrysler 156 CID (2.6L) engine must be properly timed. T F
3. A Ford 140 CID (2.3L) high-swirl combustion (HSC) engine has a shorter combustion period than an engine without HSC. T F

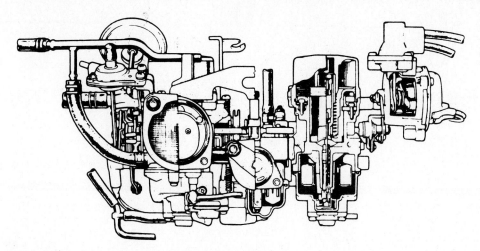

Figure 5-32. Two Side-Draft Variable Venturi Carburetors Combined with a Small Single Carburetor. (*Reprinted with Permission of Society of Automotive Engineers,* © 1983)

4. In the Ford 140 CID (2.3L) HSC engine the camshaft is mounted:
   a) in the block
   b) in the cylinder head
   c) above the rocker arms.

5. In the General Motors 173 CID (2.8L) engine, the angle between the cylinder banks is:

   a) 60°
   b) 90°
   c) 120°.

6. In the Toyota swirl-port engine, the swirl control valve is closed when the engine is operated at:
   a) heavy load
   b) moderate cruising speed
   c) extremely high speed.

6

Exhaust Systems, Turbochargers, and Intake Systems

Chapter Completion Objectives

1. Demonstrate an understanding of oxidization-type and reduction-type catalytic converters.

2. Describe the purposes of the heat riser valve.

3. Explain the process of carburetor icing.

4. List the advantages of nodular iron manifolds compared to grey cast iron manifolds.

5. List the advantages of a high-rise intake manifold.

6. Demonstrate an understanding of turbocharger operation.

7. Describe the operation of the electronic spark-retard system.

Exhaust System Components

Mufflers

The purpose of the muffler is to reduce engine exhaust noise to an acceptable level. The muffler contains a series of perforated pipes and baffles, as pictured in Figure 6-1.

The internal parts are spot-welded in the muffler to prevent rattling, and the outer shell is welded and crimped to the end plates. On most mufflers the inlet pipe has a larger diameter than the outlet pipe. The exhaust flow capacity of the muffler and the entire exhaust system must be adequate for the cubic inch displacement (CID) of the engine.

In some exhaust systems a smaller muffler is connected after the main muffler. This smaller muffler is referred to as a resonator.

Oxidization-Type Catalytic Converters

Some catalytic converters contain a "honeycombed" ceramic material that is coated with platinum and palladium, which acts as a catalyst. This type of catalytic converter is referred to as a monolith converter. The converter is connected in the exhaust system between the engine and the muffler, as indicated on the monolith converter shown in Figure 6-2.

Some catalytic converters contain pellets coated with platinum and palladium, as illustrated in Figure 6-3.

The pellet-type or the monolith-type converter oxidizes carbon monoxide (CO) and hydrocarbons (HC) into water vapor (H_2O) and carbon dioxide (CO_2). In this way the oxidization-type catalytic converter reduces emission levels of CO and HC. There must be oxygen present in the exhaust that enters this type of converter to make the converter function properly.

Air is usually pumped into the exhaust ports or into the exhaust manifold by a belt-driven air pump to supply oxygen to the catalytic converter. (Air pump systems are explained in Chapter 8.)

Two-Stage Catalytic Converters

Most cars are now equipped with two-stage catalytic converters. The conventional oxidization catalyst (COC) is located at the rear of the converter and the three-way catalyst (TWC) is positioned at the front of the converter. The two-stage catalytic converter may be a monolith- or pellet-type converter. A monolith two-stage converter is shown in Figure 6-4.

The "honeycombed" ceramic material in the TWC is coated with rhodium and platinum. The TWC reduces oxides of nitrogen (NOx) to nitrogen and oxygen. Therefore, emissions of NOx are reduced.

Air is pumped from the air pump system directly into the oxidization catalyst. On most systems this airflow occurs after the engine has been

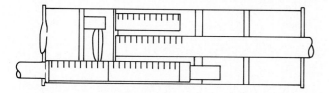

Figure 6-1. Internal Muffler Design. (*Courtesy of Chevrolet Motor Division, General Motors Corporation*)

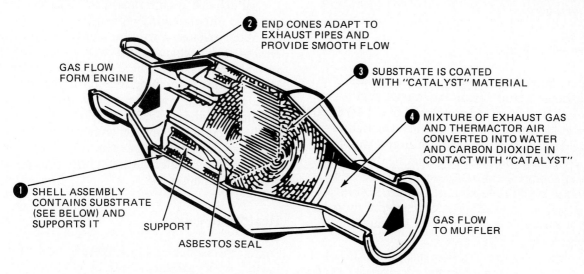

② END CONES ADAPT TO EXHAUST PIPES AND PROVIDE SMOOTH FLOW

GAS FLOW FORM ENGINE

③ SUBSTRATE IS COATED WITH "CATALYST" MATERIAL

④ MIXTURE OF EXHAUST GAS AND THERMACTOR AIR CONVERTED INTO WATER AND CARBON DIOXIDE IN CONTACT WITH "CATALYST"

① SHELL ASSEMBLY CONTAINS SUBSTRATE (SEE BELOW) AND SUPPORTS IT

SUPPORT

ASBESTOS SEAL

GAS FLOW TO MUFFLER

Figure 6-2. Monolith-Type Catalytic Converter. (*Courtesy of Ford Motor Co.*)

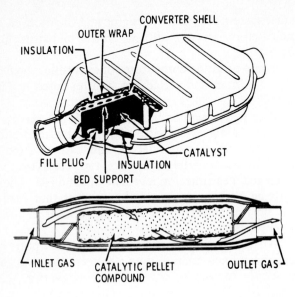

Figure 6-3.   Pellet-Type Catalytic Converter. (*Courtesy of Chevrolet Motor Division, General Motors Corporation*)

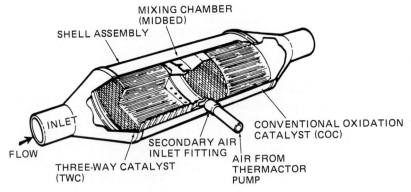

Figure 6-4.   Two-Stage Catalytic Converter. (*Courtesy of Ford Motor Co.*)

warmed up. During cold engine operation, the air pump supplies air to the exhaust ports.

Unleaded gasoline must be used with either type of catalytic converter.

Exhaust Manifolds

Exhaust manifolds are usually made of grey cast iron. Some exhaust manifolds on late-model engines are made of 70 to 90 percent nodular iron and 10 to 30 percent cast iron. These manifolds are lighter in weight and stronger than grey cast iron manifolds.

The exhaust manifold is bolted to the cylinder head and conducts exhaust gases from the exhaust ports in the head to the exhaust system. In some engines a gasket is positioned between the cylinder head and the exhaust manifold, as indicated on the four-cylinder engine in Figure 6-5.

On other engines a gasket is not required between the exhaust manifold and the cylinder head. On these applications the manufacturer may suggest

the use of a sealer between the exhaust manifold and the cylinder head. (Various types of sealers are described in Chapter 2.)

An exhaust manifold without a gasket on a V6 engine is illustrated in Figure 6-6.

Many exhaust manifolds contain such emission devices as the exhaust-gas recirculation (EGR) valve, air pipe fittings, and heated air-inlet stove and tube. Most engines with computer-controlled carburetors have an oxygen sensor threaded into the exhaust manifold, as shown in Figure 6-7. If the oxygen sensor is replaced, an anti-seize compound should be placed on the threads. (Oxygen sensors are described in Chapter 17 and emission control devices are explained in Chapter 8.)

Heat Riser Valves

Some engines have a butterfly-type heat riser valve located in the exhaust manifold. When the engine is cold, a bimetallic spring holds the heat riser valve in

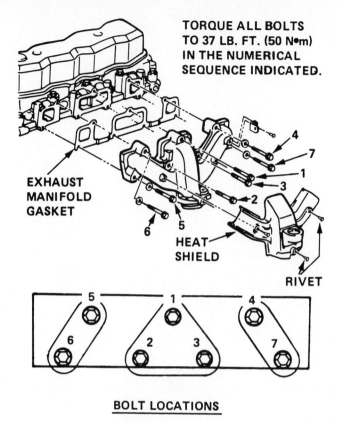

TORQUE ALL BOLTS
TO 37 LB. FT. (50 N•m)
IN THE NUMERICAL
SEQUENCE INDICATED.

EXHAUST
MANIFOLD
GASKET

HEAT
SHIELD

RIVET

BOLT LOCATIONS

Figure 6-5. Exhaust Manifold with Gasket. *(Courtesy of Chevrolet Motor Division, General Motors Corporation)*

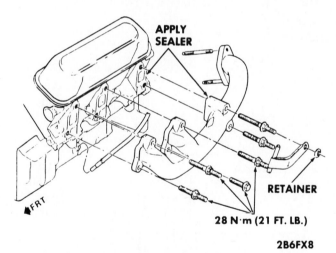

APPLY
SEALER

RETAINER

FRT

28 N·m (21 FT. LB.)

2B6FX8

Figure 6-6. Exhaust Manifold without Gasket. *(Courtesy of Chevrolet Motor Division, General Motors Corporation)*

the closed position. On a V-type engine, the heat riser valve is located between one of the exhaust manifold flanges and the exhaust pipe. When the heat riser valve is closed, some of the exhaust gas from one cylinder head is forced through the exhaust crossover passage in the intake manifold to the other

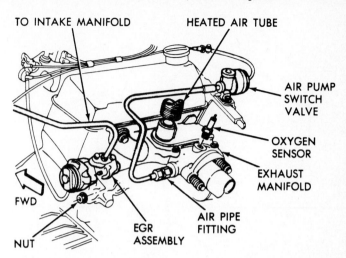

TO INTAKE MANIFOLD   HEATED AIR TUBE

AIR PUMP
SWITCH
VALVE

OXYGEN
SENSOR

EXHAUST
MANIFOLD

FWD

NUT

EGR
ASSEMBLY

AIR PIPE
FITTING

Figure 6-7. Exhaust Manifold with Oxygen and Emission-Control Components. *(Courtesy of Chrysler Canada)*

cylinder head and exhaust manifold. This exhaust flow heats the intake manifold and prevents fuel condensation on the intake manifold passages.

The exhaust crossover passage is located directly under the manifold surface below the idle mixture screws on the carburetor. Additional heat supplied to the carburetor base from the crossover passage will prevent frost from accumulating over the slow-idle ports under certain atmospheric conditions. The process of frosting at the slow-idle ports is referred to as curburetor icing. When carburetor icing occurs, the engine will not idle.

On some V-type engines the choke spring is located in a recess on top of the exhaust crossover passage in the intake manifold. Therefore, the action of the heat riser valve is essential to supply enough heat to the choke spring. Other carburetors have a hot-air type of choke with the choke spring located in a choke housing on the carburetor. On some of these applications, the heat pipe which supplies hot air to the choke housing is located in the exhaust crossover passage of the intake manifold. The exhaust flow is essential to supply sufficient heat to the choke heat pipe.

When the engine reaches normal operating temperature, the tension of the heat riser spring is reduced and the exhaust gases force the heat riser valve open. Under this condition the exhaust flow is reduced in the crossover passage. (The intake manifold and the crossover passage are discussed later in this chapter.)

A heat riser valve from a V-type engine is shown in Figure 6-8.

Many heat riser valves are vacuum operated. With this type of valve, a ported vacuum switch (PVS) is connected to the heat riser diaphragm. When

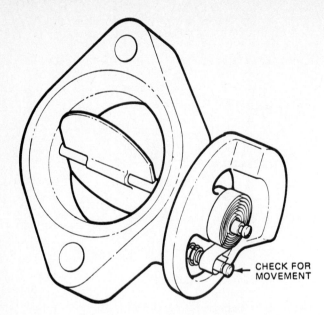

CHECK FOR
MOVEMENT

Figure 6-8. Heat Riser Valve from a V-Type Engine.
(*Courtesy of Ford Motor Co.*)

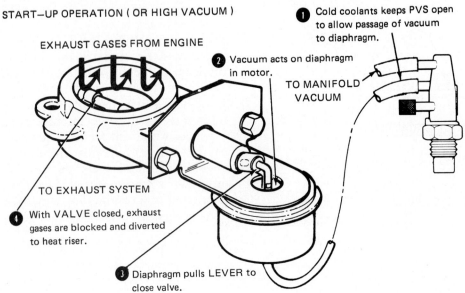

START—UP OPERATION (OR HIGH VACUUM)

EXHAUST GASES FROM ENGINE

1 Cold coolants keeps PVS open to allow passage of vacuum to diaphragm.

2 Vacuum acts on diaphragm in motor.

TO MANIFOLD VACUUM

TO EXHAUST SYSTEM

4 With VALVE closed, exhaust gases are blocked and diverted to heat riser.

3 Diaphragm pulls LEVER to close valve.

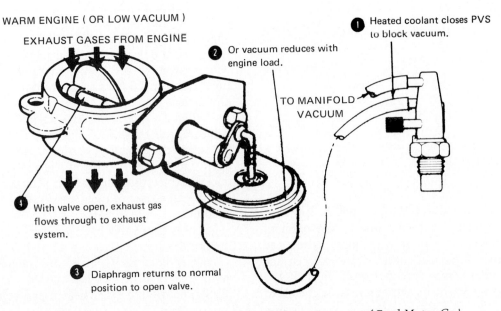

WARM ENGINE (OR LOW VACUUM)

EXHAUST GASES FROM ENGINE

1 Heated coolant closes PVS to block vacuum.

2 Or vacuum reduces with engine load.

TO MANIFOLD VACUUM

4 With valve open, exhaust gas flows through to exhaust system.

3 Diaphragm returns to normal position to open valve.

Figure 6-9. Vacuum-Operated Heat Riser Valve. (*Courtesy of Ford Motor Co.*)

the engine coolant is cold, manifold vacuum is supplied through the PVS to the heat riser diaphragm, which closes the valve. At a specific coolant temperature, the PVS shuts off the vacuum to the diaphragm, which causes the valve to open.

The operation of the vacuum-operated heat riser valve is outlined in Figure 6-9.

Complete Exhaust Systems

Purposes

One purpose of the exhaust system is to reduce engine exhaust noise to an acceptable level. The exhaust system must conduct the exhaust gases to the rear of the vehicle without allowing any exhaust leaks. Carbon monoxide (CO) is a poisonous gas if it is highly concentrated, and therefore exhaust leaks must be prevented.

The exhaust system must conduct the exhaust gases to the atmosphere without overheating any other components on the vehicle. Engine vibration must not be transmitted from the exhaust system to the chassis. Therefore, a number of flexible hangers are used to connect the exhaust system to the chassis.

If the exhaust system is equipped with a catalytic converter, the converter is responsible for reducing emission levels, as outlined previously in this chapter.

Design

An exhaust pipe is connected from the exhaust manifold to the catalytic converter. On V-type engines a crossover pipe is connected between the two exhaust manifolds and the exhaust pipe is connected from the crossover pipe to the converter. Many exhaust pipes are made of double-walled metal. An intermediate pipe is connected between the converter and the muffler, and a tail pipe is connected from the muffler to the rear of the vehicle. On some engines a one-piece exhaust pipe is connected from the exhaust manifold to the catalytic converter.

A typical exhaust system with all the necessary hangers is shown in Figure 6-10.

Some exhaust systems have a ball-type seat on the exhaust manifold and a matching flare on the exhaust pipe, as shown in Figure 6-11. On the other exhaust systems a seal or gasket is located between the crossover pipe and the manifold, as illustrated in Figure 6-12.

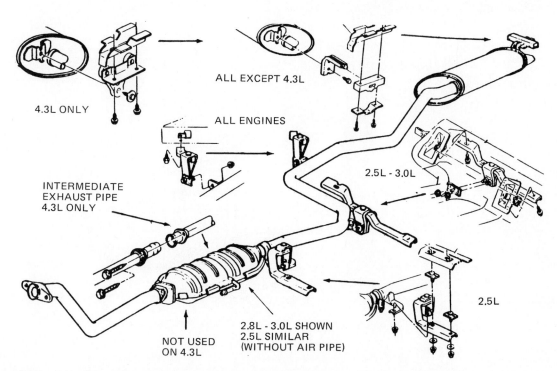

Figure 6-10.   Complete Exhaust System. (*Courtesy of Chevrolet Motor Division, General Motors Corporation*)

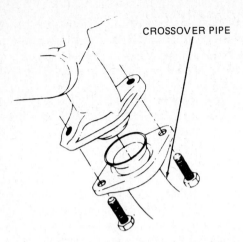

Figure 6-11. Exhaust Pipe to Manifold Connection. (*Courtesy of Pontiac Motor Division, General Motors Corporation*)

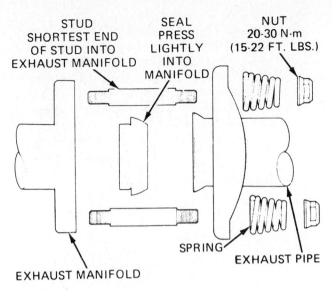

Figure 6-12. Exhaust Pipe to Manifold Seal. (*Courtesy of Chevrolet Motor Division, General Motors Corporation*)

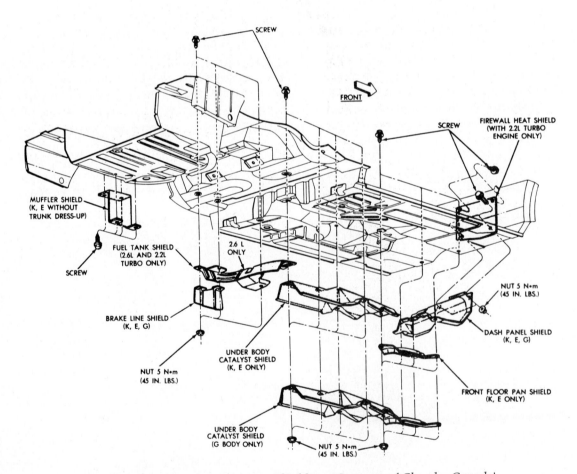

Figure 6-13. Exhaust System Heat Shielding. (*Courtesy of Chrysler Canada*)

Since the catalytic converter and other exhaust system components operate at high temperature, extensive heat shielding is required between exhaust systems and the chassis. Some vehicles also have a shield located under the catalytic converter. Typical exhaust system shielding is shown in Figure 6-13.

Stainless Steel Exhaust Systems

Some vehicles have a one-piece stainless steel exhaust system to provide longer life. All the hangers on these exhaust systems are stainless steel springs. The individual components may be replaced in this type of exhaust system by cutting off the old component and clamping the replacement component over the existing pipes.

A one-piece stainless steel exhaust system is pictured in Figure 6-14.

Intake Manifolds

Intake Manifolds with Exhaust Crossover Passage

The intake manifold passages conduct the air-fuel mixture from the carburetor, or throttle body injection assembly, to the intake ports in the cylinder head. Cast iron or aluminum may be used in the intake manifold. Intake manifold passages must provide unrestricted flow of the air-fuel mixture, so these passages are usually curved and contain no sharp bends.

An intake manifold from a V8 engine is shown in Figure 6-15, and a V6 intake manifold is illustrated in Figure 6-16.

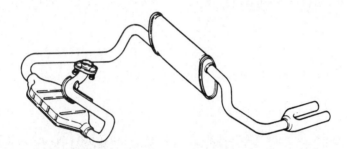

Figure 6-14.   One-Piece Stainless Steel Exhaust System. (*Courtesy of GM Product Service Training, General Motors Corporation*)

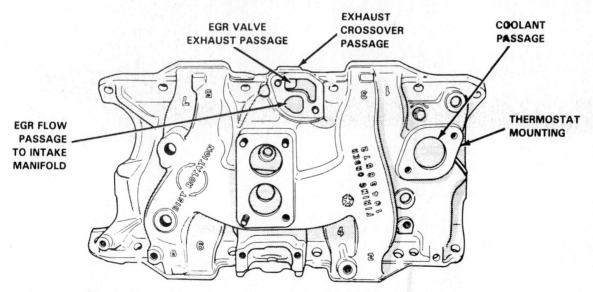

Figure 6-15.   Intake Manifold, V8 Engine with Exhaust Crossover Passage. (*Courtesy of Chrysler Canada*)

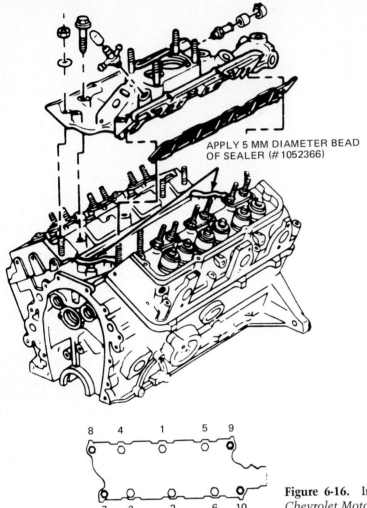

APPLY 5 MM DIAMETER BEAD
OF SEALER (# 1052366)

8 4 1 5 9

7 3 2 6 10

Figure 6-16. Intake Manifold, V6 Engine. (*Courtesy of Chevrolet Motor Division, General Motors Corporation*)

A gasket is located between each side of the intake manifold and the cylinder heads on V-type engines. Gaskets or sealer may be used between each end of the intake manifold and the engine block. A sealer is required under each end of the intake manifold in Figure 6-16.

Many V-type intake manifolds have an exhaust crossover passage, as shown in Figure 6-15. Intake manifold bolts must be tightened in the proper sequence and torqued to manufacturer's specifications.

Intake Manifold with Coolant Crossover Passages

The intake and exhaust manifolds on the Chrysler 2.2L four-cylinder engine are illustrated in Figure 6-17.

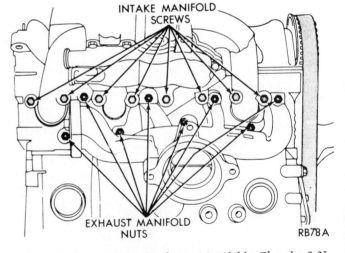

INTAKE MANIFOLD SCREWS

EXHAUST MANIFOLD NUTS

RB78A

Figure 6-17. Intake and Exhaust Manifolds, Chrysler 2.2L Engine. (*Courtesy of Chrysler Canada*)

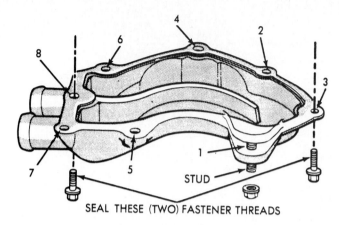

Figure 6-18. Coolant Crossover Passages in Intake Manifold. (*Courtesy of Chrysler Canada*)

The intake manifold on the Chrysler 2.2L engine has a coolant crossover passage on the intake manifold to heat the manifold. Sealer must be applied on two of the coolant crossover assembly attaching bolts, as indicated in Figure 6-18.

High-Rise Intake Manifolds

Some late-model vehicles are equipped with high-rise intake manifolds. This type of intake manifold has curved internal air passages which have improved airflow capabilities.

Engines with high-rise intake manifolds are usually equipped with port-type electronic fuel injection systems. Since these fuel systems inject the fuel at the intake ports, manifold heating and intake air heating are not required. Therefore, the heat riser valve, or coolant crossover passages, are eliminated. The heated air inlet system in the air cleaner is no longer used with a high-rise manifold. (Port-type electronic fuel injection systems are described in Chapter 18, and heated air inlet systems are explained in Chapter 8.)

When high-rise manifolds are used, engine performance and fuel economy are improved. A high-rise intake manifold is illustrated in Figure 6-19.

Air Cleaners

Most automotive air cleaners use a paper air cleaning element. This element may be checked for dirt contamination by holding a trouble lamp inside the element and looking through the element from the outside. The element can be cleaned by directing compressed air through it from the inside of the element. Replacement of the element is necessary if it still appears dirty after the cleaning operation.

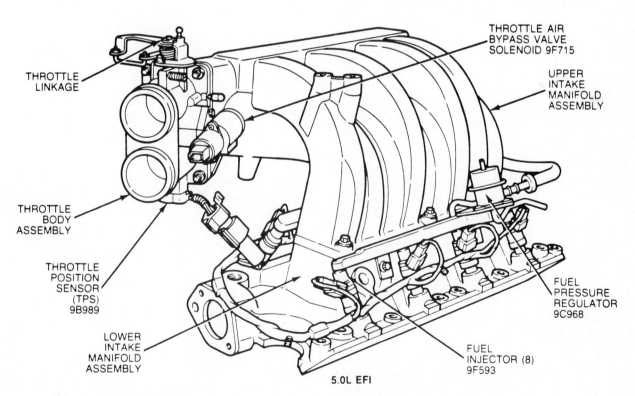

Figure 6-19. High-Rise Intake Manifold, Ford 302 CID (5.0L) Engine. (*Courtesy of Ford Motor Co.*)

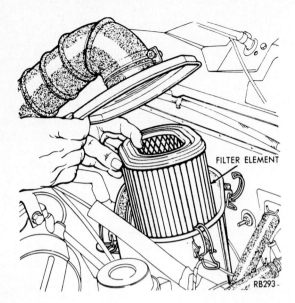

Figure 6-20. Air Cleaner Assembly. (*Courtesy of Chrysler Canada*)

The air cleaner contains the heated air inlet system and the positive crankcase ventilation (PCV) filter. (The heated air inlet system and the PCV system are explained in Chapter 8.) An air cleaner from a four-cylinder engine is shown in Figure 6-20.

Exhaust Turbochargers

Operation

In a turbocharged engine, the energy of the exhaust gases which is normally wasted is converted to mechanical energy by pressurizing the intake manifold with denser air. The exhaust gases flow past a vaned turbine wheel, causing the turbine to rotate at high speed. A shaft is connected from the turbine wheel to a vaned compressor wheel mounted in the air-intake system. The compressor wheel must rotate with the turbine wheel, and the high-speed rotation of the compressor wheel forces air into the intake manifold. This action in turn forces more air-fuel mixture into the cylinders on the intake strokes, creating higher cylinder pressures on the compression and power strokes and providing increased engine power.

The Chrysler 2.2L turbocharged engine provides 160 ft lb (217.6 Nm) of torque and 142 horsepower, a 35 percent increase in torque and a 50 percent improvement in horsepower compared to the same engine without a turbocharger. This relatively small-displacement turbocharged engine is available in

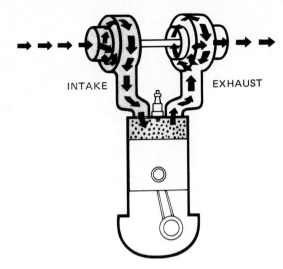

Figure 6-21. Turbocharger Operation. (*Courtesy of Chrysler Canada*)

many Chrysler front-wheel-drive cars. It provides good economy at normal cruising speeds and excellent performance when fast acceleration is required.

The basic turbocharger principle is illustrated in Figure 6-21.

On a normally aspirated non-turbocharged engine a vacuum is created in the intake manifold by the downward piston movement on the intake strokes. This manifold vacuum is used to move the air-fuel mixture through the carburetor into the cylinders. When the turbocharger pressurizes the intake manifold, more air-fuel mixture can be forced into the cylinders than in a normally aspirated engine.

Design

The main components in the turbocharger are shown in Figure 6-22. The turbine and compressor wheels turn at speeds above 100,000 revolutions per minute (rpm). An oil line supplies a continuous flow of oil from the main oil gallery to the turbocharger housing and bearings. The oil is drained from the turbocharger housing to the crankcase through an oil drain-back tube.

On the Chrysler 2.2L turbocharged engine, engine coolant is also circulated through the turbocharged housing. This coolant circulation maintains the turbocharger bearing temperature below 300°F (149°C).

When turbochargers do not have coolant circulation, excessive heat buildup after a hot engine is shut off may cause the engine oil to boil and harden in the bearings, which shortens bearing life. Seals on

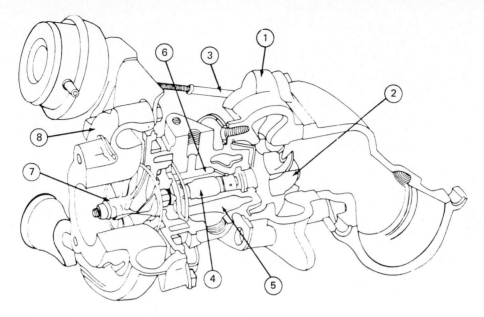

COMPONENTS OF A TURBOCHARGER

① Turbine Housing: (Hot Side)
    Directs exhaust gages to turbine wheel

② Turbine Wheel: (Hot Side)
    Driven by exhaust gages which drives
    the compressor through a shaft

③ Waste Gate:
    Limits amount of boost pressure

④ Shaft Wheel Assembly:
    Supported by bearings that float in oil

⑤ Water Passage:
    Water circulation helps cool hot side of
    turbocharger

⑥ Oil Passage:
    Lubricates and helps cool turbocharger

⑦ Compressor Wheel:
    Compresses air to be forced into intake
    manifold

⑧ Compressor Housing:
    Collects and directs pressurized air to
    intake manifold

Figure 6-22.   Turbocharger Components. (*Courtesy of Chrysler Canada*)

each side of the turbocharger shaft prevent oil from leaking into the intake or exhaust system.

In most automotive turbochargers, the center housing assembly with the shaft, bearings, seals, compressor wheel, and turbine wheel is replaced as a unit. The coolant lines connected to the turbocharger are shown in Figure 6-23.

The turbocharger housing is bolted to the exhaust manifold so that all the exhaust must flow past the turbine wheel. An exhaust pipe is connected from the turbocharger exhaust outlet to the catalytic converter. The air-intake hose is connected from the throttle body assembly to the air inlet on the compressor wheel housing. Air is forced from the compressor wheel through the air-discharge hose into the intake manifold.

The turbocharger mounting with the oil lines and coolant lines is illustrated in Figure 6-24.

Many turbocharged engines are equipped with electronic fuel injection (EFI). These engines usu-ally have fuel injectors located in the intake manifold near the intake ports. On this type of engine the turbocharger forces air into the intake manifold and the fuel is injected into the intake ports by the fuel injectors. The throttle in the throttle body assembly controls engine speed by regulating the amount of air entering the turbocharger compressor housing. A flexible hose is connected from the throttle body assembly to the air cleaner. (Refer to Chapter 18 for a description of the EFI system on the 2.2L engine.)

The turbocharger and throttle body assembly are illustrated in Figure 6-25.

Some turbocharged engines are equipped with a carburetor rather than an EFI system. On these engines the compressor housing is connected to a plenum plate under the carburetor. The compressor wheel forces the air-fuel mixture into the intake manifold.

A turbocharged engine with a carburetor is shown in Figure 6-26.

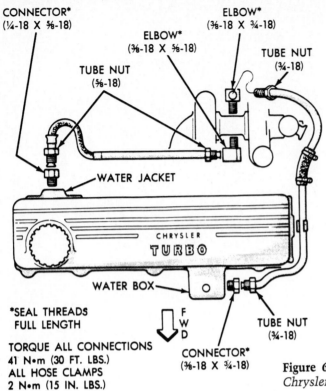

CONNECTOR*
(1/4-18 X 5/8-18)

ELBOW*
(3/8-18 X 3/4-18)

ELBOW*
(3/8-18 X 5/8-18)

TUBE NUT
(3/4-18)

TUBE NUT
(5/8-18)

WATER JACKET

CHRYSLER
TURBO

WATER BOX

FWD

TUBE NUT
(3/4-18)

CONNECTOR*
(3/8-18 X 3/4-18)

*SEAL THREADS
FULL LENGTH

TORQUE ALL CONNECTIONS
41 N•m (30 FT. LBS.)
ALL HOSE CLAMPS
2 N•m (15 IN. LBS.)

Figure 6-23. Turbocharger Coolant Lines. (*Courtesy of Chrysler Canada*)

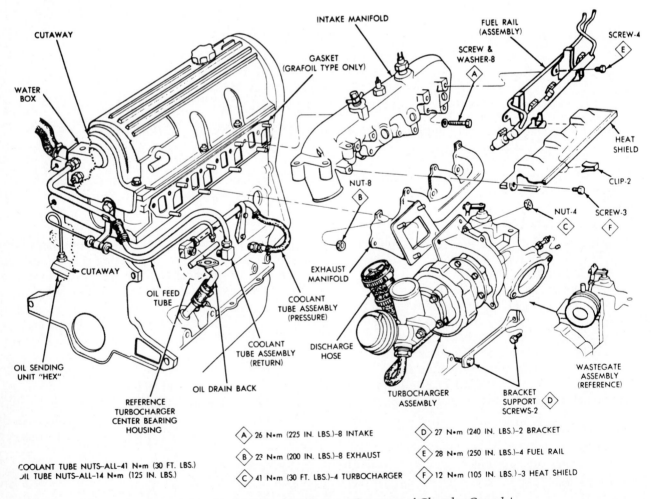

CUTAWAY

WATER BOX

INTAKE MANIFOLD

GASKET
(GRAFOIL TYPE ONLY)

SCREW &
WASHER-8

FUEL RAIL
(ASSEMBLY)

SCREW-4

Ⓔ

Ⓐ

HEAT
SHIELD

CLIP-2

NUT-8

Ⓑ

NUT-4

SCREW-3

Ⓒ

Ⓕ

EXHAUST
MANIFOLD

COOLANT
TUBE ASSEMBLY
(PRESSURE)

OIL FEED
TUBE

DISCHARGE
HOSE

COOLANT
TUBE ASSEMBLY
(RETURN)

CUTAWAY

OIL SENDING
UNIT "HEX"

OIL DRAIN BACK

REFERENCE
TURBOCHARGER
CENTER BEARING
HOUSING

TURBOCHARGER
ASSEMBLY

BRACKET
SUPPORT
SCREWS-2

Ⓓ

WASTEGATE
ASSEMBLY
(REFERENCE)

COOLANT TUBE NUTS-ALL-41 N•m (30 FT. LBS.)
OIL TUBE NUTS-ALL-14 N•m (125 IN. LBS.)

Ⓐ 26 N•m (225 IN. LBS.)-8 INTAKE

Ⓑ 23 N•m (200 IN. LBS.)-8 EXHAUST

Ⓒ 41 N•m (30 FT. LBS.)-4 TURBOCHARGER

Ⓓ 27 N•m (240 IN. LBS.)-2 BRACKET

Ⓔ 28 N•m (250 IN. LBS.)-4 FUEL RAIL

Ⓕ 12 N•m (105 IN. LBS.)-3 HEAT SHIELD

Figure 6-24. Turbocharger Mounting. (*Courtesy of Chrysler Canada*)

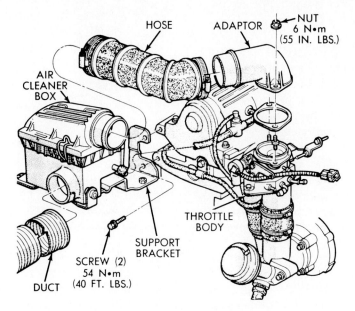

Figure 6-25. Turbocharger and Throttle Body Assembly. (*Courtesy of Chrysler Canada*)

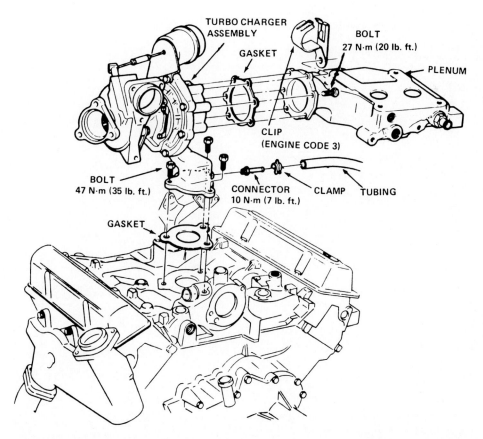

Figure 6-26. Turbocharged Engine with Carburetor. (*Courtesy of Buick Motor Division, General Motors Corporation*)

Boost Pressure Control

A wastegate poppet valve is located in the turbine housing. This valve is connected to the wastegate diaphragm by an operating rod. Boost pressure from the compressor housing is applied to the wastegate diaphragm cover. On many applications, vacuum from the throttle body assembly is applied to the spring chamber under the wastegate diaphragm. When the boost pressure reaches a preset value, the boost pressure moves the wastegate diaphragm against the spring pressure and opens the poppet valve. This allows some of the exhaust to bypass the turbine wheel, which limits the turbine speed and boost pressure.

On the Chrysler 2.2L turbocharged engine, the boost pressure is limited to 7.2 psi (49.6 kPa). This turbocharger begins to pressurize the intake manifold at 1,200 engine rpm and supplies full boost pressure at 2,050 rpm.

The wastegate diaphragm and poppet valve are pictured in Figure 6-27.

Computer Control of Boost Pressure

On many engines equipped with electronic fuel injection, the turbocharger boost pressure is controlled by the electronic control module (ECM). In this type of boost-control system, an ECM-operated solenoid is connected in the wastegate diaphragm boost pressure hose, as illustrated in Figure 6-28.

When the boost pressure reaches the maximum safe limit, the ECM energizes the wastegate solenoid. This action opens the solenoid and vents some of the boost pressure from the wastegate diaphragm to control wastegate movement and boost pressure. The ECM pulses the wastegate solenoid on and off to control boost pressure.

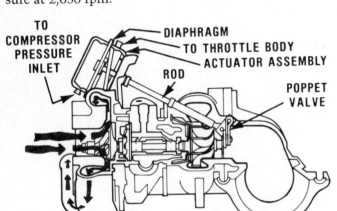

Figure 6-27. Wastegate Diaphragm and Poppet Valve. (*Courtesy of Chrysler Canada*)

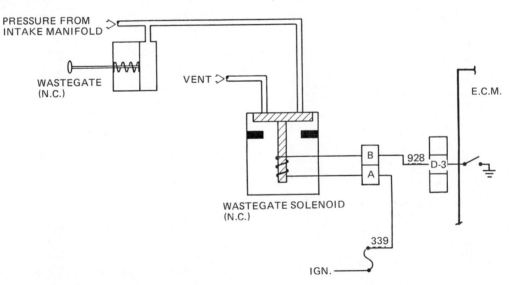

Figure 6-28. Computer-Controlled Boost Pressure. (*Courtesy of GM Product Service Training, General Motors Corporation*)

On some models, during periods of hard acceleration the ECM allows a higher boost pressure for a few seconds to improve engine performance. For example, the ECM may allow a boost pressure of 10 psi (68.9 kPa) for 10 seconds when the engine is accelerated at wide-open throttle. After ten seconds the ECM will return the boost pressure to the normal maximum limit if the engine is still operating at high speed.

(Refer to Chapter 18 for a complete description of computer systems used with electronic fuel injection.)

Boost Pressure Indicators

Most turbocharged engines have a boost indicator on the instrument panel. Some vehicles have a boost indicator light in the instrument panel which is illuminated when the turbocharger develops full boost pressure. Other applications have a second boost indicator light which is illuminated when the turbocharger begins to develop boost pressure. These indicator lights are operated by a pressure switch in the intake manifold.

Some turbocharged vehicles have a boost pressure gauge in the instrument panel, as illustrated in Figure 6-29.

Many of the components in a turbocharged engine are designed with improved durability because of the higher pressures and temperatures encountered in such engines. In the Chrysler 2.2L turbocharged engine, the following components have improved durability or performance characteristics compared to the same components in the 2.2L normally aspirated engine.

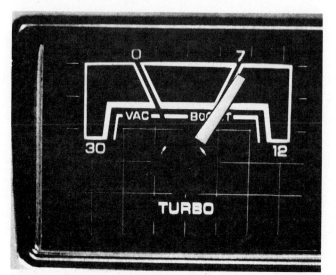

Figure 6-29. Boost Pressure Gauge. (*Courtesy of Chrysler Canada*)

1. The camshaft has reduced overlap and duration, which lowers exhaust temperature.
2. Valve springs have a higher closing rate.
3. The head gasket has improved sealing qualities.
4. Nickel alloy exhaust valves and silicon alloy intake valves are used in the turbocharged engine.
5. Dished pistons provide a compression ratio of 8.2:1 compared to a compression ratio of 9:1 on the normally aspirated engine.
6. Piston rings are the high-performance type.
7. Select-fit connecting rod and main bearings provide improved lubrication.
8. The oil pump has higher output and the tension of the bypass valve is increased.
9. High silicon alloy nodular iron is used in the exhaust manifold.
10. A higher capacity radiator is used.
11. The larger $2\frac{1}{4}$ in. (6.3 cm) diameter exhaust system has increased flow capacity.
12. The heat-shielded heavy-duty starting motor has silver-soldered electrical connections.

Electronic Spark Control (ESC) System

Design and Operation

The ESC system is connected to the General Motors high-energy ignition (HEI) system. Conventional vacuum and centrifugal advance mechanisms are used in the HEI distributor. The distributor pickup coil leads are connected to the ignition module, but these leads are also connected to the ESC controller, which is mounted under the dash on most cars. A fifth terminal on the ignition module is also connected to the ESC controller, and a ground wire is connected from the controller to the distributor housing, as shown in Figure 6-30.

A detonation sensor is mounted at the rear of the engine block or in the intake manifold. This sensor is also connected to the ESC controller. Detonation may occur in a turbocharged engine because of the higher cylinder pressures and temperature. When the engine detonates, the detonation sensor signals the controller to interfere with the pickup signal and retard the timing 4°. The ESC system can provide a total retard 20° if the engine continues to detonate. Once the detonation stops, the controller will restore the spark advance in a few seconds.

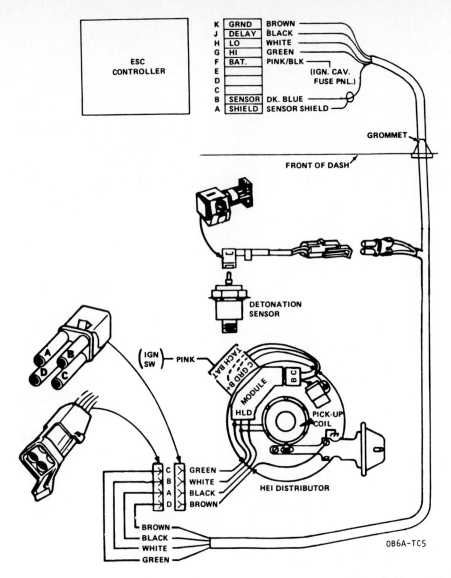

Figure 6-30. Electronic Spark Control (ESC) System. (*Courtesy of Buick Motor Division, General Motors Corporation*)

On later model vehicles, the ESC system is combined with the computer command control (3C) system. (This system is described in Chapter 17.)

The electronic fuel injection (EFI) system used in the Chrysler 2.2L turbocharged engine has a detonation sensor to retard the spark advance if the engine detonates. (Refer to Chapter 18 for a description of this system.)

(Exhaust and emission system service is explained in Chapter 5 of *Automotive Principles: Repair and Service*, Volume II.)

Test Questions

1. An oxidization-type catalytic converter changes _____ and _____ to water (H_2O) and carbon dioxide (CO_2).

2. A three-way catalyst (TWC) reduces _____ to oxygen and nitrogen.

3. Carburetor icing could be caused by a heat riser valve that always remains in the open position. T F

4. A worn seal in the turbocharger could allow oil to leak into the intake system. T F

5. When engine coolant is circulated through the turbocharger housing, the bearing temperature is kept below _____ degrees F.

6. Excessive boost pressure could be caused by a defective wastegate diaphragm. T F

7. Turbocharged engines have a _____ compression ratio than normally aspirated engines.

8. The electronic spark control (ESC) system provides an instant spark control of 20° if the engine detonates. T F

7

Computer-Controlled Diesel Injection and Emission Systems

Chapter Completion Objectives

1. Demonstrate an understanding of the four-stroke cycle diesel engine principle.
2. Explain how a diesel injection pump meters the correct amount of fuel for the engine requirements.
3. Describe the operation of an electronically controlled injection pump advance mechanism.
4. Indicate an understanding of diesel injection pumps with electronic control of fuel metering.
5. Explain the operation of injection nozzles.
6. Demonstrate an understanding of glow plug circuits.
7. Describe the operation of a computer-controlled exhaust-gas recirculation (EGR) system on a diesel engine.

Diesel Engine Principles

Diesel Ignition and Compression Ratio

There are many similarities between the four-stroke cycle diesel engine and the four-stroke cycle gasoline engine. We will consider the major differences between the two engines.

The diesel engine does not require an ignition system to ignite the air-fuel mixture in the cylinders. Instead, the diesel engine uses a very high compression ratio, which creates enough heat on the compression stroke to ignite the air-fuel mixture. The average automotive diesel engine would have a compression ratio of 22.5:1 and a cranking compression pressure of 400 psi (2,758 kPa). For every psi of compression pressure, the temperature of the air in the cylinder increases approximately two degrees F. Therefore, a compression pressure of 400 psi (2,758 kPa) would create a cylinder temperature of approximately 800°F (426°C). The ignition temperature of diesel fuel is about 750°F (398°C).

The diesel engine does not use a throttle to control engine speed. The air-intake system is unrestricted and the speed of the diesel engine is controlled by regulating the amount of fuel that is injected into the cylinders by the injection pump and injectors. Most of the components in a diesel engine are more heavily constructed than the comparable gasoline engine parts because of the higher pressure encountered in the diesel engine.

A four-cylinder automotive diesel engine is illustrated in Figure 7-1.

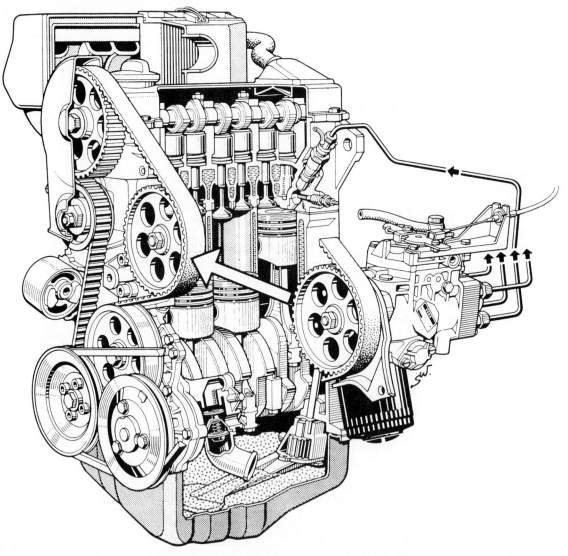

Figure 7-1. Four-Cylinder Automotive Diesel Engine. (Reference taken from SAE paper No. 770113. *Reprinted with Permission of Society of Automotive Engineers,* © *1977*)

Electronically Controlled Diesel Injection Pump

Electronic Control System

As diesel emission standards became increasingly stringent, especially in California, it was necessary to introduce diesel injection pumps that are electronically controlled. These pumps are similar to conventional pumps, but the injection advance is controlled by an electronic control unit which controls a solenoid valve in the injection pump. Input signals to the electronic control unit are the following:

1. Coolant temperature sensor.
2. Speed and crankshaft position sensor.

3. Altitude switch.
4. Injection nozzle with inductive transmitter.

On the basis of the input signals that it receives, the electronic control unit controls the pump solenoid valve to provide the precise injection advance required by the engine.

The complete injection pump electronic control system is shown in Figure 7-2.

The electronic control unit is mounted in the luggage compartment. A power relay supplies voltage to the control unit when the ignition switch is turned on. If the battery polarity is reversed, a diode in the power relay prevents the relay from closing and thus protects the electronic control unit. The power relay is illustrated in Figure 7-3.

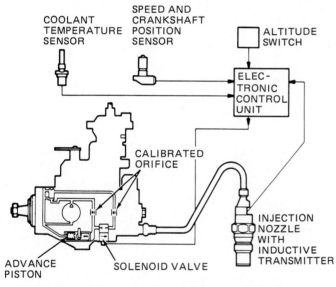

Figure 7-2. Diesel Injection Pump Electronic Control System. (*Courtesy of Ford Motor Co.*)

Fuel System

Operation

An electric lift pump delivers fuel from the fuel tank to the injection pump. A fuel conditioner is connected in the fuel line between the tank and electric pump. This conditioner contains a filter which removes contaminants such as dirt and water from the fuel. A transfer pump in the injection pump delivers fuel to the injection pump plunger. High pressure forces fuel from the pump plunger to the injection nozzles, which inject fuel into the cylinders at the right instant. Excess fuel is returned from the pump and the injectors to the fuel tank. The internal pump components are lubricated and cooled by the diesel fuel.

A complete diesel fuel system is pictured in Figure 7-4.

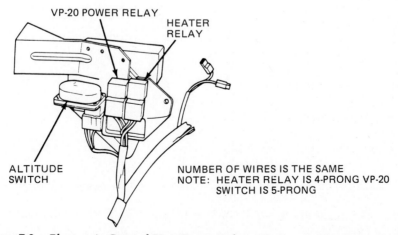

Figure 7-3. Electronic Control Unit Power Relay. (*Courtesy of Ford Motor Co.*)

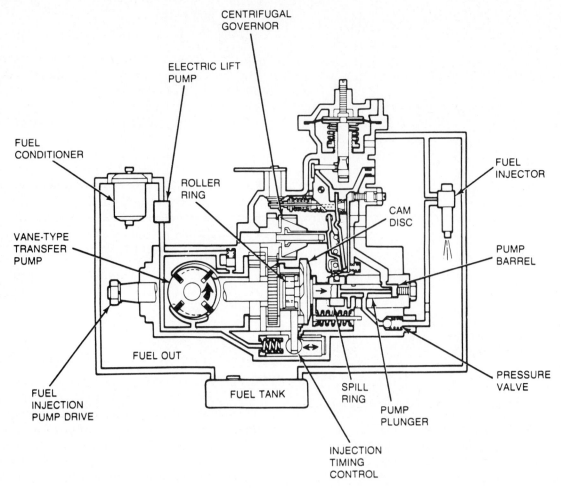

Figure 7-4. Complete Diesel Fuel System. (*Courtesy of Ford Motor Co.*)

Injection Pump

Transfer Pump

The transfer pump contains four spring-loaded vanes mounted in rotor slots. An eccentric pump cavity surrounds the outer edges of the vanes. Fuel enters the transfer pump from the lift pump, and the transfer pump forces fuel past the pressure regulating valve to the injection pump plunger. The pressure regulating valve opens at a specific pressure and returns some of the fuel to the pump inlet, which limits transfer pump pressure.

When engine speed and transfer pump speed increase, the transfer pump pressure gradually increases because of the pressure regulating valve design. A transfer pump with a pressure regulating valve is shown in Figure 7-5.

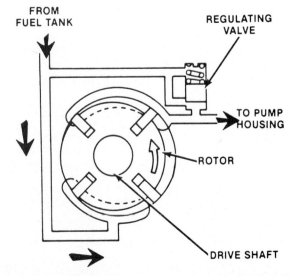

Figure 7-5. Transfer Pump and Pressure Regulating Valve. (*Courtesy of Ford Motor Co.*)

High-Pressure Pump Plunger

When the ignition switch is turned on the electric fuel shutoff plunger is lifted, which allows transfer pump pressure to force fuel into the passages in the high-pressure plunger. The transfer pump and the high-pressure plunger are rotated by the pump drive. A cam disc is mounted on the high-pressure plunger, and the cams on this disc contact rollers in a roller ring. When the low points on the cam are in contact with the rollers, the fuel flows from the transfer pump through one of the plunger fill slots into the center of the plunger.

The number of rotor fill slots corresponds to the number of engine cylinders. A return spring holds the plunger and cam disc against the rollers. As the disc high points contact the rollers, the plunger is forced ahead and the plunger seals the inlet port from the transfer pump. Forward plunger movement creates a very high fuel pressure in the center of the plunger, which forces fuel from the outlet port through the pressure valve to the injection nozzles. This extremely high fuel pressure opens the injection nozzle at the right instant, and the nozzle sprays fuel into the combustion chamber.

The clearance between the plunger and barrel is in millionths of an inch to prevent fuel leaks between the components. A series of equally spaced outlet ports is located around the plunger, and there is always one outlet port for each engine cylinder.

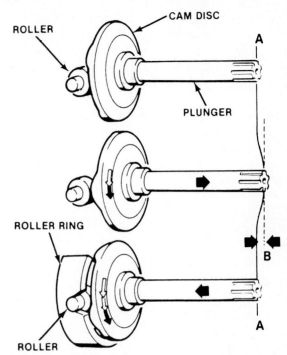

Figure 7-6. Plunger with Cam Disc, Roller, and Roller Ring. (*Courtesy of Ford Motor Co.*)

The plunger stroke is shown in Figure 7-6, and the plunger and barrel are illustrated in Figure 7-7.

The amount of fuel injected is controlled by the spill ring position, which determines the effective plunger stroke. When the plunger is moved forward,

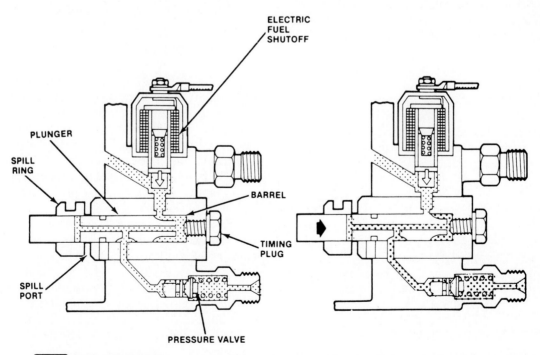

LOW PRESSURE FUEL
HIGH PRESSURE FUEL

Figure 7-7. Plunger and Barrel Fuel Passages. (*Courtesy of Ford Motor Co.*)

the vertical fuel passage in the plunger is uncovered at the edge of the spill ring, which allows fuel to be spilled from the center of the plunger. When this occurs fuel pressure decreases instantly in the plunger and the injection line, which results in injection nozzle closure.

The actual plunger stroke remains constant, but the effective plunger stroke that determines the amount of fuel delivered by the pump is controlled by the spill ring position. If the spill ring is moved toward the cam disc, the effective pump stroke, fuel delivery, and engine speed are reduced. When the spill ring is moved away from the cam disc, the effective pump stroke, fuel delivery, and engine speed are increased.

Governor

The position of the spill ring is controlled by the accelerator pedal and the governor in the pump. A linkage is connected between the accelerator pedal and the governor lever. The governor contains a group of pivoted flyweights which are rotated by a set of gears. A governor drive gear is mounted on the pump drive shaft, and the driven gear rotates the flyweights and retainer. The accelerator pedal is connected to the governor lever through the linkage and governor spring.

When the engine is idling, the governor weights, spring, and linkage position the spill ring to inject the correct amount of fuel to obtain the correct idle speed. A low-speed idle adjusting screw on the injection pump is used to adjust the idle speed, as indicated in Figure 7-8.

As the accelerator pedal is depressed, the linkage and governor spring move the spill ring away from the cam disc. This movement increases the effective plunger stroke, which injects more fuel to increase the engine speed. When the engine speed reaches the governed revolutions per minute (rpm), the outward

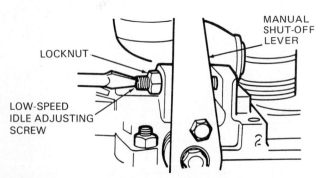

Figure 7-8.   Idle Speed Adjustment. (*Courtesy of Ford Motor Co.*)

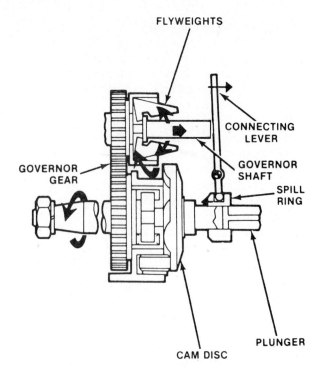

Figure 7-9.   Governor Operation. (*Courtesy of Ford Motor Co.*)

weight movement overcomes the governor spring tension and forces the lever away from the pump drive. This action moves the spill ring toward the cam disc, which reduces the effective plunger stroke and the amount of fuel injected to limit maximum engine speed.

The governor operation is shown in Figure 7-9.

Pressure Valve and Injection Lines

A pressure valve is located in each pump outlet fitting. When the spill port opens at the end of the effective plunger stroke, pressure drops rapidly in the injection line. When this occurs the pressure valve closes, which controls the negative pressure in the injection line. The pressure valve allows enough sudden pressure decrease in the injection line to cause rapid injection nozzle closure and prevent fuel dribbling at the injector.

Excessive negative pressures in the injection lines can actually tear the fuel apart and create vapor cavities in the fuel. When these vapor cavities are formed, very small particles of metal can be torn from the inside surface of the injection lines. This process is known as cavitation, and it can severely deteriorate injection lines in a short time. The pressure valve controls negative injection line pressure and prevents cavitation.

Injection lines are manufactured from high-pressure steel tubing. These lines are all the same length on a given engine. Injection lines of different lengths on the same engine would cause a slight variation in injection timing. Therefore, injection lines must never be altered in any way.

Electronic Injection Advance

A timing-control piston is mounted in a bore below the roller ring, and a pin is connected from the roller ring to the piston. Transfer pump pressure is applied to the right side of the timing-control piston, and a return spring is positioned on the opposite end of the piston.

When engine speed and transfer pump pressure increase, the increase in transfer pump pressure forces the timing control piston to the left against the spring tension. This piston movement rotates the roller ring in the opposite direction to plunger and cam disc rotation, which causes the cams to contact the rollers sooner and advance the injection timing.

The advance mechanism is illustrated in Figure 7-10.

The injection timing-advance solenoid is controlled by the electronic control unit. Some fuel moves from the advance side of the timing-control piston through the advance solenoid to the return spring side of the timing-control piston.

When the input signals inform the electronic control unit that increased injection advance is required, the electronic control unit allows the advance solenoid plunger to move upward. When this occurs, fuel flow past the advance solenoid plunger is reduced, which increases the transfer pump pressure on the timing-control piston. This pressure increase moves the timing-control piston and roller ring to provide more injection advance.

If a reduction in injection timing is necessary, the electronic control unit moves the timing-advance solenoid plunger downward. This action allows more fuel to flow from the advance side of the timing-control piston, past the advance solenoid plunger, and then to the return spring side of the timing-control piston. When this occurs, transfer pump pressure applied to the timing-control piston is reduced, which allows the roller ring and timing-control piston to move to the right. This movement reduces injection timing advance.

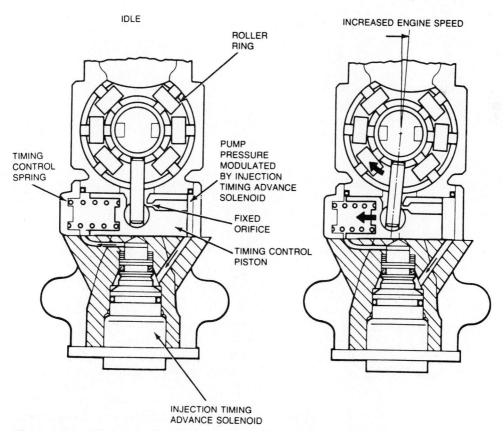

Figure 7-10.   Electronically Controlled Injection Advance Mechanism. (*Courtesy of Ford Motor Co.*)

Injection Nozzles

Design and Operation

Many automotive diesel nozzles are threaded into the cylinder head. A sealing washer seals the end of the nozzle into the cylinder head. The injection line fitting is threaded to the nozzle. A needle valve with a precision tapered tip is positioned in the spray orifice at the nozzle tip. This needle valve is seated by a pressure spring.

When the injection pump delivers high-pressure fuel to the nozzle, the needle valve is lifted against the spring tension and fuel is sprayed from the injector tip into the combustion chamber. The needle valve closes immediately when the injection pump pressure decreases.

Diesel injection nozzle construction is shown in Figure 7-11.

The clearance between the needle valve and the nozzle body is measured in millionths of an inch. Therefore, nozzles are precision devices that require careful handling. Some nozzles have several spray orifices in the tip. The actual number and size of the spray orifices will vary, depending on combustion chamber size.

Some nozzles have a valve with a tapered seat around the circumference of the valve. This type of valve opens outward into the combustion chamber and fuel sprays out around the entire seat circumference. These nozzles may be referred to as poppet nozzles. The internal design of a poppet nozzle is pictured in Figure 7-12.

An internal stop limits the maximum nozzle valve opening. Some nozzles have a return fuel line which returns excess fuel to the fuel tank.

In many automotive diesel engines, the nozzles inject fuel into a small precombustion chamber. Combustion begins in this chamber with a swirling

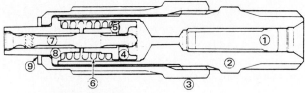

1. EDGE FILTER
2. INLET FITTING (NOZZLE HOLDER BODY)
3. BODY (CAPNUT)
4. RETAINER (COLLAR)
5. SPRING SEAT
6. SPRING
7. PINTLE VALVE (NOZZLE VALVE)
8. NOZZLE BODY
9. SEALING WASHER

Figure 7-12.   Poppet Nozzle Design. (*Courtesy of Pontiac Motor Division, General Motor Corporation*)

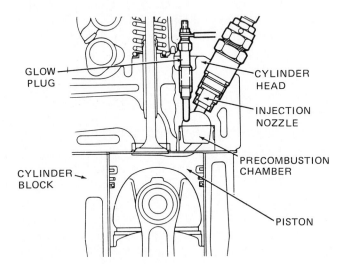

Figure 7-13.   Precombustion Chamber with Nozzle and Glow Plug. (*Courtesy of Ford Motor Co.*)

motion because of the chamber design. The burning air-fuel mixture expands with a strong swirling motion into the main combustion chamber. This action creates increased turbulence in the main combustion chamber to provide more complete burning of the air-fuel mixture.

The glow plugs are usually located in the precombustion chamber with the nozzles, as indicated in Figure 7-13.

Glow Plug Circuits

Design and Operation

Current flow through the glow plugs heats the precombustion chamber, which provides easier starting. An electronic control unit operates two relays which supply voltage to the glow plugs. The electronic control unit receives a coolant temperature

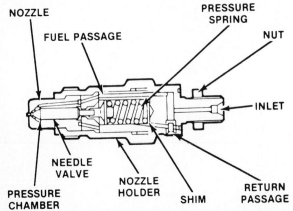

Figure 7-11.   Diesel Injection Nozzle. (*Courtesy of Ford Motor Co.*)

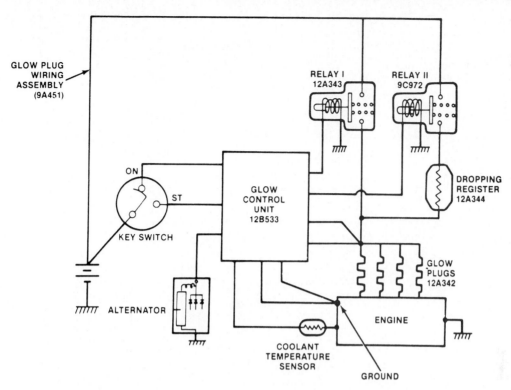

Figure 7-14. Glow Plug Circuit. (*Courtesy of Ford Motor Co.*)

signal. When the ignition switch is turned on with the coolant temperature below 86°F (30°C), the electronic control unit closes both relays. Under this condition, full voltage is supplied to the glow plugs, which heat the precombustion chambers very quickly so the engine can be started immediately.

A signal from the alternator informs the electronic control unit when the engine is started. This signal causes the electronic control unit to open relay I and keep relay II closed. A dropping resistor between relay II and the glow plugs reduces the voltage and current flow through the glow plugs. Relay II may remain closed for 30 seconds after the engine has started. The operation of relay II during this time is referred to as an after-glow period which maintains precombustion chamber temperature to prevent engine stalling.

The complete glow plug circuit is shown in Figure 7-14.

The electronic control unit will only keep relay I closed for three to six seconds after the ignition switch is turned on, whereas the length of the after-glow period will vary, depending on engine temperature. If the ignition switch is turned on and the engine is not cranked, the electronic control unit will open both relays in three to six seconds to prevent battery discharge and glow plug damage. When the coolant temperature is above 86°F (30°C), the electronic control unit will not close relay I.

The glow plug circuit shown in Figure 7-14 does

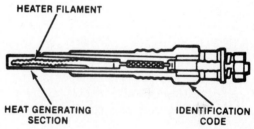

Figure 7-15. Glow Plug Design. (*Courtesy of Ford Motor Co.*)

not have an instrument panel indicator light. Some glow plug circuits have a wait period before the engine is started. These circuits have an instrument panel indicator lamp that informs the operator when to start the engine. A pulsating voltage is supplied to the glow plugs during the after-glow period in some glow plug circuits.

The internal design of a glow plug is illustrated in Figure 7-15.

Computer-Controlled Exhaust-Gas Recirculation System

Electric Circuit and Vacuum Hose Routing

The computer-controlled exhaust-gas recirculation (EGR) system is shown in Figure 7-16.

A diesel engine produces high emissions of oxide of nitrogen (NOx) during idle and off-idle opera-

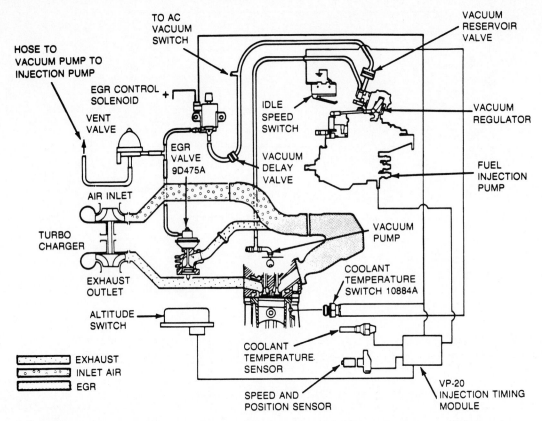

Figure 7-16. Computer-Controlled Exhaust-Gas Recirculation System. (*Courtesy of Ford Motor Co.*)

tion. Therefore, the EGR valve is open during these operating conditions. The purpose of the components in the EGR system may be summarized as follows:

1. *Temperature switch*—senses coolant temperature. This switch is closed above 172°F (78°C).

2. *Vacuum regulator*—mounted on the injection pump and operated by the pump linkage to control the EGR flow in the relation to fuel delivery.

3. *Vacuum reservoir*—prevents vacuum pulsations at the vacuum regulator.

4. *Vacuum delay valve*—delays vacuum supplied to the EGR valve to prevent sudden valve opening and improve driveability.

5. *Idle-speed switch*—informs the injection timing module when the engine is idling. The module uses this signal to control the EGR valve at idle. This switch is mounted on the injection pump.

6. *EGR control solenoid*—the injection timing module opens and closes this solenoid to supply vacuum to the EGR valve.

7. *Vacuum pump*—provides vacuum to operate the EGR valve. It is mounted beneath the rocker arm cover on the engine.

8. *Injection timing module*—controls the EGR valve operation. This module also controls injection advance, as illustrated previously in Figure 7-2.

9. *EGR valve*—when open, recirculates exhaust into the intake manifold.

10. *Speed and position sensor*—supplies an engine rpm signal to the injection timing module. This sensor is positioned on the lower left corner of the engine block.

11. *Altitude switch*—informs the injection timing module when the vehicle is operating above 9,800 ft (3,000 m) elevation.

12. *EGR vent valve*—vents the vacuum hose from the vacuum pump to the atmosphere if the EGR vacuum supply exceeds 8.6 in Hg (29 kPa).

The computer-controlled EGR system shown in Figure 7-16 and the glow plug system illustrated in Figure 7-14 are used on the Ford 2.4L turbocharged diesel engine.

Diesel Injection Pump with Computer Control of Fuel Delivery and Injection Advance

Design

The electronic programmable injection control (EPIC) injection pump has internally mounted sensors and actuators and an external microprocessor. Compared to a similar conventional diesel injection pump, the EPIC pump provides lower combustion noise with improved economy and performance. The microprocessor could easily be expanded to control the turbocharger wastegate, intercooler, and exhaust-gas recirculation (EGR).

The EPIC injection pump is lighter and more compact than a smaller conventional pump. There are only 100 parts in the EPIC injection pump, compared to 220 components in a similar conventional pump. The EPIC injection pump is designed primarily for engines in passenger cars and light trucks.

Fuel Control

In many conventional injection pumps, transfer pump pressure supplies fuel past a metering valve to the chamber between the pumping pistons in the rotor. The position of the metering valve controls the amount of fuel injected by regulating fuel delivery to the rotor pumping chamber. Rotation of the metering valve is controlled by the accelerator pedal and the governor. The pumping pistons are forced together by cams on an internal cam ring as the rotor assembly rotates.

The EPIC injection pump has angled ramps on the shoes that fit against the outer ends of the pumping pistons. These ramps match similar ramps on the pump drive shaft. Axial rotor movement varies the pumping piston position, and therefore determines the pumping chamber volume, which provides precise fuel delivery control. Transfer pump pressure supplies fuel to the rotor pumping chamber, and this same pressure also delivers fuel through an electrohydraulic actuator to the front of the rotor.

The electronic control unit controls the actuator and the amount of fuel pressure delivered to the front of the rotor. In this way the electronic control unit and the actuator control the rotor axial position to provide precise fuel delivery. A position sensor at the front of the rotor sends a signal to the electronic control unit in relation to rotor axial position.

The fuel metering control in a conventional in-

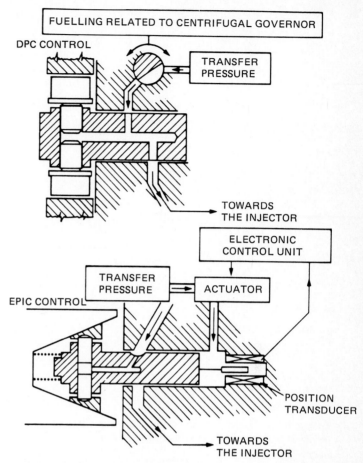

Figure 7-17. Conventional and Electronic Fuel Metering Control. (*Reprinted with Permission of Society of Automotive Engineers, © 1985*)

jection pump is compared to the EPIC pump in Figure 7-17.

Injection Timing Control

Transfer pump pressure is also supplied through another electrohydraulic actuator to the advance piston. When the input signals indicate that more injection advance is required, the electronic control unit operates the actuator to increase the transfer pump pressure supplied to the advance piston. This pressure increase moves the advance piston against the return spring pressure. This movement rotates the cam ring in the opposite direction to rotor rotation. Cam ring rotation causes the pumping piston mechanisms to strike the internal cams sooner to advance the injection timing. A position transducer on the return spring side of the advance mechanism sends an input signal to the electronic control unit in relation to advance piston movement.

BY CONTROL OF CAM POSITION

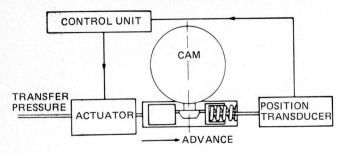

BY CONTROL OF START NEEDLE LIFT

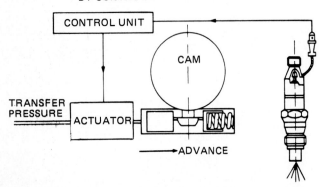

Figure 7-18. Electronic Injection Advance Control. (*Reprinted with Permission of Society of Automotive Engineers,* © 1985)

In some injection systems a sensor in the injector informs the electronic control unit when the injector plunger begins to lift. This type of sensor may be used in place of the advance piston position transducer. Both types of sensors are illustrated in the injection advance systems in Figure 7-18.

(Diesel engine service is explained in Chapter 4 of *Automotive Principles: Repair and Service,* Volume II.)

Test Questions

1. The ignition temperature of diesel fuel is approximately:
   a) 600°F.
   b) 675°F.
   c) 750°F.

2. The effective pump stroke is controlled by the:
   a) spill ring position.
   b) roller ring position.
   c) speed of plunger rotation.

3. Excessive negative pressure in diesel injection lines can result in _____ of the lines.

4. When the ignition switch is turned on and the engine coolant is cold, the electronic control unit in the glow plug circuit will close:
   a) both relays.
   b) relay I only.
   c) relay II only.

5. If the ignition switch is left on and a cold engine is not started, the electronic control unit in the glow plug circuit will:
   a) keep the glow plugs on until the battery is discharged.
   b) keep relay II closed.
   c) shut off both relays in 3 to 6 seconds.

8

Fuel Economy and Emission Control

Corporate Average Fuel Economy Standards

Energy Policy and Conservation

In the United States, the Energy Policy and Conservation Act (EPCA) gave the Secretary of Transportation a mandate to establish average fuel economy standards for major automobile manufacturers and importers with production above 10,000 cars per year. These corporate average fuel economy (CAFE) standards were established in 1978 and became increasingly stringent with each model year, as indicated in Table 8-1.

TABLE 8-1. Corporate Average Fuel Economy Standards.
(Courtesy of Chrysler Canada)

Model Year	MPG	Improvement Over 1974
1978	18.0	50%
1979	19.0	58%
1980	20.0	67%
1981	22.0	83%
1982	24.0	100%
1983	26.0	116%
1984	27.0	125%
1985	27.5	129%
1986	27.5	129%

Car manufacturers could be fined if their vehicles did not meet CAFE standards. These fines amounted to $5.00 for each tenth of a mile per gallon that their CAFE fell below that year's standard, multiplied by the number of cars produced or imported that year. The miles per gallon (MPG) rating of each vehicle is established by Environmental Protection Agency (EPA) procedures. Car manufacturers were faced with the challenge of meeting CAFE standards, as well as conforming to emission standards that also became increasingly stringent.

Methods of Improving Fuel Economy

Aerodynamics

Improving the aerodynamics of cars is a significant method of improving fuel economy. When an average automobile is travelling at 40 MPH (25 KPH), 50 percent of the engine power is used to push the air out of the way, and the percentage increases rapidly above that speed. The drag coefficient (Cd) is a measurement of the aerodynamic drag force of an auto-

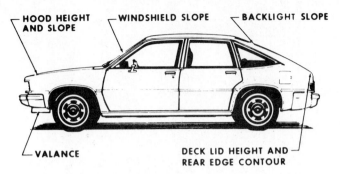

Figure 8-1. Critical Body Design Areas that Determine Drag Coefficient. (Reference taken from SAE paper No. 790724. *Reprinted with Permission of Society of Automotive Engineers,* © 1979)

mobile. Some of the critical body design areas that determine the Cd are illustrated in Figure 8-1.

Testing of aerodynamic drag is usually done by placing the car in a wind tunnel test facility in which different wind velocities are simulated. In the development of a new body style, engineers may test $\frac{1}{4}$-scale clay models, full-scale clay models, and prototype cars in the wind tunnel to develop the lowest possible Cd and still maintain an attractive body style.

Wind tunnel testing of clay models is shown in Figure 8-2, and Figure 8-3 pictures a prototype car in the wind tunnel.

The Cd on a car is improved by many small changes in body design. In the development of one typical car body, changes to the hood, roof line, and windshield molding reduced the Cd. These modifications and Cd reductions are illustrated in Figures 8-4, 8-5, and 8-6.

When the General Motors "X" body cars were developed, they had a Cd of .417 to .466, depending on the body style. If a 1980 Citation four-door hatchback is compared to its predecessor, a 1979 Nova four-door sedan, the improved Cd of the Citation provides a 1.2 MPG fuel saving using actual EPA 55/45 MPH expressway test procedures.

Electric Cooling Fans and Fan Design

Electric cooling fans use less energy than belt-driven fans, because the electric cooling fan circuit only operates the fan when engine cooling requirements are high. (Electric cooling fan circuits are explained in Chapter 3.)

Automotive engineers have done considerable testing of electric cooling fans to develop fans that require less turning power but operate quietly and provide adequate cooling. Engineers may change fan blade angles and spacing, fan motor mounting an-

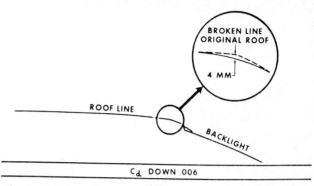

Figure 8-4. Coefficient of Drag Reduction by Roof Line Modifications. (Reference taken from SAE paper No. 790724. *Reprinted with Permission of Society of Automotive Engineers,* © *1979)*

Figure 8-2. Wind Tunnel Testing of Clay Models. (Reference taken from SAE paper No. 790724. *Reprinted with Permission of Society of Automotive Engineers,* © *1979.)*

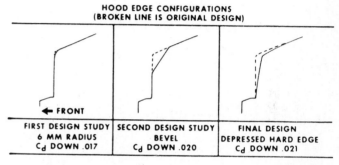

Figure 8-5. Coefficient of Drag Reduction by Hood Edge Modifications. (Reference taken from SAE paper No. 790724. *Reprinted with Permission of Society of Automotive Engineers,* © *1979)*

Figure 8-3. Wind Tunnel Testing of Prototype Cars. (Reference taken from SAE paper No. 790724. *Reprinted with Permission of Society of Automotive Engineers,* © *1979)*

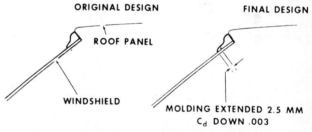

Figure 8-6. Coefficient of Drag Reduction with Windshield Molding Changes. (Reference taken from SAE paper No. 790724. *Reprinted with Permission of Society of Automotive Engineers,* © *1979)*

Tire Rolling Resistance

Fuel economy can be improved by reducing tire rolling resistance. Uniroyal Tire Company, in cooperation with General Motors, developed tires with reduced rolling resistance for the General Motors "X" body cars. These tires had reduced weight and less sidewall flexibility. The monoply tire developed for the "X" cars is compared to a conventional two-ply radial tire in Figure 8-8.

gles, mounting brackets, and shrouds to achieve these objectives.

Typical fan motor mounting angles and mounting brackets are shown in Figure 8-7.

The electric cooling fan in a 1980 "X" body Chevrolet Citation provides a .3 MPG fuel saving when this car is compared to a 1979 Nova with a belt-driven fan, as illustrated in Table 8-2.

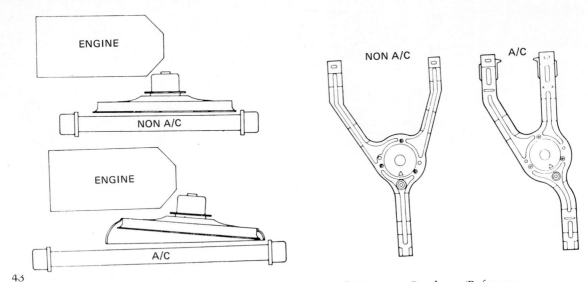

43
44 **Figure 8-7.** Electric Fan Motor Mounting Angles and Mounting Brackets. (Reference
45 taken from SAE paper No. 790722. *Reprinted with Permission of Society of Automo-*
46 *tive Engineers,* © *1979)*

TABLE 8-2. Fuel Economy Saving, 1980 Citation "X" Car Compared to 1979 Nova "X" Car. (Reference taken from SAE paper No. 790724. *Reprinted with Permission of Society of Automotive Engineers,* © *1979)*

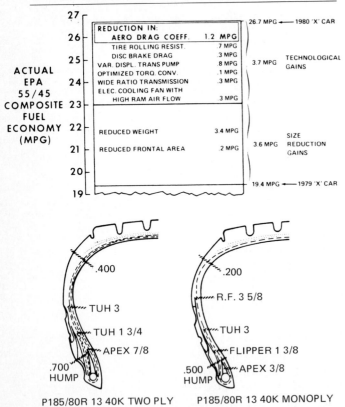

Figure 8-8. Monoply Tire and Two-Ply Tire. (Reference taken from SAE paper No. 790726. *Reprinted with Permission of Society of Automotive Engineers,* © *1979)*

The reduced tire rolling resistance on the "X" body cars provided a .7 MPG increase in fuel economy compared to a 1979 Nova with conventional tires, as shown in Table 8-2.

Variable-Displacement Automatic Transaxle Pumps

A variable-displacement oil pump is used in some automatic transaxles to increase fuel economy. This type of pump contains rotating vanes that are mounted in a movable vane ring which is connected to the rotor. A pump drive shaft is splined to the rotor and the torque converter. The vanes rotate inside a pivoted slide.

Oil pressure from the pressure regulator valve is supplied to one side of the slide, which is sealed in the pump body. A priming spring pushes the slide toward the high-output position. In this mode the longest area of the vanes is exposed to the oil that is being moved from the pump inlet to the outlet. The outlet from the oil pump is supplied to the pressure regulator valve and to the hydraulic system in the transaxle.

If oil flow demands in the transaxle are low, the pump pressure increases and moves the pressure regulating valve against its spring. This allows oil pressure to be supplied from the pressure regulating valve to the oil pump slide, which forces the slide to move against the priming spring tension. Under this condition the shorter length of the vanes is exposed to the oil that is being moved through the pump.

This reduces the pump output so that less energy is required to turn the pump. In the low-output mode, some oil will be returned from the pressure regulator valve to the oil sump, and this action limits pump pressure.

If transaxle oil flow requirements are high, the line pressure tends to decrease. This causes the pressure regulating valve spring to move the valve to the right, and a land on the valve shuts off oil pressure to the pump slide. When this occurs the priming spring moves the vane ring to the high-output position.

The variable-displacement pump is pictured in Figure 8-9.

In most automatic transaxles the oil pump operates at a constant volume. When oil flow demands are low in the transaxle, a considerable amount of oil pressure is returned from the pressure regulating valve to the transaxle sump. This type of pump requires more turning force than a variable-displacement pump.

In the General Motors "X" body cars, the variable-displacement oil pump provides a fuel saving of .9 MPG. In the same automatic transaxles, a more efficient torque converter contributes a fuel saving of .1 MPG, and more accurate matching of transmission gear ratios to engine torque and horsepower provide a .3 MPG improvement in fuel economy, as outlined in Table 8-2.

Reduced Brake Drag

Disc brakes are used on the front wheels of many vehicles. In some of these brake systems, the brake pad lining contacts the brake rotor lightly when the brakes are not applied, and this produces a slight drag on the rotors and front wheels.

Some brake caliper pistons have a special seal that twists when the brakes are applied and the piston is extended. When the brakes are released, the seal retains its original shape and pulls the piston back into the caliper. This allows a small clearance between the brake pads and the rotor, which prevents any drag on the rotor.

A quick-take-up master cylinder is required with this type of piston seal. (Refer to Chapter 25 for an explanation of the complete brake system.) The special piston seals are illustrated in Figure 8-10. The low-drag brake system provided a .3 MPG fuel saving on General Motors "X" body cars, as indicated in Table 8-2.

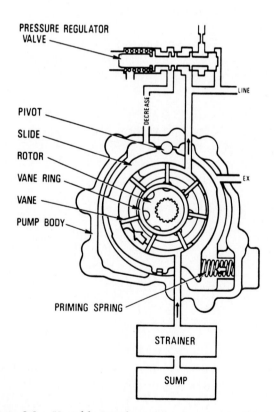

Figure 8-9. Variable-Displacement Automatic Transaxle Pump. (Reference taken from SAE paper No. 790725. *Reprinted with Permission of Society of Automotive Engineers,* © *1979)*

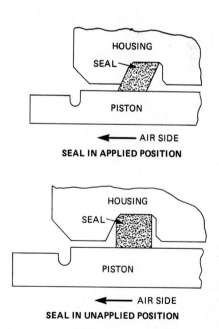

Figure 8-10. Brake Caliper Piston Seals that Provide Reduced Brake Drag. (Reference taken from SAE paper No. 790723. *Reprinted with Permission of Society of Automotive Engineers,* © *1979)*

Reduced Vehicle Weight

Reducing weight is one of the most effective methods to reduce fuel consumption. In 1980s cars, manufacturers have reduced the weight of many components. Lighter weight materials such as plastic and aluminum have been used in many body parts. Aluminum castings have replaced heavier cast iron castings in many engine components, such as intake manifolds, cylinder heads, and timing gear housings. Thinner, lighter weight glass has been used in the windows. Lightweight power steering pumps and air conditioning compressors have been introduced. One manufacturer has developed tubular stainless steel exhaust manifolds to replace the previous cast iron manifolds, which reduces weight.

The reduced weight of a 1980 General Motor "X" body car compared to a 1979 Nova provides a fuel saving of 3.4 MPG, as shown in Table 8-2.

Motor Vehicle Emissions

Regulated Emissions

Air pollution legislation usually regulates unburned hydrocarbon (HC), carbon monoxide (CO), and oxides of nitrogen (NOx) emissions from automobiles. Most emissions occur at the tailpipe of the vehicle. Since gasoline is a hydrocarbon fuel and combustion in the cylinders is never complete, HC emissions occur in the exhaust of the vehicle. Evaporative sources such as fuel tanks and carburetors also contribute to HC emissions.

Hydrogen and carbon in the gasoline combine with oxygen in the air to form a combustible air-fuel mixture in the engine cylinders. When the combustible mixture is burned in the cylinders, the resultant byproducts are CO, carbon dioxide (CO_2), carbon (C), and water (H_2O). Therefore, combustion must occur before CO will be formed.

The atmosphere contains approximately 20 percent oxygen and 80 percent nitrogen. When the temperature in the cylinders exceeds 2,500°F (1,370°C) during the combustion process, the oxygen and nitrogen combine to form NOx.

The government of California became the first official body to regulate the emission levels of new automobiles when it passed legislation in 1963 requiring positive crankcase ventilation (PCV) valves on new automobiles. The California Air Resources Board (CARB) is responsible for air quality in the state.

The Environmental Protection Agency (EPA) is in charge of federal air pollution regulation in the United States. In Canada, air quality is the responsibility of Environment Canada.

Emission Standards

Passenger Car Emission Standards

Federal and California passenger car emission standards from 1978 to the 1986 model year are compared with the uncontrolled emission levels of 1960 in Table 8-3.

Light-Duty Truck Emission Standards

A light-duty truck is defined by Title 13 of the California Administrative Code as any motor vehicle

TABLE 8-3. Emission Standards. (*Courtesy of Chrysler Canada*)

Model Year	Hydrocarbon (HC)		Carbon Monoxide (CO)		Oxides of Nitrogen (NOx)	
	California	Federal	California	Federal	California	Federal
1978	0.41	1.5	9.0	15.0	1.5	2.0
1979	0.41	0.41	9.0	15.0	1.5	2.0
1980	0.39	0.41	9.0	7.0	1.0	2.0
1981	0.39	0.41	7.0	3.4	0.7	1.0
1982	0.39	0.41	7.0	3.4	0.4	1.0
1983	0.39	0.41	7.0	3.4	0.4	1.0
1984	0.39	0.41	7.0	3.4	0.4	1.0
1985	0.39	0.41	7.0	3.4	0.7	1.0
1986	0.39	0.41	7.0	3.4	0.7	1.0
1960 (No Control)		10.6		84		4.1

TABLE 8-4. Emission Standards for Light-Duty Trucks.

| Year | Standard | Hydrocarbons (HC) | | Carbon Monoxide (CO) | Oxides of Nitrogen (NO$_x$) |
		Nonmethane	Total		
1983	California 50,000	0.39	0.41 g/mi	9.0 g/mi	0.4 g/mi
	Federal 50,000	no standard	1.7	18.0	2.3

that is rated at 6,000 lbs (2.718 kg) gross vehicle weight (GVW) or less and is designed primarily for purposes of transportation of property, or that is a derivative of such a vehicle, or that is available with special features enabling off-street or off-highway operation and use. The current federal and California emission levels for light-duty trucks are listed in Table 8-4.

Exhaust-Gas Recirculation (EGR) Valves

Conventional EGR Valves

The conventional EGR valve contains a vacuum diaphragm linked to a tapered valve. One side of the tapered valve is connected to the exhaust crossover passage in the intake manifold, and the other side is connected to the fuel passages in the intake manifold. Ported vacuum from a vacuum outlet above the throttle valve is connected to the EGR valve vacuum chamber, as illustrated in Figure 8-11, and a diaphragm spring holds the valve closed.

When the throttle is opened from the idle position, ported manifold vacuum applied to the EGR valve diaphragm opens the tapered valve. Once the

EGR valve is opened, exhaust gas flows into the intake manifold. Because of the lack of oxygen, the exhaust gas does not promote combustion in the cylinders. Recirculating exhaust gas through the EGR valve into the intake manifold lowers combustion temperature and reduces oxides of nitrogen emission levels.

Most EGR valves require 3 in. Hg (10 kPa) of vacuum applied to the diaphragm to hold the valve open. At a wide-throttle opening, the manifold vacuum drops below 3 in. Hg (10 kPa), and the diaphragm spring closes the EGR valve.

Exhaust gas must not be allowed to recirculate into the intake manifold at idle speed. Rough idling will occur if the EGR valve sticks in the open position.

Back-Pressure Transducer EGR Valve

Some EGR valves contain a built-in back-pressure transducer (BPT) valve. Exhaust-gas pressure is applied through the hollow EGR valve stem to the BPT diaphragm, as shown in Figure 8-12, and a vacuum control valve is located above the BPT diaphragm.

When the throttle is opened from the idle position, ported vacuum becomes available at the EGR

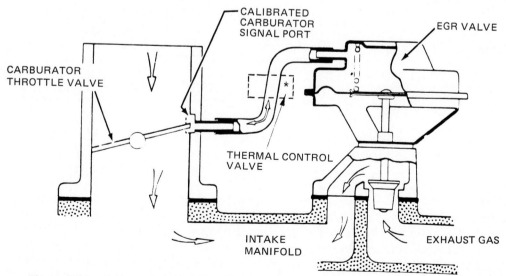

Figure 8-11. Conventional EGR Valve. (*Courtesy of GM Product Service Training, General Motors Corporation*)

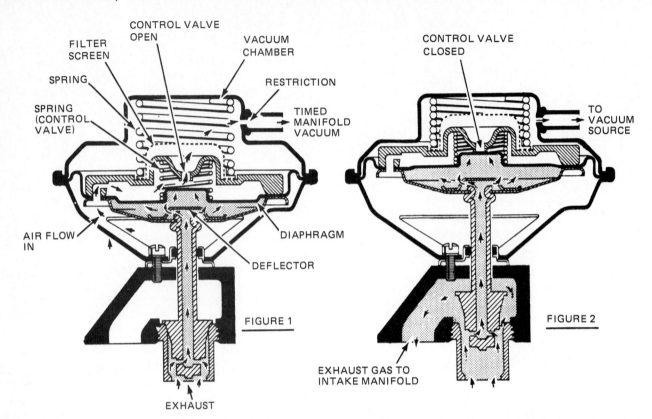

Figure 8-12.   Back-Pressure Transducer EGR Valve. (*Courtesy of Chevrolet Motor Division, General Motors Corporation*)

valve. At low speeds, the vacuum applied to the EGR valve is bled off through the control valve and vent opening, and the EGR valve remains closed. Exhaust pressure forces the BPT diaphragm upward and closes the control valve at 30 to 35 MPH (50 to 58 KPH). Once the control valve is closed, as pictured in the EGR valve on the right side of Figure 8-12, the ported manifold vacuum opens the EGR valve.

EGR Valve Control

Coolant-Controlled Ported Vacuum Switch (PVS)

Nitrous oxide emissions occur at high cylinder temperatures. While the engine is warming up, NOx emissions are low, and exhaust-gas recirculation is not required. A ported vacuum switch operated by coolant temperature is connected in the EGR vacuum hose. This switch shuts off vacuum to the EGR valve when the engine coolant is cold. When the engine coolant is above a specified temperature, the ported vacuum switch opens and supplies vacuum to the EGR valve.

A ported vacuum switch is connected in the EGR vacuum hose in Figure 8-13.

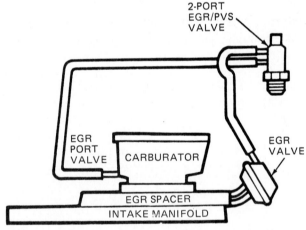

Figure 8-13.   EGR Coolant-Controlled Ported Vacuum Switch. (*Courtesy of Ford Motor Co.*)

EGR Vacuum Amplifier

Many engines have a vacuum amplifier to control the EGR valve. The intake manifold vacuum and carburetor venturi vacuum are both applied to the vacuum amplifier, as shown in Figure 8-14.

The EGR vacuum amplifier is replaced as a unit. Before the system can be diagnosed, however, the internal operation of the amplifier must be understood.

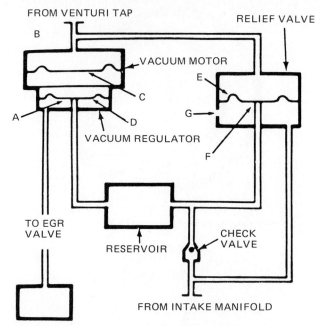

Figure 8-14. Internal Design of EGR Vacuum Amplifier. *(Courtesy of Ford Motor Co.)*

the venturi vacuum will be sufficient to lift diaphragms C and D. As diaphragm D lifts up, port A opens and allows the manifold vacuum to open the EGR valve. The venturi vacuum is applied to the upper side of diaphragm E, and manifold vacuum becomes available at the lower diaphragm chamber.

During idling or at cruising speed, manifold vacuum is higher than venturi vacuum. The higher manifold vacuum holds diaphragm E downward and valve F remains closed. At wide throttle openings, diaphragm E is lifted upward when venturi vacuum exceeds manifold vacuum. When valve F is open, the manifold vacuum in the EGR system is bled off through port G, and the EGR valve is allowed to close at wide throttle opening.

Valve A is designed with a small amount of leakage. Vacuum applied to the EGR valve should not exceed 0.5 in. Hg (1.6 kPa) at idle speed. Rough idling could result if excessive leakage at valve A were to hold the EGR valve open during idle operation.

Charge Temperature Switch and Timer

Some models have a charge temperature switch (CTS) and a CTS timer to control the EGR vacuum solenoid, as pictured in Figure 8-15.

The CTS senses the temperature of the air-fuel mixture charge in the intake manifold. When the intake charge temperature is less than 60°F (16°C), the CTS is closed and the timer keeps the solenoid en-

When the engine is idling, manifold vacuum is available through the check ball and reservoir to valve A, as shown in Figure 8-14. The manifold vacuum to the EGR valve is shut off by valve A. The venturi vacuum at port B increases in relation to engine rpm. Diaphragms C and D are interconnected. At a vehicle speed of 30 to 35 MPH (50 to 58 KPH),

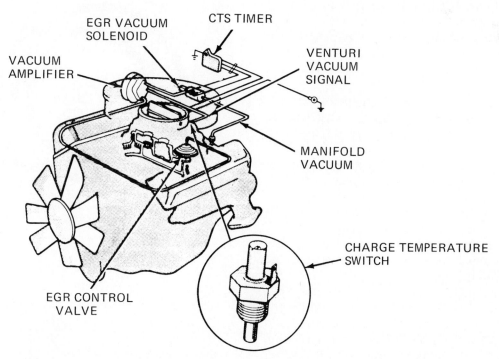

Figure 8-15. Charge Temperature Switch (CTS) and Timer. *(Courtesy of Chrysler Canada)*

ergized continuously and shuts off the vacuum to the amplifier and the EGR valve. When the intake charge temperature is greater than 60°F (16°C), the CTS is open and the timer is able to energize the vacuum solenoid and shut off the vacuum to the amplifier for 35 seconds each time the engine is started. After the engine has been running for 35 seconds, the timer de-energizes the vacuum solenoid and vacuum is applied to the amplifier.

Air-Injection Reactor (AIR) Systems

Air Pump

The main component in the air-injection system is a belt-driven air pump. Air is moved through the pump by two rotating vanes, as illustrated in Figure 8-16.

Air enters the pump through the centrifugal filter behind the pulley, and exits through the outlet at the rear of the pump. Dirt particles are cleaned from the air by the centrifugal filter, as shown in Figure 8-17.

Air System

Airflow from the pump moves through the diverter valve, hoses, one-way check valves, and piping into each exhaust port, as shown in Figure 8-18.

Some cylinder heads have internal air passages rather than external air pipes. Vehicles without catalytic converters use air injection to burn hydrocarbon (HC) emissions at the exhaust ports. Oxygen is necessary for the catalytic converter to oxidize carbon monoxide (CO) and HC into carbon dioxide (CO_2) and water vapor. In cars equipped with catalytic converters, the air pump supplies oxygen to the converter. (Catalytic converters are discussed in Chapter 8.)

In some converter-equipped vehicles, air is injected downstream into the exhaust manifold flange or converter rather than into the exhaust ports. Some air-injection systems use a switching arrangement to change air injection from the exhaust ports to a downstream location under specific operating conditions. Different types of air-injection systems are covered later in this chapter.

Airflow through the air-injection system is pictured in Figure 8-19. The one-way check valves prevent exhaust from flowing into the air system should the pump become inoperative. Notice the vacuum connection from the intake manifold to the diverter valve.

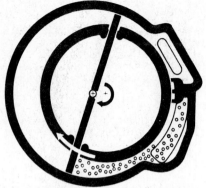

The vane is travelling from a small area into a larger area—consequently a vacuum is formed that draws fresh air into the pump.

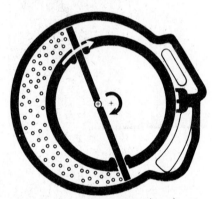

As the vane continues to rotate, the other vane has rotated past the inlet opening. Now the air that has just been drawn in is entrapped between the vanes. This entrapped air is then transferred into a smaller area and thus compressed.

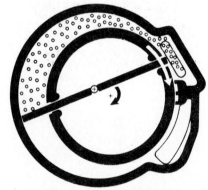

As the vane continues to rotate it passes the outlet cavity in the pump housing bore and exhausts the compressed air into the remainder of the system.

Figure 8-16. Airflow Through Air Pump. (*Courtesy of Chevrolet Motor Division, General Motors Corporation*)

The diverter valve assembly contains a pressure relief valve and a diverter valve operated by a vacuum diaphragm. The pressure relief valve limits pump pressure to 2 to 6 psi (14 to 42 kPa). Under idle, cruise, or wide-open throttle conditions, the

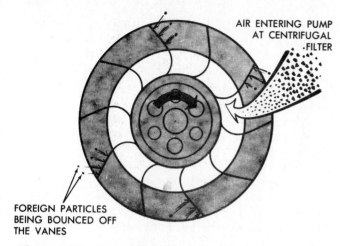

Figure 8-17. Centrifugal Filter Operation. (*Courtesy of Chevrolet Motor Division, General Motors Corporation*)

manifold vacuum is insufficient to move the diverter valve diaphragm. With the diaphragm and diverter valve in the downward position, air is allowed to flow from the pump to the exhaust ports, as illustrated in Figure 8-20.

On sudden deceleration, manifold vacuum is approximately 21 to 22 in. Hg (69 to 72 kPa), which lifts the diverter valve and diaphragm. Under this condition air is directed from the pump through the diverter valve to the atmosphere.

Sudden deceleration causes the air-fuel mixture to become richer, and thus HC and CO emissions increase. If the air pump continued pumping air into the exhaust ports on deceleration, excessive burning of HC would occur in the exhaust manifolds, and manifold backfiring would result. The diverter valve prevents manifold backfiring on deceleration by mo-

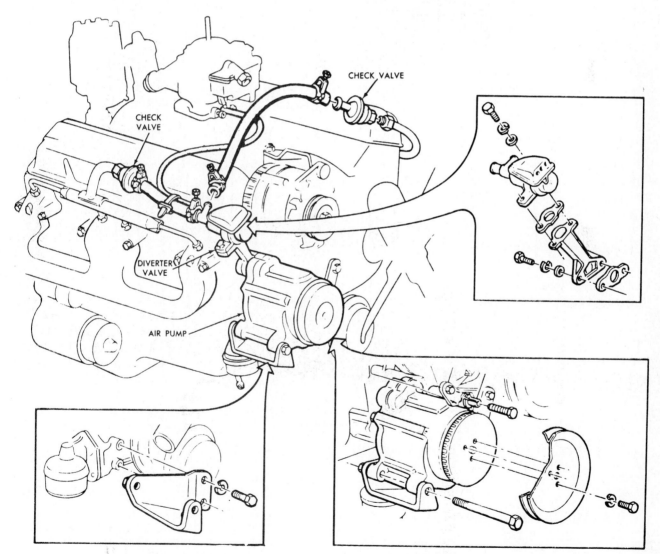

Figure 8-18. Air-Injection System. (*Courtesy of Chevrolet Motor Division, General Motors Corporation*)

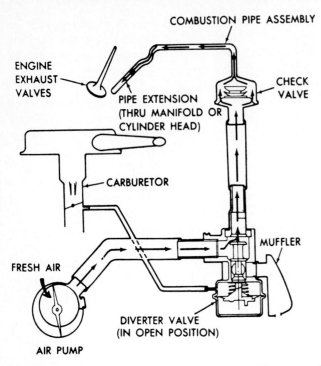

Figure 8-19. Airflow Through Air System. (*Courtesy of Chevrolet Motor Division, General Motors Corporation*)

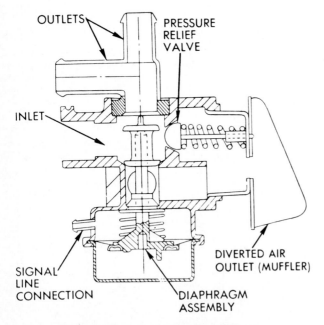

EXTERNAL MUFFLER TYPE

Figure 8-20. Diverter Valve Design. (*Courtesy of Chevrolet Motor Division, General Motors Corporation*)

mentarily directing airflow from the pump to the atmosphere.

Air-Injection System with Downstream Injection

Design

The airflow from the pump is directed to the exhaust ports or the exhaust manifold flange by the air-switching valve. A coolant-control vacuum switch in connected in the vacuum circuit to the air-switching valve, as illustrated in Figure 8-21.

Diverter Valve

Airflow is directed into the air system or bypassed to the atmosphere by the diverter valve. Under normal operating conditions, the diverter valve directs airflow from the pump into the air system, as shown in Figure 8-22.

When the engine is suddenly decelerated, high manifold vacuum pulls the diverter valve diaphragm upward. Airflow is then directed from the pump through the diverter valve to the atmosphere. The pressure relief valve limits pump pressure to a maximum of 6 psi (42 kPa) by directing excess airflow to the atmosphere. As mentioned earlier, airflow into the exhaust ports during deceleration would cause severe exhaust manifold backfiring because of excessive burning of hydrocarbon (HC) emissions.

Air-Switching Valve

When the engine coolant is cold, manifold vacuum is applied through the coolant-control vacuum switch to the air-switching valve. The air-switching valve and diaphragm move upward when the manifold vacuum is applied to the diaphragm. Airflow is then directed past the lower side of the valve to the exhaust ports, as shown in Figure 8-23.

When the engine coolant is warm, manifold vacuum to the air-switching valve diaphragm is shut off by the coolant-control vacuum switch. Under this condition the diaphragm and valve assembly is held downward by the diaphragm spring, and airflow is directed to the downstream location at the exhaust manifold flange.

Many air-injection systems on later model cars are computer controlled. (These systems are discussed in Chapter 17 and 18.)

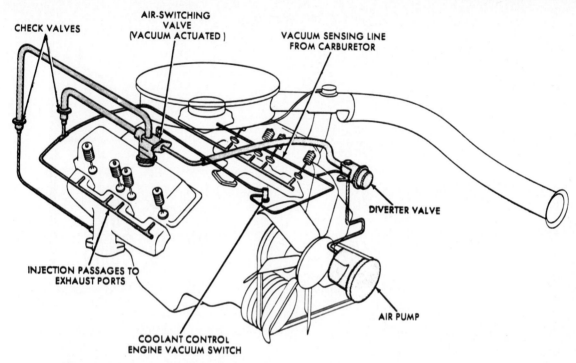

Figure 8-21. Air-Injection System with Downstream Injection. (*Courtesy of Chrysler Canada*)

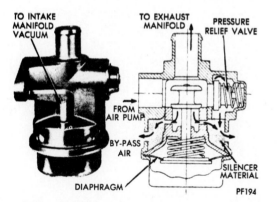

Figure 8-22. Diverter Valve. (*Courtesy of Chrysler Canada*)

Pulse Air-Injection Reactor (PAIR) Systems

Design and Operation

The pulse air-injection reactor (PAIR) system draws clean air from the air cleaner and injects the air into each exhaust port. A one-way check valve and pipe are connected from a small air tank to each exhaust port, as pictured in Figure 8-24.

Clean air is delivered from the air cleaner to the air storage tank by a connecting hose. As each ex-

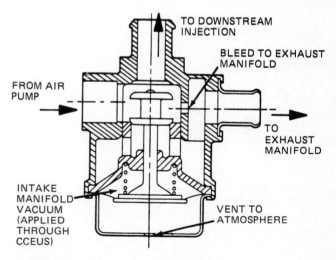

Figure 8-23. Air-Switching Valve Operation. (*Courtesy of Chrysler Canada*)

haust valve opens, high (positive) pressure occurs at the exhaust port. At the same time low (negative) pressure occurs between each positive high-pressure peak at the exhaust ports. The negative pressure opens the one-way check valve and pulls air into the exhaust port. Air injected by the PAIR system ignites and burns HC at the exhaust ports and supplies oxygen for the catalytic converter.

The PAIR system is advantageous because it

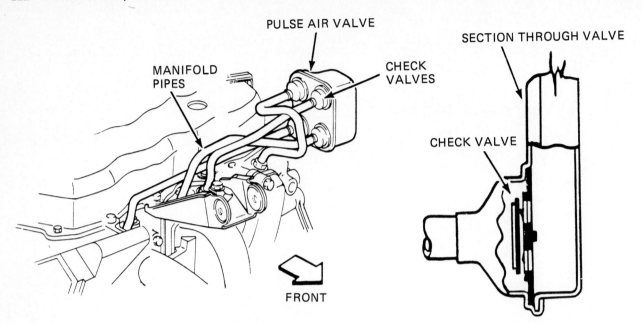

Figure 8-24. Pusle Air-Injection Reactor System. (*Courtesy of Pontiac Motor Division, General Motors Corporation*)

does not require engine power to turn a belt-driven air pump. Some similar air-injection systems use a single air tube and check valve between the air cleaner and the exhaust system. The PAIR system is most effective at low engine speeds, because there is more time between the pressure peaks in the exhaust system.

Early Fuel-Evaporation Systems

Design and Operation

A vacuum-operated power actuator is linked to the heat riser valve in the early fuel-evaporation (EFE) system, as pictured in Figure 8-25.

Manifold vacuum is routed through a thermal vacuum switch (TVS) to the power actuator. The EFE TVS may be combined with the EGR TVS, as indicated in Figure 8-26.

When the engine coolant is cold, the TVS allows vacuum to be applied to the power actuator and closes the heat riser valve. Additional exhaust gas is forced through the intake manifold crossover passage by the closed heat riser valve. Intake manifold fuel vaporization and driveability are improved by the EFE system during cold-engine operation. When the coolant is warm, the TVS shuts off the vacuum to the power actuator and thus allows the heat riser valve to open. An inoperative EFE system will cause acceleration stumbles during cold-engine operation.

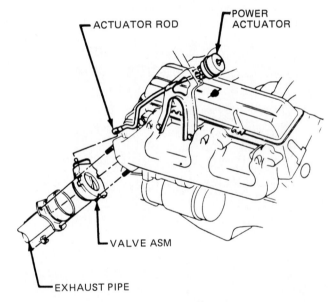

Figure 8-25. Early Fuel-Evaporation (EFE) System. (*Courtesy of Pontiac Motor Division, General Motors Corporation*)

Grid-Type EFE Systems

Some EFE systems have an electrical grid mounted in a spacer block between the carburetor and the intake manifold, as indicated in Figure 8-27. A two-stage, two-barrel carburetor with a primary and secondary throttle may be used in these systems.

The EFE electrical grid is located under the primary throttle. The EFE grid receives electrical power from the ignition switch through a coolant temper-

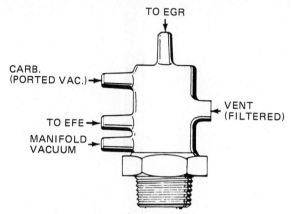

Figure 8-26. Combined EFE and EGR TVS. *(Courtesy of Oldsmobile Division, General Motors Corporation)*

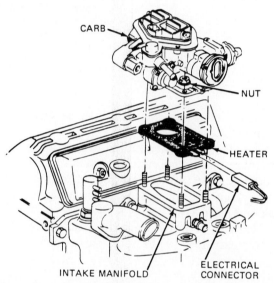

Figure 8-27. Grid-Type EFE System. *(Courtesy of Chevrolet Motor Division, General Motors Corporation)*

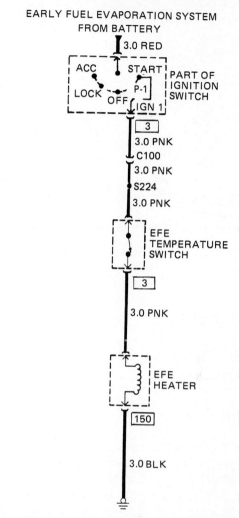

Figure 8-28. Grid-Type EFE Electrical Circuit. *(Courtesy of GM Product Service Training, General Motors Corporation)*

ature switch. When the coolant is cold, electrical power is supplied through the closed temperature switch contacts to the EFE grid, as illustrated in Figure 8-28.

Heat from the EFE grid warms the fuel vapor, improves cold driveability, and lowers emission levels. Warm engine coolant opens the EFE temperature switch contacts and stops current flow through the grid. A ground wire on the engine completes the electrical circuit from the grid to ground.

Heated Air-Inlet Systems

Design and Operation

The heated air-inlet system contains a thermostatic air bleed and a vacuum-operated air control valve

mounted in the air cleaner. An exhaust manifold heat stove is connected to the air control valve by a flexible hose, as shown in Figure 8-29.

When the air cleaner temperature is below 125°F (52°C), the thermostatic air bleed supplies manifold vacuum to the air control valve diaphragm. The air control valve is lifted upward by the manifold vacuum; this upward movement shuts off the flow of cold underhood air and allows warm air from the manifold stove into the air cleaner. Heated intake air improves cold-engine driveability. At temperatures above 125°F (52°C), the thermostatic air bleed vents the vacuum applied to the air control valve diaphragm and thus allows the air control valve to move downward. Cooler underhood air is supplied to the air cleaner by the downward position of the air control system.

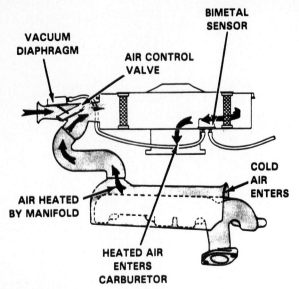

Figure 8-29. Heated Air-Inlet System. (*Courtesy of Chrysler Canada*)

Positive Crankcase Ventilation (PCV) Systems

Design

The PCV system prevents crankcase emissions from escaping to the atmosphere. Unburned HC emissions blow by the piston rings on the compression stroke. When the piston is on the power stroke, small quantities of exhaust gases escape past the

CRANKCASE "BLOW—BY" GASES

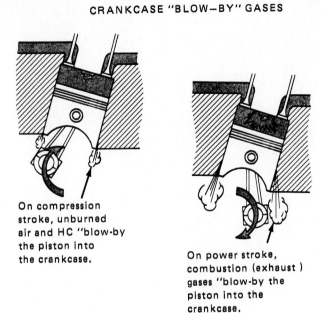

On compression stroke, unburned air and HC "blow-by" the piston into the crankcase.

On power stroke, combustion (exhaust) gases "blow-by the piston into the crankcase.

Figure 8-30. Origin of Crankcase Emissions. (*Courtesy of Ford Motor Co.*)

rings and piston into the crankcase, as illustrated in Figure 8-30.

The PCV valve is mounted in one of the rocker-arm covers and is connected through a hose to the intake manifold. A clean-air hose is connected from the air cleaner to the other rocker-arm cover, as pictured in Figure 8-31.

Clean air is drawn from the air cleaner through the clean-air hose to the rocker-arm cover and into

NORMAL ENGINE OPERATION

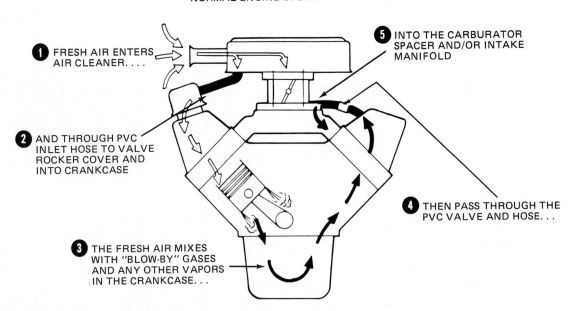

Figure 8-31. PCV System. (*Courtesy of Ford Motor Co.*)

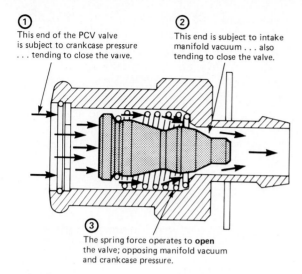

Figure 8-32. Internal Design of PCV Valve. (*Courtesy of Ford Motor Co.*)

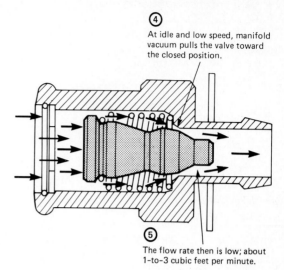

Figure 8-33. Normal Operation of PCV Valve. (*Courtesy of Ford Motor Co.*)

the crankcase. Emissions in the crankcase mix with the clean air. The manifold vacuum moves crankcase emissions and air through the PCV valve into the intake manifold, as illustrated in Figure 8-31. The PCV valve contains a tapered flow control valve. Manifold vacuum and crankcase pressure act as closing forces on the valve. Spring pressure pushes the valve toward the open position, as illustrated in Figure 8-32.

PCV System Under Normal Engine Loads

During idle or normal cruising speeds, the PCV valve is held in a reduced-flow position by high manifold vacuum, as pictured in Figure 8-33.

At idle or part throttle, crankcase emissions are reduced because of lower cylinder pressure.

PCV System Under Heavy Engine Loads

High cylinder pressure that develops when the engine is operating under heavy loads or at high speeds increases crankcase emissions. Reduced manifold vacuum at wide throttle opening allows the spring pressure to increase PCV valve opening, as illustrated in Figure 8-34.

If the engine is in normal condition, the PCV valve flow rating will adequately handle the crankcase emissions at heavy load. Crankcase emissions may exceed the PCV valve flow rating if piston ring blow-by is excessive. When the flow rating of the PCV valve is exceeded, crankcase pressure forces crankcase emissions through the clean-air hose into the air cleaner.

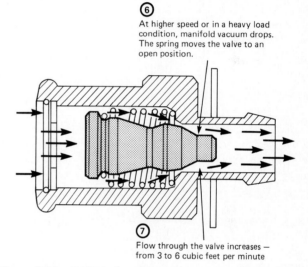

Figure 8-34. PCV Valve Operation under Heavy Engine Loads. (*Courtesy of Ford Motor Co.*)

An intake manifold backfire seats the tapered valve against the PCV valve housing and prevents the manifold from backfiring into the crankcase, as indicated in Figure 8-35. Most PCV systems have a screen on the end of the clean-air hose in the air cleaner as a backfire safety device.

Decel Emission Systems

Decel Valve

The decel valve clean-air inlet is connected to the air cleaner. When the decel valve is open, clean air flows through the decel valve into the intake mani-

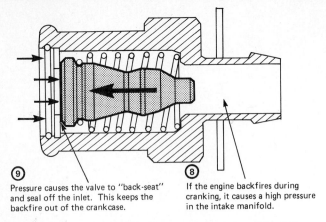

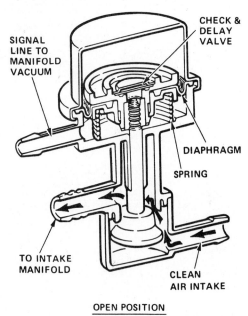

⑨ Pressure causes the valve to "back-seat" and seal off the inlet. This keeps the backfire out of the crankcase.

⑧ If the engine backfires during cranking, it causes a high pressure in the intake manifold.

Figure 8-35. PCV Valve During Backfire Conditions. (*Courtesy of Ford Motor Co.*)

CHECK & DELAY VALVE

SIGNAL LINE TO MANIFOLD VACUUM

DIAPHRAGM

SPRING

TO INTAKE MANIFOLD

CLEAN AIR INTAKE

OPEN POSITION

Figure 8-36. Decel Valve. (*Courtesy of Pontiac Motor Division, General Motors Corporation*)

fold. Under normal driving conditions, spring pressure holds the tapered valve in the closed position. On deceleration, high manifold vacuum applied to the decel valve diaphragm moves the diaphragm and valve assembly downward, as pictured in Figure 8-36.

Downward valve movement allows air to flow through the open decel valve into the intake manifold, which provides leaner air-fuel mixtures and reduced emissions on deceleration.

Electric-Assist Choke Systems

Design and Operation

The electric-assist choke system is shown in Figure 8-37. A set of oil-pressure switch contacts is connected in series between the ignition switch and the control switch. When the engine is running, oil pressure closes the switch contacts. If the engine is not running, the oil-pressure switch contacts are open, which prevents the choke spring from being relaxed if the ignition is left on with a cold engine.

Different single and dual control switches are used in the later model system. The single control switch, labeled A in Figure 8-37, is closed above 80°F (27°C) and open below 55°F (13°C). The dual control unit, labeled B in the figure, supplies partial voltage to the choke heating coil below 55°F (13°C) and full power above 80°F (27°C).

Evaporative Emission-Control Systems

Design and Operation

Fuel vapors from the fuel tank and carburetor are vented into a charcoal canister in the evaporative emission-control system. The charcoal in the canister absorbs the fuel vapors when the engine is not running. A purge hose moves fuel vapors out of the canister into the intake manifold while the engine is running. The rollover valve in the vapor line of the fuel tank prevents liquid fuel from entering the canister if the vehicle is overturned in an accident.

The complete evaporative emission-control system is illustrated in Figure 8-38.

In some systems fuel vapors are separated and returned to the fuel tank by a filter-separator and return line. The evaporative emission-control system prevents the escape of HC emissions from the fuel tank and carburetor to the atmosphere.

The canister-purge port in the carburetor is usually located above the throttle. In this type of system, canister purging occurs when the throttle is opened. A few systems have a small constant-bleed purge port below the throttles to provide some canister purging at idle speed.

Clean air flows through a fiberglass filter into the bottom of the canister when purging occurs. Periodic replacement or cleaning of the fiberglass filter is required, as shown in Figure 8-39.

Float-Bowl Vent Valves

A mechanically operated vent valve, or an electrically operated solenoid valve, controls the flow of fuel vapors from the carburetor float bowl to the canister. The mechanically operated vent valve is controlled by the throttle linkage. The valve is open when the throttles are in the idle position, as illustrated in Figure 8-40.

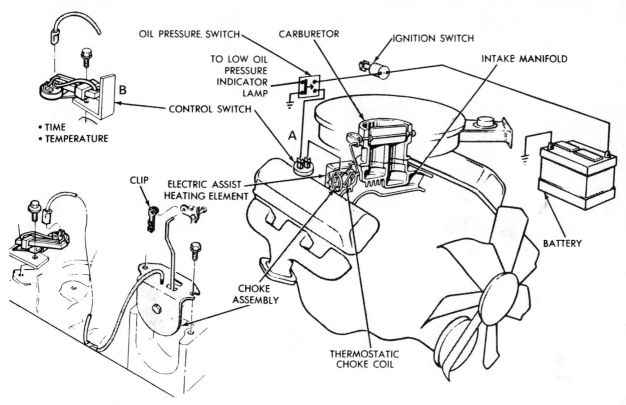

Figure 8-37. Electric-Assist Choke System. (*Courtesy of Chrysler Canada*)

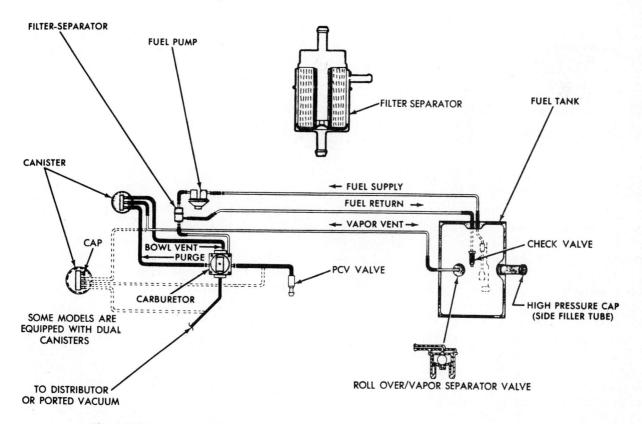

Figure 8-38. Evaporative Emission-Control System. (*Courtesy of Chrysler Canada*)

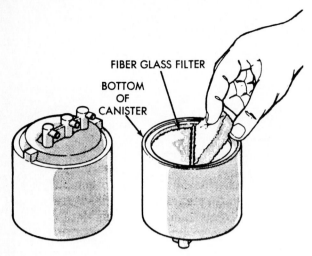

Figure 8-39. Canister Filter Replacement. (*Courtesy of Chrysler Canada*)

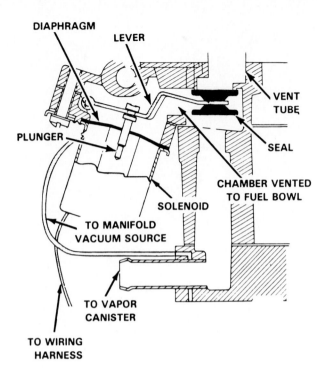

Figure 8-41. Electrically Operated Float-Bowl Vent Valve. (*Courtesy of Chrysler Canada*)

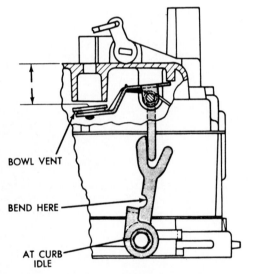

Figure 8-40. Mechanically Operated Float-Bowl Vent Valve. (*Courtesy of Chrysler Canada*)

When the vent valve is open, fuel vapors flow from the float bowl to the canister. Opening the throttle closes the vent valve.

The electrically operated vent valve solenoid is open when the ignition switch is off. This allows fuel vapors to flow from the float bowl to the canister, as shown in Figure 8-41.

When the ignition switch is turned on, the solenoid winding is energized, which closes the vent valve. Vacuum applied to the vent valve diaphragm assists the solenoid winding in closing the vent valve. Fuel vapors are vented from the float bowl to the vent tube under the air cleaner when the vent is closed.

Fuel Tank Filler Cap

A special pressure-relief filler cap is used on the fuel tank on evaporative emission-control systems. The special filler cap maintains a slight pressure in the fuel tank, which forces fuel vapors from the tank to the canister. The pressure and relief valves are safety features to prevent excessive pressure or vacuum in the fuel tank if the evaporative system malfunctions.

The pressure-vacuum filler cap is pictured in Figure 8-42.

Evaporative System with Purge Control Valve

Some evaporative systems use a purge control valve to control the flow of fuel vapors from the canister to the intake manifold. This system also has an electrically operated fuel-bowl solenoid vent valve, as pictured in Figure 8-43.

The purge control is connected to the purge hose between the canister and the intake manifold. On most systems the purge control valve is operated by spark port, or EGR port, vacuum. Hose connections to the purge control valve are shown in Figure 8-44.

The fuel-bowl solenoid vent valve is connected in the hose between the float bowl and the canister. If the ignition switch is off, the solenoid valve is de-

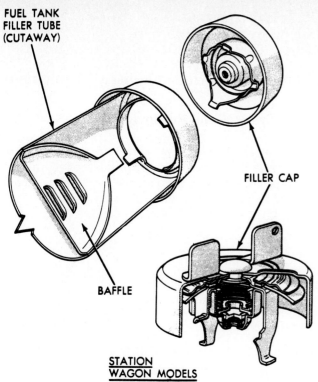

FUEL TANK
FILLER TUBE
(CUTAWAY)

FILLER CAP

BAFFLE

STATION
WAGON MODELS

Figure 8-42. Pressure-Vacuum Fuel Tank Filler Cap. (*Courtesy of Chrysler Canada*)

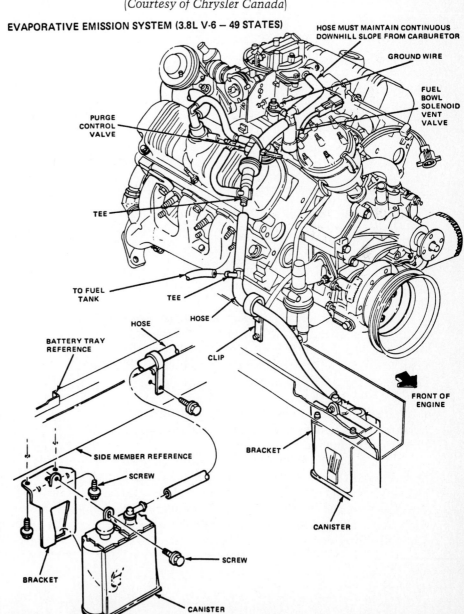

EVAPORATIVE EMISSION SYSTEM (3.8L V-6 – 49 STATES)

HOSE MUST MAINTAIN CONTINUOUS DOWNHILL SLOPE FROM CARBURETOR

GROUND WIRE

FUEL BOWL SOLENOID VENT VALVE

PURGE CONTROL VALVE

TEE

TO FUEL TANK

TEE

HOSE

HOSE

BATTERY TRAY REFERENCE

CLIP

FRONT OF ENGINE

BRACKET

SIDE MEMBER REFERENCE

SCREW

CANISTER

CANISTER

SCREW

BRACKET

CANISTER

Figure 8-43. Evaporative System with Purge Control Valve. (*Courtesy of Ford Motor Co.*)

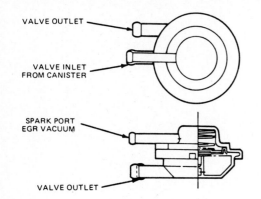

Figure 8-44. Purge Control Valve. (*Courtesy of Ford Motor Co.*)

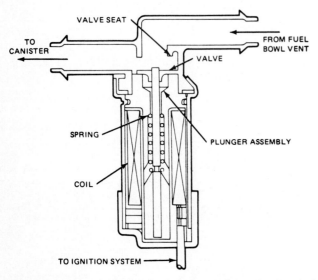

Figure 8-45. Fuel-Bowl Solenoid Vent Valve. (*Courtesy of Ford Motor Co.*)

energized, and fuel vapors can flow from the float bowl through the solenoid valve to the canister, as shown in Figure 8-45.

When the ignition switch is turned on, the solenoid valve is energized, which closes the solenoid valve and blocks the flow of fuel vapors from the float bowl to the canister. If the engine is shut off, fuel vapors from the fuel tank and the float bowl can flow into the canister.

With the engine idling, the purge control valve remains closed. Under this condition fuel vapors can flow from the fuel tank to the canister.

When the throttle is opened, vacuum is applied to the purge control valve, which opens the valve and allows vapors to be purged from the canister into the PCV hose and intake manifold. Fuel vapors also flow from the fuel tank into the intake manifold when the purge control valve is open.

Computer-Controlled Emission Equipment

Basic Systems and Advantages

On many late-model, front-wheel-drive cars, some of the emission-control equipment described in this chapter is computer controlled. Computer-controlled exhaust-emission equipment would include the following:

1. Exhaust-gas recirculation (EGR).
2. Canister purge (CANP).
3. Air-injection reactor (AIR).
4. Early fuel evaporation (EFE).

In most of these systems, the on-board computer operates a solenoid, or solenoids, to control each emission device. The computer operates each emission device in relation to the input signals received. Since the computer monitors several engine and vehicle parameters continuously, more precise control of emission equipment and improved driveability result.

The computer systems also provide precise control of ignition spark advance and of air-fuel ratio under all engine operating conditions, which also improves fuel economy, emission levels, and driveability. (These computer systems are described in Chapters 17 and 18, and computer-controlled ignition systems are explained in Chapter 13.)

Test Questions

1. The purpose of the EGR valve is to reduce _____ _____ emission levels.
2. When a conventional EGR valve is used without a vacuum amplifier, the EGR valve vacuum source is always located _____ _____ _____.
3. The BPT valve is operated by _____ _____.
4. In the EGR delay system, the delay timer and delay solenoid turn on manifold vacuum to the amplifier _____ seconds after a warm engine is started.
5. Air injection into the exhaust ports lowers _____ _____ emissions.
6. An air pump pressure of 11 psi (77 kPa) would be normal.   T F

7. An acceleration stumble during cold-engine operation could be caused by loss of vacuum to the EFE actuator diaphragm.   T F

8. Current flows through the EFE grid at normal operating engine temperatures.   T F

9. PCV valve flow decreases when the engine is accelerated from idle to 2,000 rpm.   T F

10. A dual external control switch in an electric-assist choke system supplies partial power to the choke heating coil below 55°F (13°C).   T F

9

Electricity and Electronics

Chapter Completion Objectives

1. Test for an open circuit with a 12V test light.
2. Test for a grounded circuit with a 12V test light.
3. Use a compass to test for a grounded or shorted circuit.
4. Test for a shorted condition in an electromagnet.
5. Use Ohm's Law formula to calculate volts, ohms, or amperes in a series circuit.
6. Use Ohm's Law formula to calculate volts, ohms, or amperes in a parallel circuit.
7. Calculate the total resistance in a series or parallel circuit.
8. Explain basic computer signals.
9. Demonstrate an understanding of basic computer operation.
10. Describe various data-transmission methods.

Atomic Structure

Elements

An understanding of basic electricity and electric circuits is absolutely essential before studying the new technology involved in automotive computer systems. Therefore, we have included a thorough discussion of basic electricity, electric circuits, and basic circuit diagnosis in this chapter.

An element may be defined as a liquid, a solid, or a gas that contains only type of atom. Copper is an example of an element that is widely used in automotive wiring and electrical components.

Atoms

The smallest particle into which an element can be divided and still retain its characteristics is referred to as an atom. An atom is extremely small and cannot be seen with the most powerful electron microscope that magnifies millions of times.

Compounds

A compound is a liquid, a solid, or a gas that contains two or more atoms. Water is a compound that consists of hydrogen and oxygen atoms.

Molecules

A molecule is the smallest particle of a compound in which the characteristics of the compound are maintained. A water molecule contains two hydrogen atoms and one oxygen atom, as illustrated in Figure 9-1. The chemical symbol for water is H_2O.

Parts of the Atom

At the center or nucleus of most atoms there are extremely small particles known as protons and neutrons. Arranged in different orbits, or rings, around the nucleus are other small particles called electrons. Electrons orbit around the nucleus in much the same way as the planets orbit around the sun.

Seven rings located at various distances from the nucleus represent the configuration of most atoms. The outer ring is called a valence ring, and any electrons on this ring are referred to as valence electrons. A copper atom, as shown in Figure 9-2, contains 29 protons and 35 neutrons in the nucleus, and 29 electrons orbiting around the nucleus.

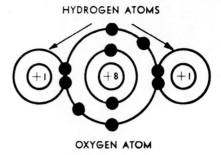

Figure 9-1. Water Molecule. (*Courtesy of Delco Remy Division, General Motors Corporation*)

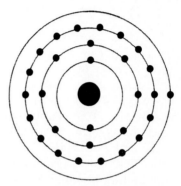

Figure 9-2. Copper Atom. (*Courtesy of Delco Remy Division, General Motors Corporation*)

The maximum number of electrons on the first ring is 2, while the second and third rings may have a maximum of 8 and 18 electrons respectively. Since a copper atom has 29 electrons, there will be 1 electron on the valence ring of the atom. The number of valence electrons is very important, because it determines the electrical characteristics of the element.

Electrons have a negative electrical charge and protons have a positive electrical charge. Neutrons do not have an electrical charge, but they add weight to the atom. If an atom is in balance, it has the same number of protons and electrons. Centrifugal force tends to move the electrons away from the atom. However, the negatively charged electrons are held in their orbits by the attraction of the positively charged protons.

Some atoms have the same number of protons and neutrons, but many of the heavier atoms have more neutrons.

A proton is 1,840 times heavier than an electron. Therefore, electrons are very light and can be moved easily from one atom to another in some elements.

Periodic Table

All the known elements are listed on the Periodic Table according to their number of protons. For ex-

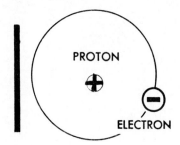

Figure 9-3. Hydrogen Atom. (*Courtesy of Delco Remy Division, General Motors Corporation*)

ample, hydrogen has 1 proton and it is number 1 in the Periodic Table. The hydrogen atom contains 1 proton and 1 electron, but it does not have any neutrons, as shown in Figure 9-3.

The atomic number of each element is determined by the location of the element on the Periodic Table. For example, oxygen has an atomic number of 8, and it is number 8 in the Periodic Table, which indicates that each oxygen atom has 8 protons and 8 electrons. Some of the other well known elements on the Periodic Table are: silver, number 47; gold, number 79; and uranium, number 92. Many Periodic Tables list 103 known elements.

Electricity

Electrical Conductors

In an element with 1, 2, or 3 valence electrons, the electrons move easily from one atom to another. Copper, silver, or gold atoms have 1 valence electron. Aluminum atoms have three valence electrons, so this element is a reasonably good conductor.

Electrical Insulators

Some elements do not conduct electricity very easily, and hence are classified as insulators. These elements have 5 or more valence electrons on each atom. When an atom has 5 or more valence electrons, they will not move easily from one atom to another.

Semiconductors

When an element has 4 valence electrons, it is classified as a semiconductor. Carbon, silicon, and germanium are in the semiconductor category. Some of these semiconductors, such as silicon, have unusual properties when combined with other elements. Sil-

icon is used in the manufacture of diodes and transistors.

Electron Movement

There are three requirements for electron movement in an electrical circuit:

1. A massing of electrons (high voltage) at one point in the circuit.
2. A lack of electrons (low voltage) at another point in the circuit.
3. A complete circuit.

A voltage, or electrical pressure difference, is created by a massing of electrons at one point in the circuit, and a lack of electrons at another point in the circuit. Chemical action in a lead-acid battery causes a massing of electrons on one set of plates, and a lack of electrons on the outer set of plates. (Battery operation is explained in Chapter 10.)

When the battery is connected to a complete circuit, electrons begin to move through the circuit from one set of battery plates to the other. The electrons are actually massed on the negative battery plates, and electron movement is from the negative battery terminal through the external circuit to the positive battery terminal. However, in the automotive industry the conventional theory is often used in which current flow is from the positive battery terminal to the negative terminal.

A basic electric circuit is illustrated in Figure 9-4, in which electrons are moving from the positive battery terminal to the negative terminal.

Only the valence electrons move from atom to atom through the conductor. When a copper atom loses a valence electron, it has an excess of one positively charged proton. This positive attraction immediately moves a negatively charged valence electron from another atom. If a copper atom receives a free valence electron, so that it has two valence electrons, one of the valence electrons, is repelled immediately to another atom. Hence, the flow of electric current can be defined as the controlled mass movement of valence electrons from atom to atom in a conductor.

Electrical Measurements

Volt

A volt is a measurement for electrical pressure difference in a circuit. If a voltmeter is connected across the terminals of a lead-acid battery, the meter may

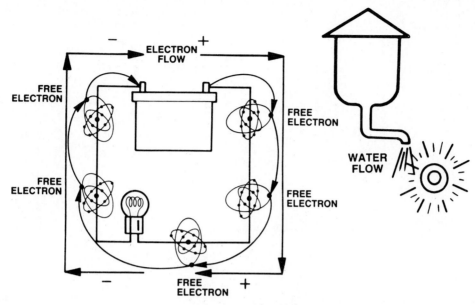

Figure 9-4. Electron Movement. (*Courtesy of Chrysler Canada*)

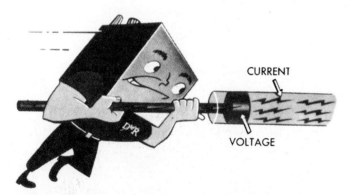

Figure 9-5. Volts in an Electric Circuit. (*Courtesy of Delco Remy Division, General Motors Corporation*)

read 12.6V. This indicates that there is 12.6V electrical pressure at one battery terminal in relation to 0V pressure at the other terminal. The electrical pressure, which is measured in volts, forces the electrons or current to flow through the circuit, as shown in Figure 9-5.

Ampere

The electron movement, or current flow, in a circuit is measured in amperes.

Ohms

Electrical resistance, or opposition to current flow, is measured in ohms (Ω). A water pipe offers a resistance to the flow of water. In much the same way, electrical components, such as light filaments, offer

resistance to the flow of current. A smaller filament containing fine wire has a higher resistance to current flow than a large filament made from heavier wire. The resistance in a light filament is compared to the resistance in a water pipe in Figure 9-6.

Ohm's Law

Ohm's Law states that the current flow in a circuit is directly proportional to the voltage and inversely proportional to the resistance. This means that an increase in voltage creates a corresponding increase in amperes, while a voltage decrease reduces the amperes. When the resistance in a circuit is increased, the amperes are reduced. If the resistance is lowered, the amperes increase.

Ohm's Law Formula

In Ohm's Law formula voltage is expressed as E, which is an abbreviation for electromotive force (EMF). Amperes are indicated by induction (I) in this formula, and ohms are represented by resistance (R). Ohm's Law formula is often expressed as

$$\frac{E}{I \times R}$$

If two values in a circuit are known, this formula may be used to calculate the unknown value. The amperes in a circuit may be determined by dividing the resistance into the volts. Therefore,

$$I = \frac{E}{R}$$

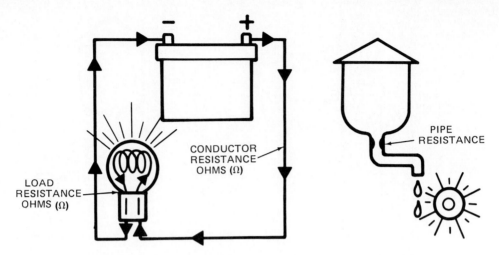

Figure 9-6.   Ohms Resistance. (*Courtesy of Chrysler Canada*)

When the voltage is unknown, it may be calculated by multiplying the amperes times the resistance. Thus

$$E = I \times R$$

The ohms in a circuit may be determined by dividing the amperes into the volts. Therefore

$$R = \frac{E}{I}$$

Types of Electric Circuits

Series Circuit

In a series circuit, the resistances are connected so that the same current flows through all the resistances, as indicated in Figure 9-7. Four facts about series circuits may be summarized as follows:

1. The total resistance is the sum of all resistances in the circuit.
2. The same amperes must flow through each resistance.
3. A specific amount of voltage is dropped across each resistance.
4. The sum of the voltage drops across each resistance must equal the source voltage.

   In the circuit shown in Figure 9-7, the total resistance would be

$$2 + 5 + 4 + 1 = 12\Omega.$$

The current flow would be

$$12V \div 12\Omega = 1 \text{ ampere}$$

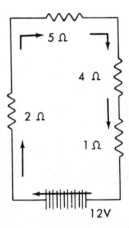

Figure 9-7.   Series Circuit. (*Courtesy of Delco Remy Division, General Motors Corporation*)

This current would flow through each resistance. The voltage drop across the resistors would be

$$1A \times 2\Omega = 2V$$
$$1A \times 5\Omega = 5V$$
$$1A \times 4\Omega = 4V$$
$$1A \times 1\Omega = 1V$$

The sum of the voltage drops across each resistance would be

$$2V + 5V + 4V + 1V = 12V$$

Parallel Circuits

In a parallel circuit, each resistance forms a separate path for current flow. The automotive electrical system has many resistances connected parallel to the battery as illustrated in Figure 9-8.

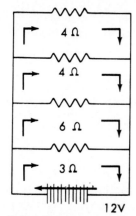

Figure 9-8. Parallel Circuit. (*Courtesy of Delco Remy Division, General Motors Corporation*)

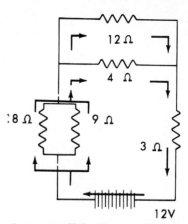

Figure 9-9. Series-Parallel Circuit. (*Courtesy of Delco Remy Division, General Motors Corporation*)

Four important facts that must be understood about a parallel circuit are the following:

1. The total resistance is always less than the lowest value resistor in the circuit.
2. The current flow in each parallel branch of the circuit is determined by the resistance in that branch, and the sum of the current flows in the branches is equal to the current flow leaving the source and returning to the source.
3. Equal full source voltage is applied to each resistance.
4. Equal full source voltage is dropped across each resistance.

The easiest way to calculate the total resistance in a parallel circuit is to determine the current flow through each parallel branch and then add the current flows to obtain the total current.

In the parallel circuit shown in Figure 9-8, the current flow through each resistor would be:

$$12V \div 3\Omega = 4A$$

$$12V \div 6\Omega = 2A$$

$$12V \div 4\Omega = 3A$$

$$12V \div 4\Omega = 3A$$

The total current flow would be

$$4A + 2A + 3A + 3A = 12A$$

Therefore, the total resistance would be

$$12V \div 12A = 1\Omega$$

Series-Parallel Circuits

Some automotive electrical circuits are series-parallel circuits. This type of circuit contains resistances that are connected in series with the parallel resistances in the circuit. The instrument panel light circuit on many cars is an example of a series-parallel circuit. Each instrument panel light is connected parallel to the battery, but a variable resistor in the headlight switch is connected in series with the panel lights. When the headlight switch control knob is rotated, the variable resistor reduces the voltage applied to the instrument panel lights, which reduces their brilliance. A series-parallel circuit is shown in Figure 9-9.

Electric Circuit Defects

Open Circuit

An open circuit may be defined as an unwanted break in an electric circuit. This defect could occur in a wire or in an electric component such as a light filament. If an open circuit occurs in a series circuit, the current flow is stopped in the entire circuit, as shown in Figure 9-10.

An open circuit in one parallel branch of a parallel circuit will only stop the current flow in the parallel branch where the defect is located, as illustrated in Figure 9-11.

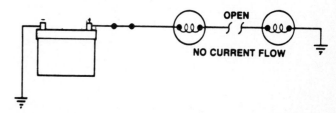

Figure 9-10. Open Circuit in a Series Circuit. (*Courtesy of Chrysler Canada*)

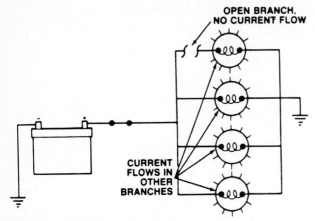

Figure 9-11. Open Circuit in a Parallel Circuit. (*Courtesy of Chrysler Canada*)

Grounded Circuit

A grounded circuit may be defined as an unwanted copper-to-metal connection. Insulation is located on the connecting wires in an electric circuit. If the insulation is worn, the copper wire may touch the metal of the vehicle chassis and create a grounded condition. When this occurs the current flows directly through the defective ground connection without flowing through the electrical components in the circuit. Under this condition excess current flow will probably burn out the fuse in the circuit.

Short Circuit

A short circuit may be defined as an unwanted copper-to-copper connection in an electrical circuit. When the insulation is worn on two adjacent wires and the wires contact each other, a short circuit is created, as illustrated in Figure 9-12.

A short circuit may cause the current to flow from one circuit into a second circuit when the

switch in the second circuit is off. (Electrical defects in electromagnets are discussed later in this chapter.)

Circuit Diagnosis

Test Meters

An ammeter is used to measure current flow in a circuit. The ammeter has a very low internal resistance and must be connected in series in the circuit. If an ammeter is connected in parallel across the terminals of a battery, the meter will be damaged by excessive current flow. The ammeter in Figure 9-13 is connected in series.

A voltmeter has very high internal resistance and must be connected in parallel, as shown in Figure 9-14.

The ohmmeter is self-powered by an internal battery. This type of meter must never be connected to a circuit in which current is flowing or the meter will be damaged. When the resistance of an electrical component is being measured, disconnect the component from the circuit and connect the ohmmeter leads to the terminals on the component, as pictured in Figure 9-15.

Most ohmmeters have several different switch positions such as ×1, ×10, and ×1,000. The ×1 switch position provides a meter scale reading of 0 to 100Ω. If the ×10 position is selected, the scale will indicate 0 to 1,000Ω. The ×1,000 position provides a meter reading of 0 to 100,000Ω.

The correct scale must be used for the resistance of the component being tested. If the resistor in Figure 9-15 has a specified value of 1.25Ω, the ×1 meter scale should be selected.

Many ohmmeters require calibration on each scale by connecting the leads together and rotating

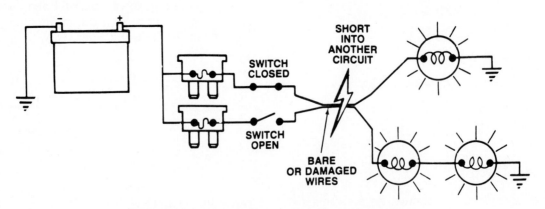

Figure 9-12. Short Circuit. (*Courtesy of Chrysler Canada*)

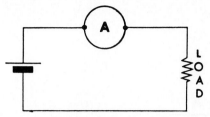

Figure 9-13. Ammeter Connected in Series. (*Courtesy of Delco Remy Division, General Motors Corporation*)

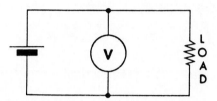

Figure 9-14. Voltmeter Connected in Parallel. (*Courtesy of Delco Remy Division, General Motors Corporation*)

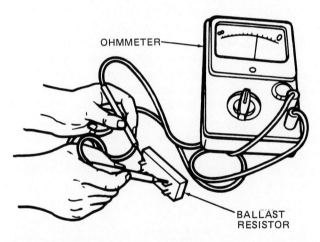

Figure 9-15. Resistance Test with Ohmmeter. (*Courtesy of Chrysler Canada*)

the calibration control until the pointer is in the 0 position.

Test for Open Circuits

A 12V test light may be used to test for an open circuit in conventional electric circuits. Do not use a 12V test light to test computer-controlled circuits, because these circuits operate on a very low current flow and the test light current may damage the computer or other components in the circuit. (Refer to Chapter 13 of *Automotive Principles: Repair and Service*, Volume II, for computer system diagnosis.)

With the switch in the circuit turned on, test for power at different locations in the circuit with the test lamp. Power will not be available immediately after the open circuit. The open-circuit test procedure is illustrated in Figure 9-16.

Test for Grounded Circuits

When a grounded-circuit test is being performed, the 12V test lamp should be installed in place of the circuit fuse and the load should be disconnected from the circuit, as shown in Figure 9-17.

If the test light is on, the circuit is grounded. The next step is to disconnect the circuit connectors starting at the load. When the test light goes out, the grounded circuit is after the connector that was disconnected last.

Compass Test for Shorted or Grounded Circuits

When this test is performed, a circuit breaker should be installed in place of the circuit fuse, then a compass should be moved along the wiring harness. Each

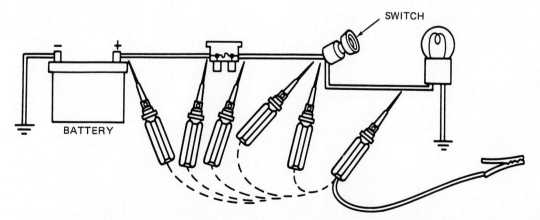

Figure 9-16. Open-Circuit Test Procedure. (*Courtesy of Chrysler Canada*)

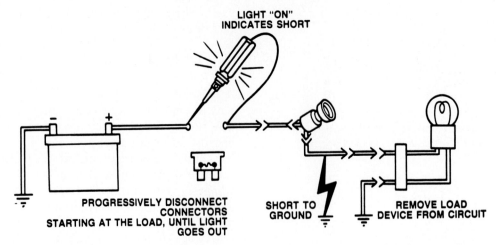

Figure 9-17. Grounded-Circuit Test Procedure. (*Courtesy of Chrysler Canada*)

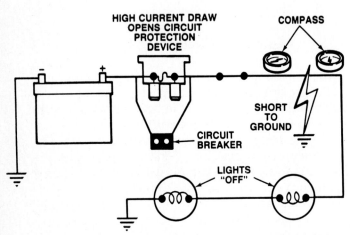

Figure 9-18. Compass Test Procedure for a Grounded or Shorted Circuit. (*Courtesy of Chrysler Canada*)

time the circuit breaker closes, the compass needle will deflect. When the compass is moved past the grounded location, the needle will no longer deflect. The same test procedure may be used to test for a shorted condition between the wires in a harness. When the shorted location in a wire is passed with the compass, the needle will no longer deflect because the current will be flowing from the shorted location to other wires that are connected into a different harness.

(The test procedure for a shorted condition in an electromagnet is discussed later in this chapter.) The compass test procedure is pictured in Figure 9-18.

Voltage Drop

When current flows through a resistance, the amount of voltage that is dropped across the resistance depends on the amount of resistance and the current flow. If the resistance increases, the voltage drop also increases. An increase in current flow also results in more voltage drop. The connecting wires in an electric circuit have a very low voltage drop across them. Excessive resistance in the wires results in a higher voltage drop across the wires.

Voltage drop is only present when current is flowing. For example, in Figure 9-10, 12V would be available up to the open circuit, because there is no current flow and therefore no voltage drop across the first lamp. The voltmeter may be used to measure voltage drop. With the current flowing in the circuit, the voltmeter may be connected across a resistor, or wire, to measure the voltage drop, as indicated in Figure 9-19.

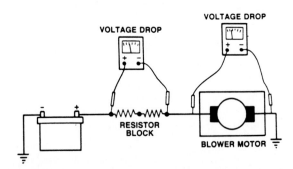

Figure 9-19. Voltmeter Connected to Measure Voltage Drop. (*Courtesy of Chrysler Canada*)

Electromagnetism

Permanent Magnets

Certain metals, such as iron, nickel, and cobalt, can be magnetized. When a metal becomes magnetized, the molecules are aligned with the poles of the mag-

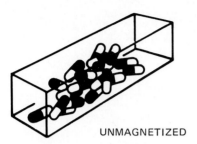

UNMAGNETIZED

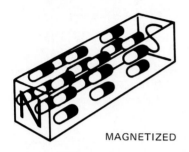

MAGNETIZED

Figure 9-20. Magnetized and Unmagnetized Metal. *(Courtesy of Chrysler Canada)*

net, whereas the molecules are randomly arranged in unmagnetized metal, as illustrated in Figure 9-20.

Hard steel retains magnetism for long periods of time; hence this type of magnet is often referred to as a permanent magnet. Soft iron loses its magnetism immediately.

An invisible field of force surrounds each magnet, with the lines of force moving from the north pole to the south pole, as pictured in Figure 9-21.

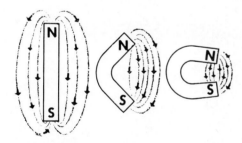

Figure 9-21. Permanent Magnets. *(Courtesy of Delco Remy Division, General Motors Corporation)*

If the permanent magnet is bent into a "U" shape, the lines of force become more concentrated, because the poles are closer together. When the unlike poles of two magnets are brought near each other, the magnets are attracted together, because the lines of force around both magnets are moving in the same direction. Like magnetic poles repel because the lines of force surrounding the magnets are moving against each other, as shown in Figure 9-22.

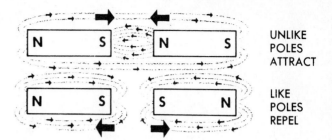

UNLIKE POLES ATTRACT

LIKE POLES REPEL

Figure 9-22. Magnetic Attraction and Repelling Action. *(Courtesy of Delco Remy Division, General Motors Corporation)*

Electromagnets

When current flows through a wire, an invisible magnetic field surrounds the wire. This field is concentric to the conductor, and an increase in current flow creates a corresponding increase in magnetic strength. The right-hand rule may be used to determine the direction of current flow. When the fingers of the right hand are placed in the direction of the lines of force surrounding the conductor, the thumb points in the direction of current flow, as indicated in Figure 9-23.

When the current flow through the conductor is reversed, the magnetic field changes direction. If two adjacent conductors have current flow through them in opposite directions, the magnetic fields are in opposite directions. Under this condition the magnetic lines of force directly between the conductors move in the same direction. This results in a concentration of magnetic lines of force in this area, so that the conductors are pushed apart, as illustrated in Figure 9-24.

If current flows through two adjacent conductors in the same direction, the magnetic fields around both conductors move in the same direction. However, in the area directly between the conductors the magnetic lines of force move in opposite directions. Magnetic lines of force moving in opposite directions in the same space cannot exist. Therefore, the magnetic fields distort and surround both conductors, which tends to pull the conductors together, as shown in Figure 9-25.

When current flows through a coil of wire, it becomes an electromagnet with a north pole and a south pole at the ends of the coil. An iron core placed in the center of the coil concentrates the lines of force.

The strength of an electromagnet is determined by the current flow through the coil and the number of turns in the coil. This magnetic strength is expressed in ampere turns, which is calculated by mul-

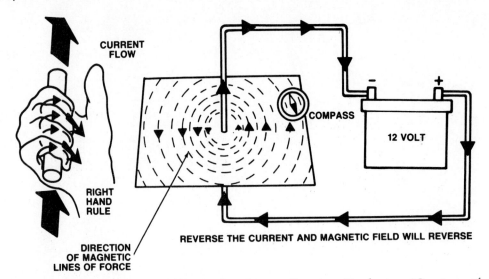

Figure 9-23. Magnetic Field Around a Current-Carrying Conductor. (*Courtesy of Chrysler Canada*)

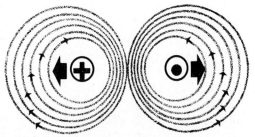

Figure 9-24. Adjacent Conductors with Current Flow in Opposite Directions. (*Courtesy of Delco Remy Division, General Motors Corporation*)

tiplying the amperes times the turns. The direction of the magnetic field around an electromagnet is determined by the direction of current flow, as illustrated in Figure 9-26.

Defects in an Electromagnet The defects in an electromagnet can be defined as follows:

1. *Open circuit*—unwanted break.
2. *Grounded circuit*—unwanted copper-to-metal connection.

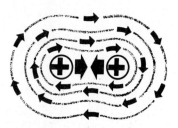

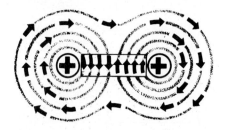

Figure 9-25. Adjacent Conductors with Current Flow in the Same Direction. (*Courtesy of Delco Remy Division, General Motors Corporation*)

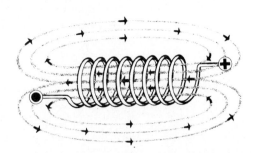

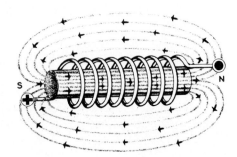

Figure 9-26. Magnetic Fields Surrounding an Electromagnet. (*Courtesy of Delco Remy Division, General Motors Corporation*)

3. *Shorted circuit*—unwanted copper-to-copper connection.

The windings in an electromagnet are coated with an insulating material that prevents the coils of wire from touching each other. Insulating paper may be located between each layer of turns. A short circuit occurs when the insulating material is melted on the coils so that some of the coils touch each other. A short circuit will have the following results:

1. Coils, or turns are less effective.
2. Resistance is reduced.
3. Current flow is increased.
4. Magnetic strength is the same as it was originally.

Reduction in the number of turns tends to decrease the magnetic strength, but the increase in current flow offsets this effect. Therefore, the magnetic strength of an electromagnet with a shorted condition will remain the same if the electromagnet is the only resistance in the circuit.

When a short circuit occurs in an electromagnet, the increased current flow usually damages some of the other components in the circuit. For example, a shorted alternator field winding may result in a damaged voltage regulator. (Refer to Chapter 11 for an explanation of the charging circuit.)

A shorted condition may be tested by connecting an ohmmeter to the electromagnet. If the coil is shorted, the resistance will be less than specified by the manufacturer.

Basic Electric Components

Wires

Stranded copper wires are used in most automotive electric circuits. The gauge size of the wire indicates the diameter of the wire. A 16-gauge wire has a smaller diameter than a 12-gauge wire, as indicated in Figure 9-27.

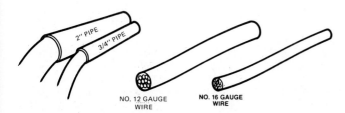

Figure 9-27. Wires Gauge Sizes. (*Courtesy of Chrysler Canada*)

The resistance of a wire is determined by its size, length, temperature, and the type of conductor. A large-diameter copper wire has less resistance than a smaller wire, and therefore the larger wire has a greater current-carrying capacity. The resistance of a wire increases with its length. Also, when the temperature of copper wire is increased, its resistance is higher.

Relays

A relay contains a set of contacts mounted above the relay core. The magnetism developed by the fine winding on the relay core controls the action of the contacts.

A relay is often connected in the horn circuit. When the horn ring is depressed, a switch in the steering wheel completes the circuit from the relay winding to ground. Under this condition the relay coil magnetism closes the contacts and current is supplied through the contacts to the horn. The lower current through the relay winding is used to control the higher current in the horn circuit, as illustrated in Figure 9-28.

Circuit Breakers, Fuses, and Fuse Panels

Circuit breakers or fuses are used as safety devices to protect electric wiring and circuit components.

A circuit breaker contains a set of contacts and a strip made from two metals. Since the two metals expand at different rates when they are heated or cooled, the bimetal strip bends when it is subjected to temperature changes. If a defect occurs, such as a grounded circuit or a short circuit, excessive current

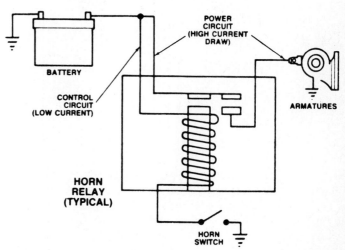

Figure 9-28. Horn Relay Circuits. (*Courtesy of Chrysler Canada*)

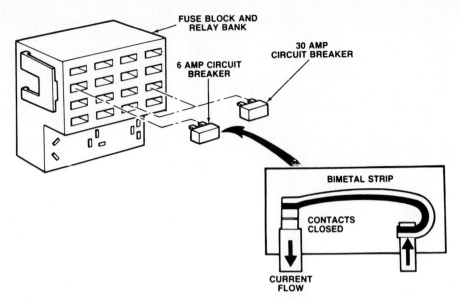

Figure 9-29. Circuit Breaker. (*Courtesy of Chrysler Canada*)

flow heats the bimetal strip and causes the contacts to open. If this action did not take place, the wires or circuit components would overheat and be damaged. When the bimetal strip cools, the contacts close again, as shown in Figure 9-29.

Older vehicles use round fuses in the fuse panel. The amp rating of each fuse and the circuit identification is stamped on the fuse panel. A fuse panel with round fuses is illustrated in Figure 9-30.

Most of today's cars use plug-in type fuses. The color code on these fuses indicates the amp rating. This code and the test procedure are explained in Figure 9-31.

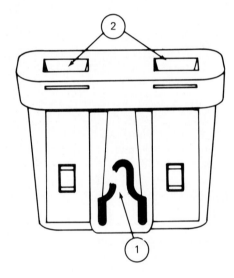

To test for blown mini-fuse
① Pull fuse out and check visually
② With the circuit activated, use a test light across the points shown

Mini-fuse color codes

Rating	Color
5 amp	Tan
10 amp	Red
20 amp	Yellow
25 amp	White

Figure 9-31. Plug-in Type Fuse. (*Courtesy of Chevrolet Motor Division, General Motors Corporation*)

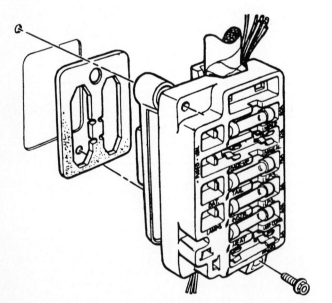

Figure 9-30. Fuse Panel with Round Fuses. (*Courtesy of Chevrolet Motor Division, General Motors Corporation*)

Other components, such as signal light flashers, horn relay, buzzers, and circuit breakers, may be plugged into the fuse panel, as indicated in Figure 9-32.

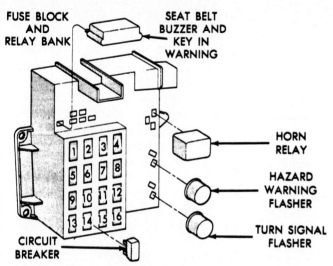

Figure 9-32. Fuse Panel with Plug-in Type Fuses. (*Courtesy of Chrysler Canada*)

Resistors

Various types of resistors are used in automotive electric circuits. Some resistors, such as ignition resistors or blower motor resistors, are made from a coil of wire. Variable resistors are used in headlight switches to reduce the brilliance of the instrument panel lights. This type of resistor may be referred to as a rheostat. Carbon resistors are used in some computers and modules.

A variety of resistors is shown in Figure 9-33.

Capacitors

Most automotive capacitors contain two aluminum foil plates that are separated by insulating paper. One plate is connected to the capacitor lead and the other plate is grounded to the case. The capacity of a capacitor is measured in farads or microfarads (MFD).

In many circuits the capacitor is used to block direct current (DC) voltage. A capacitor is used in most alternators to protect the diodes from high induced voltages. (Refer to Chapter 11 for a complete explanation of the charging circuit.) Capacitors may also be used to suppress radio interference. The primary ignition circuit on a point-type ignition system uses a capacitor to prevent point arcing and provide faster magnetic collapse in the ignition coil.

The design and basic operation of a capacitor are outlined in Figure 9-34.

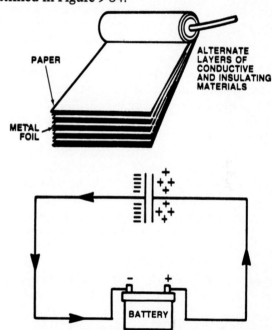

THE CAPACITOR CHARGES TO THE SOURCE VOLTAGE

Figure 9-34. Capacitor and Capacitor Operation. (*Courtesy of Chrysler Canada*)

Figure 9-33. Types of Resistors. (*Courtesy of Chrysler Canada*)

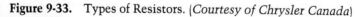

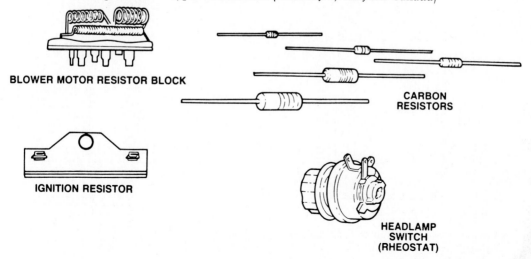

Diodes and Transistors

Diode Operation

Most diodes and transistors are made from silicon. This element is classified as a semiconductor because it has four valence electrons. If two pieces of silicon are melted together, the valence rings on the atoms join together, so that there are eight electrons on the valence rings. When this occurs a silicon crystal has been created, as pictured in Figure 9-35.

When a diode or transistor is manufactured, a silicon crystal is combined with other elements. Phosphorus is an element with five valence electrons, and boron atoms contain three valence electrons. In the diode manufacturing process, a small silicon crystal wafer is coated with boron on one side and phosphorus on the other. The wafer is then heated, and the two elements melt into the silicon. When the outer rings of the atoms join together, one excess, or free, electron will be provided for each atom of phosphorus that melts into the silicon, because there are nine valence electrons in the two elements and the maximum number of valence electrons is eight. Therefore, a negative (N-type) material which has an excess of electrons is made when silicon is combined with phosphorus, as illustrated in Figure 9-36.

When boron is combined with silicon, a positive (P-type) material with a lack of electrons is cre-ated, because the two elements have a total of seven valence electrons, and eight electrons are required to complete the valence ring. A positive-type material is shown in Figure 9-37.

Electrons flow through a diode when a positive terminal of a voltage source is connected to the positive side of the diode, and the negative source terminal is connected to the negative side of the diode. This type of connection is referred to as a forward-bias connection, as indicated in Figure 9-38.

A diode blocks electron movement when the negative source terminal is connected to the positive side of the diode and the positive source terminal is attached to the negative side of the diode. Reverse-bias is the term used for this type of connection, as indicated in Figure 9-39.

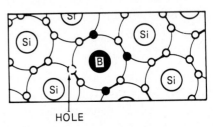

Figure 9-37.   Positive-Type Material. (*Courtesy of Delco Remy Division, General Motors Corporation*)

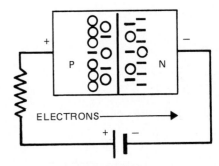

Figure 9-38.   Forward-Bias Connection. (*Courtesy of Delco Remy Division, General Motors Corporation*)

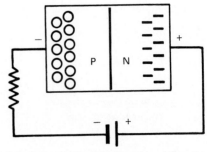

Figure 9-39.   Reverse-Bias Connection. (*Courtesy of Delco Remy Division, General Motors Corporation*)

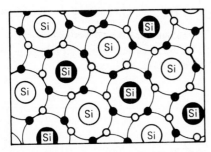

Figure 9-35.   Silicon Crystal. (*Courtesy of Delco Remy Division, General Motors Corporation*)

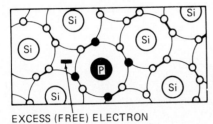

Figure 9-36.   Negative-Type Material. (*Courtesy of Delco Remy Division, General Motors Corporation*)

A diode is sometimes referred to as a P/N junction. In the forward direction, a diode only conducts a certain amount of current flow. If the current flow is above the diode rating, the diode will be damaged.

The peak inverse voltage (PIV) is the highest voltage that a diode will block in the reverse direction. If the PIV is exceeded, the diode may break down and conduct current, which will likely cause diode damage.

(Refer to Chapter 11 for an explanation of diodes in the alternator.)

Zener Diode

A zener diode breaks down at a specific voltage in the reverse direction. This type of diode is used in electronic voltage regulators and ignition modules. (Electronic regulators are explained in Chapter 11.) Zener diodes cannot be damaged by reverse current flow. A zener diode is shown in Figure 9-40.

Transistors

A transistor contains three semiconductor materials, called emitter, base, and collector. In some transistors the emitter is a P-type material, the base

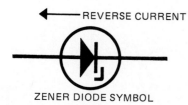

REVERSE CURRENT

ZENER DIODE SYMBOL

Figure 9-40. Zener Diode. (*Courtesy of Delco Remy Division, General Motors Corporation*)

is an N-type material, and the collector is a P-type material. This type of transistor is called a PNP transistor. An NPN transistor may also be used in many circuits. Both types of transistors and the transistor symbols are illustrated in Figure 9-41.

In order to start current flowing through a transistor, a forward-bias connection must be made from a source of voltage to the emitter and base terminals. When current begins to flow through the emitter-base circuit, a much higher current can flow through the emitter-collector circuit, as shown in Figure 9-42.

If the base circuit is opened, the free electrons in the N-type collector material are attracted to the outer edge of the collector, and a high resistance develops immediately at the base-collector junction. This stops the current flow in the emitter-collector circuit, as shown in Figure 9-43. Therefore, the low current in the base circuit can be used to control the higher current in the collector circuit. The current flow in the emitter-base circuit may be stopped by opening a switch, or a set of contacts, in the base circuit. Another method of switching off the current flow in the emitter-base circuit is to create a reverse-bias voltage at the emitter-base terminals, as illustrated in Figure 9-44.

A transistor can be defined as an electronic switch. The transistor can switch a circuit on and off much faster than a set of contacts or a mechanical switch can.

Integrated Circuits

Integrated circuits (ICs) are silicon chips that contain hundreds, or thousands, of solid-state components. Silicon crystal slices are used to manufacture ICs. A photographic printing and diffusion process

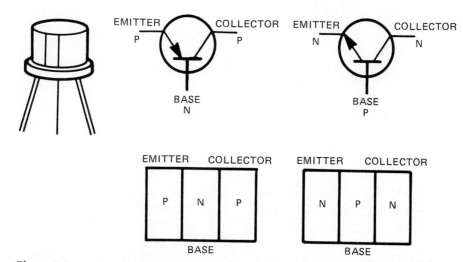

Figure 9-41. Transistors and Transistor Symbols. (*Courtesy of Chrysler Canada*)

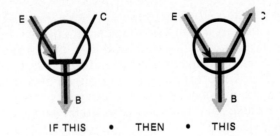

IF THIS • THEN • THIS

WITH VERY LITTLE CORRECT FLOW IN THE EMITTER-BASE
CIRCUIT, A GREATER CURRENT CAN BE ESTIMATED IN
THE EMITTER-COLLECTOR CIRCUIT

Figure 9-42.   Transistor Operation, Emitter-Base Circuit, Forward-Biased. (*Courtesy of Delco Remy Division, General Motors Corporation*)

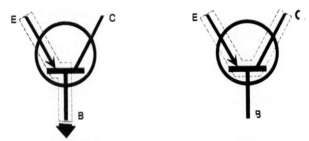

IF NO CURRENT FLOW HERE • THEN • NO CURRENT FLOW HERE

WITH NO CURRENT FLOW IN THE EMITTER-BASE CIRCUIT,
THERE IS NO CURRENT FLOW IN THE EMITTER-COLLECTOR
CIRCUIT.

Figure 9-43.   Transistor Operation with Base Circuit Open. (*Courtesy of Delco Remy Division, General Motors Corporation*)

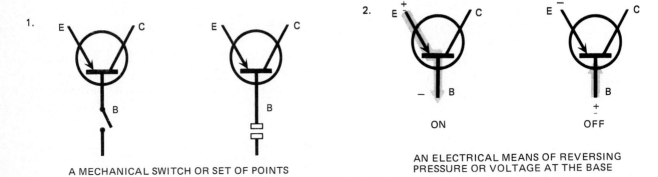

A MECHANICAL SWITCH OR SET OF POINTS

AN ELECTRICAL MEANS OF REVERSING
PRESSURE OR VOLTAGE AT THE BASE

Figure 9-44.   Methods of Switching a Transistor On and Off. (*Courtesy of Delco Remy Division, General Motors Corporation*)

is used to construct the circuits on individual chips in a slice of silicon, and the slice is cut into individual chips. One chip may contain hundreds of resistors, diodes, transistors, capacitors, and interconnecting circuits.

The IC chip is the basic building block for many electronic voltage regulators, ignition modules, and computers. The IC chip manufacturing process is shown in Figure 9-45.

A list of electric and electronic signals is provided in Figure 9-46.

Computers

Voltage Signals

The computer basics explained in this section are very important to understand prior to studying the highly technical computer systems described in later chapters.

An analog signal is continuously variable. This type of signal can be any voltage within a certain

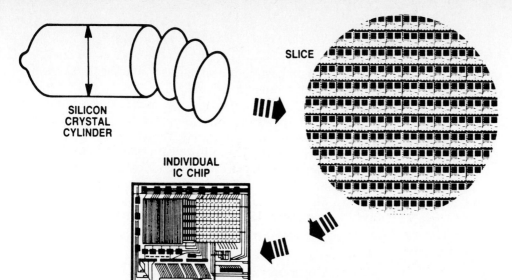

Figure 9-45. Integrated Circuit Chip Manufacturing. (*Courtesy of Chrysler Canada*)

Symbol	Name	Symbol	Name
+	POSITIVE	→→⊢	CONNECTOR
−	NEGATIVE	→	MALE CONNECTOR
ground	GROUND	>⊢	FEMALE CONNECTOR
fuse	FUSE	↓↓↓ Y Y Y	MULTIPLE CONNECTOR
circuit breaker	CIRCUIT BREAKER		DENOTES WIRE CONTINUES ELSEWHERE
capacitor	CAPACITOR		SPLICE
Ω	OHMS	J2 2	SPLICE IDENTIFICATION
resistor	RESISTOR	OPTIONAL	OPTIONAL WIRING WITH / WIRING WITHOUT
variable resistor	VARIABLE RESISTOR		THERMAL ELEMENT (BI-METAL STRIP)
series resistor	SERIES RESISTOR		"Y" WINDINGS
coil	COIL	88:88	DIGITAL READOUT
step up coil	STEP UP COIL		SINGLE FILAMENT LAMP

Symbol	Name	Symbol	Name
open contact	OPEN CONTACT		DUAL FILAMENT LAMP
closed contact	CLOSED CONTACT		L.E.D.-LIGHT EMITTING DIODE
closed switch	CLOSED SWITCH		THERMISTOR
open switch	OPEN SWITCH		GAUGE
closed ganged switch	CLOSED GANGED SWITCH	TIMER	TIMER
open ganged switch	OPEN GANGED SWITCH		MOTOR
two pole single throw switch	TWO POLE SINGLE THROW SWITCH		ARMATURE AND BRUSHES
pressure switch	PRESSURE SWITCH		DENOTES WIRE GOES THROUGH GROMMET
solenoid switch	SOLENOID SWITCH	#36	DENOTES WIRE GOES THROUGH 40 WAY DISCONNECT
mercury switch	MERCURY SWITCH	#19 STRG COLUMN	DENOTES WIRE GOES THROUGH 25 WAY STEERING COLUMN CONNECTOR
diode	DIODE OR RECTIFIER	INST PANEL #14	DENOTES WIRE GOES THROUGH 25 WAY INSTRUMENT PANEL CONNECTOR
zener diode	BY-DIRECTIONAL ZENER DIODE		

Figure 9-46. Electrical and Electronic Symbols. (*Courtesy of Chrysler Canada*)

range. For example, a throttle position sensor (TPS) provides a voltage signal that varies continuously between 0V and 5V in relation to throttle opening. (This sensor is explained in Chapter 17.)

Digital signals can only be represented by specific voltages within a specific range. For example, 1V, 2V, or 3V would be allowed in a digital signal, but 1.73V or 2.66V would not be allowed. Digital signals are used when information refers to two conditions, such as on and off or high and low. This type of signal is referred to as a digital binary signal and is limited to two voltage levels. One of these voltage levels will be a positive voltage and the other a zero voltage. The digital binary signal is a square wave signal.

An analog signal is compared to a digital binary signal in Figure 9-47.

The computer uses digital signals in a code that contains ones and zeros. One represents the high voltage of the digital signal and zero represents zero volts. Each zero and each one is referred to as a bit, and eight bits are called a word. A combination of eight binary digital signals is contained in each word, as illustrated in Figure 9-48.

Digital binary codes are used inside a computer, and also between the computer and other electronic components. Thousands of bits are used by a computer to store an infinite variety of information and communicate effectively with other system components. For example, if the air conditioner is turned on, a 10100110 may be received by the automotive computer. In response to this signal, the computer provides a slight increase in idle speed.

Computer Purpose

A computer receives information, makes decisions regarding that information, and takes some action as a result of those decisions. In performing these functions, the computer follows a detailed list of instructions called a program. Programs break each computer task down into its most basic parts. A program may contain hundreds of steps, depending on the complexity of the computer functions.

Microprocessors

The microprocessor is the "brain" of the small computer in that it does calculations and makes decisions. The other components in the computer support the microprocessor.

Memories

A microprocessor cannot store information, so a computer requires storage devices called memories. Information that is stored permanently in a computer, such as the programs that control the microprocessor, is placed in the read-only memory (ROM). The microprocessor can read instructions from the ROM, but it cannot write any new information into the ROM.

Random-access memory (RAM) is often used for temporary storage. The microprocessor can write information into the RAM and also read information out of the RAM. If the microprocessor receives information it requires to make several different decisions, the information will be written into the RAM and then read out each time it is needed.

A RAM may have a volatile, or nonvolatile memory. Volatile memory is erased when power is switched off, whereas a nonvolatile memory holds its information when power is removed. A RAM with volatile memory is connected to the battery at all times. However, if the battery becomes com-

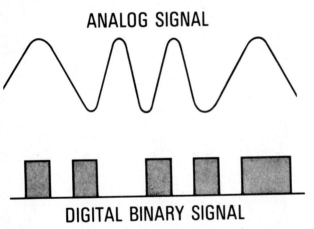

Figure 9-47.   Analog and Digital Binary Signals. (*Courtesy of GM Product Service Training, General Motors Corporation*)

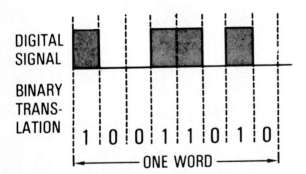

Figure 9-48.   Eight Digital Binary Codes in a Word. (*Courtesy of GM Product Service Training, General Motors Corporation*)

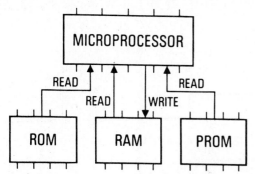

Figure 9-49. Microprocessor with Memories. (*Courtesy of GM Product Service Training, General Motors Corporation*)

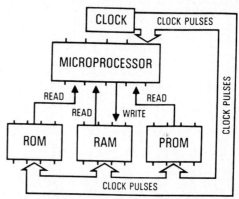

Figure 9-51. Microprocessor with Memories and Clock. (*Courtesy of GM Product Service Training, General Motors Corporation*)

pletely discharged or if the cables are removed, the RAM loses its information.

Many automotive computers contain a programmable read-only memory (PROM). This type of memory is removable from the computer, whereas ROMs and RAMs are installed permanently. The microprocessor can read information from the PROM, but it cannot write information into it. The PROM contains information that varies in each model of car. New information can be added to the PROM without changing the original program. (Refer to Chapter 17 for an explanation of computers with a PROM.)

A microprocessor with different memories is outlined in Figure 9-49.

Computer Clocks

Thus far we have seen that a computer contains a microprocessor that communicates with several memories. The language used for communication is a digital binary code which contains long strings of

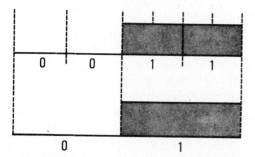

Figure 9-50. Different Digital Binary Code Messages. (*Courtesy of GM Product Service Training, General Motors Corporation*)

ones and zeros. A computer must use some method to determine when one message ends and the next information begins. For example, the computer must be able to distinguish a 01 signal from a 0011 input, as indicated in Figure 9-50.

Computers contain clock generators that provide constant, steady pulses that are one bit in length. The memories watch these clock pulses when they are sending or receiving information. Therefore, the memories and the microprocessor know how long each bit is supposed to last. In this way the computer can distinguish between a 01 and a 0011 signal.

A microprocessor with a clock and various memories is shown in Figure 9-51.

Interfaces

A computer requires interfaces to handle the incoming and outgoing information. These interfaces protect the delicate electronics in the computer from high induced voltages in electrical circuits. The interfaces also translate input and output signals. When the computer receives an analog signal, the interface converts this signal to a digital binary code for the microprocessor. If the computer controls output devices with a digital signal, the output interface translates the computer language into digital output signals.

The computer must know the operating conditions of the system that it is controlling. Various sensors are used to provide this information. These sensors usually contain thermistors or potentiometers. A thermistor is a temperature-sensitive resistor, and a potentiometer is a variable resistor. The throttle position sensor contains a potentiometer that is connected to the carburetor throttle shaft. This potentiometer sends an analog signal to the

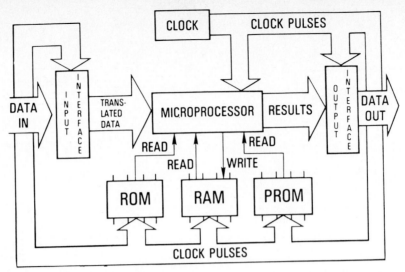

Figure 9-52. Computer with Memories, Clock, and Interfaces. (*Courtesy of GM Product Service Training, General Motors Corporation*)

computer in relation to throttle opening. Many computer systems have a thermistor in the coolant temperature sensor that sends an analog signal to the computer in relation to engine coolant temperature.

Computers send and receive signals through wires called data links. Some data links transmit data in one direction only, while other data links can transmit data in both directions. For example, the computer supplies a reference voltage to the throttle position sensor, which then transmits an output voltage signal back to the computer. Data links are also used for communication between two computers. (Refer to Chapters 17 and 18 for a complete explanation of automotive computer systems.)

A complete computer with interfaces is illustrated in Figure 9-52.

Types of Computer Data

Serial Data

Many automotive computer systems now have more than one computer. These computers use various methods to transmit data to each other. When serial data transmission is used between two computers, all the data words are sent one after the other. The computers are synchronized to the data being sent and clocked together. Serial data transmission is shown in Figure 9-53.

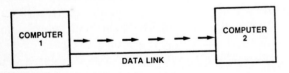

Figure 9-53. Serial Data Transmission. (*Courtesy of GM Product Service Training, General Motors Corporation*)

Duplex Serial Data

In duplex serial data transmission between two computers, a single, two-way data link is used. Serial data may be sent or received by either computer. An external clock line between the two computers controls the sending and receiving functions of each computer. When the clock pulse is high, computer 1 is programmed to send data while computer 2 listens to or receives the data. During low clock pulses, computer 2 transmits data and computer 1 receives it. Duplex serial data lines are used on some cars between the body computer module (BCM) and the electronic climate control head. (Refer to Chapters 18 and 26 for an explanation of the BCM system.)

Duplex serial data transmission is shown in Figure 9-54.

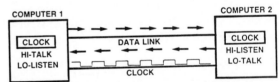

Figure 9-54. Duplex Serial Data Transmission. (*Courtesy of GM Product Service Training, General Motors Corporation*)

Peripheral Serial Bus Data

In a peripheral serial bus system, dual data links are used between two computers. One of these data links is always used to send data from computer 1 to computer 2, whereas the other data link transmits data from computer 2 to computer 1, as indicated in Figure 9-55.

Peripheral serial bus data links are used between the body control module (BCM) and the electronic control module (ECM) on some cars. (Computer sys-

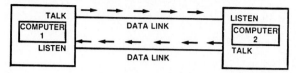

Figure 9-55. Peripheral Serial Bus Data Link. (*Courtesy of GM Product Service Training, General Motors Corporation*)

tems with an ECM, BCM, and data links are described in Chapter 18.)

Synchronous Data

Synchronous data systems have a constant data flow with regular clock pulses. In these systems, "sync" pulses occur at regular clock intervals. These sync pulses signal the computer that a new piece of data is starting. Synchronous data transmission is pictured in Figure 9-56.

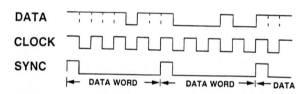

Figure 9-56. Synchronous Data. (*Courtesy of GM Product Service Training, General Motors Corporation*)

Asynchronous Data

In some computer systems, data is transmitted only when it is required, rather than being sent continuously. This type of data transmission is referred to as asynchronous data. A start pulse informs the computer that data is about to be transmitted, and a stop pulse informs the computer that data transmission is complete. The computer checks to ensure that the total word, or words, have been sent correctly. When the stop pulse is received, data transmission stops until the next start pulse signal. The asynchronous data transmission method is shown in Figure 9-57.

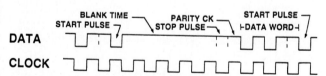

Figure 9-57. Asynchronous Data. (*Courtesy of GM Product Service Training, General Motors Corporation*)

Parallel Data

When parallel data transmission is used, separate data lines are connected from several switches to the computer. These switches may be turned on and off simultaneously to send specific data signals to the computer. Parallel data transmission is pictured in Figure 9-58.

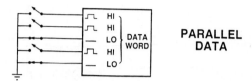

Figure 9-58. Parallel Data. (*Courtesy of GM Product Service Training, General Motors Corporation*)

Voice Synthesizers

Operation

Voice synthesizers are used in voice-alert systems to warn the vehicle operator audibly when specific abnormal conditions occur. The voice synthesizer is a microprocessor, or computer, that stores electronic voice signals in its memory. Input signals to the computer indicate abnormal conditions in each monitored system. When one of these signals is received, the computer selects the correct response from its memory. In some systems the electronic voice signals from the computer are converted into an audible message through the radio speaker nearest the driver. (Voice-alert systems are discussed in Chapter 15.)

The operation of a voice synthesizer is shown in Figure 9-59.

Test Questions

1. An atom is the smallest particle of an
   _____.
2. An element with 5 valence electrons on each atom will be a good conductor. T F
3. Name the three requirements for electron movement.
4. Electrical pressure is measured in _____.
5. When the voltage in a circuit decreases, the current flow _____.
6. If the resistance in a circuit increases, the current flow _____.

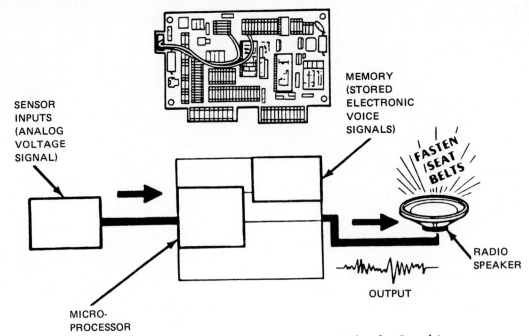

Figure 9-59.   Voice Synthesizer Operation. (*Courtesy of Chrysler Canada*)

7. A shorted circuit may be defined as an un-wanted copper-to- _____ connection.

8. When phosphorus is combined with a silicon crystal, a _____ type of material is formed.

9. The current flow in the collector circuit of a transistor is _____ than the current flow in the base circuit.

10. When the emitter-base circuit of a transistor is connected to a voltage source with a reverse-bias connection, there will be current flow in the emitter-collector circuit.   T F

11. Calculate the following values from the series circuit in Figure 9-60.

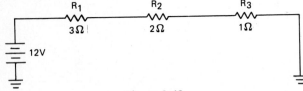

Figure 9-60.

a) total resistance
b) current flow
c) voltage drop across R1
d) voltage drop across R2
e) voltage drop across R3

12. Calculate the following values from the parallel circuit in Figure 9-61.

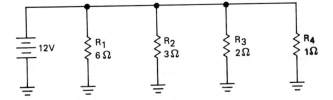

Figure 9-61.

a) current flow in R1
b) current flow in R2
c) current flow in R3
d) current flow in R4
e) total current
f) total resistance

13. An analog signal is continuously variable.   T F

14. A microprocessor can write information into a random-access memory.   T F

15. In computer language, a word represents _____ bits of information.

16. Computers use a clock generator to recognize different input signals.   T F

17. An analog signal is changed to a digital signal in the _____ of a computer.

18. Asynchronous data is transmitted continuously.   T F

19. In a peripheral serial bus system, data may be sent through the data links in both directions.   T F

10

Lead-Acid Batteries

Chapter Completion Objectives

1. Demonstrate an understanding of conventional lead-acid battery design.
2. Indicate a knowledge of electrolyte specific gravity and the effects of incorrect specific gravity.
3. Explain the factors that determine the voltage and amperes available from a lead-acid battery.
4. Describe the chemical changes that occur during battery discharging and charging procedures.
5. Explain the differences between conventional and maintenance-free batteries.
6. Demonstrate an understanding of battery ratings.
7. Explain battery counterelectromotive force (CEMF) in relation to state of charge.

Battery Design

Plates

Battery plates are built on a lead grid that resembles a coarse screen. In some grids, antimony is mixed with the lead to make the grid more rigid. Many of the maintenance-free batteries use calcium to add rigidity to the grid. A plate grid is shown in Figure 10-1.

A sponge lead (Pb) paste is adhered to the negative plate grids, and lead peroxide (PbO_2) paste is placed on the positive plate grid, as illustrated in Figure 10-2.

Figure 10-1. Plate Grid. (*Courtesy of Delco Remy Division, General Motors Corporation*)

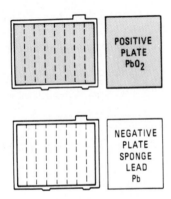

Figure 10-2. Positive and Negative Plates. (*Courtesy of Delco Remy Division, General Motors Corporation*)

Separators

Many batteries have separators made from a plastic, polyvinylchloride. some older batteries have fiberglass or rubber separators. The separators are positioned between the plates to keep the plates from touching each other. Separators contain small microscopic holes to make them porous. The porosity of the separators is very important, because the sulphuric acid content of the electrolyte has to move through the separators and contact the plates. The battery plates will only deliver electrical energy when they are in contact with a sulphuric acid solution.

Plate Groups

A plate strap is lead-burned to the grid tabs on the negative and positive plates to make a negative plate group and a positive plate group for each battery cell. The negative and positive plates are positioned alternately in the cell group, and a negative plate is located on both sides of the group. Therefore, each battery cell contains one more negative plate than positive plates. The cell group shown in Figure 10-3 has four positive plates and five negative plates.

A separator is installed between each negative and positive plate. The separators are smooth on one side and ribbed on the other. The vertical ribs always face the positive plates, which allows any material shed off the positive plates to drop into the bottom of the case. The complete group of plates and separators in a battery cell may be referred to as an element.

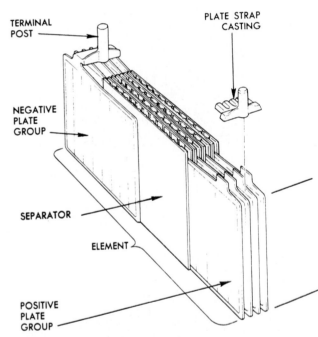

Figure 10-3. Plate Groups in a Battery Cell. (*Courtesy of Delco Remy Division, General Motors Corporation*)

Complete Battery

The negative plates in one battery cell are always connected to the positive plates in the next cell by a lead connector that goes through the partition between the cells, as shown in Figure 10-4.

A 12V battery contains six cells that are connected in series. The negative plates in the cell at one end of the battery and the positive plates in the cell at the other end are connected to posts that ex-

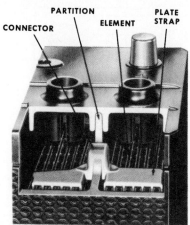

Figure 10-4. Battery Cell Connector. (*Courtesy of Delco Remy Division, General Motors Corporation*)

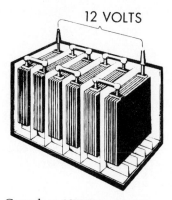

Figure 10-5. Complete 12V Battery. (*Couretsy of Delco Remy Division, General Motors Corporation*)

tend through the top of the battery, as illustrated in Figure 10-5.

Most batteries manufactured today have polypropylene cases. The battery plates rest on bridges in the bottom of the case. These bridges form sediment reservoirs which collect the material that is

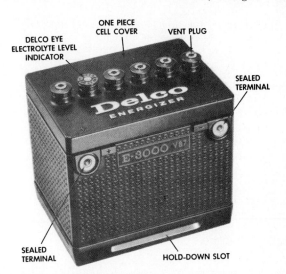

Figure 10-6. Side Terminal Battery. (*Courtesy of Delco Remy Division, General Motors Corporation*)

shed off the plates and thus prevent shedded material from shorting the plates together. Each filler cap is vented to allow the escape of gas during the charging process.

The cables from the vehicle's electrical system are connected to the battery posts. In most vehicles the negative battery post is connected to ground on the engine and the positive post is connected to the starter solenoid and other electrical circuits. Side terminals are used on some batteries rather than top-mounted terminals. This type of battery, sometimes referred to as a sealed terminal battery, is illustrated in Figure 10-6. Side terminals usually are more resistant to corrosion than top terminals.

Electrolyte

The electrolyte solution within a battery is a mixture of 36 percent sulphuric acid and 64 percent water. Specific gravity is used to compare the weight of other liquids to the weight of water. Water has a specific gravity of 1.000, and the specific gravity of sulphuric acid is 1.835. Therefore, sulphuric acid is 1.835 times heavier than an equal volume of water. The electrolyte solution has a specific gravity of 1.265, which means that a quart of electrolyte is 1.265 times heavier than a quart of water. If the electrolyte had a higher percentage of sulphuric acid and a specific gravity above 1.310, the plate grids would deteriorate rapidly. When the electrolyte is lower than 1.265 specific gravity, there is a danger of the electrolyte freezing in colder climates. If the electrolyte specific gravity is 1.220, it will freeze at $-31°$ F ($-35°$ C), as indicated in Table 10-1.

TABLE 10-1. Freezing Temperatures of Electrolyte

	Freezing Temperature	
Specific Gravity	*F*	*C*
1.100	18°	−8°
1.040	8°	−13°
1.080	−6°	−21°
1.220	−31°	−35°
1.260	−75°	−59°

Battery Operation

Fully Charged

The purposes of the battery are to supply current to the starting motor for cranking the engine and to provide current to the electrical accessories when the engine is not running or when a charging circuit fails. In a fully charged battery, the material on the positive plates is lead peroxide and the material on the negative plates is sponge lead. When these dissimilar plates are immersed in a diluted sulphuric acid solution, a massing of electrons occurs on the negative plates. Therefore, a voltage difference of 2.13V is created between the battery plates, since this is the potential difference between lead and lead peroxide. Each battery cell will have a fully charged voltage of at least 2.1V and the entire 12V battery will have 12.6V. If an electrical load is connected between the battery plates, electrons begin to move through the load because of the voltage difference between the plates, as indicated in Figure 10-7.

The total amount of current flow, or electron movement, that a fully charged battery delivers depends on the plate area in the battery. Batteries with a larger plate area deliver more current flow. The electrons are actually massed on the negative battery plate and flow through the external circuit to the positive plates. However, for illustration purposes the current is often shown to be flowing

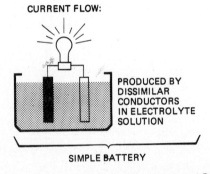

Figure 10-7. Battery Electron Movement. (*Courtesy of Delco Remy Division, General Motors Corporation*)

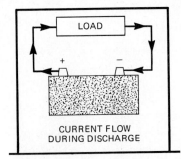

Figure 10-8. Battery Current Flow from Positive to Negative. (*Courtesy of Delco Remy Division, General Motors Corporation*)

through the external circuit from the positive battery terminal to the negative terminal, such as is pictured in Figure 10-8.

Discharge Action

When a battery is being discharged, two chemical changes occur inside the battery:

1. The sulphuric acid (H_2SO_4) molecules break up and the sulphate (SO_4) is attracted to both plates, which begins changing the plates to lead sulphate ($PbSO_4$).
2. The oxygen (O_2) breaks away from the lead peroxide (PbO_2) on the positive plates. The O_2 joins with the hydrogen (H_2) in the electrolyte to form water. Therefore, the electrolyte solution gradually changes to a higher percentage of water as the battery discharges.

The chemical changes that occur during discharge are illustrated in Figure 10-9.

Charging Action

When a battery is completely discharged, both plates change to lead sulphate ($PbSO_4$) and the electrolyte contains a much higher percentage of water (H_2O) than a fully charged battery. The lead-acid battery state of charge is completely reversible. It can be dis-

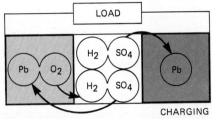

Figure 10-9. Chemical Changes during Battery Discharge. (*Courtesy of Delco Remy Division, General Motors Corporation*)

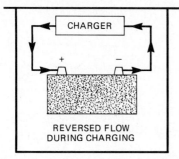

Figure 10-10. Battery Recharging. (*Courtesy of Delco Remy Division, General Motors Corporation*)

charged and charged repeatedly. A battery charger or the charging system of the vehicle can be used to force current through the battery for recharging purposes. The charging process is shown in Figure 10-10.

Repeated discharging and charging of a battery is referred to as cycling. Each time a battery is cycled, some material is shed off the plates, which shortens the life of the battery.

When a battery is being charged, two chemical changes take place inside the battery:

1. The sulphate (SO_4) breaks away from the lead (Pb) on the plates and joins with the hydrogen (H_2) in the solution to form sulphuric acid (H_2SO_4).

2. The water (H_2O) molecule breaks up and the oxygen (O_2) is attracted to the positive plates, where it joins with the lead (Pb) to form lead peroxide (PbO_2).

The charging action in a battery is shown in Figure 10-11.

When a battery is being charged, some of the oxygen (O_2) is released as a gas at the positive plates and some hydrogen (H_2) gas is given off at the negative plates. Since H_2 is explosive, sparks or flames should always be kept away from batteries, especially when they are being charged. These two gases combined form water (H_2O), and therefore the sulphate (SO_4) is never released as gas from a battery.

The voltage of a battery depends on the chemical difference between the plates. If the battery is

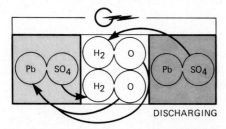

Figure 10-11. Chemical Changes while Charging. (*Courtesy of Delco Remy Division, General Motors Corporation*)

Chemical changes in battery during discharge

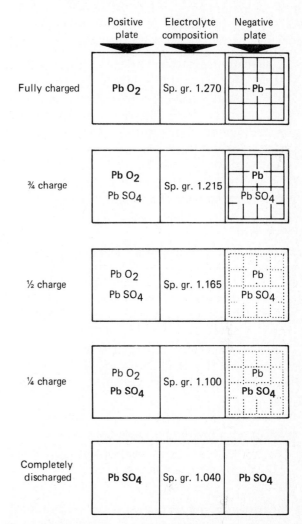

	Positive plate	Electrolyte composition	Negative plate
Fully charged	Pb O_2	Sp. gr. 1.270	Pb
¾ charge	Pb O_2 / Pb SO_4	Sp. gr. 1.215	Pb / Pb SO_4
½ charge	Pb O_2 / Pb SO_4	Sp. gr. 1.165	Pb / Pb SO_4
¼ charge	Pb O_2 / Pb SO_4	Sp. gr. 1.100	Pb / Pb SO_4
Completely discharged	Pb SO_4	Sp. gr. 1.040	Pb SO_4

Figure 10-12. Battery Discharge Summary. (*Courtesy of Delco Remy Division, General Motors Corporation*)

fully charged, the negative plates are sponge lead and the positive plates are lead peroxide. Under this condition the battery voltage is at least 12.6V. If the battery is partly discharged and some lead sulphate ($PbSO_4$) is formed on the plates, the battery voltage is reduced.

The discharge process is summarized in Figure 10-12.

Maintenance-Free Batteries

Special Features

Many batteries sold today are classified as maintenance-free batteries. Some of these batteries are sealed to prevent filler cap removal so that water cannot be added to the electrolyte. Other maintenance-free batteries have removable filler caps. The top of the battery or the filler caps are always vented to allow gas to escape. Some features of maintenance-free batteries are the following:

1. Sealed batteries have a liquid-gas separator in the battery top that returns liquid to the reservoir.

2. Plate grids are made of lead and calcium. Some grids also contain tin. These grids are sheet-rolled in the manufacturing process to provide a fine granular structure with increased strength and high corrosion resistance.

3. The lead-calcium grids protect the battery from overcharge damage. They also provide more resistance to self-discharge, and therefore shelf life is increased.

4. Separator envelopes that are open at the top and closed on three sides are placed over one set of plates. These separators may be placed on the positive or negative plates by the manufacturer, which eliminates the possibility of shedded plate material shorting the plates together.

5. When the envelope separator is used, the sediment reservoirs in the bottom of the case are eliminated. This allows the use of larger plates and provides increased electrolyte capacity.

6. A ribbed polypropylene case combines light weight with high impact strength.

7. The lead-calcium grids and separator envelopes make the battery more resistant to road shock and vibration.

All of these special features may not be found in some makes of maintenance-free batteries.

Maintenance-free batteries may have top terminals or side terminals. A maintenance-free battery with top terminals is illustrated in Figure 10-13.

Maintenance-free batteries with sealed tops have a sight glass in the battery top that is used as a test indicator. This indicator is a built-in hydrometer that indicates the battery condition.

The battery should be in the level position before the test indicator is observed. If a green dot is visible in the center of the indicator, the battery is sufficiently charged for test purposes. When the indicator appears dark with no green dot visible, the battery is discharged and should be charged and tested. The charging system should also be checked. A clear or light yellow light in the sight glass indicates that the electrolyte level is below the test indicator. This condition can be caused by excessively high charging voltage, a cracked battery case, or tipping of the battery or vehicle.

The sight glass may appear yellow after the bat-

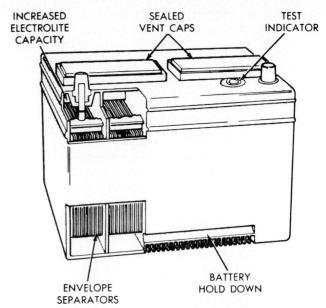

Figure 10-13. Maintenance-Free Battery. (*Courtesy of Chrysler Canada*)

tery has been in service for several years. If there is a cranking complaint and the sight glass appears yellow, the battery should be replaced and the charging system tested. Under this condition the battery should not be charged and the vehicle should not be started with a booster battery.

The sight glass and the different test indications are illustrated in Figure 10-14.

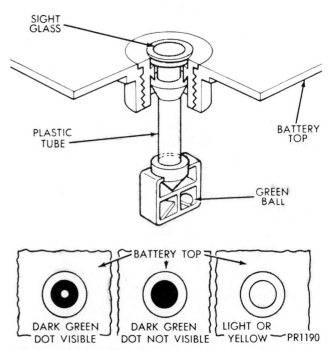

Figure 10-14. Maintenance-Free Battery Test Indicator. (*Courtesy of Chrysler Canada*)

Dry-Charged Batteries

Preparation for Service

Some batteries are shipped in a dry-charged condition and the electrolyte is added when the battery is sold. The electrolyte is supplied with the correct specific gravity of 1.265. Each battery cell should be filled to the split ring in the top of the cell, as pictured in Figure 10-15. The electrolyte level should be rechecked five minutes after the battery has been filled and the level should be brought up to the split ring indicator if necessary.

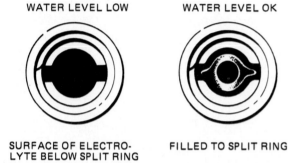

WATER LEVEL LOW   WATER LEVEL OK

SURFACE OF ELECTRO-   FILLED TO SPLIT RING
LYTE BELOW SPLIT RING

Figure 10-15. Electrolyte Level Indicator. (*Courtesy of Delco Remy Division, General Motors Corporation*)

When a voltmeter is connected to the battery terminals, if the voltage is 10V or less on a 12V battery, the battery has a defective cell and should not be put into service. If the hydrometer readings vary more than 0.030 specific gravity points between the cells, the battery should be fully charged on a slow charger.

Some suppliers of dry-charged batteries recommend that the battery be boost-charged after being filled with electrolyte if the atmospheric temperature is below 32°F (0°C), or if the battery and electrolyte temperature are below 60°F (15.5°C). The recommended boost charge on passenger car and light truck batteries would be 15 amperes for 10 minutes. A second boost charge may be necessary to bring the battery temperature above 60°F (15.5°C).

Battery Characteristics

Self-Discharge

Lead-acid batteries slowly discharge if they are not used for a long period of time. This process is called self-discharge. Self-discharge will take place faster at higher battery temperatures, as indicated in Figure

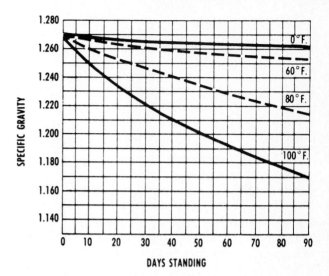

Figure 10-16. Battery Self-Discharge. (*Courtesy of Chevrolet Motor Division, General Motors Corporation*)

10-16. Therefore, batteries should be stored in a location where the temperature is cool. Self-discharge occurs faster if there is moisture on top of the battery or if the battery is placed on a cement floor. When a battery is placed in storage, its case should be clean and dry and it should not be stored directly on a cement floor.

The self-discharge chart in Figure 10-16 is for a conventional battery. Maintenance-free batteries have improved self-discharge characteristics.

Efficiency in Relation to Temperature

The battery will only function when the sulphate (SO_4) is in contact with the plate materials. When a battery is cold the electrolyte is denser and therefore does not move through the separators as quickly. This makes the battery less efficient as the temperature decreases. If the battery temperature is −20°F (−28.8°C), the battery will only produce 45 percent of the power that it had available at 80°F (26.6°C), as illustrated in Figure 10-17. As indicated in the figure, cranking the engine requires 3.5 times more power at −20°F (−28.8°C) than it did at 80°F (26.6°C). Therefore, the available battery cranking time is reduced considerably during cold-weather operation.

In cold climates, an electric battery blanket can be used to maintain the battery temperature and improve its cold-cranking power. An electric block heater can be installed in the engine block to keep the coolant and oil warmer, which reduces the power required to crank the engine. Some batteries have slightly different cold-cranking characteristics because of the variations in internal design.

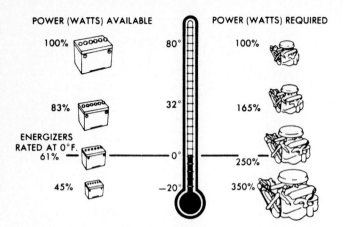

Figure 10-17.   Battery Efficiency in Relation to Temperature. (*Courtesy of Chevrolet Motor Division, General Motors Corporation*)

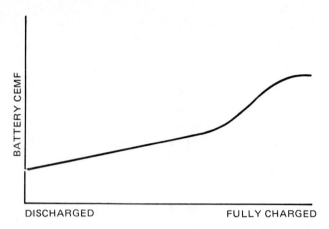

Figure 10-18.   Battery Counterelectromotive Force in Relation to State of Charge. (*Courtesy of Delco Remy Division, General Motors Corporation*)

Battery Counterelectromotive Force (CEMF)

The CEMF of a battery may be defined as the opposition that a battery offers to the flow of current. When a battery is discharged, its CEMF is low; conversely, CEMF is high in a fully charged battery.

When the battery becomes fully charged, a large number of oxygen (O_2) particles collect on the positive plates and hydrogen (H_2) particles attach to the negative plates. This occurs because the water (H_2O) molecules break up faster than the sulphate (SO_4) comes off the plates. This massing of O_2 and H_2 at the positive and negative plates raises the CEMF and the voltage of the battery so that the battery voltage is almost the same as the charging circuit voltage. Under this condition the charging amperes from the alternator to the battery are very low, which prevents overcharging of the battery. (Refer to Chapter 11 for a complete explanation of the charging circuit.) When a battery is fully charged, the increase in battery voltage may be referred to as surface charge.

Battery CEMF in relation to the state of charge is shown in Figure 10-18.

Battery Ratings

Ampere-Hour Rating

Battery ratings are used by battery manufacturers as a uniform method of classifying batteries according to their ability to deliver current under various conditions. During the ampere-hour rating with the battery temperature at 80°F (26.6°C), the battery is discharged at $\frac{1}{20}$ of the published rating for 20 hours and

the voltage should remain above 1.75V per cell. If the manufacturer rated a battery at 80 ampere hours, the battery would be discharged at 4 amperes for 20 hours. After the 20-hour discharge, if the cell voltage is above 1.75V, the battery is proven to be an 80 ampere-hour battery. This rating indicates the ability of a battery to deliver a low current flow for a long period of time.

Since batteries are usually not subjected to this type of load during normal driving conditions, this rating is not widely recognized at present.

Peak Watt Rating

Watts are calculated by multiplying amperes by volts. The peak watt rating is established by discharging the battery at different ampere rates at 0°F (−18°C) and reading the voltage at each rate. The watts are calculated for each discharge rate, and the peak watt rating is the highest wattage delivered by the battery at any discharge rate. For example, if the peak wattage occurred at a discharged rate of 400 amperes and the voltage was 8V, the peak watt rating would be 400 amperes times 8V, or 3200 watts.

This rating is not widely used today, but it may be found on some batteries still in service.

Reserve Capacity Rating

The reserve capacity rating is designed to indicate the length of time that a vehicle can be driven with the charging circuit inoperative. In this rating, the battery is discharged at 25 amperes with the battery temperature at 80°F (26.6°C). The rating is the time in minutes required to lower the voltage to 10.2V. For example, a battery with a reserve capacity rating of 110 minutes would withstand a discharge rate of 25 amperes for 110 minutes before the battery voltage decreased to 10.2V.

Cold-Cranking Rating

To obtain this rating, the battery temperature is lowered to 0°F (−18°C) and the battery is discharged at a high rate for 30 seconds. The rating is the discharge rate in amperes that is required to lower the battery voltage to 7.2V in 30 seconds. Therefore, a battery with a cold-cranking rating of 450 amperes would supply 450 amperes of current for 30 seconds before the voltage decreased to 7.2V.

Test Questions

1. If the electrolyte in a battery has a specific gravity of 1.325, the battery:
   a) will have a shorter life.

b) will deliver less total amperes.

c) may freeze in cold weather.

2. A fully charged battery cell should have a voltage of:
   a) 1.9V.
   b) 2.1V.
   c) 2.5V.

3. Describe the two chemical changes that occur when a battery is being discharged.

4. The total amperes that a warm, fully charged battery delivers depends on the _____ _____.

5. When a battery is being charged, the sulphate (SO_4) comes off the _____ and joins with the _____.

6. Sulphate (SO_4) may be given off as a gas during the charging process. T F

7. As the battery temperature decreases, the available power of the battery is reduced. T F

11

Charging Systems

Chapter Completion Objectives

1. Explain the advantages of a ribbed "V" belt compared to a conventional "V" belt.
2. Describe how the voltage is induced in the stator windings.
3. Demonstrate an understanding of rectification in wye- and delta-wound stators.
4. Explain the results of high charging system voltage.
5. Describe point-type voltage regulator operation at low, medium, and high speeds.
6. Demonstrate an understanding of electronic voltage regulator operation.
7. Explain the difference between A- and B-type electronic charging circuits.

Belts and Pulleys

"V" Belts and Pulleys

Many alternators, water pumps, air conditioning compressors, air pumps, and power steering pumps use "V" belts and pulleys. With this type of belt, the friction surfaces are on the sides of the belt. The belt should never contact the center of the pulley, and the belts and pulleys should always be inspected for wear on the friction surfaces. Belts should also be inspected for cracks, glazing, fraying, and oil contamination. An alternator will never have full output if the belt is slipping.

An alternator pulley with two "V"-type drive belts is illustrated in Figure 11-1. One view shows the pulley removed and the other shows the pulley and belts installed.

If the pulleys on belt-driven components are misaligned, the drive belt will wear prematurely. Pulley misalignment may be caused by worn mounting bolts or worn holes in the mounting brackets and alternator end housings. Bent mounting brackets can also cause pulley misalignment.

On some alternators, spacers are positioned between the mounting bracket and the end housing to align the pulley accurately. One manufacturer recommends that a 0.0078 in. (0.198 mm) spacer should be installed between the mounting bracket and the end housing if the clearance at this location is 0.008 in. (0.2 mm) or more with the alternator held toward the front of the engine. Point A in Figure 11-2 shows the location where the spacer should be installed.

Ribbed "V" Belts

The ribbed "V" belt is much wider than the conventional "V" belt and contains a series of small ribbed grooves on the underside of the belt. A comparison between the ribbed "V" belt and conventional "V" belt is given in Figure 11-3.

The ribbed "V" belt can be tightened with a tensioning pulley that applies tension to the back of the belt. One advantage of this type of belt is that the back of the belt may also be used as a drive surface if it is wrapped around a smooth pulley. Therefore, the ribbed "V" belt can be used to drive more components, and fewer tightening brackets are required than with conventional "V" belts. In Figure 11-4, a tensioner is applied to the back of the ribbed "V" belt so that the back of the belt drives the water pump. This type of belt-driven system is referred to as a serpentine belt.

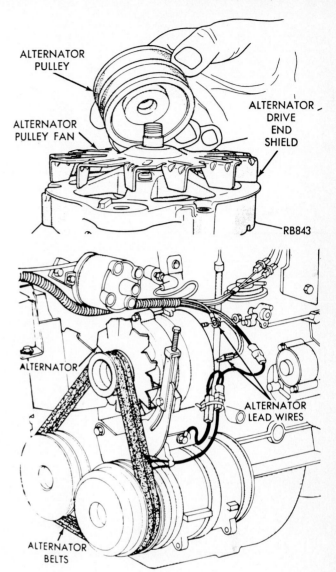

Figure 11-1. Alternator "V" Belts and Pulley. (*Courtesy of Chrysler Canada*)

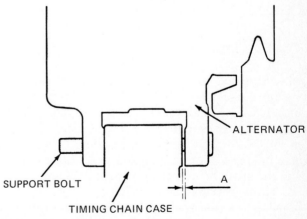

Figure 11-2. Alternator Pulley Alignment. (*Courtesy of Chrysler Canada*)

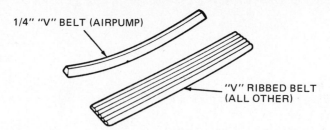

Figure 11-3. "V" Belt and Ribbed "V" Belt Comparison. (*Courtesy of Ford Motor Co.*)

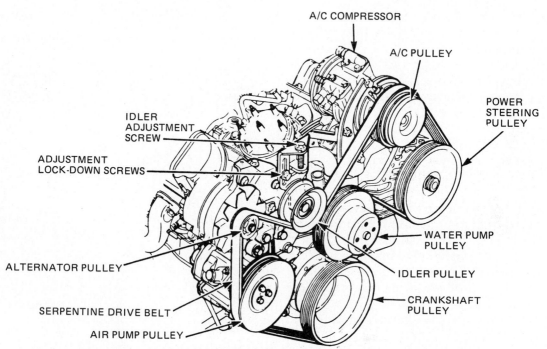

Figure 11-4. Components Driven by Ribbed "V" Belt. (Reference taken from SAE paper No. 820112. *Reprinted with Permission of Society of Automotive Engineers,* © 1982.)

Alternator Components

End Housings

The drive end housing contains a ball bearing that supports the rotor shaft. A ball bearing is also mounted in the rear end housing to support the slip ring end of the rotor shaft. Many alternators have a needle bearing in the rear end housing. This housing also contains the rectifier and heat-sink assembly and the brush holder, as illustrated in Figure 11-5.

Through bolts are installed from the rear end housing into the drive end housing to hold the alternator assembly together. The stator assembly is mounted between the two housings.

Pulley and Fan

The fan is used to move air through the alternator for cooling purposes. Many cooling fans have unequally spaced fins so that the noise of each fin cutting the air does not accumulate.

When the nut on the pulley is tightened, the cooling fan is jammed between the pulley spacer and the spacer that goes against the inner race of the drive end bearing. This forces the fan to rotate with the pulley and rotor. The pulley may be held onto the rotor shaft with a woodruff key. This key is mounted in a hole in the rotor shaft, and a groove in the pulley slides over the key. A nut and lock washer secure the pulley to the rotor shaft. The pulley contains the drive belt groove or grooves.

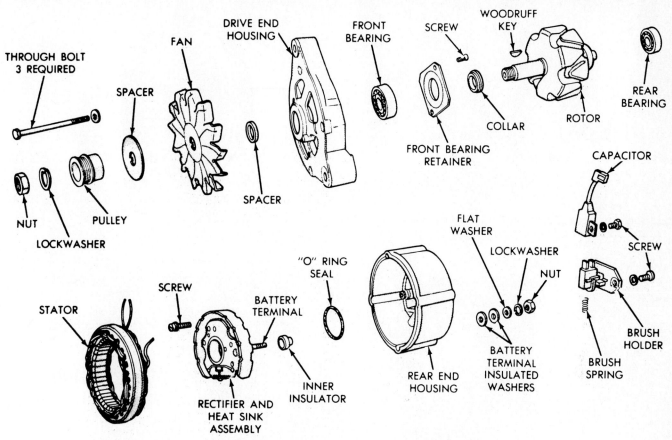

Figure 11-5. Complete Alternator. (*Courtesy of Chrysler Canada*)

A ribbed "V" belt is used on some alternator pulleys, whereas other alternators may have single or dual conventional "V" belts. Some pulleys are held onto the rotor shaft with nut and wave washer without using the woodruff key. Other pulleys are pressed onto the rotor shaft, so that a retaining nut is not required.

Rotor

The field winding is mounted on an insulated spool inside the rotor. Steel pole pieces with interlacing fingers are mounted on each side of the field winding, as shown in Figure 11-6.

The wire in the field winding is coated with an insulating material so that the turns of wire are insulated from each other. A slip ring assembly is pressed onto the rotor shaft. The two slip rings are insulated from each other and also from the rotor shaft. An insulated wire is attached to each slip ring, and these wires are connected to the ends of the field winding which extend through insulated openings in one end of the pole pieces. The assembled rotor is pictured in Figure 11-7.

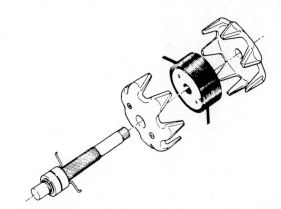

Figure 11-6. Rotor Design. (*Courtesy of Delco Remy Division, General Motors Corporation*)

Stator

The stator windings are mounted in insulated slots in the laminated metal stator frame. A stator winding that contains seven coils of wire is shown in Figure 11-8.

The number of coils in each stator winding is always matched to the number of poles on the rotor.

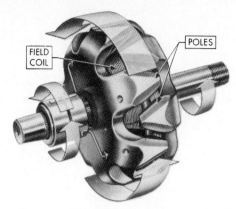

Figure 11-7.   Assembled Rotor. (*Courtesy of Delco Remy Division, General Motors Corporation*)

Figure 11-9.   Complete Wye-Wound Stator. (*Courtesy of Delco Remy Division, General Motors Corporation*)

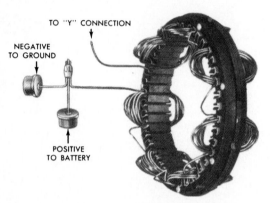

Figure 11-8.   Stator with One Winding. (*Courtesy of Delco Remy Division, General Motors Corporation*)

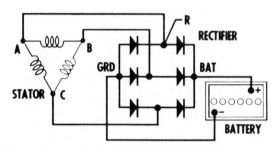

Figure 11-10.   Delta-Wound Stator. (*Courtesy of Delco Remy Division, General Motors Corporation*)

For example, if there are seven coils of wire in each stator winding, there will be fourteen poles or fingers on the rotor. In this way, all the magnetic poles on the rotor cut across all the coils in each stator winding at the same time. Therefore, maximum voltage is induced in each stator winding by the magnetic poles of the rotor.

The coils in each stator winding are interconnected so that the seven coils form one continuous winding. One positive diode and one negative diode are connected to one end of the stator winding. The other end of the stator winding is attached to a "Y" connection. The wires in each stator coil are insulated from each other.

A complete stator contains three separate windings. One end of each winding is connected to a positive diode and a negative diode, and the opposite end of each winding is connected to the "Y" connection. This type of stator winding is referred to as a wye-wound stator. A complete wye-wound stator is illustrated in Figure 11-9.

Some stator windings are connected so that all six ends of the three stator windings are connected

to the diodes. This type of stator winding is referred to as a delta-wound stator. High-output alternators are usually equipped with this type of stator. A delta-wound stator is shown in Figure 11-10.

Diodes

Today, most diodes are retained to their mounting plate or heat sink with epoxy, whereas early-model diodes had a zinc-coated copper case. The diode case is pressed into the end housing or the heat sink. (The operation of individual diodes was explained in Chapter 9.) A diode with a copper case and the diode symbol are pictured in Figure 11-11.

Three negative diodes are connected to the drive end housing, and three positive diodes are mounted on an insulated heat sink. The battery terminal of the alternator is attached to the heat sink, and a wire is connected from the positive battery cable to the battery terminal of the alternator. A capacitor is connected from the alternator battery terminal to ground.

When any relay on the vehicle is shut off, a high voltage is induced in the relay winding. If this voltage were applied through the battery wire against the diodes in the reverse direction, it would damage the

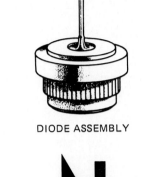

DIODE ASSEMBLY

DIODE SYMBOL

Figure 11-11. Diode Assembly and Diode Symbol. (*Courtesy of Delco Remy Division, General Motors Corporation*)

diodes. However, the capacitor protects the diodes from these high induced voltages.

The stator and diode connections with the capacitor and the field circuit are shown in Figure 11-12.

A fusible link is located in the wire that is connected to the alternator battery terminal. When the battery is installed with the correct polarity, the diodes prevent any reverse flow of current from the battery positive terminal through the diodes to ground when the engine is stopped.

If the battery polarity were reversed and the positive post were connectd to ground, extremely high current would flow through the ground to the alternator, and then through diodes in the forward direction. This current would continue to flow through the alternator battery wire to the negative battery

post. Under this condition, the extremely high current flow would burn out the fusible link in the alternator battery wire, and the diodes could be damaged. Should the battery polarity be reversed, the fusible link is designed to burn out and open the circuit to protect the diodes.

Alternator Operation

Rotor and Stator Operation

When the ignition switch is turned on, current flows through the ignition switch to the alternator field terminal. An insulated brush is connected from the field terminal to one slip ring, and in some alternators another brush is connected from the other slip ring to ground. Current flows from the field terminal through the insulated brush, field winding and slip rings, and the ground brush. The current then flows through the ground return back to the negative battery terminal.

When current flows through the field winding, a magnetic field is created around the rotor, as shown in Figure 11-13. The field current would be 3 to 6 amperes, as determined by the resistance of the field winding. High-output alternators usually have more field current than low-output alternators.

When the engine starts, the alternator belt turns the rotor assembly. The revolving magnetic field of the rotor induces a voltage in the stator windings, since these windings are mounted around the outside of the rotor.

A revolving rotor and a basic stator with one winding are shown in Figure 11-14.

The magnetic field from a north rotor pole cuts across the top side of the stator loop, and a magnetic field from a south pole moves across the lower side of the loop. Under this condition a voltage is in-

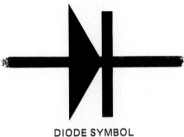

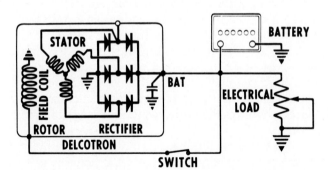

Figure 11-12. Stator and Diode Connections. (*Courtesy of Delco Remy Division, General Motors Corporation*)

Figure 11-13. Rotor Magnetic Field. (*Courtesy of Delco Remy Division, General Motors Corporation*)

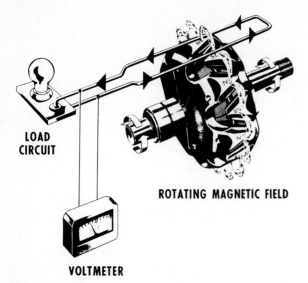

Figure 11-14.   Revolving Rotor and One Stator Winding. (*Courtesy of Delco Remy Division, General Motors Corporation*)

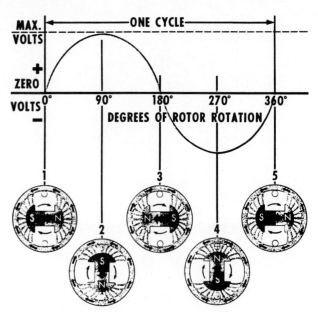

Figure 11-15.   Alternating Voltage Wave. (*Courtesy of Delco Remy Division, General Motors Corporation*)

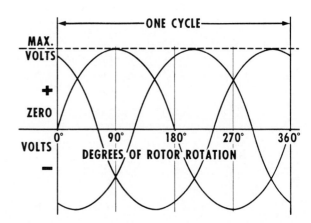

Figure 11-16.   Alternating Voltage Waveforms from Three Windings. (*Courtesy of Delco Remy Division, General Motors Corporation*)

duced in the loop and current flows through the loop in the direction of the heavy arrows shown in the diagram. In a fraction of a second, the rotor magnetic poles move past the sides of the stator winding and the voltage in the winding deceases to zero.

As the rotor continues to revolve quickly, a south magnetic pole moves under the upper side of the stator loop and a north magnetic pole is then under the lower side of the loop. When the fields from the opposite magnetic poles cut across the sides of the stator winding, the voltage in the stator is induced in the opposite direction, which causes the current to flow in the opposite direction through the load circuit. This type of voltage is called an alternating voltage, and the current flow that it produces is referred to as alternating current (AC). A direct current (DC), such as the current flow from the battery, flows in only one direction.

An alternating voltage wave is indicated in Figure 11-15, and the alternating voltage wave from three stator windings is shown in Figure 11-16.

Since the battery and electrical circuits on the vehicle must be supplied with DC, the AC in the stator windings must be changed to DC. This is the purpose of the diodes.

Diode Operation

Each end of the stator winding is connected to a pair of diodes. One of the diodes in each pair is grounded, whereas the other diode in each pair is mounted in an insulated heat-sink plate which is connected to

the alternator battery terminal battery. The magnetic poles of the rotor always cut across two stator windings at any given instant, because the stator windings are overlapped in the stator frame.

The process of changing the AC in the stator windings to DC is referred to as rectification, and one diode may be called a rectifier. In Figure 11-17, the magnetic poles of the rotor are cutting across stator windings A and B in the first stage of rectification.

The rotor magnetic fields induce 8V in windings A and B, and the voltage potential across the two windings is 16V at A and 0V at B. Current flows from the 16V source at A through the diode in the heat

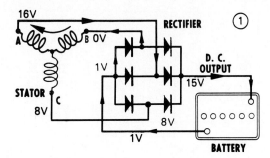

Figure 11-17. First Stage of Rectification. (*Courtesy of Delco Remy Division, General Motors Corporation*)

sink and the battery. The current returns through the ground of the vehicle and one of the diodes in the end housing to the 0V potential at B.

Notice that the 8V in winding C cannot move current through the diode in the heat sink because of the higher voltage from A that is on the battery side of the diode. Most of the voltage is dropped across the battery and the voltage in the ground return circuit is very low. However, the same amount of current is flowing through the ground circuit and in the circuit from the alternator battery terminal to the positive battery post. Note also that some voltage is dropped across a diode when it is conducting in the forward direction.

The other five stages of rectification are illustrated in Figure 11-18.

In stage 4, the opposite magnetic poles of the rotor cut across stator windings A and B, compared to the first rectification stage shown in Figure 11-17. When this occurs, the induced voltage in the windings is reversed, and the resulting current flow alternates or flows in the opposite direction. However, the diodes make the current flow through the battery in the same direction. Therefore, the diodes change the AC in the stator windings to a flow of DC for the battery and the electrical equipment.

As each pair of stator windings delivers current to the battery and electrical system, a smooth DC output appears at the alternator battery terminal, as indicated in Figure 11-19.

Delta-Connected Stator Operation

When a delta-connected stator is used, the diodes operate in the same way as explained above. As indicated in Figure 11-20, the rotor magnetic field is inducing 16V at A and 0V at B. When maximum voltage appears in winding BA, windings BC and CA are just at a changeover point. The voltage in winding BC decreases and the voltage in winding CA increases, as illustrated in the voltage waves from the

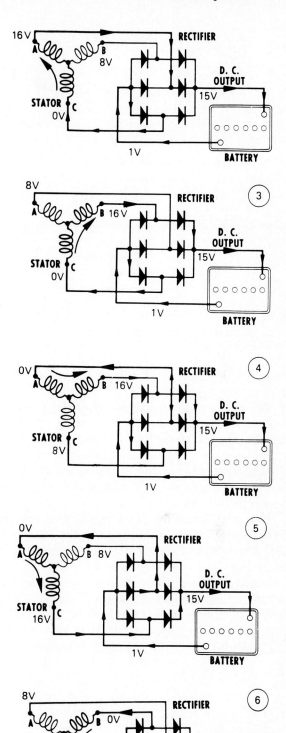

Figure 11-18. Five Remaining Stages of Rectification. (*Courtesy of Delco Remy Division, General Motors Corporation*)

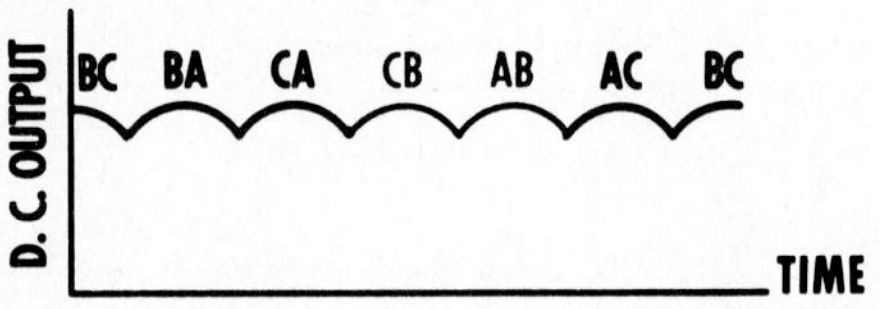

Figure 11-19. DC Output at Alternator Battery Terminal. (*Courtesy of Delco Remy Division, General Motors Corporation*)

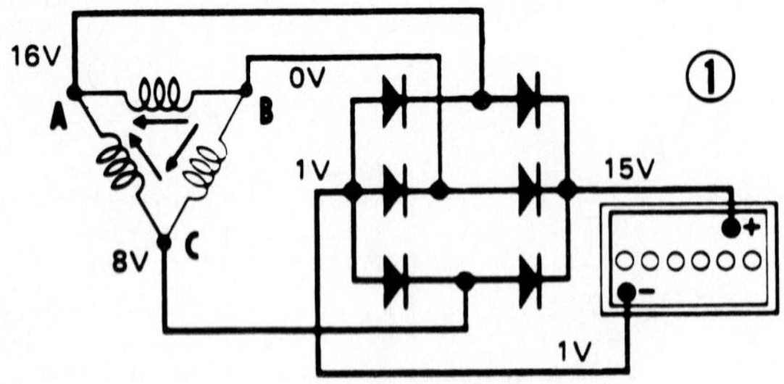

Figure 11-20. First Rectification Stage, Delta-Connected Stator. (*Courtesy of Delco Remy Division, General Motors Corporation*)

three delta-connected windings shown in Figure 11-21.

When 16V is induced in winding BA, there will be 8V in winding BC and 8V in winding CA. Therefore, the potential from B to C to A is also 16V. Current flows from A through the diode in the heat sink to the battery, and the current returns from the battery through the diode in the end housing to B, where there is 0V.

Notice that current flows in all three windings at the same time in a delta-connected stator. The other five stages of rectification are pictured in Figure 11-22.

In stage 4, the opposite rotor poles cut across the stator windings compared to stage 1. As a result, the induced voltage and the current flow in the stator windings is in the opposite direction. However, the diodes change the AC in the stator windings to DC

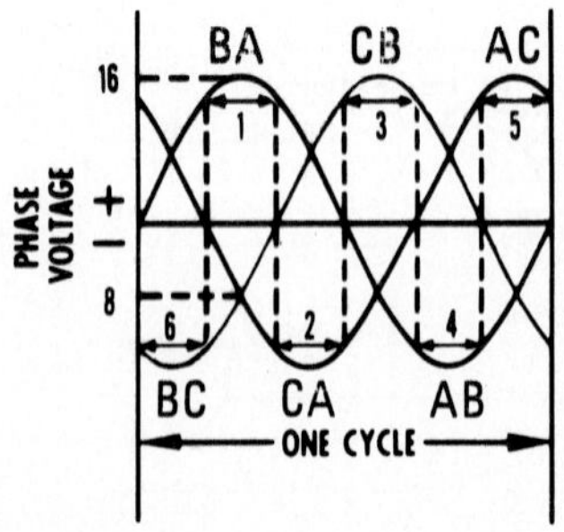

Figure 11-21. Voltage Waveforms from Delta-Connected Stator. (*Courtesy of Delco Remy Division, General Motors Corporation*)

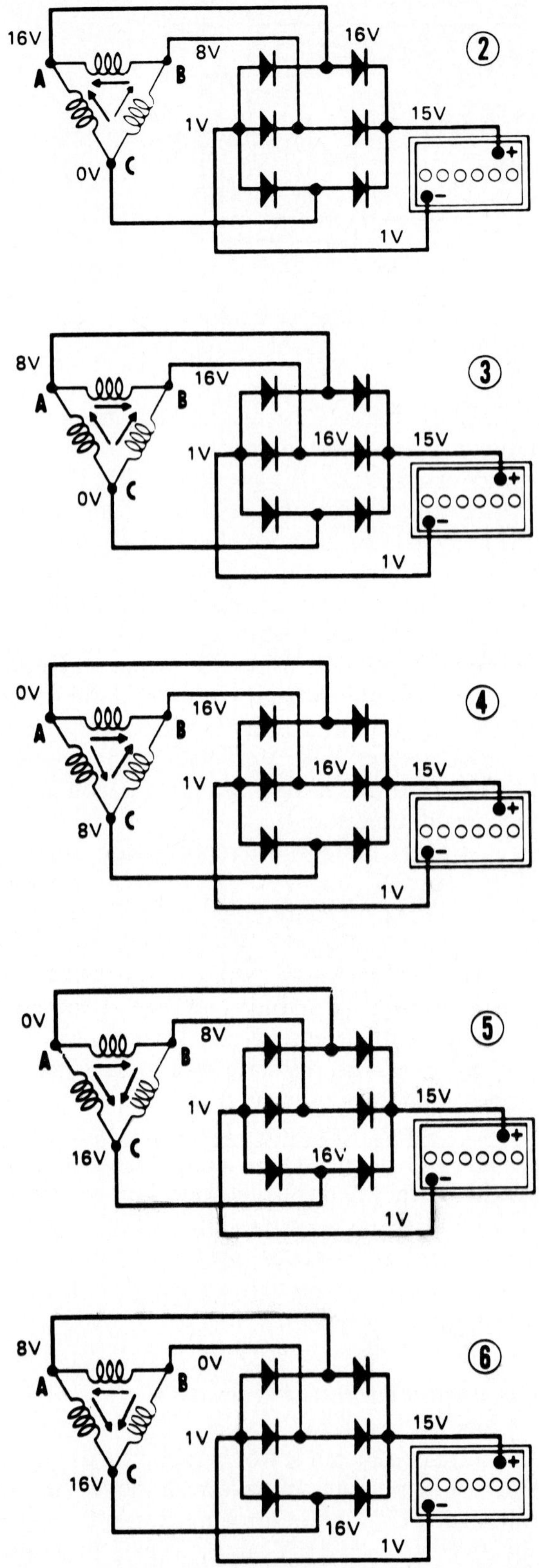

Figure 11-22. Five Remaining Stages of Rectification, Delta-Connected Stator. (*Courtesy of Delco Remy Division, General Motors Corporation*)

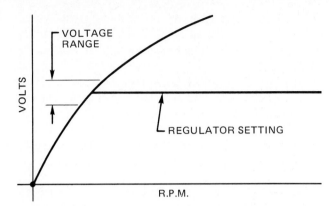

Figure 11-23. Voltage Regulation Requirements. (*Courtesy of Delco Remy Division, General Motors Corporation*)

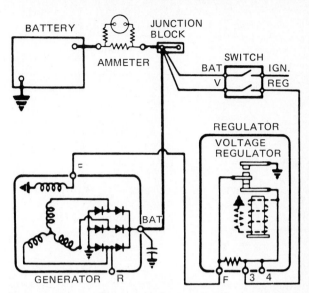

Figure 11-24. Voltage Regulator Circuit. (*Courtesy of Pontiac Motor Division, General Motors Corporation*)

for the battery and electrical equipment on the vehicle.

When the rotor speed increases with the engine speed, the voltage in the stator tends to increase. Excessive alternator voltage could force extremely high current flow through the battery and electrical circuits, which would result in severe damage to these components. Therefore, the voltage in the stator windings must be limited to protect the battery and electrical components. This is the purpose of the voltage regulator, as indicated in Figure 11-23.

Point-Type Voltage Regulators

Design and Operation

The regulator contains a dual set of vibrating contacts mounted above a relay core. One set of contacts is connected in series in the field circuit. These contacts are referred to as series contacts. The other contacts in the other set are called ground contacts. In Figure 11-24, the lower set of points are the series contacts, and the ground contacts are located above the series contacts.

The center contact is stationary, whereas the upper and lower contacts are hinged and vibrate together. However, the upper and lower contacts are insulated from each other. The fine, high-resistance winding that surrounds the voltage relay core is connected from the voltage relay frame to ground. Since the frame is part of the field circuit, alternator voltage is applied to this winding.

When the ignition switch is turned on, current flows through the switch to the regulator 3 terminal. From this point, the field current flows through the series contacts and out the F terminal to the F ter-

minal on the alternator. The current then flows through the rotor field coil to ground, which builds up a magnetic field around the rotor.

When the engine starts, the rotor magnetic field induces a voltage in the stator windings. As the engine speed and rotor speed increase, the voltage in the stator windings attempts to increase. This increase in voltage forces more current through the voltage relay winding to ground, and the increase in magnetism around the voltage relay coil pulls the points downward as the rotor speed increases.

A 14Ω resistor is connected parallel to the series points, and the field current must flow through the resistor when these points open. When the ground contacts close, the field current flows through the resistor and the contacts to ground, and the current in the alternator field coil becomes 0 amperes momentarily.

The operation of the voltage regulator is summarized in Table 11-1.

When the series contacts are closed, the only resistance in the field circuit is the field coil in the rotor. If this field coil has a resistance of 6Ω and the charging circuit voltage is 14V, the field current is 14V divided by 6Ω or 2.3 amperes. The field coil and the resistor in the regulator have a total resistance of 14Ω plus 6Ω, or 20Ω. Therefore, when the series points are open and field current flows through the resistor, the field current is 14V divided by 20Ω or .7 ampere.

The regulator points vibrate very quickly and the field current will be an average between .7 ampere and 2.3 amperes with the series points vibrating. The voltage regulator controls the field current and the

TABLE 11-1. Voltage Regulator Operation.

Speed	Contacts	Field Current	Voltage
Low	Series Contacts	2.3 Amps Contacts Closed	14V
	Vibrating	1.5 Amps Average .7 Amps Contacts Open	
Medium	Float Position	.7 Amp Continuously	14.2V
High	Ground Contacts	0 Amp Contacts Closed	14.4V
	Vibrating	.35 Amp Average .7 Amp Contacts Open	

rotor magnet strength to limit the voltage to a safe value. The difference in voltage between series contact and ground contact operation is referred to as step voltage.

Voltage Regulator with Field Relay

In some regulators, a field relay is connected with the voltage relay. This type of regulator has 4 terminals. The number 3 terminal is connected to the battery positive terminal at the horn relay, and the number 4 terminal is connected to the charge indicator bulb and parallel resistor. A wire is connected from the number 2 terminal to the alternator "R" terminal, and the "F" terminal of the regulator is connected to the "F" terminal on the alternator, as shown in Figure 11-25.

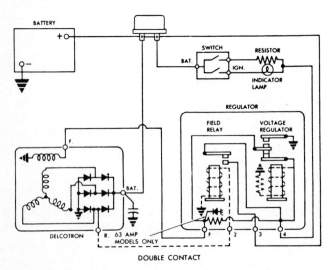

Figure 11-25. Voltage Regulator with Field Relay. (*Courtesy of Pontiac Motor Division, General Motors Corporation*)

A 10Ω resistance wire is located in the wiring harness and connected parallel to the charge indicator lamp. When the ignition switch is turned on, current flows through the charge indicator bulb and resistor to the regulator number 4 terminal. This current then flows through the series contacts and the alternator field coil to ground, and a magnetic field is created around the rotor. The resistor that is connected parallel to the charge indicator lamp allows enough field current to flow through the circuit, which provides sufficient magnetic strength around the rotor to start inducing voltage in the stator windings when the engine starts. The charge indicator lamp by itself does not supply enough initial field current when the ignition switch is turned on.

When the engine starts, the voltage at the alternator "R" terminal supplies a small amount of current through the field relay winding to ground. This closes the field relay contacts, which closes the circuit between the number 3 terminal and the voltage relay.

The voltage relay operates in the same way as explained previously. When the field relay points close, charging circuit voltage is applied to the voltage relay frame and the number 4 terminal. Since the same voltage is available at the ignition switch, the charge indicator lamp goes out because of equal voltage on each side of the lamp.

When the engine is shut off, the field relay points open the circuit between the number 3 terminal and the voltage relay to prevent battery discharge through the field circuit. The diode that is connected from the regulator "F" terminal to ground protects the series contacts from high induced voltage in the alternator field coil each time these contacts open and the field current and rotor magnetic strength are reduced.

Motorcraft Point-Type Regulator Circuit

In the Motorcraft regulator, the field relay and the voltage relay operate in the same manner as in other regulators. However, different markings are used to identify the terminals, as indicated in Figure 11-26.

The charge indicator bulb and parallel resistor are connected to the regulator "I" terminal. A wire is connected from the battery positive cable to the regulator "A" terminal. The stator ("S") terminal on the alternator is connected to the "S" terminal on the regulator, and the "F" terminal on the alternator is connected to the regulator "F" terminal.

In all the point-type regulator circuits, the voltage regulator is connected before the alternator field coil in the field circuit. The letter "B" is taken from

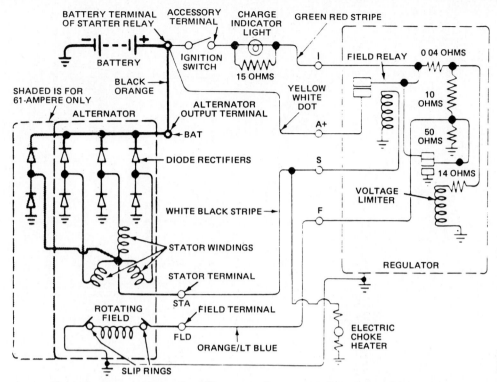

Figure 11-26. Motorcraft Voltage Regulator. (*Courtesy of Ford Motor Co.*)

the word *before* to identify these charging systems as B-type circuits. In these circuits, one alternator brush always completes the field circuit to ground. Since other charging systems use a different method of connecting the regulator in the field circuit, some means of charging circuit identification is necessary.

Integral Electronic Charging Systems

Design and Operation

In an integral electronic charging system, the electronic voltage regulator is mounted inside the alternator between the brush holder and the end housing, as illustrated in Figure 11-27.

The alternator battery terminal is connected to the positive battery cable. A charge indicator lamp is connected from the ignition switch to the number 1 terminal on the voltage regulator. The regulator number 2 terminal is also connected to the battery positive cable, as shown in Figure 11-28.

A diode trio is connected from the stator terminals to the regulator. This diode trio supplies DC to the field coil and voltage regulator while the engine is running. The brushes on both slip rings are insulated and the regulator is connected after the field coil in the field circuit. The letter "A" from the word

after is used to identify this charging system as an A-type circuit.

In the regulator the main components are the two transistors, TR1 and TR2, and the zener diode, D2. Two resistors, R2 and R3, are connected from the number 2 terminal to ground inside the regulator. When the engine is not running, there is a very low current flow of 3 to 5 milliamps from the battery positive terminal through these resistors to ground. This low current flow will not discharge the battery, even after a long period of time.

Voltage Regulator Operation with Ignition Switch On

When the ignition switch is turned on, current flows through the indicator lamp to terminal 1. When this occurs, the current flow through the field coil and regulator is as follows:

1. Current flows from terminal 1 through R1 and D1. The base-emitter circuit in TR1 is forward-biased and current flows through the base-emitter to ground.

2. When the base-emitter is forward-biased, a higher current flows through the rotor field coil and through the collector-emitter of TR1 to ground.

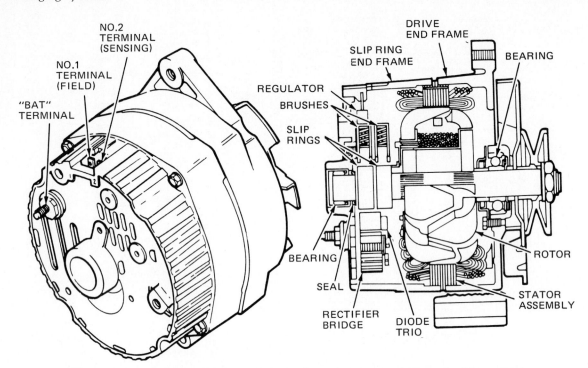

Figure 11-27. Alternator with Integral Regulator. (*Courtesy of Chevrolet Motor Division, General Motors Corporation*)

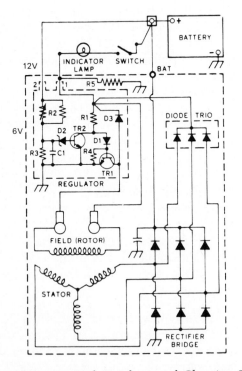

Figure 11-28. Integral Regulator and Charging System. (*Courtesy of Chevrolet Motor Division, General Motors Corporation*)

3. Current flows from the battery terminal through the number 2 terminal and R2 and R3 to ground. The voltage applied to the zener diode is 6V, as indicated in Figure 11-28. Since D2 is an 8V zener diode, it remains off and TR2 is also turned off.

If the field circuit has an open circuit, R5 will complete the indicator lamp circuit to ground, which turns on the lamp at partial brilliance to indicate the defect to the operator.

The rotor pole pieces are permanently magnetized. This residual magnetism, coupled with the electromagnetism supplied by the low current through the charge indicator lamp, magnetizes the rotor sufficiently so that the alternator begins charging.

Voltage Regulator Operation at 14V

When the engine starts, field current is supplied from the diode trio to the number 1 terminal. Under this condition 14V is supplied to the 1 terminal, and 14V is also available at the ignition switch. The charge indicator bulb remains off because of the equal voltage on each side of the bulb. If the voltage regulator limits the alternator voltage to 14.4V, the current flow through the regulator with 14V in the charging circuit would be as follows:

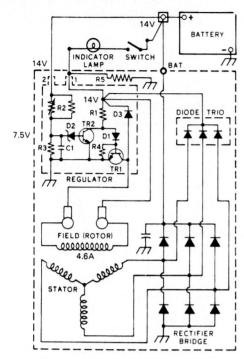

Figure 11-29. Voltage Regulator Operation 14V. (*Courtesy of Chevrolet Motor Division, General Motors Corporation*)

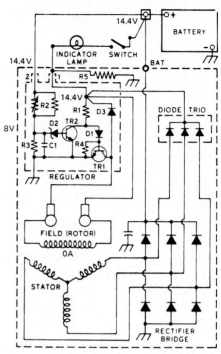

Figure 11-30. Voltage Regulator Operation at 14.4V. (*Courtesy of Chevrolet Motor Division, General Motors Corporation*)

1. Field current flows from the diode trio through R1 and D1. The base-emitter of TR1 is forward-biased and current flows through the base-emitter to ground.

2. Under this condition a higher current can flow through the field coil and through the collector-emitter to ground. Since the field coil has 3Ω resistance, the current through the field coil is 14V divided by 3Ω, or 4.66 amperes.

3. The voltage applied to the zener diode is 7.5V, as indicated in Figure 11-29, and the zener diode and TR2 remain off.

Voltage Regulator Operation at 14.4V

If the field current is at its maximum of 4.66 amperes, the strong rotor magnetic field causes the voltage to increase rapidly in the stator windings. When the voltage in the stator windings and the charging circuit reaches 14.4V, the following changes occur in the regulator:

1. With 14.4V available at the number 2 terminal, the voltage at the zener diode increases to 8V and current flows through the zener diode in the re-

verse direction. (See Chapter 9 for zener diode and transistor operation.)

2. When current flows through the zener diode, it forward-biases the base-emitter of TR2, and current flows through the base-emitter to ground.

3. Under this condition the current flow from the diode trio through R1 flows through the collector-emitter of TR2 to ground.

4. Since R1 is the only resistance in the circuit from the diode trio to ground, most of the voltage is dropped across R1. The voltage after R1 is too low to forward-bias D1 and the base-emitter of TR1. The base-emitter and the collector-emitter of TR1 turn off, and the field current in the rotor field coil attempts to drop to 0 amperes, as illustrated in Figure 11-30.

When the field current and the rotor magnetic strength decrease rapidly, the voltage in the stator windings and charging circuit is also reduced. If the voltage drops, the zener diode and TR2 turn off and TR1 turns on, which allows 4.66 amperes to flow through the field coil again. The electronic regulator cycles the field current on and off very rapidly to

TABLE 11-2. Electronic Regulator Operation.

Voltage	Zener Diode	TR2	TR1	Field Current
14V	Off	Off	On	4.66 Amps
14.4V	On	On	Off	0 Amps

control the field current and rotor magnetic strength, which limits the alternator voltage.

Table 11-2 summarizes the operation of the electronic regulator.

Temperature Compensation

In Figure 11-30, the resistor with an arrow on it in R2 is a temperature-sensitive resistor, or thermistor. When the thermistor temperature is reduced, the resistance of the thermistor increases. At normal operating temperature, the voltage drop across R2 is 6.4V, as shown in the figure.

During extremely cold temperatures, the voltage drop across R2 could be 7.4V. Under this condition 15.4V is required at the number 2 terminal to provide 8V at the zener diode. Therefore, the voltage in the stator windings and charging circuit is 15.4V. This higher charging voltage is necessary to maintain the current flow through the battery, because the battery internal resistance increases at colder temperatures. The process of providing a higher charging circuit voltage when the battery and regu-

lator are cold is referred to as temperature compensation.

The regulator must be warmed up before the voltage setting can be checked accurately.

Integral Charging Systems with Dual Stator Windings

Some Mitsubishi alternators have an integral voltage regulator and two sets of stator windings and diodes. This alternator also has a diode trio to supply DC to the field coil and voltage regulator when the engine is running. The operation of this system is similar to that explained previously. A Mitsubishi charging system is pictured in Figure 11-31.

Electronic Charging Systems with External Regulators

Design

In some electronic charging systems with an external regulator, both field terminals are insulated from ground, and the brushes are connected from the rotor slip rings to each field terminal. Since there is no internal electrical connection between the field and the stator circuits, these may be referred to as isolated field alternators.

The ignition switch is connected to one field ter-

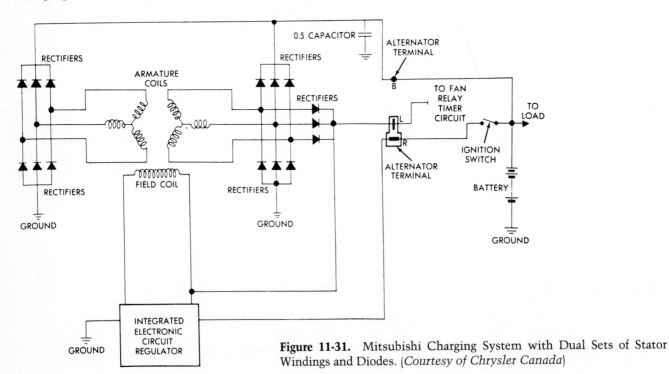

Figure 11-31. Mitsubishi Charging System with Dual Sets of Stator Windings and Diodes. (*Courtesy of Chrysler Canada*)

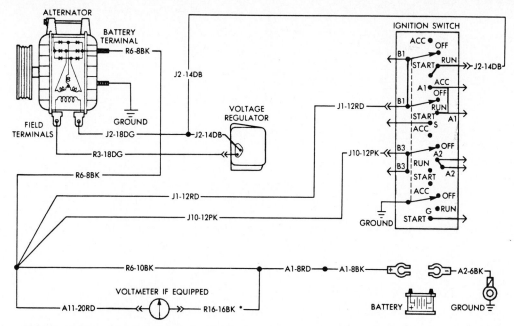

Figure 11-32. Electronic Charging System with External Regulator. (*Courtesy of Chrysler Canada*)

minal and the other field terminal is connected to the voltage regulator, as illustrated in Figure 11-32.

When the ignition switch is turned on, current flows through the rotor field coil and the regulator to ground. These charging systems may be referred to as A-type circuits, because the voltage regulator is connected *after* the field coil in the field circuit. The voltage regulator must have a resistance-free ground connection where it is mounted under the hood.

Some electronic charging systems with an external regulator have a field loads relay in the field circuit. When the ignition switch is on, or the engine is running, current flows from the ignition switch through the field loads relay winding and the starter solenoid windings to ground. This causes the relay contacts to close, which connects the battery positive cable to the alternator field terminal. The field current flows through the relay contacts rather than flowing through the ignition switch.

When the engine is being cranked, equal voltage is supplied to both sides of the field loads relay winding and the winding is not energized. This saves the starting motor from turning the magnetized rotor, which requires a certain amount of torque. When the ignition switch is turned off, the relay contacts open the circuit between the battery positive cable and the field terminal.

An electronic charging system with an external voltage regulator and a field loads relay is illustrated in Figure 11-33.

Electronic Voltage Monitor

Some charging systems with an external electronic voltage regulator have an electronic voltage monitor to operate the charge indicator lamp. If the charging system voltage is below a specific value, the voltage monitor grounds the indicator lamp. This turns the lamp on, because full voltage is available at the other lamp terminal. As the voltage in the electrical system decreases, the voltage monitor decreases the resistance in the lamp ground circuit, which increases the brilliance of the lamp. If the charging system voltage is normal, the voltage monitor opens the circuit from the indicator lamp to ground and the lamp remains off.

The voltage monitor is located behind the instrument panel, as shown in Figure 11-34.

Motorcraft Electronic Charging Systems

Design

Motorcraft electronic charging systems have an externally mounted electronic voltage regulator that is interchangeable with their point-type regulators. Therefore, the same B-type circuit is used with the point-type and electronic regulators. A Motorcraft charging system with an external electronic regulator is shown in Figure 11-35.

(Charging systems with computer monitoring, or

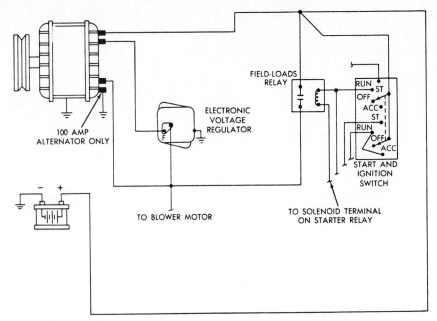

Figure 11-33. Charging Circuit with External Electronic Regulator and Field Loads Relay. (*Courtesy of Chrysler Canada*)

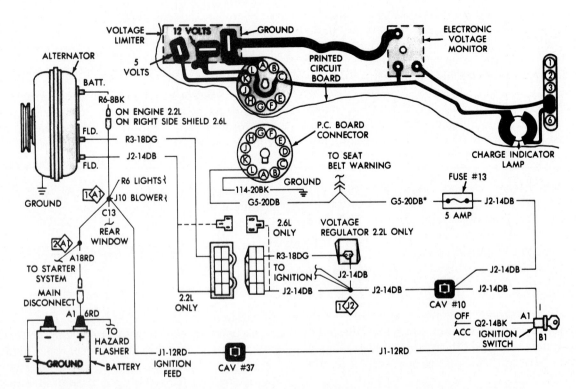

Figure 11-34. Charging System with Electronic Voltage Monitor. (*Courtesy of Chrysler Canada*)

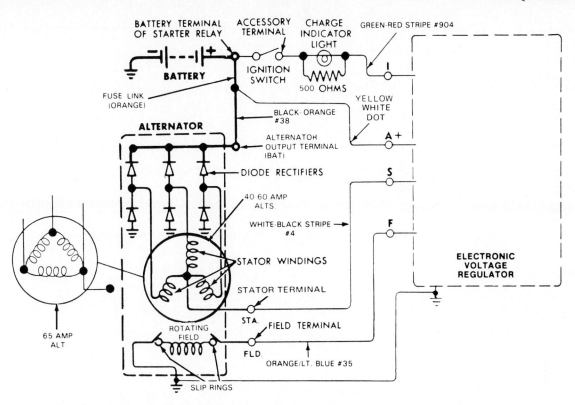

Figure 11-35. Motorcraft Electronic Voltage Regulator Circuit. (*Courtesy of Ford Motor Co.*)

computer voltage control, are explained in Chapter 18. Refer to Chapter 6 in *Automotive Principles: Repair and Service*, Volume II, for charging system service.)

Test Questions

1. If an alternator has seven coils in each stator winding, there will be _____ poles on the rotor.

2. The capacitor protects the _____ from high induced voltage.

3. The diodes change the _____ current in the stator windings to _____ current.

4. In a delta-connected stator, all six ends of the stator windings are connected to the diodes.   T   F

5. The voltage regulator limits the alternator voltage to protect the _____ and _____.

6. A voltage regulator limits the alternator voltage by controlling the:

   a) induced voltage in the field winding.

   b) field current through the field winding.

   c) rotor speed.

7. In a General Motors integral-type alternator, there is a very low current flow through the number 2 terminal with the ignition switch off.   T   F

8. In a General Motors integral-type alternator, if the zener diode is conducting current, the field current will try to drop to _____ amperes.

9. In most charging systems with the engine running, the charge indicator lamp remains off because there is:

   a) an open circuit in the lamp ground circuit.

   b) a low voltage applied to the lamp.

   c) equal voltage on each side of the lamp.

12

Starting Motors

Chapter Completion Objectives

1. Demonstrate an understanding of starting motor electromagnetic principles.
2. Explain the operation of the drive pull-in type solenoid.

3. Indicate a knowledge of various types of starter field coil circuits.

4. Demonstrate an understanding of starting motor solenoids.

5. Describe the function of starting motor drives.

Starting Motor Design and Operation

Electromagnetic Principles

In the starting motor, the field windings are wound on steel pole shoes. The field windings are made of heavy copper wire. One end of the windings is connected to the battery and the other end is connected to an insulated brush. A copper commutator bar is soldered to each end of the armature winding and this winding, or loop, is positioned between the pole shoes. The commutator bars are insulated from each other, and the insulated brush contacts one commutator bar. A ground brush completes the circuit from the other commutator bar to the ground terminal of the battery.

Current in the starter circuit flows from the battery through the field coils and armature winding and returns through the ground brush to the other battery terminal. Since the field coils are connected in series with each other and with the armature loop, the same amount of current must flow through both field coils and the armature winding.

The current flow through the armature loop creates strong magnetic fields around the sides of the loop. Since the current flow in the sides of the loop is in opposite directions, the magnetic fields around the sides of the loop will move in opposite directions, as indicated in Figure 12-1.

The current flow through the field coils creates a magnetic field between the pole shoes. The armature winding is positioned in this magnetic field, as illustrated in Figure 12-2. In the figure, the magnetic field around the upper side of the armature winding is moving in a counterclockwise direction. On the top side of this loop, the magnetic field around the armature loop is moving in the same direction as the field between the pole shoes. Therefore, the mag-

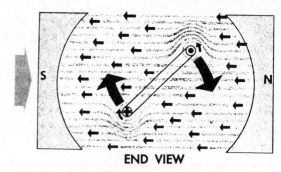

END VIEW

Figure 12-2. Magnetic Action of Fields Around the Armature Windings with Fields Between Pole Shoes. (*Courtesy of Delco Remy Division, General Motors Corporation*)

netic fields join together and a very strong magnetic force is created above this side of the armature winding.

Underneath the upper side of the armature winding, the magnetic field around the armature winding is moving in the opposite direction to the magnetic field between the pole shoes. Since magnetic fields moving in opposite directions in the same space cancel each other (this principle was explained in Chapter 9), a very weak magnetic force is created below the upper side of the armature loop.

The magnetic field around the lower side of the armature loop is moving in a clockwise direction. Below this side of the loop, the magnetic field around the loop and the field between the pole shoes are moving in the same direction, which causes a very strong magnetic force below the loop. The magnetic field above this side of the loop is cancelled out because the field around the armature loop is moving in the opposite direction to the magnetic field between the pole shoes. Since strong magnetic forces are created below the lower side of the loop and above the upper side of the loop, the armature loop is forced to rotate.

The armature windings and field windings are made of very heavy copper wire, which has a very low resistance. Therefore, the current flow in a starting motor is very high, which creates extremely strong magnetic fields around the armature windings and between the pole shoes. These strong magnetic fields cause the starting motor to develop very high torque and horsepower for its size. However, most starting motors are designed to operate only for 30 seconds at a time, and damage can result from longer cranking periods.

The torque would be very erratic in a starting motor with only one armature winding, as illustrated in Figure 12-3. A smoother, more consistent torque output results when three armature windings

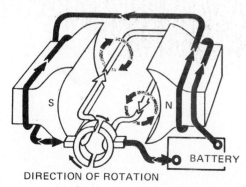

DIRECTION OF ROTATION

Figure 12-1. Starting Motor Field Coil and Armature Windings. (*Courtesy of Delco Remy Division, General Motors Corporation*)

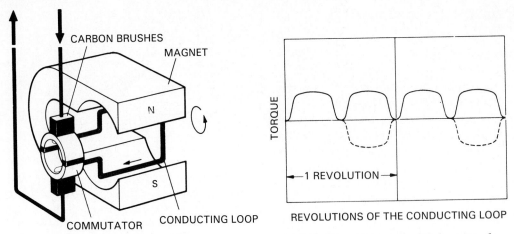

Figure 12-3. Torque Developed by One Armature Winding. (*Courtesy of Robert Bosch Corporation Sales Group*)

are used, because some of the windings will always be positioned in the magnetic field between the pole shoes. This is illustrated in Figure 12-4.

Armature Design

The armature core is made from a group of laminated metal plates that are pressed onto the armature shaft. Machined areas on each end of the shaft are supported by bushings in the end plates. The armature windings are positioned in the core slots and are insulated from the core. Insulation between each winding keeps the windings from touching each other.

A typical starter armature is shown in Figure 12-5.

Some manufacturers use a resistance cold-soldering process to connect each pair of armature windings to the copper commutator bars, as indi-

cated in Figure 12-6. Epoxy or mica is used to insulate the commutator bars from each other and from the armature shaft. The starter drive is mounted on the armature shaft splines.

Field Coils

Many automotive starting motors have four field windings held in place by metal pole shoes which are bolted to the field frame. In some starting motors the four field windings are connected in series, as illustrated in Figure 12-7.

Heavy copper wire is used in the series field coils. One end of the field windings is connected to the starter main terminal and the other end is attached to the two insulated brushes. The insulated brushes and the two ground brushes are positioned on the commutator bars by brush holders in the field frame or commutator end plate. If the brush holders

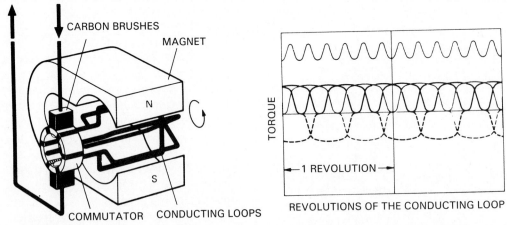

Figure 12-4. Torque Developed by Three Armature Windings. (*Courtesy of Robert Bosch Corporation Sales Group*)

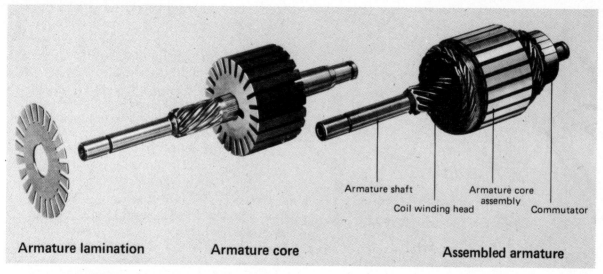

Figure 12-5. Armature Design. (*Courtesy of Robert Bosch Corporation Sales Group*)

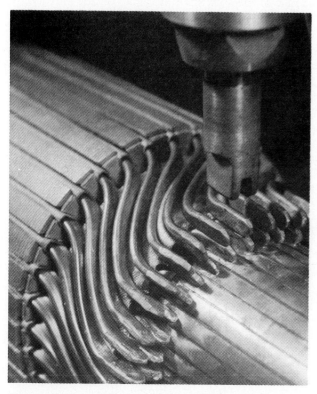

Figure 12-6. Connecting Armature Windings to Commutator Bars. (*Courtesy of Robert Bosch Corporation Sales Group*)

are attached to the end plate, a dowel pin is used to position the end plate properly on the field frame. The brush position is important because the armature windings must have current flow through them when they are located in the magnetic field between the pole shoes.

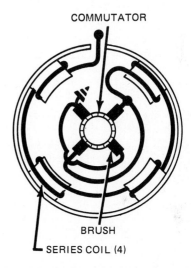

Figure 12-7. Series Field Coil Windings. (*Courtesy of Delco Remy Division, General Motors Corporation*)

The magnetic fields and armature winding position are pictured in Figure 12-8.

Adequate clearance between the armature core and the pole shoe is important. If this clearance were reduced, the core would rub on the pole shoes and the starting motor torque would be reduced. Worn starter bushings could allow the core to rub on the pole shoes. If the clearance were increased, the starting motor torque would be reduced because the additional air space would weaken the magnetic fields between the pole shoes. Therefore, metal should never be removed from an armature core. In most starting motors the clearance between the armature core and the pole shoes should be 0.040 to 0.060 in. (1.016 to 1.524 mm).

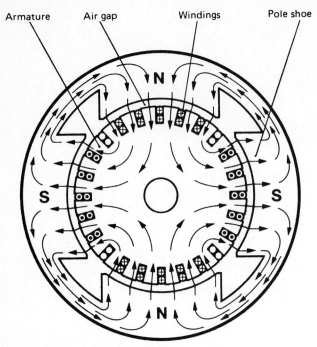

Figure 12-8. Field Coil Magnetic Fields and Armature Winding Position. (*Courtesy of Robert Bosch Corporation Sales Group*)

A complete starting motor is illustrated in Figure 12-9.

Some starting motors have three series field coils and one shunt coil, as indicated in Figure 12-10. The

shunt coil contains many turns of fine copper wire. One end of the shunt coil is connected to the main terminal and the other end of the coil is grounded.

All the field windings are insulated from the field frame. Insulation is baked on the field windings during the manufacturing process to prevent the turns of wire from touching each other. A plastic insulation on each field winding prevents contact with the field frame.

Since the shunt coil is a fixed resistance, the amount of current flow through this coil is determined by battery voltage. The load on the armature and the speed of the armature affects the current flow through the series field coils, because these coils are connected in series with the armature windings. While the starting motor is cranking the engine, the current flow through the series coils and armature windings could be 100 amperes, in which case the battery voltage would be approximately 10V because of the starting motor load on the battery.

Let us assume that each series field coil contains 10 turns of heavy copper wire. Under cranking conditions the magnetic strength of each series field coil would be 100 amperes times 10 turns, or 1000 ampere turns (AT). If the shunt coil contained 200 turns of fine copper wire, the current through this high-resistance coil would be 5 amperes with 10V applied from the battery; therefore, the magnetic strength of the shunt coil would be 200 turns times 5 amperes; or 1000 AT. The shunt coil develops the same mag-

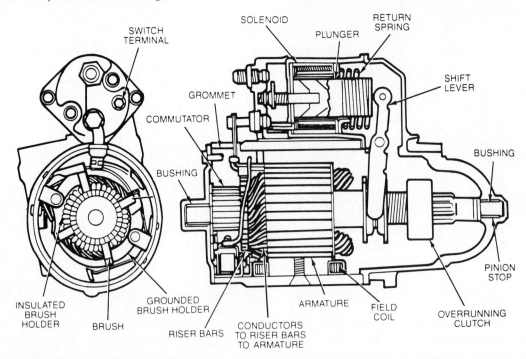

Figure 12-9. Complete Starting Motor. (*Courtesy of Chevrolet Motor Division, General Motors Corporation*)

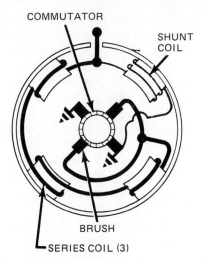

Figure 12-10. Series Field Coil and Shunt Coil Windings. (*Courtesy of Delco Remy Division, General Motors Corporation*)

netic strength as the series field coils while the starting motor is cranking the engine.

The instant that the engine starts, the armature may spin at very high speed when the engine load is removed from the starting motor and the operator keeps the ignition switch in the start position for a fraction of a second. If the armature speed becomes too high, the heavy armature windings could be thrown from their slots and the starting motor would be severely damaged. As the armature rotates at high speed through the magnetic field between the pole shoes, a voltage is induced in the armature windings which opposes the battery voltage and current flow, as indicated in Figure 12-11. This induced opposing voltage reduces the current flow through the series field coils and armature windings, which limits the free-running speed of the armature.

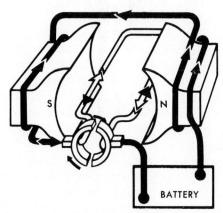

Figure 12-11. Inducing Opposing Voltage in Armature Windings. (*Courtesy of Delco Remy Division, General Motors Corporation*)

When the engine starts, the starting motor free-runs for a fraction of a second until the starter drive is pulled out of mesh with the flywheel ring gear. Under this condition the battery voltage may increase to 11.5V, because the current flow through the series field coils and armature windings is reduced to approximately 50 amperes. This results in a series field coil magnetic strength of 10 turns times 50 amperes, or 500 AT. However, since the higher battery voltage increases the current flow through the shunt coil to 8 amperes, the shunt coil magnetic strength would be 200 turns times 8 amperes, or 1600 AT. The strong magnetic field of the shunt coil induces more opposing voltage in the armature windings and further reduces the current flow through the series field coils and armature windings. Hence, the purpose of the shunt coil is to limit the maximum free-running speed of the armature and prevent the armature windings from being thrown out of their slots.

Solenoids and Relays

Magnetic-Switch Type Solenoids

Some starter circuits use a magnetic-switch type solenoid to open and close the circuit between the battery and the starting motor. This type of solenoid contains a movable plunger surrounded by a winding. In most circuits, one end of the winding is connected to ground on the solenoid case and the other end is attached to an insulated terminal in the case. This terminal is usually connected to the "start" terminal on the ignition switch.

When the ignition switch is turned to the "start" position, the solenoid winding is energized and the magnetic force of the winding pulls the plunger into the coil. This plunger action forces the heavy copper disc against the solenoid terminals. Since one solenoid terminal is connected to the positive battery terminal and another cable is connected from the other solenoid terminal to the starting motor main terminal, the solenoid disc closes the circuit between the battery positive terminal and the starting motor.

The magnetic-switch type solenoid is shown in Figure 12-12.

When the ignition switch is released from the "start" position, the solenoid winding is de-energized and the return spring forces the disc and plunger away from the terminals. On some magnetic-switch type solenoids, the plunger may be de-

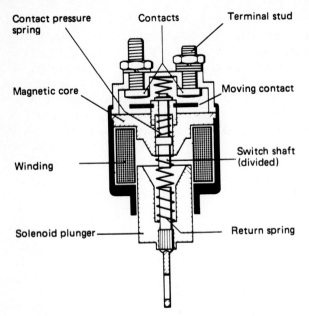

Figure 12-12. Magnetic-Switch Type Solenoid. (*Courtesy of Robert Bosch Corporation Sales Group*)

pressed manually if a defect occurs in the circuit that energizes the winding.

Drive Pull-in Type Solenoids

Many starting motors have a solenoid that pulls the starter drive gear into mesh with the flywheel ring gear and also opens and closes the circuit between the battery positive terminal and the starting motor. A pivoted shift lever is connected from the solenoid plunger to a collar on the starter drive, as illustrated in Figure 12-13.

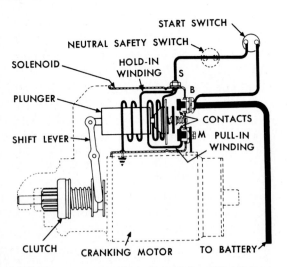

Figure 12-13. Drive Pull-in Type Solenoid. (*Courtesy of Delco Remy Division, General Motors Corporation*)

When the plunger is pulled ahead, the shift lever forces the drive gear into mesh with the flywheel ring gear. A pull-in winding and a hold-in winding are wound around the solenoid plunger. The pull-in winding usually contains heavier wire with a lower resistance than the hold-in winding. The pull-in winding is connected from the solenoid "S" terminal to the starting motor main terminal, and the hold-in winding is connected from the "S" terminal to ground.

A neutral safety switch is connected in series between the ignition switch "start" terminal and the solenoid "S" terminal. This switch is closed when the transmission selector is in the neutral or park position; it is open in all other positions. The neutral safety switch allows the engine to be started only when the transmission selector is in neutral or park.

The neutral safety switch is used on vehicles with an automatic transmission. Some vehicles with manual transmissions have a clutch safety switch that is connected in the same way as the neutral safety switch. This switch will only allow the solenoid to operate if the clutch is depressed. When the ignition switch is turned to the start position, current flows through both solenoid windings in the same direction. The combined magnetic strength of both windings pulls the plunger ahead, as indicated in the diagram in Figure 12-14.

When the solenoid plunger forces the disc against the terminals, current flows from the battery positive terminal into the starting motor and the starting motor begins to crank the engine. Under this condition battery voltage is available at the starting motor main terminal. The same battery voltage is available at the solenoid "S" terminal. Since equal voltage is now applied to both ends of the pull-in winding, current stops flowing through the winding, as shown in diagram 2 of Figure 12-14. The magnetic field of the hold-in winding is strong enough to hold the plunger in the engaged position.

When the ignition switch is released from the "start" position, current stops flowing through the "S" terminal. However, current attempts to flow from the solenoid disc through the solenoid windings to ground. When this occurs the current flow in the two windings is in opposite directions. Since the windings have the same number of turns, the magnetic force of the windings is equal but in opposite directions. Therefore, the magnetic force around the plunger is cancelled, as indicated in diagram 3 of Figure 12-14. Under this condition the disc return spring pushes the disc away from the terminals and the plunger return spring forces the plunger and starter drive back to the disengaged position.

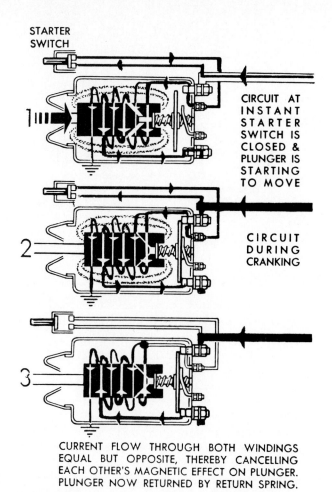

Figure 12-14. Drive Pull-in Type Solenoid Operation. (*Courtesy of Delco Remy Division, General Motors Corporation*)

Starter Relays

In some starting circuits a starter relay is connected as shown in Figure 12-15. The relay winding is connected between the "ignition switch" terminal and

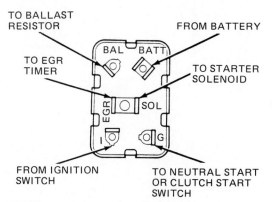

Figure 12-15. Starter Relay. (*Courtesy of Chrysler Canada*)

the "neutral start" terminal, and the relay contacts open and close the circuit between the "battery" terminal and the "starter solenoid" terminal.

When the ignition switch is placed in the "start" position and the transmission selector is in the neutral or park position, current flows through the relay winding and the neutral safety switch to ground. The relay coil magnetism closes the relay contacts and current flows through the contacts to the solenoid windings. The relay contacts also supply current to the exhaust gas recirculation (EGR) timer. (This system is discussed in Chapter 8.)

Starter Drives

Overrunning Clutch Drive

While the engine is being cranked, the starter drive connects the armature shaft to the flywheel ring gear. Once the engine starts, the drive must overrun until the solenoid pushes it out of mesh to protect the armature from excessive speed.

The gear ratio between the drive gear and the flywheel ring gear varies from 15:1 to 20:1, depending on the application. With a gear ratio of 20:1, if the armature remained connected to the flywheel ring gear with the engine running at 1,000 revolutions per minute (rpm), the armature would turn at 20,000 rpm. At this speed, the windings would be thrown from the armature slots and the armature would be destroyed. Hence, the overrunning action of the drive is very important to protect the armature.

The outer drive housing is splined to the armature shaft, and a series of steel rollers is mounted in tapered grooves in the housing. A shoulder on the drive gear pinion is positioned in the center of the rollers, as illustrated in Figure 12-16.

The starter drive is pushed into mesh with the flywheel ring gear by the solenoid shift lever. Once the drive is in mesh, the armature begins turning, which forces the outer drive housing to rotate. Under this condition the rollers are wedged in the narrow part of the tapered grooves between the outer housing and the gear collar, so that the armature also turns the drive gear and the flywheel to crank the engine. Since the armature is not turning when the drive goes into mesh, wear on the flywheel ring gear is reduced.

The shift-lever collar on the drive can slide on the outer housing against the force of the meshing spring. If the drive gear teeth jam against the ring

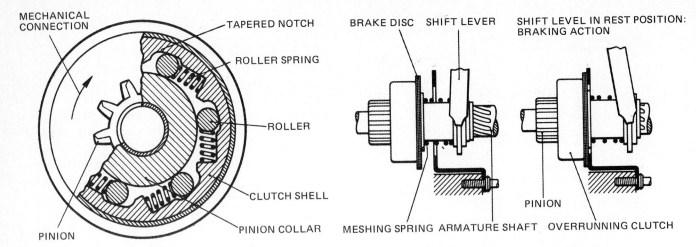

Figure 12-16.   Overrunning Clutch Drive. (*Courtesy of Robert Bosch Corporation Sales Group*)

gear teeth, the movable shift lever collar allows the solenoid plunger to keep moving ahead and the solenoid disc connects the battery positive terminal to the starting motor. When the armature begins to turn, the meshing spring pushes the drive gear into mesh with the ring gear.

Once the engine starts, the drive gear rotates faster than the outer drive housing. When this occurs, the rollers move against their return springs into the wider part of the tapered grooves. This action allows the drive gear to turn, or overrun, without turning the outer housing. Therefore, the engine cannot turn the armature at high speed. When the solenoid windings are de-energized, the shift lever forces the drive gear out of mesh with the ring gear.

The brake disc on the drive also helps to reduce the armature speed when the drive disengages.

Gear-Reduction Starters

Design

Some starting motors have a set of gears between the armature shaft and the shaft on which the drive is mounted. The gear reduction in the starting motor is necessary because of the reduced flywheel diameter on some engines. This type of starting motor has a drive pull-in type solenoid and operates in the same way as other starters.

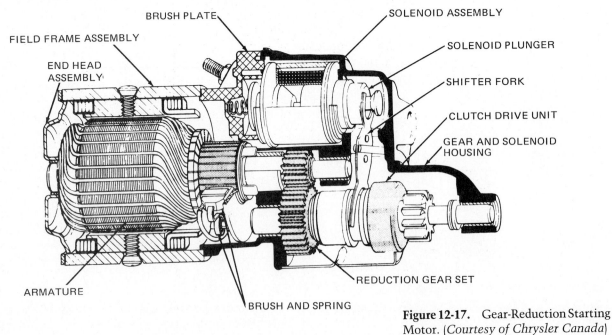

Figure 12-17.   Gear-Reduction Starting Motor. (*Courtesy of Chrysler Canada*)

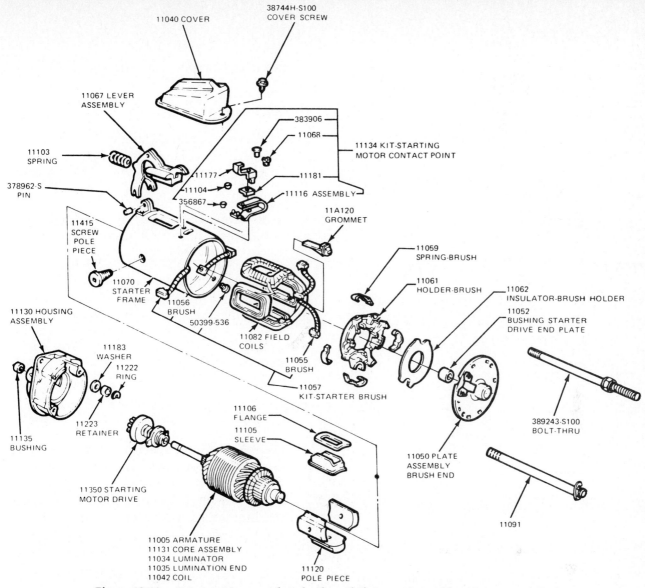

Figure 12-18. Starting Motor with Pole Shoe Shift-Lever Assembly. (*Courtesy of Ford Motor Co.*)

A gear-reduction type starting motor is shown in Figure 12-17.

Pole Shoe Shift-Lever Type Starting Motors

Design

In some starting motors, a pole shoe shift lever is used to push the drive into mesh with the flywheel ring gear. A heavy copper winding and the shunt coil are wound around the movable pole shoe. The shunt coil is connected from the main starting motor terminal to ground, and the heavy copper winding is connected from the main terminal to a set of normally closed contacts under the pole shoe shift lever.

This type of starting motor has a magnetic-switch type solenoid. When the solenoid closes and supplies current to the starting motor, most of the current flows through the heavy winding on the pole shift lever and the contacts to ground. A small amount of current also flows through the shunt coil to ground. The combined magnetic strength of both windings pulls the pole shoe shift lever down and pushes the starter drive into mesh with the flywheel ring gear. When this occurs, the pole shoe opens the contacts so that current stops flowing through the heavy winding and now flows through the other field windings and the armature windings to ground. The magnetic strength of the shunt coil holds the movable pole shoe down and the starter begins to crank the engine.

When the magnetic-switch type solenoid is de-energized, the current stops flowing through the starting motor and the return spring forces the pole

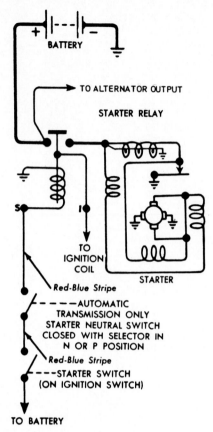

Figure 12-19. Electrical Circuit for Starter with Pole Shoe Shift Lever. (*Courtesy of Ford Motor Co.*)

shoe shift lever upward, which pulls the drive out of mesh.

A starting motor with a pole shoe shift lever is illustrated in Figure 12-18. The electrical circuit for the starter is given in Figure 12-19.

Permanent-Magnet Starting Motors

Design

Some 1986 and later model starting motors have permanent magnets in place of conventional pole shoes and field coils. The armature and field frame assembly on these starters is very small, and a planetary gear set is used to increase the armature torque.

Some permanent-magnet starting motors provide a 16 percent increase in cranking torque and a 31 percent weight reduction compared to previous starting motors. In many of these types of starting motors, roller bearings or ball bearings are used in place of brass bushings. The armature and planetary gear set are illustrated in Figure 12-20.

(Refer to Chapter 7 in *Automotive Principles: Repair and Service*, Volume II, for starting motor service.)

Test Questions

1. Describe the interaction between the magnetic fields of the armature windings and field coils that makes the armature rotate.

2. Explain how the shunt coil limits the maximum free-running armature speed.

3. List two different types of field coil windings.

4. The series field coils are connected in _____ _____ with the armature winding.

5. In a starting motor with a drive pull-in type solenoid, the armature begins to turn before the

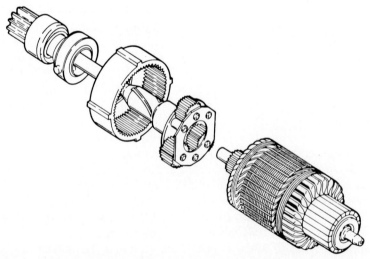

Figure 12-20. Permanent-Magnet Starting Motor Armature and Planetary Gear Set. (*Courtesy of GM Product Service Training, General Motors Corporation*)

drive is pushed into mesh with the flywheel ring gear.   T F

6. In the drive pull-in type solenoid, both windings are energized while the starting motor is cranking the engine.   T F

7. If a starter relay is used in the solenoid circuit, the current flow through the solenoid windings also flows through the relay contacts.   T F

8. One end of the shunt field coil is connected to the starter main terminal and the other end is connected to the:

    a) insulated brushes.

    b) series field coils.

    c) field frame.

9. In a starting motor with a pole shoe shift lever, when the solenoid makes contact, most of the initial current flows through the:

    a) series field coils and armature.

    b) heavy winding on the pole shoe shift lever.

    c) shunt coil.

10. In a starting motor with a pole shoe shift lever, the contacts are connected in series with the:

    a) heavy winding on the pole shoe shift lever.

    b) armature windings.

    c) shunt coil.

13

Electronic Ignition Systems

Chapter Completion Objectives

1. Demonstrate an understanding of basic electronic ignition operation.
2. Describe the difference between a hot-range spark plug and a cold-range spark plug.
3. Explain the purpose of distributor advance mechanisms.

4. Demonstrate an understanding of normal required secondary coil voltage, maximum available secondary coil voltage, and reserve secondary coil voltage.

5. Indicate a thorough knowledge of General Motors, Ford, and Chrysler electronic ignition systems.

Electronic Ignition System Components

Spark Plugs

Spark plugs contain a center electrode surrounded by an insulator. This center electrode and insulator assembly is mounted on a steel shell. A ground electrode is attached to the steel shell and positioned directly below the center electrode. Since the center electrode must withstand high temperature, it is manufactured from a nickel alloy.

The spark plug electrodes provide the gap within the combusion chamber across which high voltage arcs and ignites the air-fuel mixture. When combustion takes place in the cylinder, the heat is concentrated on the center spark plug electrode. This heat is dissipated through the insulator and the shell of the spark plug into the cylinder head. Coolant is circulated through a passage in the cylinder head which surrounds the spark plug seat. The coolant circulation conducts the heat away from the spark plug.

The heat range of a spark plug is determined by the depth of the insulator before it contacts the lower end of the spark plug shell. Spark plugs with normal, cold, and hot heat ranges are pictured in Figure 13-1.

If an engine is driven continuously at idle and low speeds, the spark plugs can become fouled with carbon because their operating temperature is too low. Under this type of driving condition, hot-range spark plugs may be required to prevent carbon fouling. When an engine is operated continuously under heavy load or high-speed conditions, extremely high temperatures may burn the spark plug electrodes. Under this type of operating condition, spark plugs with a colder heat range may be required. The heat range of the spark plugs recommended by the manufacturer for a specific engine are adequate for average driving conditions.

Spark plug gaps should always be set to the manufacturer's specifications. When spark plugs are installed, they should be tightened to the specified torque.

Spark Plug Wires

Many spark plug wires have a core which contains glass threads coated with carbon. This type of conductor in the core reduces electromagnetic interference (EMI). Vehicles equipped with computer systems must be equipped with this type of spark plug wires. (See Chapter 18 for an explanation of computer systems.)

The older type of spark plug wires had cores with stranded copper conductors. This type of spark plug wire could produce EMI, which can interfere with computer input or output signals.

The core of the spark plug wire is surrounded by insulation and a hypalon or silicone jacket, as indicated in Figure 13-2.

When spark plug wires are being removed, they should not be stretched. The spark plug boot should be rotated back and forth on the spark plug before the wire is removed from the plug.

Spark plug wires may be tested with an ohmmeter on the ×1000 scale. The wires are defective if the resistance exceeds manufacturer's specifications.

Distributors

The distributor is usually positioned in the engine block. In some overhead-cam engines, the distributor is located in the cylinder head. A bushing, or bushings, in the distributor housing support the distributor shaft. The distributor drive gear is attached to the shaft with a roll pin. In many engines this drive gear is driven by a gear on the camshaft. The

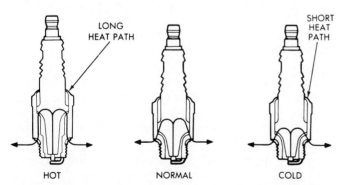

Figure 13-1.   Spark Plug Heat Range. (*Courtesy of Chrysler Canada*)

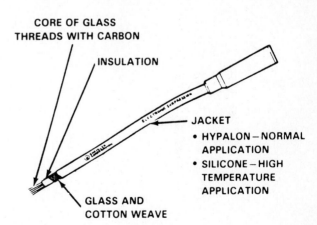

Figure 13-2.   Spark Plug Wire. (*Courtesy of Chrysler Canada*)

centrifugal advance mechanism is mounted on the upper end of the distributor shaft, and a reluctor is held on the upper end of the shaft with a roll pin. An aligning lug inside the rotor fits into a slot on top of the distributor shaft.

The pickup coil assembly is mounted on a plate in the distributor housing. A linkage from the vacuum advance is connected to the pickup plate. The pickup coil plate is designed to rotate with vacuum-advance diaphragm movement. A permanent magnet is positioned in the pickup coil. An aligning notch in the distributor cap fits into a notch in the distributor housing, so that the distributor cap can be installed in only one position. Spring clips are

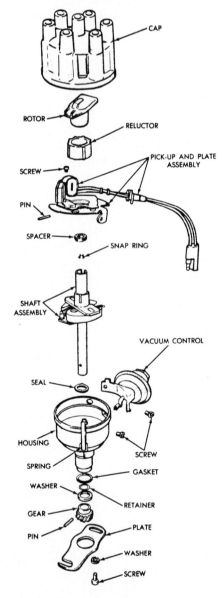

Figure 13-3. Distributor Assembly. (*Courtesy of Chrysler Canada*)

used to retain the distributor cap on top of the housing.

A complete distributor is illustrated in Figure 13-3.

Ignition Coil

A laminated iron core is located at the center of the coil windings. The secondary coil winding is wound around this iron core. This winding contains thousands of turns of very fine wire. A coating of insulating material on the wire prevents the turns of wire from touching each other.

One end of the secondary winding is connected to the secondary high-tension terminal in the coil tower, and the other end is often connected to one of the primary terminals. A primary winding is wound on top of the secondary winding. There are approximately 200 turns of wire on the primary winding, and it is much heavier wire than the secondary winding. The ends of the primary winding are connected to the two primary terminals on the top of the coil. These terminals are identified with positive (+) and negative (−) symbols.

The coil tower and winding assembly is sealed in a round metal container. This assembled coil is filled with oil to help cool the windings. The oil also prevents air space inside the coil, which would allow the formation of moisture.

A typical ignition coil is shown in Figure 13-4.

Ignition Module

The ignition module is completely sealed, so it must be replaced as a unit. Many ignition modules are bolted to the fender shield or firewall. Some ignition modules must be grounded where they are mounted, or the ignition system will be inoperative. Various wires from the electronic ignition system are connected to the module wiring harness plug.

An ignition module is pictured in Figure 13-5.

Primary Circuit Resistor

A primary circuit resistor is used in some ignition systems. This resistor is connected between the ignition switch and the positive coil terminal to provide the correct voltage and current flow in the primary circuit.

A primary circuit resistor is pictured in Figure 13-6.

Some ignition systems have a resistance wire in place of the block-type primary circuit resistor.

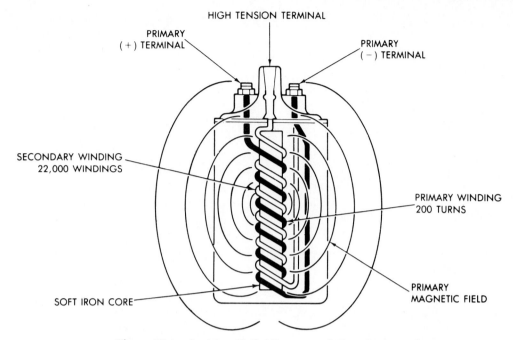

Figure 13-4. Ignition Coil. (*Courtesy of Chrysler Canada*)

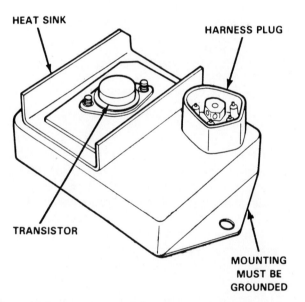

Figure 13-5. Ignition Module. (*Courtesy of Chrysler Canada*)

Complete Ignition System

In the ignition system shown in Figure 13-7, the pickup coil leads are connected to the number 4 and 5 terminals on the ignition module. The negative (−) primary coil terminal is connected to the number 2 terminal on the ignition module. Another wire is connected from ignition 1 (I1) terminal on the ignition switch to the primary circuit resistor, and also to the number 1 terminal on the ignition module.

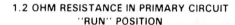

1.2 OHM RESISTANCE IN PRIMARY CIRCUIT "RUN" POSITION

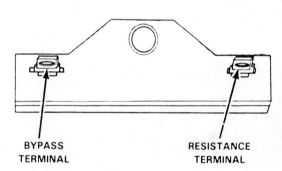

Figure 13-6. Primary Circuit Resistor. (*Courtesy of Chrysler Canada*)

The other end of the primary circuit resistor is connected to the positive (+) primary coil terminal. A wire from the ignition 2 (I2) terminal is connected to the primary circuit resistor terminal that is attached to the positive (+) primary coil connection.

The I2 terminal of the ignition switch supplies battery voltage directly to the ignition positive (+) primary coil terminal while the engine is being cranked. This maintains a higher voltage at the coil and provides an increase in primary current while the engine is being started. If the I2 ignition switch terminal did not perform this function, voltage and current would be supplied through the primary circuit resistor to the positive (+) primary coil terminal. Under this condition the voltage at the positive

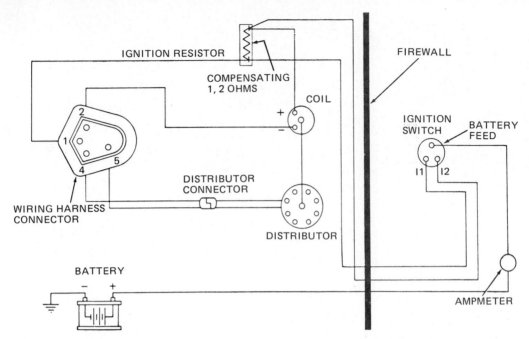

Figure 13-7. Complete Ignition System. (*Courtesy of Chrysler Canada*)

(+) primary coil terminal would be reduced and primary current flow would decrease. If the primary current flow is decreased, the magnetic field in the coil becomes weak and the maximum secondary coil voltage is low.

Electronic Ignition System Operation

Ignition Module and Pickup Coil Operation

One high point is located on the distributor reluctor for each engine cylinder. When the reluctor high points are out of alignment with the pickup coil, a weak magnetic field exists around the pickup coil, as indicated in Figure 13-8. Under this condition the module closes the primary ignition circuit and current flows though the ignition switch, resistor, primary coil winding, and the module to ground. This

current flow through the primary circuit creates a magnetic field around both coil windings.

As the distributor shaft rotates, a reluctor high point moves into alignment with the pickup coil. Since the metal reluctor tip is a better conductor for magnetic lines of force than air, the magnetic field around the pickup coil is strengthened, as pictured in Figure 13-9.

The instant that the reluctor tip begins to move out of alignment with the pickup coil, the magnetic field around the pickup coil collapses. A voltage is then induced in the pickup coil, which causes the module to open the primary circuit. When the primary circuit is opened, the magnetic field collapses across the coil windings and this induces a very high voltage in the secondary coil winding because of the large number of secondary turns. This high voltage forces current flow out the secondary coil wire to the center distributor cap terminal. From this point, the secondary current flows through the rotor, dis-

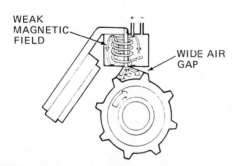

Figure 13-8. Reluctor High Point Out of Alignment with the Pickup Coil. (*Courtesy of Chrysler Canada*)

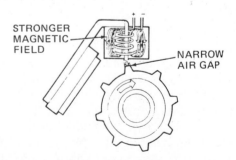

Figure 13-9. Reluctor Tip in Alignment with the Pickup Coil. (*Courtesy of Chrysler Canada*)

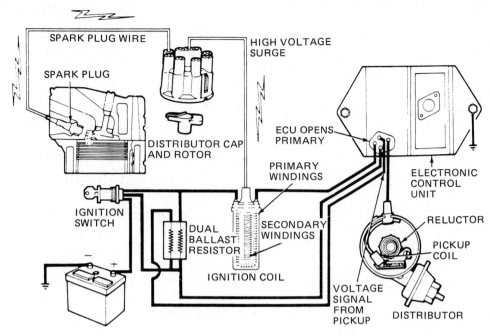

Figure 13-10 Ignition System Operation. (*Courtesy of Chrysler Canada*)

tributor cap terminal, spark plug wire, and spark plug electrodes to ground. This spark across the plug electrodes ignites the air-fuel mixture in the cylinder, which forces the piston down in the power stroke.

The purpose of the ignition system is to create a spark at each spark plug electrode gap at the right instant. Some ignition manufacturers refer to the ignition module as an electronic control unit (ECU). The operation of the ignition system is illustrated in Figure 13-10.

The purpose of the ignition module is to open and close the primary ignition circuit. When the reluctor tip moves a very short distance out of alignment with the pickup coil, the induced voltage in the pickup coil decreases. When this occurs, the ignition module closes the primary circuit and primary current flow resumes.

The ignition module must keep the primary circuit turned on long enough to allow the magnetic field to build up in the ignition coil. This "on time" for the primary circuit is referred to as dwell time. In most electronic ignition systems, the dwell time is determined electronically by the ignition module.

In the older, point-type ignition systems, the ignition points and the cam lobe opened and closed the primary circuit in place of the ignition module. A point-type distributor and ignition coil are shown in Figure 13-11.

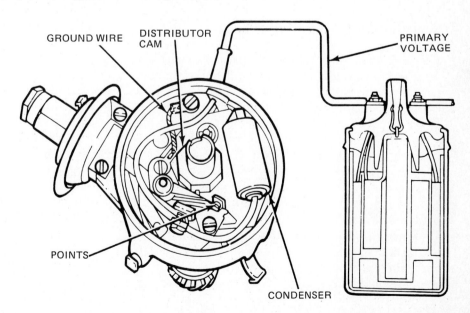

Figure 13-11. Point-Type Distributor and Ignition Coil. (*Courtesy of Chrysler Canada*)

Secondary Coil Voltage

When the engine is operating at low speeds, the required secondary ignition coil voltage is normally about 10,000V. However, many ignition coils are capable of producing a maximum secondary coil voltage of 25,000V or more. The difference between required secondary voltage and maximum secondary voltage is referred to as reserve voltage.

When the engine is operated with a wide-open throttle at high speeds or under heavy load, cylinder pressures increase. This pressure increase between the spark plug electrodes requires an increase in secondary voltage to keep firing the spark plugs.

Spark plug electrodes wear gradually from continual arcing and extreme heat. When the electrode gap becomes wider, the required secondary voltage must increase to fire the spark plug. An increase in required secondary coil voltage will also occur if additional resistance develops in the spark plug wires or the rotor gap. Hence, secondary reserve voltage is necessary to compensate for higher cylinder pressures under wide-open throttle conditions, as well as for any increase in secondary resistance.

The maximum available secondary voltage must always exceed the normal required secondary voltage. Excessive resistance at spark plug electrodes or in spark plug wires can reduce the secondary voltage reserve. The maximum secondary coil voltage may be reduced by a defective coil, low primary current, or a cracked distributor cap or rotor. If any of these defects occur, secondary misfiring may occur under hard acceleration.

Distributor Advances

Centrifugal Advance Mechanism

The centrifugal advance mechanism is attached to the distributor shaft. This advance mechanism contains pivoted advance weights which move outward when the engine and distributor shaft speed increase. The advance weight movement is controlled by two springs. When the advance weights move outward, they turn the reluctor in the same direction that the distributor shaft is rotating. This causes the reluctor tips to be aligned sooner with the pickup coil, which results in earlier spark advance at the spark plug electrodes.

When the piston speed increases, the spark must occur sooner at the spark plug electrodes in order to maintain maximum pressure on the piston from combustion. If this spark advance in relation to pis-

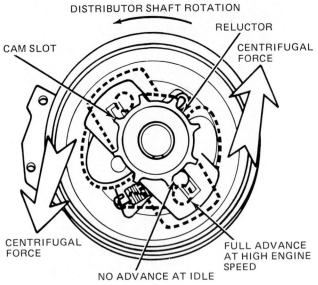

Figure 13-12. Centrifugal Advance Mechanism. (*Courtesy of Chrysler Canada*)

ton speed did not occur, the piston would move down on the power stroke before the air-fuel mixture had time to start burning, which would result in reduced engine power. Hence, the centrifugal advance mechanism advances the spark at the spark plug electrodes in relation to engine speed, as indicated in Figure 13-12.

Vacuum Advance

The vacuum advance contains a diaphragm in a sealed chamber. On some engines this chamber is connected to a ported vacuum source above the throttle, whereas in other engines the vacuum source for the vacuum advance is directly from the intake manifold.

A linkage from the vacuum-advance diaphragm is connected to the pickup coil plate. When the engine is operating at part throttle, a relatively high vacuum is applied to the vacuum-advance diaphragm. This vacuum overcomes the spring tension on the diaphragm and moves the diaphragm toward the vacuum outlet. When this occurs, the diaphragm link rotates the pickup coil plate opposite to the distributor shaft rotation, which causes the pickup coil to be aligned sooner with the reluctor tips. This pickup coil movement causes the spark to occur sooner at each spark plug electrode. Under part-throttle, light-load operating conditions, additional spark advance provides improved fuel economy and performance.

If the throttle is moved to the wide-open position, cylinder pressure and heat increase, which results in faster burning of the air-fuel mixture. Under

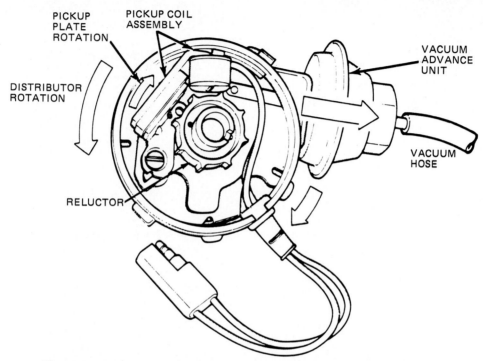

Figure 13-13. Vacuum Advance Operation. (*Courtesy of Chrysler Canada*)

this condition the spark advance must be retarded to prevent detonation. At wide-open throttle, manifold vacuum decreases and the vacuum-advance return spring moves the diaphragm toward the distributor housing, which moves the pickup coil to the retarded position. The vacuum advance controls the spark advance in relation to engine load.

On most late model cars, the distributor advances are discontinued and the spark advance is computer controlled. (Computer-controlled spark-advance systems are explained later in this chapter.)

The operation of a vacuum advance mechanism is illustrated in Figure 13-13.

General Motors High-Energy Ignition Systems

Design

Point-type ignition systems are subject to dwell and timing changes because of point rubbing block wear. High exhaust emissions are caused by dwell and timing changes. Electronic ignition systems provide more stable operation, because the dwell is determined by a solid-state module. Exhaust emissions are reduced by the increased stability of electronic ignition systems.

The High-Energy Ignition (HEI) system is self-contained in the distributor. Early-model HEI sys-

tems were equipped with conventional vacuum and centrifugal advance mechanisms. On later model HEI systems, the spark advance is controlled by the electronic control module (ECM), and the advance mechanisms are not required. A later model HEI system is shown in Figure 13-14.

Many HEI coils are mounted on top of the distributor cap; other models are externally mounted. A spring contact connects the secondary coil terminal to the center cap terminal. High voltage leakage is prevented by the seal around the center cap terminal, as illustrated in Figure 13-15. The ground terminal dissipates induced voltages from the coil frame to ground on the distributor housing.

Early-model HEI coils have the secondary winding connected from the center cap terminal to the primary winding. On later model coils, secondary windings are connected from the center cap terminal to the coil frame.

Four screws attach the coil to the distributor cap. The primary coil leads, identified as "bat" and "tach" terminals, are mounted in the distributor cap. A double connector is used on each primary terminal. One connection on the "bat" terminal is connected to the ignition switch. The "bat" terminal is also connected to the HEI module. Inner "tach" terminals are connected to the module, and the outer "tach" connection extends to the dash-mounted tachometer or diagnostic connector.

A timer core is attached to the distributor shaft. The number of teeth on the timer core matches the

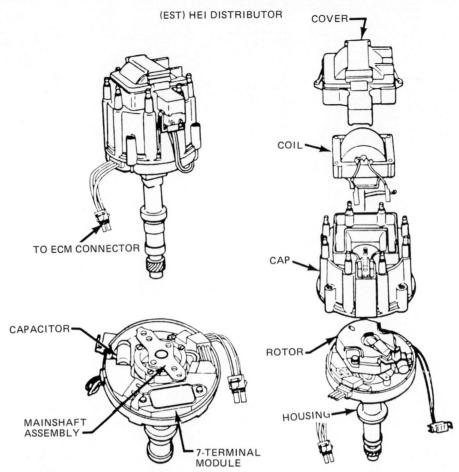

(EST) HEI DISTRIBUTOR

COVER

COIL

CAP

ROTOR

HOUSING

TO ECM CONNECTOR

CAPACITOR

MAINSHAFT
ASSEMBLY

7-TERMINAL
MODULE

Figure 13-14. High-Energy Ignition System. (*Courtesy of Pontiac Motor Division, General Motors Corporation*)

IGNITION COIL REMOVED FROM CAP

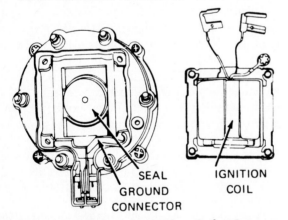

SEAL
GROUND
CONNECTOR

IGNITION
COIL

Figure 13-15. High-Energy Ignition Coil. (*Courtesy of Chevrolet Motor Division, General Motors Corporation*)

number of engine cylinders. A pickup coil assembly surrounds the timer core, and the number of teeth on the pickup pole piece matches the number of timer core teeth, as pictured in Figure 13-16.

Operation

As the timer core teeth approach alignment with the teeth on the pickup pole piece, a magnetic field builds up around the pickup coil. The resulting induced voltage in the pickup coil signals the module to turn on the primary current, as illustrated in Figure 13-17. With the ignition switch on and the distributor shaft not turning, there is no primary current flow.

When the timer core teeth begin moving out of alignment with the pole piece teeth, the magnetic field suddenly collapses across the pickup coil. When the pickup coil induced voltage signal is received, the module opens the primary circuit. When this occurs, the magnetic field collapses across the ignition coil windings and high voltage required to fire the spark plug is induced in the secondary winding.

Primary dwell time is the length of time that the primary circuit remains closed by the module. The module extends primary dwell time as engine speed increases, providing higher primary magnetic

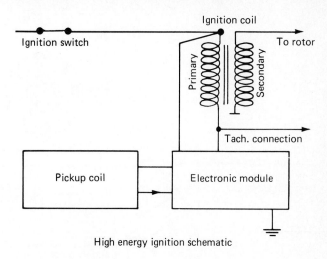

High energy ignition schematic

Figure 13-18. High-Energy Ignition, Primary Circuit Open. (*Courtesy of Chevrolet Motor Division, General Motors Corporation*)

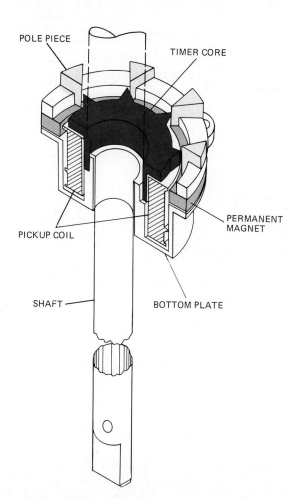

POLE PIECE

TIMER CORE

PERMANENT MAGNET

PICKUP COIL

SHAFT

BOTTOM PLATE

Figure 13-16. High-Energy Ignition Timer Core. (*Courtesy of Sun Electric Corporation*)

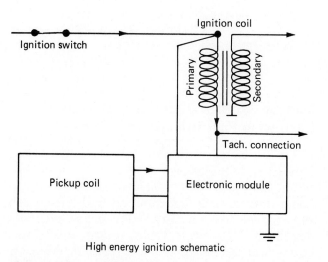

High energy ignition schematic

Figure 13-17. High-Energy Ignition Primary Current Flow. (*Courtesy of Chevrolet Motor Division, General Motors Corporation*)

strength and maximum secondary voltage. Other electronic ignition systems operate on similar basic principles, but many systems provide a constant dwell time regardless of engine rpm.

The HEI system with the primary circuit open is shown in Figure 13-18.

High-Energy Ignition Used with Computer Command Control System

Design and Operation

A seven-wire ignition module is used in the computer command control (3C) HEI system. The additional three module terminals are connected to the electronic control module (ECM). Conventional vacuum and centrifugal advance mechansims are discontinued, and the correct spark advance is supplied by the ECM in relation to the input sensor signals that it receives.

Input sensor signals from the barometric pressure sensor, manifold absolute pressure sensor, coolant temperature sensor, and the crankshaft rpm signal are used by the ECM to determine the correct spark advance, as shown in Figure 13-19.

While the engine is cranking, the pickup coil signal goes directly through the module signal converter and bypass circuit. The ECM does not affect spark advance when the engine is being started. Approximately five seconds after the engine is started, a 5V disable signal is sent from the ECM to the module. This signal opens the module bypass circuit and completes the compensated ignition spark-timing

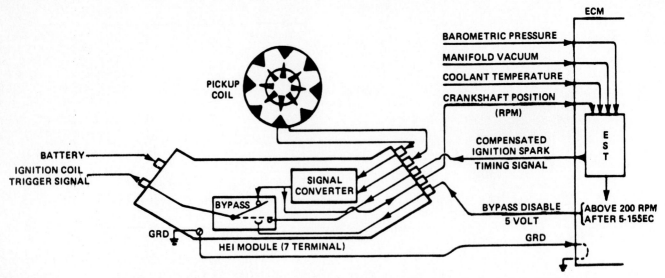

Figure 13-19. Computer Command Control High-Energy Ignition System, Start Mode. (*Courtesy of GM Product Service Training, General Motors Corporation*)

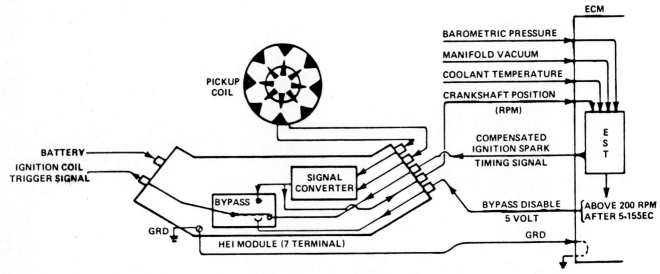

Figure 13-20. Computer Command Control High-Energy Ignition System, Run Mode. (*Courtesy of GM Product Service Training, General Motors Corporation*)

circuit from the ECM to the module, as illustrated in Figure 13-20.

The pickup coil signal now travels through the module signal converter, ECM, and the compensated ignition spark-timing circuit to the module. Ignition spark advance is controlled by the electronic spark-timing (EST) circuit in the ECM under this condition. The distributor pickup coil signal that is sent through the module to the ECM is referred to as a crankshaft position revolutions per minute (rpm) signal, because it provides the ECM with an engine speed signal. (The complete 3C system is explained in Chapter 17.)

General Motors High-Energy Ignition Used with Fuel Injection Systems

Design and Operation

Some throttle body injection systems have a conventional pickup coil and a Hall Effect switch in the distributor. The conventional pickup coil is used only while the engine is being cranked. While the engine is running, a signal is sent from the Hall Effect switch through the ECM to the HEI module. The Hall Effect switch sends a revolutions per minute

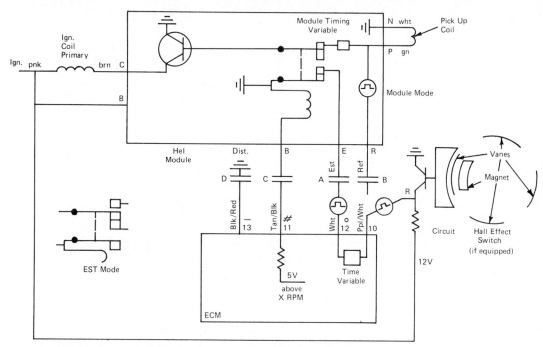

Figure 13-21.   High-Energy Ignition with Hall Effect Switch. (*Courtesy of GM Product Service Training, General Motors Corporation*)

(rpm) signal to the ECM, and the "R" terminal on the HEI module that was used on other systems for this purpose is no longer connected to the ECM, as shown in Figure 13-21.

When the engine is being cranked, the conventional pickup coil signal is sent directly to the transistor in the HEI module. A 5V disable signal is sent from the ECM through the tan/black wire and the winding in the HEI module to ground. This 5V disable signal changes the HEI module circuit into the EST mode, as shown in the illustration in the lower left-hand side of Figure 13-21. The signal from the Hall Effect switch can now travel through the ECM and the HEI module circuit to the transistor in the module.

The "time variable" circuit in the ECM varies the signal from the Hall Effect switch to provide the precise spark advance that is required by the engine. Each time a signal is received by the transistor in the HEI module, it opens the primary ignition circuit to provide magnetic collapse in the ignition coil and the high induced voltage in the secondary winding to fire the spark plug. In the EST mode, the circuit is open from the conventional pickup coil to the transistor in the HEI module. The Hall Effect switch will provide a signal each time a reflector blade that is attached to the distributor shaft rotates past the switch.

The HEI module circuit shown in Figure 13-21

is for illustration purposes; the actual module circuit would be much more complex.

Computer-Controlled Coil Ignition Systems Used with Port Fuel Injection

Design and Operation

The main components in the computer-controlled coil ignition (C³I) system are the cam sensor, crank sensor, and the electronic coil module, as pictured in Figure 13-22.

The cam sensor and the crank sensor both contain Hall Effect switches. A conventional distributor is not required with the C³I system; the cam sensor is mounted in the engine block in place of the distributor. This sensor is driven by the camshaft. The crank sensor is mounted at the front of the crankshaft, and this sensor is operated by an interruption ring attached to the crankshaft pulley.

Signals from the crank sensor inform the electronic coil module and the ECM when each piston is at top dead center (TDC). This signal is used by the ECM and the coil module for correct timing and spark advance. A signal is also sent from the cam sensor to the coil module and the ECM. This sensor generates one signal for each sensor revolution. The

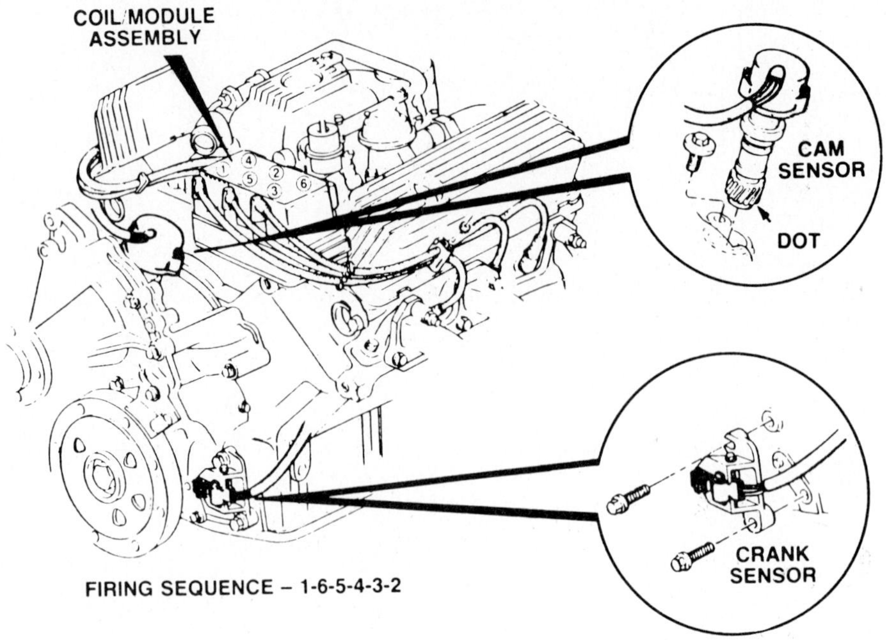

Figure 13-22. Computer-Controlled Coil Ignition System. (*Courtesy of GM Product Service Training, General Motors Corporation*)

ECM uses this signal to time the injector opening. For example, if the engine has sequential fuel injection (SFI), the ECM will begin to energize the injectors in the correct sequence when it receives the cam sensor signal.

Three ignition coils are mounted in the electronic coil module assembly, and an electronic module is located underneath the coils. The C³I system has two spark plug wires connected to each coil. On some V6 engines, spark plug wires 1 and 4, 5 and 2, and 6 and 3 are paired together. With this type of system, each coil fires both spark plugs at the same time. The wires are paired so that one spark plug is firing when the piston is on the compression stroke and the other piston is on the exhaust stroke. If a spark plug fires when the piston is on the exhaust stroke, it has no effect.

When the engine is being cranked, the crank sensor signal goes directly to the coil module, which opens the primary circuit of each coil. Once the engine starts, the crank sensor signal goes through the reference-low/reference-high circuit to the ECM. This signal is sent from the ECM through the EST circuit to the coil module. On the basis of the input signals, the ECM will vary the crank sensor signal to provide the precise spark advance required by the engine. An initial timing adjustment is not required on the C³I system.

The wiring diagram for C³I system is provided in Figure 13-23.

With the ignition switch on, voltage is supplied from terminal "P" on the coil module through the module circuit to the blue input wires on each coil primary winding. The coil module opens and closes the circuit from each primary winding to ground. When the ignition switch is turned on, voltage is supplied from terminal "M" on the coil module through terminal "H" to terminal "A" on the crank and cam sensor.

Some engines have a combined crank and cam sensor mounted at the front of the crankshaft. The wiring diagram for this circuit is shown in Figure 13-24.

A tachometer lead is connected to the coil module, and the terminal on this wire is usually located near the coil module. Only digital tachometers should be connected to the tachometer lead.

General Motors Distributorless Direct-Ignition System

Design

The distributorless direct-ignition system (DIS) is similar to the C³I system. The coils in the DIS may be replaced individually, whereas in the C³I system the coils must be replaced as a complete assembly. Figure 13-25 illustrates these two different coil assemblies.

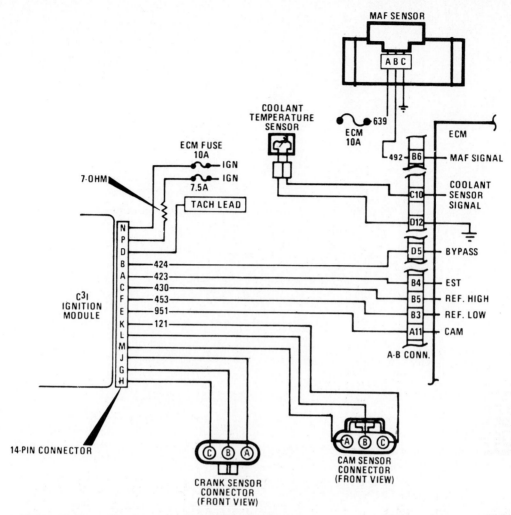

Figure 13-23.   Computer-Controlled Coil Ignition System Wiring Diagram. (*Courtesy of GM Product Service Training, General Motors Corporation*)

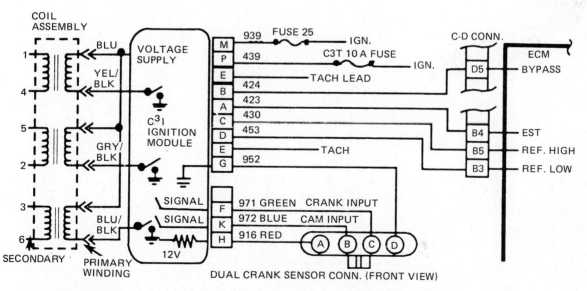

Figure 13-24.   Computer-Controlled Coil Ignition System with Combined Crank and Cam Sensor. (*Courtesy of GM Product Service Training, General Motors Corporation*)

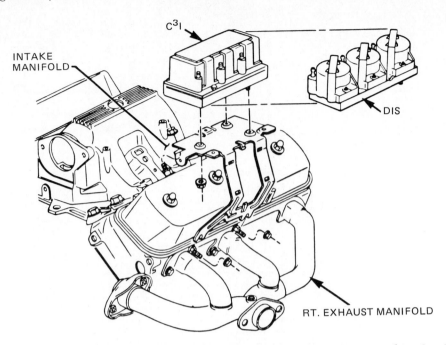

Figure 13-25. Coil Assemblies from C³I and DIS. (*Courtesy of GM Product Service Training, General Motors Corporation*)

A single crankshaft sensor is used in the DIS. The sensor is triggered by an interrupter vane on the back of the crankshaft harmonic balancer. When the interrputer vane rotates through the sensor, three vane windows generate a signal in the sensor every 120°, as indicated in Figure 13-26.

As in the C³I system, the crankshaft sensor signal in the DIS is sent through the coil module to the

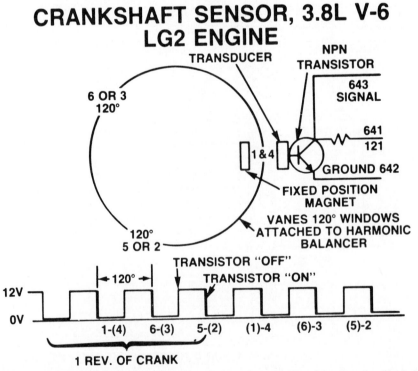

Figure 13-26. Crankshaft Sensor Signal. (*Courtesy of GM Product Service Training, General Motors Corporation*)

ECM and back to the coil module on the electronic spark-timing (EST) circuit. When this signal is received, the coil module opens the appropriate coil primary circuit and fires the spark plugs at the right instant.

The DIS system has a camshaft sensor that is mounted in the timing gear cover and is triggered by a magnetic interrupter on the camshaft gear. This signal is used by the ECM to start sequential pulsing of the fuel injectors in the intake ports.

The camshaft sensor and interrupter are shown in Figure 13-27, and the camshaft sensor signal is compared to the crankshaft sensor signal in Figure 13-28.

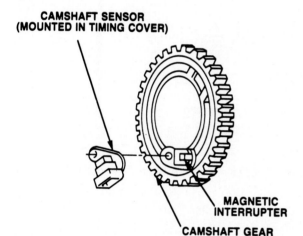

Figure 13-27. Camshaft Sensor and Magnetic Interrupter. (*Courtesy of GM Product Service Training, General Motors Corporation*)

(Refer to Chapter 18 for a description of the computer system used with C³I and DIS.) A DIS wiring diagram is illustrated in Figure 13-29.

Ford Duraspark Ignition Systems

Design

Duraspark II ignition systems have a six-wire module, and the distributor is equipped with conventional centrifugal and vacuum advance mechanisms. A Duraspark II ignition wiring diagram is illustrated in Figure 13-30.

Some Duraspark II ignition systems have a universal ignition module (UIM) which has an additional wiring harness connector that contains three wires. This extra wiring harness connector may be connected to a vacuum switch, a barometric pressure switch, or to a microprocessor control unit (MCU) system, depending on the engine application.

The vacuum switch signals the module to retard the spark advance 3° to 6° if the manifold vacuum drops below 6 in. Hg. If a barometric pressure switch is used, the signal from the switch to the module retards the timing 3° to 6° when the vehicle is operating at elevations below 2,400 ft (731 m).

When the basic timing is being checked, the additional three-wire connector on the UIM should be disconnected.

Duraspark III ignition systems have a five-wire ignition module. This ignition system is used with

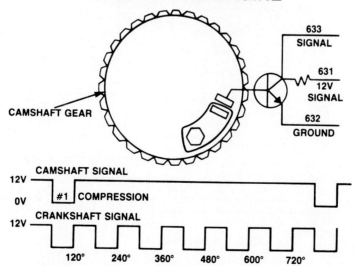

Figure 13-28. Comparison Between Camshaft and Crankshaft Sensor Signals. (*Courtesy of GM Product Service Training, General Motors Corporation*)

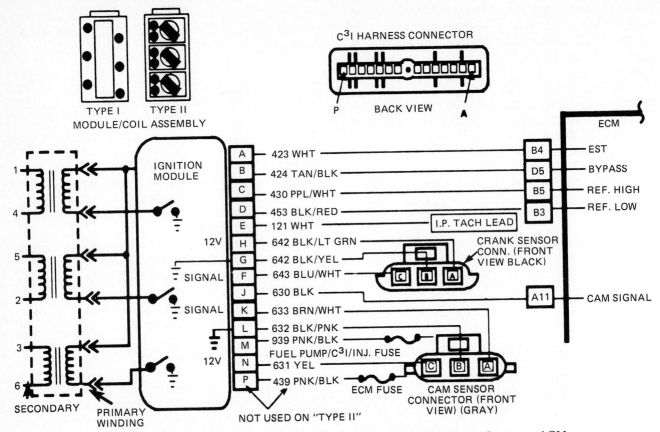

Figure 13-29. Distributorless Direct-Ignition System Wiring Diagram. (*Courtesy of GM Product Service Training, General Motors Corporation*)

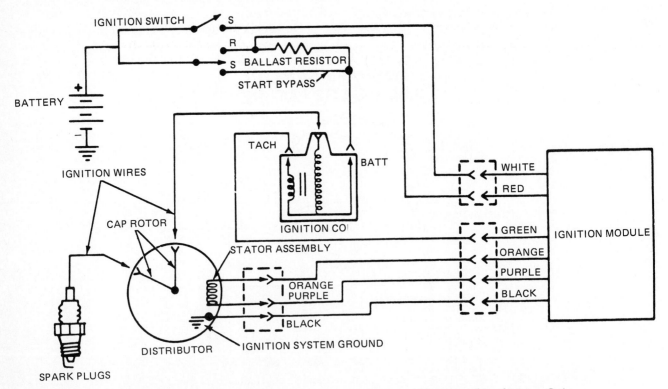

Figure 13-30. Duraspark II Ignition Wiring Diagram. (*Courtesy of Ford Motor Co.*)

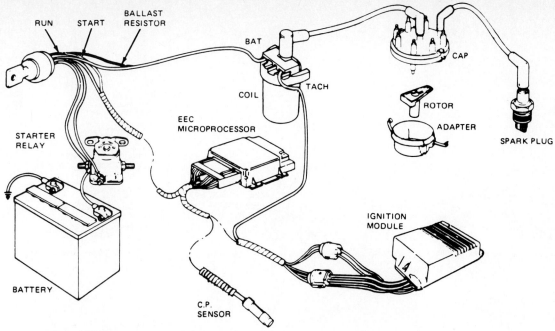

Figure 13-31. Duraspark III Ignition System with Crankshaft Pickup Assembly. (*Courtesy of Ford Motor Co.*)

the Electronic Engine Control (EEC) system. The distributor advances are not required in this system, because the spark advance is determined by the microprocessor in the EEC system.

Duraspark III ignition systems may have a pickup coil located in the distributor or a pickup assembly positioned at the front of the crankshaft. If the pickup assembly is located at the front of the crankshaft, a cam ring with four high points is located on the crankshaft pulley. When these high points rotate past the pickup, the pickup signal is sent through the microprocessor to the ignition

module. The instant this signal is received, the module opens the primary ignition circuit.

The microprocessor can vary the pickup signal to provide the precise spark advance required by the engine. This type of pickup is referred to as a crankshaft position (CP) sensor. The basic timing cannot be adjusted on a Duraspark III ignition system with a CP sensor, because the sensor cannot be rotated.

A Duraspark III system with a CP sensor is shown in Figure 13-31, and a Duraspark III ignition wiring diagram is illustrated in Figure 13-32.

Figure 13-32. Duraspark III Ignition System Wiring Diagram. (*Courtesy of Ford Motor Co.*)

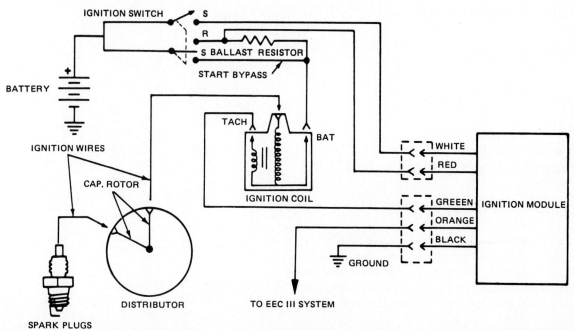

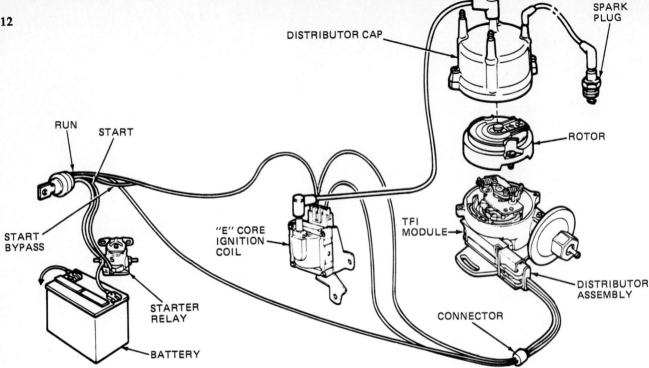

Figure 13-33. TFI Ignition System. (*Courtesy of Ford Motor Co.*)

Thick Film Integrated Ignition Systems

The thick film integrated (TFI) systems differ from other ignition systems as follows:

1. A TFI module is attached to the distributor housing. Module circuitry increases dwell time as engine speed increases.

2. TFI ignition coil windings are set in epoxy. An iron frame surrounds the coil windings.

3. The primary circuit resistance wire normally connected between the ignition switch and the coil primary winding is eliminated on TFI systems.

4. Pickup coil leads are connected to the TFI module inside the distributor housing.

A TFI ignition system is shown in Figure 13-33, and a TFI distributor is pictured in Figure 13-34.

Thick Film Integrated Ignition Systems Used with Electronic Engine Control IV

Design and Operation

TFI ignition systems are used with all Electronic Engine Control (EEC IV) systems. The distributor in the EEC TFI ignition system is similar to the distributor that is used with the conventional TFI ignition system. A Hall Effect device is used in place of the

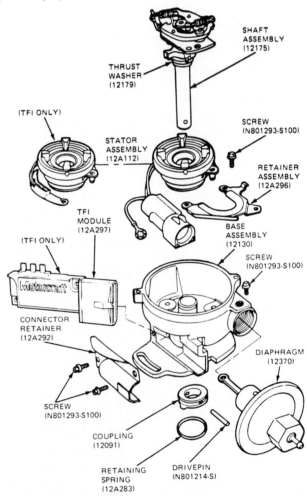

Figure 13-34. TFI Distributor. (*Courtesy of Ford Motor Co.*)

conventional pickup coil in the distributor. This device is referred to as a profile ignition pickup (PIP).

The EEC IV TFI distributor is illustrated in Figure 13-35.

EEC IV TFI ignition systems use a six-wire TFI module. The primary ignition circuit is connected to the module in the same way as it is on the conventional TFI ignition systems. However, the EEC IV TFI ignition system has three extra wires that are connected from the module to the electronic control assembly (ECA), as shown in Figure 13-36.

The electrical ground circuit between the ECA

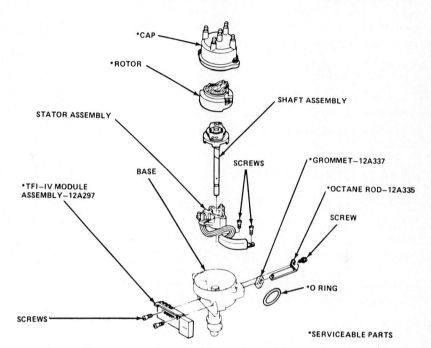

Figure 13-35. EEC IV TFI Distributor. (*Courtesy of Ford Motor Co.*)

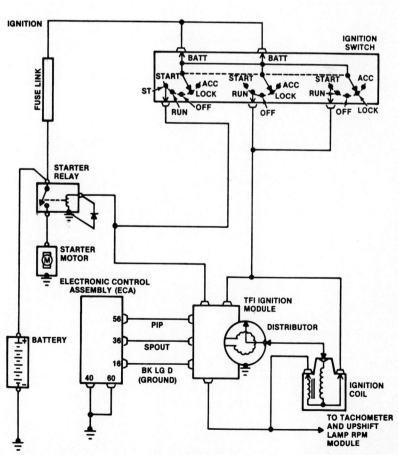

Figure 13-36. EEC IV TFI Ignition Wiring Diagram. (*Courtesy of Ford Motor Co.*)

and the TFI module is provided by circuit number 16. A PIP signal is sent from the Hall Effect device to the ECA through circuit number 56. This signal informs the ECA when each piston is at 10 degrees before top dead center (BTDC). The ECA provides a spark output (SPOUT) signal through circuit number 36 to the TFI module, which provides the precise spark advance that is required by the engine under all operating conditions. This eliminates the need for conventional spark-advance mechanisms on the EEC IV TFI distributor.

Chrysler Electronic Ignition Systems

Electronic Ignition Circuits

Chrysler-built vehicles with electronic ignition have four- or five-terminal modules, and these systems were equipped with conventional distributor advances. An electronic ignition system with a five-terminal module is shown in Figure 13-37, and the ignition circuit with the four-terminal module is illustrated in Figure 13-38.

Electronic Lean-Burn and Electronic Spark-Advance Ignition Systems

In the electronic lean-burn (ELB) systems or electronic spark-advance (ESA) systems, the spark advance is computer controlled and the conventional distributor advances are discontinued. A centrifugal advance was used in some ELB distributors.

In many ELB systems, two pickup coils were located in the distributor. The start pickup signal provided a signal to the computer while the engine was being cranked, and the run pickup signal was used once the engine started.

A diagram of an ELB system is provided in Figure 13-39.

In the ESA systems, single or dual pickup coils may be used in the distributors on V8 engines, depending on the year of the vehicle. On four-cylinder ESA systems, a single Hall Effect pickup is used in the distributor. In early-model ESA systems, the computer only controlled the spark advance, whereas in later systems the air-fuel ratio and other functions are computer controlled.

An early-model ESA system with a single pickup coil and a single ignition resistor is shown in Figure

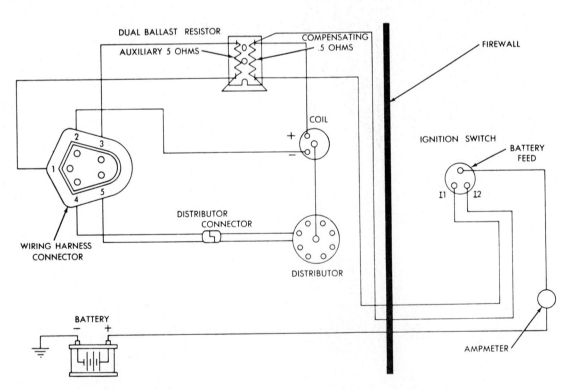

Figure 13-37. Chrysler Electronic Ignition System with Five-Terminal Module. (*Courtesy of Chrysler Canada*)

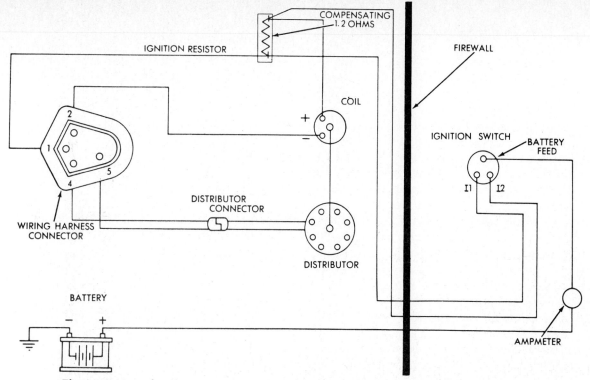

Figure 13-38. Chrysler Electronic Ignition System with Four-Terminal Module. (*Courtesy of Chrysler Canada*)

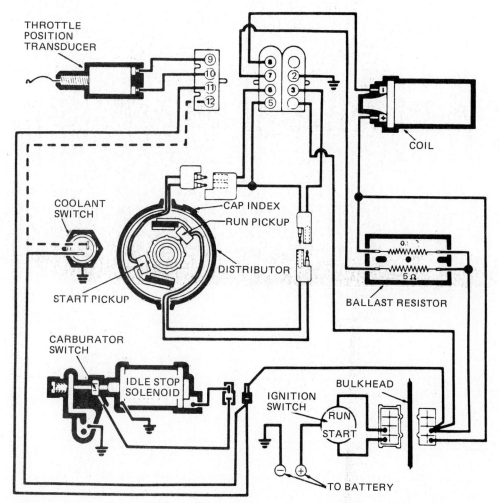

Figure 13-39. Chrysler Electronic Lean-Burn System. (*Courtesy of Chrysler Canada*)

13-40. A later model ESA system with a computer-contolled oxygen (O_2) feedback carburetor system from a 2.2L four-cylinder engine is shown in Figures 13-41 and 13-42.

The ESA system with the O_2 feedback carburetor, or electronic fuel injection (EFI), is used on many front-wheel-drive Chrysler cars. (These systems are explained in Chapter 17 and 18.) An ignition resistor is not used in the primary circuit of these ESA systems. The Hall Effect switch in the distributor provides a signal to the computer each time the shutter blade on the rotor moves through the switch. A synchronizer ("sync") pickup is located in the distributor with the Hall Effect switch if this system is used on the multi-port EFI system. The "sync" pickup signal is used for fuel system control.

A distributor with a Hall Effect switch is pictured in Figure 13-43.

A metal tab on the rotor grounds the shutter blade to the distributor shaft. If the ground tab does not contact the shaft, the engine will not start. (Elec-tronic ignition system service is explained in Chapter 8 of *Automotive Principles: Repair and Service*, Volume II.)

Test Questions

1. In an HEI system, the dwell remains constant regardless of the engine rpm.   T F

2. In a 3C HEI system, the pickup coil signal is sent through the ECM to the ignition module when the engine is running.   T F

3. When an HEI distributor has a Hall Effect switch and a conventional pickup coil, the signal from the Hall Effect switch is used:

   a) when the engine is being cranked.

   b) when the engine is running.

   c) only when the engine is running above 1,200 rpm.

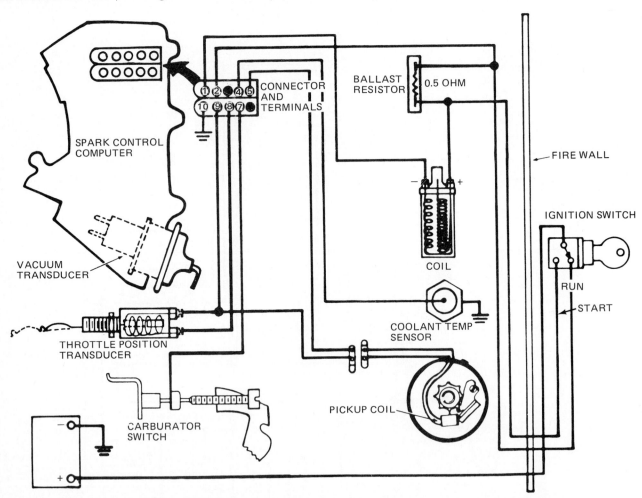

Figure 13-40.   Chrysler Electronic Spark Advance with Single Pickup Coil. (*Courtesy of Sun Electric Corporation*)

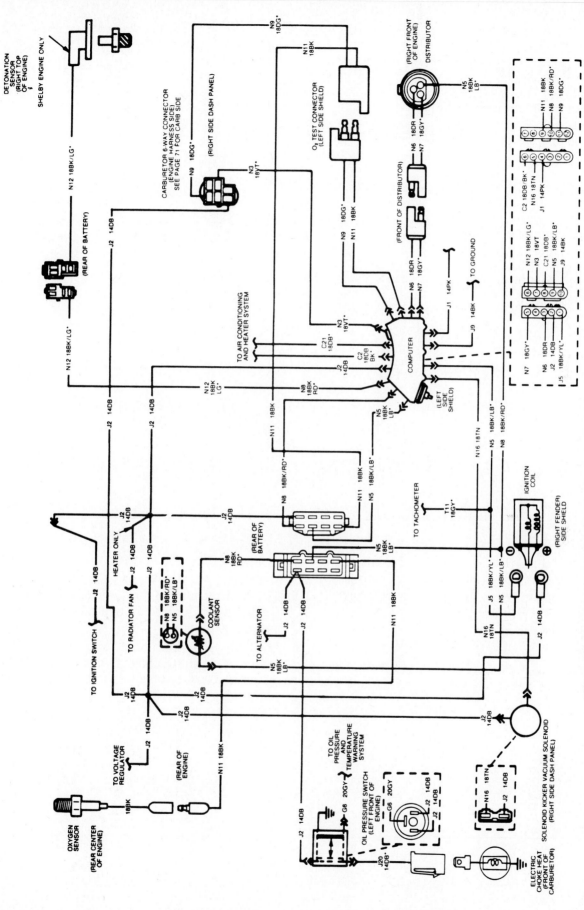

Figure 13-41. Electronic Spark-Advance System with Oxygen Feedback Carburetor System. (*Courtesy of Chrysler Canada*)

217

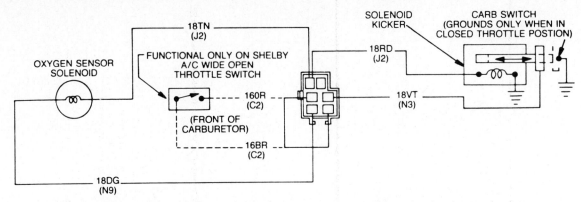

Figure 13-42. Carburetor Wiring Diagram for Oxygen Feedback Carburetor System. (*Courtesy of Chrysler Canada*)

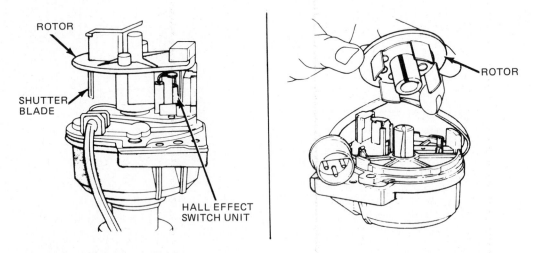

Figure 13-43. Distributor with Hall Effect Switch. (*Courtesy of Chrysler Canada*)

4. When a vacuum switch is connected to the additional three-wire connector on a Ford universal ignition module (UIM), the vacuum switch signal causes the module to:

a) retard the timing if the vacuum is below 6 in. Hg.

b) retard the timing if the vacuum is above 15 in. Hg.

c) advance the timing if the vacuum is below 6 in. Hg.

5. The basic timing is not adjustable on a Ford Duraspark III ignition system with a crankshaft position (CP) sensor.   T F

6. In a Chrysler distributor with a Hall Effect switch, if the shutter blade is not grounded to the distributor shaft the engine will fail to start.   T F

14

Cruise Controls, Vacuum Pumps, and Windshield Wiper Motors

Chapter Completion Objectives

1. Demonstrate an understanding of electronic and vacuum-operated cruise controls.
2. Indicate a knowledge of electric and belt- or gear-driven vacuum pumps.
3. Understand shunt field windshield wiper motors.
4. Display a knowledge of permanent-magnet windshield wiper motors and pulse-type permanent-magnet wiper motors.
5. Explain the operation of an integral windshield washer mechanism.

Electronic Cruise Control

Components

Control Switch   The control switch is used to select the various operating modes. This switch is located on the end of the signal light lever, as pictured in Figure 14-1.

Vehicle Speed Sensor Buffer Amplifier   The vehicle speed sensor (VSS) buffer amplifier is connected to the speedometer. This sensor sends a digital 12V vehicle speed signal to the electronic controller. On some vehicles, a permanent-magnet (PM) speed sensor mounted in the transaxle is used in place of the speed sensor buffer amplifier.

A speed sensor buffer amplifier is shown in Figure 14-2.

Electronic Controller   The controller receives input signals from the speed sensor and the mode con-

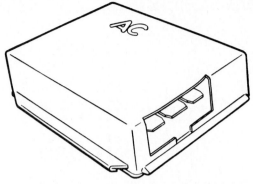

Figure 14-3.   Electronic Controller. (*Courtesy of Pontiac Motor Division, General Motors Corporation*)

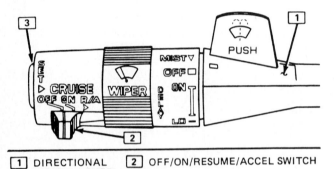

1	DIRECTIONAL SIGNAL LEVER	2	OFF/ON/RESUME/ACCEL SWITCH
		3	SET/COAST SWITCH

Figure 14-1.   Cruise Control Switch. (*Courtesy of Pontiac Motor Division, General Motors Corporation*)

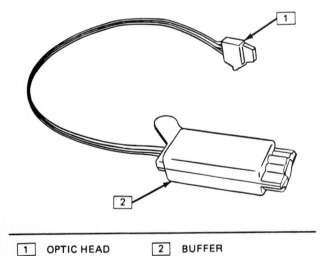

1	OPTIC HEAD	2	BUFFER

Figure 14-2.   Vehicle Speed Sensor Buffer Amplifier. (*Courtesy of Pontiac Motor Division, General Motors Corporation*)

trol switches. A position signal is sent from the servo to the controller. In response to these inputs, the digital/analog integrated circuit in the controller provides the necessary output signals to the vacuum and vent solenoid valves in the servo. The electronic controller is illustrated in Figure 14-3.

Servo Unit   The servo contains a vacuum-operated diaphragm that is connected to the throttle with a bead chain or a cable. A normally open solenoid in the servo vents the diaphragm chamber to the atmosphere, and a normally closed solenoid is used to supply vacuum to the diaphragm chamber. The electronic controller operates these two solenoids to supply a specific vacuum to the servo diaphragm, which holds the throttle in the right position to maintain the selected vehicle speed. A variable-inductance position sensor is also located in the servo, as indicated in Figure 14-4.

Vacuum Release Valve   The vacuum release valve vents the servo diaphragm chamber to the atmosphere when the brakes are applied. This venting action occurs with a small amount of brake pedal movement, in the "free travel" of the brake pedal. The cruise control is released quickly when the servo diaphragm chamber is vented.

The vacuum release valve is mounted on a bracket above the brake pedal arm. When the brakes are released, a button on the valve contacts the brake pedal arm to hold the release valve closed.

Vehicles with a lockup torque converter have a combination vacuum release valve and converter clutch electric switch. This switch releases the converter lockup clutch when the brakes are applied.

A vacuum release valve is shown in Figure 14-5.

Combination Cruise/Stoplight Switch   A set of contacts in the cruise/stoplight switch opens the circuit from the cruise switch to the electronic controller when the brakes are applied. This action as-

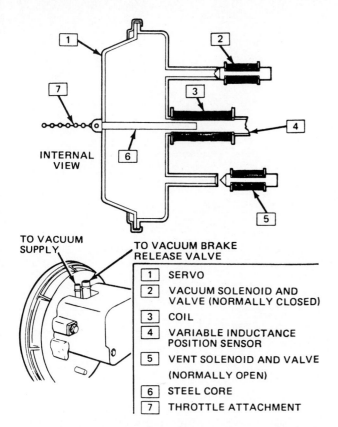

INTERNAL
VIEW

TO VACUUM
SUPPLY

TO VACUUM BRAKE
RELEASE VALVE

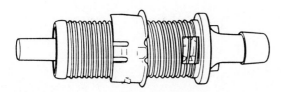

1	SERVO
2	VACUUM SOLENOID AND VALVE (NORMALLY CLOSED)
3	COIL
4	VARIABLE INDUCTANCE POSITION SENSOR
5	VENT SOLENOID AND VALVE (NORMALLY OPEN)
6	STEEL CORE
7	THROTTLE ATTACHMENT

Figure 14-4. Servo Unit. (*Courtesy of Pontiac Motor Division, General Motors Corporation*)

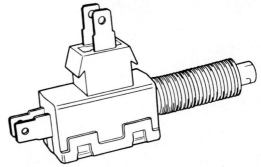

Figure 14-5. Vacuum Release Valve. (*Courtesy of Chevrolet Motor Division, General Motors Corporation*)

sures immediate cruise release in addition to the vacuum release valve action. A separate set of contacts in the switch supplies voltage to the stoplights when the brakes are applied.

On vehicles with manual transaxles, a clutch switch replaces the cruise switch operated by the brake pedal. This switch results in cruise release when the clutch is depressed. With either type of switch, the cruise remains disengaged after the brake pedal, or clutch pedal, is released.

A combination cruise/stoplight switch is illustrated in Figure 14-6.

Accumulator The accumulator is a vacuum storage tank that stores vacuum to maintain satisfactory cruise operation when the manifold vacuum is low

Figure 14-6. Combination Cruise/Stoplight Switch. (*Courtesy of Chevrolet Motor Division, General Motors Corporation*)

at wide-open throttle. A cruise vacuum system is shown in Figure 14-7.

Electronic Cruise Control Operation

General Operation The cruise control is engaged when the cruise switch on the signal light lever is moved to the "on" position and the "set" push button on the end of the lever is depressed and released. A low-speed inhibit feature in the controller prevents cruise engagement below 25 MPH (40 KPH). The system may be disengaged by moving the switch to the "off" position or by depressing the brake pedal. On vehicles with manual transaxles, the clutch pedal must be depressed rather than the brake pedal.

When the brake pedal is depressed to disengage the cruise system, the resume/accelerate (R/A) button may be pushed momentarily to return the vehicle to the previously set cruise speed at a controlled rate. Under this condition the controller remembers the last set speed.

If the R/A button is held for more than one second, the cruise system reverts to the accelerate mode. In this mode the vehicle accelerates at a controlled rate. The cruise set speed will be the speed at which the R/A button is released.

A lower cruise set speed may be selected by depressing the set/coast button on the end of the signal light lever. When this action is taken, the vehicle will coast down at a controlled rate and the new set cruise speed will be the speed at which the set/coast button is released. (The cruise control switch was shown in Figure 14-1.)

If the R/A button is tapped quickly with the cruise control engaged, the cruise control set speed will increase 1 MPH (1.6 KPH). This action may be repeated up to ten times to achieve a 10 MPH (16 KPH) increase in cruise set speed. After ten taps of the R/A switch have been completed, the system must be reset to a new speed to continue this func-

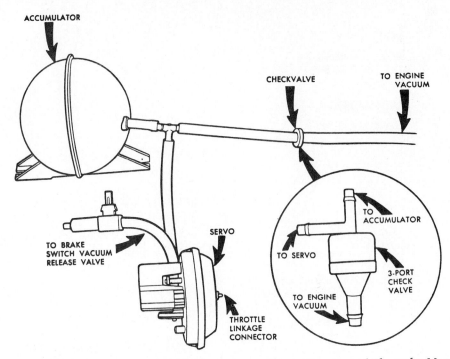

Figure 14-7. Cruise Vacuum System with Accumulator. (*Courtesy of Chevrolet Motor Division, General Motors Corporation*)

tion. This feature is referred to as a "tap-up" function.

When the cruise control system is at a set speed, if the set/coast button is tapped, the cruise set speed will decrease 1 MPH (1.6 KPH). This action may be repeated until the vehicle speed decreases to 25 MPH (40 KPH). The term "tap-down" is applied to this function.

Servo and Controller Modes

Steady-Speed Cruise Mode   In this mode the controller energizes the vent solenoid and de-energizes the vacuum solenoid. When this occurs the vacuum is trapped in the servo diaphragm and the diaphragm maintains the throttle position.

Maintain Vehicle Speed Modes   If the vehicle starts up a hill in the cruise mode, the vehicle speed will start to decrease. When this occurs the controller energizes the vacuum solenoid, which increases the vacuum in the servo diaphragm chamber so that vehicle speed is maintained. Under this condition the vent solenoid remains energized and closed.

If the vehicle begins to go downhill, the vehicle speed will try to increase. Under this condition the controller de-energizes the vent solenoid and vents the servo diaphragm chamber to the atmosphere. This action decreases the vacuum applied to the diaphragm, which allows the throttle to move toward

the closed position and maintain the cruise set speed. During this mode the vacuum solenoid is de-energized and closed.

Vacuum-Operated Cruise Control

Design

The speedometer cable is connected to the servo in a vacuum-operated cruise control. One speedometer cable is connected from the servo to the transaxle and another is connected from the servo to the speedometer. The servo diaphragm chamber is connected to the intake manifold vacuum, and the servo diaphragm is attached to the throttle with a cable. A multi-function cruise control switch is mounted on the signal light lever, and a brake switch, or clutch switch, is connected into the cruise control electrical circuit.

The complete cruise control system is shown in Figure 14-8.

Operation

When the vehicle is operating at speeds above 30 MPH (50 KPH), if the speed-set button is depressed, current flows through the brake release valve wind-

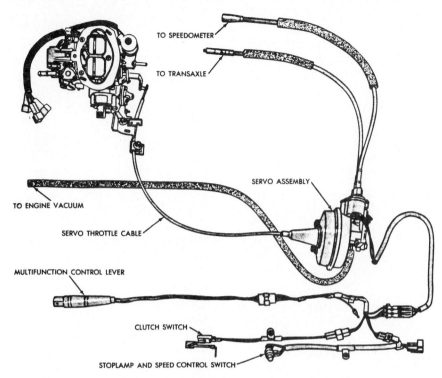

Figure 14-8. Cruise Control System. (*Courtesy of Chrysler Canada*)

ing and the governor switch contacts to ground. Under this condition the brake release valve closes and seals the diaphragm chamber, as indicated in Figure 14-9.

When the speed-set button is depressed, the locking coil current flow is stopped and the locking coil armature is released. This action enables the governor to push the locking coil armature core into the exact required speed position, because the gov-

ernor is rotated by the speedometer cable, as shown in Figure 14-10.

Release of the speed-set button results in locking coil current, which attracts the armature against the core. Since the vacuum control valve is attached to the armature, it is also locked to the core, as indicated in Figure 14-11.

The top of the vacuum control valve is centered between the vacuum port and a vent port. Therefore, once the valve is locked to the core, the governor

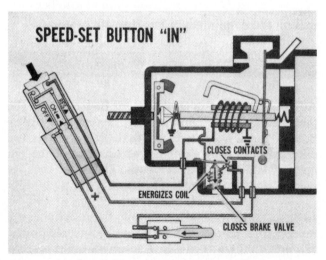

Figure 14-9. Speed-Set Button Depressed. (*Courtesy of Chrysler Canada*)

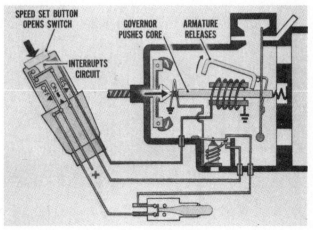

Figure 14-10. Governor and Locking Coil Action with Speed-Set Button Depressed. (*Courtesy of Chrysler Canada*)

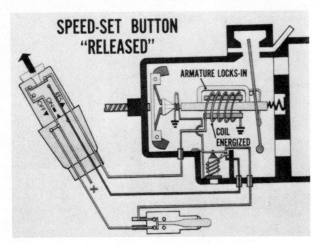

Figure 14-11. Governor and Locking Coil Action with Speed-Set Button Released. (*Courtesy of Chrysler Canada*)

positions the valve to supply a specific amount of vacuum in the diaphragm chamber. This specific vacuum moves the servo diaphragm and holds the throttle in the exact position to maintain the vehicle at the set cruise speed.

When the vehicle starts going up a hill, it begins to slow down. A slight decrease in vehicle speed also reduces the cruise control governor speed. Under this condition the governor allows the vacuum control valve to seal off the vent port and increase the vacuum port opening, which increases the vacuum in the diaphragm chamber. When this occurs the diaphragm pulls the throttle open further to maintain the vehicle speed, as illustrated in Figure 14-12.

When the vehicle begins descending a hill, its speed increases. When this occurs the increased governor speed moves the vacuum control valve toward the vacuum port. This action restricts the vacuum applied to the diaphragm chamber and increases the vent port opening. Under this condition diaphragm

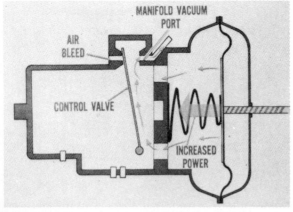

Figure 14-12. Vacuum Control Valve, Increase Speed Mode. (*Courtesy of Chrysler Canada*)

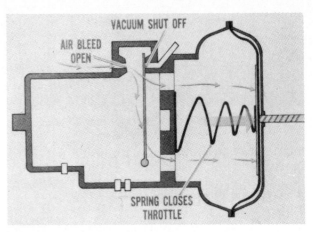

Figure 14-13. Vacuum Control Valve Position, Decrease Speed Mode. (*Courtesy of Chrysler Canada*)

chamber vacuum is reduced and the diaphragm spring moves the diaphragm and throttle toward the closed position, which prevents the vehicle speed from increasing, as shown in Figure 14-13.

If the brake pedal is depressed, the brake switch opens the circuit through the brake release valve winding. This opens the brake release valve and dumps the diaphragm chamber vacuum, which allows the cruise control to be disengaged. However, the current flow through the locking coil is maintained and the armature remains locked to the core in the exact previous speed-set position.

If the control switch is rotated to the resume position, after the brakes are released current will flow through the brake release valve winding and the governor contacts to the ground. This action closes the brake release valve and seals the diaphragm chamber. Under this condition the vacuum slowly pulls the diaphragm back to the previous speed-set position. The resume button only requires momentary rotation, because the current will continue to flow through the brake switch contacts and the brake release valve contacts and winding once these contacts close.

If the vehicle is operating below 30 MPH (50 KPH), the governor switch contacts open, which prevents the brake release valve from closing. This action prevents cruise control operation.

Electric Vacuum Pumps

System Design

The electric vacuum pump inlet is connected to the power brake booster, and the pump outlet is connected to the inlet manifold. If the manifold vacuum drops below 13.9 in. Hg (47 kPa), the controller in the pump starts the pump. The pump brings the vacuum up to 13.9 in. Hg (47 kPa) in five to ten seconds to ensure positive brake booster operation. A vacuum switch located in the pump inlet hose operates a warning lamp on the instrument panel when the vacuum drops below a specific level.

The charcoal filter in the outlet hose prevents fuel vapors from entering the pump. A vacuum switch and an electronic controller in the pump turn the pump on and off in response to the vacuum signal.

When the engine is operating under high vacuum conditions at moderate throttle openings, manifold vacuum is applied to the brake booster and the vacuum pump. Under this condition a check valve in the pump prevents vacuum leaks. If a low-vacuum signal causes the pump to start, the vacuum at the pump inlet maintains the vacuum at the brake booster. When the pump is operating it exhausts from the outlet to the intake manifold.

The pump location and complete pump system are illustrated in Figure 14-14. The vacuum and electrical connections to the pump are shown in Figure 14-15.

Belt- and Gear-Driven Vacuum Pumps

Design and Operation

Some engines have a belt- or gear-driven vacuum pump to maintain the vacuum supply to the vacuum-operated equipment on the vehicle. These pumps have a cam which causes the diaphragm to pulsate and create a vacuum. Since diesel engines have low intake manifold vacuum, they are usually equipped with a vacuum pump. Smaller gasoline engines often operate at wider throttle openings, and thus a vacuum pump is required.

A belt-driven vacuum pump is illustrated in Figure 14-16, and a gear-driven pump is shown in Figure 14-17.

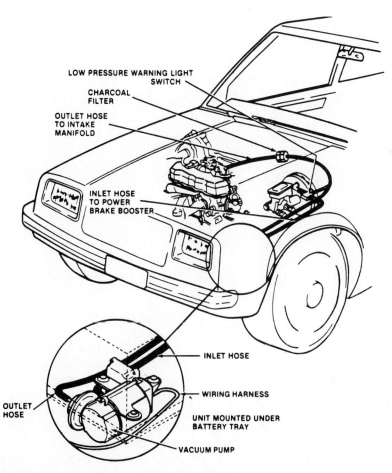

Figure 14-14.   Electric Vacuum Pump System. (*Courtesy of Delco Products Division, General Motors Corporation*)

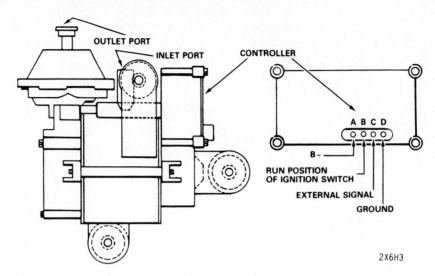

Figure 14-15. Electrical and Vacuum Connections to Electric Vacuum Pump. (*Courtesy of Pontiac Motor Division, General Motors Corporation*)

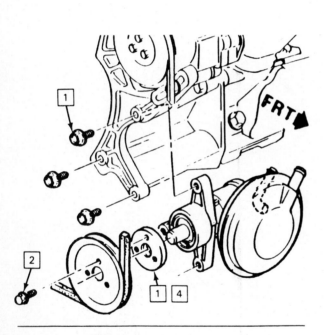

1	HUB
2	27 N·m (20 FT. LBS.)
3	10 N·m (7 FT. LBS.)
4	HUB MUST BE PRESSED FLUSH WITH END OF PUMP SHAFT

Figure 14-16. Belt-Driven Vacuum Pump. (*Courtesy of Pontiac Motor Division, General Motors Corporation*)

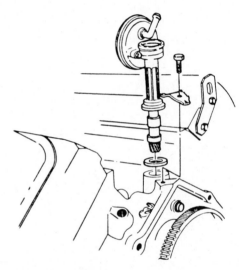

Figure 14-17 Gear-Driven Vacuum Pump. (*Courtesy of Chevrolet Motor Division, General Motors Corporation*)

Shunt Field Windshield Wiper Motors

Design and Operation

Some windshield wiper motors have a series field coil and a shunt field coil. Other shunt field wiper motors have two series field coils and two shunt coils. The operation of the wiper motor is controlled by a switch on the instrument panel. When this switch is placed in the low-speed position, current flows through the relay winding and the center low-speed contacts in the switch. The relay coil magnetism closes the relay contacts, which results in current flow through these contacts and the series field and armature windings to ground. This current flow results in armature rotation and windshield wiper movement, because the armature is connected through a gear set to the wiper control arms. In the low-speed position, some current also flows from the series field coil through the shunt coil and right low-speed contacts in the switch. Shunt coil current results in higher induced opposing voltage in the armature windings, and therefore reduced armature speed.

The wiper motor armature and shunt coil operate on the same electric principles as the starting motor. (Refer to Chapter 12 for an explanation of starting motors.)

A shunt field wiper motor and instrument panel switch are illustrated in Figure 14-18.

When the wiper switch is moved to the high-speed position the center switch contacts continue to ground the relay winding, but the right contacts open the shunt coil circuit. Under this condition

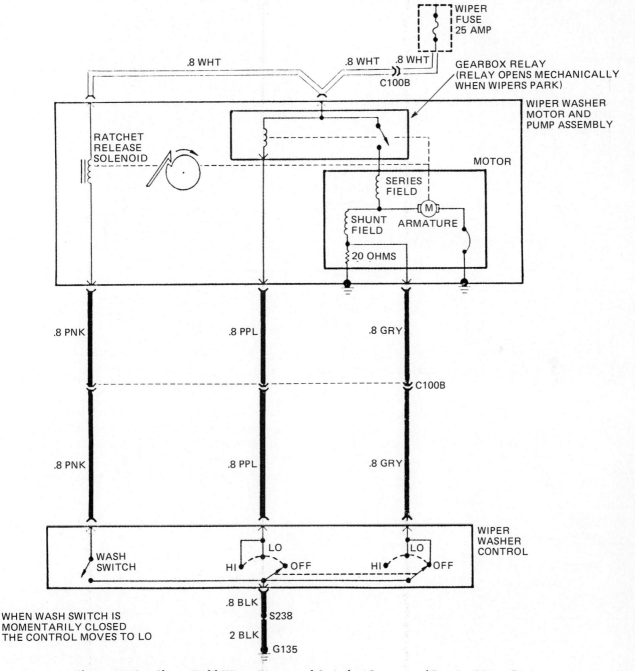

Figure 14-18.   Shunt Field Wiper Motor and Switch. (*Courtesy of Pontiac Motor Division, General Motors Corporation*)

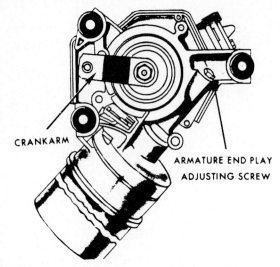

Figure 14-19. External Features of Shunt Field Wiper Motor (*Courtesy of Chevrolet Motor Division, General Motors Corporation*)

current flows through the shunt coil and the resistor in the wiper motor to ground, which reduces shunt coil current flow. This action results in less induced opposing voltage in the armature windings and increased armature speed.

Battery voltage is supplied through the wiper fuse to the wiper motor input terminals; therefore, the wipers will operate with the ignition switch in the off position.

The external features of a shunt field wiper motor are shown in Figure 14-19.

Park Cycle

When the wiper switch is moved to the off position, the circuit through the dash switch to ground is opened. In this position, the low- and high-speed terminals are connected together and current flows through the shunt field, dash switch contacts, and

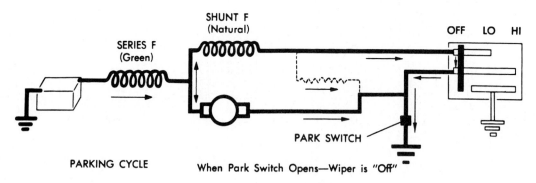

Figure 14-20. Wiper Motor and Control Switch Park Circuit. (*Courtesy of Pontiac Motor Division, General Motors Corporation*)

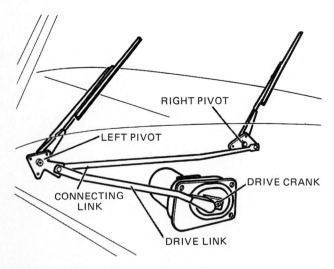

Figure 14-21. Wiper Motor with Connecting Links, Pivots, and Blades. (*Courtesy of Chrysler Canada*)

park switch to ground. Current also flows through the series field, armature, and part switch to ground, as indicated in Figure 14-20.

When the wiper blades reach the park position, a cam on the wiper motor output gear opens the park switch and the motor stops.

A complete wiper system with the motor connecting links, pivots, and blades is illustrated in Figure 14-21.

Depressed Park Wipers

Some wiper systems are designed with a depressed park feature which causes the wiper blade to park about 4 in. (10 cm) below the windshield so that the wiper blades are not visible in the park position. In this type of wiper motor, current is normally supplied from the wiper switch to the series field coil and the armature windings. Current is also supplied through the wiper switch to the shunt coil.

Two resistors in the wiper switch are used to control the shunt coil current and provide three wiper motor speeds. Wiper motor speed is faster when the switch places the highest resistance in the shunt field current. Wiper speed is reduced if the switch supplies full voltage to the shunt coil, because shunt coil current and induced opposing voltage in the armature windings increase.

If the wiper switch is moved to the off position, the wiper switch supplies voltage through the park switch and the armature windings in the original direction. However, current also flows through the park switch, series field coil, and shunt field coil to ground. This current flow through the field coils is reversed in relation to the field current when the motor is operating normally, as pictured in Figure 14-22.

The reversed field current results in reversed magnetic fields. Since the armature current is in the same direction but the magnetic fields are reversed, the armature rotation is reversed. This action causes a cam on the wiper motor crank arm to change position and lengthen the drive arm $\frac{1}{4}$ in. (6.35 mm), which causes the wiper blades to move 4 in. (10 cm) down off the windshield. When the wiper blades reach the depressed park position, the output gear cam opens the park switch and stops the motor.

In some depressed-park wiper motors, the park switch is designed so that the wiper blades complete one wipe across the windshield after the wiper switch is turned off. This is referred to as an anti-streak feature.

The crank arm cam action is illustrated in Figure 14-23.

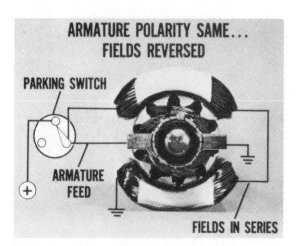

Figure 14-22. Depressed-Park Wiper Motor Park Cycle. (*Courtesy of Chrysler Canada*)

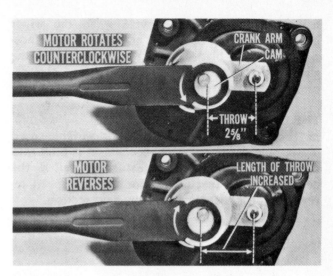

Figure 14-23. Depressed-Park Wiper Motor Crank Arm Action. (*Courtesy of Chrysler Canada*)

Permanent-Magnet Wiper Motors

Design and Operation

Many wiper motors have permanent-magnet type fields rather than wound field coils. This type of wiper motor has a low-speed brush and a high-speed brush to control motor speed, as indicated in Figure 14-24.

When the wiper switch is moved to the high-speed position, current flows from the switch input terminal through the high-speed terminal to the high-speed brush. From this point, current flows through the armature windings and the ground brush. Since the high-speed brush is not directly opposite the ground brush, current flows only through some of the armature windings. Armature speed is limited by induced opposing voltage in the armature windings. This induced opposing voltage is only effective in the armature windings through which current is flowing. Therefore, if current flows only through some of the armature windings, the armature speed increases.

In the low-speed mode, current flows from the low-speed switch terminal through the low-speed brush, armature windings, and ground brush. Since the low-speed brush is directly opposite the ground brush, current flows through more armature windings in the low-speed mode compared to the high-speed mode. The induced opposing voltage is now effective in more armature windings, and armature speed is reduced.

The upper park switch contacts are normally closed. When the off position is selected, current

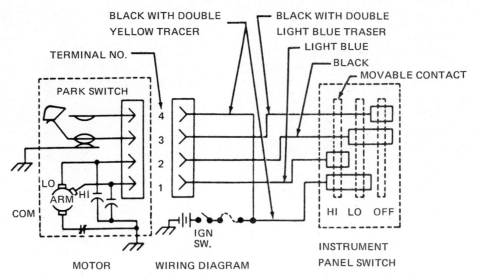

Figure 14-24. Permanent-Magnet Wiper Motor Circuit. (*Courtesy of Buick Motor Division, General Motors Corporation*)

flows from the ignition switch, park switch, low-speed brush, armature windings, and ground brush. This action causes the motor to operate at low speed until the output gear cam opens the park switch when the wipers are in the park position. In the park position, the lower park switch connects the low-speed brush to ground. When this brush and the ground brush are both grounded, the armature stops instantly.

Most wiper motors have a circuit breaker connected between the ground brush and the motor ground. This circuit breaker protects the motor and wiring harness from high current flow and possible damage if the motor draws excessive current because of electrical or mechanical defects.

Permanent-Magnet Pulse Wiper System

Operation

The pulse wiper motor contains an electronic printed circuit board that is permanently mounted in the motor cover. An integral flex-vane washer motor is also mounted in the motor cover, as indicated in Figure 14-25.

A delay switch can be moved from "min" to "max" in the delay mode. This switch action results in a wiper pause of 0 to 25 seconds at the end of each wiper blade sweep. In the pulse mode, the wiper motor operates at low speed.

The electronic printed circuit board also con-

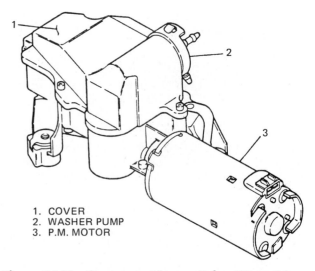

1. COVER
2. WASHER PUMP
3. P.M. MOTOR

Figure 14-25. Permanent-Magnet Pulse Wiper Motor. (*Courtesy of Buick Motor Division, General Motors Corporation*)

trols the washer pump operation. When the "wash" button is pushed for less than 1 second, the pump will provide $2\frac{1}{2}$ seconds of fluid flow, followed by 6 seconds of dry wiper operation. If the "wash" button is depressed for more than 1 second, the wash mode is continued as long as the button is held, followed by 6 seconds of dry wiper operation. The motor also operates in the conventional low- and high-speed positions.

A permanent-magnet pulse-type wiper motor circuit is illustrated in Figure 14-26.

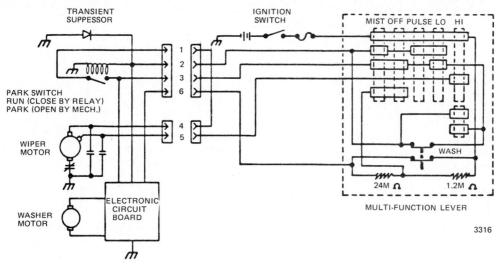

Figure 14-26. Permanent-Magnet Pulse Wiper Circuit. (*Courtesy of Buick Motor Division, General Motors Corporation*)

Windshield Washers

Design and Operation

Some windshield washer pumps are mounted in the bottom of the washer fluid reservoir. When the "wash" button is depressed, the electrically driven pump delivers fluid through the washer hoses to the nozzles, which may be mounted on the wiper arms as shown in Figure 14-27. Other washer systems have nozzles mounted near the wiper blades.

Regardless of the nozzle location, the nozzles must be adjusted to direct fluid on the windshield, as pictured in Figure 14-28.

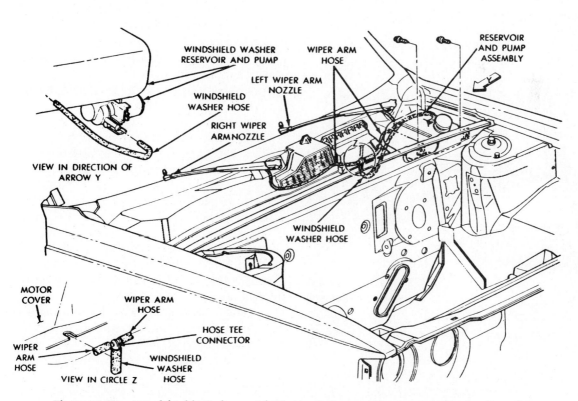

Figure 14-27. Windshield Washers with Reservoir Pump. (*Courtesy of Chrysler Canada*)

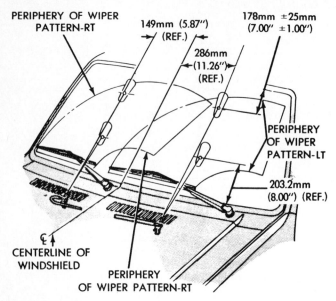

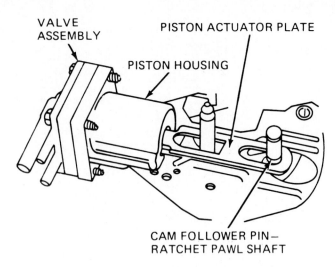

Figure 14-30.   Washer Pump Cam Follower Pin. (*Courtesy of Chevrolet Motor Division, General Motors Corporation*)

Figure 14-28.   Washer Nozzle Adjustment. (*Courtesy of Chrysler Canada*)

Integral Washer Pumps

Design and Operation   Some windshield washer pumps are driven by a cam or gear connected to the wiper motor drive gear. In this type of pump, a ramp on the back of a notched plastic gear catches on the pump arm tang and holds the pump arm in the retracted position, as illustrated in Figure 14-29.

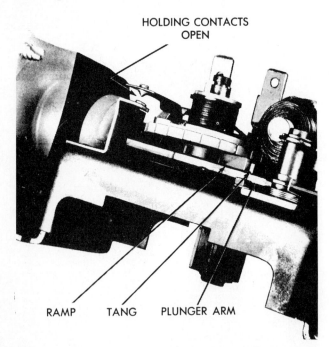

Figure 14-29.   Pump Arm in Retracted Position. (*Courtesy of Pontiac Motor Division, General Motors Corporation*)

In the retracted position, the cam follower pin is driven back and forth in the pump arm slot, but the pump arm or plate remains stationary, as pictured in Figure 14-30.

Battery voltage is applied to the washer relay coil. When the "wash" button is depressed, current flows through the relay coil and washer switch to ground. The relay coil magnetism attracts the relay armature and lifts the armature lock tang out of the notched gear slot. Upward armature motion allows the pawl to start catching on the notched gear teeth, which rotates the gear. This rotation allows the ramp on the back of the gear to release the pump plate tang and the pump spring drives the pump plate forward, which pumps fluid from the pump outlet valve. The cam follower pin now pulls the pump plate back and fluid is moved from the reservoir through the pump inlet valve, as indicated in Figure 14-31.

After one revolution of the notched plastic gear, the ramp holds the pump plate in the retracted position and the armature lock tang drops into the slot in the notched gear. This action locks the gear and allows the relay armature to drop down into its original position. When this occurs, the pump washer cycle is ended.

The armature and pawl are illustrated in Figure 14-32, and the complete washer pump assembly is pictured in Figure 14-33.

(Cruise control, vacuum pump, and wiper motor servicing and diagnosis are explained in Chapter 9 of *Automotive Principles: Repair and Service*, Volume II.)

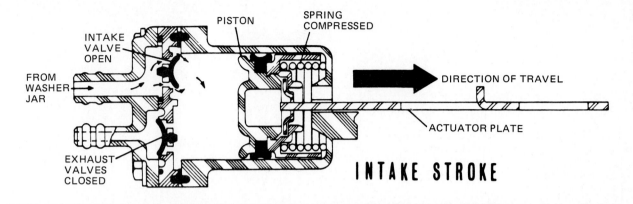

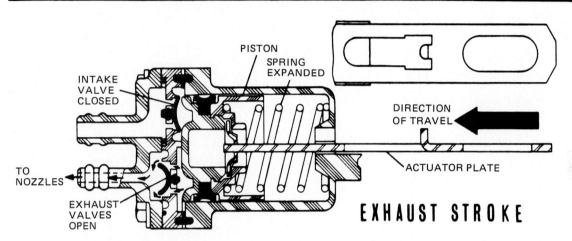

Figure 14-31.   Washer Pump Action. (*Courtesy of Chevrolet Motor Division, General Motors Corporation*)

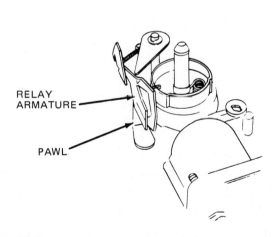

Figure 14-32.   Washer Pump Armature and Pawl. (*Courtesy of Chevrolet Motor Division, General Motors Corporation*)

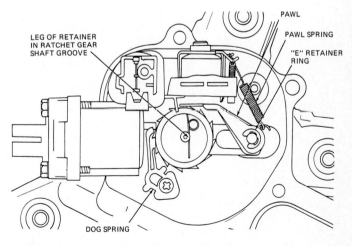

Figure 14-33.   Complete Washer Pump Assembly. (*Courtesy of Chevrolet Motor Division, General Motors Corporation*)

Test Questions

1. In an electronic cruise control, the controller and the servo increase engine speed when the servo:

   a) vent valve is closed and vacuum valve is open.

   b) vent and vacuum valves are open.

   c) vent valve is open and vacuum valve is closed.

2. If the brake pedal is depressed with the electronic cruise engaged, the resume feature may be used by:

   a) depressing the set button for 1 second.

   b) depressing the set button for 5 seconds.

   b) depressing the set button for 8 seconds.

3. In a vacuum-operated cruise control, the governor is driven by the speedometer cable.   T F

4. When a vacuum-operated cruise control is engaged, the brake release valve is closed.   T F

5. In a shunt field wiper motor, if the shunt field current is increased the armature speed will:

   a) increase.

   b) decrease.

   c) remain the same.

6. In a permanent-magnet wiper motor, current flows through more armature windings in the low-speed mode than in the high-speed mode.   T F

7. The outlet of the electric vacuum pump is connected to the:

   a) brake booster.

   b) vacuum storage tank.

   c) intake manifold.

8. The delay switch in the pulse-type windshield wiper system can vary the wiper pause from:

   a) 0 to 10 seconds.

   b) 0 to 25 seconds.

   c) 0 to 50 seconds.

9. When the windshield washer button is depressed on an integral washer pump system, the washer relay coil is energized.   T F

15

Instrument Panels, Voice-Alert Systems, and Trip Computers

Chapter Completion Objectives

1. Demonstrate an understanding of conventional instrument panel gauges and indicator lights.

2. Indicate a knowledge of light circuits.
3. Understand liquid crystal displays and vacuum fluorescent displays.
4. Display an understanding of voice-alert systems.
5. Describe the functions of a trip computer.

Conventional Instrument Clusters and Gauges

Instrument Clusters

Conventional instrument clusters may contain gauges or indicator lights that display various engine or vehicle operating conditions to the driver. Instru-

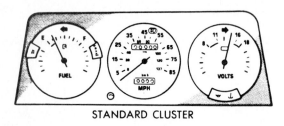

STANDARD CLUSTER

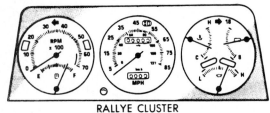

RALLYE CLUSTER

Figure 15-1. Instrument Clusters with Gauges. (*Courtesy of Chrysler Canada*)

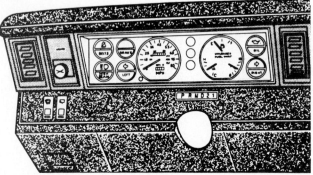

Figure 15-2. Instrument Cluster with Gauges and Indicator Lights. (*Courtesy of Chrysler Canada*)

ment clusters with gauges are shown in Figure 15-1, and an instrument cluster with indicator lights and gauges is illustrated in Figure 15-2.

Most instrument clusters have a printed circuit board to interconnect the various gauges or lights electrically. Plug-in type connectors are used to connect the vehicle wiring harness to the printed circuit board, as indicated in Figure 15-3.

Instrument Voltage Regulator

When gauges are used in an instrument cluster, an instrument voltage regulator (IVR) may be used to limit the voltage supplied to the gauges. The IVR contains a set of vibrating contacts. One of these contacts is mounted on a bimetal strip which is surrounded by a heating coil. Current flow through the heating coil heats the bimetal strip, which causes the strip to bend and open the points. This action reduces the voltage supplied to the gauges. When the bimetal strip cools, the points close.

The IVR supplies a pulsating 5 to 7V to the gauges regardless of the input voltage, which provides more stable gauge operation. A basic IVR circuit is pictured in Figure 15-4.

If the IVR is not grounded, it will supply full voltage to the gauges, which would result in damage to the gauges. Therefore, an instrument cluster with an IVR must always have a ground connection before the ignition switch is turned on.

Thermal Electric Gauges

Design and Operation

Thermal electric gauges contain a bimetal strip surrounded by a heating coil. This bimetal strip is connected to the pivoted gauge pointer. The heating coil is connected in series between the IVR and the gauge

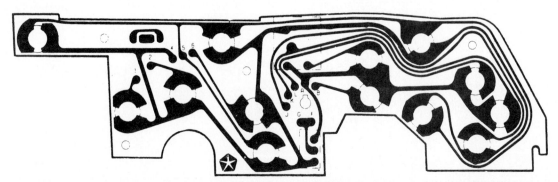

Figure 15-3. Instrument Cluster Printed Circuit Board. (*Courtesy of Chrysler Canada*)

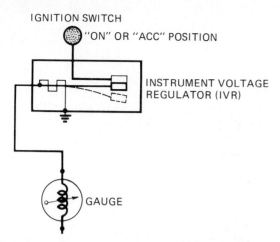

Figure 15-4. Instrument Voltage Regulator. (*Courtesy of Ford Motor Co.*)

sending unit, which contains a variable resistor. A thermal electric gauge circuit is pictured in Figure 15-5.

When the fuel level increases in the fuel tank, the sending unit float moves the sliding contact on the variable resistor to a lower resistance position. This action increases the current flow through the indicator heating coil and the sending resistor, which heats the bimetal strip. As this strip is heated, it bends and pushes the gauge pointer over to provide a higher reading. All thermal electric gauges operate in the same way. The temperature sending unit contains a sensing element that provides less resistance

as the unit is heated. The radio choke prevents radio static which could result from the vibrating contacts in the IVR.

Instrument Cluster Indicator Lights

Operation

When indicator lights are used to sense various engine functions, the sending switches contain an on/off switch which opens and closes the circuit from the indicator bulb to ground. Full system voltage is supplied to the input side of the indicator bulbs. The oil pressure sending unit contains a set of normally closed contacts attached to a diaphragm. When the ignition switch is turned on, current flows through the oil indicator light and the sending contacts to ground. If the engine is started and the oil pressure exceeds 3 to 7 psi (20.6 to 48.2 kPa), the oil pressure applied to the sending switch diaphragm opens the contacts and the oil light goes out. If the engine is running and the oil pressure drops below the value given above, the sending switch contacts close and the oil light comes on.

An instrument cluster with indicator lights and a thermal electric fuel gauge is shown in Figure 15-6.

The temperature sending switch contains a bimetal strip and a set of contacts. When the coolant temperature reaches 230°F (110°C) the bimetal strip

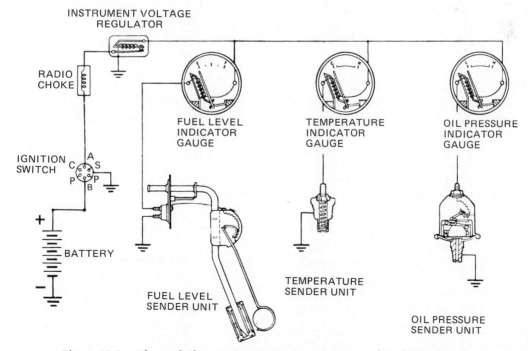

Figure 15-5. Thermal Electric Gauge Circuit. (*Courtesy of Ford Motor Co.*)

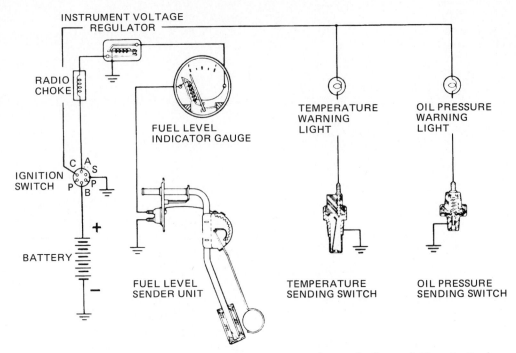

Figure 15-6. Instrument Cluster with Indicator Lights and Thermal Electric Fuel Gauge. (*Courtesy of Ford Motor Co.*)

bends and closes the contacts, which illuminates the temperature warning light.

Electromagnetic Gauges

Design and Operation

Electromagnetic gauges contain two electromagnets, and a permanent magnet is attached to the gauge pointer. The variable resistor in the tank sending unit is connected in series with the empty coil. A movable contact on the sending unit resistor and the full coil are both connected to ground. When the fuel tank is empty, sending unit resistance is low and current flows through the empty coil and the sending unit resistor to ground. The empty coil magnetism attracts the permanent magnet on the gauge pointer, so that the pointer moves to the empty position, as indicated in Figure 15-7.

A full fuel tank results in high sending unit resistance. Under this condition current flows through the empty coil and the full coil to ground, because the sending unit resistance is higher than the full coil resistance. Since the full coil has more turns than the empty coil, the full coil has a stronger magnetic field, which attracts the gauge pointer to the full position.

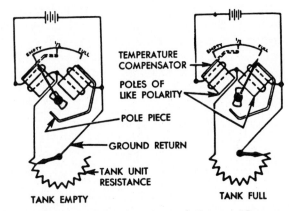

Figure 15-7. Electromagnetic Fuel Gauge. (*Courtesy of Pontiac Motor Division, General Motors Corporation*)

Light Circuits

Headlight Circuit

Many headlight circuits have a circuit breaker mounted in the headlight switch. The dimmer switch directs current flow to the low-beam or high-beam filaments in the headlights when the light switch is turned on, as indicated in Figure 15-8.

The headlight circuit in Figure 15-8 has two outer headlights which contain low- and high-beam

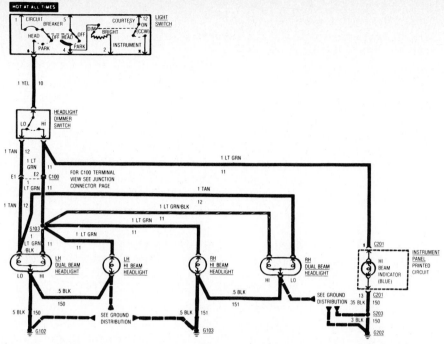

Figure 15-8. Headlight Circuit. (*Courtesy of Pontiac Motor Division, General Motors Corporation*)

filaments and two inner headlights which have high-beam filaments. The two inner headlights are not used on some vehicles.

Some 1986 and later model cars have four headlights with single low-beam filaments in the outer headlights and single high-beam filaments in the inner headlights. Some of these later model cars have replaceable headlight bulbs rather than sealed headlight units.

Tail Lights, License Lights, and Marker Lights

A tail light fuse in the fuse block supplies voltage to the tail light terminal on the headlight switch. When the headlight switch is extended to the first or second position, voltage is supplied to the tail lights, license lights, and marker lights. Many tail light bulbs contain the tail light and stoplight filaments, as indicated in Figure 15-9.

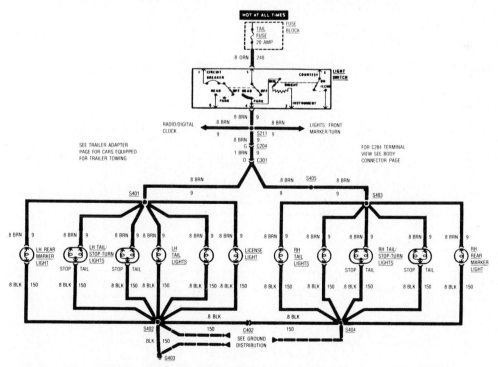

Figure 15-9. Tail Light, License Light, and Marker Light Circuits. (*Courtesy of Pontiac Motor Division, General Motors Corporation*)

Signal Light and Stoplight Circuits

When the ignition switch is turned on, voltage is available through the turn signal fuse and flasher to the signal light switch. When the signal light switch is moved to the left-turn position, current flows through the switch to the left-front and rear signal light bulbs and the left-turn indicator bulb to ground. Current also flows through the left-front marker bulb to ground.

One of the signal light flasher contacts is mounted on a bimetal strip which is surrounded by a heating coil. When the current flow heats the bimetal strip, the flasher produces a pulsating action similar to the instrument voltage limiter. A specific number of signal light flashes per second is provided by the pulsating action of the flasher.

The signal light fuse, flasher, switch, and front lights are illustrated in Figure 15-10.

In many signal light systems, the rear signal lights and stoplights use the same bulb filaments.

When the signal light lever is moved to the right-turn position, current flows through the switch to the right signal light bulbs, indicator bulb, and marker bulb. The flasher provides the necessary pulsating action for the right signal lights. If the hazard signal switch is turned on, voltage is supplied to all the signal light bulbs through the hazard flasher and signal light switch.

When the brake pedal is depressed with the signal light lever in the center position, voltage is supplied through the brake light switch and signal light switch contacts to the rear stoplights and signal lights. When the brakes are applied with the signal lights flashing on one side, voltage is supplied through the brake light switch and signal light contact to the stoplights on the opposite side of the vehicle.

A rear lighting diagram is given in Figure 15-11. Point A in the diagram indicates where the rear wiring is connected to point A on the front wiring diagram in Figure 15-10.

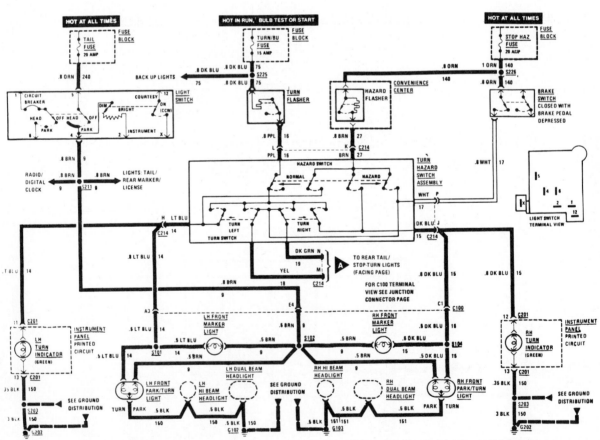

Figure 15-10.   Signal Lights, Front-End Lighting. (*Courtesy of Pontiac Motor Division, General Motors Corporation*)

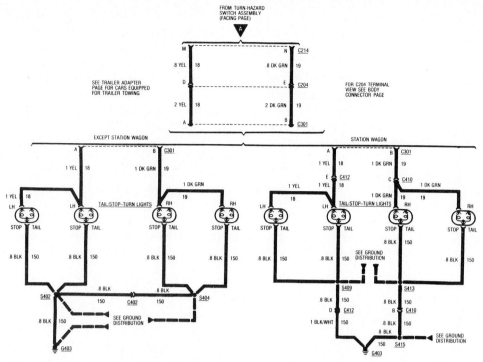

Figure 15-11. Signal Lights, Rear-End Lighting. (*Courtesy of Pontiac Motor Division, General Motors Corporation*)

Types of Electronic Instrumentation Displays

Light-Emitting Diodes

A light-emitting diode (LED) is a diode that emits light as electric current flows through it. Small dot-

ted segments are arranged in the LED display so that numbers and letters can be formed when selected segments are turned on. The LEDs usually emit red light and can be seen easily in the dark; however, they are less visible in direct sunlight. The tachometer on the electronic instrument cluster in Figure 15-12 has 36 LEDs.

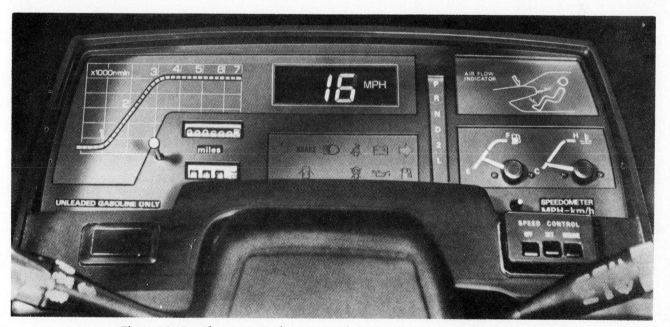

Figure 15-12. Electronic Tachometer with LEDs. (*Courtesy of Chrysler Canada*)

Liquid Crystal Displays

The liquid crystal display (LCD) uses polarized light from a nematic liquid crystal to display numbers and characters. An LCD display uses extremely low electrical power, but it requires backlighting to be viewed in the dark.

A complete LCD instrument display is illustrated in Figure 15-13. The retainer is made of heat-resistant mineral and glass-filled polyester and provides a closely dimensioned support for the LCD cells. A dark background is used on the nematic LCDs, and active areas change from dark to clear when they are energized. Polarizers in the LCDs provide the proper balance of contrast, transmission, and hue. The protective matte film on the front surface of the LCDs reduces reflections and provides resistance to scratches and chemicals.

A thin polycarbonate transflector is mounted behind the LCD to provide color. The front surface of the transflector is silk-screened with translucent fluorescent inks which make use of front-incident ambient light and rear-incident backlighting to obtain proper day and night intensity levels.

Backlighting is achieved with the use of clear acrylic light pipes. Light entrance areas and special optical patterns on the rear surfaces of the light pipes provide optimum backlighting balance and intensity. White polycarbonate reflectors are placed behind the light pipes to use the light escaping from their rear surfaces.

Hundreds of individual electrical connections

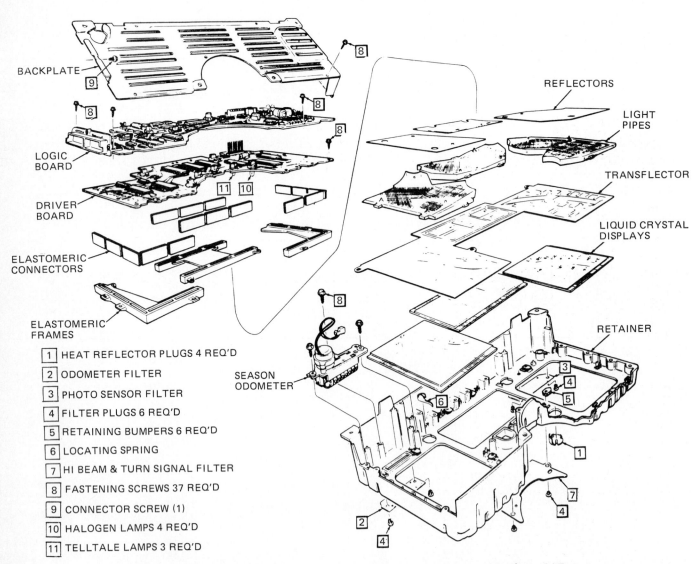

BACKPLATE
LOGIC BOARD
DRIVER BOARD
ELASTOMERIC CONNECTORS
ELASTOMERIC FRAMES
REFLECTORS
LIGHT PIPES
TRANSFLECTOR
LIQUID CRYSTAL DISPLAYS
RETAINER
SEASON ODOMETER

1 HEAT REFLECTOR PLUGS 4 REQ'D
2 ODOMETER FILTER
3 PHOTO SENSOR FILTER
4 FILTER PLUGS 6 REQ'D
5 RETAINING BUMPERS 6 REQ'D
6 LOCATING SPRING
7 HI BEAM & TURN SIGNAL FILTER
8 FASTENING SCREWS 37 REQ'D
9 CONNECTOR SCREW (1)
10 HALOGEN LAMPS 4 REQ'D
11 TELLTALE LAMPS 3 REQ'D

Figure 15-13. Liquid Crystal Display Components. (Reference taken from SAE paper No. 830041. *Reprinted with Permission of Society of Automotive Engineers, © 1983*)

are made through the elastometric connectors which make contact between the indium tin oxide conductor pads on the LCDs to corresponding contacts on the driver board.

The driver board contains eight static LCD driver integrated circuits (ICs), which are individually responsible for driving 32 LCD segments.

The microprocessor on the logic board receives input data from various sensors and switches and then determines whether each LCD segment should be on or off. A 12-pin connector is used to connect the logic board to the driver board, whereas a 24-pin and a 36-pin connector complete the electrical connections between the microprocessor and the electrical system.

The inputs to the microprocessor in the LCD instrument cluster and the output control functions are outlined in block form in Figure 15-14.

The front of the LCD instrument cluster is pictured in Figure 15-15. The switch and telltale console which is mounted near the LCD instrument cluster is shown in Figure 15-16.

The LCD instrument cluster is continuously backlit by four halogen lamps. Their intensity is automatically controlled by pulse width modulation to provide proper display intensity under varied natural lighting conditions. A photocell in the upper-left corner senses natural light conditions, and the microprocessor then determines the correct pulse width cycle for the halogen lamps, which provides the proper LCD display intensity.

When the ignition switch is turned on, the LCD cluster is lit at full intensity for two seconds and all the LCD segments are activated. During this time the microprocessor measures all inputs so it can display them immediately after the initialization sequence. The driver may adjust the brilliance of the LCD display by rotating the rheostat on the headlight switch.

Liquid Crystal Display Functions

Vehicle Speed

The speedometer displays vehicle speed in both digital and analog bar graph form. Metric or English values may be selected on the LCD displays with the Metric/English switch on the switch and telltale console. The yellow digital speedometer display indicates speed from 0 to 157 miles per hour (MPH) or 0 to 255 kilometers per hour (KPH). A green 41-segment bar graph with white graphics displays speed from 5 to 85 MPH (8 to 137 KPH). A multipole per-

manent-magnet speed sensor in the transaxle provides a speed signal to the LCD microprocessor.

The odometer is driven with a stepper motor. A trip odometer is updated every 0.1 mile (mi) or 0.1 kilometer (km). This odometer counts from 0 to 999.9 mi (or km), and then from 1,000 to 4,000 mi (1,000 to 6,436 km). The trip odometer is set on zero when the reset button is depressed.

Engine Speed

The tachometer displays engine revolutions per minute (rpm) in analog and digital forms. Yellow digits will display engine speed from 0 to 7,000 rpm. A 31-segment bar graph is green from 0 to 4,300 rpm, yellow to 5,100 rpm, and red to 6,000 rpm. Vehicle speed and engine speed displays are updated 16 times per second. An input signal from the high-energy ignition (HEI) module is used by the microprocessor to control the tachometer displays.

Oil Pressure and Temperature

The driver can select an oil pressure or oil temperature reading on the LCD cluster with the selector switch on the switch and telltale console. Oil pressure displays range from 0 to 80 psi (0 to 560 kPa), while oil temperature displays read from 149° to 320°F (65° to 160°C). When the oil temperature exceeds 300°F (149°C), an out-of-normal-limits warning is activated on the oil display.

Coolant Temperature and Volts

Coolant temperature or a voltage reading can be selected on the LCD display when the appropriate selector button is depressed on the switch and telltale console. Coolant temperature is displayed from 104° to 302°F (40° to 150°C), and electrical system voltage is displayed in the 11.5 to 16.5V range. When coolant temperature exceeds 255°F (124°C), an out-of-normal-limits warning is shown on the temperature display.

Fuel Economy

Instant or average fuel economy is displayed in the lower-right LCD quadrant. This display indicates miles per gallon (MPG) or liters per 100 kilometers (L/100 km). Speed sensor pulses are counted by the LCD microprocessor to determine the distance travelled.

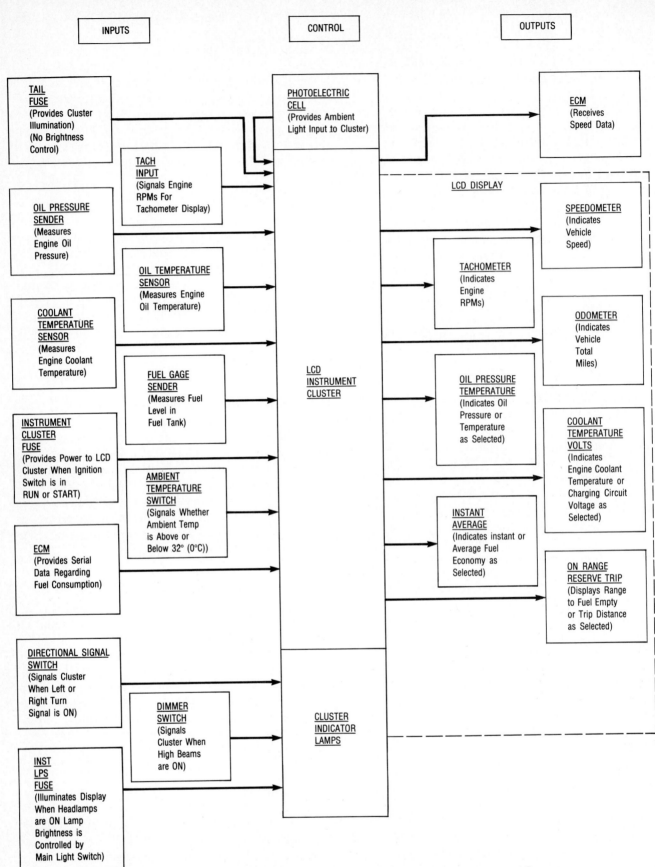

Figure 15-14. Inputs and Outputs, LCD Instrument Cluster Microprocessor. (*Courtesy of Chevrolet Motor Division, General Motors Corporation*)

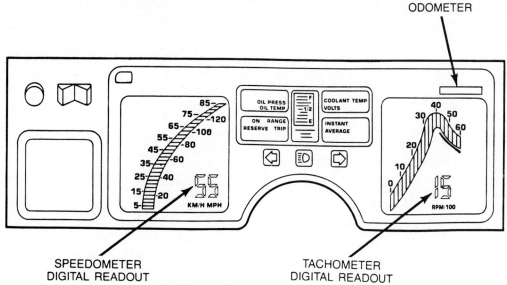

Figure 15-15.   LCD Instrument Cluster. (*Courtesy of Chevrolet Motor Division, General Motors Corporation*)

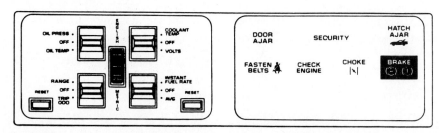

Figure 15-16.   Switch and Telltale Console Used with LCD Instrument Cluster. (Reference taken from SAE paper No. 830041. *Reprinted with Permission of Society of Automotive Engineers,* © 1983)

The electronic control module (ECM) on the vehicle controls the fuel system. (Refer to Chapter 17 for an explanation of the ECM.) A serial data link from the ECM to the LCD microprocessor provides the necessary information regarding the amount of fuel consumed. This signal is updated each 0.675 second, and the instant fuel economy display is updated each 0.75 second. Average fuel economy is computed from the distance travelled and the fuel used since the reset button was depressed.

Fuel Level

An illuminated bar graph fuel gauge is located in the center of the LCD cluster. When the fuel tank is full, all the bars are brightly illuminated. As the fuel level is lowered in the tank, the bars gradually fade out from the top down. An amber low-fuel warning light is activated when only two bars remain illuminated. When this occurs, the lower left reading in the LCD display switches from trip distance, or range, to a display of the distance travelled with the low-fuel warning activated. Miles or kilometers may be displayed in this reserve fuel mode. When two bars are left illuminated on the fuel gauge, the range display will read zero. At higher levels in the fuel tank, the range display indicates the distance that may be travelled on the fuel remaining in the tank.

If the vehicle is operating in the reserve fuel mode, the driver can display the trip odometer reading for 5 seconds by selecting "off" or "range" and then switching to "trip odometer." After 5 seconds this display changes back to display the distance travelled since the low-fuel warning was activated.

Vacuum Fluorescent Displays

Operation

A vacuum fluorescent display (VFD) generates its light by the same basic principles as a television picture tube. In the VFD a heated filament emits electrons which strike a phosphorescent material and emit a blue-green light. The filament is a resistance wire that is heated by electric current. A coating on the heated filament emits electrons which are accelerated by the electric field of the accelerating grid. The anode is charged with a high voltage, which attracts the electrons from the grid. A VFD computer supplies high voltage to the specific anode segments needed to emit light for any given message.

The operating principles of a VFD are shown in Figure 15-17.

The brightness of the VFD may be intensified by increasing the voltage on the accelerating grid. Another method of controlling VFD brilliance is pulse width timing. When this method is used, the VFD is turned on and off very rapidly. A shorter on-time dims the display, whereas a longer on-time increases the brilliance.

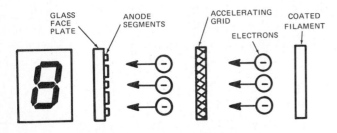

VACUUM FLUORESCENT DISPLAY (VFD)

Figure 15-17.   Vacuum Fluorescent Display Principles. *(Courtesy of Chrysler Canada)*

Shock can damage a VFD display; therefore, they must be handled with care.

A typical VFD is pictured in Figure 15-18.

Chrysler 11-Function Voice-Alert System

Operation

This system provides audible messages through the radio speaker regarding eleven vehicle conditions. The messages that may be provided are the following:

1. Your headlights are on.
2. Don't forget your keys.
3. Your washer fluid is low.
4. Your fuel is low.
5. Your electrical system is malfunctioning. Prompt service is required.
6. Your parking brake is on.
7. A door is ajar.
8. Please fasten your seat belts.
9. Your engine is overheating. Prompt service is required.
10. Your engine oil pressure is low. Prompt service is required.
11. All monitored systems are functioning.
12. Thank you.

Message number 1 is heard after the following sequence of events.

1. The driver's door is closed.
2. The headlights are turned on.
3. The ignition switch is turned on and off.

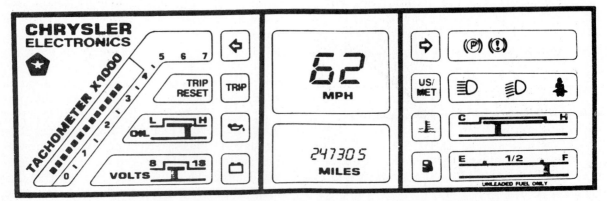

Figure 15-18.   Vacuum Fluorescent Display. *(Courtesy of Chrysler Canada)*

4. The key is removed from ignition switch.

5. The driver's door is opened.

Message number 5 occurs if the charging system is below 11.75 volts and the engine is running above idle speed for several minutes. Message number 9 is heard if the engine temperature is above 270°F (132°C) for one minute and engine speed is above idle for one minute. Message number 10 is provided if the oil pressure is low for a minimum of two seconds and the engine is running. Forward vehicle motion is necessary, in addition to the other applicable conditions, before messages number 6, 8, or 11 are heard. Message number 7 is provided if a door is ajar and the vehicle is in forward or reverse motion.

The heart of the electronic voice-alert system is a microprocessor, or module, mounted above the glove compartment. A switch or sensor located in each monitored component sends the necessary input signal to the module. If an unsatisfactory signal is received, the control module provides the appropriate message. Forward and reverse vehicle motion signals are provided by a speed sensor and the backup light switch.

A volume control is located on the underside of the module. The on/off switch on the module cancels the voice signal if the switch is moved toward the rear of the vehicle. This switch is accessible through an opening at the top right inside the glove box. A pulsating beep is provided before the audible message, and a tone follows the message. The on/off module switch only cancels the audible message.

The voice-alert module is accessible through the glove box opening after the glove box has been removed, as indicated in Figure 15-19.

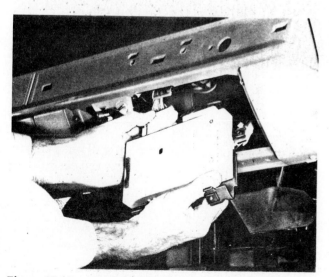

Figure 15-19.   Voice-Alert Module. (*Courtesy of Chrysler Canada*)

Chrysler 24-Function Monitor and Voice-Alert System

Operation

The 24-function message center is referred to as an Electronic Monitor. This system provides the driver with visual and audible warnings. Visual messages are presented on a two-line, ten-character blue-green vacuum fluorescent display. Orange- and lemon-colored symbols are activated simultaneously. Audible messages are provided by a voice synthesis microprocessor.

The monitor system contains an electronic monitor module with two vacuum fluorescent displays and an electronic voice-alert microprocessor or module. The monitor module is located in the center dash area, and the voice-alert module is located above the glove box.

This system is capable of displaying and verbalizing 24 warning conditions of the vehicle. The actual number of warning conditions varies depending on the vehicle options. Messages displayed and verbalized include three categories as follows:

1. *Safety*: Passenger door ajar, driver door ajar, hatch ajar, fasten seat belts.

2. *Operation*: Oil pressure low, engine temperature high, fuel level low, transmission pressure low, voltage low.

3. *Convenience*: Coolant level low, brake fluid low, disc brake pads worn, washer fluid low, rear washer fluid low, engine oil level low, headlight out, brake lamp out, tail lamp out, parking brake engaged, keys in ignition, exterior lights on.

The electronic monitor module senses various defective conditions from the inputs. When a defective condition exists, this module displays a warning message and sends a tone and talk signal to the voice-alert module. This causes the voice-alert module to generate a short tone and provide the appropriate audible message. When more than one defect exists, the same sequence is followed for each fault and each message is displayed for 4 seconds. If the defect is driver-correctable, the monitor module signals the voice-alert module to provide a "thank-you" tone.

The voice-alert module does not generate tones through the radio speaker, as in the 11-function system. Instead, an external sound transducer in the voice-alert module provides the tone signals. If the radio is on, the radio is interrupted and the audible messages are delivered through the radio speaker, as in the 11-function system.

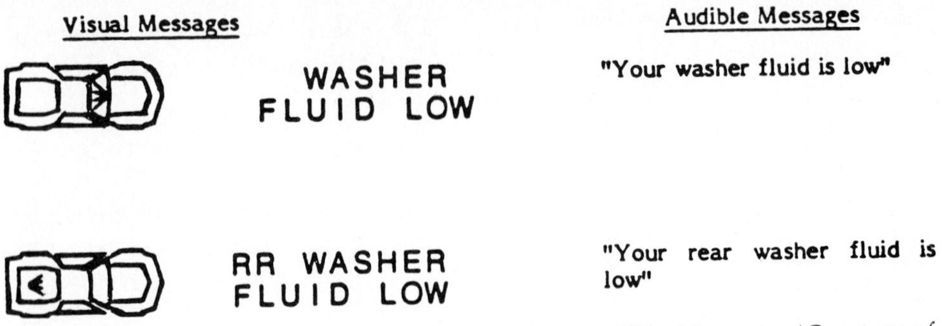

Visual Messages   **Audible Messages**

    WASHER   "Your washer fluid is low"
                        FLUID LOW

                        RR WASHER   "Your rear washer fluid is
                        FLUID LOW   low"

Figure 15-20. Visual Messages and Corresponding Audible Messages. (*Courtesy of Chrysler Canada*)

Two visual messages and audible messages are shown in Figure 15-20.

Requirements to Obtain Messages

A "keys in ignition" or "exterior lamps on" message is provided if these conditions are present and the driver's door is opened with the ignition switch in the off, lock, or "acc" positions. The audible message is followed by a pulsating tone for "keys in ignition," or a continuous tone for "exterior lamps on," and the tones continue until the condition is corrected.

A "fasten seat belts" message is provided for 6 seconds when the ignition switch is turned on. It continues to be displayed if the driver's seat belt is not buckled, or until the car has been moved 16 to 24 in. (40.6 to 60.9 cm), at which time the audible message is given.

The "monitored systems OK" message is provided when the ignition switch has been on for 6 seconds and no defects have been found.

Some visual messages, such as "park brake engaged," all "door ajar" messages, and "trunk or hatch ajar," are displayed when the ignition switch is on and the corresponding fault is sensed. The audible message is provided with the visual message after the vehicle has been moved 16 to 24 in. (40.6 to 60.9 cm). When the fault is corrected, a short "thank-you" tone is heard.

Faults in the following systems result in visual and audible messages if the ignition switch is on and the defective condition has been sensed for 15 seconds: "washer fluid low," "rear washer fluid low," "fuel level low," "coolant level low," "brake fluid low," "disc brake pads worn." After the defective condition has been corrected, the ignition switch must be turned off to clear these messages from the monitor module.

Any lamp message, such as "headlamp out," "tail lamp out," or "brake lamp out," are displayed and heard if the ignition switch is on and the fault has been sensed for 3.5 seconds. Correction of the fault clears the failure message.

A "low oil pressure" message is provided if low oil pressure is sensed and the engine rpm is between 300 and 1,500 rpm. The failure message is cleared when the fault is corrected

The "engine temperature high" message is displayed and heard when the engine temperature is sensed high and engine rpm is above 300 for 30 seconds. A second-level audible message is heard after the same fault conditions are present for 60 seconds. The failure message is cleared when the fault is corrected or the engine speed drops below 300 rpm.

A "voltage low" audible and visual message is given if the battery voltage is below 12.35V and the engine speed is above 1,500 rpm for 15 seconds. The ignition switch must be turned off after the fault is corrected to clear this message.

When the transmission pressure is sensed low for 15 seconds and the engine speed is above 300 rpm with the vehicle not in reverse, a "low transmission pressure" audible and visual message is provided. The ignition switch must be turned off after the correction procedure to clear this message.

An "engine oil level low" audible and visual message is provided if the monitor module is powered by the time-delay relay (TDR) only and the engine oil level is sensed low. The TDR supplies power to the monitor module for a specific time period after the ignition is turned off. This message is also given with the ignition on and the TDR still on. The ignition switch must be turned off after the condition is corrected to clear the message.

A system-check button is located on front of the monitor. When this button is pushed twice within a 5-second interval, the system is muted and a mute-engaged message is displayed for 4 seconds. This message is only visual. The system may also be muted with the switch on the voice-alert module, as in the 11-function system. The functions of other

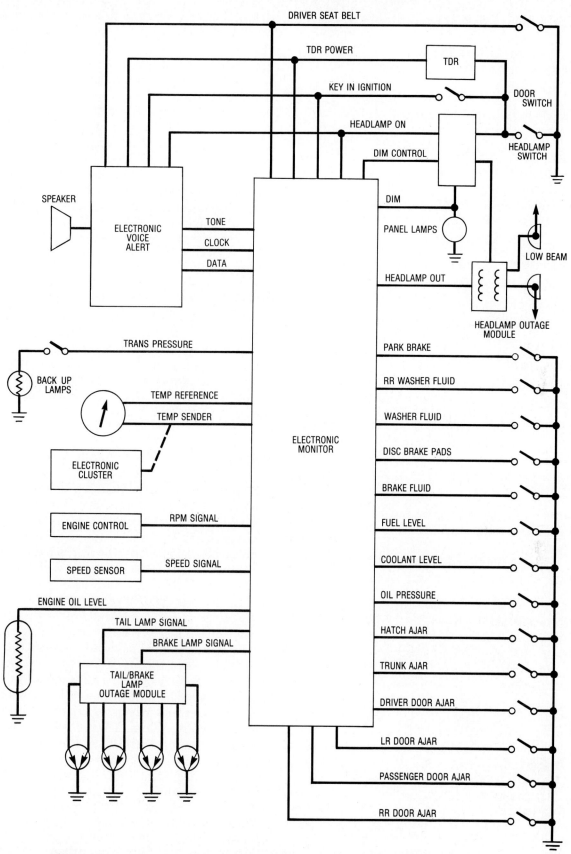

Figure 15-21. Chrysler 24-Function Monitor and Voice-Alert System. (*Courtesy of Chrysler Canada*)

voice-alert systems would be similar to the Chrysler systems.

The complete 24-function system is illustrated in Figure 15-21.

Chrysler Electronic Navigator

Functions

Most trip computers provide similar functions. The Chrysler trip computer, referred to as an electronic navigator, provides the following functions:

1. Miles until empty.
2. Estimated time to arrival and time of arrival.
3. Distance to destination.
4. Time, day, month, and date.
5. Present and average miles per gallon.
6. Fuel consumed.
7. Average speed.
8. Miles travelled.
9. Elapsed driving time.

The main components in the electronic navigator system are illustrated in Figure 15-22.

Inputs

The electronic navigator supplies the driver with trip information that is not supplied by standard instrumentation.

A "vehicle speed" and "distance travelled" signal is supplied from the speed sensor to the module

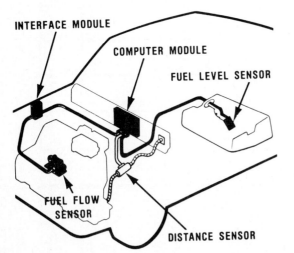

Figure 15-22. Electronic Navigator System Components. (*Courtesy of Chrysler Canada*)

in the navigator. This speed sensor signal is also used in the electronic fuel injection (EFI) system and the electronic voice-alert system. (The EFI system is explained in Chapter 18.)

An input signal regarding the amount of fuel consumed is sent from the logic module in the EFI system to the navigator module. On some trip computer systems, this signal is generated by a fuel sensor in the fuel line. The fuel gauge sending unit in the fuel tank sends an input signal to the navigator module in relation to the amount of fuel in the tank. This signal is transmitted on the G4 circuit.

The navigator control buttons and wiring diagram are illustrated in Figure 15-23.

Range Function

When the RANGE button is pressed, the navigator digital display indicates the number of miles that can be driven on the fuel remaining in the tank. The navigator module multiplies the amount of fuel in the tank by the projected fuel mileage to provide this calculation. An update of the range reading is provided every few seconds by the navigator module as fuel is used out of the tank.

Distance to Destination Function

The distance to destination (DEST) must be set before this function will operate. When the DEST is entered, the driver presses the DEST button and then presses the SET button within 5 seconds. This action causes the navigator display to indicate 0 miles. At this time, the DEST is entered with the appropriate numbered navigator buttons. When the SET button is pressed, the navigator module begins the countdown of distance travelled. The maximum distance setting is 9,999 miles (16,091 km). After the DEST is entered, the navigator displays the remaining DEST when the DEST button is pressed. When the destination is reached, the navigator displays "trip completed," followed by several audible tones.

The electronic navigator system is connected to the voice-alert system. The navigator displays U.S. or metric readings if the US/M button is pressed.

Time Function

When the engine is started or the TIME button is pressed, the navigator continuously displays the time of day, day of week, month of year, and day of month. The display can be reset by pressing the

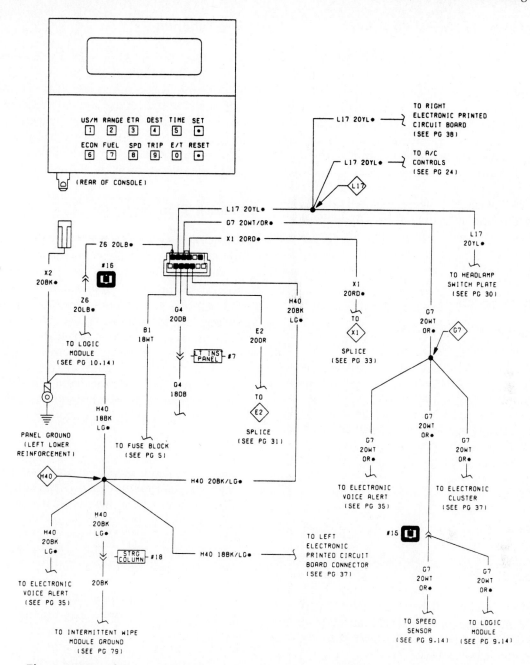

Figure 15-23.   Electronic Navigator Control Buttons and Wiring Diagram. (*Courtesy of Chrysler Candad*)

TIME button followed by the SET button within 5 seconds. When this action is taken, an arrow appears on the display which indicates that the hours are to be set. The hour display is advanced if the RESET button is pressed, or the US/M button will back up the display. After the hour display has been set, the SET button is pressed again and the arrow points to the minute display. The same procedure may be used to advance or back up each display. When the min-

utes are set, the procedure is repeated for day, month, and date. When the entire time display is correct, the SET button is pressed a final time to establish the readings.

Any portion of the time display may be bypassed if the SET button is pressed until the arrow indicates the time function that requires setting. If the battery has been disconnected, the time display will require setting.

Estimated Time of Arrival Function

When the estimated time of arrival (ETA) button is pressed, the navigator displays the estimated driving time to destination for 5 seconds. After this time, the display switches to continuous reading of time and date of arrival at a previously entered destination. If the vehicle is operating at normal or high speeds, the navigator module calculates the ETA from the current vehicle speed. At low vehicle speeds, the module uses the trip average speed to make this calculation. If the ETA exceeds 100 hours, "trip over 100 hours" is displayed. When the destination has been passed, "trip completed" appears on the display.

Economy Function

If the economy (ECON) button is pressed, the average miles per gallon (MPG) since the last reset will be displayed for 5 seconds. After this time the display indicates the present MPG, and this reading is updated continuously. The navigator module will begin a new average MPG calculation if the RESET button is pressed while the average MPG is displayed. Updating of the average MPG reading occurs every 16 seconds, whereas the present MPG display is updated every 2 seconds.

Fuel Function

When the FUEL button is pressed, the navigator display indicates the number of gallons consumed since the last reset. The highest possible display reading is 999.9 gallons, and the display is updated every few seconds. A new fuel-consumed calculation is started if the RESET button is pressed within 5 seconds after the FUEL button is pressed.

Speed Function

When the speed (SPD) button is pressed, the average miles per hour (MPH) since the last reset is displayed. This reading is updated every 8 seconds, and the highest display is 85 MPH. If the RESET button is pressed within 5 seconds after the SPD button is pressed, a new average MPH calculation is initiated. Since low-speed ETA calculations are based on the average speed, the driver may wish to reset the average speed after the DEST is entered.

Trip Function

If the TRIP button is pressed, the navigator display indicates the accumulated trip miles since the RESET button was pressed. The maximum displayed mileage is 999.9 miles, and this reading is updated every .5 second. When this mileage is reached, the display returns to zero. A new trip mileage calculation is initiated if the RESET button is pressed within 5 seconds after the TRIP button is pressed.

Elapsed Time Function

When the elapsed time (E/T) button is pressed, the amount of driving time since the RESET button was pressed is indicated on the navigator display. The highest reading is 99 hours and 59 minutes. After this time is reached, the reading returns to zero. During the first hour after the RESET button has been pressed, the E/T is displayed in minutes and seconds. After this time, hours and minutes are shown on the E/T display. If the RESET button is pressed within 5 seconds after the E/T button is pressed, a new E/T calculation is initiated.

Reset Function

The reset button is used as previously described to clear various functions and begin new calculations. All trip information may be cleared simultaneously if the RESET button is pressed twice within 5 seconds after any of the following buttons are pressed: ECON, FUEL, SPD, TRIP, E/T. When this action is taken, the navigator display indicates "trip reset" for 5 seconds.

The instrument panel pictured in Figure 15-24 contains an electronic instrument cluster, electronic navigator, and the message center for the 24-function monitor and voice-alert system.

(Refer to Chapter 10 in *Automotive Principles: Repair and Service*, Volume II, for servicing and diagnosis of instrument panels, voice-alert systems, and trip computers. Refer to Chapter 18 for a description of an instrument panel cluster and lighting system that is interconnected with a body computer module (BCM).)

Test Questions

1. An instrument voltage regulator (IVR) limits the voltage supplied to the gauges to:

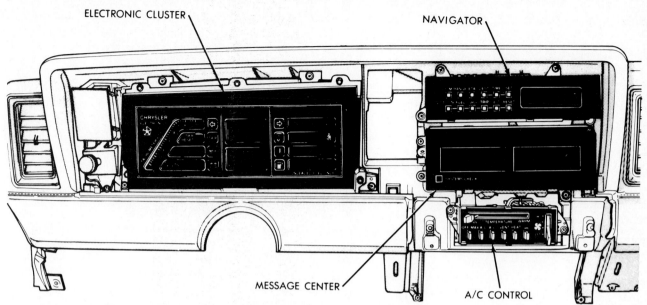

Figure 15-24. Instrument Panel with Electronic Cluster, Navigator, and Message Center. (*Courtesy of Chrysler Canada*)

a) 2 to 3V.

b) 5 to 7V.

c) 8 to 9V.

2. When the current flow increases through the winding in a thermal electric gauge, the gauge reading is higher.   T F

3. If the engine oil pressure is 15 psi (103 kPa), the oil indicator light will be on.   T F

4. A liquid crystal display (LCD) instrument cluster requires backlighting.   T F

5. In the LCD instrument cluster shown in Figure 15-15, the low-fuel warning light is activated when:

a) two bars are lit on the fuel gauge.

b) three bars are lit on the fuel gauge.

c) four bars are lit on the fuel gauge.

6. The brightness of a vacuum fluorescent display may be intensified by increasing the voltage applied to the _____ _____.

7. If the battery is disconnected, the navigator will maintain the correct time.   T F

8. If an instrument voltage regulator (IVR) is not grounded, it will result in:

a) damage to the gauges.

b) low gauge readings.

c) damage to the gauge wiring harness.

9. An input signal regarding the amount of fuel consumed is sent to the navigator module from the:

a) electric fuel pump.

b) logic module or fuel flow sensor.

c) fuel injectors.

10. The navigator displays the time function when the engine is started.   T F

16

Gasoline Fuel Systems

Chapter Completion Objectives

1. Describe volatility, octane rating, and air-fuel ratio as they relate to gasoline.
2. Define detonation and preignition.
3. Understand mechanical and electric fuel pumps.
4. Demonstrate a knowledge of the six carburetor systems.
5. Display an understanding of electric choke circuits.

Gasoline

Chemical Composition and Combustion

Any substance that contains only one type of atom is referred to as an element. For example, copper (CU) contains only CU atoms. The atom may be defined as the smallest particle into which an element can be divided and still retain its characteristics.

A compound is a substance which contains two or more types of atoms. The smallest particle of a compound is called a molecule. Gasoline is a compound that contains hydrogen and carbon atoms. Its chemical symbol is C_8H_{15}, which means that each molecule of gasoline contains 8 carbon atoms and 15 hydrogen atoms.

A precise quantity of gasoline must be mixed with oxygen in the air to ensure that combustion in the combustion chambers will be as complete as possible. When one gallon of gasoline is burned, 9,000 gallons of air are required to mix with the gasoline. Since this air-fuel ratio of 9,000:1 would be inconvenient to work with, it has been simplified. Air weighs 1 pound (lb) [.453 kilograms (kg)] per 100 gallons. Gasoline weighs approximately 6 lbs. (2.7 kg) per gallon. Therefore, 90 lbs. (40.7 kg) of air are required to burn 6 lbs. (2.7 kg) of gasoline. The gasoline air-fuel ratio may be expressed as 15:1, because 15 lbs. (6.7 kg) of air are required to burn 1 lb (.453 kg) of gasoline, as illustrated in Figure 16-1.

The preceding figures are approximate; the ideal air-fuel ratio is actually 14.7:1. Although the air-fuel ratio is varied by the carburetor according to operating requirements, such as for cold-start conditions,

the ideal ratio must be maintained to achieve satisfactory engine performance and economy. A lean air-fuel ratio of 18:1 contains an excessive amount of air in relation to the amount of gasoline. A rich air-fuel ratio of 10:1 would contain an excessive quantity of fuel in relation to the amount of air. The ideal air-fuel ratio may be referred to as the stoichiometric ratio.

When combustion of the air-fuel mixture takes place, the byproducts are carbon, carbon dioxide (CO_2), carbon monoxide (CO), and water. A small amount of oxides of nitrogen (NOx) is also formed as a result of the combustion process. [See Chapter 8 for a complete discussion of CO, NOx, and unburned hydrocarbons (HC), which are major automotive pollutants.]

Volatility

The ease with which a liquid vaporizes is referred to as its volatility. The volatility of a simple compound, such as water, is found by increasing the temperature of the water until it boils. A liquid that boils at a low temperature has high volatility, and one that boils at a high temperature has low volatility. A heavy oil with a boiling point of 600°F (315°C) has very low volatility. Water has relatively high volatility, because it boils at 212°F (100°C).

Gasoline is actually a blend of different hydrocarbon compounds which have boiling points that vary from 85°F (30°C) to 437°F (225°C). When gasoline is refined from crude oil, the various hydrocarbon compounds must be blended together to obtain the desired volatility.

Gasoline refiners will change the volatility of their gasoline in relation to climatic conditions. The gasoline that is sold in colder climates will have a greater percentage of highly volatile hydrocarbons to provide easier engine starting in cold weather. In hotter climates, gasoline must contain a higher percentage of less volatile hydrocarbons to avoid vapor lock in the fuel lines. Vapor lock occurs when the gasoline in the fuel lines changes to a vapor because of extremely high fuel line temperatures. Since automotive fuel pumps are designed to pump liquid gasoline, the engine will stop running when vapor forms in the fuel lines.

Correct gasoline volatility is also necessary to obtain satisfactory engine performance and economy. If the volatility of the gasoline is too low, the carburetor will not vaporize the gasoline properly and the fuel will condense on the intake manifold passages. Engine performance and economy will be

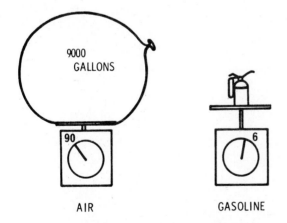

9000 GALS. ARE NEEDED TO BURN 1 GAL.
90 LBS. ARE NEEDED TO BURN 6 LBS.
15 LBS. ARE NEEDED TO BURN 1 LB.

Figure 16-1. Gasoline Air-Fuel Ratio. (*Courtesy of Chevrolet Motor Division, General Motors Corporation*)

reduced because liquid gasoline will not burn in the combustion chambers. If liquid gasoline enters the combustion chambers, it may get past the piston rings into the crankcase and contaminate the lubricating oil.

Detonation and Preignition

The burning of the air-fuel mixture is initiated when the spark occurs at the spark plug electrodes. The air-fuel mixture should burn progressively across the combustion chamber, as illustrated in Figure 16-2.

Under certain conditions combustion will begin normally but the remaining air-fuel mixture will suddenly explode before the flame front reaches the unburned mixture, as indicated in Figure 16-3. This sudden explosion drives the piston against the cylinder wall with a terrific force and causes severe engine knocking. This is referred to as detonation. Some of the causes of detonation are: extremely high intake air temperature, excessive carbon buildup in the cylinders, or a fuel with a low octane rating.

If the spark occurs too soon at the spark plug electrodes, the burning air-fuel mixture will try to drive the piston back down in the compression stroke. This process is referred to as preignition, and it could be caused by the initial timing being too far advanced. Preignition may also be caused by carbon buildup in the cylinder, which can become ex-

tremely hot and ignite the air-fuel mixture before the spark occurs at the spark plug electrodes.

Detonation and preignition both result in a knocking sound from the engine and can cause damage to engine components, such as pistons and connecting rod bearings.

Compression Ratio

The compression ratio is the ratio of the volume in the cylinder when the piston is at bottom dead center (BDC) compared to the cylinder volume with the piston at top dead center (TDC). For example, if the cylinder volume is 45 cubic inches (cu in.) [733 cubic centimeters (cm^3)] with the piston at BDC and 5 cu in. (81 cm^3) when the piston is at TDC, the compression ratio is 9:1. Higher compression ratios increase the pressure in the cylinders on the compression and power strokes, which causes an increase in engine power. Detonation is more likely to occur with higher compression ratios because the increased cylinder pressures cause higher temperatures in the combustion chambers.

Octane Rating

The octane rating of gasoline indicates the detonation qualities of the fuel. When gasoline has a higher octane rating, it has improved anti-knock, or anti-

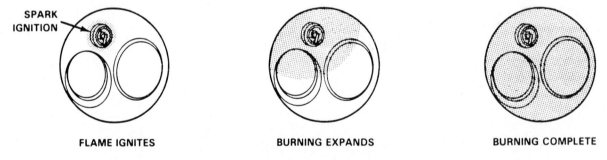

Figure 16-2.   Normal Combustion. (*Courtesy of Chrysler Canada*)

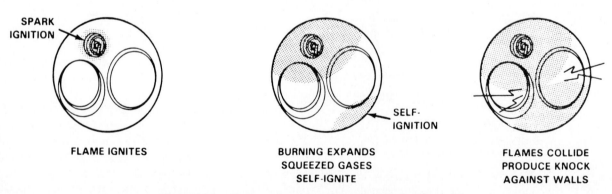

Figure 16-3.   Detonation. (*Courtesy of Chrysler Canada*)

detonation, qualities. Two reference fuels, isooctane and heptane, are used in the octane rating process. Isooctane is extremely resistant to detonation and heptane detonates very easily.

To establish the octane rating for a fuel, a specially designed engine with a variable compression ratio is operated on the fuel being rated, and the compression ratio is increased until a specific severity of detonation occurs. A mixture of the two reference fuels is used to fuel the test engine until the same severity of detonation is experienced under identical operating conditions. The percentage of isooctane in the fuel mixture that produced identical detonation conditions is the octane rating of the gasoline being tested. If a mixture of 90 percent isooctane and 10 percent heptane produces identical detonation conditions, the gasoline being tested has an octane rating of 90.

The research octane number (RON) is calculated with the variable compression test engine operating at low speed and cooler intake air temperatures, while the motor octane number (MON) is determined with the engine operating at higher speed and increased inlet air temperature. The MON is always lower than the RON. The advertised or road octane number is the average of the RON and MON. For example, if a gasoline has a MON of 84 and a RON of 92, it has a road octane rating of 88.

Tetraethyl lead is added to regular leaded gasoline to prevent the fuel from detonating. However, leaded gasoline usually causes the catalytic converter to be inoperative once the vehicle has been driven for a few hundred miles. Hence, unleaded gasoline must be used in vehicles that are equipped with catalytic converters. The road octane rating of unleaded gasoline is 87 to 91, and regular leaded gasoline may have an octane rating of 87 to 89. Engines that are designed for unleaded gasoline, or regular leaded gasoline, will usually have compression ratios of 8:1 to 8.5:1. Premium unleaded gasoline will have a road octane rating of 90 to 92, and it could be used in engines with compression ratios as high as 9.3:1.

Unleaded gasolines require additional refining processes, which involves higher costs. In some states or provinces, refiners are allowed to add very small quantities of manganese to increase the octane rating of unleaded gasoline. Environmental regulations prevent the use of manganese in other locations. If manganese is used as a fuel additive, the spark plugs develop carbon deposits that are reddish brown in color.

Refining standards and octane ratings vary among states because of climatic conditions, altitudes, and environmental regulations.

Mechanical Fuel Pumps

Design and Operation

The mechanical fuel pump contains a pivoted rocker-arm and lever assembly that is linked to a diaphragm, as illustrated in Figure 16-4.

The fuel pump is bolted to the side of the engine block, and the rocker arm is operated by a camshaft lobe. An inlet valve and an outlet valve are mounted in a sealed chamber above the diaphragm. When the cam lobe moves the rocker arm inward toward the pump housing, the diaphragm is pulled down by the rocker arm and lever, which creates a vacuum above the diaphragm. The pressure difference between atmospheric pressure above the fuel in the tank and vacuum in the fuel pump causes the fuel to move from the tank through the inlet line and valve into the area above the diaphragm. (See Chapter 8 for an explanation of fuel tank venting systems.)

When the lowest portion of the cam lobe is against the rocker arm, it returns to the original position so that the diaphragm is forced upward by the diaphragm spring (item 6 in Figure 16-4). Under this condition pressure is exerted on the fuel above the diaphragm, which forces the inlet valve to close and opens the outlet valve to allow the fuel to flow through the outlet line to the carburetor. The fuel pump pressure is determined by the diaphragm spring. When the required level of fuel is present in

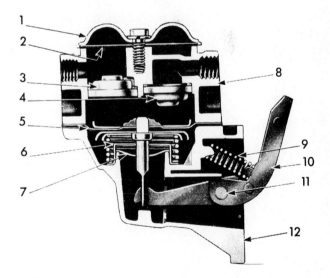

1. Pulsator Cover
2. Pulsator Diaphragm
3. Outlet Valve
4. Inlet Valve
5. Diaphragm Assembly
6. Diaphragm Spring
7. Oil Seal
8. Fuel Cover
9. Rocker Arm Return Spring
10. Rocker Arm and Lever Assembly
11. Pivot Pin
12. Pump Body

Figure 16-4. Mechanical Fuel Pump. (*Courtesy of Chevrolet Motor Division, General Motors Corporation*)

the carburetor float bowl, the needle valve in the carburetor closes and prevents any further flow of fuel from the pump. (The carburetor float system is described later in this chapter.) When the carburetor needle valve closes, the pressure in the outlet fuel line increases and holds the diaphragm down against the diaphragm spring.

The diaphragm rod is slotted where it is connected to the lever assembly. When the diaphragm is held downward, the lever moves up and down the diaphragm rod slot, but does not move the diaphragm. Therefore, the fuel pump pressure is limited to 4 to 7 psi (27.6 to 48.2 kPa). When fuel is used out of the carburetor float bowl, the needle valve opens and allows fuel to flow from the fuel pump to the carburetor. Under this condition the pressure in the outlet line decreases, and the diaphragm moves upward, which causes the fuel pump to return to its normal pumping operation.

The rocker-arm return spring keeps the rocker arm in constant contact with the camshaft lobe. A broken return spring would cause the rocker arm to clatter against the camshaft lobe. The pulsator diaphragm smooths out the pulsations in fuel pump pressure.

Electric Fuel Pumps

Design and Operation

Most electric fuel pumps are mounted with the fuel gauge sending unit in the fuel tank, as pictured in

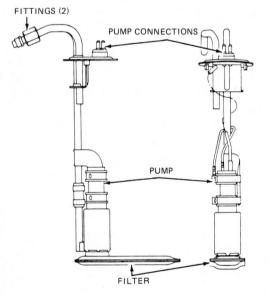

Figure 16-5.   Electric Fuel Pump. (*Courtesy of Ford Motor Co.*)

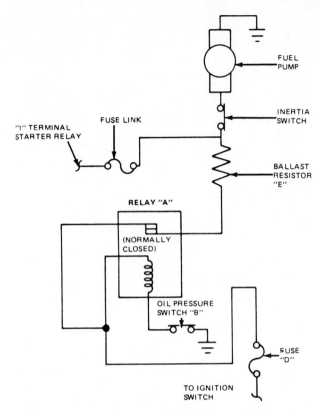

Figure 16-6.   Electric Fuel Pump Circuit. (*Courtesy of Ford Motor Co.*)

Figure 16-5. The impeller in the pump is driven by an electric motor. The pump assembly must be replaced as a unit.

While the engine is being cranked, full battery voltage is supplied from the "I" terminal of the starter relay through the fuse link and inertia switch to the fuel pump motor, as shown in Figure 16-6. When the engine starts, oil pressure switch "B" closes and current flows through the winding in relay "A" and the oil pressure switch to ground. This closes the points in relay "A" so that a reduced voltage is supplied through the ballast resistor and the inertia switch to the fuel pump motor.

If the vehicle is involved in a collision, the inertia switch opens the circuit to the fuel pump motor as a safeguard against fire.

Carburetor Principles

Vacuum

Airflow through a pipe creates a pressure drop within the pipe that is proportional to the speed of the air. To measure the difference between atmospheric pressure and the pressure within the pipe, a U-tube

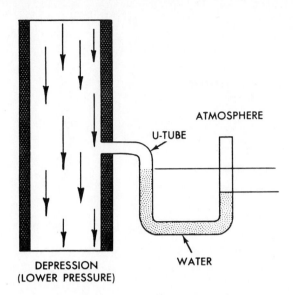

Figure 16-7. Measurement of Pressure Difference. (*Courtesy of Chevrolet Motor Division, General Motors Corporation*)

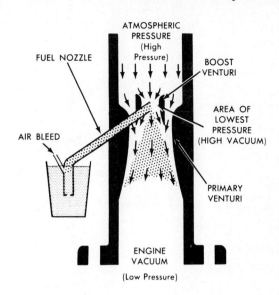

Figure 16-8. Venturi Principle. (*Courtesy of Chevrolet Motor Division, General Motors Corporation*)

that is partially filled with water may be inserted into the pipe, as illustrated in Figure 16-7. The difference in pressure, referred to as vacuum, is expressed by measuring the distance in inches between the two heads of water. Atmospheric pressure forces the water in the U-tube toward the low pressure area, or vacuum.

Low vacuum is usually expressed in inches of water, but high vacuum, such as manifold vacuum, is usually measured in inches of mercury (in. Hg) because mercury is $13\frac{1}{2}$ times heavier than water and thus provides a more convenient way for measuring larger pressure differences. In the metric system, vacuum, or pressure difference, is expressed in kilopascals (kPa).

Venturi Principle

A venturi is formed by a narrow area in the air passage through the carburetor. The venturi increases the air velocity and thus creates a pressure drop, or vacuum, in the venturi area. Most carburetors have a boost venturi inside the main venturi which creates a higher vacuum than the main venturi alone.

The air velocity and the vacuum in the venturi increase in proportion to engine speed. The fuel nozzle is positioned in the boost venturi, and the fuel is moved out of the nozzle by atmospheric pressure above the fuel in the bowl and vacuum in the venturi. An air bleed in the fuel nozzle partially atomizes the fuel before it is discharged into the venturi, as indicated in Figure 16-8.

Atomization and Vaporization

Gasoline must be mixed with oxygen in the air to form a combustible mixture. Before gasoline can be used as fuel for an engine, it must be atomized—that is, broken into fine particles—so it can be mixed with air. This process of mixing the fuel with air is referred to as vaporization, and it will occur only when the liquid absorbs enough heat to boil. For example, as a tea kettle is heated on a stove, heat is transferred to the water, which raises its temperature until the boiling point is reached. When the water boils, it changes to water vapor and is carried off in the atmosphere in gaseous form. At sea level water boils at 212°F (100°C), but at higher altitudes less heat is required for water to boil because the atmospheric pressure is reduced.

As mentioned previously, gasoline is discharged from the fuel nozzle in a carburetor as a partially atomized air-fuel mixture. The air velocity at the fuel nozzle breaks the fuel into smaller particles, and this fuel vapor is drawn into the intake manifold by manifold vacuum and atmospheric pressure outside the carburetor. Manifold vacuum is created by the movement of the pistons on the intake strokes. The throttle controls engine speed by regulating the amount of air entering the cylinders. The highest manifold vacuum is available when the throttle is closed, and vacuum decreases as the throttle opens. Since the pressure in the intake manifold is much less than atmospheric pressure, the boiling point of the gasoline is lowered considerably.

Heat from the incoming air and the intake manifold surface also assists in vaporizing the fuel. Com-

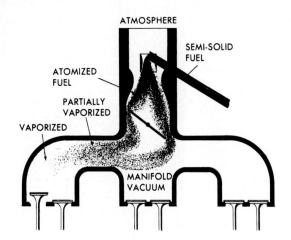

Figure 16-9. Fuel Vaporization. (*Courtesy of Chevrolet Motor Division, General Motors Corporation*)

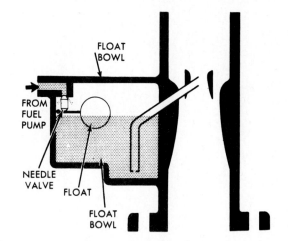

Figure 16-10. Float System Single-Barrel Carburetor. (*Courtesy of Chevrolet Motor Division, General Motors Corporation*)

plete fuel vaporization is the result of several factors, such as intake air temperature, fuel temperature, manifold vacuum, and intake manifold temperature. Anything that reduces any one of these factors will adversely affect fuel vaporization, and hence reduce fuel economy and increase exhaust emissions.

Fuel vaporization in the intake manifold is illustrated in Figure 16-9.

Single-Barrel Carburetor Systems

A single-barrel carburetor contains a single venturi and throttle valve. This type of carburetor is used on smaller engines.

Float System

The purpose of the float system is to maintain a precise level of fuel in the float bowl at all times. All the other systems in the carburetor depend on this precise level of fuel for proper operation. A pivoted float, usually made of plastic or hollow copper, is mounted in the float bowl. As fuel flows from the fuel pump past the needle valve into the float bowl, the float rises with the level of fuel. When the required fuel level is reached, the float closes the needle valve, which stops the fuel flow from the fuel pump into the float bowl. As fuel is used out of the float bowl, the float moves downward and opens the needle valve, which allows more fuel to enter the float bowl from the fuel pump.

The operation of the float system is illustrated in Figure 16-10.

Float bowls are vented internally to the top of the carburetor under the air cleaner. This area of the carburetor is referred to as the air horn. Under normal conditions the internal bowl vent supplies atmospheric pressure above the fuel in the float bowl. If the air cleaner becomes restricted, the vacuum increases inside the air cleaner element and in the venturi. This would tend to enrich the air-fuel ratio, but the internal bowl vent supplies reduced pressure to the float bowl, so that the air-fuel ratio is not affected by the partially restricted air cleaner.

The float bowl may be vented to a charcoal canister to relieve fuel bowl vapors under certain operating conditions. (See Chapter 8 for a discussion of charcoal canister venting systems.) A float bowl that is vented to the air horn and to the charcoal canister is illustrated in Figure 16-11.

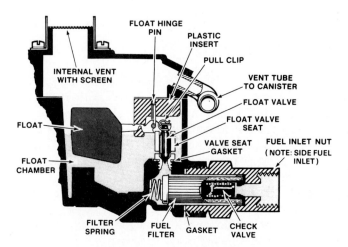

Figure 16-11. Float Bowl Vents. (*Courtesy of Chevrolet Motor Division, General Motors Corporation*)

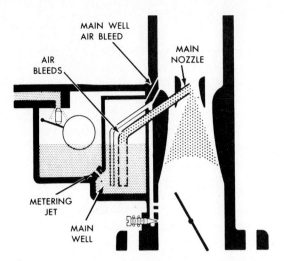

Figure 16-12. Main System. (*Courtesy of Chevrolet Motor Division, General Motors Corporation*)

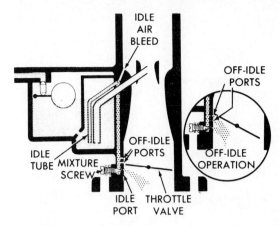

Figure 16-13. Idle System. (*Courtesy of Chevrolet Motor Division, General Motors Corporation*)

Main System

When the throttle is partially open, the fuel is moved out the main nozzle by the venturi vacuum and atmospheric pressure above the fuel in the float bowl. Fuel flows from the float bowl through the metering jet to the main well. The same level of fuel is maintained in the float bowl and the main well. A high-velocity stream of air enters the main well air bleed and the air bleeds in the main nozzle to atomize the fuel, as indicated in Figure 16-12.

The amount of fuel that flows through the main system is determined by the metering jet size, float level, and venturi vacuum. These three items in the carburetor are calibrated to provide an air-fuel ratio of 14.7:1. The main system delivers fuel continuously when the engine is operating from part throttle to full throttle.

Idle System

When the engine is idling, the throttle valve is almost closed. Fuel is moved out the idle port by manifold vacuum below the throttle and atmospheric pressure above the fuel in the float bowl. The fuel flows from the main well through the idle tube past the idle air bleed and off-idle ports to the idle port. Airflow into the idle passage from the idle air bleed and the off-idle ports atomizes the fuel, as pictured in Figure 16-13.

The idle air bleed prevents fuel from flowing through the idle system after the engine is shut off. A calibrated opening in the end of the idle tube delivers the correct amount of fuel to the idle system.

The mixture screw adjusts the amount of air and fuel that flows through the idle circuit in relation to the small amount of air that rushes past the throttle. The mixture screw has a right-hand thread. Clockwise rotation of the mixture screw moves the screw inward, which results in a leaner air-fuel ratio. A richer air-fuel ratio is obtained by rotating the screw in a counterclockwise direction.

When the throttle is opened slightly from the idle position, manifold vacuum is applied to the off-idle ports, and fuel flows from the idle port. If the throttle is opened further, venturi vacuum increases and fuel begins to flow from the main nozzle. Further opening of the throttle results in a lower manifold vacuum at the idle and off-idle ports, so that fuel stops flowing through the idle system.

Accelerator Pump System

If the throttle is opened suddenly from the idle position, an extreme increase in airflow through the carburetor occurs. However, the fuel flow will not react as quickly as the airflow, because the fuel is much heavier than air. This tends to create a lean air-fuel ratio on sudden acceleration, and the engine may hesitate, or stumble, if the mixture is not enriched. The accelerator pump discharges a stream of fuel into the venturi area to prevent hesitation at low-speed acceleration. The pump linkage is connected to the throttle, and the plunger is forced downward when the throttle is opened. This exerts a pressure on the fuel under the plunger, so that the fuel is forced past the discharge check ball and out the discharge passage into the venturi. This process is shown in Figure 16-14.

The pump plunger has a collapsible stem. The

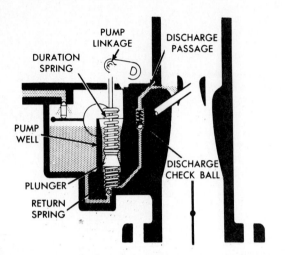

Figure 16-14. Accelerator Pump System. (*Courtesy of Chevrolet Motor Division, General Motors Corporation*)

pump linkage pushes the duration spring downward, which creates a gradual downward force on the plunger head. Thus, the duration spring provides a longer period of time for the pump stroke.

If the throttle is moved from the part-throttle to the idle position, the throttle linkage moves the pump plunger upward. Under this condition the discharge ball seats and keeps the discharge passage filled with fuel. A vacuum under the plunger unseats the inlet ball to allow fuel flow from the bowl into the pump well under the plunger. The spring above the discharge ball prevents venturi vacuum from lifting the ball and moving the fuel out of the discharge passage at high engine speeds.

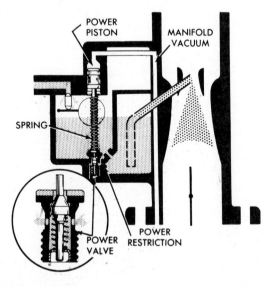

Figure 16-15. Power System. (*Courtesy of Chevrolet Motor Division, General Motors Corporation*)

Power System

Vacuum is supplied from the intake manifold to the top of the power piston as shown in Figure 16-15.

When the engine is operating at idle speed or at part throttle, high manifold vacuum holds the power piston upward and the power valve remains closed. If the throttle is more than 75 percent open, manifold vacuum is reduced and the spring forces the power piston downward, which opens the power valve. This allows fuel to flow through the power valve and power restriction into the main system in addition to the fuel flow through the metering jet. The power circuit supplies a richer air-fuel ratio to maintain engine power under heavy engine load or at high speed.

Choke System

When starting a cold engine, a very rich air-fuel mixture is required because a high percentage of the fuel condenses on the cold intake manifold surface. In the choke system the thermostatic coil is linked to the choke valve. This coil is a bimetallic strip that contains two different metals fused together. Because the two metals expand at different rates, the thermostatic coil unwinds as it cools and closes the choke valve. When the engine is cranked with the choke valve closed, the manifold vacuum that is present directly under the choke valve moves additional fuel out the main nozzle to enrich the air-fuel ratio. The vacuum diaphragm unit is also linked to the choke valve, as shown in Figure 16-16.

When the engine is started, the vacuum diaphragm is seated by manifold vacuum, which pulls the choke valve open a small distance to prevent an air-fuel mixture that is too rich. As the choke spring is heated from the surface of the exhaust manifold, the spring winds up and allows the choke valve to open.

A fast-idle cam with a series of steps is also linked to the choke valve. When the choke valve is closed, the fast-idle cam is lifted so the highest step is positioned under the fast-idle lever, or fast-idle screw, as outlined in Figure 16-17.

The fast-idle cam holds the throttle open when a cold engine is being started, and provides the correct fast-idle speed once the engine starts.

In some choke systems the choke spring is mounted in a housing attached to the carburetor. A hot-air type of choke may be used on these applications. Manifold vacuum is supplied through a passage in the carburetor casting to the choke housing.

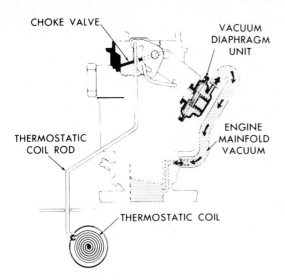

Figure 16-16. Choke System. (*Courtesy of Chevrolet Motor Division, General Motors Corporation*)

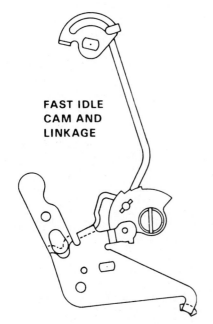

FAST IDLE CAM AND LINKAGE

Figure 16-17. Fast-Idle Cam. (*Courtesy of Chevrolet Motor Division, General Motors Corporation*)

A heat pipe is connected to the exterior of the housing. In many applications this heat pipe is mounted in the exhaust crossover passage of the intake manifold.

A clean-air pipe is usually connected from the air horn area at the top of the carburetor to the heat pipe. When the engine is running, the manifold vacuum in the choke housing pulls air through the heat pipe and choke housing into the intake manifold. The air is heated as it passes through the heat pipe, so that heat is applied to the choke spring.

In this type of choke, if an exhaust leak occurs into the heat pipe, the choke housing will become contaminated with moisture and carbon. It is also essential that this type of choke system does not have any vacuum leaks.

Some choke springs are heated electrically. (This type of choke is explained later in this chapter.) A hot-air type of choke with a heat pipe is illustrated in Figure 16-18.

Rochester Varajet Dual-Stage Two-Barrel Carburetor Systems

Secondary Main System

A dual-stage two-barrel carburetor has two venturis and throttle valves. A linkage is connected from the primary throttle to the secondary throttle. When the primary throttle is approximately half open, the linkage begins to force the secondary throttle open, and both throttles reach the wide-open position at the same time. Figure 16-19 illustrates the secondary main system and the power system.

The secondary air valve is held in the closed position by a light spring. When the secondary throttles begin to open, the air valve is opened by air velocity. The air valve opening is proportional to the secondary throttle opening. Fuel flows through the secondary fuel pickup passage and secondary metering jet into the airstream. The secondary air bleed atomizes the fuel before it flows out of the metering jet. The secondary metering rod is attached to the air valve, and the thinner part of the metering rod is placed in the jet as the air valve moves to the open position. This provides fuel delivery in relation to opening of the air valve and secondary throttle.

The secondary calibration screw positions the metering rod in relation to the air valve. This screw is factory adjusted and its adjustment should not be altered when the carburetor is being serviced.

Primary Main System

A pair of boost venturis is positioned in the primary venturi, as illustrated in Figure 16-20.

Fuel flow in the main system is through the main metering jet, main well, and the main discharge nozzle. The air bleeds in the main well atomize the fuel before it is discharged from the main nozzle. A small amount of fuel flows past the part-throttle calibration screw into the main system. This

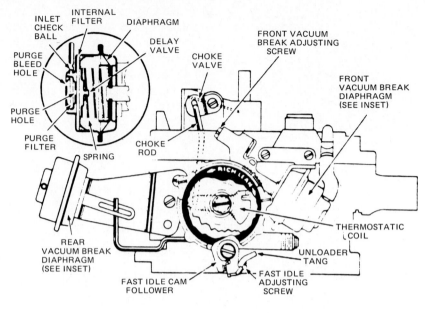

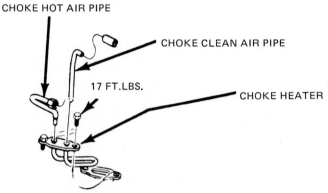

Figure 16-18. Hot-Air Choke with Heat Pipe. (*Courtesy of Oldsmobile Division, General Motors Corporation*)

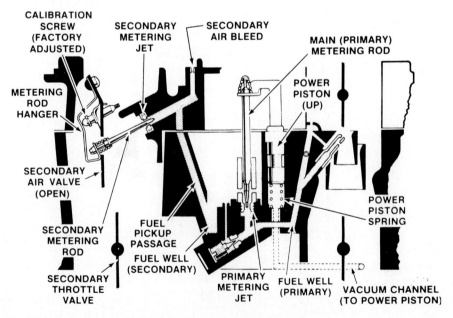

Figure 16-19. Secondary Main System and Power System. (*Courtesy of Pontiac Motor Division, General Motors Corporation*)

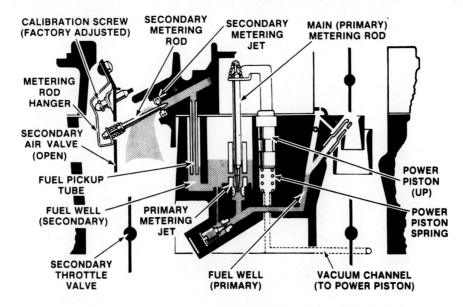

Figure 16-20. Primary Main System. (*Courtesy of Pontiac Motor Division, General Motors Corporation*)

screw is adjusted at the factory to obtain more accurate air-fuel ratios and reduce exhaust emissions.

A steel plug is inserted on top of the part-throttle calibration screw, and this plug should not be removed while the carburetor is being serviced.

(The computer controlled Varajet carburetor is explained in Chapter 17.)

Power System

When the throttle is in the idle or part-throttle position, the power piston is held downward by high manifold vacuum. Under this condition the thicker part of the metering rod is positioned in the main jet, and the air-fuel ratio will be approximately 14.7 : 1. When the primary throttle is more than 75 percent open, manifold vacuum decreases and allows the spring to move the power piston upward. This action places the thinner part of the metering rod in the main jet, which enriches the air-fuel ratio to provide additional engine power.

Float System

The float system is conventional in design. As illustrated in Figure 16-21, the float bowl is vented internally to the air horn and externally to the charcoal canister.

If the filter becomes completely plugged, the filter spring allows fuel pump pressure to force the filter away from the inlet nut, so that fuel continues

to flow into the float bowl. This prevents the engine from stopping because of fuel starvation. The check valve in the filter prevents fuel from draining out of the carburetor if the vehicle is rolled over in an accident and the fuel line is broken.

Idle System

Fuel flow in the idle system is through the main metering jet, idle tube, idle channel restriction, and idle discharge hole. The idle channel restriction gives the air and fuel a swirling action to assist in atomizing the fuel. The lower idle air bleed is positioned at the lower edge of the venturi, and it discharges some fuel from the idle system while the main system is in operation. When the throttle is opened from the idle position, fuel is discharged from the off-idle port and then from the lower idle air bleed and the main nozzle to provide a smooth transition from the idle system to the main system.

A steel plug is driven into the opening at the end of the idle mixture screw. This plug may be removed if an idle mixture adjustment is necessary.

The hot-idle compensator is located on top of the carburetor, as shown in Figure 16-22. The hot-idle compensator is operated by a bimetallic strip. When the engine is at normal operating temperature, the hot-idle compensator valve is held closed by the bimetallic strip. During extremely hot idle or hot shutdown conditions, the bimetallic strip opens the valve and allows additional air past the valve into the intake manifold. This offsets the enriching ef-

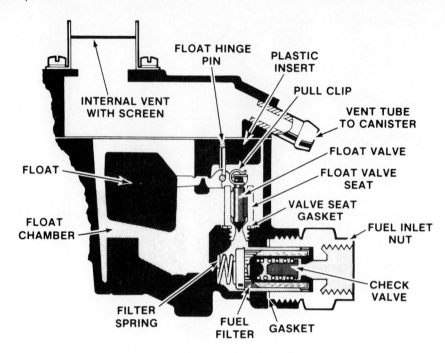

Figure 16-21.   Float System. (*Courtesy of Pontiac Motor Division, General Motors Corporation*)

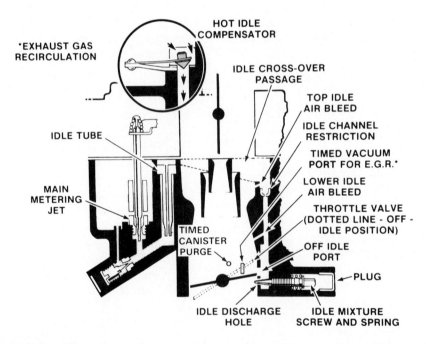

Figure 16-22.   Idle System. (*Courtesy of Pontiac Motor Division, General Motors Corporation*)

fect of fuel vapors that come out of the main nozzle due to fuel boiling in the main well. The hot-idle compensator valve must be closed when the idle speed or idle mixture is being adjusted.

Two vacuum ports above the throttle are connected to the charcoal canister and the exhaust gas recirculation (EGR) valve. (These systems will be discussed in Chapter 8.)

Accelerator Pump System

The cup on the accelerator pump plunger has a small amount of vertical movement. When the plunger is moved upward by the throttle linkage, the cup unseats and allows fuel to flow past the cup into the pump well that is underneath the plunger. If the plunger is forced downward by the throttle linkage,

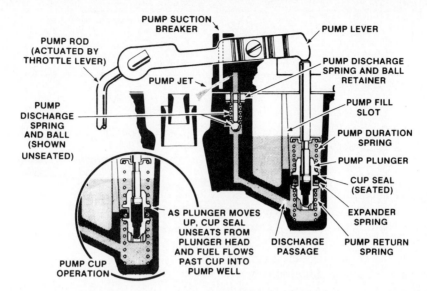

Figure 16-23. Accelerator Pump System. (*Courtesy of Pontiac Motor Division, General Motors Corporation*)

the cup seats on the plunger head, which prevents fuel from escaping through the cup seal to the float bowl. Downward movement of the pump plunger forces fuel past the discharge ball and out the pump jet, as pictured in Figure 16-23.

Choke System

An electrically heated choke is used in the Varajet carburetor. Electric current flowing through a ceramic resistor in the choke cover supplies heat to the thermostatic coil. As illustrated in Figure 16-24, two terminals are connected between the terminal plate and the ceramic resistor.

When the temperature of the choke cover is below 50°F (10°C), electrical contact is made from the terminal plate through one of the terminals to a small area in the ceramic resistor. The current flow through the resistor heats the thermostatic coil, which allows the choke to open gradually. If the temperature is above 70°F (21°C), the bimetallic snap disc forces the second terminal to make contact between the terminal blade and the ceramic resistor. This allows current to flow through a larger area of the ceramic resistor, which increases the heat on the thermostatic spring and opens the choke faster to reduce exhaust emissions. The electric circuit to the choke terminal blade is connected from the ignition switch through a set of contacts in the oil pressure switch. An oil indicator light in the instrument panel is connected to the electrical circuit between the oil-pressure switch and the choke heater, as shown in Figure 16-25.

When the ignition switch is turned on, current

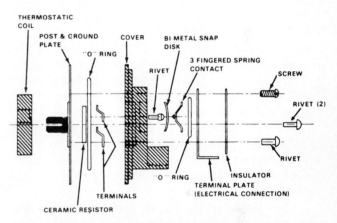

Figure 16-24. Electric Choke. (*Courtesy of Delco Products Division, General Motors Corporation*)

flows through the oil indicator light and the choke heater to ground. Because the oil indicator bulb has high resistance, this current flow will be very low and will not heat the choke spring enough to open the choke if the ignition switch is left on without starting a cold engine. When the engine is started, the oil-pressure switch contacts close and supply full battery voltage to the choke heater. Under this condition a higher current flows through the choke heater, which heats the choke spring and causes the choke to open. When the oil-pressure switch closes, the oil light goes out, because equal voltage is supplied to each side of the light. If the engine oil pressure is very low and the engine is running, the switch contacts will not close and the oil indicator light circuit will be completed to ground through the choke heater. This illuminates the oil indicator light to warn the driver that a problem exists.

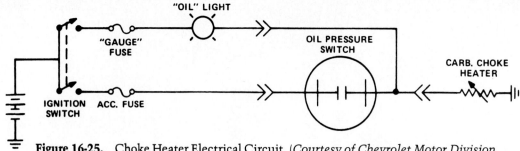

Figure 16-25. Choke Heater Electrical Circuit. (*Courtesy of Chevrolet Motor Division, General Motors Corporation*)

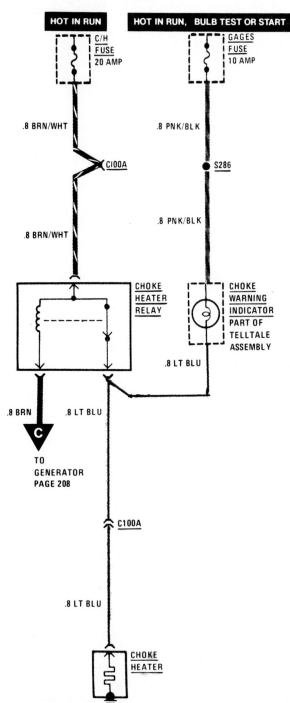

Figure 16-26. Electric Choke Circuit with Choke Heater Relay and Choke Warning Light. (*Courtesy of Pontiac Motor Division, General Motors Corporation*)

A choke heater relay is connected in some electric choke circuits. When the ignition switch is turned on, current flows through the relay winding, the number 1 terminal, and the field circuit of the integral alternator to ground. The relay coil magnetism holds the relay contacts open. Under this condition current flows through the choke warning light and the choke heater to ground, so that the light is illuminated. Once the engine starts and the alternator begins charging, equal voltage is supplied to both ends of the relay winding, which stops the current flow through the winding and causes the points to close. When this occurs, full voltage is supplied through the relay contacts to the choke heater. Equal voltage is supplied to both sides of the choke warning light because of the closed relay contacts, and the light is not illuminated.

In this type of circuit, a defective alternator can cause an inoperative electric choke, because the relay contacts will not close with the engine running. If this occurs, the choke warning light is illuminated.

The electric choke circuit with a choke heater relay and choke warning light is illustrated in Figure 16-26.

The electric choke does not require a gasket between the choke cover and the choke housing. The choke thermostatic coil is linked to the choke valve, as indicated in Figure 16-27.

A vacuum-break diaphragm is also linked to the choke valve. When a cold engine is started, manifold vacuum seats the diaphragm, which pulls the choke valve open a small amount to prevent a rich air-fuel ratio while the engine is warming up. The vacuum-break diaphragm is also linked to the secondary air valve. When the secondary throttle begins to open, manifold vacuum decreases and the vacuum-break diaphragm stem slowly extends. The linkage to the secondary air valve prevents the valve from opening too quickly, which could result in a lean air-fuel ratio and hesitation in engine operation.

Some carburetors have a secondary vacuum-break diaphragm, as illustrated in Figure 16-28. Manifold vacuum is usually supplied through a coolant temperature switch to the secondary vacuum-

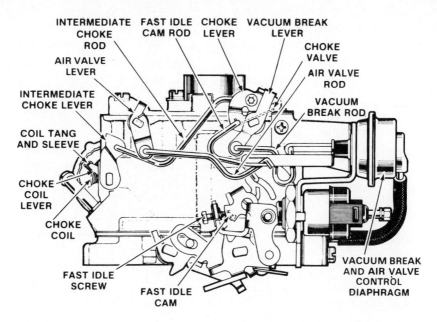

Figure 16-27. Choke System. (*Courtesy of Pontiac Motor Division, General Motors Corporation*)

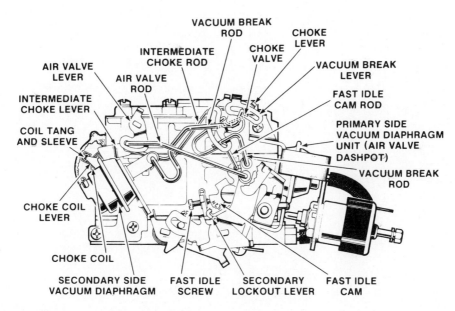

Figure 16-28. Secondary Vacuum Break Diaphragm. (*Courtesy of Pontiac Motor Division, General Motors Corporation*)

break diaphragm. When the engine coolant reaches a specific temperature, manifold vacuum seats the secondary vacuum-break diaphragm, which pulls the choke open further to improve exhaust emissions while the engine is warming up.

(Refer to Chapter 11 in *Automotive Principles: Repair and Service*, Volume II, for carburetor adjustments and service.)

Test Questions

1. The ideal gasoline air-fuel ratio is _____.

2. When one gallon of gasoline is burned, _____ gallons of air are required to mix with the gasoline.

3. If the volatility of gasoline is too high, _____ _____ may occur in the fuel lines.

4. The road octane rating of premium unleaded gasoline would be _____ to _____.

5. An open circuit in the inertia switch in the electric fuel pump circuit would result in an inoperative fuel pump.   T F

6. A decrease in manifold vacuum affects fuel vaporization in the intake manifold.   T F

7. The accelerator pump system prevents _____ at low-speed acceleration.

8. When the engine is operating at wide-open throttle, additional fuel is supplied to the main system from the _____ system.

9. In the Varajet carburetor, both throttles open simultaneously.   T F

10. In the Varajet electric choke, a constant current flows through the ceramic resistor as the engine warms up.   T F

11. Battery voltage is supplied to the Varajet electric choke with the ignition switch on and the engine not running.   T F

17

Computer Systems with Computer-Controlled Carburetors

Chapter Completion Objectives

1. Understand General Motors computer command control (3C) systems.

2. Demonstrate a knowledge of Ford electronic engine control IV (EEC IV) systems with computer-controlled carburetors.

3. Indicate an understanding of Chrysler computer systems with oxygen (O_2) feedback carburetors.

General Motors Computer Command Control (3C) System

Electronic Control Module (ECM)

The computer used with the 3C system is referred to as an electronic control module (ECM). A removable programmable read-only memory (PROM) is located in the ECM, as illustrated in Figure 17-1.

The ECM is the control center of the 3C system. It constantly monitors information it receives from the various sensors and provides commands for performance of the correct functions. Specific information about each vehicle is programmed into the PROM, so the ECM can be tailored to meet the requirements of the specific combination of engine, transmission, and differential within a particular vehicle. The ECM receives signals from the following devices:

1. Oxygen (O_2) sensor.
2. Throttle position sensor (TPS).
3. Coolant temperature sensor.
4. Manifold absolute pressure (MAP) and barometric pressure (baro) sensors.
5. Vehicle speed sensor (VSS).
6. Distributor pickup coil, crankshaft position, revolutions per minute (rpm).

The ECM, in turn, controls the following:

1. Mixture-control (MC) solenoid.
2. Electronic spark-timing (EST) system.
3. Exhaust-gas recirculation (EGR) value.
4. Air-injection reactor (AIR) pump.

5. Torque-converter clutch (TCC) lockup.
6. Early fuel-evaporation (EFE) system.
7. Idle-speed control (ISC) motor.

Sources of ECM Input

Oxygen (O_2) Sensor An exhaust-gas oxygen (O_2) sensor is located in one of the exhaust manifolds. Rich air-fuel ratios supply fuel to mix with all the oxygen entering the engine. Rich air-fuel ratios create low oxygen levels in the exhaust because excess fuel mixes with all the oxygen entering the engine. When lean mixtures are used, oxygen levels in the exhaust are high because of the lack of fuel entering the cylinders.

Exhaust gas is applied to the outside of the oxygen-sensing element, and atmospheric pressure is supplied to the inside of the sensing element, as shown in Figure 17-2.

Rich mixtures and low levels of oxygen in the exhaust cause the sensing element to generate higher voltage, as shown in Figure 17-3.

High levels of oxygen in the exhaust and lean air-fuel mixtures result in low oxygen sensor voltage because high oxygen levels are present on both sides of the sensing element. The oxygen sensor signal to the ECM is used to control the air-fuel ratio in the carburetor.

Unleaded gasoline must be used for satisfactory oxygen sensor operation.

Throttle Position Sensor (TPS) The throttle position sensor is in a variable resistor operated by the

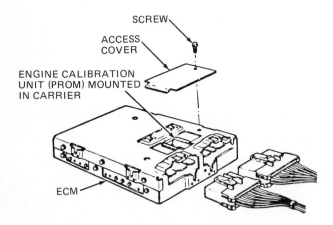

Figure 17-1. Electronic Control Module (ECM). (*Courtesy of GM Product Service Training, General Motors Corporation*)

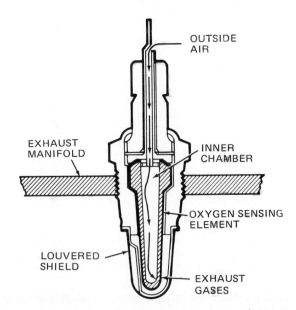

Figure 17-2. Oxygen (O_2) Sensor. (*Courtesy of GM Product Service Training, General Motors Corporation*)

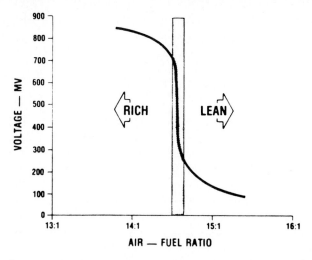

Figure 17-3. Oxygen Sensor Voltage Output. (*Courtesy of Sun Electric Coporation*)

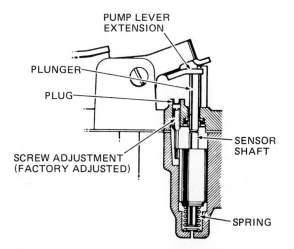

Figure 17-4. Throttle-Position Sensor (TPS). (*Courtesy of Chevrolet Motor Division, General Motors Corporation*)

accelerator pump linkage, as illustrated in Figure 17-4.

A reference voltage is supplied to the TPS from the ECM. The TPS output varies in relation to throttle opening. At wide-open throttle and sudden acceleration, the TPS signal calls for mixture enrichment.

Coolant Temperature Sensor The resistance of the coolant sensor varies in relation to coolant temperature. The ECM operating mode is selected from the coolant sensor signal. Open-loop operation occurs during engine warm-up, when a richer mixture is necessary. In the open-loop mode, the ECM maintains the carburetor mixture. Closed-loop operation occurs when the coolant sensor reaches a predetermined temperature.

The ECM controls the air-fuel ratio in response to an oxygen sensor signal in the closed-loop mode.

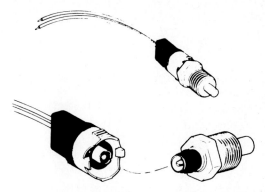

Figure 17-5. Coolant Temperature Sensor. (*Courtesy of Pontiac Motor Division, General Motors Corporation*)

The ECM may also use the coolant sensor signal to assist in regulating ignition, air injection, and exhaust-gas recirculation.

Figure 17–5 illustrates a coolant temperature sensor.

Manifold Absolute Pressure Sensor On many systems, the manifold absolute pressure (MAP) sensor is combined with the barometric pressure (baro) sensor, while a few systems have separate MAP and baro sensors. A reference voltage is supplied to the MAP sensor from the ECM, as illustrated in Figure 17-6.

The voltage output signal from the MAP sensor to the ECM varies in relation to manifold vacuum. Spark control is managed by the ECM in response to the MAP sensor signal. Other ECM functions may be affected by the MAP sensor signal.

Vehicle Speed Sensor (VSS) The speedometer cable rotates a reflector blade past a light-emitting diode and photocell in the VSS, as shown in Figure 17-7.

Reflector blade speed and VSS output signal are

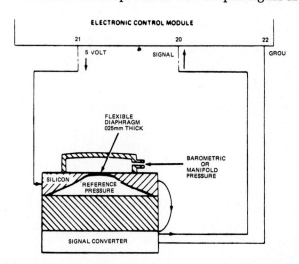

Figure 17-6. Manifold Absolute Pressure Sensor. (*Courtesy of GM Product Service Training, General Motors Corporation*)

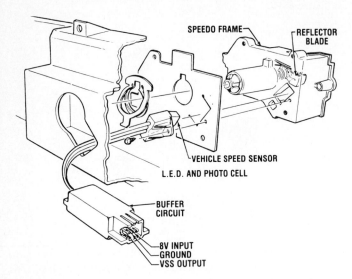

Figure 17-7. Vehicle Speed Sensor. (*Courtesy of GM Product Service Training, General Motors Corporation*)

directly proportional to vehicle speed. The ECM controls torque-converter clutch lockup from the VSS signal.

ECM Control Functions

Mixture-Control Solenoid Management The 3C carburetor contains a mixture-control (MC) solenoid that is controlled by the ECM. The MC solenoid is spring-loaded in the upward position. When the ECM energizes the solenoid winding, the plunger moves downward. This plunger movement controls a tapered valve in the main system and an air bleed in the idle system. Fuel for the main system is supplied through the lean-mixture screw. Some fuel for the main system is also supplied through the tapered valve on the MC solenoid plunger and the rich-mixture screw, as shown in Figure 17-8.

When the ignition switch is turned on, voltage is supplied to one end of the MC solenoid winding. The other end of the winding is connected to the ECM. If the oxygen sensor provides a rich signal to the ECM, the ECM grounds the MC solenoid winding. When this occurs, the MC solenoid plunger moves downward and the tapered value closes, which shuts off the fuel flow through the rich-mixture screw. This action results in a leaner air-fuel mixture. A lean-oxygen sensor signal to the ECM causes the ECM to de-energize the MC solenoid winding. This causes upward plunger movement and additional fuel flow through the tapered valve and rich-mixture screw into the main system; thus, a richer air-fuel mixture is provided.

The ECM energizes the MC solenoid winding 10 times per second, and the "on time" of the winding can be varied by the ECM to maintain the air-fuel ratio at 14.7 : 1 under most operating conditions.

Air is bled into the idle system past the top of the MC solenoid plunger. Upward plunger movement results in reduced airflow into the idle system and a richer air-fuel mixture. If the solenoid plunger is moved downward by the ECM, additional air flows into the idle system and a leaner air-fuel mixture results. Therefore, the ECM and the MC solenoid control the air-fuel mixture in the idle system or main system.

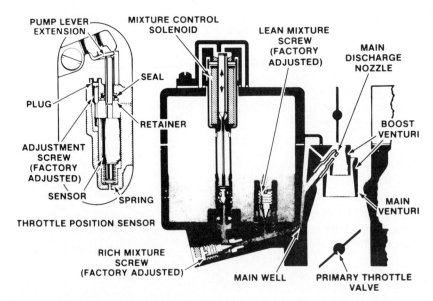

Figure 17-8. Main System with Mixture-Control Solenoid. (*Courtesy of GM Product Service Training, General Motors Corporation*)

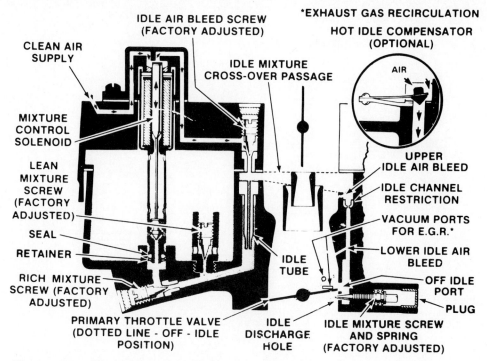

Figure 17-9. Idle System with Mixture-Control Solenoid. (*Courtesy of GM Product Service Training, General Motors Corporation*)

The MC solenoid and the idle system are illustrated in Figure 17-9.

Most defects in the MC solenoid, oxygen sensor, or the ECM will result in upward movement of the MC solenoid plunger, which causes a rich air-fuel mixture and excessive fuel consumption.

The MC solenoid shown in Figures 17-8 and 17-9 is from a Varajet carburetor. This type of MC solenoid plunger is not adjustable. (Refer to Chapter 16 for an explanation of conventional Varajet carburetors.)

Ignition Management Conventional distributor advances are discontinued in the 3C system and the ignition spark advance is controlled by the ECM. (Refer to Chapter 13 for a description of 3C ignition systems.)

Torque-Converter Clutch Lockup A lockup type converter contains a pressure plate with a narrow strip of friction material attached to the front of the plate. This plate is splined to the turbine assembly, as indicated in Figure 17-10.

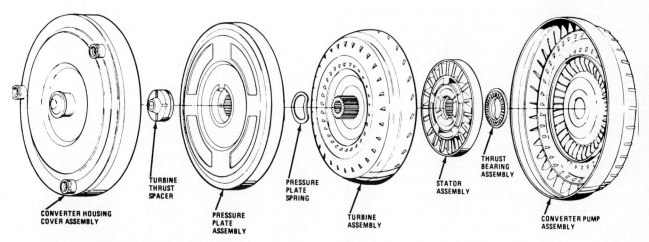

Figure 17-10. Lockup Torque Converter. (*Courtesy of Chevrolet Motor Division, General Motors Corporation*)

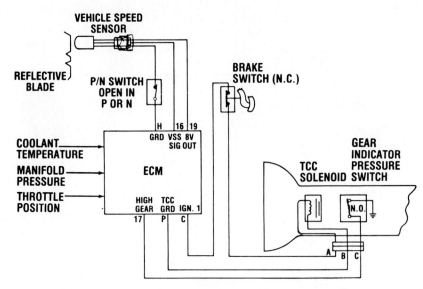

Figure 17-11. Torque Converter Clutch Circuit. (*Courtesy of GM Product Service Training, General Motors Corporation*)

Converter lockup takes place when oil enters the converter hub and forces the friction disc against the front of the converter. In the lockup mode, the flywheel is connected through the front of the converter to the friction disc, turbine, and transmission input shaft. The converter becomes unlocked when oil is directed through the hollow input shaft and the friction disc is forced away from the front of the converter. Oil flow to the converter is controlled by an apply valve in the transmission. The apply valve is controlled by the TCC solenoid.

When the vehicle reaches a predetermined speed in high gear, the computer grounds the TCC solenoid winding. Once the TCC solenoid is energized, a hydraulic bleed port in the direct clutch circuit closes, and the direct clutch oil pressure rises. The increase in oil pressure moves the converter apply valve and directs oil in the converter hub to lock up the converter. Other input signals to the computer may affect TCC lockup, as indicated in Figure 17-11.

Early Fuel-Evaporation (EFE) Management The heat riser valve in the EFE system is operated by a vacuum diaphragm, as shown in Figure 17-12. A cold coolant sensor signal causes the ECM to energize the EFE solenoid and apply vacuum to the power actuator. If the heat riser valve is closed, the intake manifold becomes heated as exhaust gas is forced through the intake manifold crossover passage. The ECM deactivates the EFE solenoid at a specific coolant temperature and allows the heat riser valve to open. The EFE vacuum is also supplied to the air-injection system, as illustrated in Figure 17-13.

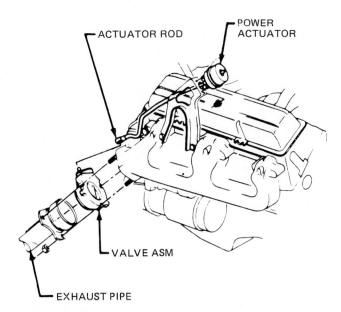

Figure 17-12. Early Fuel-Evaporation (EFE) System. (*Courtesy of GM Product Service Training, General Motors Corporation*)

Air-Injection Reactor (AIR) Management The AIR system supplies air from the air pump to the exhaust ports or to the catalytic converter, as illustrated in Figure 17-14.

Airflow to the exhaust ports lowers emission levels during warm-up and reduces oxygen sensor and converter warm-up time. Oxygen is necessary for converter operation once the converters have reached operating temperature.

A divert valve and a switching valve are used to control airflow from the AIR pump. During engine

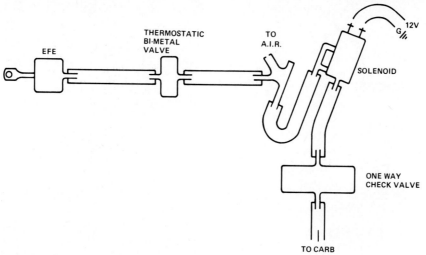

Figure 17-13. Early Fuel-Evaporation Vacuum Circuit. *(Courtesy of GM Product Service Training, General Motors Corporation)*

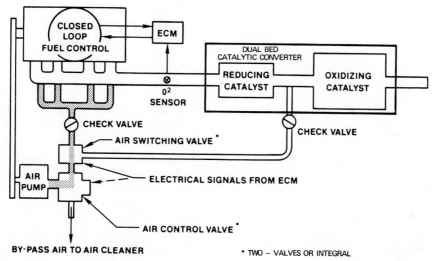

Figure 17-14. Air-Injection Reactor System. *(Courtesy of Pontiac Motor Division, General Motors Corporation)*

warm-up, the ECM de-energizes the divert valve solenoid winding and enables AIR pump pressure to move the divert valve diaphragm and spool valve upward. Air from the pump is diverted to the air cleaner when the spool valve is in the upward position, as indicated in Figure 17-15.

When the ECM energizes the divert solenoid winding, the solenoid valve shuts off AIR pump pressure applied to the divert valve diaphragm, and the diaphragm and spool valve are able to move to the downward position. As a result, air is directed from the AIR pump to the air-switching valve. High manifold vacuum on deceleration can lift the divert valve diaphragm and cause air from the pump to exhaust to the air cleaner.

When the engine coolant is cold, vacuum from the EFE system is applied to the lower air-switching valve vacuum port, which shuts off the flow of air from the AIR pump to the air-switching valve diaphragm. As a result, the diaphragm and spool valve remain in the downward position, and air from the AIR pump is directed to the exhaust ports. Vacuum to the lower air-switching valve port is shut off when the coolant is warm and AIR pump pressure can force the diaphragm and spool valve upward. The flow of air through the air-switching valve will be directed to the converter when the spool valve is in the upward position, as indicated in Figure 17-16.

Manifold vacuum applied to the upper air-switching valve port could lift the diaphragm and

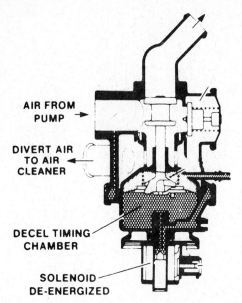

Figure 17-15. Air-Injection System Reactor (AIR) Divert Valve. (*Courtesy of GM Product Service Training, General Motors Corporation*)

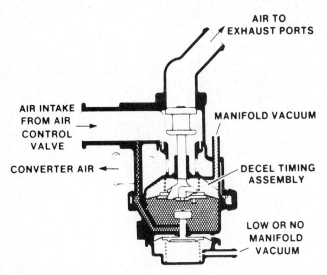

Figure 17-16. Air-Switching Valve. (*Courtesy of GM Product Service Training, General Motors Corporation*)

spool valve on deceleration with a cold engine. Air will be directed momentarily to the converters to prevent manifold backfiring.

Exhaust-Gas Recirculation (EGR) Management The EGR valve directs exhaust from the exhaust system to the intake manifold and lowers NOx emissions. Vacuum to the EGR valve is controlled by a solenoid operated by the ECM. The ECM shuts off EGR vacuum when the coolant is cold by energizing the solenoid. Warm engine coolant conditions signal the ECM to deactivate the solenoid and thus allow vacuum to the EGR valve. The vacuum port

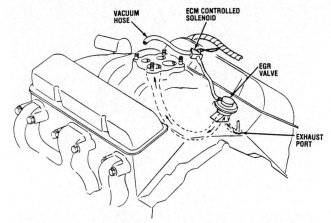

Figure 17-17. Exhaust-Gas Recirculation (EGR) Valve. (*Courtesy of GM Product Service Training, General Motors Corporation*)

connected to the EGR system is always above the throttles. Vacuum should never be applied to the EGR valve until the throttles are opened. An EGR valve that is open at idle speed will cause rough idling.

Figure 17-17 illustrates the EGR valve and the vacuum control circuit.

Idle-Speed Control (ISC) Management The idle-speed control (ISC) motor is a small, reversible motor that is operated by the ECM to control idle speed. When the engine coolant is cold, the fast-idle cam determines the fast-idle speed. The ISC motor extends slightly more than normal when a cold signal is sent from the coolant temperature sensor to the ECM. The air conditioner clutch switch signals the ECM to maintain engine idle speed when the air conditioning compressor clutch is engaged. If the transmission selector is moved from drive to park, the park-neutral switch signals the ECM to reduce idle speed to specifications. The reference signal from the distributor sends a revolutions-per-minute (rpm) signal to the ECM as long as the engine is running. A low battery voltage signal to terminal ''R'' on the ECM causes the ECM to increase idle speed to assist in recharging the battery.

When a hot signal is received from the coolant temperature sensor, the ECM that extends the ISC motor plunger and increases the idle speed so that the engine temperature decreases.

The ISC motor does not require adjusting, because the ECM determines the correct idle postion. A tang on the throttle level contacts the ISC motor plunger and closes a throttle switch in the ISC motor. The throttle switch is connected to the ECM, and the ECM will not control the ISC motor unless the throttle switch is closed.

The system must be in the closed-loop mode be-

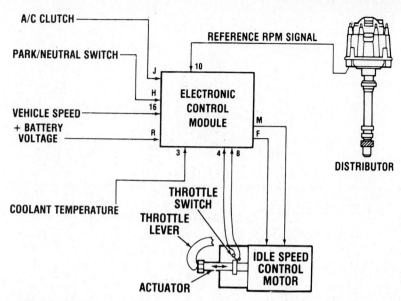

Figure 17-18. Idle-Speed Control Motor. (*Courtesy of GM Product Service Training, General Motor Corporation*)

fore the ECM will control the ISC motor. During a cylinder output test, the coolant sensor must be disconnected to put the system in open-loop operation; otherwise the ISC motor will try to correct the drop in speed as each cylinder is shorted out.

The ISC motor and related ECM circuit are shown in Figure 17-18.

Ford Electronic Engine Control IV Systems Used with 2.3L High-Swirl Combustion Engine

Electronic Control Assembly

The computer in the electronic engine control IV (EEC IV) system is referred to as an electronic control assembly (ECA). Input signals from various sensors are sent to the ECA, which in turn performs specific output functions. When the ignition switch is turned on, current flows through the power relay winding to ground. The coil magnetism closes the relay contacts and voltage is supplied through these contacts to the ECA, as indicated in Figure 17-19. An ECA is illustrated in Figure 17-20.

Sources of ECA Input

Many of the same input sensors, such as the exhaust-gas oxygen (EGO) sensor, engine coolant temperature (ECT) sensor, throttle position sensor (TPS),

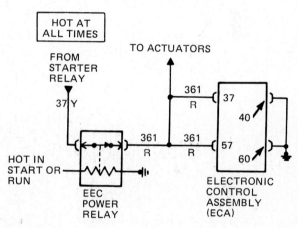

Figure 17-19. Power Relay Circuit. (*Courtesy of Ford Motor Co.*)

manifold absolute pressure (MAP) sensor, and the A/C clutch compressor signal, are similar to the sensors in other systems. The exhaust-gas recirculation (EGR) position sensor is a variable resistor that sends a signal to the ECA in relation to EGR valve position. A Hall Effect switch in the distributor is referred to as a profile ignition pickup (PIP). (The PIP with the EEC IV ignition system is explained in Chapter 13.) All of the inputs and outputs in the EEC IV system are displayed in Figure 17-21.

Output Control Functions

Air-Fuel Ratio Control The feedback control solenoid (FCS) contains an electrically operated vacuum solenoid with a movable plunger. The FCS controls

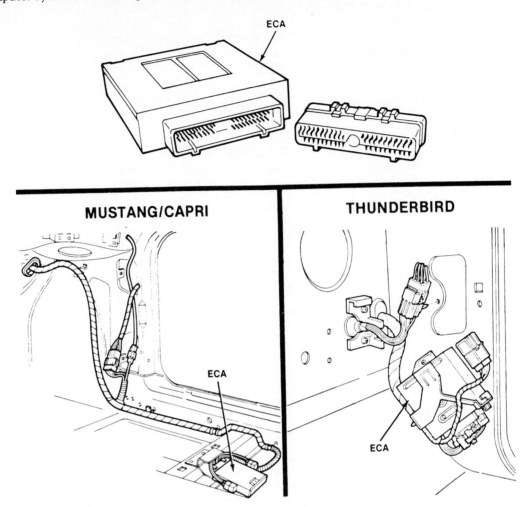

Figure 17-20. Electronic Control Assembly. (*Courtesy of Ford Motor Co.*)

the amount of vacuum that is supplied to the carburetor diaphragm, as well as the amount of air that is bled into the idle circuit, as shown in Figure 17-22.

The ECA energizes the FCS winding 10 times per second. Output vacuum from the FCS to the carburetor diaphragm varies from 2 to 5 in. Hg. Output vacuum is very low when the winding is not energized; energizing the winding causes the output vacuum to increase. The ECA varies the "on time" of the FCS winding to supply the correct output vacuum and an air-fuel ratio of 14.7:1.

If the oxygen sensor provides a rich mixture signal, the ECA energizes the FCS winding, which increases the output vacuum from the FCS to the carburetor diaphragm. The increase in output vacuum lifts the carburetor diaphragm and actuator, which allow the feedback metering valve to reduce the fuel flow to the main system. A lean oxygen sensor signal results in reduced FCS winding "on time" and

reduced output vacuum, which allows the carburetor diaphragm and actuator to move downward. This action opens the feedback metering valve and supplies more fuel to the main system, as indicated in Figure 17-23.

When the FCS supplies more vacuum to the carburetor diaphragm, it also supplies more air to the idle system, which results in a leaner air-fuel mixture if the engine is idling. The idle feedback air bleed is shown in Figure 17-24.

Thick-Film Integrated Ignition [The thick-film integrated (TFI)ignition and spark-advance control are discussed in Chapter 13.]

Throttle Kicker Solenoid When the air conditioner is turned on, the ECA energizes a throttle kicker solenoid (TKS), and vacuum is supplied through the solenoid to the throttle kicker actuator on the carburetor. This action increases the idle speed. The

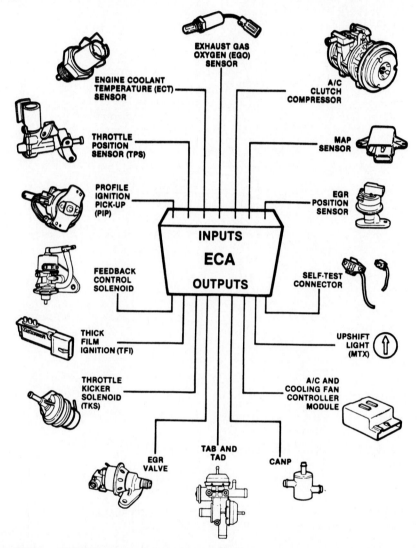

Figure 17-21.   EEC IV Inputs and Outputs, 2.3L High-Swirl Combustion (HSC) Engine. *(Courtesy of Ford Motor Co.)*

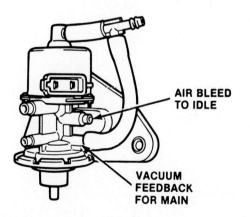

Figure 17-22.   Feedback Control Solenoid. *(Courtesy of Ford Motor Co.)*

ECA may energize the TKS under other operating conditions, such as when engine coolant is cold. However, the fast-idle cam still provides the correct fast-idle speed during engine warm-up.

Exhaust-Gas Recirculation   The ECA operates two solenoids in the vacuum system connected to the exhaust-gas recirculation (EGR) valve. If more EGR flow is required, the ECA supplies power to both solenoids. When this occurs the vent solenoid closes and the vacuum solenoid opens, which supplies more vacuum to the EGR valve.

When the input signals inform the ECA that the EGR flow should be reduced, the ECA opens the circuit to both solenoids. Under this condition the EGR control solenoid closes and the EGR vent solenoid

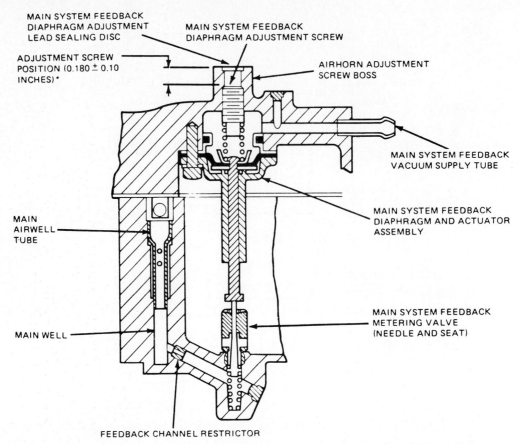

Figure 17-23.   Feedback Diaphragm of Actuator. (*Courtesy of Ford Motor Co.*)

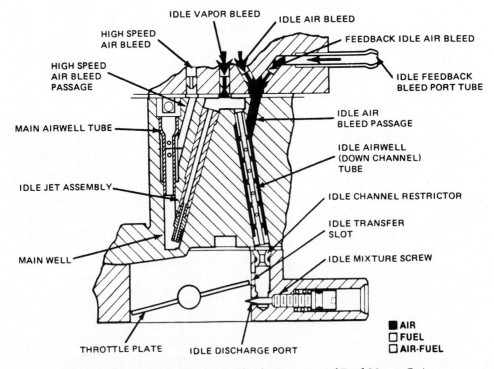

Figure 17-24.   Idle Feedback Air Bleed. (*Courtesy of Ford Motor Co.*)

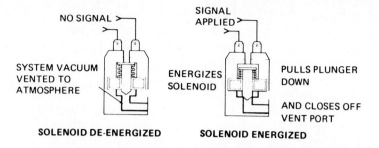

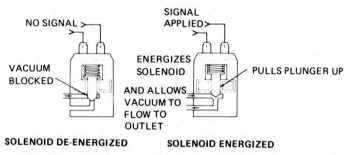

Figure 17-25.   EGR Control Solenoid and Vent Solenoid. (*Courtesy of Ford Motor Co.*)

opens, which vents the vacuum in the system and allows the EGR valve to close.

EGR control solenoid and vent solenoid operation are illustrated in Figure 17-25.

Thermactor Pump Air Control   The ECA operates the dual air control solenoids to control the thermactor pump airflow. Vacuum applied to the thermactor air bypass (TAB) valve and thermactor air divert (TAD) valve is turned on and off by the dual air control solenoids. The thermactor pump airflow has three possible routings:

1. Downstream, in which air is injected into the catalytic converter.

2. Upstream, in which air is injected into the exhaust ports.

3. Bypass, in which air is bypassed to the atmosphere.

In the bypass mode, the ECA de-energizes the TAB and TAD solenoids. Under this condition vacuum is not applied to the TAB or TAD valves, and airflow from the pump is bypassed to the atmosphere. The bypass mode is diagrammed in Figure 17-26.

The bypass mode occurs during periods of prolonged idle, under wide-open throttle conditions, or when the oxygen sensor signal is extremely low.

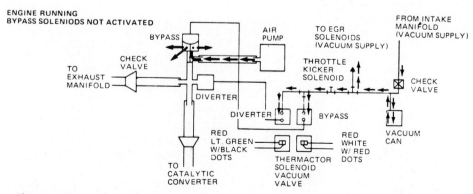

Figure 17-26.   Thermactor Pump Airflow Bypassed to Atmosphere. (*Courtesy of Ford Motor Co.*)

When the engine coolant is cold, the ECA energizes the TAB and TAD solenoids and manifold vacuum is applied through the solenoids to the TAB and TAD valves. Under this condition thermactor pump air is diverted to the exhaust ports, as indicated in Figure 17-27. This results in lower hydrocarbon (HC) emissions during the engine warm-up period.

When the input sensors signal the ECA to provide downstream injection, the ECA energizes the TAB solenoid and de-energizes the TAD solenoid. Manifold vacuum is maintained through the TAB solenoid to the TAB valve, but the manifold vacuum to the TAD solenoid is shut off. When this occurs, the thermactor pump airflow is diverted to the catalytic converter, as illustrated in Figure 17-28.

Canister Purging The ECA energizes the canister-purge (CANP) solenoid, which controls the flow of fuel vapors from the canister to the intake manifold. Activation of the CANP solenoid by the ECA occurs when the following conditions are present.

1. Engine coolant temperature is in the normal operating range.

2. Engine revolutions per minute (rpm) is above a calibration value.

3. The time since the engine was started is above a calibration value.

4. The engine is not in the closed-throttle mode.

Upshift Light On vehicles equipped with manual transaxles, the upshift light is illuminated by the ECA when an upshift to the next highest gear will provide optimum fuel economy.

Self-Test Connector Diagnostic procedures are performed when a voltmeter or digital tester is connected to the self-test connector. (Diagnosis of Ford EEC IV systems with computer-controlled carburetors or fuel injection is explained in Chapter 13 of *Automotive Principles: Repair and Service*, Volume II.)

Air Conditioner (A/C) and Cooling Fan Controller Module A cooling fan and A/C controller module is used with the EEC IV system on the 2.3L engine to control the operation of the cooling fan and the A/C compressor clutch. The module is mounted

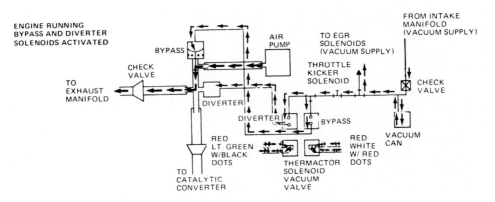

Figure 17-27. Thermactor Pump Airflow Diverted to Exhaust Ports. (*Courtesy of Ford Motor Co.*)

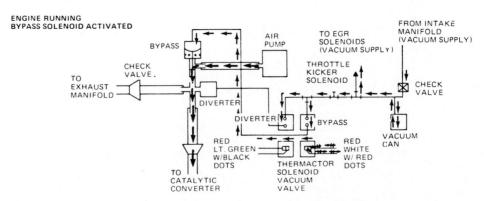

Figure 17-28. Thermactor Pump Airflow Diverted to Catalytic Converter. (*Courtesy of Ford Motor Co.*)

under the right side of the instrument panel. Input signals are sent to the module from the coolant temperature switch, the ECA, and the stop lamp switch. The stop lamp switch signal is used only on vehicles that are equipped with an automatic transaxle (ATX). Output signals from the module control the operation of the engine cooling fan and the A/C compressor clutch, as illustrated in Figure 17-29.

When the module receives a signal from the clutch cycling pressure switch, the module sends an output signal to apply the A/C compressor clutch. During periods of wide-open throttle (WOT) operation, the ECA applies an input signal to the module that disables the signal to the compressor clutch. This WOT signal from the ECA also de-energizes the cooling fan motor if the engine coolant temperature is below 210°F (97°C). The coolant temperature switch applies a ground signal to the module if the coolant temperature exceeds 210°F (97°C). This ground signal overrides the WOT signal from the ECA and prevents the cooling fan from shutting off.

The ECA also contains a time-out feature for the WOT signal. After approximately 30 seconds, the WOT signal is stopped even if the WOT condition is still present. However, slow recycling from WOT to part throttle and back to WOT will shut off the compressor clutch again for 30 seconds.

When the brake pedal is applied on vehicles that are equipped with an automatic transaxle (ATX), an input signal is sent from the brake lamp switch to the module. This will result in a disable signal being sent from the module to the cooling fan and the A/C compressor clutch for 3 to 5 seconds to prevent engine stalling on deceleration. Disabling the compressor clutch and the cooling fan at WOT provides more engine power.

Control Modes   The crank mode is used by the ECA while the engine is being cranked or if the engine stalls and the ignition switch is left in the start position. When the engine is being cranked, fuel control is in the open-loop mode and the ECA sets ignition timing at 10 to 15 degrees before top dead center (BTDC). The EGR solenoids are not energized and therefore the EGR valve is closed. Thermactor air is upstream to the exhaust ports and the canister purge system is off. The crank mode is a special program that is used to aid engine starting.

The underspeed mode is used to provide additional fuel enrichment and increased airflow to the

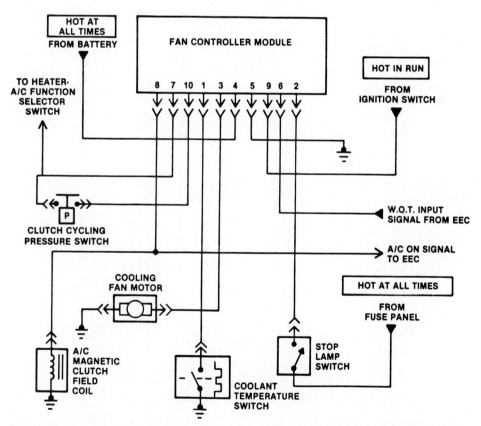

Figure 17-29.   Cooling Fan and A/C Compressor Controller Module. (*Courtesy of Ford Motor Co.*)

engine to help it recover from a stumble. If the engine speed drops below 600 rpm, the ECA enters the underspeed mode. Operation in this mode is similar to the crank mode.

In the closed-throttle mode, the various input sensor signals are evaluated by the ECA and the ECA determines the correct air-fuel ratio and ignition timing. As long as the exhaust-gas oxygen (EGO) sensor signal is maintained, the system remains in closed loop mode. If the EGO sensor cools off and its signal is no longer available the system goes into open-loop operation. The ECA activates the throttle kicker system if the engine coolant is above a predetermined temperature or if the air conditioning is on. The throttle kicker will also be activated for a few seconds after the engine is started. During the closed-throttle mode, the EGR valve and the canister-purge system are turned off. The closed-throttle mode is used during idle operation or deceleration.

The part-throttle mode is entered during moderate cruising speed conditions. In this mode the system operates in closed-loop mode as long as the EGO sensor signal is available. The throttle kicker is activated to provide a dashpot function when the engine is decelerated. The ECA activates the EGR solenoids and the EGR valve opens.

At wide-open throttle, the system switches to open-loop operation, and the ECA operates the feedback solenoid to provide a slightly richer air-fuel ratio. To improve engine performance, the WOT signal from the ECA to the fan controller module causes the module to shut off the cooling fan and the A/C clutch.

When an electrical defect occurs that prevents the ECA from performing its normal modes of operation, the system enters the limited operation strategy (LOS) mode.

A complete wiring diagram of the EEC IV sys-

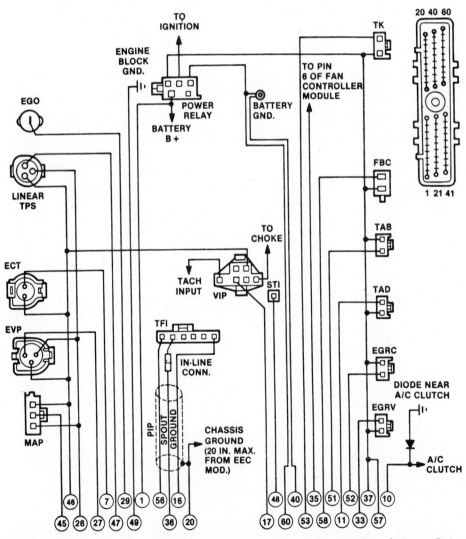

Figure 17-30. EEC IV 2.3L Engine Wiring Diagram. (*Courtesy of Ford Motor Co.*)

tem used on the 2.3L HSC engine is provided in Figure 17-30.

Ford Electronic Engine Control IV (EEC IV) Systems Used with 2.8L V6 Engines

Input Sensors

Many of the same sensors are used on the EEC IV system on the 2.8L V6 engine and the 2.3L engine. The knock sensor, idle tracking switch (ITS), air charge temperature (ACT) sensor, and the neutral/start switch are additional input signals on the 2.8L V6 engine.

The knock sensor sends a signal to the ECA if the engine begins to detonate. When the ECA receives this signal it retards the ignition spark advance. The amount of retard depends on the severity and duration of the detonation. The maximum amount of retard is 8 degrees.

The idle tracking switch (ITS) is an integral part of the idle-speed control motor. This switch signals the ECA when the throttle is closed. When the throttle is closed, the ITS switch is open. Under this condition the ECA operates the idle-speed control motor to control the idle speed. When the throttle is

opened, the ITS switch closes and the ECA no longer operates the idle-speed control motor.

The air charge temperature (ACT) sensor is mounted in the air cleaner. This sensor sends a signal to the ECA in relation to the air-intake temperature. The ACT sensor signal is used by the ECA to control the choke opening when the air-intake temperature is cold. Once the engine is warmed up, the ACT signal is used by the ECA to control idle speed. When the air-intake temperature is below 55°F (13°C), the ACT signal causes the ECA to direct thermactor air to the atmosphere.

The neutral/start switch signal is used on vehicles that are equipped with an automatic transaxle. This switch is closed when the transaxle is in neutral or park, and open in all other transaxle selector positions. When the ECA receives a signal from the neutral/start switch that indicates the transaxle selector is in neutral or park, it increases the idle speed 50 rpm to improve idle quality.

All of the input signals and output controls in the EEC IV system on the 2.8L V6 engine are illustrated in Figure 17-31.

Output Controls

The EEC IV system on the 2.8L engine uses many of the same output controls that are used on the EEC IV system on the 2.3L engine. Additional output

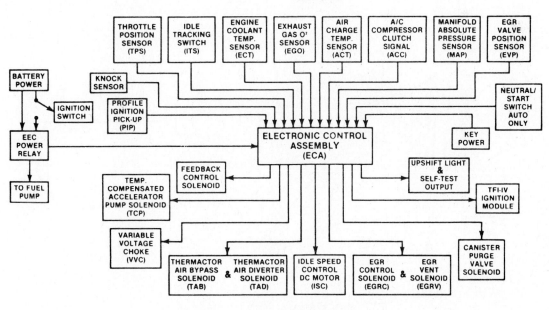

Figure 17-31.   EEC IV Input Signals and Output Controls on 2.8L V6 Engine. (*Courtesy of Ford Motor Co.*)

controls on the 2.8L engine would include the temperature-compensated accelerator pump (TCP) solenoid, variable voltage choke (VVC), and the idle-speed control (ISC) motor. A different type of feedback control (FBC) solenoid is used with the 2150A two-barrel carburetor on the 2.8L V6 engine. The ECA operates the FBC plunger, which controls the amount of airflow into the idle and main circuit air-bleed passages, as pictured in Figure 17-32.

When the exhaust-gas oxygen (EGO) sensor signals the ECA that the air-fuel ratio is too rich, the ECA operates the FBC solenoid plunger to allow more air into the idle and main circuits to provide a leaner air-fuel ratio. The ECA operates the FBC solenoid to maintain an air-fuel ratio of 14.7:1 when the engine is at normal operating temperature and the system is operating in closed-loop mode.

The temperature-compensated accelerator pump (TCP) allows delivery of full pump capacity to improve cold engine performance, and a lesser pump capacity during warm engine operation. The TCP contains a bypass bleed valve that is operated by a vacuum diaphragm. A vacuum solenoid that is controlled by the ECA applies vacuum to the vacuum diaphragm in the TCP. When the engine coolant is cold, the vacuum solenoid shuts off the vacuum applied to the TCP and thus allows the bypass valve to remain closed. Under this condition full accelerator pump capacity is delivered through the accelerator

pump system. The TCP system is illustrated in Figure 17-33.

At normal engine coolant temperature, the ECA energizes the TCP solenoid and applies vacuum to the TCP diaphragm. When this occurs the bypass valve opens and some fuel is returned past the bypass valve to the float bowl each time the engine is accelerated.

The variable voltage choke (VVC) is an electric choke that is controlled by the ECA and a solid-state power relay. A variable duty cycle is used by the ECA and power relay to control the opening of the choke. The VVC and the power relay are pictured in Figure 17-34.

As the air-intake temperature decreases, the ECA and the power relay reduce the "on time" of the voltage that is supplied to the choke. This allows the choke to remain on longer. When the choke cover temperature is above 80°F (27°C), the ECA and the power relay supply voltage to the choke continuously to keep it open.

The idle-speed control (ISC) motor is a direct current (DC) electric motor that is used to control idle speed after the choke is open. An ISC motor is shown in Figure 17-35.

A conventional fast-idle cam that is operated by the choke spring provides fast idle speed when the engine coolant is cold. The ISC motor will not move past preset limits, nor will it move if the idle track-

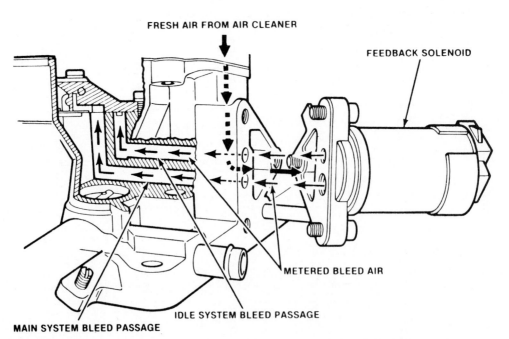

FRESH AIR FROM AIR CLEANER

FEEDBACK SOLENOID

METERED BLEED AIR

IDLE SYSTEM BLEED PASSAGE

MAIN SYSTEM BLEED PASSAGE

Figure 17-32. Feedback Control (FBC) Solenoid, 2.8L V6 Engine. (*Courtesy of Ford Motor Co.*)

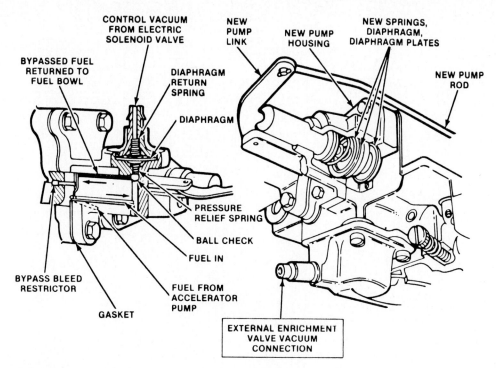

Figure 17-33. Temperature-Compensated Accelerator Pump (TCP). (*Courtesy of Ford Motor Co.*)

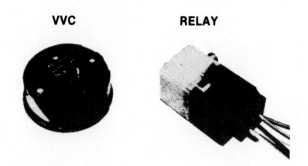

Figure 17-34. Variable Voltage Choke (VVC) and Power Relay. (*Courtesy of Ford Motor Co.*)

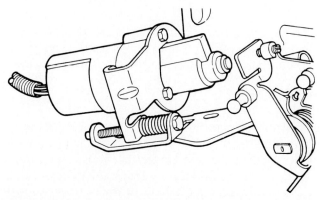

Figure 17-35. Idle-Speed Control (ISC) Motor. (*Courtesy of Ford Motor Co.*)

ing switch (ITS) signal to the ECA indicates that the throttle is not in the idle position. When the engine is shut off, the ISC motor retracts and closes the throttle to prevent the engine from dieseling. After the engine stops running, the ISC motor extends to its maximum travel for restart purposes.

A time-delay circuit in the power relay supplies voltage to the ECA for 10 seconds after the ignition switch is turned off. This allows the ECA to extend the ISC motor after the ignition switch is turned off. When the engine is started, the ISC motor is extended for a brief period of time to provide a faster idle speed. The time period when the ISC motor is extended depends on coolant temperature. Under cruising-speed conditions the ISC motor is extended to provide a dashpot action when the engine is decelerated. If the engine overheats, or if the battery voltage is low, the ECA operates the ISC motor to increase the idle speed. The idle speed is also increased by the ISC motor if the air conditioner is turned on, or if the automatic transaxle is placed in neutral or park.

Most of the solenoids and relays in the EEC IV system are located behind a plastic cover on the firewall or in the fender shield. The ECA is located in the passenger compartment under the right kick-pad.

A complete wiring diagram of the EEC IV sys-

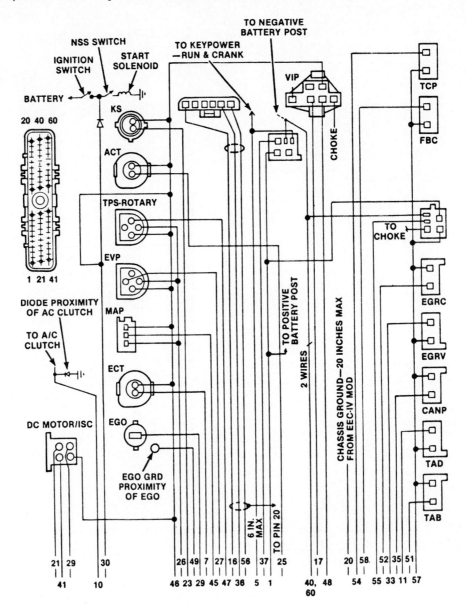

Figure 17-36.   EEC IV Wiring Diagram, 2.8L V6 Engine. (*Courtesy of Ford Motor Co.*)

tem that is used on the 2.8L V6 engine is illustrated in Figure 17-36.

Chrysler Oxygen Feedback Carburetor System

Operation

In the oxygen (O₂) feedback carburetor system, the electronic control computer controls the "on time" of the carburetor feedback solenoid winding. When the oxygen sensor sends a signal to the electronic fuel-control computer indicating an excessively rich air-fuel ratio, the computer increases the "on time" of the carburetor feedback solenoid and provides a leaner mixture in the main carburetor system, as illustrated in Figure 17-37.

The return spring on the carburetor feedback solenoid holds the solenoid plunger in the upward position. When the electronic fuel-control computer energizes the carburetor feedback solenoid winding, the solenoid plunger is held in the downward position. If the oxygen sensor sends a lean air-fuel ratio signal to the electronic fuel-control computer, the

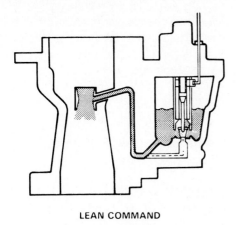

LEAN COMMAND

Figure 17-37 Carburetor Feedback Solenoid, Lean Command. (*Courtesy of Chrysler Canada*)

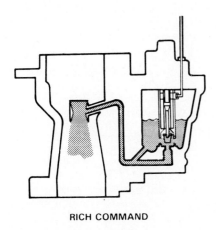

RICH COMMAND

Figure 17-38. Carburetor Feedback Solenoid, Rich Command. (*Courtesy of Chrysler Canada*)

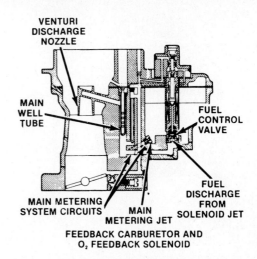

FEEDBACK CARBURETOR AND O₂ FEEDBACK SOLENOID

Figure 17-39. Feedback Solenoid with Air Bleed to Idle Circuit. (*Courtesy of Chrysler Canada*)

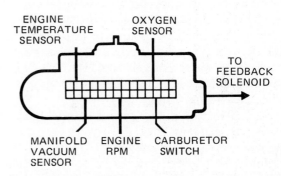

Figure 17-40. Computer Input Sensor Signals. (*Courtesy of Chrysler Canada*)

computer decreases the "on time" of the solenoid winding. This allows the solenoid plunger to remain in the upward position for a longer period of time, thus providing a richer air-fuel ratio, as shown in Figure 17-38.

The carburetor feedback solenoid also controls the airflow into the idle system. Downard movement of the solenoid plunger results in an increase in airflow into the idle system, so that a leaner air-fuel ratio is provided at idle speed. The airflow into the idle system is reduced when the solenoid plunger is in the upward position; therefore a richer air-fuel ratio occurs at idle speed.

The air bleed from the top of the solenoid plunger into the idle circuit is illustrated in Figure 17-39.

In the closed-loop mode, the electronic fuel-control computer operates the carburetor feedback solenoid in response to the oxygen sensor signal to provide an air-fuel ratio of 14.7:1. The electronic fuel-

control computer and the electronic spark-advance computer are combined in one unit. The input sensors signals that are used by the combined computers are pictured in Figure 17-40.

The air pump system uses an air-switching valve to direct the airflow from the pump to the exhaust ports when the engine coolant is cold. The air-switching valve directs airflow from the air pump to the catalytic converters when the engine is at normal operating temperature. A coolant-controlled vacuum switch applies manifold vacuum to the air-switching valve when the engine coolant is cold. (The operation of this air-switching system was explained in Chapter 8.)

On some engines that are equipped with an oxygen feedback system, the electronic fuel-control computer operates a vacuum solenoid winding to control the manifold vacuum that is applied to the air-switching valve. When the engine coolant is cold, the electronic fuel-control computer energizes the vacuum solenoid winding and thus allows vacuum through the solenoid to the air-switching valve.

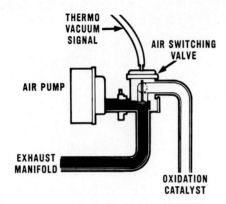

Figure 17-41. Air-Switching Valve Operation. (*Courtesy of Chrysler Canada*)

When manifold vacuum is applied to the air-switching valve, the airflow from the pump is directed to the exhaust manifold as shown in Figure 17-41.

The electronic fuel-control computer de-energizes the vacuum solenoid when the engine coolant is at normal operating temperature. Under this condition the vacuum solenoid shuts off the vacuum applied to the air-switching valve, and the airflow from the pump is directed through the air-switching valve to the catalytic converter.

(An explanation of the ignition system and complete wiring diagrams for the Chrysler O_2 feedback system are provided Chapter 13.)

(Refer to Chapter 12 in *Automotive Principles: Repair and Service*, Volume II, for servicing and diagnosis of computer systems with computer-controlled carburetors.)

Test Questions

Questions on 3C Systems

1. When the air-fuel ratio becomes richer, the oxygen sensor voltage_____.

2. Leaded gasoline may be used in a vehicle that has an oxygen sensor in the exhaust system.　T　F

3. If the electronic control module (ECM) increases the "on time" of the mixture control solenoid winding, the air-fuel ratio becomes ____.

4. Airflow from the air pump should be directed to the catalytic converter when the engine is operating at normal temperature and light-load, cruising-speed conditions.　T　F

Questions on Electronic Engine Control Systems

5. On an EEC IV system used on a 2.3L engine, the cooling fan and air conditioning compressor clutch are operated by the _____ _____ _____.

6. The upshift light is turned on when a shift to the next highest gear will provide optimum ____ _____ _____.

7. The temperature-compensated accelerator pump supplies more fuel when the engine is:
   a) operating at normal temperature.
   b) overheated.
   c) operating during warm-up.

8. When the temperature decreases, the duty cycle of the variable voltage choke:
   a) decreases.
   b) remains the same.
   c) increases.

Questions on Chrysler Feedback Systems

9. If the electronic fuel-control computer receives a rich-mixture signal from the oxygen sensor, it will _____ the "on time" of the carburetor feedback solenoid.

10. The manifold vacuum that is applied to the air-switching valve is controlled by a coolant-controlled vacuum switch or a _____ _____ vacuum solenoid.

11. If the airflow is directed from the air pump to the exhaust manifold with the engine at normal temperature, the oxygen sensor signal indicates a _____ air-fuel ratio.

18

Computer-Controlled Fuel-Injection Systems

Chapter Completion Objectives

1. Demonstrate an understanding of General Motors throttle body and port fuel injection systems.
2. Display a knowledge of General Motors computer systems with body computer modules.
3. Indicate an understanding of Chrysler computer systems with throttle body or port injection.
4. Show a thorough comprehension of Ford electronic engine control IV (EEC IV) systems with fuel injection.

General Motors Throttle Body Injection Systems

Throttle Body Injection Assemblies

In a throttle body injection system, the carburetor is replaced with a throttle body injector assembly. This assembly may contain a single injector, as illustrated in Figure 18-1. When a single injector is used, the injection system is referred to as electronic fuel injection (EFI) or throttle body injection (TBI).

Some large-displacement engines have dual injectors in the throttle body assembly, as shown in Figure 18-2.

Such systems are referred to as digital fuel injection (DFI) or digital electronic fuel injection (DEFI). Other throttle body injection systems use a pair of single injectors that are spaced in an offset position on a special intake manifold, as pictured in Figure 18-3. When offset single injectors are used, the injection system is called crossfire injection (CFI).

Regardless of the type of throttle body injector assembly used, the internal structure is similar. Gasoline is forced into the fuel inlet from the fuel pump and then flows past the injector(s) to the pressure regulator. When fuel pressure reaches 10 psi (69 kPa), the pressure regulator spring is compressed, the pressure regulator valve opens, and any excess fuel is returned to the fuel tank. Pressurized fuel surrounds the injectors at all times, as illustrated in Figure 18-4.

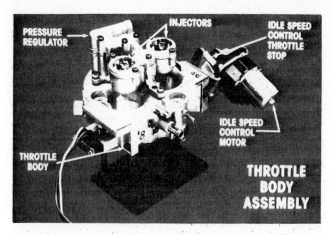

Figure 18-2. Digital Fuel Injection (DFI) Throttle Body Injector Assembly. (Reference taken from SAE paper No. 800164. *Reprinted with Permission of Society of Automotive Engineers,* © *1980*)

A return spring on the injector plunger holds the injector closed. The injector opens when the solenoid coil surrounding the plunger is energized by the electronic control module (ECM). When the injector opens, fuel is sprayed into the airstream above the throttles, as shown in Figure 18-5. The ECM varies the open time of the injector to control the amount of fuel injected.

Complete Fuel System

A twin-turbine fuel pump is mounted in the fuel tank with the gauge sending unit. The fuel pump forces fuel through the filter under the vehicle to the throttle body injector assembly. Excess fuel from the injector assembly flows through the return fuel line to the fuel tank, as illustrated in Figure 18-6.

The ECM energizes the fuel pump relay winding when the ignition switch is turned on, and the relay points close. Thus, battery voltage is allowed to go through the relay points to the fuel pump, which then supplies fuel to the injectors. If no attempt is made to start the vehicle within two seconds from the time the ignition switch is turned on, the ECM de-energizes the fuel pump relay winding and the relay points open the circuit to the fuel pump. The ECM energizes the fuel pump relay winding as long as the engine is running.

An alternate circuit is provided through a special set of oil pressure switch contacts to the fuel pump, as illustrated in Figure 18-7.

If the fuel pump relay becomes defective, power is still supplied to the fuel pump through the oil pressure switch contacts. This makes it possible to drive the vehicle when the pump relay is defective.

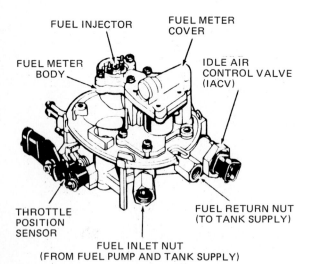

Figure 18-1. Throttle Body Injection (TBI) Assembly. (*Courtesy of GM Product Service Training, General Motors Corporation*)

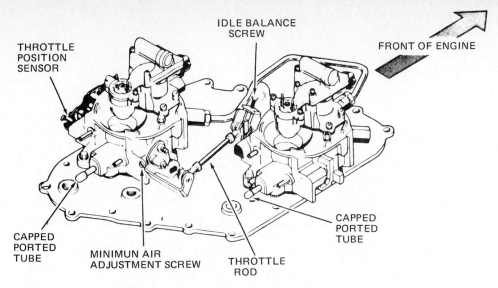

Figure 18-3. Crossfire Injection (CFI) Throttle Body Injector Assembly. (*Courtesy of Chevrolet Motor Division, General Motors Corporation*)

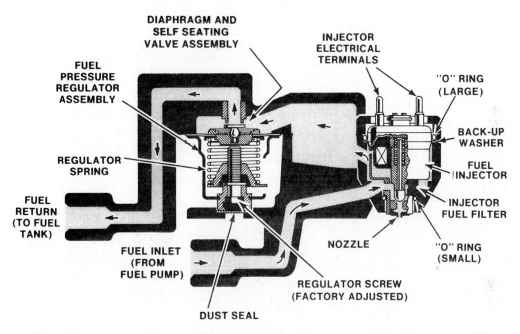

Figure 18-4. Internal Design of Throttle Body Injector Assembly. (*Courtesy of GM Product Service Training, General Motors Corporation*)

Throttle Body Injection (TBI) System Components

The electronic control module (ECM) is the "brain" of the TBI system. The ECM receives information from the sensors and performs the necessary control functions. A removable programmable read-only memory (PROM) is installed in the ECM, as pictured in Figure 18-8. The PROM contains calibration data for each engine, transmission, and rear axle ratio. This information will always be retained in the permanent memory of the PROM.

Special tools are available for PROM removal and replacement. The technician must be careful to install the PROM in the correct position, and to be

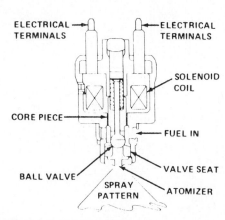

Figure 18-5. Injector Assembly. (*Courtesy of GM Product Service Training, General Motors Corporation*)

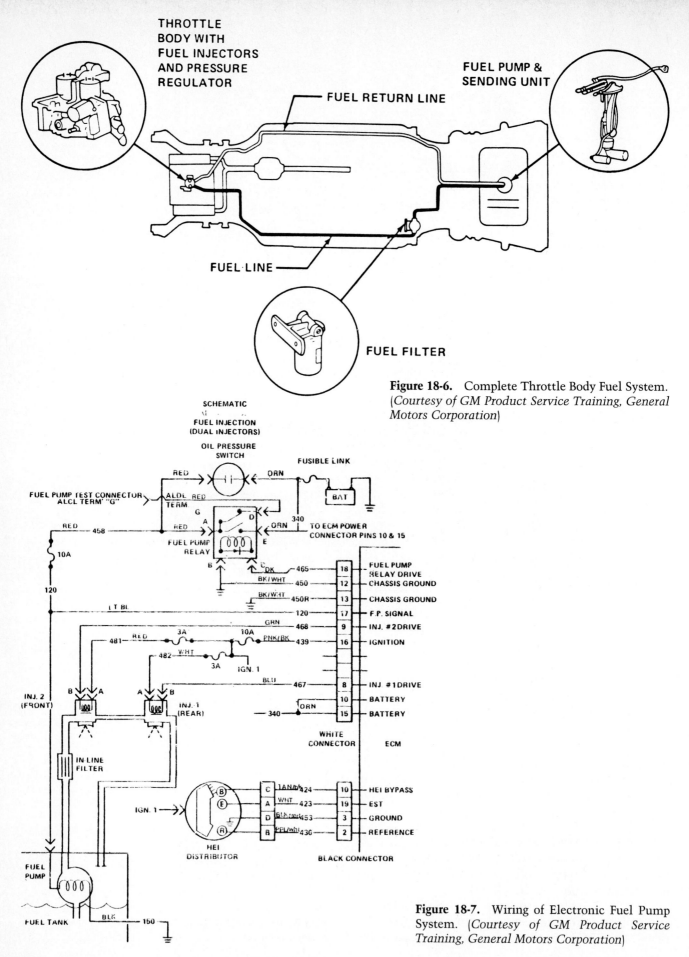

THROTTLE
BODY WITH
FUEL INJECTORS
AND PRESSURE
REGULATOR

FUEL PUMP &
SENDING UNIT

FUEL RETURN LINE

FUEL LINE

FUEL FILTER

Figure 18-6. Complete Throttle Body Fuel System.
(*Courtesy of GM Product Service Training, General Motors Corporation*)

SCHEMATIC
FUEL INJECTION
(DUAL INJECTORS)

OIL PRESSURE
SWITCH

FUSIBLE LINK

RED   ORN

FUEL PUMP TEST CONNECTOR
ALCL TERM "G"   ALDL   RED
                       TERM.
                          G   D

RED   RED   A   D
RED   458   E
                       ORN   TO ECM POWER
                          340   CONNECTOR PINS 10 & 15

10A   FUEL PUMP
               RELAY

120   B   C   DK   465   18   FUEL PUMP
                          BK/WHT 450   12   RELAY DRIVE
                                                 CHASSIS GROUND
                          BK/WHT 450R   13   CHASSIS GROUND
          LT BL   120   17   F.P. SIGNAL
                          GRN   468   9   INJ. #2 DRIVE
481   RED   3A   10A   PNK/BK   439   16   IGNITION
482   WHT   IGN. 1
           3A
                          BLU   467   8   INJ. #1 DRIVE
B   A   A   B   10   BATTERY
INJ. 2   340   15   BATTERY
(FRONT)   INJ. 1   ORN
             (REAR)
                          WHITE
                          CONNECTOR   ECM

IN-LINE
FILTER

                    C   TAN/blk 424   10   HEI BYPASS
                    A   WHT   423   19   EST
IGN. 1   D   BLK/red 453   3   GROUND
                    B   PPL/wht 430   2   REFERENCE
                    HEI
                    DISTRIBUTOR   BLACK CONNECTOR

FUEL
PUMP

FUEL TANK   BLK   150

Figure 18-7. Wiring of Electronic Fuel Pump System. (*Courtesy of GM Product Service Training, General Motors Corporation*)

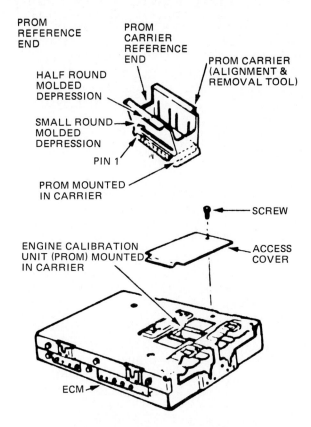

PROM REFERENCE END

PROM CARRIER REFERENCE END

PROM CARRIER (ALIGNMENT & REMOVAL TOOL)

HALF ROUND MOLDED DEPRESSION

SMALL ROUND MOLDED DEPRESSION

PIN 1

PROM MOUNTED IN CARRIER

SCREW

ENGINE CALIBRATION UNIT (PROM) MOUNTED IN CARRIER

ACCESS COVER

ECM

Figure 18-8. Electronic Control Module (ECM) with Programmable Read-Only Memory (PROM). (*Courtesy of GM Product Service Training, General Motors Corporation*)

sure not to bend the pins on the PROM during installation. An alignment notch is used to position the PROM correctly, as shown in Figure 18-8.

The most important electronic components of the TBI systems are:

1. Manifold absolute pressure (MAP) sensor.
2. Barometric pressure (baro) sensor.
3. Throttle position sensor (TPS).
4. Coolant temperature sensor (CTS).
5. Manifold air temperature (MAT) sensor.
6. Oxygen (O_2) sensor.
7. Distributor reference pulses.
8. Vehicle speed sensor (VSS).
9. Park–Neutral (P–N) switch.
10. Air conditioning clutch switch.

All the components listed above may not be used in every throttle body injection system.

The input sensors are basically the same as the sensors used in the computer command control (3C) system. (See Chapter 17 for a complete description of the 3C system.)

Electronic Control Module (ECM) Control Functions

Fuel The ECM maintains the correct air-fuel ratio of 14.7:1 by controlling the time that the injectors are open. The ECM varies the open time or "on time" of the injectors from 1 to 2 milliseconds at idle, and from 6 to 7 milliseconds at wide-open throttle. As the "on time" of the injector increases, the amount of fuel injected increases proportionately.

The injectors are operated by the ECM in two different modes: synchronized, and nonsynchronized. In the synchronized mode, the injector is energized by the ECM each time a distributor reference pulse is received by the ECM. On systems with dual throttle body injectors, the injectors are pulsed alternately. In the nonsynchronized mode of operation, the injectors are energized every 12.5 or 6.5 milliseconds, depending on the application. This pulse time is controlled by the ECM and is independent of distributor reference pulses.

The nonsynchronized pulses take place under the following conditions:

1. When the injector "on time" becomes less than 1.5 milliseconds.
2. During the delivery of prime pulses that are used to charge the intake manifold with fuel when the engine is being started or just before starting.
3. During acceleration, when a rich air-fuel ratio is required.
4. During deceleration, when a lean air-fuel ratio is required.

If the engine coolant is cold, the ECM delivers "prime pulses" to the injector when the engine is being cranked and the throttle is less than 80 percent open. This eliminates the need for a conventional choke. As the coolant temperature decreases, the ECM increases the "on time" or pulse width of the injector. At −33°F (−36°C) coolant temperature, the ECM increases the injector pulse width to provide an air-fuel ratio of 1.5:1 for cold-start purposes. If dual throttle body injectors are used, the ECM may energize both injectors simultaneously during the prime pulses.

Should a cold engine become flooded, the ECM has the capability to clear this condition. To clear a flooded engine, the driver must depress the accelerator pedal to the wide-open position. The ECM then reduces the injector pulse width to deliver an air-fuel ratio of 20:1. This ratio is maintained as long as the throttle is held wide open and the engine speed is below 600 rpm.

When the engine is running at a speed above 600 rpm, the system enters the open-loop mode. In this mode the ECM ignores the signal from the oxygen (O_2) sensor and calculates the injector pulse width on the basis of the input signals from the coolant temperature sensor (CTS) and the manifold absolute pressure (MAP) sensor. During the open-loop mode, the ECM analyzes the following information before it enters the closed-loop mode:

1. Oxygen sensor voltage output (must be present).

2. Temperature of the CTS sensor (must be at or above normal).

3. The time that has elapsed from engine start-up (a specific period is required).

When the ECM is satisfied with the input signals, the system enters the closed-loop mode. In this mode the ECM modifies the injector "on time" on the basis of the signal from the O_2 sensor to provide the ideal air-fuel ratio of 14.7:1.

If the engine is accelerated suddenly, the manifold vacuum decreases rapidly. The ECM senses the increase in throttle opening from the TPS sensor and the decrease in manifold vacuum from the MAP sensor. When the ECM receives input signals indicating sudden acceleration of the engine, it increases the injector "on time" to provide a slightly richer air-fuel ratio. This acceleration enrichment prevents hesitation when the engine is accelerated.

If the engine is decelerated, a leaner air-fuel ratio is required to reduce CO and HC emission levels. A sudden increase in manifold vacuum occurs when the engine is decelerated. The ECM senses engine deceleration from the MAP sensor signal and the TPS sensor input. When the ECM receives signals indicating engine deceleration, it reduces the injector "on time" to provide a leaner air-fuel ratio and prevent high emissions of CO and HC.

If a defect occurs in the system that makes it impossible for the ECM to operate in the normal modes, a throttle body backup (TBB) circuit in the ECM takes over operation of the injectors. When the TBB circuit is in operation, the "on time" of the injectors is increased so that the air-fuel ratio is richer than normal, but the vehicle can be driven until the necessary repairs are made.

Electronic Spark Timing (EST) The spark advance is controlled by the ECM in response to the input signals that it receives. (Refer to Chapter 13 for a complete description of ignition systems used with General Motors fuel injection systems.)

Exhaust Gas Recirculation (EGR) The ECM controls a vacuum solenoid that is used to open and close the vacuum circuit to the EGR valve. The ECM

energizes the vacuum solenoid and shuts off the vacuum to the EGR valve when the coolant temperature is below 150°F (64°C) or when the engine is operating at idle speed, under heavy load, or at wide-open throttle. Under part-throttle conditions with the coolant temperature above 150°F (64°C), the ECM de-energizes the solenoid and allows vacuum to open the EGR valve.

The EGR solenoid and related circuit are shown in Figure 18-9.

Canister Purge Vapors from the fuel tank are collected in the charcoal canister. The ECM operates a solenoid in the purge hose between the canister and the intake manifold, as illustrated in Figure 18-10.

The ECM operates the purge solenoid and allows canister purging when the engine coolant temperature is warm, the throttle is above idle speed, and the vehicle speed is above 10 MPH (16 KPH).

Idle Speed On some throttle body injection systems, the ECM operates an idle-speed control (ISC) motor to control idle speed under slow- or fast-idle conditions. The same ISC motor is used in some

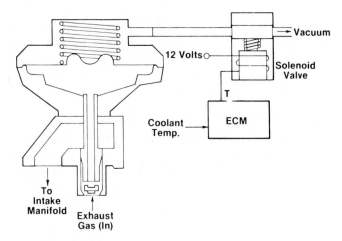

Figure 18-9. EGR Solenoid Circuit. (*Courtesy of GM Product Service Training, General Motors Corporation*)

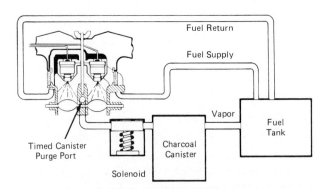

Figure 18-10. Canister-Purge Solenoid Circuit. (*Courtesy of GM Product Service Training, General Motors Corporation*)

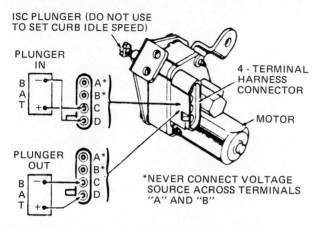

Figure 18-11. Idle-Speed Control (ISC) Motor. (*Courtesy of GM Product Service Training, General Motor Corporation*)

computer command control (3C) systems. An ISC motor and the motor test procedure are illustrated in Figure 18-11.

Some throttle body injection systems use an idle air control (IAC) motor to control idle speed. The IAC motor is operated by the ECM and controls idle speed by opening or closing an air passage into the intake manifold. Airflow through the IAC passage bypasses the throttle, as shown in Figure 18-12.

The IAC motor is used to control idle speed. If the coolant temperature sensor (CTS) sends a signal to the ECM that indicates cold engine coolant, the ECM operates the IAC motor and opens the IAC passage to increase the idle speed. When the engine is at normal operating temperature, the IAC motor provides a faster idle speed for a few seconds each time the engine is started.

When dual throttle body assemblies are used, as in the crossfire injection system, an IAC motor is located in each throttle body assembly.

Air Injection   The air injection reactor (AIR) system is basically the same for throttle body injection systems or computer command control (3C) systems. (See Chapter 17 for a description of 3C AIR systems.) A complete AIR system is illustrated in Figure 18-13.

The ECM operates two electric solenoids in the air control valve and air-switching valve to control

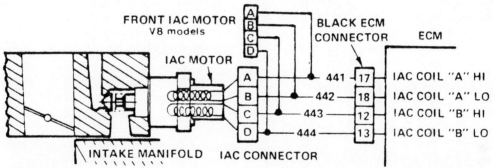

Figure 18-12. Idle Air Control (IAC) Motor. (*Courtesy of GM Product Service Training, General Motors Corporation*)

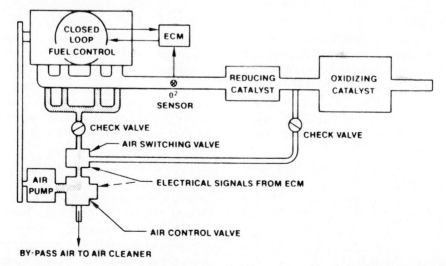

Figure 18-13. Air Injection Reactor (AIR) System. (*Courtesy of GM Product Service Training, General Motors Corporation*)

airflow from the air pump to the air cleaner, exhaust ports, or catalytic converter. On many throttle body injection systems, the ECM operates the air control valve to bypass air to the cleaner for a few seconds each time the engine is started. Once the engine has been running for a brief period, the air control valve directs the airflow from the air pump to the air-switching valve. During the engine warm-up time, the air-switching valve directs airflow from the air pump to the exhaust ports. When the coolant reaches normal operating temperature and the system enters the closed-loop mode, the air-switching valve directs the airflow from the pump to the catalytic converter.

Torque-Converter Clutch The vehicle speed sensor (VSS) signal is used by the ECM to control the torque converter lockup time. The VSS and the torque-converter clutch system are the same on the throttle body injection systems and computer command control (3C) systems. (See Chapter 17 for a description of the VSS and torque-converter clutch in the 3C system.) When the VSS on throttle body injection systems sends a speed signal above 35 MPH (56 KPH) to the ECM, the ECM will maintain the idle air control motors in the extended position. A defective VSS can cause erratic idling.

General Motors Port Fuel Injection

Fuel System

The port fuel injection (PFI) system has individual injectors located in the intake manifold ports. Air injection pumps and heated air-inlet systems are not required with the PFI systems. When the PFI system is used on turbocharged engines, it may be referred to as a sequential fire injection (SFI) system.

There are many similarities between the PFI and SFI systems. One of the most important differences between the two systems is that in the PFI system, all the injectors are energized by the electronic control module (ECM) once for each crankshaft revolution, whereas in the SFI system the injectors are energized individually.

A naturally aspired 186 CID (3.0L) V6 engine with PFI is shown in Figure 18-14.

The electric fuel pump circuit is basically the same as the circuit used on the General Motors throttle body injection systems. (An explanation of the fuel pump circuit was provided earlier in this chapter.) Fuel is forced through the fuel filter and accumulator to the injector fuel rail by the electric

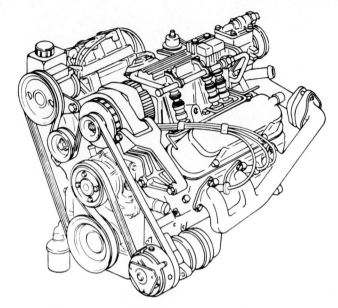

Figure 18-14. Non-Turbocharged V6 Engine with PFI. (*Courtesy of GM Product Service Training, General Motors Corporation*)

fuel pump. An "O" ring seal is located on each end of the injectors to seal the injectors to the fuel rail and the intake manifold. The pressure regulator limits the fuel pressure to 26 to 46 psi (179 to 317 kPa), and excess fuel is returned from the regulator through the fuel return line to the tank.

The fuel system components are shown in Figure 18-15.

A vacuum hose is connected from the lower side of the pressure regulator diaphragm to the intake manifold, as shown in Figure 18-16.

When the engine is idling, manifold vacuum will be 16 to 18 in. Hg (54 to 61 kPa). This low pressure is applied to the injector tips in the intake manifold. When manifold vacuum is applied to the pressure regulator, less fuel pressure is required to force the diaphragm and valve downward and the fuel system pressure will be limited to 26 to 28 psi (179 to 193 kPa). As the throttle approaches the wide-open position, manifold vacuum will be 2 to 3 in. Hg (6.8 to 10 kPa), and this increase in pressure will be sensed at the injector tips. If the manifold vacuum applied to the regulator diaphragm is only 2 to 3 in. Hg (6.8 to 10 kPa), fuel pressure will have to increase to force the diaphragm and valve downward, and fuel system pressure will increase to 33 to 38 psi (227 to 262 kPa). When the intake manifold pressure increases at wider throttle openings, the pressure regulator increases the fuel pressure at the injectors to maintain a constant pressure drop across the injectors and provide more precise air-fuel ratio control.

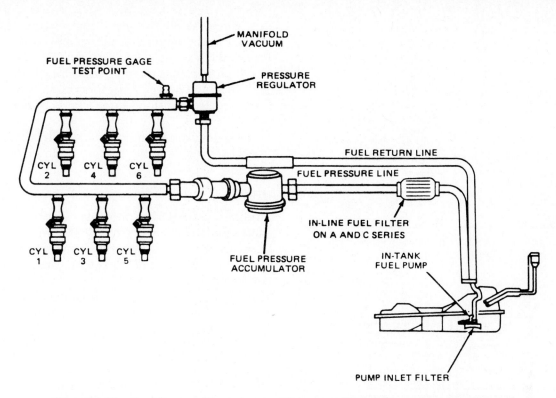

Figure 18-15. Fuel System Components. (*Courtesy of Buick Motor Division, General Motors Corporation*)

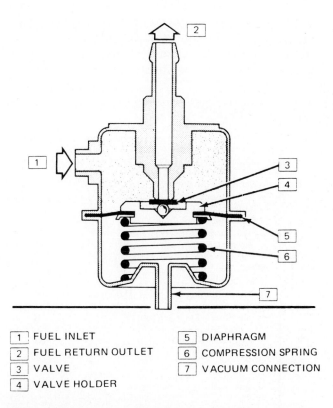

1 FUEL INLET	5 DIAPHRAGM
2 FUEL RETURN OUTLET	6 COMPRESSION SPRING
3 VALVE	7 VACUUM CONNECTION
4 VALVE HOLDER	

Figure 18-16. Pressure Regulator. (*Courtesy of Buick Motor Division, General Motors Corporation*)

Electronic Control Module (ECM)

The ECM is located under the instrument panel and is similar in appearance to those used with throttle body injection systems. Removable programmable read-only memory (PROM) and calibration package (CALPAK) units are located under an access cover in the ECM, as indicated in Figure 18-17. The CALPAK unit allows fuel delivery if other parts of the ECM are damaged.

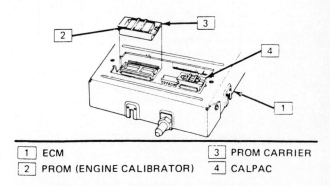

1 ECM	3 PROM CARRIER
2 PROM (ENGINE CALIBRATOR)	4 CALPAC

Figure 18-17. ECM with PROM and CALPAK Units. (*Courtesy of Buick Motor Division, General Motors Corporation*)

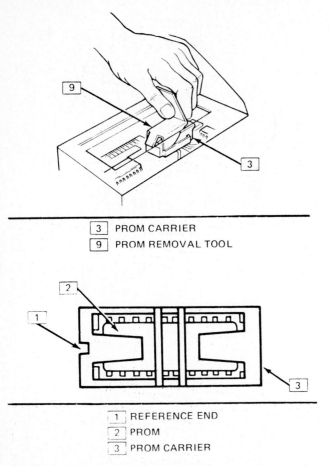

| 3 | PROM CARRIER |
| 9 | PROM REMOVAL TOOL |

1	REFERENCE END
2	PROM
3	PROM CARRIER

Figure 18-18. PROM and CALPAK Removal and Replacement. (*Courtesy of Buick Motor Division, General Motors Corporation*)

When the PROM unit is replaced, it must be installed in the original direction and the connectors must not become bent. The removal and replacement procedure is pictured in Figure 18-18.

When the ECM connectors are being removed or installed, the ignition switch should be in the off position.

The operating conditions sensed by the ECM and the systems that it controls are listed in Table 18-1.

Inputs

Similarities to Other Systems   The throttle position sensor (TPS), oxygen (O_2) sensor, coolant temperature sensor, manifold absolute pressure (MAP) sensor, and the park/neutral switch are similar to the sensors used on General Motors 3C and throttle body injection systems. (Refer to Chapter 17 for an explanation of these sensors in the 3C systems.)

Mass Airflow (MAF) Sensor   The MAF sensor is used in place of the MAP sensor on many engines. Turbocharged engines always use an MAF sensor. The MAF sensor is located in the air intake between the air cleaner and the throttle body assembly, as indicated in Figure 18-19.

The MAF sensor contains a resistor that measures the temperature of the incoming air. A heated film in the sensor is a nickel grid coated with Kapton, a high-temperature resistant material. An electronic module in the top of the sensor maintains the temperature of the heated film at 167°F (75°C). If

TABLE 18-1. ECM Operating Conditions Sensed and Systems Controlled.
(*Courtesy of GM Product Service Training, General Motors Corporation*)

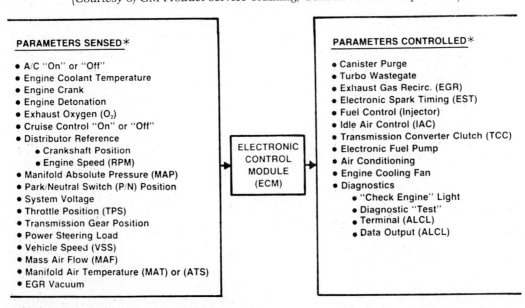

PARAMETERS SENSED*

- A/C "On" or "Off"
- Engine Coolant Temperature
- Engine Crank
- Engine Detonation
- Exhaust Oxygen (O_2)
- Cruise Control "On" or "Off"
- Distributor Reference
    - Crankshaft Position
    - Engine Speed (RPM)
- Manifold Absolute Pressure (MAP)
- Park/Neutral Switch (P/N) Position
- System Voltage
- Throttle Position (TPS)
- Transmission Gear Position
- Power Steering Load
- Vehicle Speed (VSS)
- Mass Air Flow (MAF)
- Manifold Air Temperature (MAT) or (ATS)
- EGR Vacuum

ELECTRONIC CONTROL MODULE (ECM)

PARAMETERS CONTROLLED*

- Canister Purge
- Turbo Wastegate
- Exhaust Gas Recirc. (EGR)
- Electronic Spark Timing (EST)
- Fuel Control (Injector)
- Idle Air Control (IAC)
- Transmission Converter Clutch (TCC)
- Electronic Fuel Pump
- Air Conditioning
- Engine Cooling Fan
- Diagnostics
    - "Check Engine" Light
    - Diagnostic "Test"
    - Terminal (ALCL)
    - Data Output (ALCL)

*NOT ALL SYSTEMS USED ON ALL ENGINES.

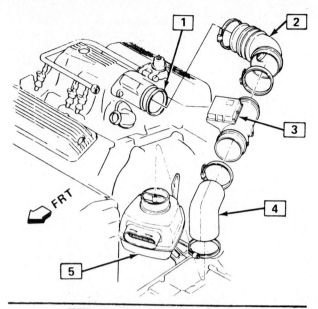

1 THROTTLE BODY ASM.
2 REAR AIR INTAKE DUCT
3 MASS AIR FLOW (MAF) SENSOR
4 INT. AIR INTAKE DUCT
5 AIR CLEANER ASM.

Figure 18-19. MAF Sensor Location. (*Courtesy of Buick Motor Division, General Motors Corporation*)

more energy is required to maintain the heated film at 167°F (75°C), the incoming mass of air has increased. This information is sent to the ECM, and the ECM uses this input to provide a very precise air-fuel ratio control. The MAF sensor is shown in Figure 18-20.

Vehicle Speed Sensor (VSS) The VSS is a signal generator located in the transaxle. It is rotated mechanically and generates an electrical signal in rela-

Figure 18-20. MAF Sensor. (*Courtesy of GM Product Service Training, General Motors Corporation*)

tion to vehicle speed. This signal is sent through the VSS signal buffer to the ECM, as indicated in Figure 18-21.

Knock Sensor A knock sensor is used on some PFI systems. The knock sensor signal is sent through the electronic spark control (ESC) module to the ECM. When the engine detonates, the knock sensor signal to the ESC module and ECM causes the ECM to retard the spark advance. The knock sensor circuit is shown in Figure 18-22.

Exhaust-Gas Recirculation (EGR) Vacuum Diagnostic Switch The ECM operates a vacuum solenoid which applies vacuum to the EGR valve. When vacuum is applied to the EGR valve, the EGR vacuum diagnostic switch signals the ECM that the EGR valve is operating. If the EGR valve is operating when the necessary input signals are not present, the

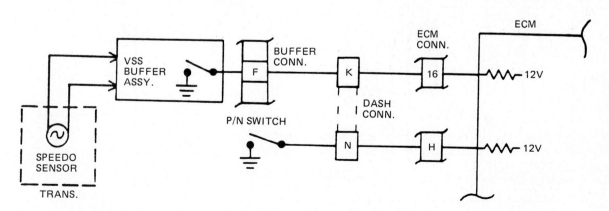

Figure 18-21. VSS Sensor. (*Courtesy of Buick Motor Division, General Motors Corporation*)

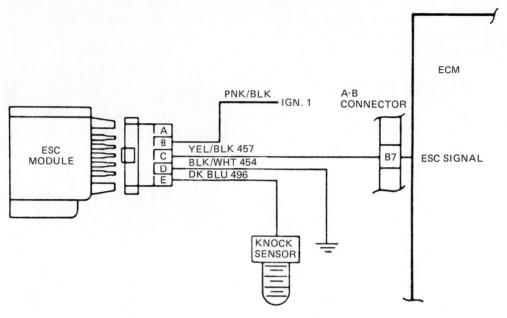

Figure 18-22. Knock Sensor Circuit. (*Courtesy of GM Product Service Training, General Motors Corporation*)

EGR vacuum diagnostic switch signals the ECM and a diagnostic code 32 is set in the ECM memory.

The EGR vacuum diagnostic switch and the EGR solenoid circuits are illustrated in Figure 18-23.

Manifold Air Temperature (MAT) Sensor   Some PFI systems use a MAT sensor which sends a signal to the ECM in relation to the temperature of the air in the intake manifold or in the air cleaner.

Distributor Reference Signal   Many PFI systems use the same ignition system as General Motors 3C systems. (These ignition systems were described in Chapter 13.) The distributor reference signal from the high-energy ignition (HEI) module to the ECM is

used as a crankshaft position signal and engine speed signal.

ECM Outputs

Spark Advance   When the engine is running, the distributor pickup coil signal is sent through the HEI module and the distributor reference circuit to the ECM. This pickup signal travels through the electronic spark timing (EST) circuit in the ECM and then out to the HEI module through the EST wire. When the HEI module receives this pickup signal through the EST wire, it switches off the primary ignition circuit. This results in collapse of the mag-

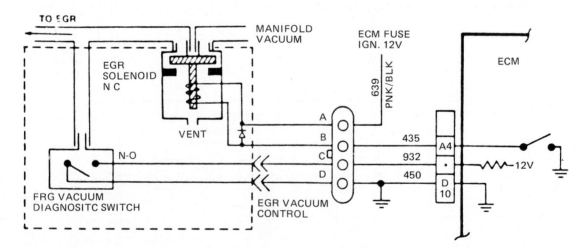

Figure 18-23. EGR Vacuum Diagnostic Switch and Solenoid. (*Courtesy of GM Product Service Training, General Motors Corporation*)

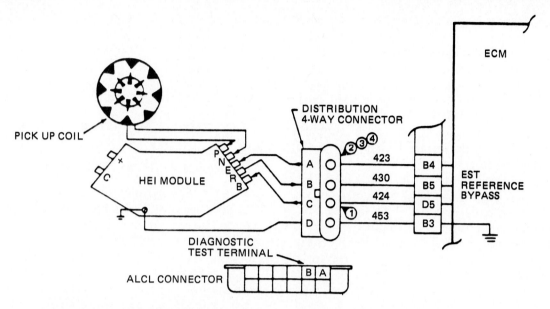

Figure 18-24. HEI Module and EST Circuit in ECM. (*Courtesy of GM Product Service Training, General Motors Corporation*)

netic field in the ignition coil so that the spark plugs are fired. The EST circuit in the ECM varies the pickup coil signal to provide the exact spark advance required by the engine.

Figure 18-24 illustrates the spark advance control circuit.

[Refer to Chapter 13 for General Motors high-energy ignition (HEI) systems and computer-controlled coil ignition (C³I) systems.]

Coolant Fan   Several different coolant fan circuits are used on PFI-equipped vehicles. In these circuits the ECM operates the coolant fan under certain conditions. One coolant fan circuit is outlined in Figure 18-25. The system shown does not have a timer to operate the fan after the engine is turned off.

Some heavy-duty cooling systems have an optional cooling fan located beside the standard fan. The low-speed fan relay winding is grounded by the

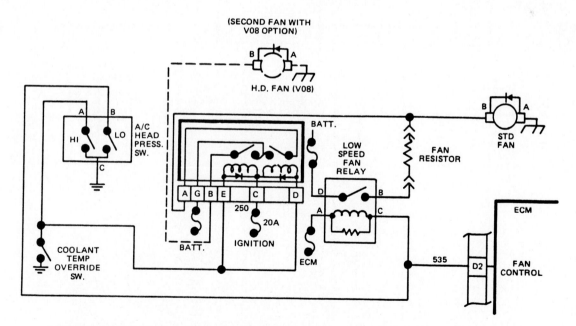

Figure 18-25.   Coolant Fan Circuit without Timer. (*Courtesy of GM Product Service Training, General Motors Corporation*)

ECM when the coolant temperature is above 208°F (98°C), the air conditioning (A/C) system pressure is below 260 psi (1,793 kPa), and the vehicle speed is below 45 MPH (72 KPH). The "LO" contacts in the A/C head pressure switch ground the low-speed fan relay contacts when A/C is turned on and the pressure is above 260 psi (1,793 kPa). When the low-speed fan relay contacts are closed, voltage is supplied through the resistor to the standard fan motor, which causes the fan to run at low speed.

If the coolant temperature exceeds 223°F (106°C), the coolant temperature override switch closes, which grounds both windings in the dual contact relay. One set of points supplies voltage to the standard fan and the other contacts complete the circuit to the heavy-duty fan, so that fans operate at high speed. When the A/C is on and the pressure in the system exceeds 300 psi (2,068 kPa) and "HI" contacts in the A/C head pressure switch close, which grounds both windings in the dual relay and causes both fans to operate at high speed. The standard fan operates at low speed when terminals A and B are connected in the assembly line communications link (ALCL).

The low-speed fan relay is mounted behind a plastic panel on the firewall with most of the other relays in the PFI system, and the dual relay is located near the brake booster.

Some coolant fan circuits have a timer that is used to operate the coolant fan after the engine is shut off. This type of circuit has one coolant fan that operates at two speeds. This type of circuit is illustrated in Figure 18-26.

The ECM will operate the coolant fan at low speed if the following conditions are present.

1. Coolant temperature above 208°F (98°C).
2. Vehicle speed under 45 MPH (72 KPH).
3. A/C system pressure under 260 psi (1,793 kPa).

The A/C head pressure switch "LO" contacts close and operate the coolant fan at low speed when the A/C system pressure exceeds 260 psi (1,793 kPa). When the coolant temperature exceeds 223°F (106°C), the coolant temperature switch closes which energizes the high-speed relay winding and supplies full voltage through the high-speed relay contacts to the coolant fan motor. This causes the coolant fan to operate at high speed. If the A/C system pressure exceeds 300 psi (2,068 kPa), the "HI" contacts in A/C head pressure switch close, which also causes the coolant fan to operate at high speed.

When the ignition is turned off and the coolant temperature is above 223°F (106°C), the coolant temperature override switch remains closed, which grounds the timer relay winding. This supplies full voltage to the coolant fan motor through the timer relay contacts so that the coolant fan operates at high

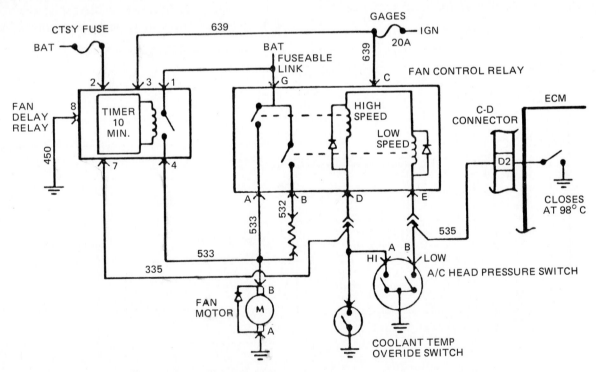

Figure 18-26. Coolant Fan Circuit with Timer. (*Courtesy of GM Product Service Training, General Motors Corporation*)

speed. The coolant fan is shut off after ten minutes by the timer, or when the coolant temperature drops below 223°F (106°C), and the coolant temperature override switch contacts open.

A/C Compressor Clutch   When the A/C control switch is turned on and the cycling switch is closed, voltage is supplied to terminal B8 on the ECM and to the A/C clutch-control relay contacts. Under this condition the ECM grounds the A/C clutch-control relay winding so that the relay contacts close, which supplies voltage to the A/C compressor clutch winding. If the power steering (P/S) pressure is high, such as when a full turn of the steering is completed, the P/S signal causes the ECM to open the A/C clutch-control relay winding circuit. When this occurs the relay contacts open and the compressor clutch is disengaged. The ECM also disengages the compressor clutch when the engine is operating at wide-open throttle (WOT).

Figure 18-27 shows the compressor clutch circuit.

Idle Air Control (IAC) Motor   The ECM operates the IAC motor on the throttle body assembly to control idle speed under all operating conditions. (This motor was explained earlier in this chapter in the section on General Motors throttle body injection systems.) The IAC motor connections to the ECM are illustrated in Figure 18-28.

Transmission Converter Clutch (TCC)   The purpose of the TCC system is to eliminate power loss in the torque converter when the vehicle is operating at moderate cruising speed. (This system was explained in Chapter 17.) The ECM grounds the apply solenoid winding and engages the TCC when the engine is operating at normal temperature under light-load conditions and above a specific road speed with the transmission in third or fourth gear. The TCC engagement speed may vary, depending on the engine and transmission. Figure 18-29 illustrates the TCC circuit.

Canister Purge   When the following conditions are present, the ECM operates a solenoid that allows fuel

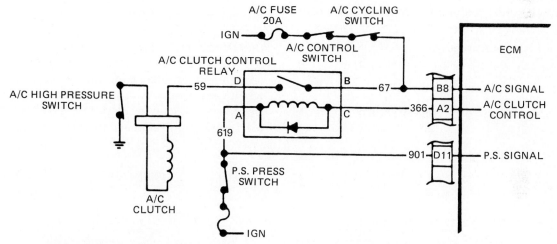

Figure 18-27.   Compressor Clutch Circuit. (*Courtesy of GM Product Service Training, General Motors Corporation*)

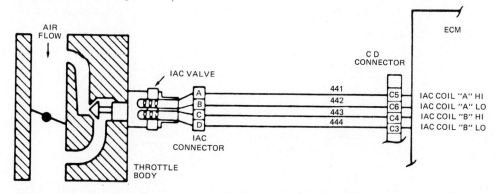

Figure 18-28.   IAC Motor Circuit. (*Courtesy of GM Product Service Training, General Motors Corporation*)

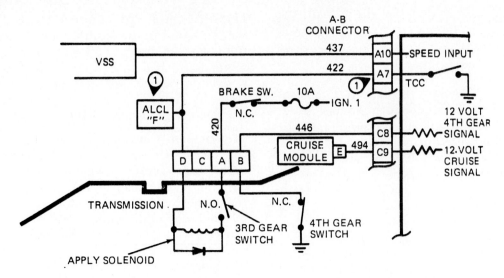

Figure 18-29. TCC Circuit. (*Courtesy of Buick Motor Division, General Motors Corporation*)

vapors to be purged from the canister into the intake manifold:

1. Engine has been running for more than one minute.
2. Coolant temperature is above 165°F (80°C).
3. Vehicle speed is above 10 MPH (16 KPH).
4. Throttle is above idle speed.

The canister-purge circuit is shown in Figure 18-30.

Fuel The ECM controls the pulse width of the injectors to provide the precise air-fuel ratio required by the engine. When the engine is at normal operating temperature and the engine is operating at idle speed or moderate cruising speed, the ECM controls the air-fuel ratio at, or very close to, the stoichiometric value of 14.7:1. The ECM provides mixture enrichment by increasing the injector pulse width when the engine coolant is cold, at wide-open throttle, and on sudden acceleration. To lower emission levels and improve fuel economy, the ECM stops en-

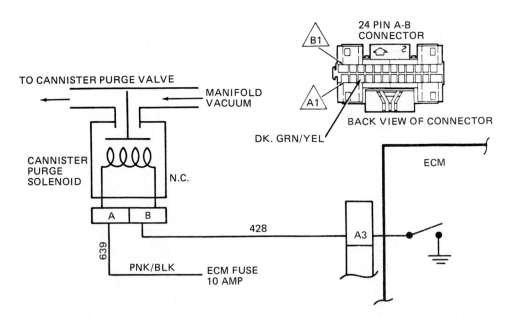

Figure 18-30. Canister-Purge Circuit. (*Courtesy of Buick Motor Division, General Motors Corporation*)

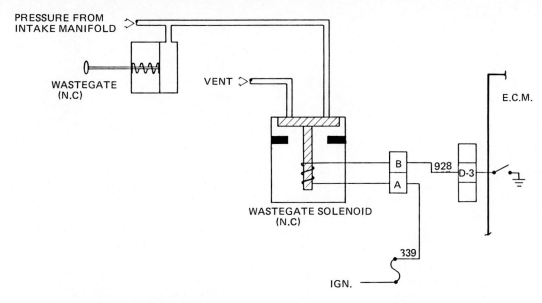

Figure 18-31. Wastegate Solenoid Circuit. (*Courtesy of GM Product Service Training, General Motors Corporation*)

ergizing the injectors when the engine is decelerated.

Turbo Wastegate The ECM operates a solenoid to limit the turbo boost pressure on turbocharged engines. When the ECM energizes the wastegate solenoid, some of the pressure supplied to the wastegate diaphragm is vented through the solenoid, which lowers the boost pressure. The ECM then closes the wastegate solenoid. The ECM uses the MAF sensor and engine speed signals to limit the boost pressure to approximately 7.8 psi (55.5 kPa). (Turbocharger operation is explained in Chapter 6.) The wastegate solenoid circuit is illustrated in Figure 18-31.

General Motors Tuned Port Injection

Design

The tuned port injection (TPI) system is used on some 5.7L (350 CID) and 5.0L (305 CID) V8 engines. These engines have an air plenum and tubular runners in the intake manifold which provide smooth, unobstructed airflow into the cylinders. The TPI system is similar to a PFI system with a fuel injector located in each intake port. A manifold air temperature (MAT) sensor is used in the TPI system, and a separate cold-start injector is operated by the ECM to inject additional fuel when a cold engine is being started.

An engine with a TPI system is illustrated in Figure 18-32.

General Motors Computer Systems with Body Computer Module and Serial Data Line

System Design

Many 1986 and later model General Motors cars are equipped with a body computer module (BCM) and a serial data line which interconnects the ECM, BCM, instrument panel cluster (IPC), electronic climate control (ECC), voice/chime module, and heater ventilation and air conditioning (HVAC) programmer. The serial data line between these components is referred to as an 800 circuit, as indicated in Figure 18-33.

A permanent connector in the assembly line diagnostic link (ALDL) is part of the serial data line. The ALDL is similar to the ALCL in other systems. Since the serial data line is bidirectional, the system will still function if the permanent connector is removed from the ALDL. The serial data line may be compared to a conference call telephone connection. When data is being transmitted between two components, the other components can "listen" to the data transmission. For example, as the ECM sends data to the BCM, such as A/C clutch status, coolant temperature, and engine speed, the other compo-

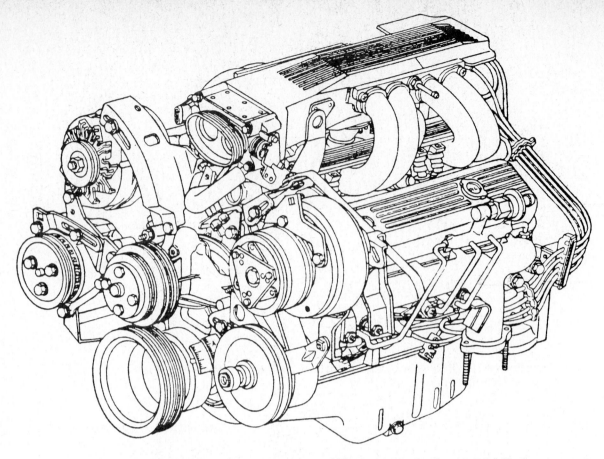

Figure 18-32. Tuned Port Injection System. (*Courtesy of GM Product Service Training, General Motors Corporation*)

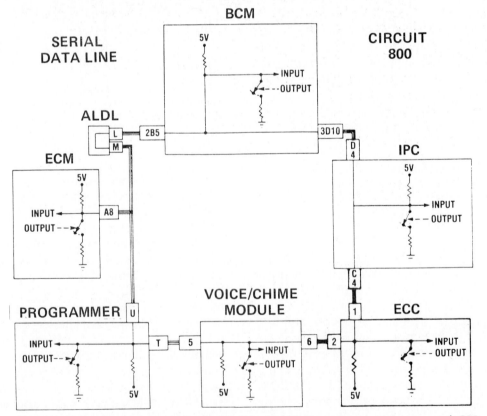

Figure 18-33. Serial Data Line and Interconnected Components. (*Courtesy of GM Product Service Training, General Motors Corporation*)

nents have access to this information. The IPC uses the engine speed information to display engine revolutions per minute (rpm) for the driver.

Electronic Control Module Functions

The electronic control module (ECM) is similar to the ECM in other port fuel injection (PFI) systems. The ECM's input and output control functions are listed in Table 18-2, and the location of the ECM along with its related inputs and outputs are given in Figure 18-34.

The inputs and output control functions are similar to the ones described previously in this chapter, and the fuel system and fuel pump relay circuit are basically the same as those used in the PFI systems discussed earlier. Sequential energizing of the injectors is provided by the ECM. Since the electric cooling fan circuit in systems with a data line is somewhat different compared to previous systems, this circuit is provided in Figure 18-35.

On vehicles equipped with a heavy-duty cooling system, a high-speed pusher fan is located in front of the radiator in addition to the conventional two-speed fan behind the radiator.

The operation of the cooling fan circuit may be summarized as follows:

1. At 208°F (98°C) coolant temperature, the ECM grounds the low-speed fan relay winding. This closes the relay contacts and supplies voltage through the relay contacts and the resistor to the low-speed fan motor. The resistor lowers the voltage at the motor, which results in low-speed fan operation.

2. Low-speed fan operation also occurs when the low-pressure contacts close in the A/C head pressure switch, before the ECM grounds the low-speed fan relay winding. These low-pressure contacts close when the A/C refrigerant pressure reaches 260 psi (1,793 kPa).

3. The coolant temperature override switch closes and grounds both high-speed fan relays when the coolant temperature reaches 226°F (108°C). When this occurs, both relay contacts close, and the standard fan relay supplies voltage directly to the low-speed fan, while the pusher fan relay supplies voltage to the pusher fan. This results in high-speed operation of both fans.

4. If the A/C head pressure switch high-pressure contacts close at 300 psi (2,068 kPa) refrigerant pressure, before the coolant temperature override switch closes, both high-speed fan relay windings are grounded through the high-pressure contacts, so that both fans operate at high speed.

A distributorless direct ignition system (DIS) is used in these systems. The DIS has a different camshaft position sensor and coil assembly as compared to the computer-controlled coil ignition C³I systems. (These ignition systems are described in Chapter 13.) The ECM terminals and the voltage readings at each terminal are provided in Figure 18-36.

Central Power Supply

The central power supply (CPS) supplies 12V and 7V to the BCM, IPC, voice/chime module, and other electronic components regardless of input voltage

TABLE 18-2. ECM Input and Output Control Functions.
(Courtesy of GM Product Service Training, General Motors Corporation)

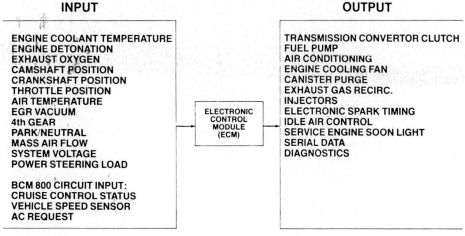

INPUT	OUTPUT
ENGINE COOLANT TEMPERATURE	TRANSMISSION CONVERTOR CLUTCH
ENGINE DETONATION	FUEL PUMP
EXHAUST OXYGEN	AIR CONDITIONING
CAMSHAFT POSITION	ENGINE COOLING FAN
CRANKSHAFT POSITION	CANISTER PURGE
THROTTLE POSITION	EXHAUST GAS RECIRC.
AIR TEMPERATURE	INJECTORS
EGR VACUUM	ELECTRONIC SPARK TIMING
4th GEAR	IDLE AIR CONTROL
PARK/NEUTRAL	SERVICE ENGINE SOON LIGHT
MASS AIR FLOW	SERIAL DATA
SYSTEM VOLTAGE	DIAGNOSTICS
POWER STEERING LOAD	
BCM 800 CIRCUIT INPUT:	
CRUISE CONTROL STATUS	
VEHICLE SPEED SENSOR	
AC REQUEST	

ELECTRONIC CONTROL MODULE (ECM)

312   Computer-Controlled Fuel-Injection Systems

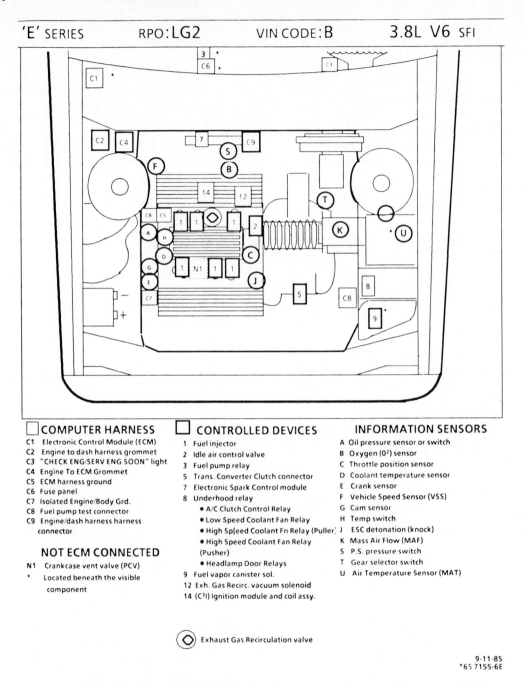

Figure 18-34. Location of ECM and Related Inputs and Outputs. (*Courtesy of Olds-mobile Division, General Motors Corporation*)

variations. This 12V supply is available continuously from the battery through the CPS to the BCM, IPC, and voice/chime module to maintain the computer memories and operate the IPC. When the ignition switch is off, the 12V supply operates the voice/chime module.

The 7V circuits are used for the BCM and IPC software. This 7V power supply is reduced to 5V by the BCM and then sent out as a reference voltage to the BCM input sensors. These 7V circuits will only

function when the CPS turns them on. This occurs when the CPS receives a "wake-up" signal from the BCM.

The ground circuits from the BCM, IPC, HVAC programmer, voice/chime module, and the EEC panel are completed through the CPS. This ground circuit is connected directly to the negative battery terminal. Therefore, these ground circuits are not shared with any other components, so that electromagnetic interference (EMI) is reduced. The CPS

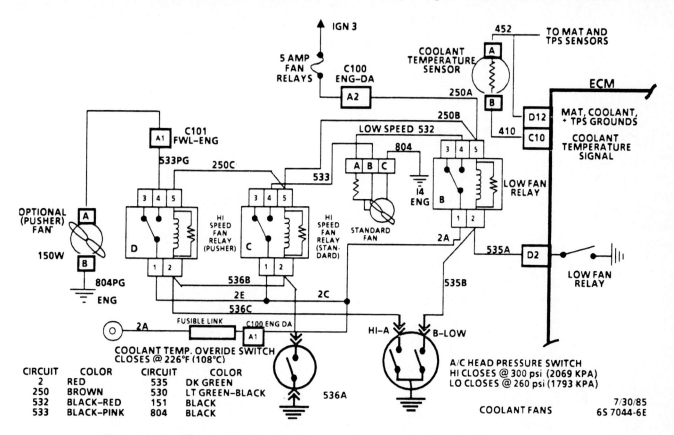

Figure 18-35. Electric Cooling Fan Circuit. (*Courtesy of Oldsmobile Division, General Motors Corporation*)

output voltages and ground circuits are illustrated in Figure 18-37.

Normally the BCM triggers the CP "wake-up" circuit when it receives an input signal from a door handle switch when a door is opened. On cars without illuminated entry, this input signal is supplied from the doorjamb switch. Alternate input signals could also trigger the wake-up circuit, as indicated in Figure 18-38.

When the BCM receives a wake-up signal from a door handle switch, the BCM supplies 12V to the CPS. This causes the CPS to activate the various 7V circuits to the BCM, IPC, and voice/chime module.

The BCM and the CPS are usually located under the dash. The locations of the BCM and the CPS are pictured in Figure 18-39, and the locations of the BCM, ECM, HVAC module, and voice/chime module are shown in Figure 18-40.

Body Computer Module

General Functions The body computer module (BCM) is the center of communications for the multiple computer system. It performs the following functions:

1. Controls the electronic climate control system.
2. Controls the cruise control system.
3. Controls the fuel level display and performs fuel data calculations.
4. Controls vehicle status messages such as the "door ajar" warning.
5. Provides vehicle speed data.
6. Remembers and updates odometer information.
7. Provides transaxle shifter position data for display. (This feature was not available on 1986 early production models.)
8. Calculates English/metric conversions for display.
9. Controls the courtesy lights, including the optional illuminated entry.
10. Controls the optional twilight sentinel.
11. Controls instrument panel dimming.
12. Recognizes and compensates for BCM system failures and stores diagnostic codes which can be displayed for diagnostic purposes.

The BCM functions above are for a 1986 Toronado; however, the BCM functions vary, depending

ECM CONNECTOR IDENTIFICATION

This ECM voltage chart is for use with a digital voltmeter to further aid in diagnosis. The voltages you get may vary due to low battery charge or other reasons, but they should be very close.

THE FOLLOWING CONDITIONS MUST BE MET BEFORE TESTING:

- Engine at operating temperature • Engine idling in closed loop (for "Engine Run" column)
- Test terminal not grounded • ALCL tool not installed • A/C Off

	VOLTAGE				
	KEY "ON"	ENG. RUN	OPEN CKT.	CIRCUIT	PIN
④	.01	B+	0	FUEL PUMP RELAY	A1
⑤	.01	0	0	A/C CLUTCH CONTROL	A2
	B+	B+	0	CANISTER PURGE CONTROL	A3
	B+	B+	0	EGR SOLENOID	A4
	.79	B+	0	SERVICE ENGINE SOON LIGHT	A5
	B+	B+	B+	IGN #1 (ISO)	A6
	B+	B+	B+	TCC CONTROL	A7
	2.3 3.6	2.3 3.6	3.7	SERIAL DATA	A8
	5.0	4.9	5.0	DIAG. TERM	A9
①	B+	B+	B+	VSS SIGNAL	A10
	0	6.8	0	CAM HIGH	A11
	0	.02	0	GROUND	A12
				NOT USED	C1
				NOT USED	C2
	.86 11.8	12.3	3.8 10.5	IAC-B-LO	C3
	.86 11.8	.86	B+ .5	IAC-B-HI	C4
	.86 11.8	.86	B+ .5	IAC-A-HI	C5
	.86 11.8	12.3	.5 B+	IAC-A-LOW	C6
				NOT USED	C7
	0	0	B+	4TH GEAR SIGNAL	C8
				NOT USED	C9
②	2.24	1.75	5.0	COOLANT TEMP SIGNAL	C10
	2.2	1.75	5.0	AIR TEMP	C11
	B+	B+	0	INJECTOR 6	C12
	.45	.45	0	TPS SIGNAL	C13
	5.0	4.9	5.0	TPS 5V REF	C14
	B+	B+	0	INJECTOR 2	C15
	B+	B+	.5	B+	C16

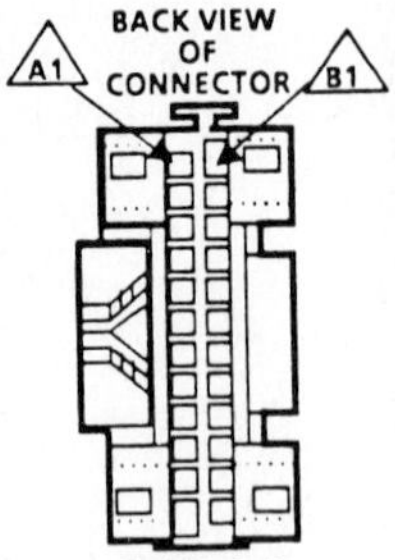

BACK VIEW OF CONNECTOR A1 B1

24 PIN A-B CONNECTOR

WHEN TWO VALUES ARE GIVEN, THE VOLTAGE SIGNAL WILL CYCLE BETWEEN THE TWO VALUES

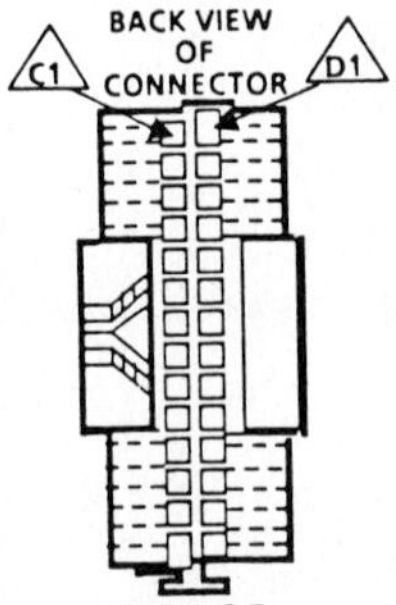

BACK VIEW OF CONNECTOR C1 D1

32 PIN C-D CONNECTOR

	VOLTAGE				
PIN	CIRCUIT	KEY "ON"	ENG RUN	OPEN CKT.	
B1	NOT USED				
B2	NOT USED				
B3	CRANK REF LOW	0	.0	3.0	
B4	EST CONTROL	.04	1.2	0	
B5	CRANK REF HI	0	4.0	0	
B6	MASS AIR FLOW SENSOR SIGNAL	2.0 3.5	2.6	5.0	③
B7	ESC SIGNAL	9.2	9.2	0	
B8	NOT USED				
B9	NOT USED				
B10	PARK/NEUTRAL SW. SIGNAL	.0	.0	B+	
B11	NOT USED				
B12	INJECTOR 5	B+	B+	0	
D1	GROUND	.0	.0	.0	
D2	COOLING FAN CONTROL	B+	1.57	.45	
D3	NOT USED				
D4	NOT USED				
D5	EST BYPASS SIGNAL	.0	3.75 4.85	.0	
D6	GRND (O₂) LOW	0	0	1,8	
D7	O₂ SENSOR SIGNAL	.42	.25 1.0	.42	③
D8	NOT USED				
D9	EVRV FBK SIGNAL	B+	B+	B+	
D10	GROUND	.0	.0	.0	
D11	POWER STEERING SW SIGNAL	B+	B+	0	
D12	MAT (AIR TEMP) & COOLANT TPS GROUND	.0	0	.0	
D13	NOT USED				
D14	INJECTOR 1	B+	B+	0	
D15	INJECTOR 3	B+	B+		
D16	INJECTOR 4	B+	B+	0	

① Varies from .60 to battery voltage depending on position of drive wheels.
② Normal operating temperature.
③ Varies
④ 12 V only for first 2 seconds unless engine is cranking or running.
⑤ 6.62 with A/C On (System will not reenergize if fuel rail pressure is high)

8-8-85
6S7008-6E

Figure 18-36. Electronic Control Module (ECM) Terminal Identification. (*Courtesy of Oldsmobile Division, General Motors Corporation*)

on the application and year of vehicle. (Refer to Chapter 26 for the electronic climate control system and related BCM circuits.)

Cruise Control Operation In vehicles equipped with a BCM, the cruise control operates the same as was explained in Chapter 14; however, the BCM takes over the functions of the external electronic controller. A cruise set-speed display appears on the IPC when the cruise is engaged, resumed, or the speed is changed. The BCM receives input signals from the cruise on/off switch, set/coast switch, and resume/accelerate switch on the turn-signal lever. These normally open switches provide a voltage input signal to the BCM when they are closed by the driver. If the brake pedal is depressed, the brake switch opens, and in response to this signal the BCM deactivates the cruise control. Other inputs are the vehicle speed sensor (VSS) and ECM-to-BCM communications on the serial data circuit which the

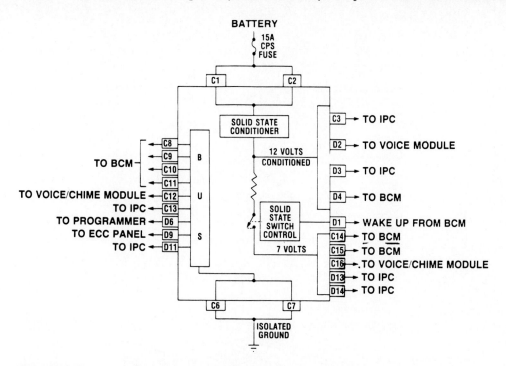

Figure 18-37. Central Power Supply Output Voltages and Ground Circuits. (*Courtesy of GM Product Service Training, General Motors Corporation*)

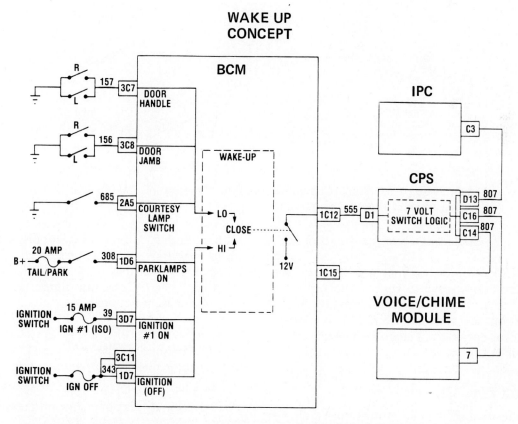

Figure 18-38. Wake-Up Circuit to Body Computer Module and Central Power Supply. (*Courtesy of GM Product Service Training, General Motors Corporation*)

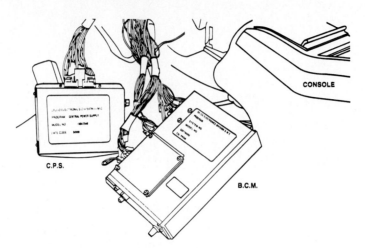

Figure 18-39. Body Computer Module (BCM) and Central Power Supply (CPS) Location. (*Courtesy of GM Product Service Training, General Motors Corporation*)

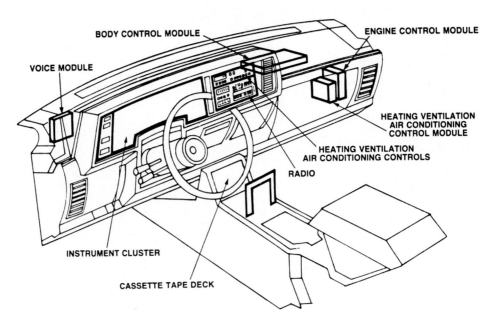

Figure 18-40. Module and Computer Location. (*Courtesy of GM Product Service Training, General Motors Corporation*)

BCM uses for vehicle speed and gear-position information.

The BCM operates the vent and vacuum solenoids in the cruise servo to control the servo vacuum and the cruise set speed. Information is also supplied from the servo to the BCM to monitor cruise control operation. The cruise control circuit is shown in Figure 18-41.

Instrument Panel Cluster

General Information The instrument panel cluster (IPC) contains a microprocessor that communicates with the rest of the system through the serial data

circuit. Both vacuum fluorescent displays and incandescent telltale bulbs are used in the IPC. (Refer to Chapter 15 for an explanation of vacuum fluorescent displays.) The IPC vacuum fluorescent displays are used for these functions:

1. Digital speedometer.
2. Odometer information.
3. Bar-graph display of system voltage.
4. Bar-graph display of engine coolant temperature.
5. Bar-graph display of engine oil pressure.
6. Bar-graph display of fuel level.
7. PRNDL indicator for transaxle gear range selec-

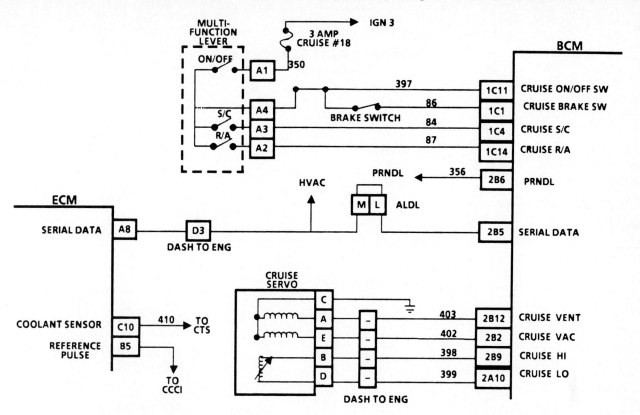

Figure 18-41. Cruise Control Circuit. (*Courtesy of GM Product Service Training, General Motors Corporation*)

tion. (This was not available on early 1986 production.)

Vacuum fluorescent indicators are used for these items:

1. Turn-signal indicators.
2. High-beam indicator.
3. "Lights on" indicator.
4. "Cruise on" indicator.

Driver-requested functions are:

1. Bar-graph tachometer display.
2. Fuel and trip information.

When the ignition switch is turned on, all segments of the IPC are illuminated for a few seconds, as indicated in the top diagram in Figure 18-42. After the initial IPC display, each bar graph will have brightly illuminated bars to provide specific indications. For example, when the fuel tank is half full, the bars on the fuel gauge are brightly illuminated to the center position on the fuel gauge. The IPC information center display has a 20-character vacuum fluorescent dot matrix display with these messages available:

1. Fuel level
2. Engine hot
3. Low coolant
4. Low refrigerant
5. Electrical problem
6. Generator problem
7. Low brake fluid
8. Park brake
9. Low washer fluid
10. Lighting problem
11. A/C system problem
12. Low oil pressure
13. Right door open
14. Left door open
15. Both doors open
16. Headlamp out
17. Tail lamp out
18. Park lamp out
19. Stop lamp out
20. Lamp fuse out
21. Cruise set speed

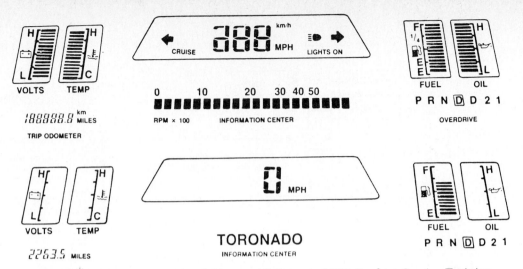

Figure 18-42. Instrument Panel Cluster. (*Courtesy of GM Product Service Training, General Motors Corporation*)

The following messages are provided by incandescent telltale lamps:

1. Security
2. Fasten belts
3. Service engine soon
4. Brake
5. Lights on

Switch panels on each side of the IPC supply driver-initiated inputs to the IPC. The left switch panel is shown in Figure 18-43, and the right switch panel is pictured in Figure 18-44.

Figure 18-43. Left Switch Panel. (*Courtesy of GM Product Service Training, General Motors Corporation*)

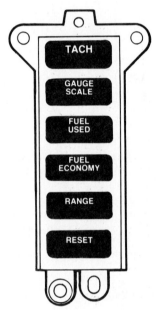

Figure 18-44. Right Switch Panel. (*Courtesy of GM Product Service Training, General Motors Corporation*)

Left Switch Panel Operation The odo/trip button switches the mileage display from season odometer to trip odometer. When this button is pressed a second time, the mileage display changes back to season odometer.

When the trip-reset button is pressed, the trip odometer resets to zero.

The English/metric button is used to switch the IPC and electronic climate control (ECC) displays from English to metric units for speed, distance, fuel consumption, and temperature.

A vacuum fluorescent display check is initiated when the driver presses the system monitor button. This button is also used to acknowledge messages in the information center and redisplay these messages.

The left switch panel also contains the headlight and park light switches, the panel dimming switch, and the twilight sentinel control switch.

Right Switch Panel Operation When the driver presses the tach button, the tachometer display appears in the information center.

The gauge scale button switches the fuel-level gauge from full scale to an expanded $\frac{1}{4}$ tank scale. After a specific length of time, the display changes back to full scale.

When the fuel-used button is pressed, the information center displays the amount of fuel used since the last driver-requested reset.

Pressing the fuel-economy button causes fuel consumption information to be displayed in the information center. Either instant fuel economy or average fuel economy since the last reset may be displayed.

The range button allows the driver to request fuel range information. This value is based on the amount of fuel in the tank and the average fuel economy during the last 25 miles (40 km) of driving.

The reset button allows the driver to reset the fuel-used and average fuel economy readings to zero, depending on which reading is displayed in the information center.

Specific Instrument Panel Cluster Functions

Data Communicating Serial data from the BCM is the most important input to the IPC. The IPC controls its displays on the basis of the information received from the BCM on the serial data link. If this input information from the BCM is not available, the IPC will not function and "Electrical Problem" is displayed in the information center.

An IPC wiring diagram which includes the serial data link to the BCM is shown in Figure 18-45.

Speedometer and Odometer Operation The permanent-magnet type vehicle speed sensor (VSS) is located in the transaxle. This sensor generates an AC voltage pulse that is proportional to vehicle speed. A buffer circuit in the BCM changes this signal into a

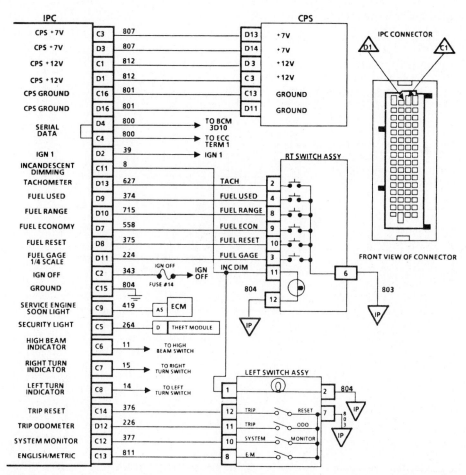

Figure 18-45. Instrument Panel Cluster Wiring Diagram. (*Courtesy of GM Product Service Training, General Motors Corporation*)

DC square-wave digital signal. The BCM communicates the vehicle speed information to the IPC on the serial data circuit, and a decoder in the IPC decodes this information before the IPC microprocessor illuminates the speedometer display.

The BCM counts the VSS signal pulses to calculate mileage for the season odometer display. This total accumulated mileage is continuously written into the BCM's electronically erasable programmable read-only memory (EPROM). If battery voltage is removed from the BCM, this information is retained in the EPROM. The BCM also uses VSS input to operate the trip odometer, but this information is stored in the BCM's random access memory (RAM).

Removal of battery voltage from the BCM results in the loss of trip odometer information. The IPC will only display either season odometer information or trip odometer information at one time. As mentioned previously, this selection is made by pressing the odo/trip button.

The IPC and BCM circuits reltated to speedometer and odometer operation are illustrated in Figure 18-46.

Park/Reverse/Neutral/Drive/Low Display The park/reverse/neutral/drive/low (PRNDL) display in the IPC is activated from the ignition-off circuit to the IPC. This circuit supplies voltage to the IPC when

the ignition switch is in the "off" or "run" position. Service and towing considerations require this display with the ignition off. In this ignition switch position, all other IPC displays are not illuminated.

The gear selector connections to the BCM and ECM are shown in Figure 18-47.

Voltage Display The BCM monitors voltage directly from the ignition 1 circuit and compares this voltage to stored value limits. A digital signal from the BCM communicates this voltage information to the IPC, where the signal is decoded. On the basis of this information, the IPC microprocessor decides how many segments to illuminate on the voltage bar graph.

Coolant Temperature and Oil Pressure Displays The input signals sent to the ECM by the coolant temperature sensor affect many ECM outputs. The ECM transmits this information to the BCM on the serial data line, and the BCM repeats this signal and sends it to the IPC. The BCM also uses coolant temperature information for A/C system control. When the IPC microprocessor receives this coolant temperature information, it compares this value to its stored program to decide how many segments of the coolant temperature bar graph should be illuminated.

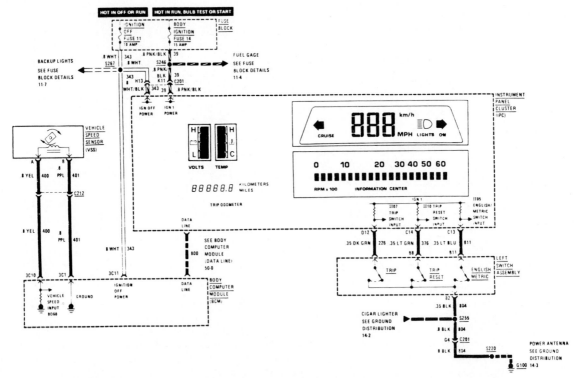

Figure 18-46. Instrument Panel Cluster and Body Computer Module Circuits Related to Speedometer and Odometer Operation. (*Courtesy of GM Product Service Training, General Motors Corporation*)

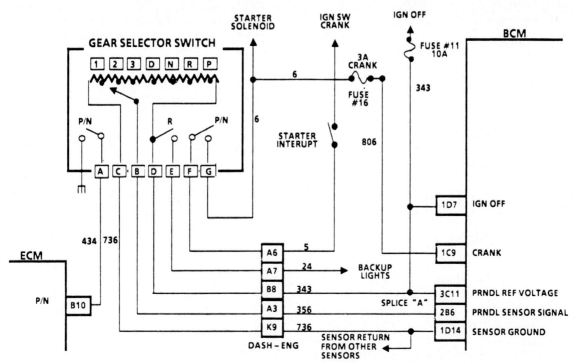

Figure 18-47. Gear Selector Switch Circuit to Body Computer Module and Electronic Control Module. (*Courtesy of GM Product Service Training, General Motors Corporation*)

An oil pressure sensor in the oil gallery near the oil filter sends an input signal to the BCM in relation to oil pressure. This information is converted to a digital signal by the BCM and then sent to the IPC. When this information is received, the IPC compares it to the stored program before deciding how many bars to illuminate in the oil pressure bar graph.

Some early production models had an off/on type of oil pressure switch. On these models the IPC illuminates half of the oil pressure bar-graph segments as long as minimum oil pressure is available.

Tachometer Display   An engine speed signal is sent from the distributorless direct ignition system (DIS) module to the ECM. This signal is used by the ECM to control some of its output functions. The ECM sends this signal to the BCM on the serial data line, and the IPC "eavesdrops" on this ECM-to-BCM information. If the driver has pressed the tach button, the IPC uses the engine speed signal to accurately illuminate the tach display.

Fuel Data Calculation   The fuel-tank sending unit sends an input signal to the BCM in relation to the fuel level in the tank. Sending unit resistance varies with fuel level, and the BCM measures the voltage drop across the sending unit. A distance-travelled calculation is completed by the BCM from the vehicle speed sensor (VSS) signal.

The ECM sends injector pulse-width and flow-

rate information to the BCM. On the basis of these inputs, the BCM determines fuel consumption and supplies this data to the IPC on the serial data line. When the driver requests any fuel data function, the IPC uses the information from the BCM to provide the correct display. The fuel-tank sending unit signal to the BCM is also used by the IPC to illuminate the fuel-gauge bar graph.

The BCM and IPC circuits related to fuel data displays are illustrated in Figure 18-48.

Lamp Monitor Operation   The lamp monitor circuits provide lamp-out messages on the information center. Four circuits are connected between the BCM and the lamp monitor module. These circuits are: "headlamp out," "tail lamp out," "stop lamp out," and "park lamp out." When all the lamps are working normally, the lamp monitor module connects these circuits to ground, which causes a low circuit voltage. The input circuit from each lamp switch is connected through two equal resistance wires to the lamp monitor module. Output wires from these same lamp monitor module terminals are connected to the appropriate lamps.

The lamp monitor circuit for the front and rear exterior lamps is shown in Figure 18-49.

If a lamp burns out, an open circuit is created and the voltage increases at the lamp monitor module terminal to which the burned-out lamp is con-

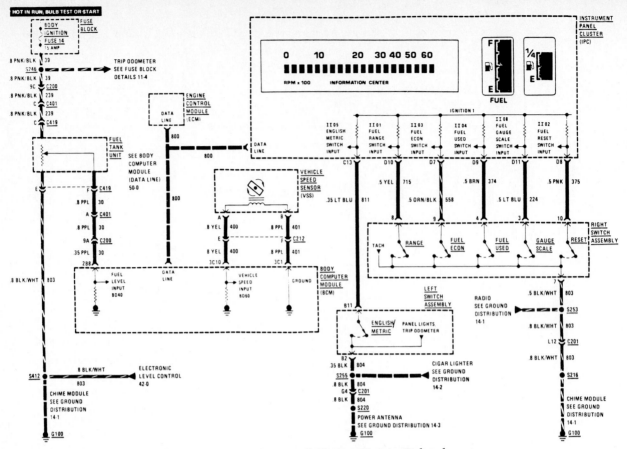

Figure 18-48. Body Computer Module and Instrument Panel Cluster Circuits Related to Fuel Data Display. (*Courtesy of GM Product Service Training, General Motors Corporation*)

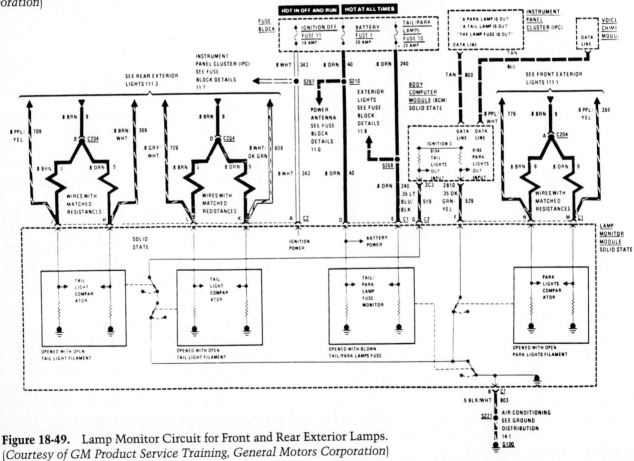

Figure 18-49. Lamp Monitor Circuit for Front and Rear Exterior Lamps. (*Courtesy of GM Product Service Training, General Motors Corporation*)

nected. This voltage increase causes the lamp monitor module to open the appropriate lamp-out circuit from the BCM. This action results in the appropriate lamp-out communication from the BCM to the IPC, and the IPC microprocessor displays the message in the information center.

Twilight Sentinel Operation The twilight sentinel system keeps the exterior lights on for an adjustable length of time after the ignition switch is turned off. This system is operated by the twilight delay control on the left switch panel. When this switch is off, the lights and headlamp doors operate manually through the headlamp switch.

If the twilight sentinel delay control is moved away from the off position, a variable resistance in the control is connected in series with the twilight photocell. The twilight photocell is a photoresistor that senses ambient light, and its resistance increases in dark conditions. Both the delay control and photocell are connected to the BCM. The BCM senses the voltage drop across the photocell and the delay control. If the delay control is on and the pho-

tocell resistance is above a specific value because of dark conditions, the BCM turns the lights on. The BCM performs this function by grounding twilight headlamp relay and twilight park lamp relay windings. When this occurs, the headlamps, park lamps, and headlamp doors are turned on, just as though the driver-controlled headlamp switch had been turned on. When the ignition switch is turned off, the BCM keeps the lights on for a specific length of time, which is adjustable with the twilight delay control.

The twilight sentinel circuit is illustrated in Figure 18-50.

Illuminated Entry Battery voltage is applied directly through a fuse to the courtesy light bulbs, and the circuit is completed from each bulb through the courtesy light relay contacts to ground. These contacts are normally open. Voltage is also applied through the same fuse to the courtesy light relay winding, and the circuit from this winding is completed to ground through the BCM.

Normally open switches are located in the door locks and doorjambs. If an exterior door handle is

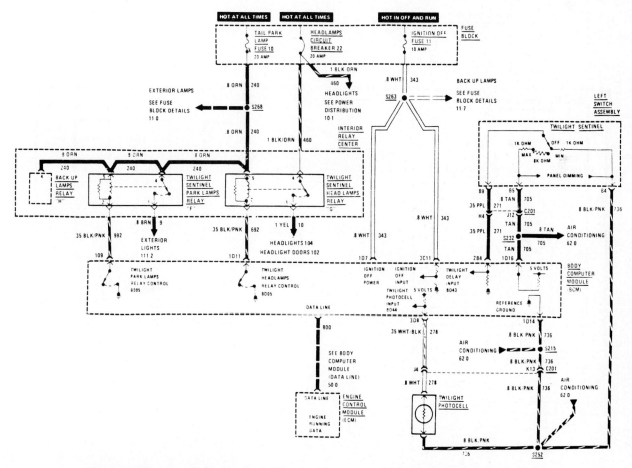

Figure 18-50. Twilight Sentinel Circuit. (*Courtesy of GM Product Service Training, General Motors Corporation*)

pushed, the door lock switch closes and signals the BCM to ground the courtesy light relay winding. This turns on the interior courtesy lights, which remain on for 20 seconds. If the door is opened, the doorjamb switch signals the BCM to keep the courtesy lights on. When the door is closed, the courtesy lights go out immediately when the ignition switch is turned to the run position.

The twilight photocell input signal to the BCM affects the operation of the courtesy lights. On a bright, sunny day, this signal informs the BCM that the courtesy lights are not required. Under this condition the BCM does not ground the courtesy light relay winding.

The courtesy light circuit is illustrated in Figures 18-51 and 18-52.

Panel Dimming The BCM controls the illumination of the left and right switch panels, as well as the radio, electronic climate control (ECC), and ashtray lights. Dimming of these lights is also controlled by the BCM in response to the input signal from the panel-dimming control in the left switch

panel. When the ignition switch is turned on, a 5V signal is supplied from the BCM to the panel-dimming control. The potentiometer in the panel-dimming switch is grounded through the BCM. As the panel-dimming control is moved toward the dim position, the voltage signal decreases from the switch to the BCM. When this signal is received, the BCM dims the switch panel and display panel illumination.

A pulse width modulated (PWM) signal is sent from the BCM to the ECC panel and the radio on circuit 724 to control the intensity of the vacuum fluorescent displays (VFDs) in these components. When the BCM increases the "on time" of the PWM signal, VFD intensity increases. The 724 circuit from the BCM to the EEC panel and the radio is shown in Figure 18-53.

The BCM also sends a panel-dimming signal on the serial data line to the IPC. The IPC microprocessor uses the signal to control the intensity of the VFD in the IPC. A PWM signal is also sent from the IPC to the incandescent illumination bulbs in the left and right switch panels, ashtray, and faceplates

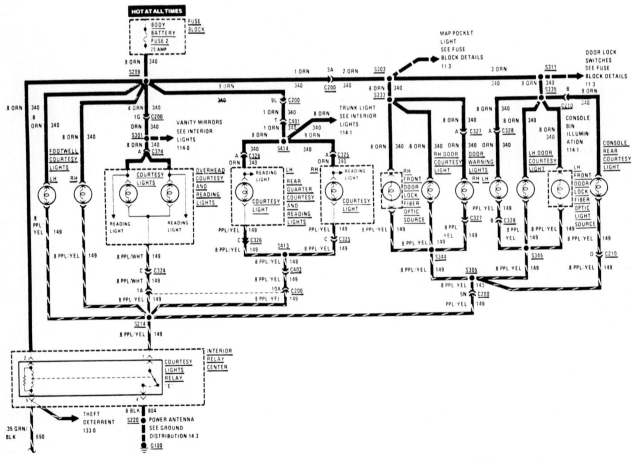

Figure 18-51. Illuminated-Entry Courtesy Light Circuit. (*Courtesy of GM Product Service Training, General Motors Corporation*)

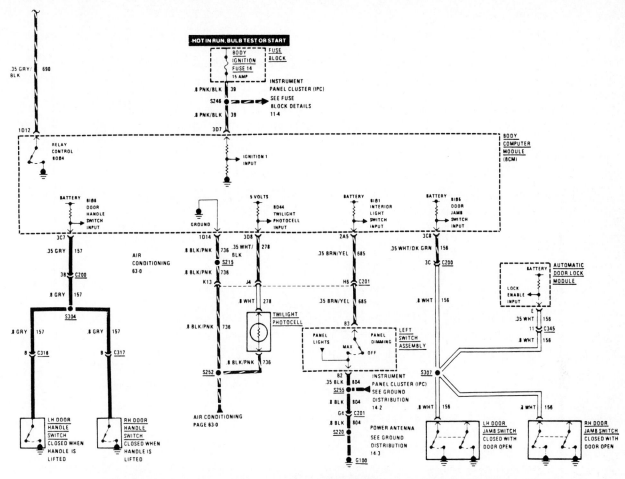

Figure 18-52. Illuminated-Entry Courtesy Light Circuit (Continued). (*Courtesy of GM Product Service Training, General Motors Corporation*)

in the EEC panel, radio, and tape deck to control the intensity of these bulbs. This circuit is given in Figure 18-54.

Charging Circuit Monitor Many 1986 and later model General Motors vehicles have a new Delco Remy integral alternator. The integral regulator in this alternator has four terminals. A phase ("P") terminal on the regulator may be used as a speed or tachometer signal. The "L" terminal is connected to the charge indicator bulb and parallel resistor. This terminal may also be connected to the BCM. The field ("F") monitor terminal is connected to the BCM, and the sense ("S") terminal is connected to the positive battery terminal.

When the ignition switch is turned on, voltage is supplied through the charge indicator bulb and the BCM to the "L" terminal and the lamp driver in the regulator. This causes the transistor to turn on, which allows current to flow from the battery terminal through the transistor and the alternator field coil to ground. When the engine is started, the regulator controls the field current and limits the alternator voltage. (Electronic regulator operation was explained in Chapter 11.)

While the alternator is charging, the regulator cycles the field current on and off, and this cycling signal is applied from the "F" terminal to the BCM. This signal informs the BCM if a defect occurs in the charging circuit, in which case trouble codes are set in the BCM memory. (Refer to Chapter 13 in *Automotive Principles: Repair and Service*, Volume II, for diagnosis of this computer system.)

The integral alternator circuit is shown in Figure 18-55, and the connections between the BCM and the regulator are illustrated in Figure 18-56.

Voice/Chime Warning System Some General Motors vehicles are equipped with a chime module, while others have an optional voice/chime module. The chime module provides chime warnings and the voice/chime module gives voice warnings through the left-front radio speaker along with the chime warnings.

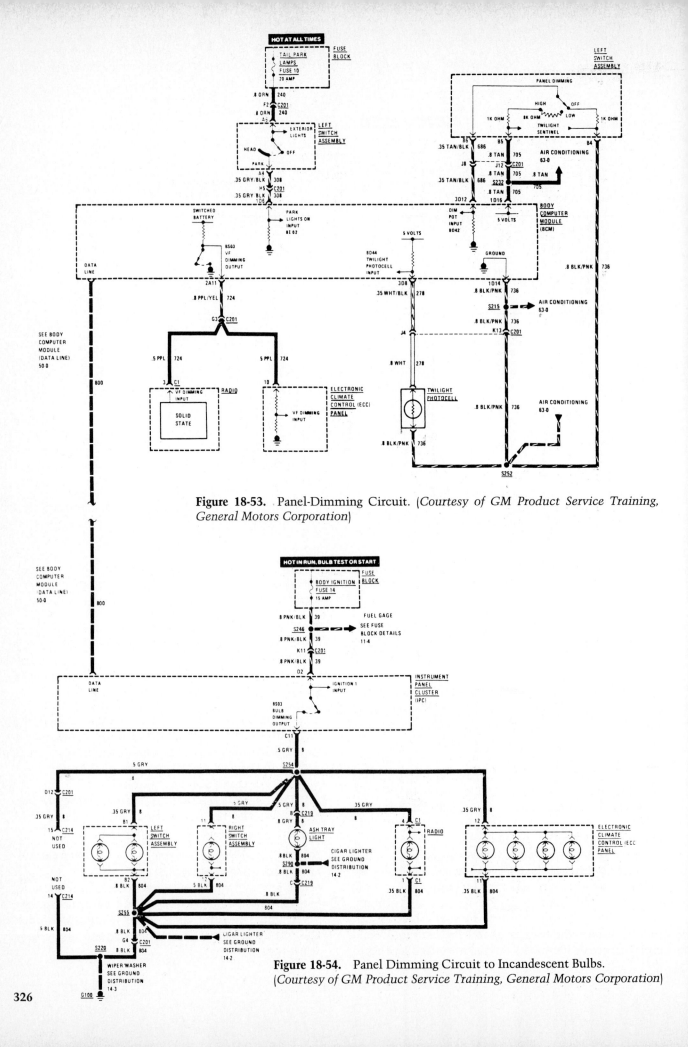

Figure 18-53. Panel-Dimming Circuit. (*Courtesy of GM Product Service Training, General Motors Corporation*)

Figure 18-54. Panel Dimming Circuit to Incandescent Bulbs. (*Courtesy of GM Product Service Training, General Motors Corporation*)

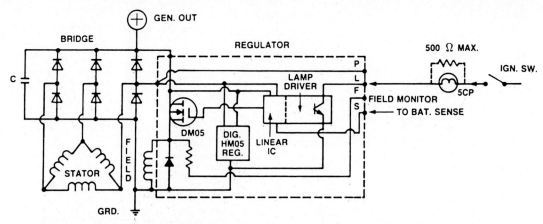

Figure 18-55. Integral Charging Circuit. (*Courtesy of GM Product Service Training, General Motors Corporation*)

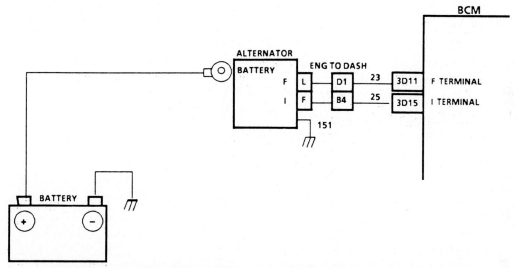

Figure 18-56. Integral Voltage Regulator to Body Computer Module Connections. (*Courtesy of GM Product Service Training, General Motors Corporation*)

When the BCM receives an input signal that indicates a driver warning is necessary, it sends a signal to the IPC on the serial data circuit and the IPC displays a visual warning on the information center. At the same time, the BCM signals the chime or voice/chime warning. The following chime warnings and information center displays are available:

1. *Left door open*—continuous slow chime.
2. *Right door open*—continuous slow chime.
3. *Both doors open*—continuous slow chime.
4. *Headlamp out*—five-second medium chime.
5. *Tail lamp out*—five-second medium chime.
6. *Park lamp out*—five-second medium chime.
7. *Stop lamp out*—five-second medium chime.
8. *Lamp fuse out*—five-second medium chime.

9. *Low washer fluid*—five-second slow chime.
10. *A/C system problem*—five-second fast chime.
11. *Generator problem*—five-second fast chime.
12. *Electrical problem*—five-second fast chime.
13. *Fasten seat belt*—five-second slow chime.

The chime module circuit is illustrated in Figure 18-57.

When the vehicle is equipped with a voice/chime module, the BCM inputs and voice/chime warnings are the following:

1. *Lights on*—voice warning with continuous fast chime.
2. *Key in ignition*—voice warning with continuous fast chime.

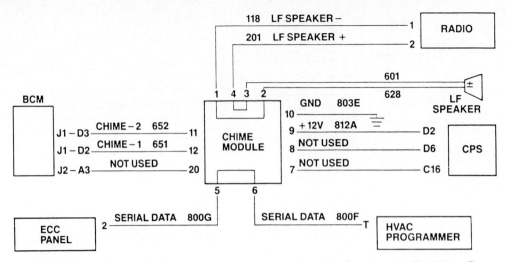

Figure 18-57. Chime Module Circuit. (*Courtesy of GM Product Service Training, General Motors Corporation*)

3. *Engine hot*

   a) First warning—voice warning to turn off A/C, with continuous fast chime.

   b) Second warning—voice warning to idle engine in park, with continuous fast chime and information center display.

   c) Third warning—voice warning to turn off ignition switch, with continuous fast chime and information center display.

   d) Fourth message—voice message that engine temperature has returned to normal.

4. *Parking brake*—voice warning with continuous medium chime and information center display.

5. *Brake fluid level*—voice warning with continuous fast chime and information center display.

6. *Engine oil pressure*—voice warning with continuous medium chime and information center display.

The same wiring harness connector fits the chime module and voice/chime module. A voice/chime module circuit is shown in Figure 18-58.

Relay Centers Many General Motors vehicles have two relay centers. One of these centers is usually located under the hood and the other is positioned under the dash or in the console. Each relay is identified on a decal in the relay cover. A fuse panel may

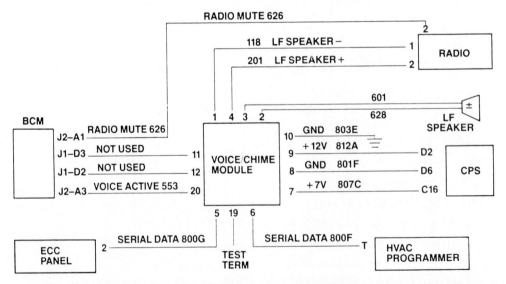

Figure 18-58. Voice Chime Module Circuit. (*Courtesy of GM Product Service Training, General Motors Corporation*)

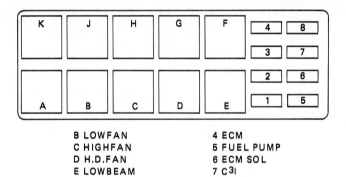

B LOWFAN
C HIGHFAN
D H.D.FAN
E LOWBEAM
H HORN

4 ECM
5 FUEL PUMP
6 ECM SOL
7 C31

Figure 18-59. Relay Center and Fuse Panel. (*Courtesy of GM Product Service Training, General Motors Corporation*)

be located with the relay center, as pictured in Figure 18-59.

The BCM wiring varies, depending on the make of car. A typical BCM wiring diagram is illustrated in Figure 18-60.

General Motors Computer Systems with Graphic Control Center

General Functions

Buick Riviera models manufactured in 1986 and later have a computer system in which many of the displays are shown on a graphic control center

CIR DESC	WIRE COL	CKT NO	CKT NO	WIRE COL	CKT DESC
CRUISE BRAKE SW	BRN	86	801	BLK/RED	CPS GROUND
BRAKE FLD LEV SW	TAN/WHT	33	651	PPL/YEL	CHIME 1
STOP LAMP OUT	PPL/WHT	549	652	PPL/WHT	CHIME 2
C.C. SET/COAST SW	DK BLU	84	733	LT BLU	MIX DR. WIPER
PARK BRAKE SW	TAN/WHT	233	801	BLK/RED	CPS GROUND
SPARE			308	GRA/BLK	PARKLAMPS ON
SPARE			343	WHT	IGNITION OFF
HEADLAMPS ON	YEL	10			SPARE
CRANK INPUT	LT GRN	80	992	BLK/PNK	TWILIGHT PK REL
CPS 12 VOLT	RED/WHT	812A	760	PPL/WHT	BLOWER CONTROL
CRUISE ON/OFF	GRA/WHT	397	692	BLK/PNK	TWILIGHT H/L REL
CPS WAKE-UP	DK BLU/WHT	555	690	GRA/BLK	COURTESY LT REL
SPARE					SPARE
C.C. RESUME/ACCEL	GRA/BLK	87	736	BLK/PNK	5V RETURN (GND)
CPS 7 VOLT	PPL/WHT	807	801	BLK/RED	CPS GROUND
CPS 7 VOLT	PPL/WHT	807	705	TAN	5V REFERENCE
RADIO MUTE	DK GRN/ORN	626			SPARE
IN CAR TEMP	DK GRN/WHT	734	402	LT GRN	CRUISE VAC ON
VOICE ACTIVE	TAN/WHT	553			SPARE
WASHER FLUID LEV	BLK/WHT	99	271	PPL	TWILIGHT DELAY
COURTESY LT SW	BRN/YEL	685	800A	TAN	SERIAL DATA
SPARE			356	GRA/BLK	PRNDL
HEADLAMP OUT	DK BLU/YEL	539			SPARE
CPS GROUND	BLK/RED	801	30	PPL	FUEL LEVEL WIPER
SPARE			398	TAN	CRUISE SERVO HI
CRUISE SERVO LO	LT BLU/BLK	399	529	DK GRN/YEL	PARK LAMP OUT
VF DIMMING	PPL/YEL	724			SPARE
SPARE			403	DK BLU/WHT	CRUISE VENT ON
VSS RETURN	PPL	401			SPARE
SPARE					SPARE
TAILLAMP OUT	LT BLU/BLK	519			SPARE
VSS TO ECM	BRN	437	731	GRA/RED	A/C LO SIDE TEMP
SPARE			732	DK BLU	A/C HI SIDE TEMP
SUNLOAD SENSOR	LT BLU/YEL	590			SPARE
DOOR HANDLE SW	GRA	157	39	PNK/BLK	IGNITION REF
DOOR JAMB SW	WHT/DK GRN	156	278	WHT/BLK	TWI PHOTOCELL
SPARE			313	LT GRN	OIL PRESSURE
VSS FEED	YEL	400	800	TAN	SERIAL DATA
IGNITION OFF	WHT	343	23	GRA/WHT	GEN F TERMINAL
DRIVER DOOR AJAR	GRA/BLK	147	686	TAN/BLK	DIM CONTROL
KEY IN IGNITION	LT GRN	80	69	GRA	COOLANT LEVEL
PASS. DOOR AJAR	BLK/ORN	158	735	LT GRN/BLK	OUTSIDE TEMP
SEAT BELT SW	BLK/PNK	238	25	BRN	GEN I TERMINAL
PARK SIGNAL	LT GRN/BLK	275	721	WHT	LO REF PRESSURE

6E OLDS

Figure 18-60. Body Computer Module Wiring. (*Courtesy of GM Product Service Training, General Motors Corporation*)

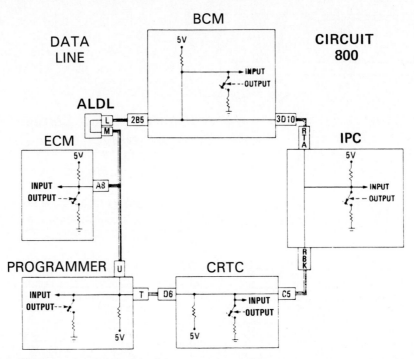

Figure 18-61. Serial Data Line 800 Circuit. (*Courtesy of GM Product Service Training, General Motors Corporation*)

(GCC). These systems also have a BCM, ECM, IPC, and an HVAC programmer. The GCC contains a cathode ray tube (CRT) and a CRT controller (CRTC). This controller is interconnected with the other microprocessors through the 800 circuit serial data line, as indicated in Figure 18-61.

The ECM and BCM inputs and outputs are sim-

ilar to those explained previously in this chapter, and the serial data line and central power supply (CPS) also operate in the same way as in the other systems. A chime module is controlled from the IPC, as indicated in Figure 18-62.

The IPC contains a microprocessor that controls the vacuum fluorescent displays (VFDs). A switch

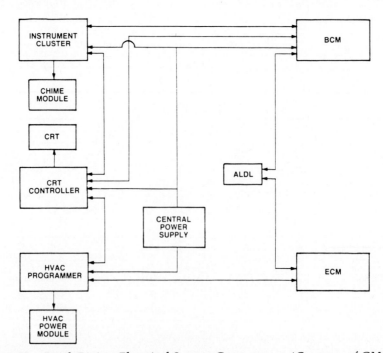

Figure 18-62. Buick Riviera Electrical System Components. (*Courtesy of GM Product Service Training, General Motors Corporation*)

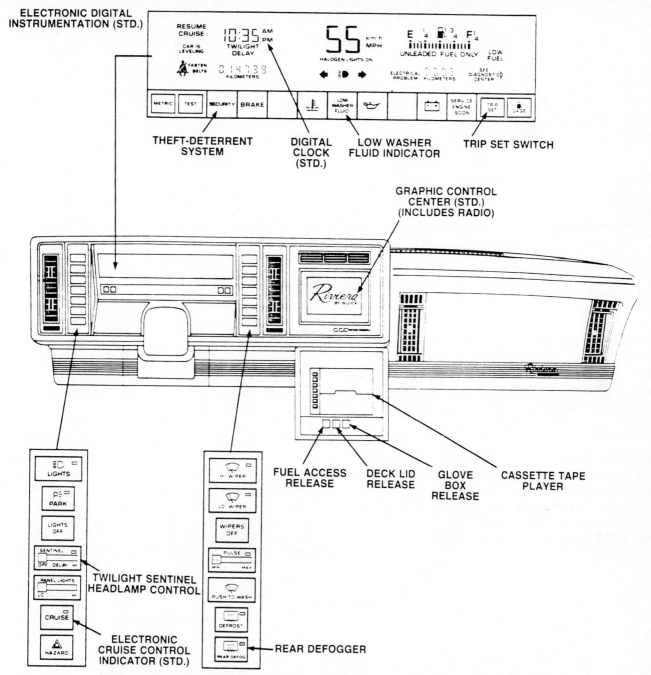

Figure 18-63. Buick Riviera Instrument Panel Cluster with Switch Pods and Graphic Control Center. (*Courtesy of GM Product Service Training, General Motors Corporation*)

pod is located on each side of the IPC. The IPC, switch pods, and GCC are shown in Figure 18-63.

Graphic Control Center Displays

Display Operation When a vehicle door is opened, the CRT in the GCC illuminates, as illustrated in Figure 18-64. An invisible mylar switch panel is placed over the CRT screen. This switch panel contains ultra-thin wires which are row- and column-encoded. The titles of the six available display pages are illuminated around the CRT screen. If the driver touches a display page title, the ultra-thin wires make contact in that area and the CRT controller displays the requested page in response to that input signal.

CLIMATE   SUMMARY   RADIO

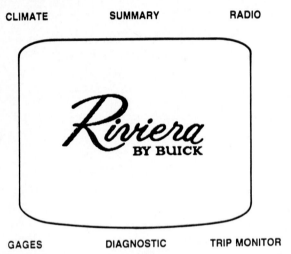

GAGES   DIAGNOSTIC   TRIP MONITOR

Figure 18-64. Initial Graphic Control Center Display. (*Courtesy of GM Product Service Training, General Motors Corporation*)

CLIMATE   SUMMARY   RADIO

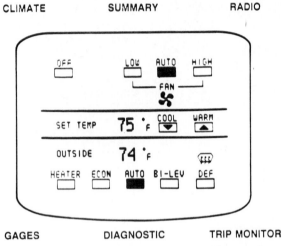

GAGES   DIAGNOSTIC   TRIP MONITOR

Figure 18-66. Graphic Control Center Climate-Control Page. (*Courtesy of GM Product Service Training, General Motors Corporation*)

Summary-Display Page After the driver's door has been closed for 30 seconds, the GCC switches from the initial display to the summary page if the driver has not made any GCC request. The summary page provides partial radio controls, partial A/C controls, partial diagnostic display, and the clock, as pictured in Figure 18-65.

Climate-Control Page If the driver selects the climate-control page, all the A/C control switches appear on the CRT with inside and outside temperature displays. The fan symbol rotates on the display and its speed increases in relation to the blower speed. The climate-control page is illustrated in Figure 18-66.

Trip-Monitor Page Three pages are available in the trip-monitor function. If the driver selects "trip monitor," page 1 is displayed, which indicates fuel economy, range, and average fuel economy, as shown in Figure 18-67.

When the driver touches "trip computer" on page 1 of the trip monitor, page 2 of the trip monitor appears. This page may be used to enter the distance to a destination, in which case the GCC calculates the estimated time of arrival based on average speed. The third trip monitor page is selected when "trip data" is touched on the first page. This page displays fuel consumption, average fuel economy, average speed, and elapsed time.

CLIMATE   SUMMARY   RADIO

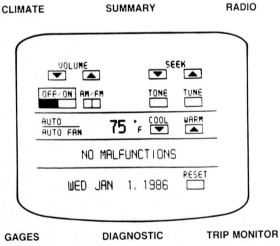

GAGES   DIAGNOSTIC   TRIP MONITOR

Figure 18-65. Graphic Control Center Summary Page. (*Courtesy of GM Product Service Training, General Motors Corporation*)

CLIMATE   SUMMARY   RADIO

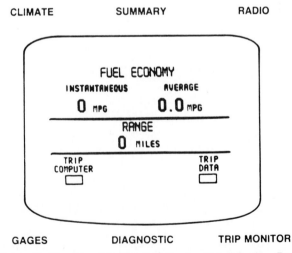

GAGES   DIAGNOSTIC   TRIP MONITOR

Figure 18-67. Graphic Control Center Trip-Monitor Page. (*Courtesy of GM Product Service Training, General Motors Corporation*)

Diagnostic Page The diagnostic page monitors these five main areas:

1. Electrical.
2. Power train.
3. Brakes.
4. Vehicle.
5. Lamps.

If there are no defects in these areas, the diagnostic page appears. This page is shown in Figure 18-68.

The driver may touch any of these five main areas on the CRT for additional diagnoses. If the electrical category is selected, these systems are checked:

1. Engine controls.
2. ECM and related circuits.
3. Instrument cluster controls.
4. Charging system.

When the power train diagnosis is requested, engine temperature, and oil pressure are diagnosed. The brake diagnosis displays the status of the brake fluid level and the parking brake system. If the vehicle diagnosis is selected, these parameters are checked:

1. Climate control system.
2. Driver and passenger doors ajar.
3. Fuel level.
4. Washer fluid level (optional).

An optional lamp diagnosis may be available. If this selection is made, the headlamps, tail lamps, and parking lamps are monitored. (Refer to Chapter 13 in *Automotive Principles: Repair and Service,* Volume II, for diagnosis of computer systems.)

Radio Page The driver may preset five AM and FM stations with the radio-page display. These five stations are displayed above the five preset switches. Adjustments for tone, fade, and the five-band graphic equalizer may be adjusted on additional pages, depending on the type of radio. The radio page is pictured in Figure 18-69.

Gauges Page A "gauges page" request will provide bar-graph displays of the following information:

1. Engine speed.
2. Coolant temperature.
3. Battery voltage.
4. Oil pressure (optional).

The gauges page is shown in Figure 18-70.

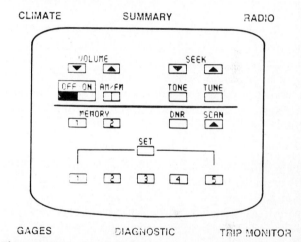

Figure 18-69. Graphic Control Center Radio Page. (*Courtesy of GM Product Service Training, General Motors Corporation*)

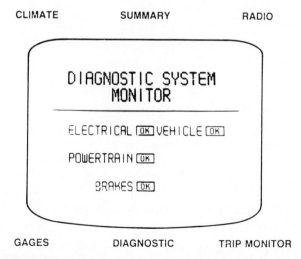

Figure 18-68. Graphic Control Center Diagnostic Page. (*Courtesy of GM Product Service Training, General Motors Corporation*)

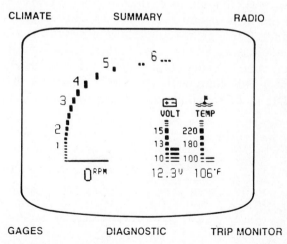

Figure 18-70. Graphic Control Center Gauges Page. (*Courtesy of GM Product Service Training, General Motors Corporation*)

Chrysler Single-Point Electronic Fuel Injection (EFI) Used on 2.2L Engine

Modules

Power Module The power module is located in the left-front fender well, behind the battery. Adequate cooling for the electronic components in the module is supplied by intake air flowing through the module before it enters the air cleaner. The power module supplies an 8V signal to the logic module and the distributor pickup. A ground circuit for the automatic shutdown (ASD) relay is provided in the power module. When this ground circuit is completed, the ASD relay supplies voltage to the electric fuel pump, logic module, ignition coil positive terminal, and the injector and ignition coil drive circuits in the power module.

The power module controls the operation of the fuel injector by opening and closing the injector ground circuit. Another function of the power module is to open and close the circuit from the coil negative terminal to ground, which operates the ignition system. Commands from the logic module used to control the power module are illustrated in Figure 18-71.

Logic Module The logic module is located inside the vehicle behind the right front kickpad. This module supplies a 5V signal to the sensors in the system, and it also receives input signals from the sensors and the distributor pickup. On the basis of all the input signals received, the logic module sends the appropriate spark-advance schedule to the power module under all engine operating conditions, and the power module opens the primary ignition circuit at the right instant to provide the correct spark advance. The logic module also commands the power module to supply the right injector pulse width, or "on time," to maintain engine performance, economy, and emission levels. Other functions of the logic module include the operation of the exhaust-

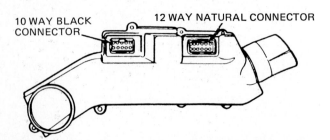

Figure 18-71. Power Module. (*Courtesy of Chrysler Canada*)

gas recirculation (EGR) and canister-purge solenoids, and the automatic idle speed (AIS) motor.

The logic module has the capability to test many of its own input and output circuits. If a fault is found in a major system, a fault code is stored in the logic module for future reference. This fault code can be displayed to the service technician by a flashing power-loss light on the instrument panel, or by a digital reading on a tester which can be connected to the system.

The logic module places the system in a "limp-in" mode if an unacceptable signal is received from the manifold absolute pressure sensor, throttle position sensor, or coolant sensor. In this mode the logic module ignores some of the sensor signals and maintains the spark advance and injector pulse width to keep the engine running, but fuel economy and performance decrease. In the "limp-in" mode, the logic module illuminates the power-loss light.

The logic module is shown in Figure 18-72.

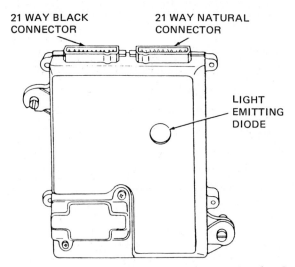

Figure 18-72. Logic Module. (*Courtesy of Chrysler Canada*)

Switch Inputs

Park/Neutral Safety Switch This switch supplies information to the logic module which is used by the module to control the automatic idle speed (AIS) motor and provide the correct idle speed in all transmission selector positions. The park/neutral safety switch signal to the logic module may affect spark advance to some extent.

Electric Backlite (EBL) Switch When the EBL is turned on, the logic module operates the AIS motor to increase throttle opening slightly to compensate for the additional alternator load on the engine.

Brake Switch In the event that the logic module does not receive a signal from the electric idle switch, the brake light switch is used to sense idle throttle position.

Air Conditioning Switch If this switch is activated, the logic module operates the AIS motor to increase idle speed.

Air Conditioning Clutch Switch When the air conditioning clutch engages, the logic module activates the AIS motor to give a one-time kick to maintain engine speed and prevent variations in idle speed. The switch inputs to the logic module are shown in Figure 18-73.

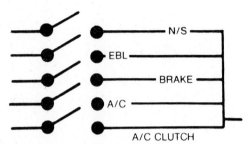

Figure 18-73. Switch Inputs to Logic Module. (*Courtesy of Chrysler Canada*)

Sensor Inputs

Manifold Absolute Pressure (MAP) Sensor The MAP sensor sends a signal to the logic module in relation to manifold vacuum and barometric pressure. A reference voltage of 5V is applied from the logic module to the sensors. The MAP sensor sends a voltage signal of 0.3V to 4.9V to the logic module. This voltage signal is 4.9V at zero vacuum, and it may be as low as 0.3V at maximum vacuum.

When engine load increases, manifold vacuum decreases, and this signal is sent from the MAP sensor to the logic module. When the signal is received, the logic module commands the power module to increase the injector pulse width and supply additional fuel to the engine. As manifold vacuum increases, the MAP sensor signal causes the logic and power modules to shorten the injector pulse width and supply less fuel to the engine.

The logic module uses the information from the MAP sensor and other inputs to determine the correct spark-advance schedule under all engine operating conditions. A MAP sensor is pictured in Figure 18-74.

Throttle Position Sensor The throttle position sensor is a variable resistor connected to the throttle shaft on the throttle body assembly. As the throttle

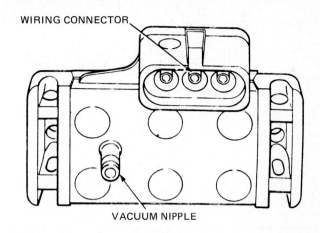

Figure 18-74. Manifold Absolute Pressure (MAP) Sensor. (*Courtesy of Chrysler Canada*)

is opened, a signal of 0.16V to 4.7V is sent from the sensor to the logic module. This signal and other sensor information is used by the logic module to adjust the air-fuel ratio to meet various conditions during acceleration, deceleration, wide-open throttle, and idle.

Oxygen Sensor The oxygen sensor is very similar to the oxygen sensor in the 3C system. (Refer to Chapter 17 for a description of this sensor.) This sensor generates a signal from 0V to 1V as the air-fuel ratio becomes richer. The oxygen sensor signal is used by the logic module along with other sensor data to provide the air-fuel ratio for optimum engine performance, economy, and emission levels. When there is a need for additional fuel enrichment, such as on sudden acceleration, the MAP sensor and throttle position sensor signals may override the oxygen sensor signal.

Coolant Temperature Sensor The coolant temperature sensor is mounted in the thermostat housing. The resistance values of the resistive element vary from 11,000Ω at −4°F (−20°C) to 800Ω at 195°F (90.5°C). Along with other input data, the coolant sensor signal is used by the logic module in the scheduling of idle speeds, air-fuel ratio, and spark-advance curves for all engine operating conditions. When the engine is cold, idle speed is increased, the air-fuel ratio is enriched, and the spark-advance curve is altered to improve cold-engine performance.

Vehicle Speed Sensor The vehicle speed sensor is located in the speedometer cable. This sensor contains an on/off microswitch that generates eight pulses per revolution of the speedometer cable. The vehicle speed sensor signal and the throttle position sensor signal are interpreted by the logic module to tell the difference between closed-throttle decelera-

Figure 18-75. Vehicle Speed Sensor. (*Courtesy of Chrysler Canada*)

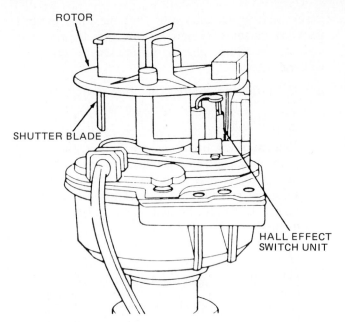

Figure 18-76. Hall Effect Distributor Pickup. (*Courtesy of Chrysler Canada*)

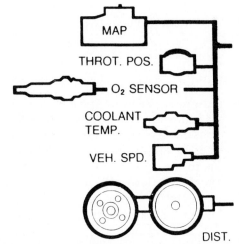

Figure 18-77. Sensor Inputs to Logic Module. (*Courtesy of Chrysler Canada*)

tion and normal idle speed with the vehicle not in motion. During deceleration, the logic module operates the AIS motor to maintain a slightly higher idle speed and reduced emissions.

The vehicle speed sensor is illustrated in Figure 18-75.

Distributor Pickup Signal   A Hall Effect switch unit is used in the distributor pickup assembly. Four metal shutter blades, one for each cylinder, are attached to the bottom of the distributor rotor. Each time one of these shutter blades rotates through the magnetic field of the Hall Effect switch, a pulse signal is generated by the switch. This pulse signal is sent to the logic module and the power module.

When the distributor pickup signal is received, the power module grounds the automatic shutdown (ASD) relay winding, which supplies voltage to the fuel pump, ignition coil positive terminal, and the injector drive and coil drive circuits of the power module. If the distributor pickup signal is not present or is not correct, the ASD relay is not energized by the power module.

The logic module uses the distributor pulse signals as speed information to help determine the spark advance. Piston position is also determined by the logic module from the distributor pulse signal. The logic module signals the power module to operate the injector when the piston position signal is received from the distributor pickup.

A distributor with the Hall Effect switch and shutter blade is shown in Figure 18-76. All the sensor inputs to the logic module are shown in Figure 18-77.

(A complete explanation of Chrysler electronic ignition systems is provided in Chapter 13.)

Automatic Shutdown (ASD) Relay

Operation   When the ignition switch is turned on, voltage is supplied through the J2 circuit to the power module, and the power module supplies 8V to the logic module and the distributor pickup. The power module also supplies voltage through the fused J2 (FJ2) circuit to the ASD relay. When this

occurs, the power module grounds the ASD relay winding and voltage is supplied through the relay contacts to the electric fuel pump, logic module, and coil positive terminal. When the ASD relay closes, the injector drive and ignition coil drive circuits are activated in the power module.

When the ASD relay closes, the logic module commands the power module to send a single "prime shot" of fuel to the engine. This is accomplished by the power module grounding the injector winding for a brief instant. If the engine is not cranked within $\frac{1}{2}$ second, the power module opens the circuit from the ASD relay winding to ground and the relay contacts open the circuit to the fuel pump, logic module, and the coil positive terminal.

If the power module does not sense battery voltage and distributor pulses at the rate of 60 revolutions per minute (rpm) within $\frac{1}{2}$ second after the first distributor pulse, the power module opens the circuit from the ASD relay winding to ground. This causes the relay contacts to open and the voltage supplied to the electric fuel pump, logic module, and coil positive terminal to be shut off. The power module also opens the circuit to the injector and deactivates the ignition coil drive circuit in the module.

The ASD relay is a safety feature that shuts down the fuel pump and the ignition system if the vehicle is involved in an accident and the ignition switch is left on.

The power module will ground the ASD relay winding continuously while the module receives distributor pulses at a rate above 60 rpm. This keeps the ASD relay contacts closed so that voltage is supplied through the relay contacts to the circuits mentioned previously.

The ASD relay is located under the right front kickpad with the logic module and MAP sensor. The ASD relay and the entire EFI system are illustrated in Figure 18-78.

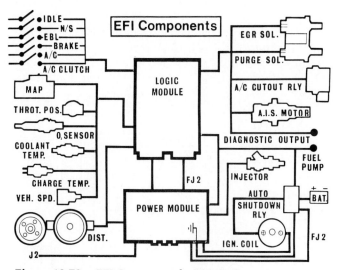

Figure 18-78. EFI System with ASD Relay. (*Courtesy of Chrysler Canada*)

Fuel System Components

Electric Fuel Pump The roller-vane type of fuel pump is driven by a permanent magnet electric motor. A check valve on the inlet side of the pump limits the maximum pump pressure to 120 psi (827 kPa) if the fuel system becomes completely plugged or restricted. Another check valve in the pump outlet

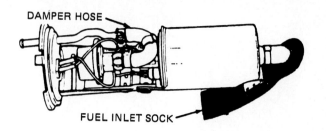

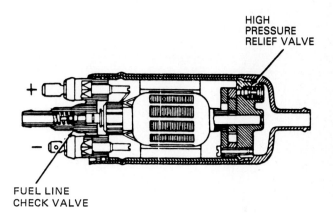

Figure 18-79. Electric Fuel Pump. (*Courtesy of Chrysler Canada*)

prevents any movement of fuel in either direction when the pump is not in operation. A 70-micron filter is provided by the fuel inlet sock on the pump inlet, which prevents water and other foreign particles from entering the fuel system.

The fuel pump is shown in Figure 18-79.

The electric fuel pump and the fuel gauge sending unit are located in separate openings in the fuel tank. A swirl tank surrounds the fuel pump in the fuel tank. The return fuel line is connected from the throttle body assembly to the swirl tank. Excess fuel is returned continuously from the throttle body assembly to the swirl tank while the engine is running. The swirl tank pictured in Figure 18-80 provides a supply of fuel at the pump inlet during all driving conditions.

The fuel flows through a low-pressure orifice in the end of the return hose, and this creates a slight low-pressure area at the end of the hose. This causes increased fuel flow from the main fuel tank to the swirl tank. A return-line check valve prevents fuel flow from the tank into the return line if the vehicle is rolled over in an accident.

In-Line Fuel Filter In addition to the filter sock on the pump inlet, a 50-micron in-line fuel filter, as shown in Figure 18-81, is located near the fuel tank under the vehicle.

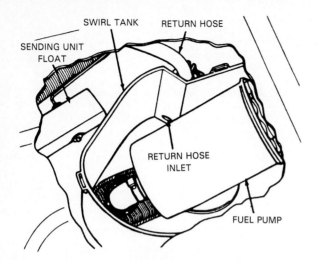

Figure 18-80.   Swirl Tank. (*Courtesy of Chrysler Canada*)

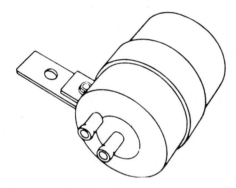

Figure 18-81.   In-Line Fuel Filter. (*Courtesy of Chrysler Canada*)

Throttle Body Assembly   The throttle body assembly contains the injector, pressure regulator, automatic idle speed (AIS) motor, throttle position sensor, and throttle valve. The fuel pump supplies fuel through the in-line filter to the injector and pressure regulator. When pump pressure reaches 36 psi (248 kPa), the pressure regulator diaphragm is forced downward by the fuel pressure so that excess fuel is returned from the pressure regulator through the return line to the fuel tank, as illustrated in Figure 18-82.

Special high-pressure fuel hoses and clamps are used in the EFI system. A vacuum hose is connected from the area above the throttle in the throttle body to the pressure regulator spring chamber. Since the injector tip is mounted above the throttle, this tip is subjected to venturi vacuum, which increases with engine speed. Therefore, a pressure decrease occurs at the injector tip at wide-open throttle. When this occurs, the pressure regulator vacuum signal assists the fuel pressure to move the regulator diaphragm downward. This moves the diaphragm downward at a lower pressure compared to the idle speed when there is no vacuum applied to the pressure regulator. Thus, fuel pressure to the injector is decreased when pressure at the tip of the injector is decreased at high speed, and a constant pressure drop of 35 psi (248 kPa) is maintained across the injector.

The injector has a winding surrounding the movable plunger. Voltage is supplied to the injector winding from the power module, and the module also grounds the other end of the injector winding to

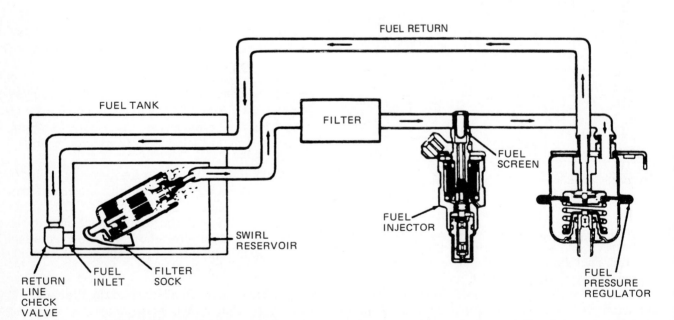

Figure 18-82.   Fuel System with Injector and Pressure Regulator. (*Courtesy of Chrysler Canada*)

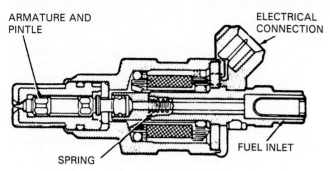

Figure 18-83. Injector Design. (*Courtesy of Chrysler Canada*)

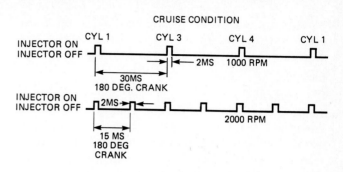

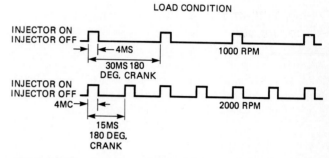

Figure 18-84. Injector Pulse Width. (*Courtesy of Chrysler Canada*)

energize the injector. The internal design of the injector is shown in Figure 18-83.

Air enters the throttle body assembly from the air cleaner. When the injector is energized fuel is sprayed from the injector into the airstream above the throttle.

Output Control Functions

Fuel Injection Control The power module energizes the injector once for each piston intake stroke. The amount of fuel delivered by the injector is determined by the pulse width, or "on time" of the injector. The pulse width is measured in milliseconds (MS), and the fuel flow from the injector increases in relation to the pulse width. Input data received by the logic module indicates the engine fuel requirements. The logic module commands the power module to supply the precise injector pulse width to meet these fuel requirements.

As indicated in Figure 18-84, the pulse width will be 2 MS at 1,000 rpm cruise conditions, and the entire injector on/off time is 30 MS.

When the engine is operating at 2,000 rpm cruise conditions, the entire injector on/off time is only 15 MS because the crankshaft is turning much faster. Under this condition the injector pulse width is still 2 MS, but more fuel is delivered by the injector because the injector is being energized every 15 MS. When the engine is operating under heavy load at 1,000 or 2,000 rpm, the injector pulse width is increased to 4 MS.

The logic module and the power module will supply the correct pulse width to maintain engine performance, economy, and emission levels under all operating conditions. When the engine is being started, the injector is energized twice for each piston intake stroke. The injector pulse width is increased when the engine is started when cold to provide the necessary mixture enrichment.

Under certain operating conditions the system will operate in open-loop mode. In this mode, the oxygen sensor signal is ignored by the logic module and the module maintains the air-fuel ratio at a predetermined value. The system remains in open-loop mode under the following conditions:

1. Cold engine, until the oxygen sensor generates a signal.
2. Park/neutral idle operation.
3. Wide-open throttle operation.
4. Deceleration conditions.
5. Oxygen sensor signal is not available for a specified period of time.

The system operates in the closed-loop mode when the following conditions are present:

1. Coolant temperature is above a specified value.
2. Start-up delay timer in the logic module has timed out.
3. Oxygen sensor is generating a valid signal to the logic module.
4. Vehicle is operating under drive/idle or cruise conditions.

Ignition Spark-Advance The logic module determines the precise spark-advance requirements by interpreting data from the distributor rpm signal, MAP sensor, and coolant temperature sensor. When the engine is cold, the logic module increases the spark advance for improved engine performance. The logic module commands the power module to open the primary ignition circuit at the right instant to provide the precise spark advance required by the engine.

Idle Speed Control While the engine is being started, the logic module positions the automatic idle speed (AIS) motor to provide easy starting without the driver having to touch the accelerator pedal. When the engine is cold, the logic module positions the AIS motor to provide the correct cold fast-idle speed. The AIS motor allows more air to flow past the motor plunger into the intake manifold to increase the idle speed. This airflow bypasses the throttle, as indicated in Figure 18-85.

The AIS motor provides the correct idle speed when the air conditioner is on, and the correct throttle opening when the engine is decelerating.

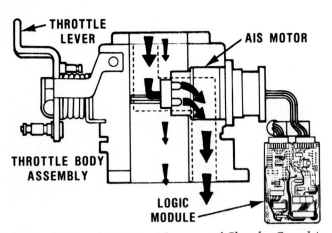

Figure 18-85. AIS Motor. (*Courtesy of Chrysler Canada*)

Exhaust-Gas Recirculation (EGR) Control The logic module energizes a vacuum solenoid in the EGR vacuum system. If the solenoid is energized, it shuts off vacuum to the EGR valve. A de-energized solenoid allows vacuum to pass through the solenoid to the EGR system. The solenoid is energized at speeds below 1,200 rpm, wide-open throttle operation, or when the coolant temperature is below 70°F (21°C). During all other engine operating conditions, the solenoid is de-energized and vacuum is supplied through the solenoid to the backpressure transducer.

If the vehicle speed is below 30 to 35 miles per hour (MPH) (48 KPH), the backpressure transducer vents the vacuum in the EGR system. Above this speed, the exhaust pressure closes the vacuum bleed in the transducer and vacuum is supplied to open the EGR valve.

The EGR valve and the backpressure transducer are shown in Figure 18-86.

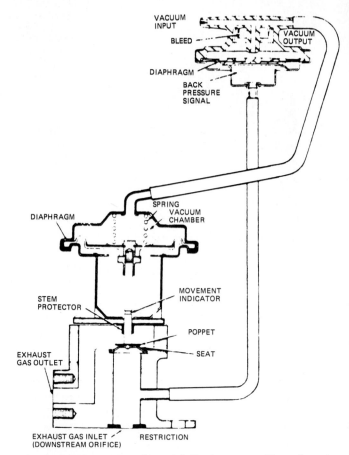

Figure 18-86. EGR Valve with Backpressure Transducer. (*Courtesy of Chrysler Canada*)

Canister-Purge Control The logic module operates a solenoid connected in the vacuum hose to the canister-purge valve. When engine temperature is below 180°F (82°C), the logic module energizes the solenoid, which shuts off vacuum to the canister-purge valve. Above this coolant temperature, the solenoid is de-energized, which supplies vacuum through the solenoid to the purge-control valve. Under this condition the canister is purged through a port in the throttle body.

The canister-purge solenoid and the EGR solenoid are located with the diagnostic connector under a cover on the fender well, as illustrated in Figure 18-87.

Air Conditioning Control When the throttle approaches the wide-open position and the throttle position sensor voltage is above a specific value, the logic module de-energizes the air conditioning (A/C) wide-open throttle (WOT) cutout relay, and the relay contacts open the circuit to the A/C compressor clutch. If the throttle is in the idle or cruising speed range, the logic module energizes the A/C WOT cutout relay and the relay contacts close, which sup-

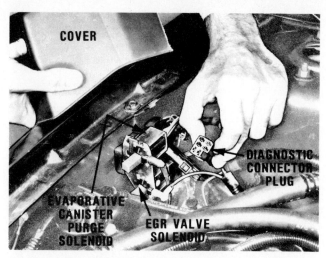

Figure 18-87. Canister Purge and EGR Solenoids with Diagnostic Connector. (*Courtesy of Chrysler Canada*)

plies voltage to the A/C compressor clutch. If the engine speed drops below 500 rpm, the logic module de-energizes the A/C WOT cutout relay and opens the circuit to the compressor clutch. This prevents the engine from stalling under unusual conditions. If the engine is being cranked and the air conditioning is turned on, the logic module does not engage the compressor clutch until the engine speed exceeds 500 rpm.

The A/C WOT cutout relay is located beside the starter relay near the battery. The complete wiring diagrams for the logic module and power module are shown in Figures 18-88 and 18-89.

Later Model Chrysler Electronic Fuel Injection

System Changes

The wiring diagrams in Figures 18-88 and 18-89 are for 1984 models. In the 1985 model year, several changes were made to the EFI system. In these newer systems, the automatic shutdown (ASD) relay is contained in the power module, and the logic module provides necessary signals to the power module for ASD relay control, charging system control, radiator fan control, and wastegate control on turbocharged engines. An external alternator voltage regulator is no longer required. A battery temperature sensor is located in the power module, and a battery charge signal is also sent to the power module. The power module operates a radiator fan control relay and a solenoid for turbo wastegate control. In addi-

tion, some new fault codes which apply to the battery and charging system have been added.

In the 1986 model year, a redesigned throttle body assembly is used. This assembly contains an improved fuel injector and a throttle body temperature sensor. Since the pressure regulator limits fuel pressure to 14.5 psi (100 kPa), vapors may form in the fuel system. When this occurs the air-fuel mixture becomes leaner. If the throttle body temperature increases to the point at which fuel vapors occur, the throttle body temperature sensor signals the logic module to supply a slightly richer air-fuel ratio.

The throttle body assembly with the temperature sensor is illustrated in Figure 18-90 and the improved injector design is shown in Figure 18-91.

Wiring diagrams for 1986 single-point EFI systems are provided in Figures 18-92 through 18-96.

Chrysler Multi-Point Electronic Fuel Injection (EFI) Used on 2.2L Turbocharged Engine

Modules and Inputs

Operation The logic module and the power module are very similar to the modules used in the single-point throttle body injection system, but they are not interchangeable. Since the modules perform basically the same functions as they did in the single-point EFI system, we will describe only the differences in the multi-point system.

Inputs The same inputs are used in the multi-point EFI system with the addition of a detonation sensor and a charge temperature sensor. If the engine detonates, the detonation sensor signals the power module to retard the spark advance until detonation stops. The charge temperature sensor sends a signal to the logic module in relation to the temperature of the air-fuel mixture in the intake manifold. This signal acts as a backup for the coolant temperature sensor if the coolant temperature sensor fails.

All the inputs and output control functions in the multi-point EFI systems are illustrated in Figure 18-97.

The distributor in the multi-point EFI system has a reference pickup and a synchronizer ("sync") pickup. The reference pickup is the same as the Hall Effect switch used in the single-point EFI system.

Information data regarding engine speed and crankshaft position is supplied to the logic module by the reference pickup signal. The logic module uses this information with the other input data to

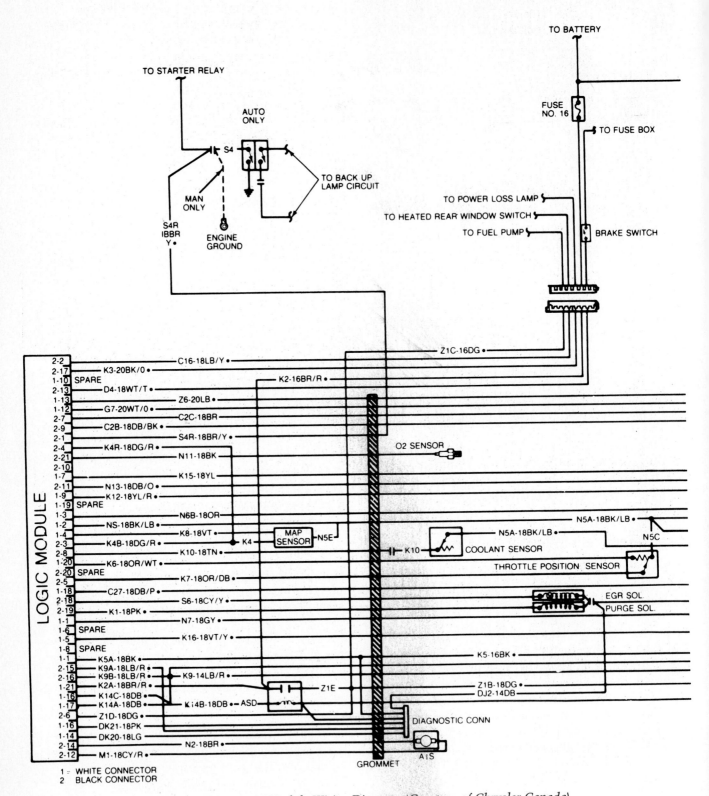

Figure 18-88. Logic Module Wiring Diagram. (*Courtesy of Chrysler Canada*)

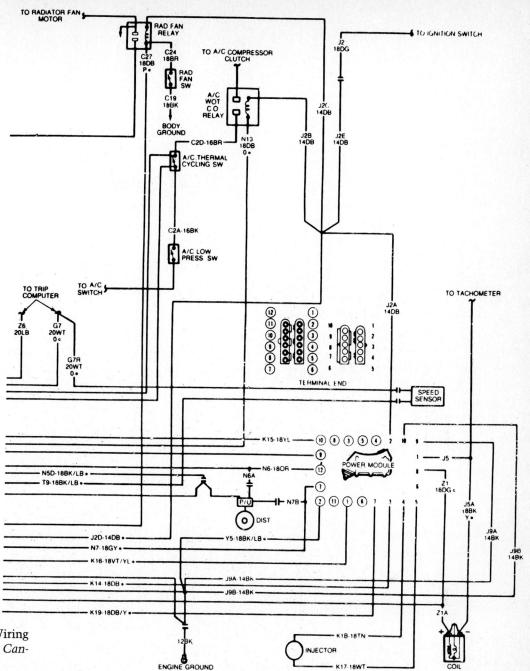

Figure 18-89. Power Module Wiring Diagram. (*Courtesy of Chrysler Canada*)

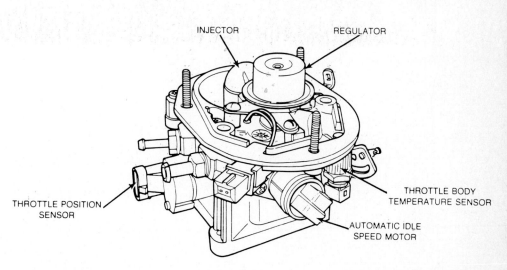

Figure 18-90. Throttle Body Assembly with Temperature Sensor. (*Courtesy of Chrysler Canada*)

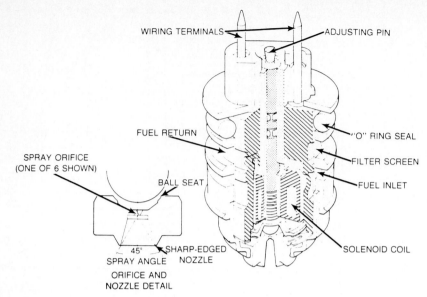

WIRING TERMINALS — ADJUSTING PIN

FUEL RETURN

"O" RING SEAL

FILTER SCREEN

FUEL INLET

SPRAY ORIFICE
(ONE OF 6 SHOWN)

BALL SEAT

SOLENOID COIL

45°
SPRAY ANGLE

SHARP-EDGED
NOZZLE

ORIFICE AND
NOZZLE DETAIL

Figure 18-91. Improved Injector Design. (*Courtesy of Chrysler Canada*)

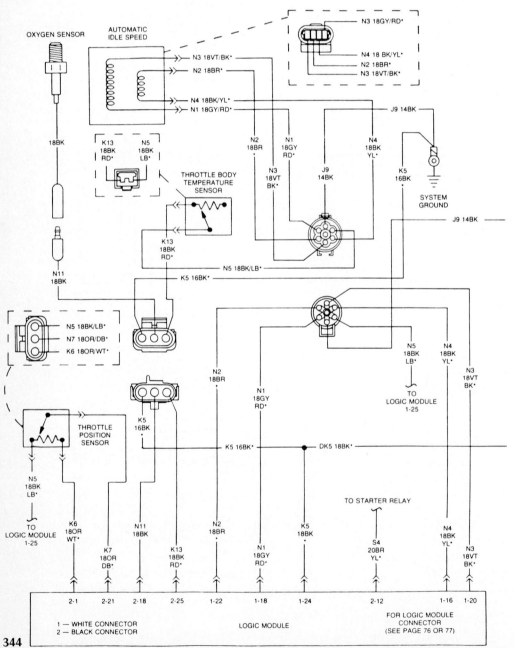

Figure 18-92. Logic Module Wiring. (*Courtesy of Chrysler Canada*)

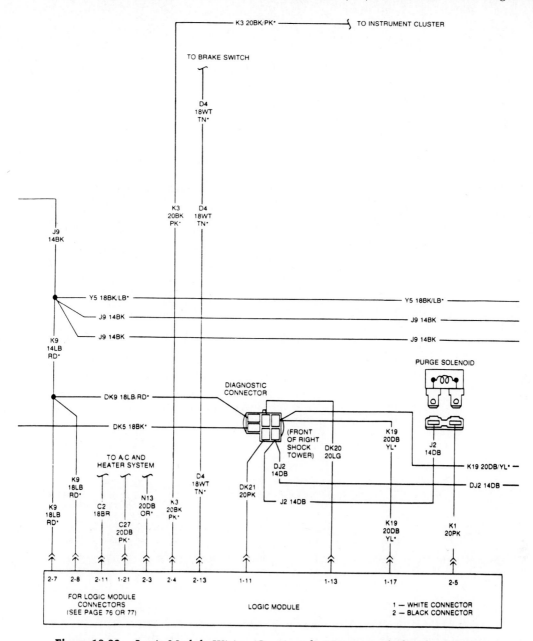

Figure 18-93. Logic Module Wiring (Continued). (*Courtesy of Chrysler Canada*)

determine the correct spark advance and injector pulse width. The "sync" pickup is mounted under the pickup plate, and a notched "sync" ring attached to the distributor shaft rotates through the pickup. This signal from the "sync" pickup tells the logic and power modules which pair of injectors to turn on and which pair to turn off. If the engine speed exceeds 6,600 rpm, the logic module shuts off the fuel until the speed drops to a safe 6,100 rpm.

The reference pickup and "sync" pickup are pictured in Figure 18-98.

Output Control Functions

Fuel-Injection Control All the output control functions in the multi-point EFI system are the same as the single-point EFI system with the exception of fuel-injection control. In the multi-point system, a single injector is placed in each intake port in the intake manifold rather than having one injector in the throttle body assembly. The injectors are similar to the injector in the single-point system. The power module energizes injectors 1 and 2 and injectors 3

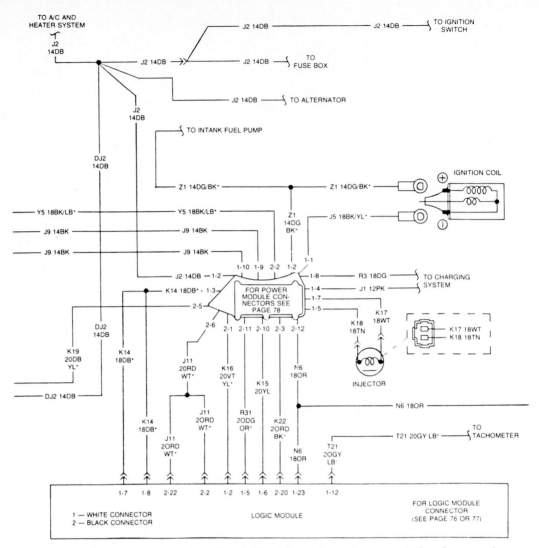

Figure 18-94.   Power Module and Logic Module Wiring. (*Courtesy of Chrysler Canada*)

and 4 in pairs. Each pair of injectors is energized once for every two crankshaft revolutions. The four injectors located in the intake manifold are shown in Figure 18-99.

The logic module commands the power module to provide the precise injector pulse width to supply the exact air-fuel ratio required by the engine. The pressure regulator maintains a constant pressure drop of 55 psi (379 kPa) across the injectors in the multi-point system. Many of the other components in the multi-point EFI system are similar to the components in the single-point system. The changes on the 1985 single-point system also apply to the multi-point system. These changes were explained under the single-point system, and they pertain to the alternator voltage regulator, battery charge and temperature signals, and the automatic shutdown relay.

Fault codes and wiring diagrams vary, depending on the year of vehicle.

Wiring diagrams for 1986 multi-point EFI systems are provided in Figures 18-100 through 18-105.

Ford Electronic Engine Control IV (EEC IV) Systems Used with 2.3L Turbocharged Engine

Input Sensors

The 2.3L turbocharged engine has an EEC IV system with electronic fuel injection (EFI). This system uses many of the same input sensors that are used in other EEC IV systems. A vane meter that contains

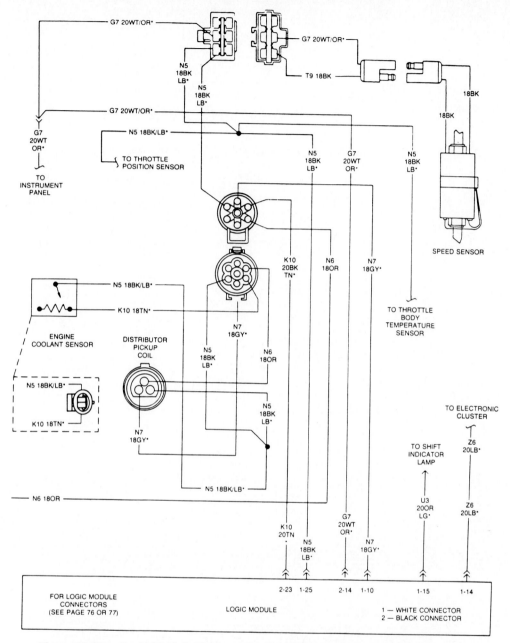

Figure 18-95.   Logic Module Wiring (*Continued*). (*Courtesy of Chrysler Canada*)

two sensors is used in this system. These sensors are referred to as the vane airflow (VAF) sensor and the vane air temperature (VAT) sensor. The vane meter is located in the engine air-intake system, as illustrated in Figure 18-106.

All the airflow into the engine must travel through the vane meter. The airflow rotates a vane that is mounted on a pivot pin in the meter body, as pictured in Figure 18-107.

The movement of the vane is proportional to the volume of airflow through the air-intake system. The

VAF sensor is a variable resistor which has a sliding contact that is attached to the vane shaft. The electronic control assembly (ECA) applies a 5V reference voltage to the VAF sensor. As the vane shaft rotates, it moves the sliding contact on the variable resistor. The voltage output signal from the VAF sensor to the ECA varies between 0V and 5V. A higher volume of airflow produces a higher voltage output signal from the VAF sensor.

The VAF sensor in the vane meter is shown in Figure 18-108.

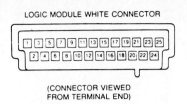

(CONNECTOR VIEWED
FROM TERMINAL END)

CAV	CIRCUIT	GAUGE	COLOR	FUNCTION
1				
2	K16	20	VT/YL*	INJECTOR CONTROL TO POWER MODULE
3				
4				
5	R31	20	DG/OR*	ALTERNATOR FIELD CONTROL TO POWER MODULE
6	K15	20	YL	IGNITION CONTROL TO POWER MODULE
7	K14	18	DB*	FUSED J2 FROM POWER MODULE
8	K14	18	DB*	FUSED J2 FROM POWER MODULE
9				
10	N7	18	GY*	DISTRIBUTOR PICKUP SIGNAL
11	DK21	20	PK	DIAGNOSTIC CONNECTOR
12	T21	20	GY/LB*	TACHOMETER SIGNAL
13	DK20	20	LG	DIAGNOSTIC CONNECTOR
14	Z6	20	LB*	FUEL MONITOR OUTPUT SIGNAL
15	U3	20	OR/LG*	SHIFT INDICATOR LIGHT
16	N4	18	BK/YL*	AUTOMATIC IDLE SPEED MOTOR
17	K19	20	DB/YL*	AUTO SHUTDOWN RELAY CONTROL
18	N1	18	GY/RD*	AUTOMATIC IDLE SPEED MOTOR
19				
20	N3	18	VT/BK*	AUTOMATIC IDLE SPEED MOTOR
21	C27	20	DB/PK*	RADIATOR FAN RELAY CONTROL
22	N2	18	BR*	AUTOMATIC IDLE SPEED MOTOR
23	N6	18	OR	8 VOLT SUPPLY FROM POWER MODULE
24	K5	18	BK*	SENSOR GROUND
25	N5	18	BK/LB*	SENSOR GROUND

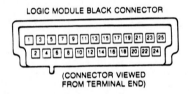

(CONNECTOR VIEWED
FROM TERMINAL END)

CAV	CIRCUIT	GAUGE	COLOR	FUNCTION
1	K6	18	OR/WT*	5 VOLT SUPPLY FOR THROTTLE POSITION SENSOR
2	J11	20	RD/WT*	DIRECT BATTERY FEED FROM POWER MODULE
3	N13	20	DB/OR*	A/C CUTOUT RELAY CONTROL
4	K3	20	BK/OR*	POWER LOSS LAMP CONTROL
5	K1	20	PK*	PURGE SOLENOID CONTROL
6				
7	K9	18	LB/RD*	POWER GROUND
8	K9	18	LB/RD*	POWER GROUND
9				
10				
11	C2	18	BR	AIR CONDITIONING CLUTCH SIGNAL
12	S4	20	BR/YL*	PARK/NEUTRAL SWITCH SIGNAL
13	D4	18	WT/TN*	BRAKE SWITCH SIGNAL
14	G7	20	WT/OR*	SPEED SENSOR SIGNAL
15				
16				
17				
18	N11	18	BK	OXYGEN SENSOR SIGNAL
19				
20	K22	20	RD/BK*	BATTERY TEMPERATURE SIGNAL FROM POWER MODULE
21	K7	18	OR/DB*	THROTTLE POSITION SIGNAL
22	J11	20	RD/WT*	DIRECT BATTERY SENSE VOLTAGE FROM POWER MODULE
23	K10	20	TN*	ENGINE COOLANT TEMPERATURE SIGNAL
24				
25	K13	18	BK/RD*	THROTTLE BODY TEMPERATURE SIGNAL

Figure 18-96. Logic Module Terminal Identification. (*Courtesy of Chrysler Canada*)

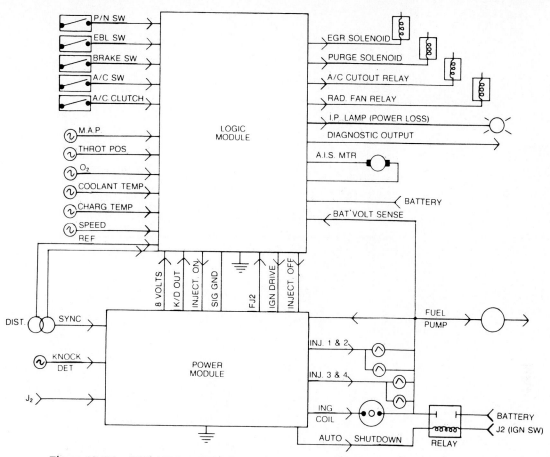

Figure 18-97. Multi-Point EFI System Components. (*Courtesy of Chrysler Canada*)

A vane air temperature (VAT) sensor is also located in the vane meter. The ECA calculates a mass airflow value from the VAT and VAF sensor signals. This value is used by the ECA to provide the correct air-fuel ratio of 14.7:1. The VAT sensor in the vane meter is shown in Figure 18-109.

Some EEC IV systems have a three-wire exhaust-gas oxygen (EGO) sensor in place of the single-wire sensor. This three-wire sensor has an internal electric heater to improve sensor response time. An air charge temperature sensor is used in some systems on 2.3L engines.

The input sensors and output controls in the EEC IV system on the 2.3L turbocharged engine are pictured in Figure 18-110.

Output Controls

An exhaust-gas recirculation (EGR) solenoid controls the vacuum that is applied to the EGR valve. The EGR solenoid shuts off the vacuum to the EGR valve if the engine coolant is cold, or when the engine is operating at idle speed or wide-open throttle

(WOT). At all other operating conditions, the ECA energizes the EGR solenoid, which applies vacuum to the EGR valve.

The throttle body assembly contains the throttle valve, throttle position sensor (TPS), and the throttle air bypass valve solenoid, as illustrated in Figure 18-111.

The fuel injectors are mounted in the intake ports, and there is no fuel delivered to the throttle body assembly. The throttle air bypass valve solenoid is operated by the ECA. When the ECA increases the voltage that is supplied to the solenoid, the throttle air bypass valve opening increases, thus allowing additional air to bypass the throttle valve and increase the engine idle speed. The throttle air bypass valve controls both the cold fast-idle speed and the idle speed at normal engine temperatures. There are no curb-idle or fast-idle adjustments on the throttle air bypass valve solenoid.

While the engine is being cranked, the ECA moves the throttle air bypass valve to the fully open position. This allows "no touch starting," which means the engine can be started at any temperature without touching the throttle. Each time the engine

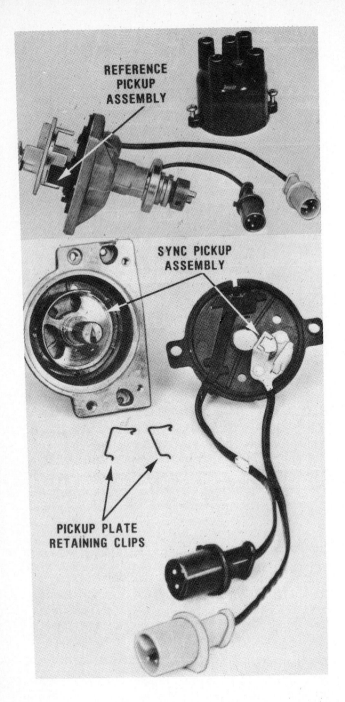

REFERENCE PICKUP ASSEMBLY

SYNC PICKUP ASSEMBLY

PICKUP PLATE RETAINING CLIPS

Figure 18-98. Reference and "Sync" Pickup Assemblies. (*Courtesy of Chrysler Canada*)

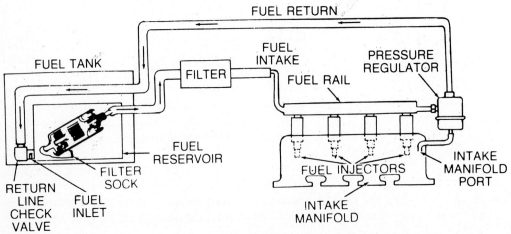

FUEL RETURN

FUEL TANK

FILTER

FUEL INTAKE

FUEL RAIL

PRESSURE REGULATOR

FUEL RESERVOIR

FILTER SOCK

RETURN LINE CHECK VALVE

FUEL INLET

FUEL INJECTORS

INTAKE MANIFOLD PORT

INTAKE MANIFOLD

Figure 18-99. Multi-Point EFI Fuel System. (*Courtesy of Chrysler Canada*)

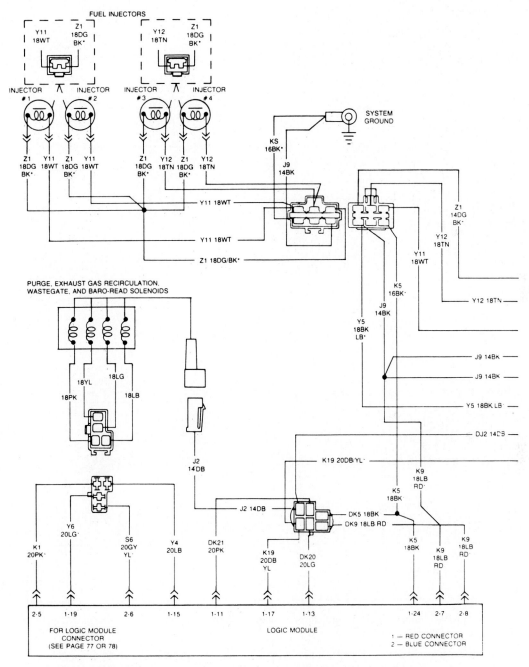

Figure 18-100.   Logic Module Wiring Chrysler Multi-Point EFI Systems. (*Courtesy of Chrysler Canada*)

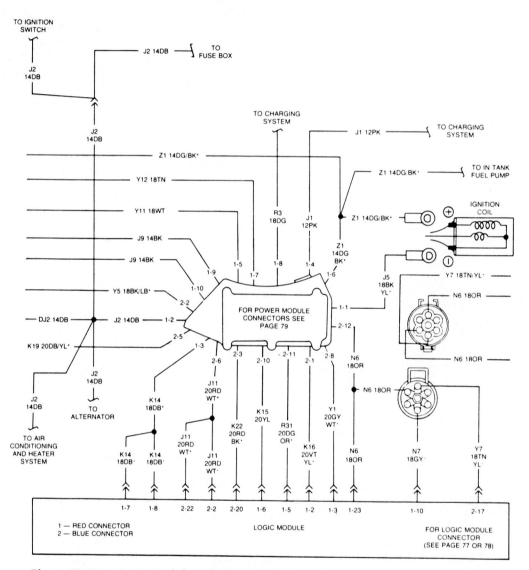

Figure 18-101. Logic Module and Power Module Wiring. (*Courtesy of Chrysler Canada*)

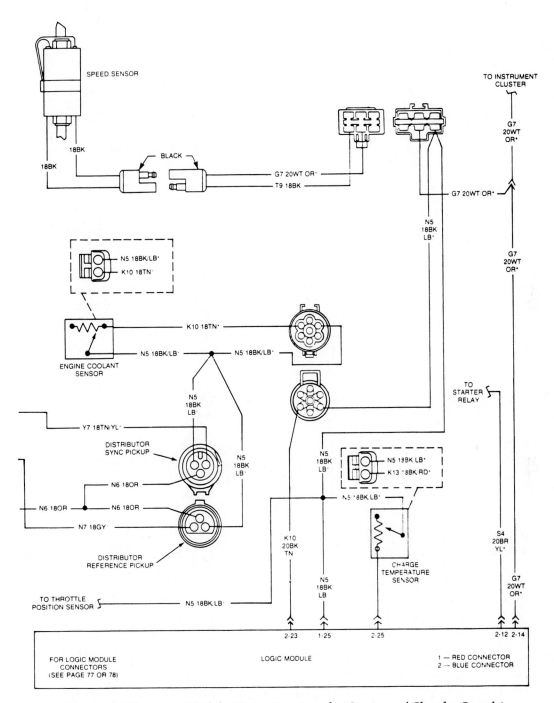

Figure 18-102. Logic Module Wiring (Continued). (*Courtesy of Chrysler Canada*)

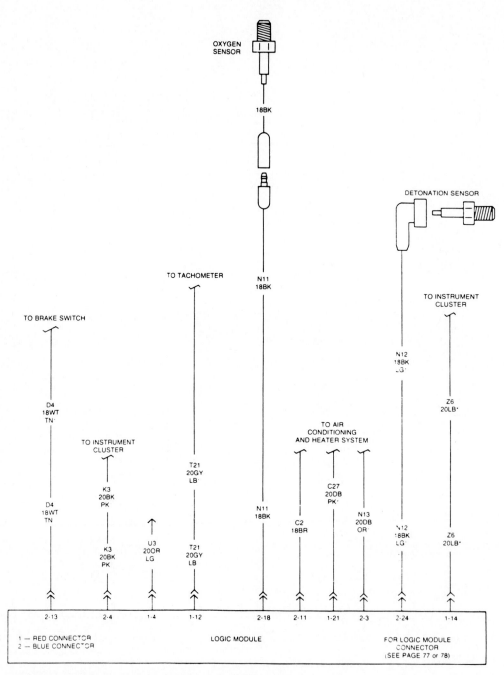

Figure 18-103. Logic Module Wiring (Continued). (*Courtesy of Chrysler Canada*)

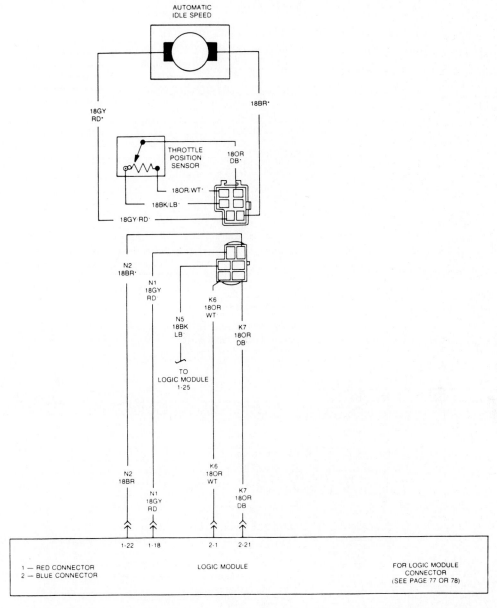

Figure 18-104. Logic Module Wiring (Continued). (*Courtesy of Chrysler Canada*)

LOGIC MODULE RED CONNECTOR

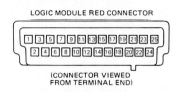

(CONNECTOR VIEWED
FROM TERMINAL END)

CAV	CIRCUIT	GAUGE	COLOR	FUNCTION
1	—			
2	K16	20	VT·YL·	INJECTOR CONTROL (1-2) TO POWER MODULE
3	Y1	20	GY WT·	INJECTOR CONTROL (3-4) TO POWER MODULE
4	—			
5	R31	20	DG OR	ALTERNATOR FIELD CONTROL TO POWER MODULE
6	K15	20	YL	IGNITION CONTROL TO POWER MODULE
7	K14	18	DB·	FUSED J2 FROM POWER MODULE
8	K14	18	DB	FUSED J2 FROM POWER MODULE
9	—			
10	N7	18	GY	DISTRIBUTOR REFERENCE PICKUP SIGNAL
11	DK21	20	PK	DIAGNOSTIC CONNECTOR
12	T21	20	GY LB	TACHOMETER SIGNAL
13	DK20	20	LG	DIAGNOSTIC CONNECTOR
14	Z6	20	LB	FUEL MONITOR OUTPUT SIGNAL
15	Y4	20	LB	BARO READ SOLENOID CONTROL
16	N4	18	BK YL	AUTOMATIC IDLE SPEED MOTOR
17	K19	20	DB YL	AUTO SHUTDOWN RELAY CONTROL
18	N1	18	GY RD	AUTOMATIC IDLE SPEED MOTOR
19	Y6	20	LG	WASTEGATE SOLENOID CONTROL
20	N3	18	VT BK	AUTOMATIC IDLE SPEED MOTOR
21	C27	20	DB PK	RADIATOR FAN RELAY CONTROL
22	N2	18	BR	AUTOMATIC IDLE SPEED MOTOR
23	N6	18	OR	8 VOLT SUPPLY FROM POWER MODULE
24	K5	18	BK	SENSOR GROUND
25	N5	18	BK LB	SENSOR GROUND

LOGIC MODULE RED CONNECTOR

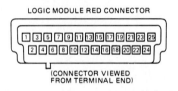

(CONNECTOR VIEWED
FROM TERMINAL END)

CAV	CIRCUIT	GAUGE	COLOR	FUNCTION
1	K6	18	OR/WT·	5 VOLT SUPPLY FOR THROTTLE POSITION SENSOR
2	J11	20	RD/WT·	DIRECT BATTERY FEED FROM POWER MODULE
3	N13	20	DB/OR·	A/C CUTOUT RELAY CONTROL
4	K3	20	BK/PK·	POWER LOSS LAMP CONTROL
5	K1	20	PK·	PURGE SOLENOID CONTROL
6	S6	20	GY/YL·	EGR SOLENOID CONTROL
7	K9	18	LB/RD·	POWER GROUND
8	K9	18	LB/RD·	POWER GROUND
9	—			
10	—			
11	C2	18	BR	AIR CONDITIONING CLUTCH SIGNAL
12	S4	20	BR/YL·	PARK/NEUTRAL SWITCH SIGNAL
13	D4	18	WT/TN·	BRAKE SWITCH SIGNAL
14	G7	20	WT/OR·	SPEED SENSOR SIGNAL
15	—			
16	—			
17	Y7	18	TN/YL·	DISTRIBUTOR SYNC PICKUP SIGNAL
18	N11	18	BK	OXYGEN SENSOR SIGNAL
19	—			
20	K22	20	RD/BK·	BATTERY TEMPERATURE SIGNAL FROM POWER MODULE
21	K7	18	OR/DB·	THROTTLE POSITION SIGNAL
22	J11	20	RD/WT·	DIRECT BATTERY SENSE VOLTAGE FROM POWER MODULE
23	K10	20	TN·	ENGINE COOLANT TEMPERATURE SIGNAL
24	N12	18	BK/LG·	DETONATION SENSOR SIGNAL
25	K13	18	BK/RD·	CHARGE TEMPERATURE SENSOR SIGNAL

Figure 18-105. Logic Module Terminal Identification. (*Courtesy of Chrysler Canada*)

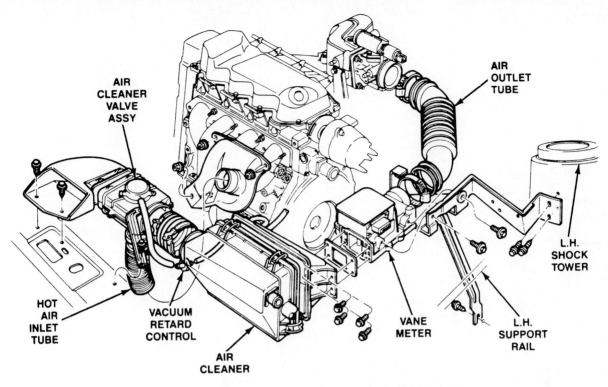

Figure 18-106.   Vane Meter Location. (*Courtesy of Ford Motor Co.*)

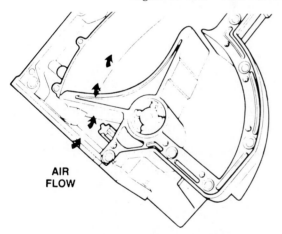

Figure 18-107.   Vane Meter Air Vane. (*Courtesy of Ford Motor Co.*)

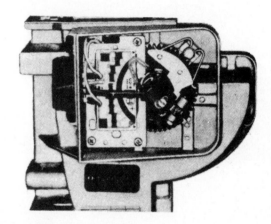

Figure 18-108.   Vane Airflow (VAF) Sensor. (*Courtesy of Ford Motor Co.*)

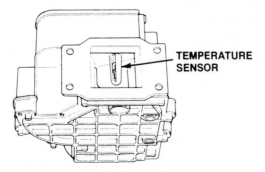

Figure 18-109.   Vane Air Temperature Sensor. (*Courtesy of Ford Motor Co.*)

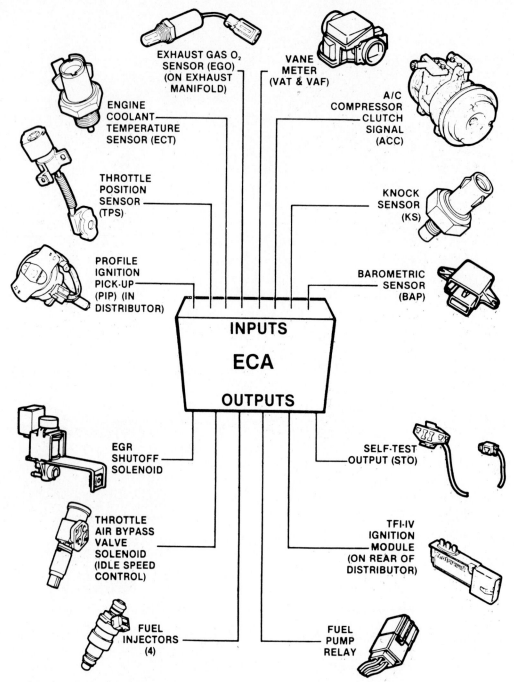

Figure 18-110.   Wiring Diagram for EEC IV System Used on 2.3L Turbocharged Engine. *(Courtesy of Ford Motor Co.)*

is started, the throttle air bypass valve provides fast idle speed for a period of time. This time period increases as engine coolant temperature decreases. The throttle air bypass valve solenoid provides the same functions as the throttle kicker or idle speed control motor on other systems.

Airflow through the throttle air bypass valve is illustrated in Figure 18-112.

Fuel System

The EEC IV system with electronic fuel injection (EFI) has a low-pressure electric pump mounted in the fuel tank and a high-pressure electric pump located on the right frame rail, as shown in Figure 18-113.

When the ignition switch is turned on, the ECA

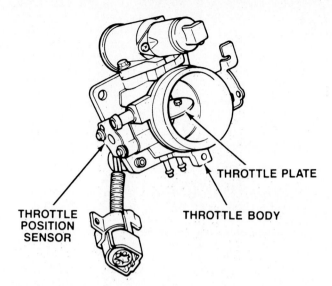

Figure 18-111. Throttle Body Assembly. (*Courtesy of Ford Motor Co.*)

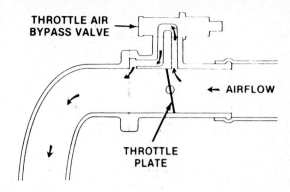

Figure 18-112. Throttle Air Bypass Valve Operation. (*Courtesy of Ford Motor Co.*)

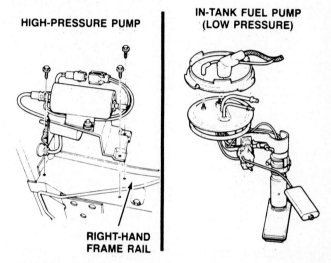

Figure 18-113. Fuel Pumps for EEC IV System with EFI. (*Courtesy of Ford Motor Co.*)

grounds the fuel pump relay winding and the relay contacts close to provide power to the fuel pumps, as shown in Figure 18-114.

If the engine is not cranked within one second, the ECA opens the circuit from the fuel pump relay to ground and the relay contacts open the circuit to the fuel pumps. The dual fuel pumps are capable of supplying fuel at 100 psi (690 kPa). A fuel filter is mounted near the high-pressure pump in the frame rail.

Fuel is delivered from the fuel pumps to the fuel rail and the pressure regulator. The fuel rail, pres-

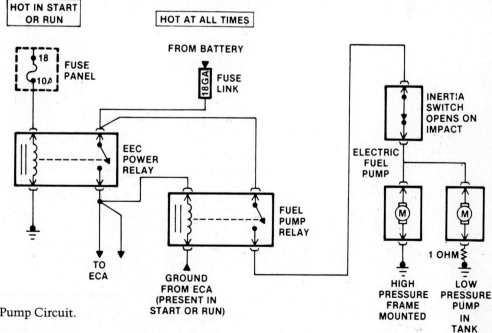

Figure 18-114. Electric Fuel Pump Circuit. (*Courtesy of Ford Motor Co.*)

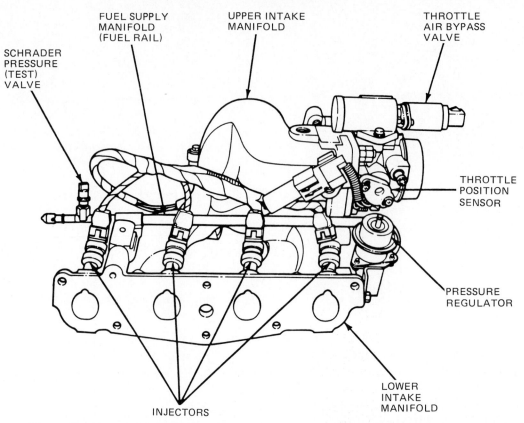

Figure 18-115.   Fuel Rail with Pressure Regulator and Injectors. (*Courtesy of Ford Motor Co.*)

sure regulator, and the injectors are mounted on the intake manifold, as shown in Figure 18-115.

When the pressure in the fuel rail reaches 39 psi (269 kPa) the pressure regulator diaphragm is forced upward, which opens the valve so that excess fuel returns to the fuel tank, as illustrated in Figure 18-116.

A vacuum hose is connected from the intake manifold to the top of the pressure regulator. This vacuum signal maintains a constant pressure drop across the injectors during all intake manifold vacuum conditions.

When the engine is idling, high manifold vacuum is applied to the upper side of the pressure regulator diaphragm and the diaphragm can be forced upward at 39 psi (269 kPa). At high engine speeds, the turbocharger pressurizes the intake manifold to 8 psi (55 kPa), and this pressure is applied to upper side of the pressure regulator diaphragm. Under this condition, 50 psi (345 kPa) is required to move the diaphragm upward and fuel pressure to the injectors is maintained at this higher value.

When the intake manifold pressure increases at high speeds, the increase in fuel pressure maintains the same pressure difference across the injectors.

The injectors are mounted in the intake ports of the intake manifold. Each injector contains an electric solenoid that is energized by the ECA. The amount of fuel that each injector delivers is determined by the "on time" of the injector, because there is a constant pressure across the injector. A cutaway view of an injector is illustrated in Figure 18-117.

The ECA controls the "on time" of the injectors to provide the precise air-fuel ratio that is required by the engine under all operating conditions. When

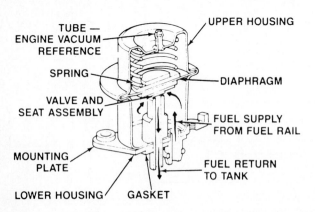

Figure 18-116.   Pressure Regulator Design. (*Courtesy of Ford Motor Co.*)

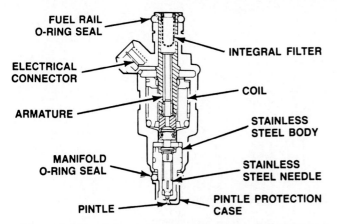

Figure 18-117. Injector Design. (*Courtesy of Ford Motor Co.*)

the ignition switch is turned on, current flows from the switch through the power relay winding to ground. This action closes the relay contacts, which supplies voltage to the injectors, the solenoids in the system, and ECA terminals 37 and 57.

Some power relays have a time-delay feature that causes the relay to remain closed for ten seconds after the ignition switch is turned off. This action allows the ECA to position the throttle air bypass valve for no-touch starting.

The injectors for cylinders 1 and 2 and the injectors for cylinders 3 and 4 are connected in parallel electrically, as shown in the wiring diagram in Figure 18-118.

The ECA energizes each pair of injectors when it completes the circuit from the injectors to ground

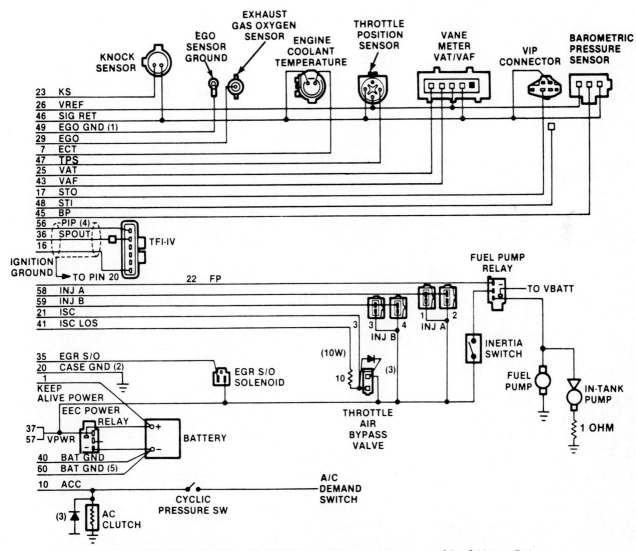

Figure 18-118. EEC IV with EFI Wiring Diagram. (*Courtesy of Ford Motor Co.*)

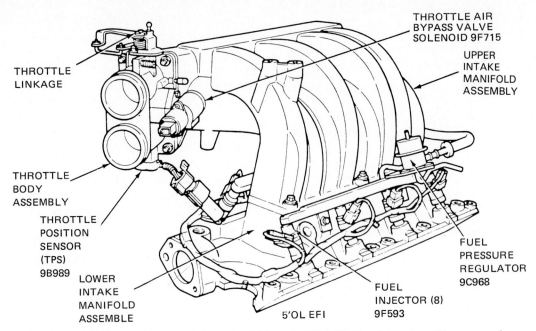

Figure 18-119. High-Rise Intake Manifold with EFI 5.0L Truck Engine. (*Courtesy of Ford Motor Co.*)

through the ECA. When the engine is decelerated in the closed-throttle mode, the ECA does not energize the injectors. This provides reduced emission levels and improved fuel economy during deceleration. The injectors are energized again when the engine speed drops to a predetermined rpm. Enrichment of the air-fuel ratio on a cold engine is provided by increasing the "on time" of the injectors, and this eliminates the need for a conventional choke.

If the engine becomes flooded, the condition can be cleared by depressing the throttle to the wide-open position while cranking the engine. When the ECA receives a wide-open throttle signal from the throttle position sensor (TPS), the ECA stops energizing the injectors while the engine is being cranked. This clears the flooded condition, and as soon as the engine starts on the excess fuel in the intake manifold, the ECA begins energizing the injectors again.

Ford Electronic Engine Control IV (EEC IV) Systems Used with 5.0L Engines

Design

The EEC IV systems used with 5.0L engines have injectors located in each intake port. These engines are equipped with high-rise intake manifolds, as shown in Figures 18-119 and 18-120.

Figure 18-120. High-Rise Intake Manifold with EFI 5.0L Car Engine. (*Courtesy of Ford Motor Co.*)

Some 5.0L engines have sequential fuel injection (SFI), in which each injector is grounded individually through the ECA, as shown in Figure 18-121.

On 5.0L engines with electronic fuel injection (EFI), injectors 2, 3, 6, and 7 are connected and

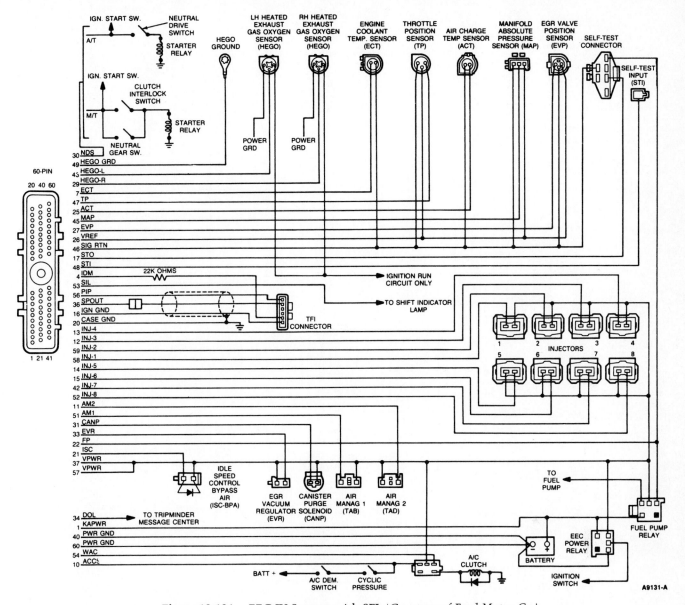

Figure 18-121. EEC IV System with SFI. *(Courtesy of Ford Motor Co.)*

grounded through the ECA. Injectors 1, 4, 5, and 8 also share a common ground through the ECA. This system is illustrated in Figure 18-122.

On some EFI systems, injectors 1, 4, 6 and 7 are connected and injectors 2, 3, 5, and 8 share a common connection. These groups of injectors are grounded through the ECA. The ECA grounded the eight injectors simultaneously on early systems, whereas on later systems the ECA grounds the groups of injectors individually.

While many of the same sensors are used on the SFI and EFI systems, there are some differences. The SFI systems have an oxygen (O₂) sensor in each exhaust manifold. These three-wire sensors contain an electric heater to provide faster heating. The EGR

valve position (EVP) sensor sends a signal to the ECA in relation to EGR valve position. On the EFI system, the inferred mileage sensor (IMS) sends a signal to the ECA at 22,500 miles (36,209 km). When this signal is received, the ECA modifies its calibration slightly. The IMS is located under the left side of the instrument panel.

A profile ignition pickup (PIP) signal is sent from the distributor pickup to the ECA. This signal is modified by the ECA and sent to the distributor module on the spark output (SPOUT) circuit to provide the spark advance required by the engine. An ignition diagnostic monitor (IDM) circuit is connected to terminal 4 on the ECA.

If a difference occurs in the PIP and SPOUT sig-

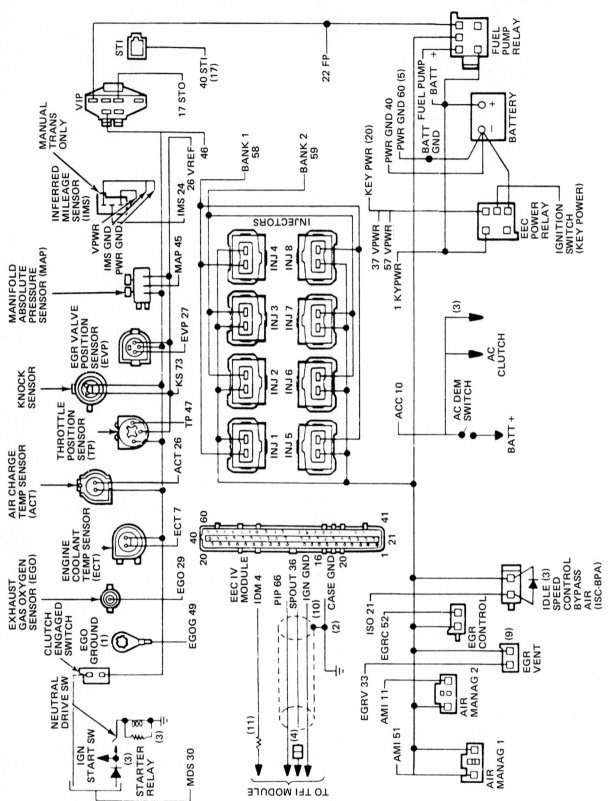

Figure 18-122. EEC IV System with EFI. (*Courtesy of Ford Motor Co.*)

STANDARD
ARMATURE

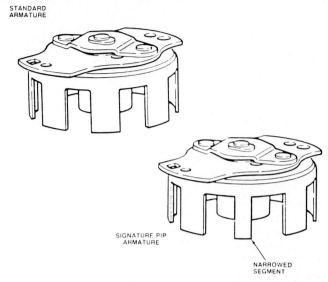

SIGNATURE PIP
ARMATURE

NARROWED
SEGMENT

Figure 18-123.   Signature PIP Armature. (*Courtesy of Ford Motor Co.*)

nals because of defects in the wires or ECA, the IDM circuit will place diagnostic codes 14 and 18 in the ECA.

(Refer to Chapter 13 in *Automotive Principles: Repair and Service*, Volume II, for complete EEC IV diagnosis.)

On the SFI systems, a signature PIP armature is used in the distributor. This armature is shown in Figure 18-123.

The signature PIP armature has one narrow blade segment that informs the ECA when number 1 piston is approaching top dead center (TDC). The ECA uses this signal to properly time and fire the injectors. The signature PIP armature must not be interchanged with other armatures.

Some EEC IV systems have a throttle body injection assembly. On a four-cylinder engine, this assembly contains a single injector, whereas on a V6 or V8 engine dual injectors are used. This type of EEC IV system is referred to as central fuel injection (CFI), as shown in Figure 18-124.

Cruise Control

On some EEC IV systems, such as those used on Taurus and Sable models, the cruise control module is integrated into the ECA. The inputs and outputs on the integrated vehicle speed control (IVSC) system are shown in Figure 18-125.

The operation of the IVSC system is similar to the electronic cruise control system described in Chapter 14. Self-diagnostics related to the IVSC system are contained in the ECA. (Refer to Chapter 13

in *Automotive Principles: Repair and Service*, Volume II, for EEC IV and IVSC diagnosis.)

Integrated Relay Control Module

The integrated relay control module provides control of the cooling fan, A/C clutch, and fuel pump. On previous EEC IV systems, these functions were controlled by separate relays.

An integrated relay control module is illustrated in Figure 18-126. A wiring diagram for this module is provided in Figure 18-127.

When the A/C switch is turned on, a signal is sent through the cyclic pressure switch to a solid-state relay in the integrated control module. A signal is also sent from the cyclic pressure switch to the ECA. The solid-state relay energizes the A/C clutch. If the throttle is wide open, a signal is sent from the ECA through the wide-open throttle A/C cutoff (WAC) circuit to the solid-state relay. This signal prevents A/C clutch operation.

If the ECA input signals indicate that cooling fan operation is necessary, the ECA grounds the electric drive fan (EDF) relay winding. This closes the EDF relay contacts so that voltage is supplied through the resistor and the contacts to the cooling fan motor. When increased cooling fan speed is required, the ECA grounds the high-speed electric drive fan (HEDF) relay winding so that full voltage is supplied through the relay contacts to the cooling fan.

When the ignition switch is turned on, a signal is sent from the ignition switch to the relay drive unit in the integrated relay control module. As a result of this signal, the relay drive unit grounds the power relay winding, which closes the relay contacts and supplies voltage to ECA terminals 37 and 57, the fuel pump relay winding, and the EDF relay windings. The ECA grounds the fuel pump relay winding, which closes the contacts and supplies voltage through the inertia switch to the electric fuel pump. If the engine is not cranked within one second, the ECA opens the fuel pump relay winding circuit and stops the pump.

Pressure Feedback Electronic EGR System

In some applications, such as the 3.0L V6 engine, there is a pressure feedback electronic EGR system. The main components in this system are the pressure feedback EGR valve, electronic vacuum regulator, and the pressure feedback electronic EGR sensor. These are illustrated in Figure 18-128.

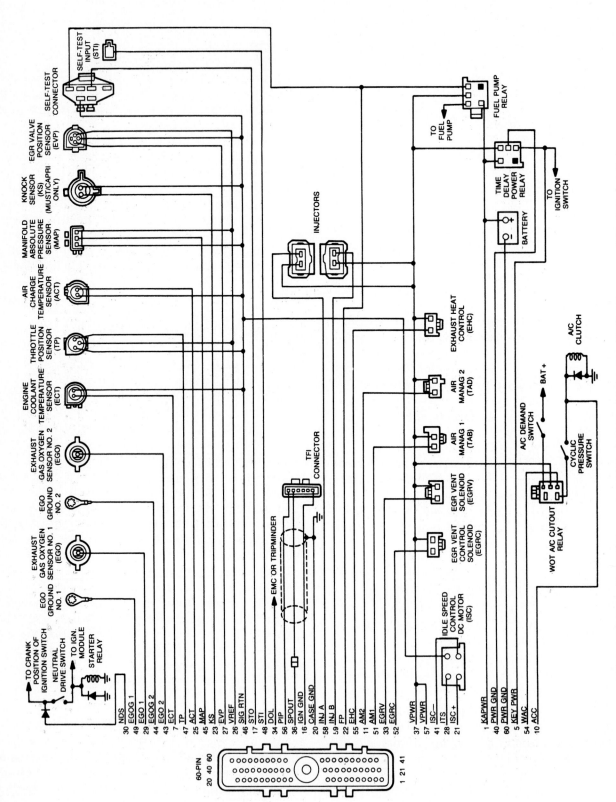

Figure 18-124. EEC IV System with Central Fuel Injection (CFI). (*Courtesy of Ford Motor Co.*)

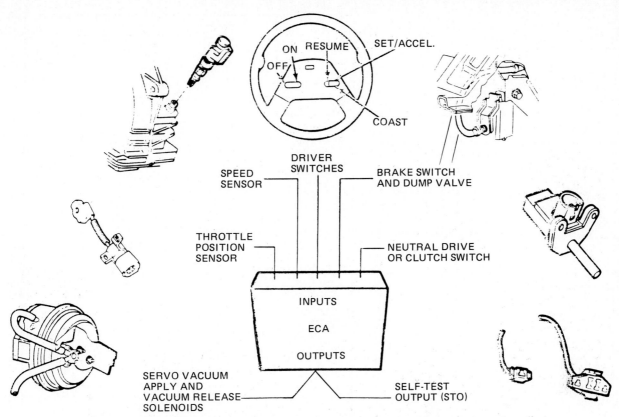

Figure 18-125.   Integrated Vehicle Speed Control System. (*Courtesy of Ford Motor Co.*)

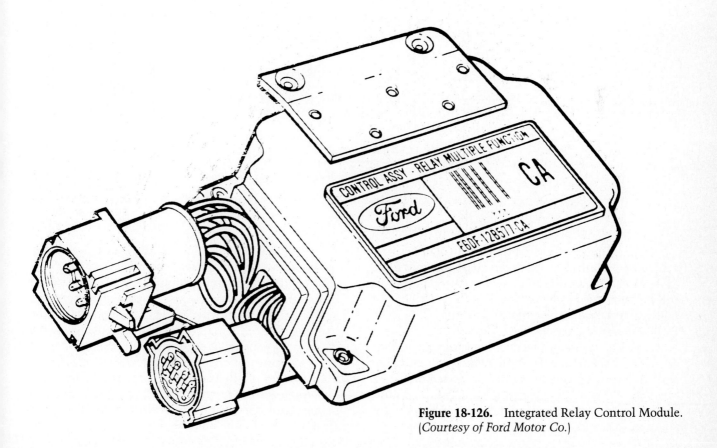

Figure 18-126.   Integrated Relay Control Module. (*Courtesy of Ford Motor Co.*)

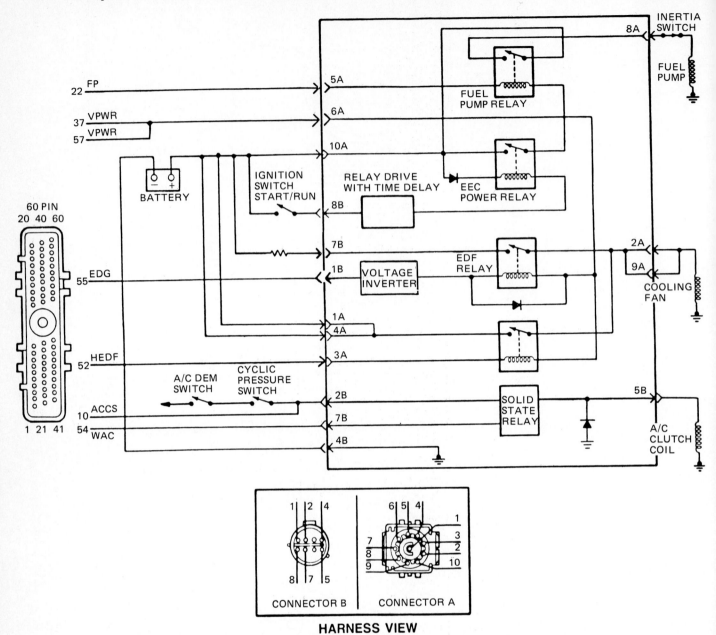

Figure 18-127.   Integrated Relay Control Module Wiring Diagram. (*Courtesy of Ford Motor Co.*)

Exhaust pressure is supplied through a metering orifice to a controlled pressure chamber under the EGR valve. A metal tube connects this chamber to the pressure feedback electronic sensor. When the EGR valve is open, the exhaust pressure in the controlled pressure chamber decreases as EGR flow increases. The pressure feedback electronic sensor sends a signal to the ECA in relation to the controlled chamber pressure. A duty-cycle output is sent from the ECA to the electronic vacuum regulator, and this regulator supplies the correct amount of vacuum to the EGR valve.

The ECA matches the EGR flow rate in relation to the input sensor signals. The ECA compares controlled pressure chamber input signal to the amount of pressure that should exist in this chamber for a specific engine operating mode. If the pressure in the chamber does not match the required pressure, the ECA adjusts the position of the EGR valve.

A diagram of the pressure feedback electronic EGR system is illustrated in Figure 18-129. (Service and diagnosis of electronic fuel injection systems is explained in Chapter 13 of *Automotive Principles: Repair and Service*, Volume II.)

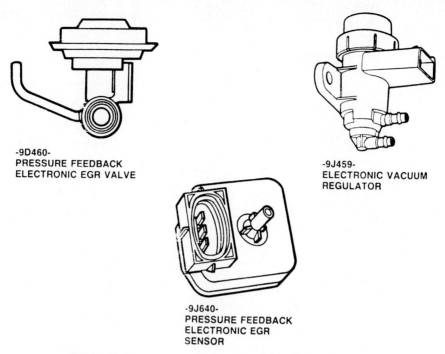

-9D460-
PRESSURE FEEDBACK
ELECTRONIC EGR VALVE

-9J459-
ELECTRONIC VACUUM
REGULATOR

-9J640-
PRESSURE FEEDBACK
ELECTRONIC EGR
SENSOR

Figure 18-128. Pressure Feedback Electronic EGR System Components. (*Courtesy of Ford Motor Co.*)

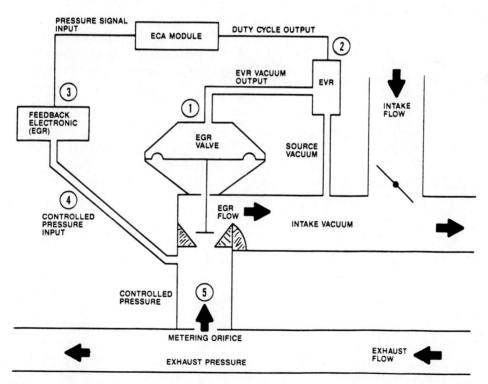

Figure 18-129. Pressure Feedback Electronic EGR System. (*Courtesy of Ford Motor Co.*)

Test Questions

Questions on General Motors Computer Systems

1. The amount of fuel that is injected is determined by the injector _____ _____.

2. When the ignition switch is on and no attempt is made to start the engine, the fuel pump runs until the battery is discharged.   T F

3. In the open-loop mode, the electronic control module ignores the oxygen sensor signal.   T F

4. Cold fast-idle speed is controlled by the idle air control (IAC) motor.   T F

Questions on Chrysler Electronic Fuel Injection (EFI) Systems

5. The automatic shutdown (ASD) relay remains closed when the ignition switch is on and the engine is not running.   T F

6. When the power-loss light is on, the EFI system is in the _____ mode.

7. Battery voltage is supplied to the electric fuel pump through the _____ _____ relay contacts.

8. In the single-point EFI system, the pressure regulator limits the fuel pump pressure to _____ psi.

9. An in-line fuel filter is located in the engine compartment.   T F

10. The power module increases the injector pulse width when engine load is increased.   T F

11. The automatic idle speed (AIS) motor increases the idle speed by allowing more _____ to bypass the throttle.

12. In the multi-point EFI system, the power module energizes the injectors individually.   T F

Questions on Ford Electronic Engine Control (EEC IV)

13. The vane air temperature (VAT) sensor sends a signal to the ECA in relation to:
    a) intake air temperature.
    b) coolant temperature.
    c) air-fuel mixture temperature.

14. While the engine is being cranked, the ECA moves the throttle air bypass valve to the _____ _____ position.

15. The high-pressure fuel pump is located in the fuel tank.   T F

16. When a cold engine is flooded, the condition may be corrected by:
    a) turning off the ignition switch and waiting ten seconds.
    b) pushing the throttle wide open while the engine is cranked.
    c) leaving the throttle in the idle position while the engine is cranked.

17. When a signature profile ignition pickup (PIP) armature is used, the signal from the narrow blade segment is used by the ECA to:
    a) supply the correct spark advance.
    b) control the basic timing.
    c) time and fire the injectors.

18. In a pressure feedback electronic EGR system, an exhaust pressure signal is sent from the controlled pressure chamber to the:
    a) pressure feedback electronic sensor.
    b) electronic vacuum regulator.
    c) EGR valve.

19. The low-speed and high-speed electric drive fan (EDF) relays are contained in the integrated relay control module.   T F

19

Differentials and Drive Shafts

Chapter Completion Objectives

1. Understand differential action.
2. Demonstrate a knowledge of the purpose of each differential component.
3. Indicate an understanding of pinion bearing and side bearing preload and the importance of these preloads to differential life.
4. Show a knowledge of limited-slip differentials.
5. Understand drive shafts, universal joints, and constant velocity joints.

Differentials

Design and Operation

A differential contains four gears mounted in a case assembly. Two of these gears are referred to as side gears; the other gears are called pinion gears. The side gears are splined to the drive axle shafts so that the axle shafts turn when the side gears rotate. A pinion shaft is mounted in the center of the pinion gears, and the gears are free to rotate on this shaft. Each end of the pinion shaft fits into a differential case bore, with the pinion gears in mesh with the side gears. The ring gear is bolted to the differential case, and the drive pinion gear is meshed with the ring gear.

Most rear-wheel-drive passenger cars have a hypoid-type drive pinion and ring gear. In this type of gear set, the drive pinion is mounted well below the center line of the ring gear. Hypoid-type gears have curved teeth which provide a wiping action while meshing. This type of gear set has several teeth in mesh to absorb the driving force and provide for quiet running. The inner end of the ring gear teeth is referred to as the toe; the outer end of the teeth is called the heel. The shape of the ring gear teeth on the drive side is convex; the coast side has a concave shape.

A spiral bevel-type drive pinion and ring gear is used in some differentials. In this type of gear set, the drive pinion center intersects with the center line of the ring gear. Solid rear axle housings which support the vehicle weight are used in rear-wheel-drive vehicles. These axle housings may be integral-type or removable carrier-type. An integral-type rear housing has the differential carrier housing integral with the axle housing, as indicated in Figure 19-1.

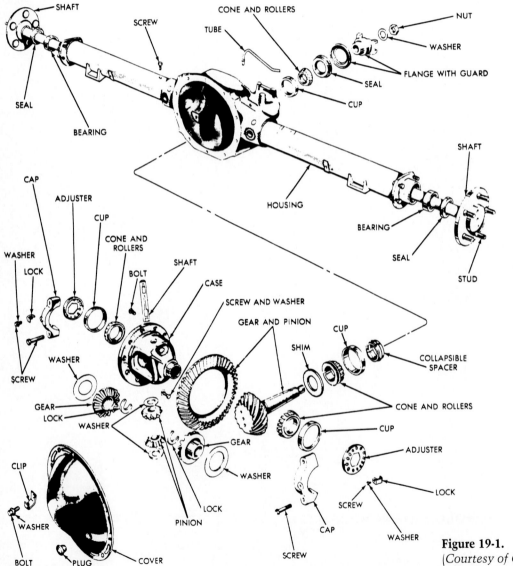

Figure 19-1. Integral-Type Differential. *(Courtesy of Chrysler Canada)*

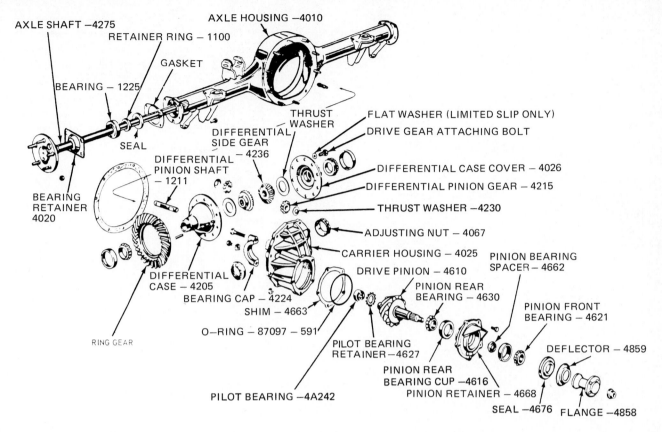

AXLE SHAFT —4275

RETAINER RING — 1100

GASKET

BEARING — 1225

AXLE HOUSING —4010

SEAL

DIFFERENTIAL
SIDE GEAR
—4236

DIFFERENTIAL
PINION SHAFT
—1211

THRUST
WASHER

BEARING
RETAINER
4020

DIFFERENTIAL
CASE — 4205

BEARING CAP — 4224

SHIM — 4663

O—RING — 87097 — 591

RING GEAR

PILOT BEARING —4A242

FLAT WASHER (LIMITED SLIP ONLY)

DRIVE GEAR ATTACHING BOLT

DIFFERENTIAL CASE COVER — 4026

DIFFERENTIAL PINION GEAR — 4215

THRUST WASHER —4230

ADJUSTING NUT — 4067

CARRIER HOUSING — 4025

DRIVE PINION — 4610

PINION REAR
BEARING — 4630

PINION BEARING
SPACER — 4662

PINION FRONT
BEARING — 4621

DEFLECTOR — 4859

PILOT BEARING
RETAINER —4627

PINION REAR
BEARING CUP —4616

PINION RETAINER — 4668

SEAL —4676   FLANGE —4858

Figure 19-2. Removable Carrier-Type Differential Housing. (*Courtesy of Ford Motor Co.*)

In a removable carrier-type differential housing, the differential carrier housing may be removed from the front of the axle housing as illustrated in Figure 19-2.

The drive pinion is supported by two tapered roller bearings in the differential carrier housing. These roller bearings are pressed onto the drive pinion shaft, and the bearing cups are pressed into the differential carrier housing. A drive pinion shaft seal prevents lubricant leaks around the pinion shaft. The drive shaft is bolted to the drive pinion flange, which is splined to the drive pinion shaft. A nut retains the flange to the drive pinion. Many differentials have a collapsible spacer between the tapered roller bearings which sets the bearing preload as the pinion nut is tightened. This type of spacer is shown in Figure 19-1.

A shim is positioned between the inner bearing and the drive pinion shaft. This shim is available in different thicknesses in order to adjust pinion depth and obtain proper tooth contact between the pinion and ring gears. This type of shim also is illustrated in Figure 19-1. In some differentials, a shim is located between the pinion retainer and the differential carrier housing to adjust pinion depth. Figure 19-2 shows a shim in this location.

The differential case is supported by two roller bearings in the carrier housing. Removable bearing caps retain the bearing cups to the differential carrier housing. Bearings of this type are referred to as side bearings. Threaded adjusters may be positioned behind each side bearing cup to adjust side bearing preload and tooth contact and backlash between the ring gear and pinion gear. This type of side bearing adjuster is illustrated in Figure 19-1. Other differentials have shims behind the side bearing cups in place of the threaded adjusters, as shown in Figure 19-3.

The outer ends of the drive axles are supported on roller bearings in the axle housing. Axle seals are located at the outer ends of the axle shafts. The axle shafts are splined to the differential side gears.

Helical ring gears are used in many transaxles in front-wheel-drive cars. (Refer to Chapter 20 for a description of these types of differentials.)

Differential Action

When the vehicle is driven straight ahead, torque is transmitted from the drive shaft to the drive pinion, ring gear, and differential case. Torque is then trans-

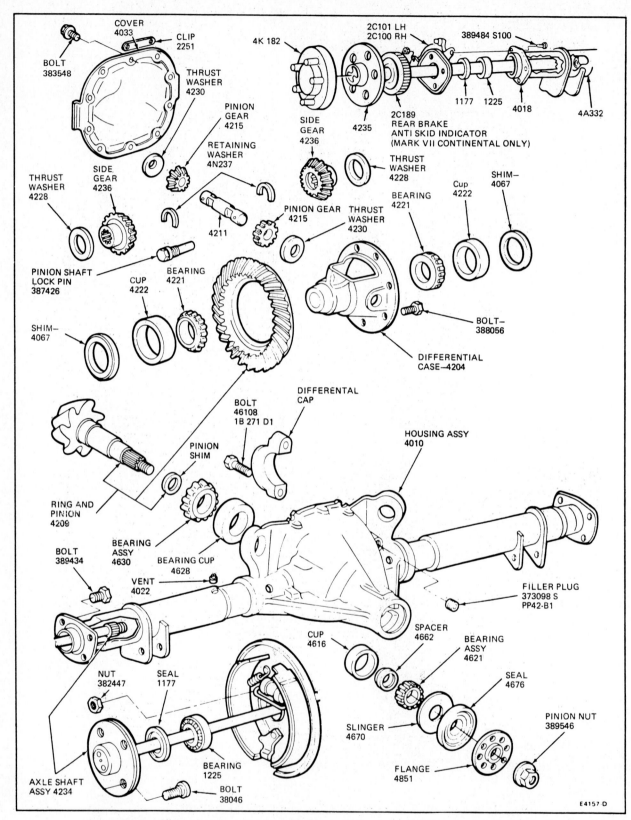

Figure 19-3. Differential with Adjusting Shims Behind the Side Bearings. (*Courtesy of Ford Motor Co.*)

mitted through the pinion shaft in the differential case to the pinion gears, side gears, and axle shafts, which drives the rear wheels. Since both rear wheels are turning at the same speed and have equal traction, the pinion gears do not rotate, because the input force on the pinion gears is equally divided between the side gears. As a result of this action, the pinion gears rotate with the case but do not rotate on the pinion shaft, as indicated in Figure 19-4.

When the vehicle turns a corner, the outer wheel must travel faster and further than the inner wheel, as indicated in Figure 19-5.

As the inner wheel slows down during a turn, the speed of the inner drive axle and side gear also reduces. Under this condition the pinion gears act as balancing levers in that they maintain equal tooth loads on both side gears but allow unequal rotating speeds of the side gears and drive axles. If the vehicle speed remains constant and the inner wheel slows

down to 90 percent of the differential case speed, the outer wheel speed increases to 110 percent of the differential case speed, as indicated in Figure 19-6.

If engine torque is supplied from the drive shaft to the drive pinion, the pinion teeth contact the convex or drive side of the ring gear teeth. Under coasting or braking conditions, the concave side of the ring gear teeth attempts to drive the pinion gear. Under severe acceleration, the drive pinion tries to climb up the ring gear, which raises the front of the differential. A rubber bumper on top of the differential carrier housing prevents the housing from hitting the chassis under this condition.

When torque is applied from the drive pinion gear to the ring gear, the angle on the gear teeth tends to drive the pinion gear ahead, whereas during coasting or braking the pinion gear is driven to the rear. If the drive pinion gear is allowed to move back and forth, the gear teeth and bearings will wear rapidly. Therefore, pinion bearing preload is extremely important.

Nonhunting or partial hunting pinion and ring gears are used in some differentials. These gear teeth are lapped during the manufacturing process so that certain teeth on the pinion gear always mesh with specific ring gear teeth. Therefore, timing marks on this type of gear set must be aligned when the differential is assembled. Hunting-type gear sets do not require timing mark alignment.

All types of drive pinion gears and ring gears must be replaced as a set. The ratio of drive pinion to ring gear is matched to the size of engine, type of transmission, and vehicle weight. (Gear ratios are explained in Chapter 20.)

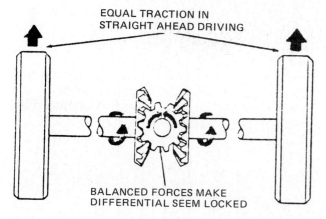

Figure 19-4. Pinion and Side Gear Action with Equal Traction on Both Drive Wheels. (*Courtesy of General Motors Corporation*)

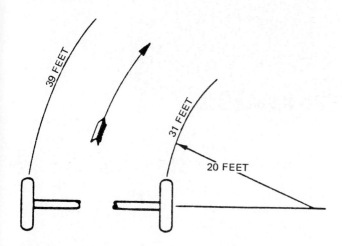

Figure 19-5. Inner and Outer Wheel Distance During a Turn. (*Courtesy of General Motors Corporation*)

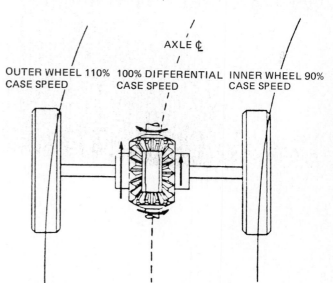

Figure 19-6. Inner and Outer Wheel Speed During a Turn. (*Courtesy of General Motors Corporation*)

Limited-Slip Differentials

Design and Operation   In a conventional differential, if one rear wheel spins on an icy road surface, the other rear wheel does not revolve, which prevents the vehicle from moving.

In a limited-slip differential, three friction discs located behind each side gear have external tabs con-

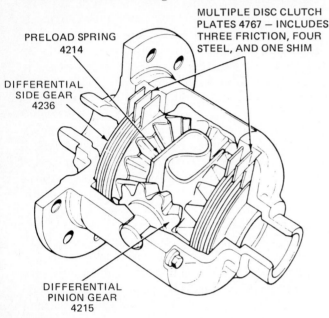

PRELOAD SPRING
4214

DIFFERENTIAL
SIDE GEAR
4236

MULTIPLE DISC CLUTCH
PLATES 4767 – INCLUDES
THREE FRICTION, FOUR
STEEL, AND ONE SHIM

DIFFERENTIAL
PINION GEAR
4215

Figure 19-7.   Limited-Slip Differential. (*Courtesy of Ford Motor Co.*)

nected to the differential housing. Four steel plates are positioned alternately with the friction discs. These plates have internal splines connected to the side gear hubs. A preload spring between the side gears supplies initial force to both clutch sets, as illustrated in Figure 19-7.

If one rear wheel begins to spin on an icy road surface while the opposite rear wheel remains stationary, torque is transmitted through the clutch set to the wheel with the most traction. This provides a combined driving effort to both rear wheels. Hence, limited-slip differentials provide improved rear wheel traction on slippery road surfaces.

A disassembled view of the clutch sets in a limited-slip differential is shown in Figure 19-8.

Some limited-slip differentials are equipped with cone clutches in place of clutch discs, as illustrated in Figure 19-9.

Drive Shafts

Design and Operation

The drive shaft transmits engine torque from the transmission to the differential. Drive shafts are made of tubular steel with a cross-and-roller type universal ("U") joint at each end. The "U" joints are necessary because the transmission output shaft and

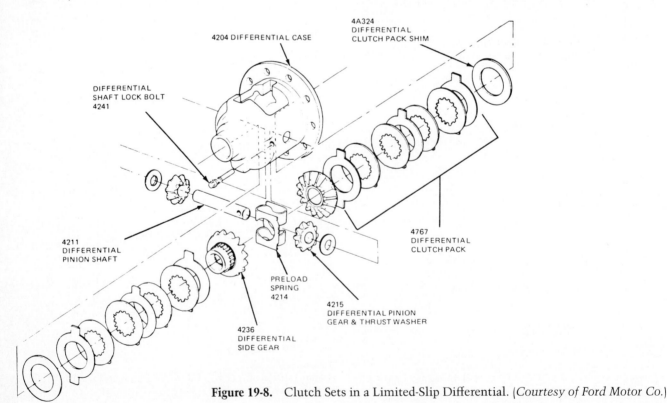

4A324
DIFFERENTIAL
CLUTCH PACK SHIM

4204 DIFFERENTIAL CASE

DIFFERENTIAL
SHAFT LOCK BOLT
4241

4211
DIFFERENTIAL
PINION SHAFT

4236
DIFFERENTIAL
SIDE GEAR

PRELOAD
SPRING
4214

4215
DIFFERENTIAL PINION
GEAR & THRUST WASHER

4767
DIFFERENTIAL
CLUTCH PACK

Figure 19-8.   Clutch Sets in a Limited-Slip Differential. (*Courtesy of Ford Motor Co.*)

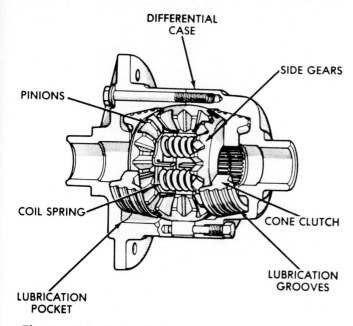

Figure 19-9. Limited-Slip Differential with Cone Clutches. (*Courtesy of Chrysler Canada*)

the differential drive pinion flange are not in a direct line with one another.

Since the differential is continually moving up and down because of irregularities in the road surface, the "U" joint angles must change continually. When the differential moves up or down, the distance changes between the differential and the transmission. Thus, a splined sliding yoke is necessary between the front of the drive shaft and the transmission output shaft.

The front of the drive shaft with the yoke and "U" joint is pictured in Figure 19-10.

The sliding yoke on the front of the drive shaft is splined to the transmission output shaft. The outside yoke surface fits into a seal and bushing in the transmission extension housing. The bushings on the rear "U" joint are clamped to the differential drive pinion flange as shown in Figure 19-11.

Universal Joints

The universal ("U") joint cross has four machined ends that are spaced 90° from each other. Needle bearings in the "U" joint bushings fit on these machined ends. Seals are located on each "U" joint bushing, and the needle bearings are permanently lubricated. Some replacement "U" joints have a grease fitting in the cross. One pair of "U" joint bushings fits into circular openings in the drive shaft ends and the other pair of bushings fits into the drive pinion yoke on the rear joint, or into the sliding yoke on the front joint. Snap-type retainers hold the bushings in place. The "U" joints must pivot freely to prevent drive line vibration and noise.

If a "U" joint is located on each end of the drive shaft, and the transmission output shaft speed is constant, the speed of the drive shaft increases and decreases. Even if the drive shaft and transmission output shaft are turning at the same speed, the drive shaft speed will fluctuate. This is due to the continuous change in the angle between the sliding yoke on the transmission output shaft and the drive shaft. The drive shaft speed increases and decreases twice for each drive shaft revolution, which can cause drive line vibrations.

Some drive shafts contain a constant-velocity "U" joint, which is actually two "U" joints with a

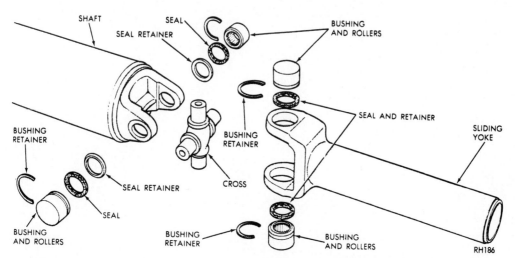

Figure 19-10. Drive Shaft Front Universal Joint and Sliding Yoke. (*Courtesy of Chrysler Canada*)

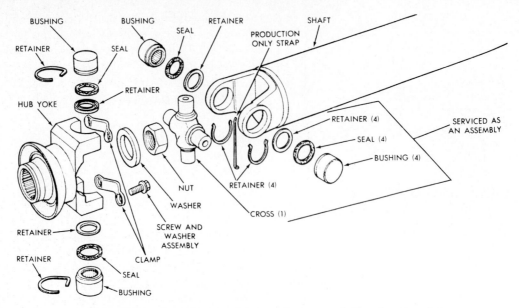

Figure 19-11.   Rear Universal Joint. (*Courtesy of Chrysler Canada*)

short center yoke between them. A ball on the end of the drive shaft fits into a socket in the rear flanged yoke, as illustrated in Figure 19-12.

In a constant-velocity "U" joint, both "U" joint yokes are lined up on the same plane. In this type of joint, fluctuation in the drive shaft speed is cancelled out by the action of the rear joint. Therefore, the constant-velocity joint provides smoother drive

shaft action with reduced vibration. Correct drive shaft angles are very important to keep the drive line vibration free.

(Drive shaft and differential service including drive shaft angle measurements are explained in Chapter 15 of *Automotive Principles: Repair and Service*, Volume II.)

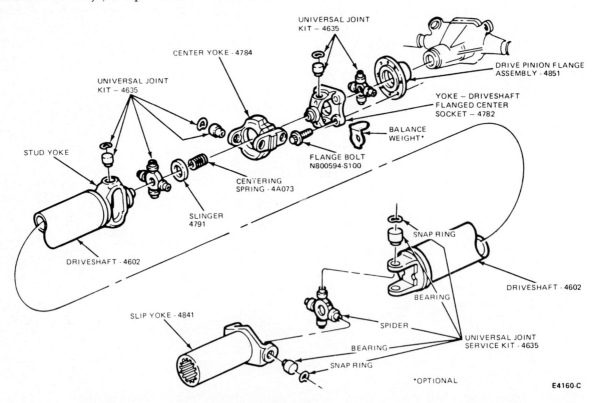

Figure 19-12.   Constant-Velocity Universal Joint. (*Courtesy of Ford Motor Co.*)

Test Questions

1. The drive sides of the differential ring gear teeth have a _____ shape.

2. When a vehicle is completing a turn, if the outside rear wheel is turning at 120 percent of the differential case speed, the inside gear wheel is turning at:
   a) 60 percent of the differential case speed.
   b) 80 percent of the differential case speed.
   c) 90 percent of the differential case speed.

3. When the engine is accelerating hard, the front of the differential tends to:
   a) move downward.
   b) remain level.
   c) lift upward.

4. With a limited-slip differential, if one rear wheel spins on an icy road surface while the opposite rear wheel remains stationary, the differential transfers torque to the rear wheel with the most traction. T F

5. When the transmission output shaft speed is constant, the drive shaft speed is also constant.   T F

6. Constant-velocity universal joints:
   a) tend to increase drive line vibration.
   b) have two universal joints on the same plane.
   c) improve rear wheel traction.

20

Manual Transaxles, Transmissions, and Drive Axles

Chapter Completion Objectives

1. Indicate an understanding of various types of bearings.
2. Understand conventional and hydraulic clutch operation.
3. Demonstrate a knowledge of different types of gears, gear ratios, and synchronizer assemblies.

4. Display an understanding of manual transaxles and transmissions.
5. Show a comprehension of various types of wheel bearings.
6. Understand drive axle design on front-wheel-drive vehicles.

Bearings

Types of Bearings

Bearings are classified as plain bearings or antifriction bearings. Various types of bearings in each classification are illustrated in Figure 20-1.

Bearing Load Forces

The load force on a bearing is radial or axial. Some bearings are subjected to both types of loads. Radial loads are applied in a vertical direction and axial loads are exerted in a horizontal direction, as indicated in Figure 20-2.

Plain Bearings

Advantages   The advantages of plain bearings are:

1. They require little space.
2. They are inexpensive.
3. They operate quietly.
4. They are of rigid construction.

Disadvantages   Plain bearings have the following disadvantages:

1. They operate under high friction.
2. They require continuous lubrication because they cannot be packed with lubricant.

Antifriction Bearings

Advantages   Antifriction bearings have the following advantages:

1. They operate under low friction.
2. They can be packed with lubricant to reduce the frequency of lubrication.
3. Their many different designs provide versatility.

Disadvantages   Antifriction bearings have the following disadvantages as compared to plain bearings:

1. They require more space.
2. They are noisier.
3. They are more expensive.
4. They are less rigid.

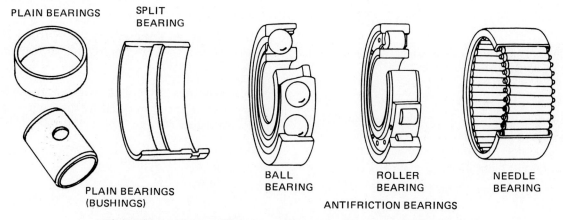

Figure 20-1.   Types of Bearings. (*Courtesy of Deere and Company.*)

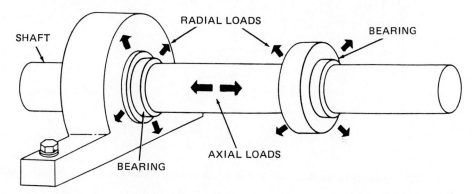

Figure 20-2.   Bearing Load Forces. (*Courtesy of Deere and Company*)

Ball Bearing Design   Ball bearings are used in many automotive applications. Some ball bearings are packed with grease, with a seal located on each side of the bearing races to keep dirt out of the bearing and to hold the lubricant in the bearing. Other ball bearings are open on one side of the race but have a shield on the other side. This type of bearing is lubricated from the component reservoir where it is mounted, and the shield prevents the entry of contaminants.

The components in a ball bearing are identified in Figure 20-3.

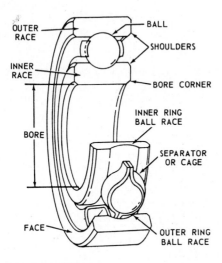

Figure 20-3. Ball Bearing Components. (*Courtesy of Deere and Company.*)

Tapered Roller Bearings   Tapered roller bearings are used as front wheel bearings and in other automotive applications. Components in this type of bearing are shown in Figure 20-4.

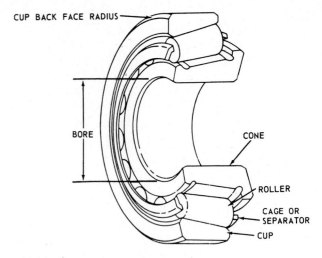

Figure 20-4. Tapered Roller Bearing Components. (*Courtesy of Deere and Company.*)

Bearing Load Application

Ball Bearings   Some types of bearings are designed to withstand only radial loads, while others will carry radial or axial loads. An axial load is also referred to as a thrust load. Various types of ball bearings and the loads they will withstand are illustrated in Figure 20-5.

Roller Bearings   Different types of roller bearings and the loads they withstand are shown in Figure 20-6.

Needle Bearings   Needle bearings may be designed to withstand radial or axial (thrust) loads, as illustrated in Figure 20-7.

Plain Bearings   Most plain bearings are designed to accept radial loads, although some plain bearings

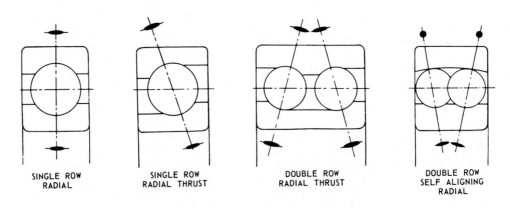

SINGLE ROW RADIAL   SINGLE ROW RADIAL THRUST   DOUBLE ROW RADIAL THRUST   DOUBLE ROW SELF ALIGNING RADIAL

Figure 20-5.   Types of Ball Bearings and Related Loads. (*Courtesy of Deere and Company.*)

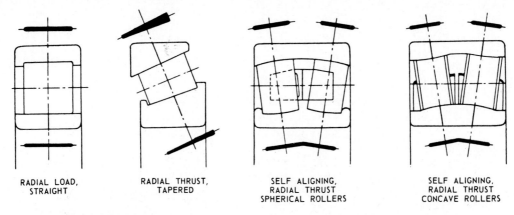

Figure 20-6.   Types of Roller Bearings and Related Loads. (*Courtesy of Deere and Company.*)

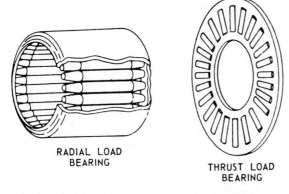

Figure 20-7.   Radial Load and Axial (Thrust) Load Needle Bearings. (*Courtesy of Deere and Company.*)

have a lip on each side so that they can withstand both radial and axial loads. (Plain bearings are described in Chapter 2.)

Clutch Component Design and Operation

Clutch-Driven Plate Assembly

Friction materials are riveted on each side of the clutch plate. These materials are made from asbestos and cotton fibers impregnated with resin or copper. The friction materials are referred to as clutch facings. When the clutch is applied, the facings are jammed between the pressure plate and the machined flywheel surface. The clutch hub is splined to the transaxle input shaft, so that engine torque is transmitted from the flywheel through the clutch plate to the input shaft. Rivets are used to attach the facing materials to the wave spring plate between the facings, which cushions the clutch applications.

Torsional springs are mounted in openings in the wave spring plate and the clutch hub. Engine torque is transmitted from the clutch facings through the torsional springs to the clutch hub. Torsional springs dampen engine vibrations that would otherwise be transferred to the transaxle.

Clutch components are pictured in Figure 20-8.

Pressure Plate and Cover Assembly

The pressure plate and cover assembly contains a pressure plate with a machined surface. When the clutch is applied, the machined surface is forced against the clutch facing material by the pivoted diaphragm spring. The pressure plate cover is bolted to the flywheel.

Release Bearing

The clutch release bearing is a sealed ball bearing mounted on a sleeve. This release bearing and sleeve is moved back and forth on the input shaft retainer extension by a fork that is connected through a linkage to the clutch pedal. When the clutch pedal is depressed to release the clutch, the linkage forces the release bearing toward the flywheel. This movement forces the diaphragm spring fingers toward the flywheel. When this occurs, the diaphragm spring pivots under the pressure plate cover, causing the outer edge of the diaphragm spring to move away from the flywheel and release the clutch facings. When the clutch facings are released, the flywheel and pressure plate continue to rotate, but the clutch plate and input shaft remain stationary.

The clutch components in the applied and released positions are shown in Figure 20-9.

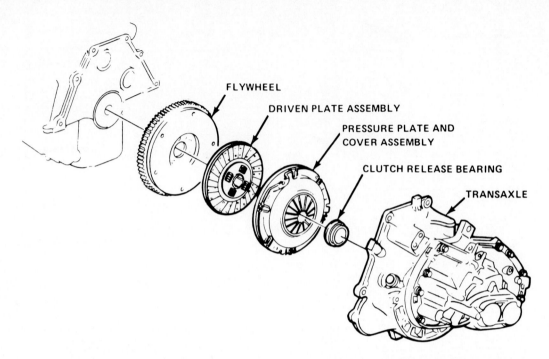

Figure 20-8. Clutch Components. (*Courtesy of Pontiac Motor Division, General Motors Corporation*)

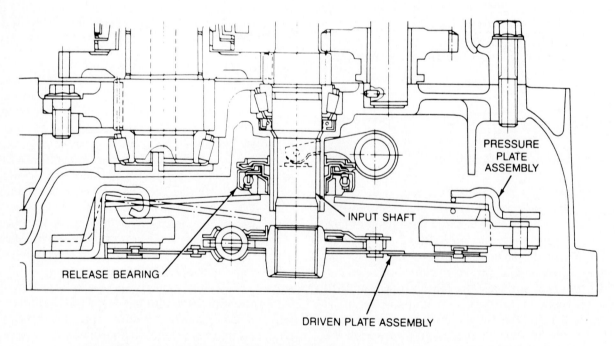

Figure 20-9. Pressure Plate in the Applied and Released Positions. (*Courtesy of Pontiac Motor Division, General Motors Corporation*)

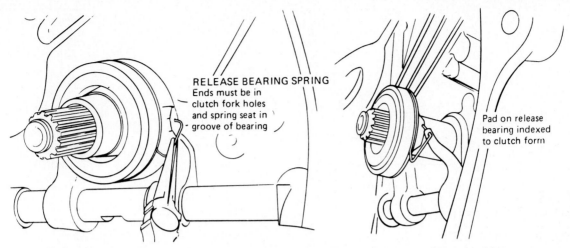

Figure 20-10. Clutch Release Bearing Retaining Springs. (*Courtesy of Pontiac Motor Division, General Motors Corporation*)

The outer end of the transaxle input shaft is mounted in a bushing pressed into the rear of the crankshaft. Some clutch release bearings are retained on the release fork with a spring, as indicated in Figure 20-10.

Hydraulic Clutch Systems

Master Cylinder

In the hydraulic clutch system, an actuator rod is connected from the clutch pedal to the master cylinder as illustrated in Figure 20-11.

When the clutch pedal is depressed, the linkage forces the plunger up the master cylinder bore. In the first $\frac{1}{32}$ in. (0.793 mm) of pedal travel, the valve seal at the end of the master cylinder bore closes the port to the fluid reservoir. As the clutch pedal is depressed further, the plunger movement forces fluid from the master cylinder outlet through a pipe to the slave cylinder. The master cylinder is pictured in Figure 20-12.

Slave Cylinder

When fluid is forced into the slave cylinder, the piston in this cylinder is forced outward. This move-

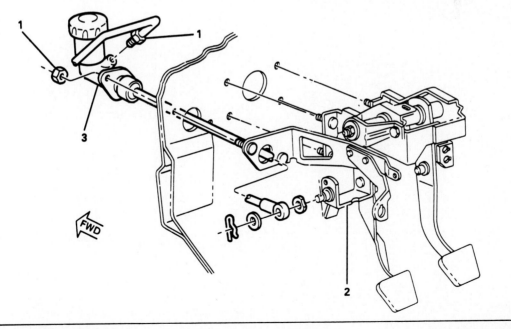

1 — NUT, 17 N•m (13 FT. LB.)   2 — CLUTCH PEDAL ASSEMBLY   3 — CLUTCH MASTER CYLINDER

Figure 20-11. Hydraulic Clutch Pedal Linkage. (*Courtesy of Pontiac Motor Division, General Motors Corporation*)

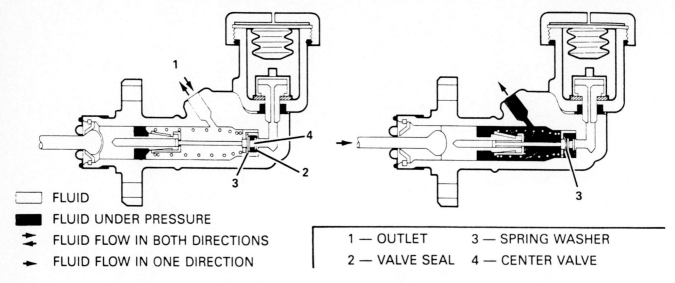

FLUID

FLUID UNDER PRESSURE

FLUID FLOW IN BOTH DIRECTIONS

FLUID FLOW IN ONE DIRECTION

1 — OUTLET	3 — SPRING WASHER
2 — VALVE SEAL	4 — CENTER VALVE

Figure 20-12. Hydraulic Clutch Master Cylinder. (*Courtesy of Pontiac Motor Division, General Motors Corporation*)

ment operates the clutch fork lever to release the clutch. The slave cylinder and its related components are shown in Figure 20-13.

If the clutch pedal is released, fluid pressure in the slave cylinder causes fluid to move back into the master cylinder. Final movement of the master cylinder plunger opens the valve seal opening so that fluid flows from the reservoir into the master cylinder bore.

Manual Transaxle and Transmission Gears

Types

Transaxle gears can be helical or straight spur-cut. Helical gears have teeth that are cut at an angle to the center line of the gear. This type of gear always has more than one tooth in mesh at once. When gear

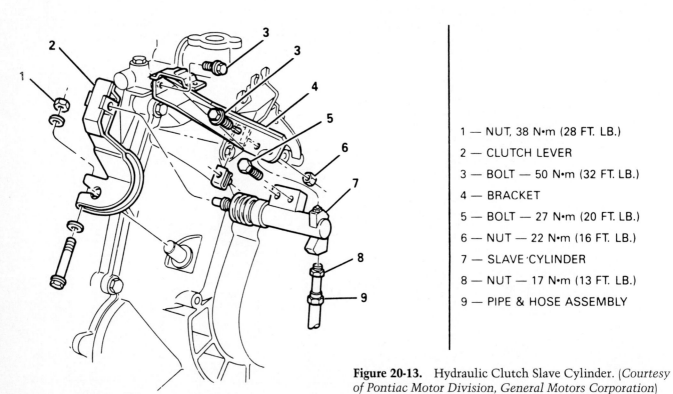

1 — NUT, 38 N•m (28 FT. LB.)

2 — CLUTCH LEVER

3 — BOLT — 50 N•m (32 FT. LB.)

4 — BRACKET

5 — BOLT — 27 N•m (20 FT. LB.)

6 — NUT — 22 N•m (16 FT. LB.)

7 — SLAVE CYLINDER

8 — NUT — 17 N•m (13 FT. LB.)

9 — PIPE & HOSE ASSEMBLY

Figure 20-13. Hydraulic Clutch Slave Cylinder. (*Courtesy of Pontiac Motor Division, General Motors Corporation*)

teeth are angled, they create a wiping action as they engage or disengage with other gear teeth. This wiping action provides quieter operation. The disadvantage of helical gears is that they create axial thrust. Axial thrust on the helical gears usually is absorbed by spacer washers.

A straight spur-cut gear has teeth that are parallel to the gear center line. These gears are noisier than helical gears; however, they do not create axial thrust.

Gears may have internal or external teeth. An external gear has the teeth arranged around its outer circumference. An internal gear is a ring-type gear with teeth around its inner circumference.

Gear teeth have a drive and a coast side. When torque is applied to a gear set during engine acceleration, the sides of the gear teeth in contact with each other are called the drive side. On deceleration, the gear teeth sides in contact are called the coast side.

Constant-mesh gears are those that have teeth that always remain in mesh with each other. Synchronizers are used to engage or disengage constant-mesh gears.

Backlash refers to the amount that one gear in a meshed pair of gears can move while the other gear is held stationary. Some backlash is necessary to allow for proper lubrication and heat expansion. However, excessive backlash indicates that a gear is worn.

A complete gear set from a manual four-speed transaxle is pictured in Figure 20-14. One pair of gears in the figure is spur-cut and the others are helical.

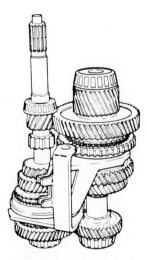

Figure 20-14. Heilical and Spur-Cut Gears, Four-Speed Manual Transaxle. (*Courtesy of Pontiac Motor Division, General Motors Corporation*)

Gear Ratios

When a small gear drives a larger gear, a gear reduction provides an increase in torque and a decrease in output shaft speed. If a large gear drives a smaller gear, an overdrive condition exists which reduces torque and increases output shaft speed.

Gear ratio refers to the ratio between the drive and driven gears. Gear ratios are determined by dividing the number of drive gear teeth into the number of teeth on the driven gear. If the drive gear has 10 teeth and the driven gear has 30 teeth, the gear ratio is 3:1. When a drive gear with 10 teeth is in mesh with a driven gear which has 8 teeth, the gear ratio is $8 \div 10$, or .8:1.

In the five-speed manual transaxle shown in Figure 20-15, the first-speed drive gear on the input shaft is much smaller than the first-speed driven gear on the output shaft. Therefore, a gear reduction is provided in first gear. In the same transaxle, the fifth-speed drive gear is larger than the fifth-speed driven gear, which provides an overdrive ratio in fifth gear.

Gear reduction is necessary to increase engine torque and overcome vehicle inertia when the car is starting off from a stationary position. At normal cruising speed in fifth gear, the overdrive gear ratio increases output shaft speed. Therefore, the engine slows down to maintain normal cruising speed in fifth gear, which results in fuel savings.

If torque is transmitted through two gear ratios, the total gear ratio is calculated by multiplying the two ratios. For example, in the transaxle in Figure 20-15, the first speed gear ratio is 3.29:1. Assuming a differential ratio of 3.56:1, the total gear ratio in first gear would be 11.71:1. The formula for this calculation is

$$\frac{\text{Driven}}{\text{Drive}} \times \frac{\text{Driven}}{\text{Drive}} = \text{Total Ratio}$$

Synchronizer Assemblies

Design and Operation

Synchronizer assemblies contain a hub that is splined to a transmission shaft. An internally splined sleeve is meshed with external splines on the hub. This sleeve contains an external groove in which a shifter fork is mounted. A tapered stop ring with external teeth is mounted on each side of the sleeve. Three spring-loaded winged struts are mounted in the hub, and high points on the struts

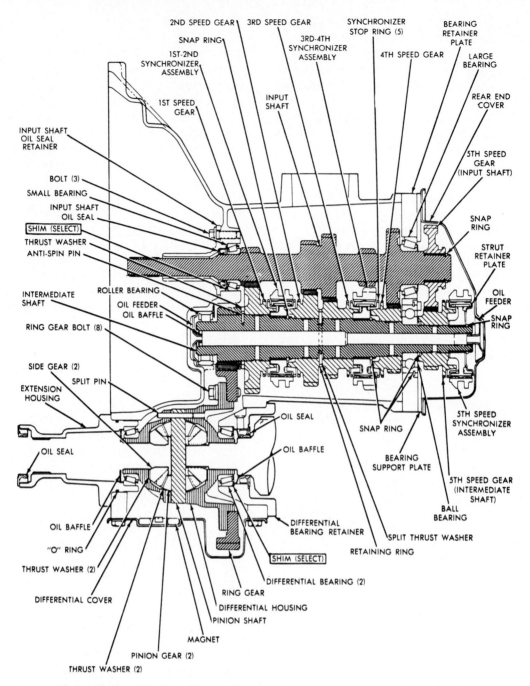

Figure 20-15. Five-Speed Manual Transaxle. (*Courtesy of Chrysler Canada*)

catch in the sleeve grooves to center the sleeve on the hub. When a transmission shift is made, the sleeve is moved by the shifter fork. This movement forces the taper on the stop ring against the taper on the gear. The stop ring brings the gear to the same speed as the shaft and synchronizer assembly, and further sleeve movement engages the sleeve splines with the gear splines. When this action occurs, the gear is connected to the shaft through the synchronizer hub. The purpose of the synchronizer assembly is to allow gear shifting without gear clashing.

Stop rings may be referred to as blocker rings in some transaxles. Two synchronizer assemblies from a four-speed manual transaxle are shown in Figure 20-16.

Synchronizer components should not be interchanged from one synchronizer to another. If the winged struts have a dot on one end, that end must face toward the clutch.

Figure 20-17 shows a disassembled view of a synchronizer assembly. The correct assembly procedure is provided in Figure 20-18.

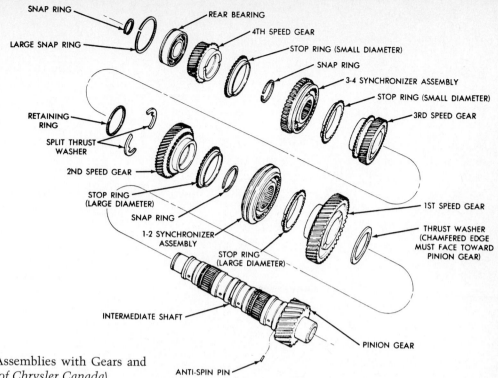

Figure 20-16. Synchronizer Assemblies with Gears and Intermediate Shaft. (*Courtesy of Chrysler Canada*)

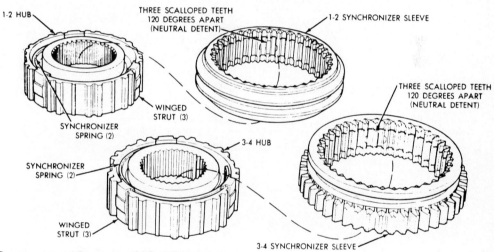

Figure 20-17. Synchronizer Components. (*Courtesy of Chrysler Canada*)

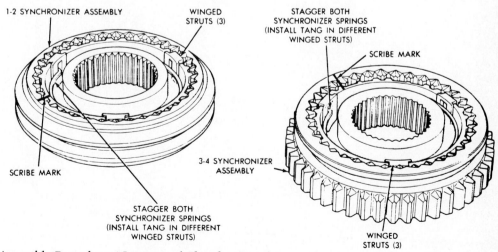

Figure 20-18. Synchronizer Assembly Procedure. (*Courtesy of Chrysler Canada*)

Five-Speed Manual Transaxle

Power Flow in Neutral

When the engine is running with the gearshift in neutral and the clutch engaged, the input gear (shaft) turns because it is splined with the clutch hub. When the 1–2 and 3–4 synchronizers are in the neutral position, power does not flow to the output gear.

In the neutral position, the input shaft, first speed gear, second speed gear, and fifth speed gear rotate. The neutral position is illustrated in Figure 20-19.

First Gear Power Flow

In first gear, the 1–2 synchronizer sleeve is moved to the right to engage the first speed blocker ring and the first gear. Since the 1–2 synchronizer hub is

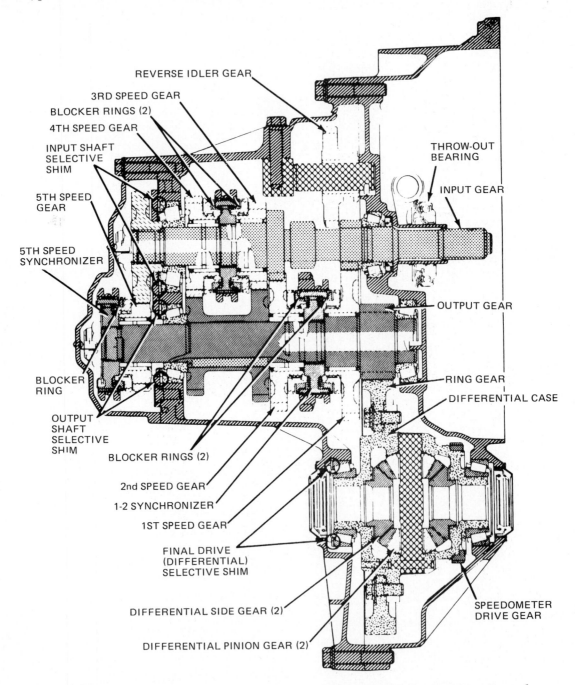

Figure 20-19.   Neutral Position. (*Courtesy of GM Product Service Training, General Motors Corporation*)

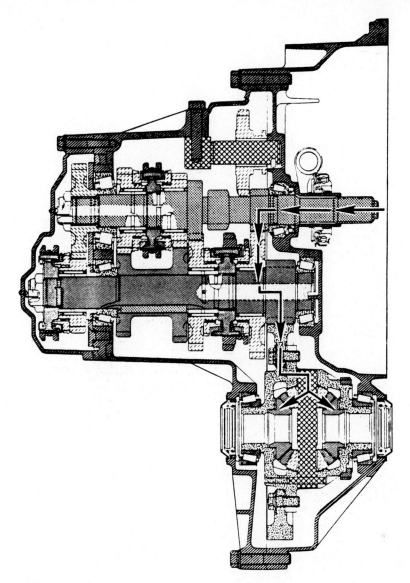

Figure 20-20.   First-Gear Power Flow. (*Courtesy of GM Product Service Training, General Motors Corporation*)

splined to the output shaft, engine torque is now transmitted from the input gear through the first speed gear and 1–2 synchronizer hub to the output gear and the differential ring gear. Torque is applied from the differential to the drive axles. In the first-gear position, speed synchronizers 3–4 and 5 are in the neutral position, as indicated in Figure 20-20.

Second-Gear Power Flow

In second gear, the 1–2 synchronizer sleeve is moved to the left so that it engages with the second speed blocker ring and the second speed gear. Under this condition torque is transmitted from the input shaft through the second speed gear and the 1–2 synchro-

nizer hub to the output shaft, differential ring gear, and drive axles. Speed synchronizers 3–4 and 5 remain in the neutral position in second gear, as shown in Figure 20-21.

Third-Gear Power Flow

When third gear is selected, the 1–2 synchronizer is moved to the neutral position and the 3–4 synchronizer is moved to the right. This action engages the synchronizer sleeve with the third speed blocker ring and gear. Since the 3–4 synchronizer hub is splined to the input shaft, torque is applied from the input shaft through the 3–4 synchronizer hub and third speed gear. This gear is in mesh with a correspond-

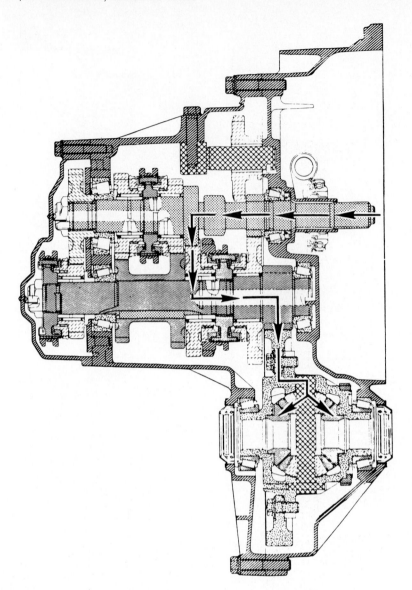

Figure 20-21. Second-Gear Power Flow. (*Courtesy of GM Product Service Training, General Motors Corporation*).

ing gear on the output shaft. Therefore, torque is transmitted from the third speed gear to the output gear, differential ring gear, and drive axles, as pictured in Figure 20-22.

Fourth-Gear Power Flow

In fourth gear, the 3–4 synchronizer sleeve is moved to the left, which engages the sleeve with the fourth speed blocker ring and gear. When this occurs, torque is applied from the input shaft through the synchronizer hub and fourth speed gear to the output gear,

differential ring gear, and drive axles, as illustrated in Figure 20-23.

Fifth-Gear Power Flow

When fifth speed is selected, the 1–2 and 3–4 synchronizer are in neutral and the fifth speed synchronizer is moved to the right. Under this condition torque is transmitted from the input shaft through the fifth speed gear and synchronizer hub to the output shaft, because the hub is splined to the output shaft. Torque is applied from the output shaft to the

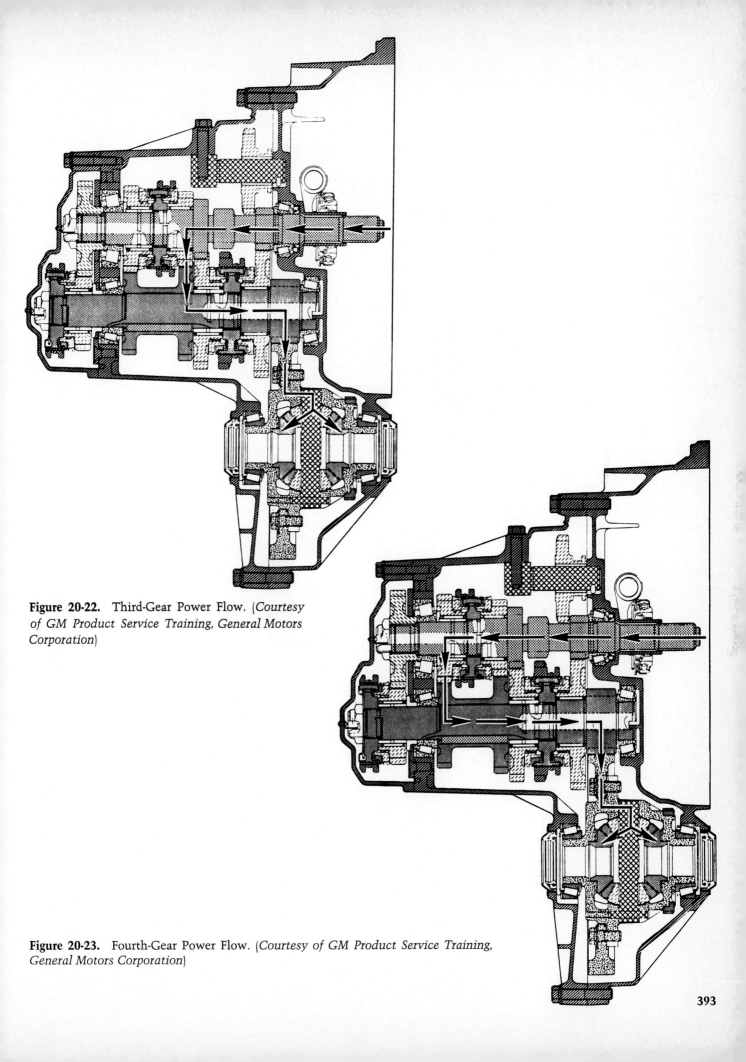

Figure 20-22. Third-Gear Power Flow. (*Courtesy of GM Product Service Training, General Motors Corporation*)

Figure 20-23. Fourth-Gear Power Flow. (*Courtesy of GM Product Service Training, General Motors Corporation*)

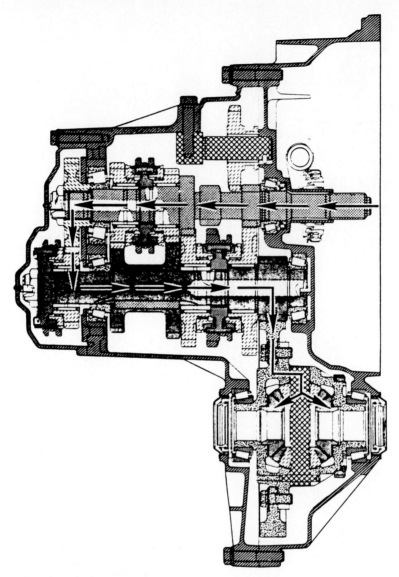

Figure 20-24. Fifth-Gear Power Flow. (*Courtesy of GM Product Service Training, General Motors Corporation*)

differential ring gear and drive axles, as indicated in Figure 20-24.

Reverse-Gear Power Flow

When the gearshift is placed in reverse, all three synchronizers are in neutral and the reverse idler gear is moved to the left. The reverse idler gear meshes with a gear on the input shaft and outer teeth on the 1–2 synchronizer sleeve. This action allows torque to be transmitted from the input shaft through the reverse idler gear to the 3–4 synchronizer sleeve. As indicated in Figure 20-25, the reverse idler gear causes the output shaft to turn in the reverse direction.

Rotation of the transaxle shafts and the differ-

ential is viewed from the front of the transaxle, or right side of the vehicle. In the forward gears, the engine and input shaft turn clockwise and the output shaft turns counterclockwise, because one of the input shaft gears is in direct contact with a gear on the output shaft. Counterclockwise output shaft rotation results in clockwise rotation of the differential ring gear and front wheels, which drives the vehicle ahead. In reverse, the clockwise rotation of the output shaft drives the differential ring gear and front wheels counterclockwise, which causes the vehicle to back up.

A four-speed transaxle is similar to a five-speed transaxle, except that the fifth speed gear and synchronizer are not used in the four-speed unit.

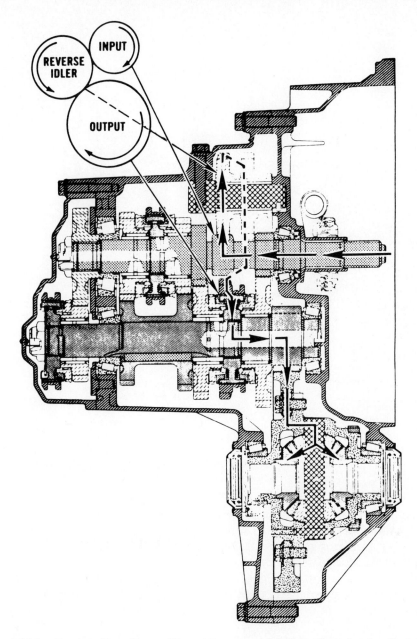

Figure 20-25. Reverse-Gear Power Flow. (*Courtesy of GM Product Service Training, General Motors Corporation*)

Gear Ratios

Transmission gear ratios vary, depending on the engine power, vehicle weight, and other variables. A typical five-speed manual transaxle has the following gear ratios:

First gear	3.29 : 1
Second gear	2.08 : 1
Third gear	1.45 : 1
Fourth gear	1.04 : 1
Fifth gear	0.72 : 1
Reverse gear	3.14 : 1

Differential gear ratio	3.05 : 1 or 3.56 : 1
Overall top gear ratio	2.20 : 1 or 2.57 : 1

The fifth gear provides an overdrive gear ratio. To obtain the overall top gear ratio, multiply the fifth gear ratio by the differential gear ratio.

Differential

The complete differential shown in Figure 20-26 is from the five-speed transaxle illustrated in Figures 20-19 through 20-25. The differential components are identified in Table 20-1.

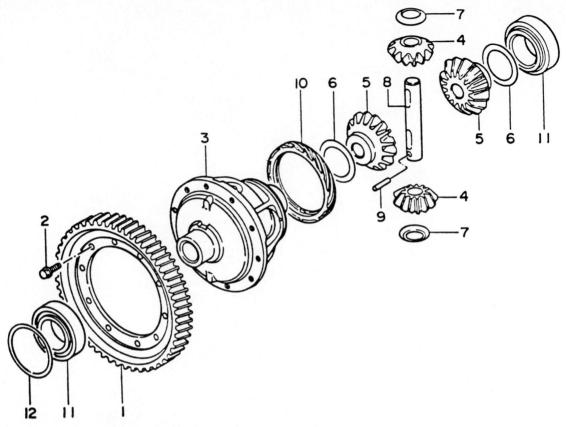

Figure 20-26. Complete Differential from Five-Speed Transaxle. (*Courtesy of GM Product Service Training, General Motors Corporation*)

Power flow in the transaxle is from the output shaft to the differential ring gear. Since the ring gear is bolted to the differential case, the case and pinion gear shaft must rotate with the ring gear. The pinion gears transmit torque to the side gears and the drive axles. (Refer to Chapter 19 for a complete description of differential action and differentials used in rear-wheel-drive cars.)

Complete Transaxle

Internal Components

All the internal transaxle components are pictured in Figure 20-27, and various parts are identified in Table 20-2.

TABLE 20-1. Differential Components.
(*Courtesy of GM Product Service Training, General Motors Corporation*)

1	5.529	5.529	GEAR, diff ring (3.19 Ratio)	94249539	1	8942495393
OR	5.529	5.529	GEAR, diff ring (3.45 Ratio)	94249537	1	8942495373
OR	5.529	5.529	GEAR, diff ring (3.83 Ratio)	94249540	1	8942495403
2	5.531	5.531	BOLT, ring gear	94250108	10	8942501080
3	5.510	5.510	CASE, diff	94244546	1	8942445464
4	5.526	5.526	GEAR, diff pinion	00463060	2	8004630600
5	5.528	5.528	GEAR, diff side	14004854	2	8140048542
6	5.543	5.543	WASHER, side gear thrust	00362025	2	8003620251
7	5.542	5.542	WASHER, pinion thrust	00463061	2	8004630610
8	5.517	5.517	SHAFT, diff pinion	00463062	1	8004630620
9	5.518	5.518	PIN, lock, pinion shaft	94250109	1	8942501090
10	4.343	4.343	GEAR, speed drive	94249541	1	8942495410
11	5.536	5.536	BEARING, differential	94249542	2	8942495420
12	5.537	5.537	SHIM, brg., diff side T=1.00 (0.039″)	94249544	1	8942495440

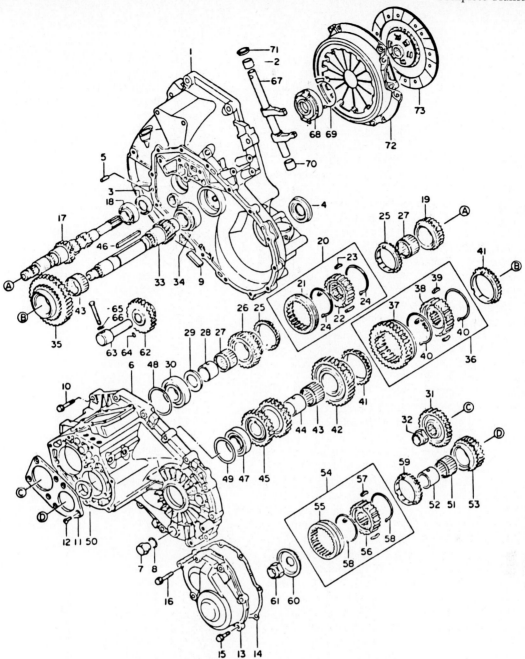

Figure 20-27. Transaxle Components. (*Courtesy of GM Product Service Training, General Motors Corporation*)

TABLE 20-2. Transaxle Component Identification.
(*Courtesy of GM Product Service Training, General Motors Corporation*)

1	0.683	0.683	HOUSING, clutch and diff	94241733	1		8942417334
2	0.799	0.799	BUSH, clutch shaft	94249519	1		8942495190
3	4.354	4.354	SEAL, oil, input shaft	94249521	1	@1	8942495211
4	6.061	6.061	SEAL, oil, drive shaft	90129860	2	@1	8901298600
5	4.317	0.685	PIN, straight knock	94008215	2		9081610200
6	4.103	4.103	CASE, transaxle	94241729	1		8942417295
7	4.103	4.105	PLUG, drain	94022501	1		9096620050
8	4.105	4.105	PACKING, o-ring, plug	94020128	1	@1	9097205600
9	4.105	4.105	MAGNET, case	94249524	1		8942495240

TABLE 20-2. *Continued*

10	4.104	4.104	BOLT, housing to case	94250103	14		8942501030
11	4.412	4.412	RETAINER, bearing	94249526	1		8942495260
12	4.104	4.412	SCREW, retainer to trans. case	94248159	7		8942481590
13	4.317	4.317	COVER, rear	94249527	1		8942495270
14	4.318	4.318	PACKING, case to rear cover	94249530	1	@1	8942495300
15	4.319	4.319	BOLT, rear cover to trans. case	94250105	3		8942501050
16	4.319	4.319	BOLT, rear cover to trans. case	94250106	4		8942501060
17	4.412	4.412	SHAFT, input	94249561	1		8942495611
18	4.355	4.355	BEARING, input shaft, front	94249564	1		8942495640
19	4.415	4.415	GEAR ASM., 3rd., input	94249568	1		8942495681
20	4.380	4.380	SYNCHRONIZER ASM, 3rd & 4th (Incl. key no. 21-24)	94249573	1		8942495730
21	N.S.S.	N.S.S.	SLEEVE, syn. 3rd & 4th. part of syn. asm.	N.P.N.	1		8942495742
22	N.S.S.	N.S.S.	HUB, clutch, 3rd & 4th, part of syn. asm.	N.P.N.	1		8942495751
23	4.384	4.384	INSERT, 3rd & 4th	94249576	3		8942495760
24	4.384	4.384	SPRING, insert, 3rd & 4th	94249577	2		8942495770
25	4.383	4.383	RING, blocking, 3rd & 4th	94249580	2		8942495802
26	4.415	4.415	GEAR ASM., 4th, input	94249582	1		8942495821
27	4.355	4.355	BEARING, needle, 3rd & 4th	94249586	2		8942495860
28	4.376	4.376	COLLAR, needle bearing, 4th gear	94249587	1		8942495870
29	4.415	4.415	WASHER, thrust, 4th gear	94249588	1		8942495880
30	4.408	4.408	BEARING, input, rear	94249610	1		8942496100
31	4.415	4.415	GEAR, 5th., input	94249612	1		8942496121
32	4.422	4.422	NUT, 5th. gear	94250111	1		8942501110
33	4.403	4.403	SHAFT, output (3.19 Ratio)	94249616	1		8942496161
OR	4.403	4.403	SHAFT, output (3.45 Ratio)	94249614	1		8942496141
OR	4.403	4.403	SHAFT, output (3.83 Ratio)	94249617	1		8942496171
34	6.311	6.311	BEARING, output shaft, front	94249619	1		8942496190
35	4.417	4.417	GEAR ASM., 1st, output	94249620	1		8942496201
36	4.380	4.380	SYNCHRONIZER ASM., 1st & 2nd (Incl. key no. 37-40)	94249624	1		8942496240
37	N.S.S.	N.S.S.	GEAR, rev. & sleeve, part of syn. asm.	N.P.N.	1		8942496251
38	N.S.S.	N.S.S.	HUB, clutch, rev. part of syn. asm.	N.P.N.	1		8942496262
39	4.384	4.384	INSERT, 1st & 2nd	94249627	3		8942496270
40	4.384	4.384	SPRING, insert, 1st & 2nd	94249628	2		8942496280
41	4.383	4.383	RING, blocking, 1st & 2nd	94249631	2		8942496313
42	4.415	4.415	GEAR ASM., 2nd., output	94249633	1		8942496332
43	4.355	4.355	BEARING, 1st & 2nd	94249637	2		8942496370
44	4.376	4.376	COLLAR, needle bearing, 2nd. gear	94249638	1		8942496380
45	4.415	4.415	GEAR, output, 3rd & 4th	94249640	1		8942496402
46	4.417	4.417	KEY, feather, 3rd & 4th	94008504	1		9080308630
47	4.408	4.408	BEARING, output, rear	94249643	1		8942496430
48	4.376	4.376	SHIM, bearing, input shaft T=2.44 (0.096")	94249589	1		8942495890
49	4.416	4.416	SHIM, bearing, output shaft T=2.44 (0.096")	94249644	1		8942496440
50	4.415	4.415	WASHER, thrust, 5th gear	94249744	1		8942497440
51	4.355	4.422	BEARING, needle, 5th gear	94249586	1		8942495860
52	4.376	4.415	COLLAR, needle brg., 5th gear	94249587	1		8942495870
53	4.415	4.415	GEAR ASM., output, 5th.	94249746	1		8942497461
54	4.380	4.380	SYNCHRONIZER ASM., 5th. gear (Incl. key no. 55-58)	94249749	1		8942497490
55	N.S.S.	N.S.S.	SLEEVE, syn. 5th. part of syn. asm.	N.P.N.	1		8942497502
56	N.S.S.	N.S.S.	HUB, clutch, 5th gear, part of syn. asm.	N.P.N.	1		8942497511
57	4.384	4.384	INSERT, 5th.	94249576	3		8942497560
58	4.384	4.384	SPRING, insert, 5th.	94249577	2		8942495770
59	4.383	4.383	RING, blocking, 5th.	94249580	1		8942495802
60	4.412	4.412	PLATE, stopper, insert	94249752	1		8942497520
61	4.422	4.412	NUT, sleeve & hub	94250111	1		8942501110

TABLE 20-2. (*Continued*)

62	4.430	4.430	GEAR ASM., idler, rev.	94249753	1		8942497531
63	4.433	4.433	SHAFT, idler, rev.	94100543	1		8941005430
64	4.302	4.302	PIN, straight	94008156	1		9081504080
65	4.302	4.302	BOLT, idler shaft, rev.	94002405	1		9028510500
66	4.665	4.302	GASKET, idler shaft	94000373	1	@1	9095714100
67	0.795	0.795	SHAFT ASM., clutch fork	94251465	1		8942514650
68	0.799	0.799	BEARING, clutch release	94249782	1		8942497820
69	0.805	0.805	SPRING, release bearing	94251599	1		8942515990
70	0.799	0.799	BUSH, clutch shaft	94249519	1		8942495190
71	0.805	0.805	SEAL, clutch shaft	94253509	1	@1	8942535090
OR	0.805	0.805	SEAL, clutch shaft (FEDERAL)	00474679	1	@1	8004746790
72	0.863	0.863	PLATE ASM., clutch pressure	94253236	1		8942532360
73	0.886	0.866	DISC ASM., clutch, w/facing	94253238	1		8942532380

NOTE: @1 Also included in REPAIR KIT, t/axle overhaul.

Gear Shifter Mechanism

The complete gear shifter mechanism is illustrated in Figure 20-28, and its components are identified in Table 20-3.

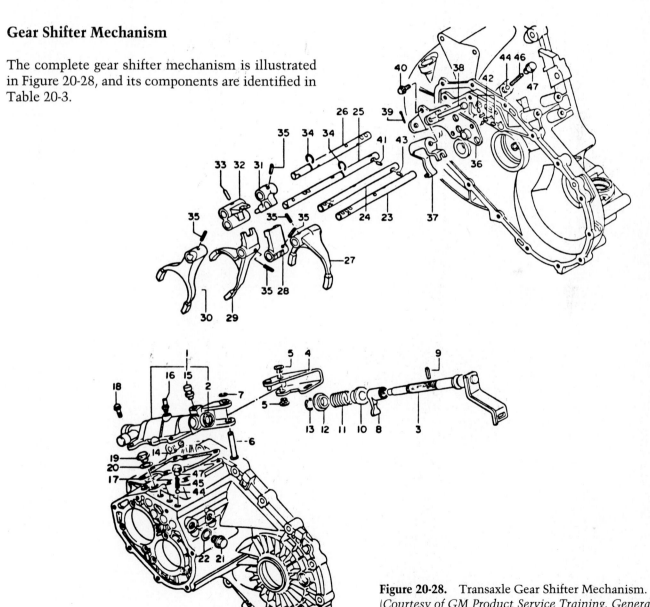

Figure 20-28. Transaxle Gear Shifter Mechanism. (*Courtesy of GM Product Service Training, General Motors Corporation*)

TABLE 20-3. Transaxle Gear Shifter Mechanism Components.
(Courtesy of GM Product Service Training, General Motors Corporation)

1	4.020	4.020	BOX SUB ASM., quadrant, shift cont. (Incl. key no. 2-4)	94259516	1		8942595161
2	4.027	4.027	SEAL, oil quadrant box	94249503	1	@1	8942495030
3	4.030	4.030	LEVER ASM., shift, external	94100650	1		8941006500
4	4.030	4.030	LEVER ASM., select, external	94257461	1		8942574610
5	4.032	4.032	BUSH, select lever	94249510	2		8942495100
6	4.032	4.032	PIN, select lever	94250117	1		8942501170
7	4.040	4.032	RING, snap, select lever	94000082	1		9091854060
8	4.027	4.027	LEVER, shift, internal	94249512	1		8942495123
9	4.027	4.027	PIN, spring, internal lever	94250113	1		8942501130
10	4.027	4.027	SEAT, spring, select stop	94257826	1		8942578260
11	4.027	4.027	SPRING, select stop, 1st & 2nd	94100490	1		8941004900
12	4.027	4.027	SEAT, spring, select stop	94257825	1		8942578250
13	4.027	4.027	RING, snap, spring seat	94000049	1		9091804160
14	4.020	4.020	PIN, knock, quadrant box	94250119	2		8942501190
15	4.104	4.104	VENTILATOR, air, quadrant box	94255649	1		8942556490
16	4.027	4.027	STUD, neutral position set	94259519	1		8942595191
17	4.015	4.015	GASKET, quadrant box	94249518	1	@1	8942495180
18	4.012	4.012	BOLT, quadrant box	94250104	4		8942501040
19	4.075	4.075	PLUG, screw	94252142	1		8942521420
20	4.075	4.075	GASKET, plug	94020241	1	@1	9099201770
21	4.075	4.302	PLUG, screw	94252142	2		8942521420
22	4.075	4.075	GASKET, plug	94020241	2	@1	9099201770
23	4.309	4.309	SHAFT, arm, gear shift, 1st & 2nd	94249755	1		8942497550
24	4.309	4.309	SHAFT, arm, gear shift, 3rd & 4th	94253912	1		8942539120
25	4.309	4.309	SHAFT, arm, gear shift, 5th	94257918	1		8942579180
26	4.309	4.309	SHAFT, arm, gear shift, rev.	94257919	1		8942579190
27	4.303	4.303	FORK, shift, 1st & 2nd	94249759	1		8942497592
28	4.303	4.303	BLOCK, shift, 1st & 2nd	94249760	1		8942497600
29	4.303	4.303	FORK, shift, 3rd & 4th	94249761	1		8942497613
30	4.303	4.303	FORK, shift, 5th	94249762	1		8942497621
31	4.303	4.303	LEVER, shift, rev.	94249763	1		8942497630
32	4.303	4.303	BLOCK, shift, rev. & 5th	94257920	1		8942579201
33	4.307	4.307	PIN, lock, rev. & 5th	94024689	1		5335340020
34	4.307	4.307	RING, snap,	94030673	2		5095880190
35	4.303	4.307	PIN, spr., shift arm	94020061	5		9096785430
36	4.302	4.302	BRACKET, fulcrum, rev. lever	94249771	1		8942497710
37	4.302	4.302	LEVER, shift, rev.	94249772	1		8942497720
38	4.302	4.302	PIN, fulcrum brkt., rev. shift	94250115	1		8942501150
39	4.302	4.302	COTTER PIN, split, fulcrum pin	94008069	1		9081020150
40	4.302	4.302	BOLT, fulcrum brkt.	94250107	4		8942501070
41	4.302	4.302	PIN, lock, 5th shaft	94250114	1		8942501140
42	4.307	4.307	PIN, inter lock	94024689	3		5335340020
43	4.302	4.302	PIN, lock, 3rd & 4th shaft	94250116	1		8942501160
44	4.311	4.311	BALL, detent, gear shift	94030683	4		9000970090
45	4.311	4.311	SPRING, detent ball	94251507	3		8942515070
46	4.311	4.311	SPRING, detent ball, rev.	94251508	1		8942515080
47	4.307	4.307	PLUG, detent spring	94251509	4		8942515091

NOTE: @1 Also included in REPAIR KIT, t/axle overhaul.

Manual Transaxle Compared to Manual Transmissions

Three-Speed Transmission

In a manual transmission that is used in a rear-wheel-drive car, the differential is located at the rear of the vehicle and the transmission is mounted on the engine flywheel housing. A drive shaft connects the transmission to the differential. The transaxle is a lighter, more compact unit.

In a manual transmission, the input and output shafts are mounted on the same horizontal plane. A machined extension on the front of the output shaft is mounted in needle bearings in the center of the input shaft. Therefore, the input shaft can rotate independently from the output shaft. A synchronizer hub is mounted on the front of the output shaft.

The power flow in each gear of a three-speed manual transmission is shown in Figure 20-29.

Four-Speed Manual Transmission

The power flow in each gear of a manual four-speed transmission is illustrated in Figure 20-30.

Five-Speed Manual Transmission

The gears and synchronizer assemblies from a five-speed manual transmission are illustrated in Figure 20-31.

Wheel Bearings

Front Wheel Bearings

Some front-wheel-drive vehicles have front wheel bearing and hub assemblies that are bolted to the steering knuckles. The bearings are lubricated and sealed, and the complete bearing and hub assembly is replaced as a unit. Each front drive axle has splines that fit into matching splines inside the bearing hubs.

A wheel bearing and hub assembly is shown in Figure 20-32, and the drive axle is shown installed in Figure 20-33.

Some front suspension systems have a sealed bearing that is pressed into the steering knuckle. The wheel hub is pressed into the inner bearing race, and the drive axle is splined into the hub. These bearings

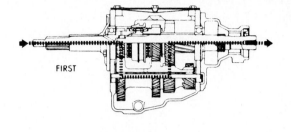

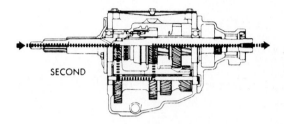

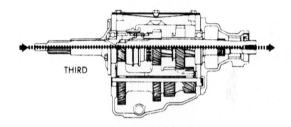

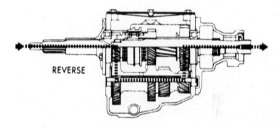

Figure 20-29. Power Flow Manual Three-Speed Transmission. *(Courtesy of Buick Motor Division, General Motors Corporation)*

may contain two rows of ball bearings, or two tapered roller bearings. In this type of installation, the drive axle hub nut torque supplies the correct bearing preload.

A steering knuckle with a pressed-in bearing is illustrated in Figure 20-34.

Other front-wheel-drive vehicles have two separate tapered roller bearings mounted in the steering knuckles. The bearing races are pressed into the steering knuckle, and seals are located in the knuckle on each side of the bearing. Correct bearing preload is supplied by the hub nut torque.

A steering knuckle with two separate tapered roller bearings is illustrated in Figure 20-35.

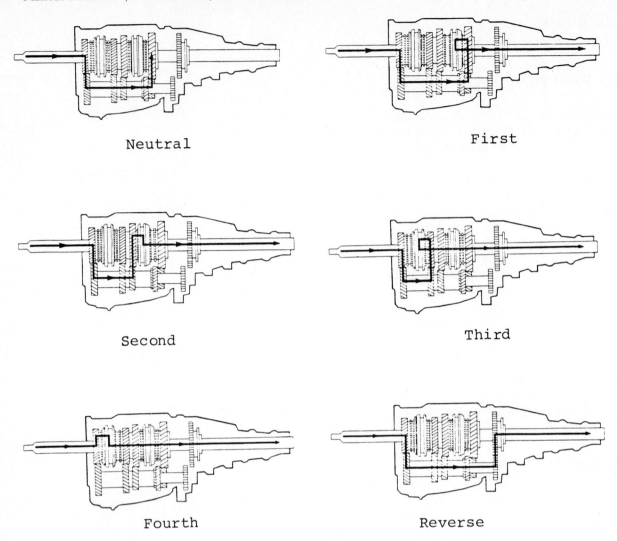

Neutral

First

Second

Third

Fourth

Reverse

Figure 20-30. Power Flow Manual Four-Speed Transmission. (*Courtesy of Buick Motor Division, General Motors Corporation*)

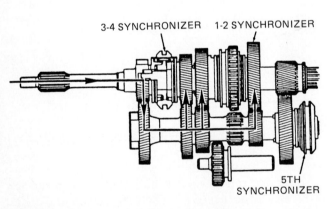

Figure 20-31. Five-Speed Manual Transmission. (*Courtesy of GM Product Service Training, General Motors Corporation*)

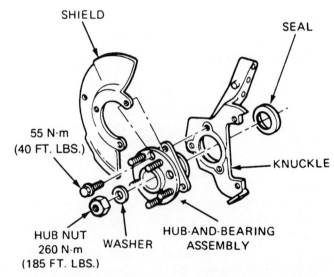

Figure 20-32. Wheel Bearing and Hub Assembly. (*Courtesy of Pontiac Motor Division, General Motors Corporation*)

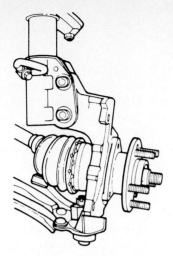

Figure 20-33. Front Drive Axle Installed in Wheel Bearing Hub. (*Courtesy of Pontiac Motor Division, General Motors Corporation*)

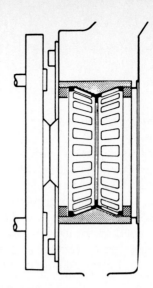

Figure 20-34. Steering Knuckle with Pressed-In Bearing. (*Courtesy of Chrysler Canada*)

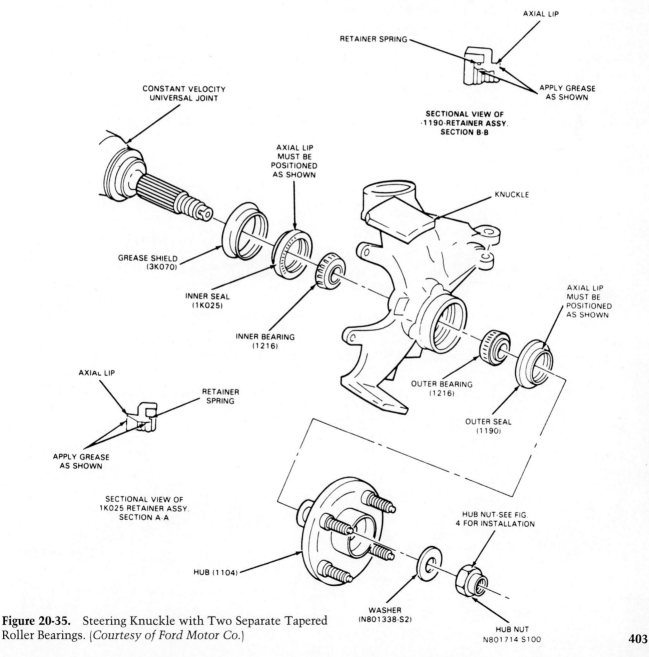

AXIAL LIP

RETAINER SPRING

APPLY GREASE AS SHOWN

SECTIONAL VIEW OF -1190-RETAINER ASSY. SECTION B-B

CONSTANT VELOCITY UNIVERSAL JOINT

AXIAL LIP MUST BE POSITIONED AS SHOWN

KNUCKLE

GREASE SHIELD (3K070)

INNER SEAL (1K025)

INNER BEARING (1216)

AXIAL LIP MUST BE POSITIONED AS SHOWN

OUTER BEARING (1216)

OUTER SEAL (1190)

AXIAL LIP

RETAINER SPRING

APPLY GREASE AS SHOWN

SECTIONAL VIEW OF 1K025 RETAINER ASSY. SECTION A-A

HUB NUT-SEE FIG. 4 FOR INSTALLATION

HUB (1104)

WASHER (N801338-S2)

HUB NUT
N801714 S100

Figure 20-35. Steering Knuckle with Two Separate Tapered Roller Bearings. (*Courtesy of Ford Motor Co.*)

Drive Axles

Types of Drive Axle Systems

In many front-wheel-drive vehicles, the engine is mounted transversely with the transaxle located behind the engine. Since the transaxle is not centered in the vehicle chassis, the right drive axle must be longer than the left drive axle. (Right and left sides of the vehicle are determined from the driver's seat.)

An unequal-length drive axle system with a solid left axle shaft and a tubular right axle shaft is pictured in Figure 20-36.

Under hard acceleration, the engine lifts up on the engine mounts. When this occurs in an unequal-length drive axle system, the angle on the long drive axle changes more than the angle on the short drive axle. This causes the vehicle to pull to one side, or "torque steer."

An equal-length drive axle system is used in some front-wheel-drive vehicles to prevent torque steer. This system has short, solid drive axles of equal length on each side, and an intermediate shaft

on the right side. A cardan "U" joint is connected on the inner end of the intermediate shaft, and a bearing and bracket support the outer end of the shaft. The bearing and bracket assembly is bolted to the engine block. The inner end of the "U" joint is splined to the differential side gear, and the inner end of the drive axle is splined to the intermediate shaft. A weight is clamped to the left drive axle shaft to reduce vibration noise.

The unequal-length drive axle system is used with normally aspirated engines, whereas the equal-length drive axle system, illustrated in Figure 20-37, is used with some turbocharged engines.

Types of Drive Axle Joints

Some front drive axles have an outer constant velocity (CV) joint with six steel balls in a cage and an inner tripod joint, as pictured in Figure 20-38. Other front drive axles have an inner and outer CV joint, as shown in Figure 20-39.

The outer drive axle joint is splined to the front wheel hub, and the inner joint is splined to the dif-

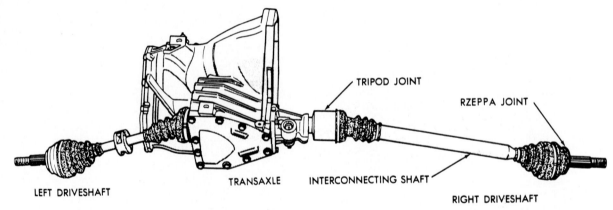

Figure 20-36. Unequal-Length Front Drive Axle System. (*Courtesy of Chrysler Canada*)

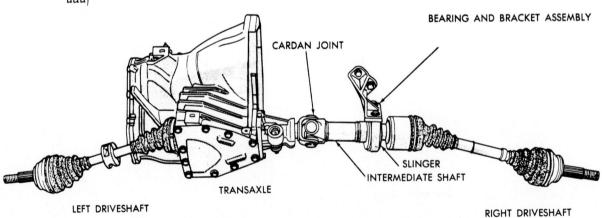

Figure 20-37. Equal-Length Drive Axle System. (*Courtesy of Chrysler Canada*)

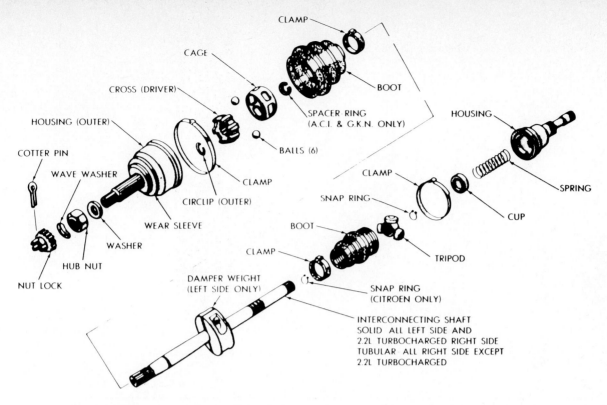

Figure 20-38. Front Drive Axle with Outer Constant Velocity Joint and Inner Tripod Joint. (*Courtesy of Chrysler Canada*)

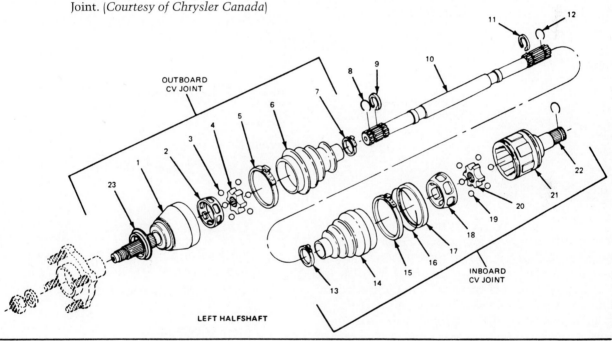

LEGEND:

1. OUTER BEARING RACE AND STUB SHAFT ASSEMBLY
2. BEARING CAGE
3. BALL BEARINGS (6)
4. INNER BEARING RACE
5. BOOT CLAMP (LARGE)
6. BOOT
7. BOOT CLAMP (SMALL)
8. CIRCLIP
9. STOP RING
10. INTERCONNECTING SHAFT
11. STOP RING

12. CIRCLIP
13. BOOT CLAMP (SMALL)
14. BOOT
15. BOOT CLAMP (LARGE)
16. BEARING RETAINER (MTX 5-SPEED ONLY)
17. BEARING RETAINER (MTX 4-SPEED AND ATX)
18. BEARING CAGE
19. BALL BEARINGS (6)
20. INNER BEARING RACE
21. OUTER BEARING RACE AND STUB SHAFT ASSEMBLY
22. CIRCLIP
23. DUST SEAL

Figure 20-39. Front Drive Axles with Two Ball-Type Constant Velocity Joints. (*Courtesy of Ford Motor Co.*)

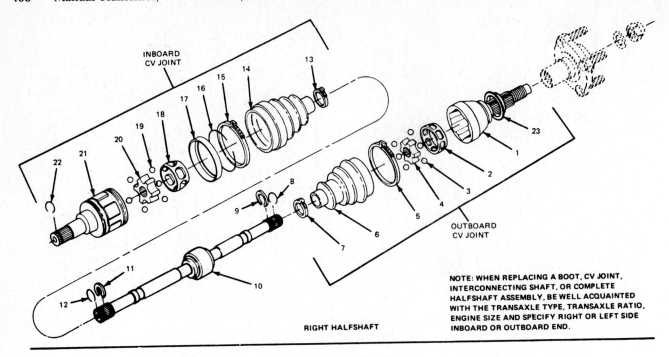

INBOARD CV JOINT

OUTBOARD CV JOINT

RIGHT HALFSHAFT

NOTE: WHEN REPLACING A BOOT, CV JOINT,
INTERCONNECTING SHAFT, OR COMPLETE
HALFSHAFT ASSEMBLY, BE WELL ACQUAINTED
WITH THE TRANSAXLE TYPE, TRANSAXLE RATIO,
ENGINE SIZE AND SPECIFY RIGHT OR LEFT SIDE
INBOARD OR OUTBOARD END.

LEGEND:

1. OUTER BEARING RACE AND
   STUB SHAFT ASSEMBLY
2. BEARING CAGE
3. BALL BEARINGS (6)
4. INNER BEARING RACE
5. BOOT CLAMP (LARGE)
6. BOOT
7. BOOT CLAMP (SMALL)
8. CIRCLIP
9. STOP RING
10. INTERCONNECTING SHAFT
11. STOP RING

12. CIRCLIP
13. BOOT CLAMP (SMALL)
14. BOOT
15. BOOT CLAMP (LARGE)
16. BEARING RETAINER (MTX 5-SPEED ONLY)
17. BEARING RETAINER (MTX 4-SPEED AND ATX)
18. BEARING CAGE
19. BALL BEARINGS (6)
20. INNER BEARING RACE
21. OUTER BEARING RACE AND STUB SHAFT
    ASSEMBLY
22. CIRCLIP
23. DUST SEAL

Figure 20-39 (Continued)

ferential side gear. When the front wheels turn, the outer joint must pivot fore and aft. This joint must also pivot vertically as the front wheel moves up and down due to road surface irregularities. Vertical and lateral movement is also available in the inner joint as the front wheel moves up and down.

In a rear-wheel-drive vehicle, the drive shaft turns at the same speed as the transmission output shaft, because the drive shaft is ahead of the differential. The front drive axles in a front-wheel-drive vehicle rotate at approximately $\frac{1}{3}$ of the drive shaft speed in a rear-wheel-drive car, because the drive axles turn at the same speed as the differential ring gear.

(Manual transaxle and drive axle service is explained in Chapter 16 of *Automotive Principles: Repair and Service*, Volume II.)

Test Questions

1. Axial load on a bearing is applied in a _____ direction.

2. A tapered roller bearing will carry:

   a) axial loads only.

   b) radial loads only.

   c) axial and radial loads.

3. In a hydraulic clutch, the clutch lever is operated by the _____.

4. If a drive gear has 9 teeth and the driven gear has 5 teeth, the gear ratio is:

   a) .43:1.

   b) .55:1.

   c) .65:1.

5. If a transaxle second-speed gear ratio is 2.08:1, and the differential ratio is 3.05:1, the total gear ratio is second gear will be:

   a) 6.34:1.

   b) 7.28:1.

   c) 7.96:1.

6. In the forward gears, the transaxle output shaft rotates in a _____ direction.

7. When a five-speed manual transaxle is in reverse, the 1–2 and 3–4 synchronizers are in the neutral position.   T F

8. The inner end of the front drive axle is splined to the:

   a) differential ring gear case.

   b) differential side gear.

   c) differential pinion gear.

9. The outer end of the front drive axle is splined to the:

   a) front wheel bearing inner race.

   b) front wheel hub.

   c) steering knuckle.

10. On many front wheel bearings, the hub nut torque applies the _____ _____ preload.

11. In an unequal-length drive axle system, the angles of the right and left drive axles are the same when the engine is accelerating hard.   T F

21

Automatic Transaxles and Transmissions

Chapter Completion Objectives

1. Demonstrate an understanding of torque converters.
2. Indicate a knowledge of planetary gear operation and ratios.
3. Understand clutch and band operation.
4. Display a knowledge of clutch and band applications in a three-speed automatic transaxle or transmission.
5. Show an understanding of the hydraulic circuits in a Chrysler automatic transaxle.
6. Understand oil pumps and governors.

Torque Converters

Design

A torque converter contains three basic elements: the impeller pump (driving member), the turbine (driven member), and the stator (reaction member). The converter cover is welded to the pump to seal these three members in an oil-filled housing. Bolts are used to attach the converter cover to the flexplate, which is bolted to the crankshaft. Therefore, the converter cover and pump must rotate with the engine whenever the engine is operating. The turbine is splined to the transaxle input shaft, and the stator is connected to the reaction shaft support through an overrunning clutch.

A torque converter is shown in Figure 21-1.

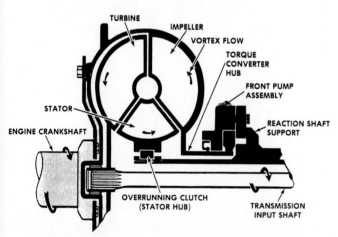

Figure 21-1. Torque Converter Components. (*Courtesy of Chrysler Canada*)

Operation

The torque converter acts as a fluid coupling to connect engine power through the transmission fluid to the transaxle gear train. Another function of the converter is to multiply engine torque when additional performance is desired.

When the engine is running and the impeller pump is spinning, the pump picks up oil at its center, and centrifugal force causes the oil to be discharged between the blades at the pump rim. The oil is spinning in a clockwise direction as it leaves the impeller pump blades. As the oil strikes the turbine blades, the turbine is forced to rotate.

If the engine is idling, the force of the fluid leaving the impeller pump is not great enough to turn the turbine. This allows the vehicle to stand still when the engine is idling and the transaxle is in

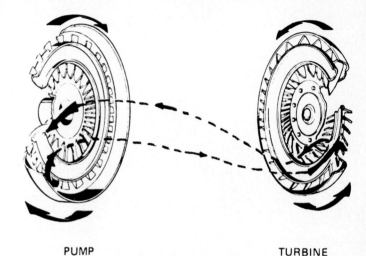

PUMP   TURBINE

Figure 21-2. Impeller Pump and Turbine Operation. (*Courtesy of Hydra-matic Division of General Motors Corporation*)

gear. When engine speed increases slightly, the fluid thrown from the impeller pump creates more force on the turbine blades and the turbine begins to rotate. Power from the turbine is transmitted through the transaxle gear train to the drive axles and front wheels, which causes the vehicle to move. The force of the fluid striking the turbine blades causes the turbine to rotate in the same direction as the impeller pump, as indicated in Figure 21-2.

The turbine blades are curved in the opposite direction to the impeller pump blades. After the fluid has imparted its force to the turbine, it follows the contour of the turbine shell and blades, so that it leaves the turbine in a counterclockwise direction. Since the direction of the fluid is opposite to the engine and impeller pump rotation, its force would work against the engine rotation if it were allowed to strike the impeller pump blades.

Stator Operation

The stator is mounted between the impeller pump and the turbine. Its purpose is to redirect the fluid returning from the turbine so that the fluid moves in a clockwise direction as it reenters the impeller pump. The force of the oil from the impeller pump tries to rotate the stator in a counterclockwise direction, but the roller clutch in the stator prevents the stator from turning in this direction. This one-way roller clutch is connected between the stator blades and the stationary reaction shaft support, as illustrated in Figure 21-3.

When the fluid from the impeller pumps strikes the curved stator blades, the fluid is redirected in a clockwise direction, causing the fluid flow from the

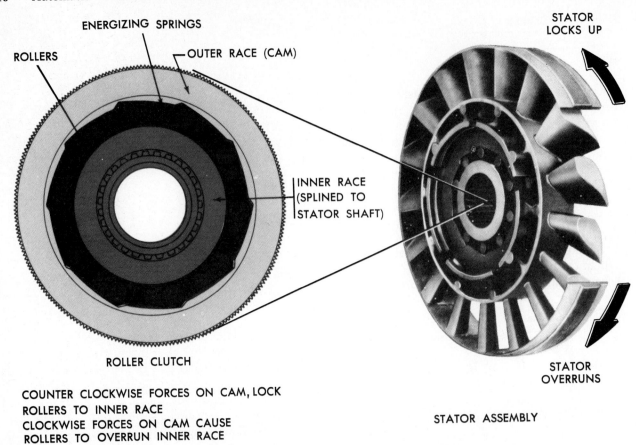

ROLLERS

ENERGIZING SPRINGS

OUTER RACE (CAM)

STATOR LOCKS UP

INNER RACE (SPLINED TO STATOR SHAFT)

ROLLER CLUTCH

STATOR OVERRUNS

COUNTER CLOCKWISE FORCES ON CAM, LOCK
ROLLERS TO INNER RACE
CLOCKWISE FORCES ON CAM CAUSE
ROLLERS TO OVERRUN INNER RACE

STATOR ASSEMBLY

Figure 21-3. Stator and Roller Clutch Design. (*Courtesy of Hydra-matic Division of General Motors Corporation*)

stator to the impeller pump to assist the engine in rotating the impeller pump. This multiplies the engine torque, as pictured in Figure 21-4.

When the engine is operating at full throttle with the transaxle in gear and the vehicle standing still, the torque converter multiplies engine torque by approximately 1.95:1. The flow of fluid from the impeller pump through the turbine and stator is referred to as vortex flow.

As the turbine and vehicle speed increase, the direction of the fluid leaving the turbine changes so that the fluid begins striking the back of the turbine blades. This action causes the roller clutch to release and allow the stator to rotate in a clockwise direction with the impeller pump and the turbine. Once the stator begins to rotate, there is no torque multiplication in the converter. Under this condition the impeller pump and the turbine rotate at the same speed and act as a fluid coupling to transmit engine torque to the transaxle input shaft.

Stator action with the roller over-running is shown in Figure 21-5.

Once the stator is over-running, there is very lit-

tle vortex fluid flow. Under this condition most of the fluid flow in the converter becomes rotary flow. Since the converter is a fluid unit, it acts as a natural shock absorber and provides smooth shifting.

A torque converter will absorb only a given amount of engine torque. For example, when the throttle is opened, the engine speed increases until the engine torque reaches converter torque capacity. When this occurs, the engine speed stabilizes and the converter slips. This condition is referred to as the converter stall speed.

The converter torque capacity must be matched to the engine torque. If the converter torque capacity is too low, the engine will operate at a higher speed before the converter can transmit maximum torque. If the converter is too large, the engine will not be able to drive the impeller pump at a speed that permits the converter to deliver maximum torque.

The engine and converter should be matched so the engine delivers maximum torque at the converter stall speed. The service technician should not alter the converter-engine match provided by the manufacturer.

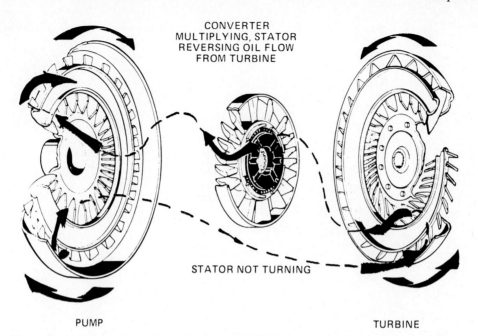

CONVERTER
MULTIPLYING, STATOR
REVERSING OIL FLOW
FROM TURBINE

STATOR NOT TURNING

PUMP   TURBINE

Figure 21-4. Stator Operation. (*Courtesy of Hydra-matic Division of General Motors Corporation*)

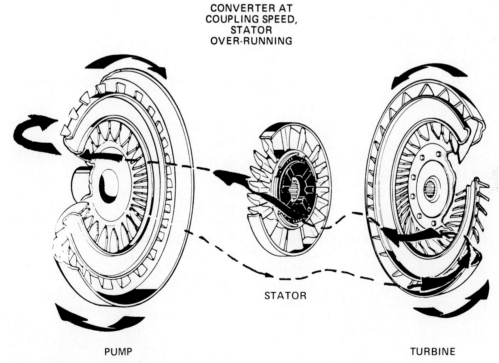

CONVERTER AT
COUPLING SPEED,
STATOR
OVER-RUNNING

STATOR

PUMP   TURBINE

Figure 21-5. Stator Operation with Roller Clutch Over-Running. (*Courtesy of Hydra-matic Division of General Motors Corporation*)

Lockup Torque Converters

Some car manufacturers, such as Chrysler Corporation, do not use lockup converters in transaxles for front-wheel-drive cars. However, other manufacturers, such as General Motors, do have lockup converters on these vehicles.

The lockup converter operates like a conventional converter, except that it has a friction disc between the turbine and the cover. This friction disc

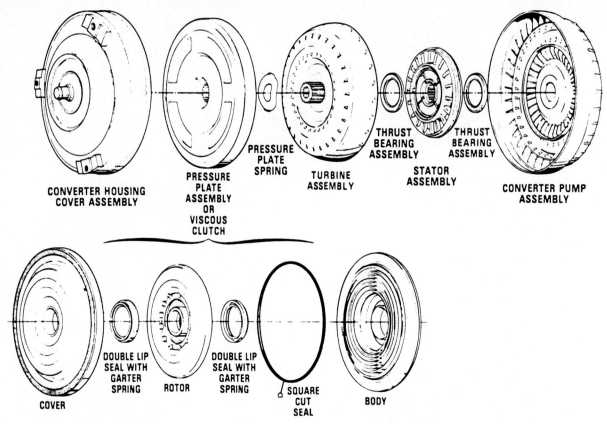

Figure 21-6.   Lockup Converter with Friction Pressure Pressure Plate or Viscous Silicone Clutch. (*Courtesy of GM Product Service Training, General Motors Corporation*)

is splined to the turbine. In direct drive (high) at normal cruising speed, the friction disc is forced against the converter cover, which locks the cover to the turbine and input shaft. This action eliminates converter slippage and provides a slight increase in fuel economy. Lockup conditions vary, depending on the type of transaxle.

Some converters have a sealed disc filled with a viscous silicone fluid in place of the friction disc. (Since the lockup conditions are computer controlled on many vehicles, the operation of this type of converter was explained in Chapter 17.) A lockup converter with a friction pressure plate or viscous silicone clutch is shown in Figure 21-6.

Planetary Gears

Design

A planetary gear set contains a sun gear that is in mesh with four planetary pinion gears mounted in a planet carrier. An annulus, or internal gear, is also

in mesh with the planet pinion gears, as indicated in Figure 21-7.

Planetary gear sets are very versatile and can be designed to provide a wide variety of gear ratios. When planetary gears are used, one member must be held while another member provides the input torque, and the third member acts as an output to transmit the torque to the differential. The sun gear

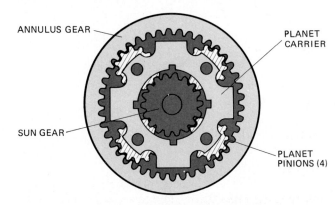

Figure 21-7.   Planetary Gear Set. (*Courtesy of Chrysler Canada*)

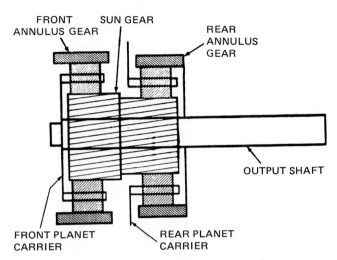

Figure 21-14. Two Planetary Gear Sets with Common Sun Gear. (*Courtesy of Chrysler Canada*)

nents are held in the retainer by a snap ring. The driving discs are lined with a friction material and have internal serrations mounted on the hub splines. The driven plates have external tangs mounted in the clutch retainer slots. These plates do not have any lining, and the driven and driving discs are placed alternately in the clutch assembly. When the clutch is not applied, the discs are free to move between each other.

The components in a multiple disc clutch assembly are shown in Figure 21-15.

When fluid pressure is applied behind the apply piston, the piston is forced against the pressure plate. This pressure forces the clutch discs together, and the hub and retainer connect through the discs. In the left clutch assembly in Figure 21-16, the clutch piston is applied with a force of 70 psi (483 kPa).

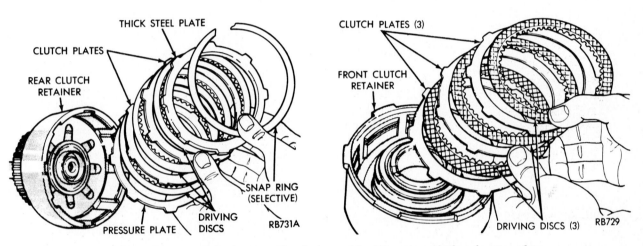

Figure 21-15. Multiple-Disc Clutch Assembly. (*Courtesy of Chrysler Canada*)

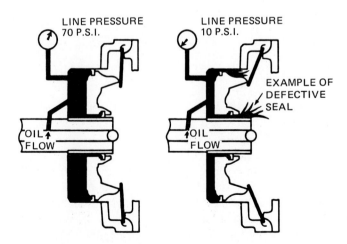

Figure 21-16. Clutch Piston Fluid Pressure. (*Courtesy of Chrysler Canada*)

Internal and external seals on the apply piston contain the fluid behind the piston. In the right clutch assembly in Figure 21-16, leaking internal and external seals allow the fluid to leak past the piston. This reduces the apply pressure and results in clutch slippage. A pressure test can be used to diagnose leaking clutch piston seals.

Bands

Transaxle bands are made of flexible steel with a friction lining on the inner surface. These bands are used to hold components such as clutch retainers or drums in a stationary position. One end of the band is anchored to the transaxle case; the other end is connected to a strut and apply lever. A servo piston

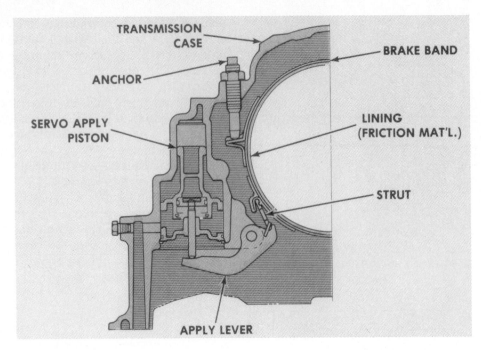

Figure 21-17.   Band and Servo Piston. (*Courtesy of Chrysler Canada*)

pin is mounted against the apply lever, as indicated in Figure 21-17.

If fluid pressure is applied behind the servo piston, the piston pushes the apply lever, which tightens the band on the clutch drum. This action prevents rotation of the clutch drum. When the fluid pressure is relieved behind the servo piston, the band is released and the clutch drum is free to rotate.

Many automatic transaxles have a kickdown band and low-reverse band. When the kickdown band is applied, it holds the sun gear stationary, as pictured in Figure 21-18.

Servo pistons have a steel or plastic ring around their outer circumference to seal the transmission fluid behind the piston. If the low-reverse band is applied, it will lock the rear planet carrier as indicated in Figure 21-19.

Many automatic transaxles have two sets of multiple-disc clutches, as shown in Figure 21-19. If the front clutch is applied, the input shaft is connected to the sun gear. Application of the rear clutch connects the input shaft to the front annulus, or internal gear. When both clutches are applied, the sun gear and the front annulus gear are locked together.

An over-running clutch is connected between the low-reverse drum and the transmission case. The low-reverse drum is connected to the rear planet carrier. The over-running clutch contains a series of rollers mounted in tapered grooves in the outer clutch race. These rollers are spring-loaded toward

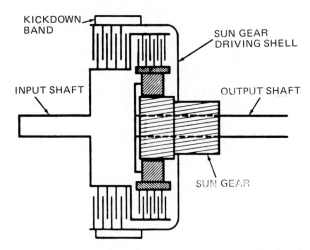

Figure 21-18.   Kickdown Band. (*Courtesy of Chrysler Canada*)

the narrow end of the tapered groove and positioned against the machined surface of the inner race as illustrated in Figure 21-20.

If the inner race is rotated in a clockwise direction, the rollers move against their springs into the wide part of the tapered groove. Under this condition the inner race is freewheeling. When an attempt is made to turn the inner race counterclockwise, the rollers jam between the inner race and the narrow area of their grooves. This action locks the inner race and prevents it from turning counterclockwise.

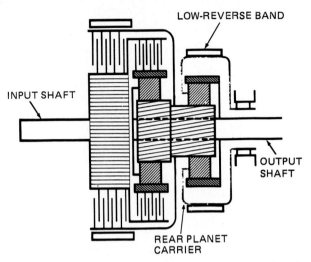

Figure 21-19. Low-Reverse Band. (*Courtesy of Chrysler Canada*)

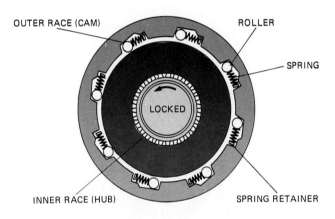

Figure 21-20. Over-Running Clutch. (*Courtesy of Chrysler Canada*)

Clutch and Band Applications

Drive Breakaway (Low) and Manual Low

When the gear selector is placed in the "D" position, the rear clutch is applied, which transmits engine torque from the input shaft to the front annulus gear. The front planet carrier and the rear annulus gear are connected to the output shaft.

Before the vehicle starts moving, the front planet carrier is held stationary by the output shaft and drive train. Therefore, the front annulus gear drives the planet pinion gears clockwise, which causes the sun gear to rotate counterclockwise. The sun gear tries to rotate the rear planet carrier counterclockwise. However, the over-running clutch prevents counterclockwise rotation of the rear planet carrier, and the sun gear drives the rear annulus gear in a clockwise direction. Since the rear annulus gear is connected to the output shaft, the vehicle is driven forward. A gear reduction is obtained because the small sun gear is driving the larger rear annulus gear.

In manual low, the low-reverse band is applied with the rear clutch. This action prevents the over-running clutch and the rear planet carrier from becoming freewheeling if the engine is decelerating in manual low, thus providing engine braking on deceleration.

The power flow through the planetary gear sets is the same in drive breakaway, or manual low. Manual low is selected when the gear selector is placed in the "L" position.

Some car manufacturers refer to the front gear set as the input unit, and the rear gear set as the reaction unit.

The power flow through the planetary gear sets in drive breakaway, or manual low, is shown in Figure 21-21.

Drive Second or Manual Second

When the transaxle upshifts into second, the kickdown band is applied with the rear clutch. This band application locks the sun gear, and the front annulus gear therefore drives the planet carrier clockwise. Since the front planet carrier is connected to the output shaft, the vehicle is driven forward. A gear reduction is provided because the smaller annulus gear is driving the larger planet carrier.

If manual second is selected with the gear selector, the path of power flow remains the same. However, in this gear selector position, higher pressures are provided for band and clutch applications.

The power flow through the planetary gear sets in drive second is shown in Figure 21-22.

Drive Direct (High)

When the transaxle upshifts into high, the front clutch and the rear clutch are both applied. Since the front clutch is connected from the input shaft to the sun gear, and the rear clutch is connected to the front annulus gear, the sun gear and the annulus gear are locked together. This action causes the gear set to rotate as a unit with a 1:1 ratio.

The power flow in drive direct is shown in Figure 21-23.

Reverse

If the gear selector is placed in reverse, the front clutch and the low-reverse band are applied. Since the front clutch connects the input shaft to the sun gear, this gear is driven in a clockwise direction. Clockwise sun gear rotation causes the rear annulus gear to rotate counterclockwise, because the rear planet carrier is locked by the low-reverse band. Counterclockwise rotation of the rear annulus gear and output shaft drives the vehicle in reverse. Since the small sun gear is driving the larger annulus gear, a gear reduction is provided.

The power flow in reverse is pictured in Figure 21-24.

Many automatic transaxles and transmissions have the same clutch and band application in each gear.

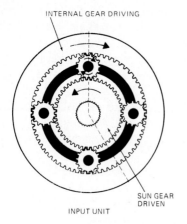

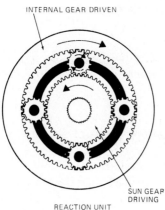

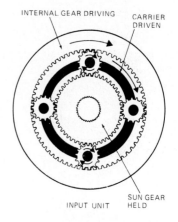

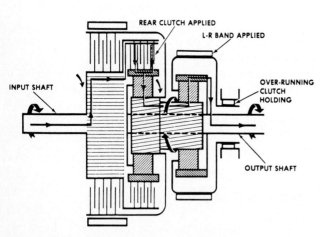

Figure 21-21.   Power Flow in Drive Breakaway or Manual Low. (*Courtesy of Chrysler Canada*)

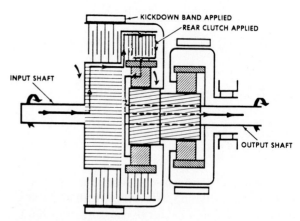

Figure 21-22.   Power Flow in Drive Second. (*Courtesy of Chrysler Canada*)

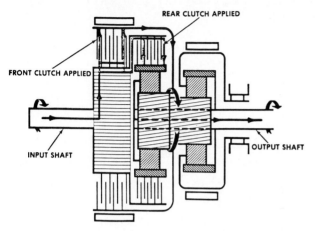

Figure 21-23. Power Flow in Drive Direct. (*Courtesy of Chrysler Canada*)

Oil Pump

Design and Operation

Many automatic transaxles have a gear-type oil pump mounted in the front of the transaxle. The internal gear has two lugs that fit into matching slots in the torque converter hub. Therefore, the engine drives the oil pump through the torque converter.

An oil pump in the installed position and a disassembled oil pump are illustrated in Figure 21-25.

A gasket is positioned between the pump and the transaxle case and an "O" ring seals the outer circumference of the pump to the case. The converter hub is sealed to the pump with a lip-type seal in the front of the pump. As the pump rotates, a low-pres-

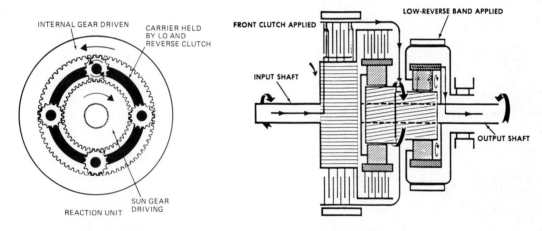

Figure 21-24. Power Flow in Reverse. (*Courtesy of Chrysler Canada*)

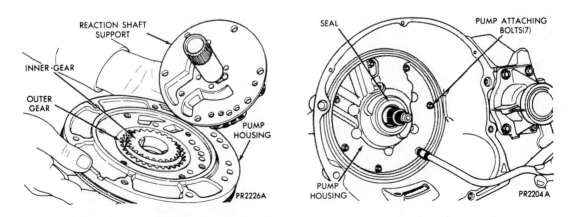

Figure 21-25. Installed Oil Pump and Disassembled Oil Pump. (*Courtesy of Chrysler Canada*)

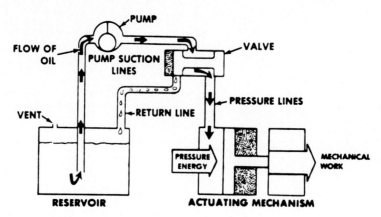

Figure 21-26.   Oil Pump and Pressure Regulator Valve. (*Courtesy of Chrysler Canada*)

sure area, or vacuum, is created in the pump. Since atmospheric pressure is available above the fluid in the transaxle reservoir, the pressure difference results in fluid flow from the reservoir to the pump.

High-pressure fluid is delivered from the pump outlet to a pressure regulator valve. This valve limits the pump pressure by returning some of the fluid flow to the reservoir. Regulated line pressure is supplied from the pressure regulator valve to operate the actuating mechanisms in the transaxle, as indicated in Figure 21-26.

(Refer to Chapter 24 for basic hydraulic principles.)

Governors

Design and Operation

The governor contains a primary valve and a secondary valve mounted in the valve body. The governor valve body is mounted on the governor support attached to the transfer shaft, so that the governor ro-

tates with the transfer shaft. The primary valve does not have a spring, but the secondary valve is spring-loaded against the transfer shaft.

A governor assembly is shown in Figure 21-27.

When the transaxle gear selector is placed in the "D" position with the engine running and the vehicle stopped, line pressure is applied from the pressure regulator valve through a screen to the center groove in the primary valve. This pressure centers the primary valve. Line pressure is also available at the secondary valve.

When vehicle speed increases, the transfer shaft and governor speed also increase. Centrifugal force moves the primary valve outward, which allows line pressure to be metered into the outer primary valve groove. This pressure from the primary valve outer groove is referred to as governor pressure. As governor speed increases, governor pressure reacts against the primary valve outer groove to control the valve movement.

At a specified speed, centrifugal force moves the secondary valve outward, which supplies a metered pressure from the secondary valve to the inner pri-

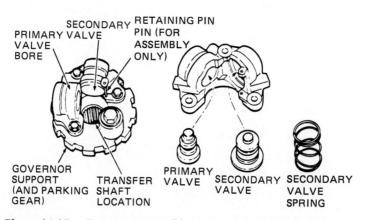

Figure 21-27.   Governor Assembly. (*Courtesy of Chrysler Canada*)

PRIMARY STAGE   SECONDARY STAGE

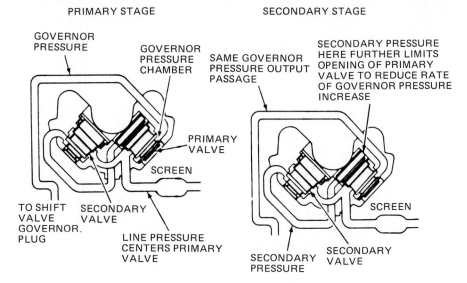

Figure 21-28. Governor Operation. (*Courtesy of Chrysler Canada*)

mary valve groove. This action reduces outward pri- mary valve movement, so the governor pressure from the primary valve outer groove is controlled ac- curately.

Governor operation is explained in Figure 21-28.

Governor pressure is applied to one end of the shift valves in the valve body. This pressure causes shift valve movement and transaxle upshifts as the vehicle speed increases.

The transfer shaft is connected between the transaxle output shaft and the differential. A trans- fer shaft gear is in mesh with the output shaft gear, and the differential pinion gear is attached to the in- ner end of the transfer shaft.

A complete transaxle is shown in Figure 21-29.

Hydraulic Circuits

Neutral or Park

The manual valve is moved by a linkage connected to the transaxle gear selector. When the transaxle is in neutral or park with the engine running, fluid flows through the hydraulic circuits as follows:

1. Fluid is forced from the pump to the pressure reg- ulator valve. When this occurs, the valve is moved to the right against its spring, which al- lows some fluid to return to the reservoir. This valve movement limits the pump pressure.

2. Fluid flows from the pressure regulator valve through the switch valve, converter, and trans-

axle cooler. Fluid is also supplied to the front clutch lubrication system.

3. Line pressure is supplied to the throttle valve, and throttle pressure is supplied from the throttle valve to other components.

4. Pressure is supplied from the manual valve to the left end of the pressure regulator valve.

5. The manual valve moves when the gear selector is changed from neutral to park. This action causes the check ball above the regulator valve to change its position, which changes the source of pressure from the manual valve to the left end of the pressure regulator.

The hydraulic circuits in neutral and park are shown in Figure 21-30.

Drive Breakaway

When the gear selector is moved to the "D" posi- tion, manual valve movement allows fluid to be sup- plied from the manual valve to the rear clutch, which results in clutch application. Fluid pressure is also supplied from the manual valve to the governor and the accumulator. The clutch application is cushioned by the accumulator. Governor pressure is available at the governor plugs of the shift valves and the shuttle valve. Fluid pressure is supplied from the manual valve to the throttle valve; throttle pressure is supplied from the throttle valve to the right end of the shift valves, and to the throttle plug on the shuttle valve.

The drive breakaway hydraulic circuit is illus- trated in Figure 21-31.

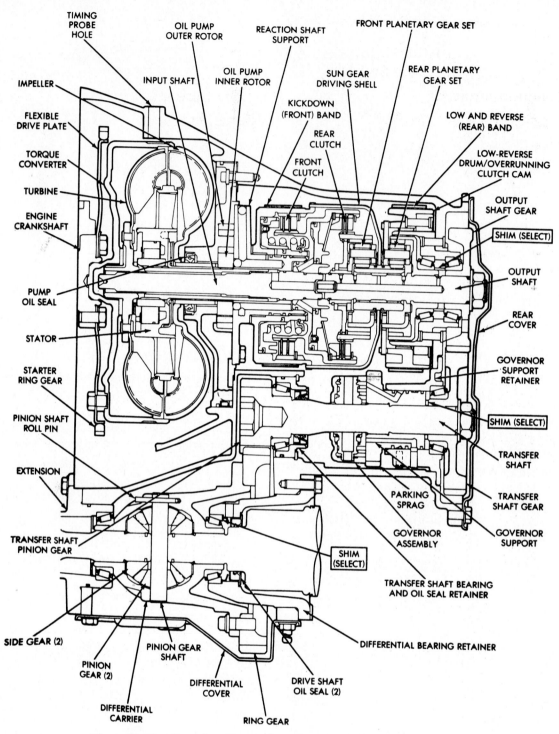

Figure 21-29.   Complete Transaxle. (*Courtesy of Chrysler Canada*)

Manual Low

If the gear selector is moved to the low, or 1, position, manual valve movement supplies fluid pressure through the governor plug of the 1–2 shift valve to the rear servo. This action applies the low-reverse band, and fluid pressure is also supplied to the rear clutch. The fluid pressure from the manual valve to the right side of the 1–2 shift valve governor plug prevents an upshift, regardless of vehicle speed. The remainder of the manual low hydraulic circuit is similar to the drive breakaway hydraulic circuit, as shown in Figure 21-32.

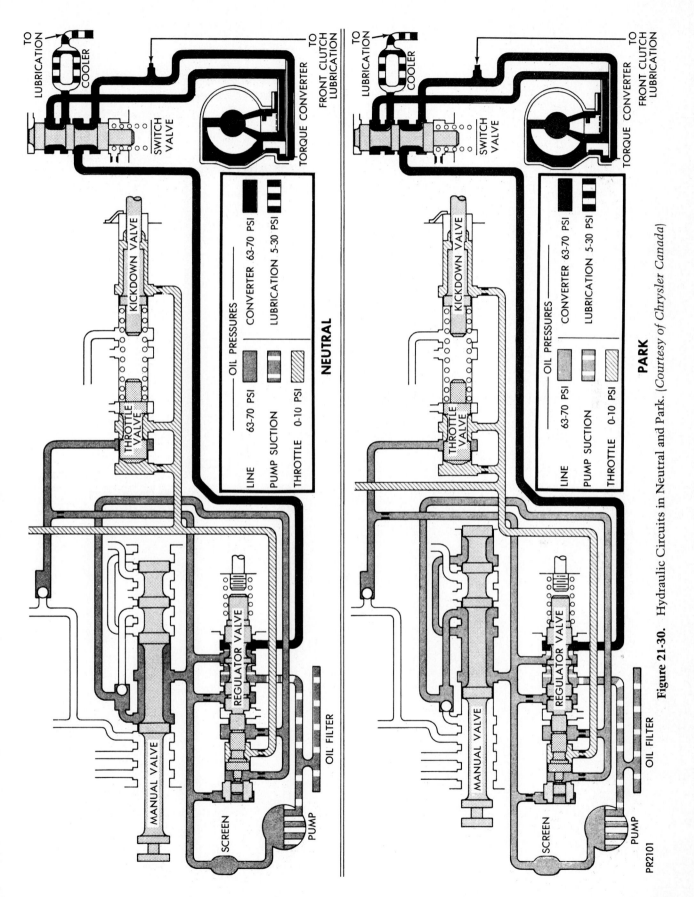

Figure 21-30. Hydraulic Circuits in Neutral and Park. *(Courtesy of Chrysler Canada)*

PR2101

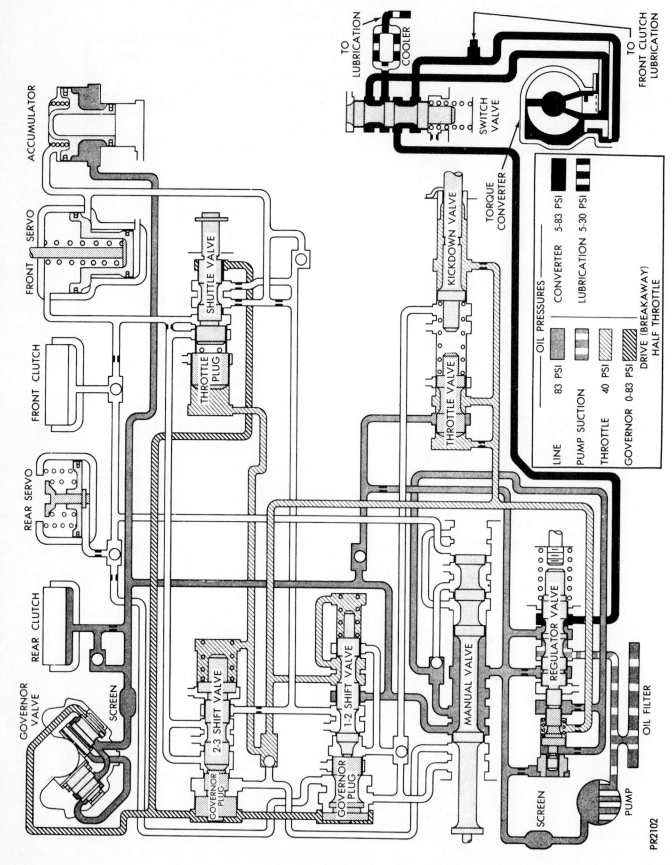

Figure 21-31. Drive Breakaway Hydraulic Circuit. (*Courtesy of Chrysler Canada*)

ACCUMULATOR

FRONT SERVO

FRONT CLUTCH

REAR SERVO

REAR CLUTCH

GOVERNOR VALVE

SCREEN

SHUTTLE VALVE

THROTTLE PLUG

2-3 SHIFT VALVE

GOVERNOR PLUG

1-2 SHIFT VALVE

GOVERNOR PLUG

MANUAL VALVE

REGULATOR VALVE

SCREEN

OIL FILTER

PUMP

KICKDOWN VALVE

THROTTLE VALVE

TORQUE CONVERTER

SWITCH VALVE

TO LUBRICATION

COOLER

TO FRONT CLUTCH LUBRICATION

— OIL PRESSURES —

CONVERTER 5-83 PSI

LUBRICATION 5-30 PSI

LINE 83 PSI

PUMP SUCTION

THROTTLE 40 PSI

GOVERNOR 0-83 PSI

DRIVE (BREAKAWAY) HALF THROTTLE

PR2102

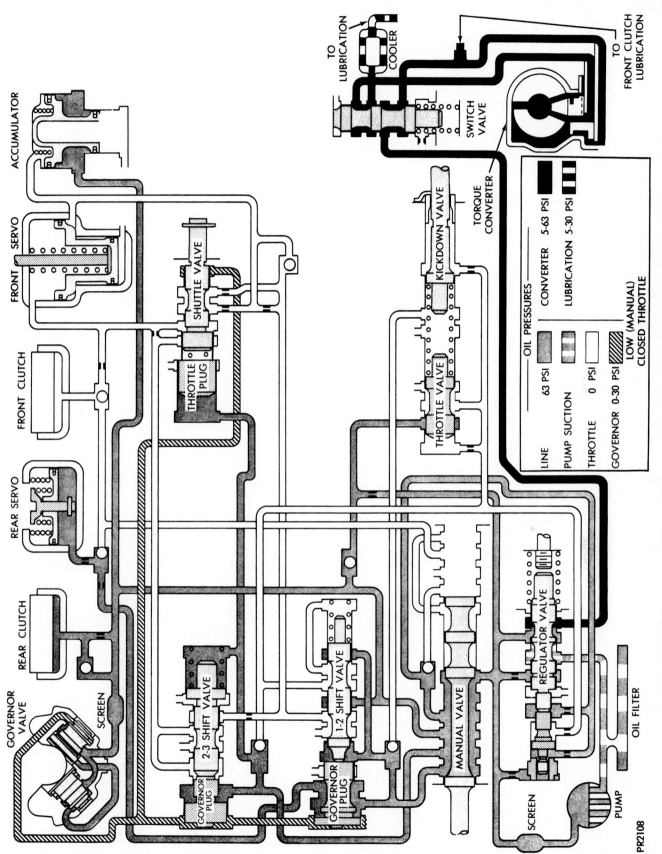

Figure 21-32. Manual Low Hydraulic Circuit. (*Courtesy of Chrysler Canada*)

425

Drive Second

When the vehicle reaches a certain speed in drive breakaway, governor pressure moves the governor plug and 1–2 shift valve against its spring tension and the throttle valve pressure. Movement of the 1–2 shift valve supplies fluid pressure from the manual valve through the 1–2 shift valve to the front servo and the upper end of the accumulator piston. This fluid pressure at the front servo applies the kickdown band, and fluid pressure is also supplied to the rear clutch. Fluid pressure above the accumulator piston assists the spring to move the piston downward, which cushions the band application.

The drive second hydraulic circuit is pictured in Figure 21-33.

If the manual second, or 2, gear selector position is selected, manual valve movement supplies fluid pressure to the right side of the 2–3 shift valve governor plug. This action prevents a 2–3 transaxle upshift.

Drive Direct

When a specific vehicle speed and throttle opening are reached, governor pressure moves the 2–3 shift valve and governor plug against the spring tension and throttle pressure. This movement supplies fluid pressure from the manual valve through the 1–2 shift valve, and the 2–3 shift valve to the front clutch. Since both clutches are applied, the transaxle is in direct drive, or high. The same fluid pressure is supplied to the front clutch and the top of the front servo piston. This pressure assists the servo piston spring to force the piston downward, which releases the kickdown band.

Fluid pressure under the front servo piston is relieved through the shuttle valve to the circuit between the shift valves. The shuttle valve and line restrictions control the speed of pressure release, and thus control shift quality. Governor pressure is applied to the right side of the shuttle valve, whereas throttle pressure is applied to the throttle plug in the shuttle valve bore.

The direct drive hydraulic circuit is illustrated in Figure 21-34.

Kickdown

The kickdown valve is operated by a cable connected to the throttle linkage. A spring is connected between the kickdown valve and the throttle valve. When the throttle is opened, the kickdown valve is moved to the left, which increases the spring pressure and also moves the throttle valve to the left. Line pressure is supplied to the throttle valve, and throttle pressure is supplied from the throttle valve to the pressure regulator valve, shift valves, and the shuttle valve throttle plug.

When the engine is idling, throttle pressure is low. As the throttle is opened and the kickdown valve and throttle valve move to the left, throttle pressure increases. Full throttle pressure is obtained when the throttle valve is moved to the left end of its bore.

Since throttle pressure is applied to one of the pressure regulator valve lands, this pressure moves the pressure regulator valve to increase line pressure as throttle opening increases. The throttle pressure supplied to the shift valves delays the upshifts at wider throttle openings.

When the vehicle is operating at moderate speed in direct drive, if the throttle is opened beyond a specific point, throttle pressure forces the 2–3 shift valve to the left against the governor pressure. This movement shuts off fluid pressure from the front clutch and supplies fluid pressure to the front servo, which results in a 3–2 kickdown into second. Under this condition the fluid pressure from the front clutch is exhausted past the check ball below the clutch and the manual valve, as indicated in Figure 21-35.

At higher vehicle speeds, the throttle pressure cannot overcome governor pressure on the 2–3 shift valve, and thus a 3–2 kickdown is not available.

If the vehicle is operating at low speed and the throttle is moved to the wide-open position, throttle pressure moves the kickdown valve to the left directly against the throttle valve. This action directs throttle pressure past the kickdown valve to the right end of the 1–2 shift valve. Below a specific speed, throttle pressure overcomes governor pressure on the 1–2 shift valve, which results in a wide-open throttle kickdown into drive breakaway, or low.

Reverse

When the gear selector moves the manual valve to the reverse position, fluid pressure is supplied from the manual valve to the rear servo and the front clutch, which provides reverse operation. Fluid pressure from the manual valve to the left end of the pressure regulator valve is shut off. Therefore, the spring and throttle pressure moves the pressure regulator valve to the left, which restricts fluid return

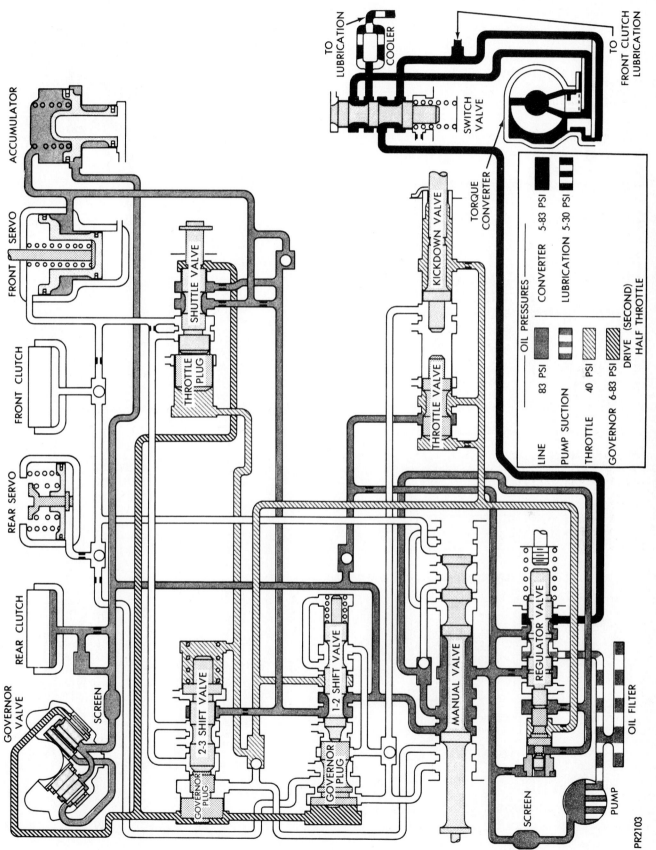

Figure 21-33. Drive Second Hydraulic Circuit. (*Courtesy of Chrysler Canada*)

427

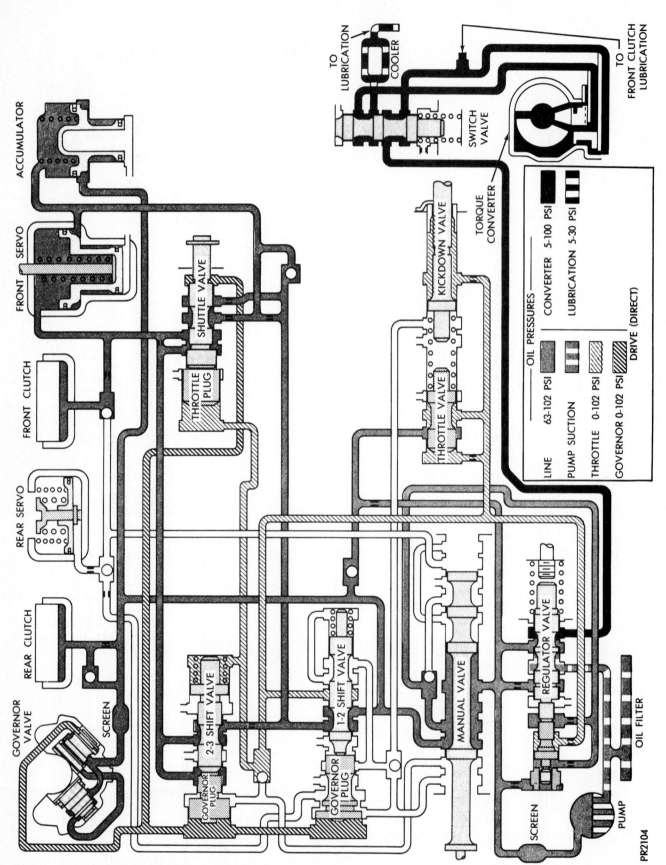

Figure 21-34. Drive Direct Hydraulic Circuit. (*Courtesy of Chrysler Canada*)

428

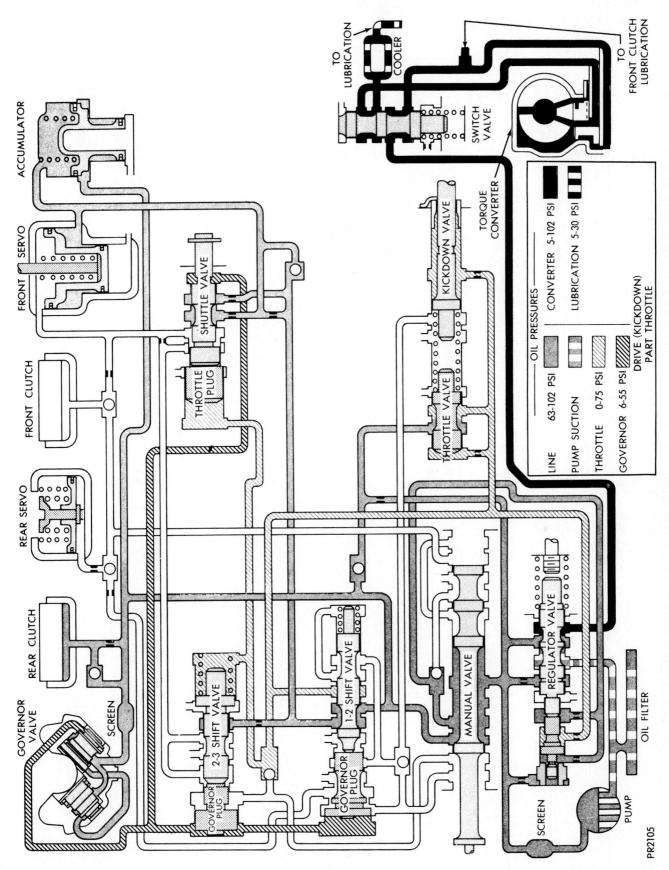

Figure 21-35. Drive Kickdown Part-Throttle Hydraulic Circuit. *(Courtesy of Chrysler Canada)*

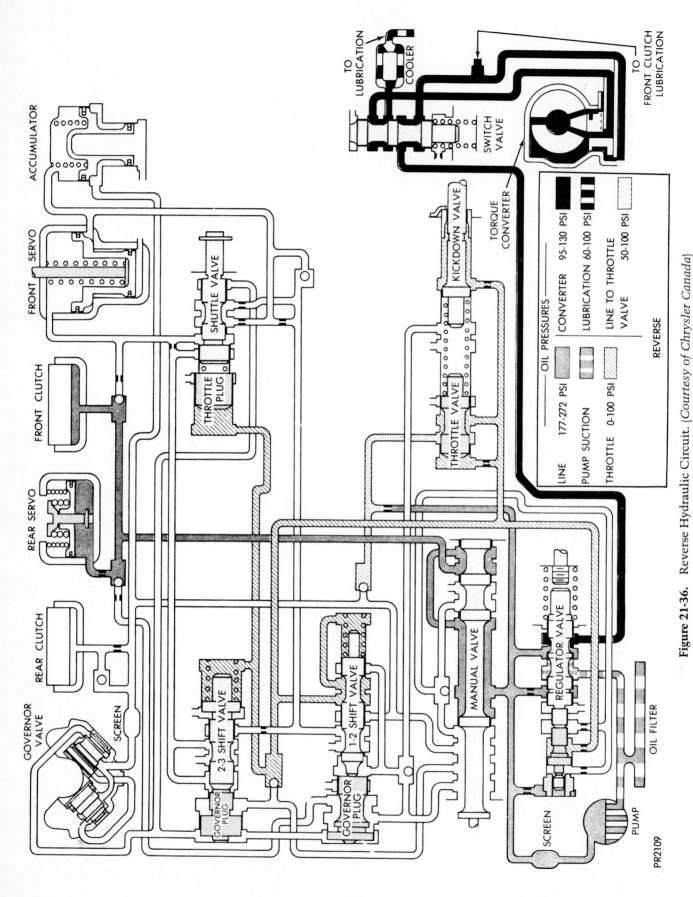

Figure 21-36. Reverse Hydraulic Circuit. *(Courtesy of Chrysler Canada)*

ACCUMULATOR

FRONT SERVO

FRONT CLUTCH

REAR SERVO

REAR CLUTCH

GOVERNOR VALVE

SCREEN

SHUTTLE VALVE

THROTTLE PLUG

2-3 SHIFT VALVE

GOVERNOR PLUG

1-2 SHIFT VALVE

GOVERNOR PLUG

MANUAL VALVE

REGULATOR VALVE

SCREEN

OIL FILTER

PUMP

KICKDOWN VALVE

THROTTLE VALVE

TORQUE CONVERTER

SWITCH VALVE

COOLER

TO LUBRICATION

TO FRONT CLUTCH LUBRICATION

OIL PRESSURES

LINE	177-272 PSI	CONVERTER 95-130 PSI
PUMP SUCTION		LUBRICATION 60-100 PSI
THROTTLE 0-100 PSI		LINE TO THROTTLE VALVE 50-100 PSI

REVERSE

PR2109

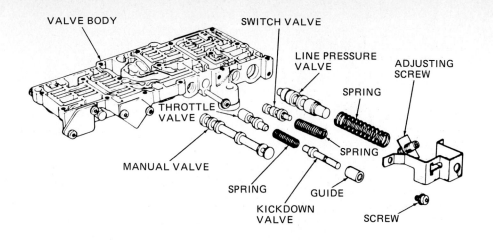

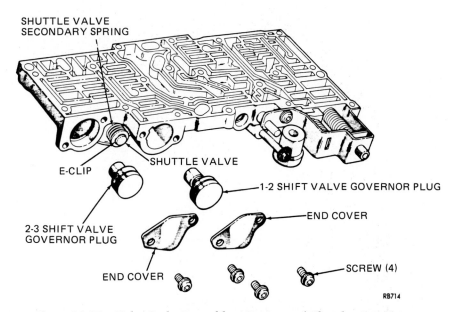

Figure 21-37. Valve Body Assembly. (*Courtesy of Chrysler Canada*)

to the reservoir and increases line pressure, as shown in Figure 21-36.

A valve body assembly and some of the valves are shown in Figure 21-37. Location of the steel check balls in the valve body is pictured in Figure 21-38.

The hydraulic circuits illustrated in this chapter are from a Chrysler automatic transaxle. Other transaxles or transmissions have similar hydraulic circuits, but differences are found in each make.

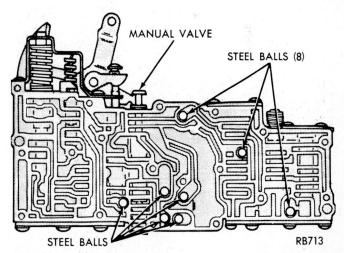

Figure 21-38. Steel Check Ball Location in Valve Body. (*Courtesy of Chrysler Canada*)

Four-Speed Automatic Transmission Clutch and Band Application

Drive Range First Gear

Many rear-wheel-drive vehicles are equipped with a four-speed automatic overdrive transmission, and some front-wheel-drive cars have a four-speed automatic overdrive transaxle. This type of transmission or transaxle allows the engine to run at lower rpm in the overdrive range, which improves fuel economy.

In the General Motors Hydra-matic THM 700-

R4 transmission, the forward clutch steel plates are tanged to the input housing and the composition face plates are splined to the forward clutch outer race. When the forward clutch is applied, a clutch piston in the input housing supplies pressure to the clutch plates. An input shaft is splined to the input housing and the converter turbine. The forward clutch is used to connect and disconnect power input from the torque converter to the transmission gear train.

A forward clutch assembly is illustrated in Figure 21-39.

An input roller clutch is connected between the forward clutch and the input sun gear. As mentioned previously, the forward clutch composition plates are splined to the input roller clutch outer race. The input roller clutch cam is splined to the input sun gear. When the forward clutch is applied, the input roller clutch forces the input sun gear to rotate as fast as the input housing. However, when needed, the roller clutch will allow the sun gear to rotate faster than the input housing.

In drive range first gear, the forward clutch is applied and the engine torque is supplied through this clutch and the input roller clutch to the sun gear. The input internal gear is connected to the reaction carrier in the reaction gear set, and the low roller clutch prevents these two components from turning counterclockwise. Therefore, engine torque is applied from the input sun gear to the input carrier and the output shaft. Since the smaller sun gear is driving the input carrier, a gear reduction of approximately 3.06:1 is provided.

Drive range first gear operation is shown in Figure 21-40.

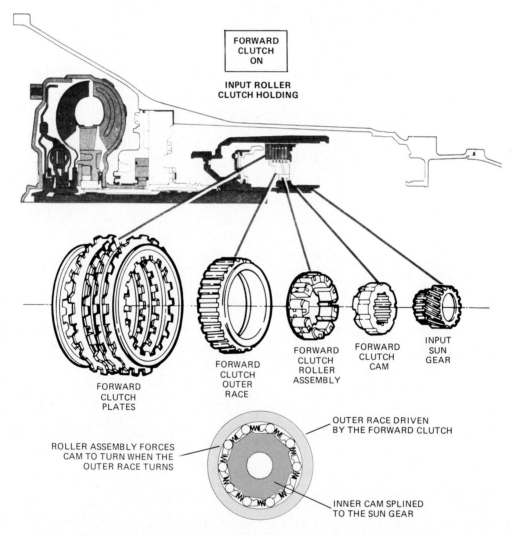

Figure 21-39. Forward Clutch Assembly. (*Courtesy of Hydra-matic Division of General Motors Corporation*)

DRIVE RANGE - FIRST GEAR

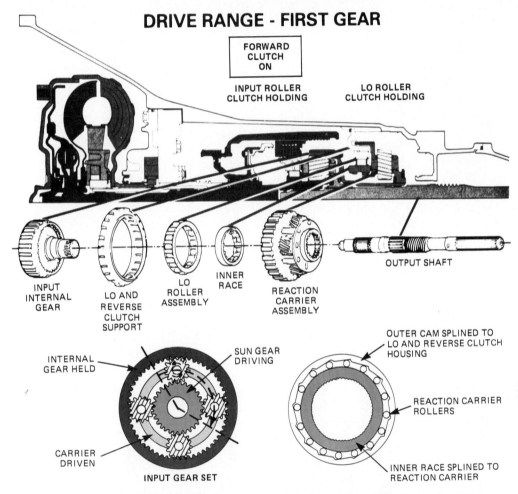

Figure 21-40. Drive Range First Gear Operation. (*Courtesy of Hydra-matic Division of General Motors Corporation*)

Drive Range Second Gear

In drive range second gear, the 2–4 band is applied with the forward clutch. The reaction sun shell is splined to the reaction sun gear. This shell is also connected to the reverse input drum. When the 2–4 band is applied, the reverse input drum, reaction sun shell, and the reaction sun gear are locked. Engine torque is transmitted through the forward clutch and input roller clutch to the input sun gear. The input carrier is driven in reduction and transmits torque to the output shaft and reaction internal gear. Clockwise rotation of the reaction internal gear drives the reaction carrier and pinion gears to rotate clockwise around the stationary reaction sun gear. Since the smaller reaction internal gear is driving the larger reaction carrier, a gear reduction of 1.44:1 is provided.

When studying the operation of this transmis-

sion, remember that the input sun gear and the reaction sun gear are two separate gears.

Drive second operation is illustrated in Figure 21-41.

Drive Range Third Gear

In drive range third gear, the forward clutch and the 3–4 clutch are applied. The forward clutch composition plates are splined to the input roller clutch and sun gear, whereas the 3–4 clutch composition plates are splined to the input internal gear. Since both of these clutch input housings are splined to the input shaft, the input internal gear and the input planet carrier are locked together when both clutches are applied. This locking action causes the input gear set to rotate as a unit with a 1:1 direct drive ratio, as shown in Figure 21-42.

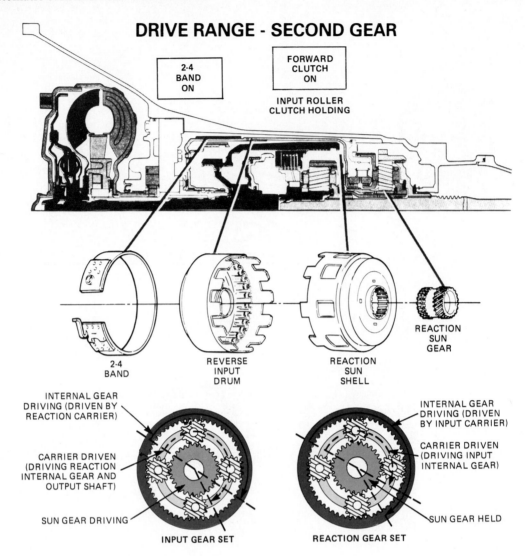

DRIVE RANGE - SECOND GEAR

| 2-4 BAND ON | FORWARD CLUTCH ON |

INPUT ROLLER CLUTCH HOLDING

2-4 BAND

REVERSE INPUT DRUM

REACTION SUN SHELL

REACTION SUN GEAR

INTERNAL GEAR DRIVING (DRIVEN BY REACTION CARRIER)

CARRIER DRIVEN (DRIVING REACTION INTERNAL GEAR AND OUTPUT SHAFT)

SUN GEAR DRIVING

INPUT GEAR SET

INTERNAL GEAR DRIVING (DRIVEN BY INPUT CARRIER)

CARRIER DRIVEN (DRIVING INPUT INTERNAL GEAR)

SUN GEAR HELD

REACTION GEAR SET

Figure 21-41. Drive Range Second Gear Operation. (*Courtesy of Hydra-matic Division of General Motors Corporation*)

Drive Range Overdrive

In overdrive, the forward clutch, 3–4 clutch, and 2–4 clutch band are applied. Engine torque is transmitted from the input shaft through the 3–4 clutch to the input internal gear and the reaction planet carrier. The 2–4 band application locks the reaction sun gear. Under this condition torque is transmitted through the reaction planet carrier, which drives the reaction internal gear and output shaft, since the reaction sun gear is locked. When the larger reaction planet carrier drives the smaller reaction internal gear, an overdrive ratio of .70:1 is provided, as illustrated in Figure 21-43.

In overdrive, the input carrier drives the input sun gear faster than the input housing, because the input carrier is connected to the output shaft. Under this condition the input roller clutch overruns and the input gear set is ineffective.

Reverse

When reverse is selected, the reverse input clutch and the low-reverse clutch are applied. The low-reverse clutch holds the reaction planet carrier stationary. Engine torque is transmitted through the reverse input clutch and the reverse input drum to the

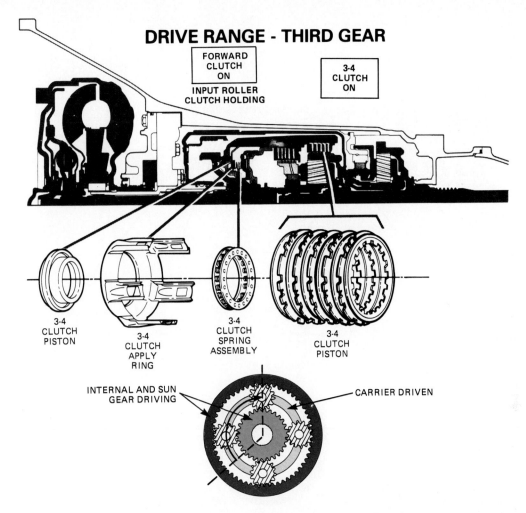

Figure 21-42.   Drive Range Third Gear Operation. (*Courtesy of Hydra-matic Division of General Motors Corporation*)

reaction sun gear, and this gear rotates in clockwise direction. Since the reaction planet carrier is locked, the reaction sun gear drives the reaction internal gear and output shaft counterclockwise, as shown in Figure 21-44.

Manual Third

In manual third gear, the overrun clutch is applied with the forward clutch and the 3–4 clutch. This action prevents the input roller clutch from overrunning, which prevents a 3–4 upshift. In manual third gear, engine braking is provided in first, second, or third gears, because the input carrier cannot turn faster than the input sun gear with the overrun clutch applied.

Manual third operation is shown in Figure 21-45.

(An explanation of automatic transaxle service is provided in Chapter 17 of *Automatic Principles: Repair and Service*, Volume II.)

Test Questions

1. A torque converter multiplies torque when the stator is freewheeling.   T F
2. The overrunning clutch is connected between the stator and the _____ _____ in the torque converter.
3. In planetary gear set, if the planet carrier is held with the sun gear as the input and the annulus gear as the output, a:

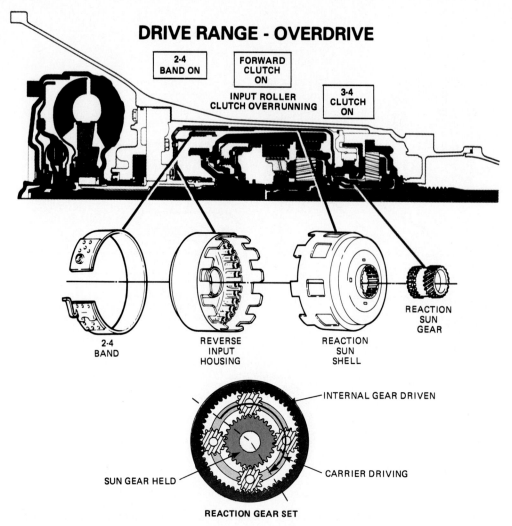

DRIVE RANGE - OVERDRIVE

2-4 BAND ON

FORWARD CLUTCH ON

INPUT ROLLER CLUTCH OVERRUNNING

3-4 CLUTCH ON

2-4 BAND

REVERSE INPUT HOUSING

REACTION SUN SHELL

REACTION SUN GEAR

INTERNAL GEAR DRIVEN

SUN GEAR HELD

CARRIER DRIVING

REACTION GEAR SET

Figure 21-43. Drive Range Overdrive Operation. (*Courtesy of Hydra-matic Division of General Motors Corporation*)

a) forward gear reduction is provided.

b) reverse gear reduction is provided.

c) 1:1 forward gear ratio is provided.

4. In a planetary gear set, if the sun gear is held with the planet carrier as the input and the annulus gear as the output, a:

a) forward gear reduction is provided.

b) reverse overdrive gear ratio is provided.

c) forward overdrive gear ratio is provided.

5. When the transaxle is in drive breakaway, the:

a) rear clutch is applied.

b) front clutch is applied.

c) low-reverse band is applied.

6. If both front and rear clutches are applied, the transaxle will be in:

a) reverse.

b) drive second.

c) drive direct.

7. A transaxle 1–2 upshift occurs when _____ pressure overcomes _____ pressure on the 1–2 shift valve.

8. A 3–2 downshift may be obtained when the transaxle is in drive direct, regardless of vehicle speed.

T F

9. In the General Motors Hydra-matic 700-R4 transmission, list three components applied in overdrive.

REVERSE

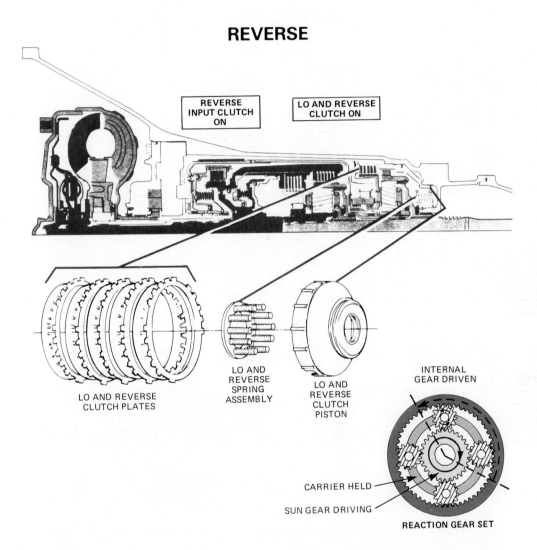

Figure 21-44. Reverse Operation. (*Courtesy of Hydra-matic Division of General Motors Corporation*)

MANUAL THIRD

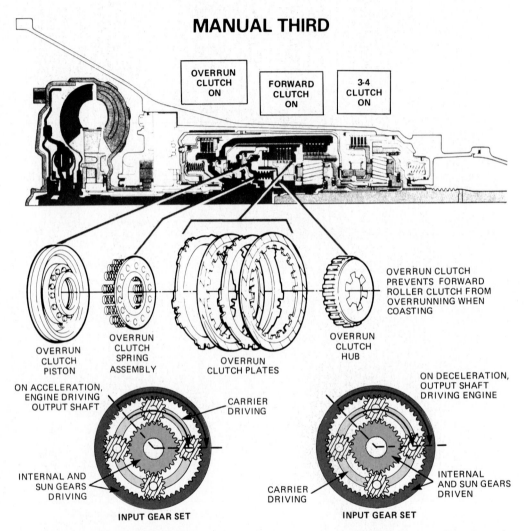

| OVERRUN CLUTCH ON | FORWARD CLUTCH ON | 3-4 CLUTCH ON |

OVERRUN CLUTCH PISTON

OVERRUN CLUTCH SPRING ASSEMBLY

OVERRUN CLUTCH PLATES

OVERRUN CLUTCH HUB

OVERRUN CLUTCH PREVENTS FORWARD ROLLER CLUTCH FROM OVERRUNNING WHEN COASTING

ON ACCELERATION, ENGINE DRIVING OUTPUT SHAFT

CARRIER DRIVING

ON DECELERATION, OUTPUT SHAFT DRIVING ENGINE

INTERNAL AND SUN GEARS DRIVING

CARRIER DRIVING

INTERNAL AND SUN GEARS DRIVEN

INPUT GEAR SET

INPUT GEAR SET

Figure 21-45. Manual Third Gear Operation. (*Courtesy of Hydra-matic Division of General Motors Corporation*)

22

Four-Wheel-Drive Systems

Chapter Completion Objectives

1. Understand four-wheel (4W) drive systems.
2. Indicate a knowledge of transfer cases.

3. Show an understanding of front drive axle hubs.
4. Display a knowledge of electronically controlled 4W drive systems.

Four-Wheel-Drive Components

Complete System

In a 4W drive system, a front drive axle drives the front wheels and a conventional rear axle drives the rear wheels. A transfer case transfers engine torque from the transmission to the front and rear axles. Conventional drive shafts are connected between the transfer case and the front and rear drive axles.

A front drive axle is shown in Figure 22-1, and a complete 4W drive system is illustrated in Figure 22-2.

Transfer Case

The transfer case input shaft is connected to the output shaft from the transmission. A planetary gear set connected to the input shaft enables the transfer case to provide a gear reduction. One output shaft is connected to the rear drive axle, and a second output shaft is connected to the front drive axle. A drive chain is connected from a drive sprocket on the rear axle output shaft to a driven sprocket on the front

axle output shaft. Shifter forks are connected to the planetary gear set and a synchronizer assembly on the rear axle output shaft. Some transfer cases have a lockup clutch in place of the synchronizer assembly. The input shaft and output shafts are mounted on bearings in the transfer case.

A complete transfer case is shown in Figure 22-3.

Transfer Case Power Flow in Neutral When the transfer case is in neutral, the shifting mechanism positions the members of the planetary gear set so that they are disconnected from the rear axle output shaft. Therefore, this gear set can rotate without transmitting torque to the output shafts, as indicated in Figure 22-4.

Transfer Case Power Flow in High-Range Two-Wheel Drive In high-range two-wheel (2W) drive (2H), the shifter fork moves the planet carrier rearward, so the planetary gears are locked to the planetary gear cage. This action prevents rotation of the planetary pinion gears on their axes, and the entire gear set must now turn as a unit. This provides a 1:1 gear ratio. The other shifter fork is positioned so the lockup clutch is disconnected. Therefore, torque is not transferred from the drive sprocket through the

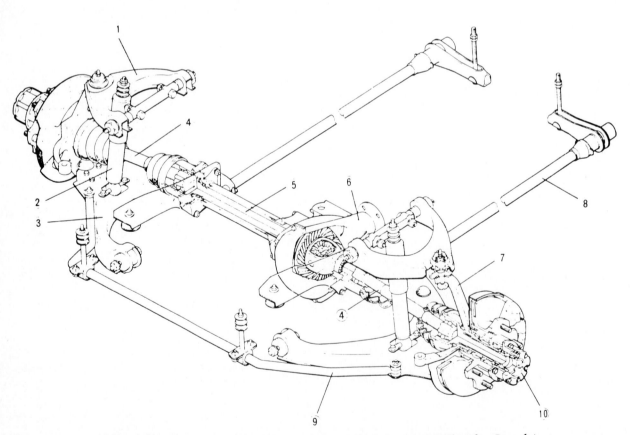

Figure 22-1. Front Drive Axle, 4W Drive System. *(Courtesy of Chrysler Canada)*

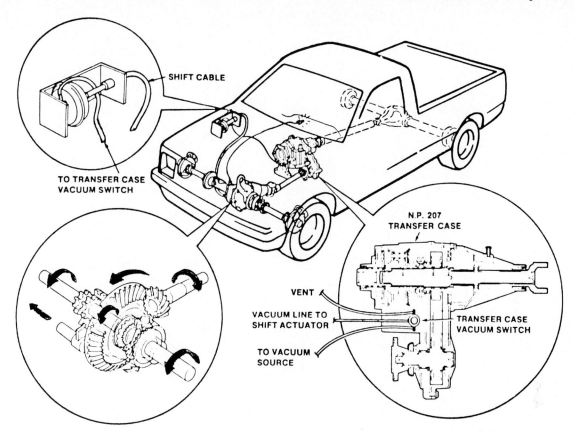

Figure 22-2. Complete 4W Drive System. *(Courtesy of Chevrolet Motor Division, General Motors Corporation)*

drive chain to the driven sprocket on the front axle output shaft.

The 2H transfer case power flow is illustrated in Figure 22-5.

Transfer Case Power Flow in High-Range 4W Drive In high-range 4W drive (4H), the planetary gear set remains in the same position as it does in 2H. However, in 4H the rear shifter fork moves the lockup clutch so the drive sprocket is connected to the rear axle output shaft. Therefore, torque is transmitted from the drive sprocket through the drive chain to the driven sprocket and front axle output shaft, so that engine torque drives the front and rear wheels.

The 4H transfer case power flow is illustrated in Figure 22-6.

Transfer Case Power Flow in Low-Range 4W Drive In low-range 4W drive (4L), the lockup clutch remains engaged, but the front shifter fork moves the planet carrier and annulus gear forward until the annulus gear is connected to the locking plate. When this occurs, the power flow is from the input shaft through the sun gear and planetary pinion gears to both output shafts. Since the smaller sun gear is driving the larger planet carrier, a gear reduction is provided.

The 4L transfer case power flow is illustrated in Figure 22-7.

Full-Time Transfer Case A differential assembly is located in the rear axle output shaft in the full-time transfer case. In this type of transfer case, gear reduction is provided by conventional gears rather than a planetary gear set. In the normal low or high ranges, the power flow goes through the differential assembly. Therefore, the front and rear wheels may rotate independently of each other if one wheel is on a slippery surface.

In either low or high range, the four-wheel-drive gear selector may be located in the lock position. This action locks the differential so that the front and rear wheels cannot rotate independently of each other. A gear shaft pattern from this type of transfer case is shown in Figure 22-8, and a full-time transfer case is illustrated in Figure 22-9.

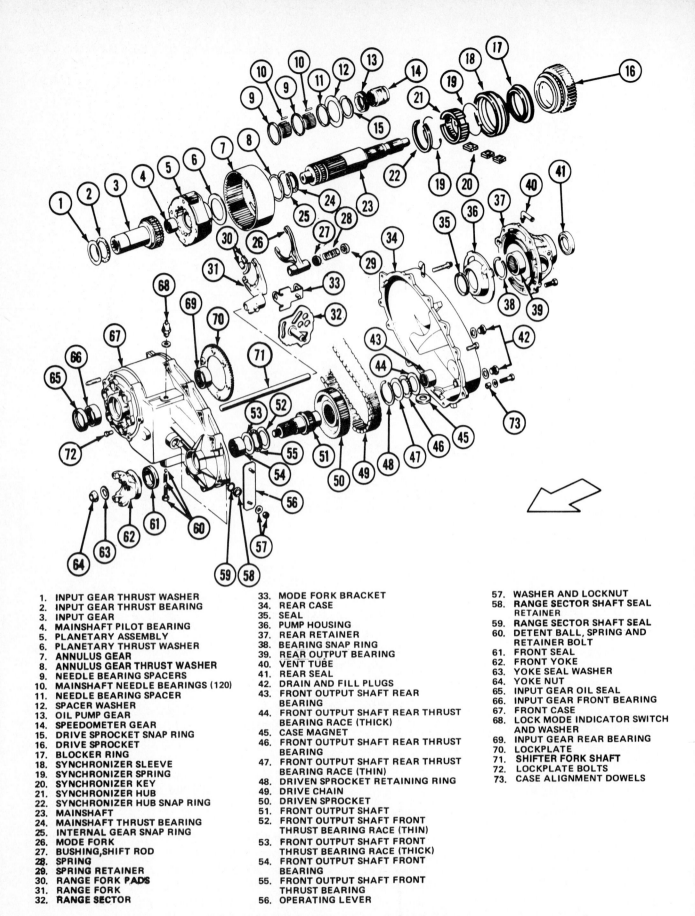

1. INPUT GEAR THRUST WASHER
2. INPUT GEAR THRUST BEARING
3. INPUT GEAR
4. MAINSHAFT PILOT BEARING
5. PLANETARY ASSEMBLY
6. PLANETARY THRUST WASHER
7. ANNULUS GEAR
8. ANNULUS GEAR THRUST WASHER
9. NEEDLE BEARING SPACERS
10. MAINSHAFT NEEDLE BEARINGS (120)
11. NEEDLE BEARING SPACER
12. SPACER WASHER
13. OIL PUMP GEAR
14. SPEEDOMETER GEAR
15. DRIVE SPROCKET SNAP RING
16. DRIVE SPROCKET
17. BLOCKER RING
18. SYNCHRONIZER SLEEVE
19. SYNCHRONIZER SPRING
20. SYNCHRONIZER KEY
21. SYNCHRONIZER HUB
22. SYNCHRONIZER HUB SNAP RING
23. MAINSHAFT
24. MAINSHAFT THRUST BEARING
25. INTERNAL GEAR SNAP RING
26. MODE FORK
27. BUSHING, SHIFT ROD
28. SPRING
29. SPRING RETAINER
30. RANGE FORK PADS
31. RANGE FORK
32. RANGE SECTOR

33. MODE FORK BRACKET
34. REAR CASE
35. SEAL
36. PUMP HOUSING
37. REAR RETAINER
38. BEARING SNAP RING
39. REAR OUTPUT BEARING
40. VENT TUBE
41. REAR SEAL
42. DRAIN AND FILL PLUGS
43. FRONT OUTPUT SHAFT REAR
    BEARING
44. FRONT OUTPUT SHAFT REAR THRUST
    BEARING RACE (THICK)
45. CASE MAGNET
46. FRONT OUTPUT SHAFT REAR THRUST
    BEARING
47. FRONT OUTPUT SHAFT REAR THRUST
    BEARING RACE (THIN)
48. DRIVEN SPROCKET RETAINING RING
49. DRIVE CHAIN
50. DRIVEN SPROCKET
51. FRONT OUTPUT SHAFT
52. FRONT OUTPUT SHAFT FRONT
    THRUST BEARING RACE (THIN)
53. FRONT OUTPUT SHAFT FRONT
    THRUST BEARING RACE (THICK)
54. FRONT OUTPUT SHAFT FRONT
    BEARING
55. FRONT OUTPUT SHAFT FRONT
    THRUST BEARING
56. OPERATING LEVER

57. WASHER AND LOCKNUT
58. RANGE SECTOR SHAFT SEAL
    RETAINER
59. RANGE SECTOR SHAFT SEAL
60. DETENT BALL, SPRING AND
    RETAINER BOLT
61. FRONT SEAL
62. FRONT YOKE
63. YOKE SEAL WASHER
64. YOKE NUT
65. INPUT GEAR OIL SEAL
66. INPUT GEAR FRONT BEARING
67. FRONT CASE
68. LOCK MODE INDICATOR SWITCH
    AND WASHER
69. INPUT GEAR REAR BEARING
70. LOCKPLATE
71. SHIFTER FORK SHAFT
72. LOCKPLATE BOLTS
73. CASE ALIGNMENT DOWELS

Figure 22-3. Complete Transfer Case. (*Courtesy of Chevrolet Motor Division, General Motors Corporation*)

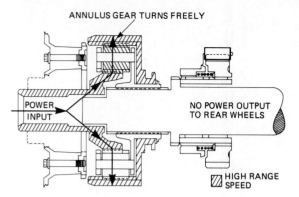

Figure 22-4. Transfer Case Power Flow in Neutral. *(Courtesy of Ford Motor Co.)*

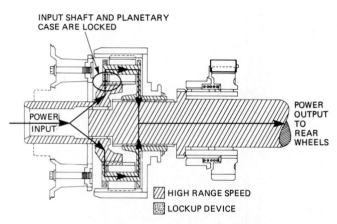

Figure 22-5. Transfer Case Power Flow in High-Range 2W Drive. *(Courtesy of Ford Motor Co.)*

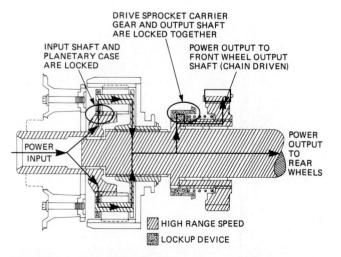

Figure 22-6. Transfer Case Power Flow in High-Range 4W Drive. *(Courtesy of Ford Motor Co.)*

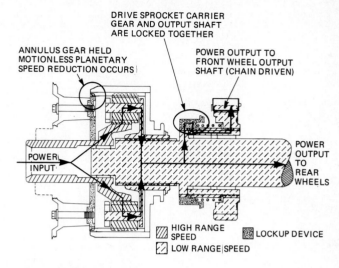

Figure 22-7. Transfer Case Power Flow in Low-Range 4W Drive. *(Courtesy of Ford Motor Co.)*

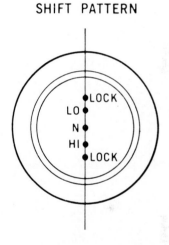

SHIFT PATTERN

Figure 22-8. Gear Shift Pattern, Full-Time Transfer Case. *(Courtesy of Ford Motor Co.)*

Front Drive Axle Hubs

Freewheeling Front Drive Axle Hubs

The freewheeling front hubs allow the hubs to be disconnected from the front axles during 2W drive operation to reduce torque loss. When the hub control handle is turned to the "lock" position, the follower moves along a groove in the control handle until the clutch fits the inner hub splines. Since the clutch is always in mesh with the freewheeling hub body, the clutch then connects the drive axle to the freewheeling hub, as illustrated in Figure 22-10.

If the hub control handle is turned to the "free" position, the follower moves along the control han-

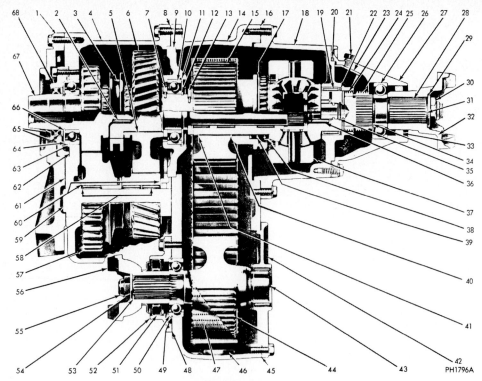

Fig. 1—203 Transfer Case—Cross Section View

LEGEND FOR FIG. 1

1. Adapter
2. Input Drive Gear Pilot Bearings
3. Range Selector Sliding Clutch
4. Range Selector Housing
5. Low Speed Gear Bushing
6. Low Speed Gear
7. Thrust Washer and Locating Pin
8. Gasket, Range Selector Housing to Intermediate Housing
9. Input Bearing Retainer
10. Input Bearing
11. Input Bearing Retaining Ring (Large)
12. Input Bearing Retaining Ring (Small)
13. Thrust Washer, Locating Pin, Lubricating Washer and Retaining Ring
14. Intermediate (Chain) Housing
15. Drive Shaft Sprocket
16. Gasket, Intermediate Housing to Differential Housing
17. Sliding Lock Clutch
18. Differential Housing
19. Rear Output Front Bearing
20. "O" Ring, Differential Housing to Rear Output Shaft Housing
21. Vent

22. Oil Seal, Rear Output Front Bearing
23. Oil Seal, Vent
24. Oil Pump
25. Speedometer Drive Gear
26. Rear Output Rear Bearing
27. Rear Output Shaft Housing
28. Rear Output Shaft
29. Washer, Rear Output
30. Nut, Rear Output
31. Rubber Washer, Rear Output
32. Rear Output Yoke
33. Oil Seal, Rear Output Bearing
34. Shim Pack
35. Input Shaft "O" Ring Seal
36. Input Shaft Roller Bearings
37. Differential Carrier Assembly
38. Spring Cup Washer
39. Lockout Clutch Spring
40. Rear Retaining Ring, Drive Shaft Sprocket
41. Front Retaining Ring, Drive Shaft Sprocket
42. Front Output Rear Bearing Cover
43. Front Output Rear Bearing
44. Front Output Drive Sprocket

45. Gasket, Front Output Rear Bearing Cover
46. Magnet
47. Drive Chain
48. Gasket, Front Output Bearing Retainer
49. Front Output Bearing Outer Retaining Ring
50. Front Output Bearing
51. Front Output Shaft Seal
52. Front Output Bearing Retainer
53. Rubber Spline Seal
54. Washer, Front Output
55. Nut, Front Output
56. Front Output Yoke
57. Countergear
58. Countergear Spacers and Bearings
59. Countergear Shaft
60. Countergear Thrust Washer
61. Gasket, Adapter to Selector Housing
62. Gasket, Input Bearing Retainer
63. Input Bearing Outer Ring
64. Input Gear Bearing
65. Input Gear Seals
66. Input Bearing Retaining Ring
67. Input Gear
68. Input Gear Bearing Retainer

Figure 22-9. Full-Time Transfer Case. *(Courtesy of Chrysler Canada)*

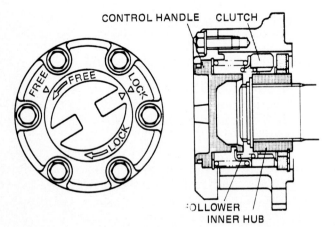

Figure 22-10. Freewheeling Front Hub in Locked Position. *(Courtesy of Chrysler Canada)*

dle groove until the clutch is disconnected from the inner hub splines. This action separates the freewheeling hub body from the drive axle, as indicated in Figure 22-11.

A complete disassembled freewheeling hub is illustrated in Figure 22-12.

Automatic Locking Front Drive Axle Hubs

In the "auto" position, the automatic locking mechanism provides a freewheeling hub for hard surface driving and automatically engages itself when four-wheel-drive is needed. The hub may be rotated manually to the "lock" position for off-road operation

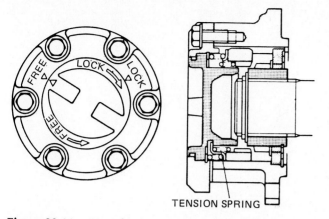

Figure 22-11. Freewheeling Front Hub in Free Position. *(Courtesy of Chrysler Canada)*

where continuous lockup on the front hubs is required.

An automatic locking front drive axle hub is shown in Figure 22-13.

Transfer Case Shift Controls

Electronic Shift Control

Some transfer cases are shifted with a gear shift and mechanical linkage. An electronically controlled shift mechanism is used on other models. The latter type of shift mechanism has a touch control panel in the roof console, as shown in Figure 22-14.

The 4 × 4 push button below the vehicle silhouette on the control panel selects either 2H or 4H positions, and the push button light is illuminated in 4H. The Low Range push button above the vehicle silhouette is used to select the 4L position, and the 4L light indicates this range selection. A shift in or out of low range can occur only when the automatic transmission in neutral and the vehicle is stopped or moving below 3 MPH. Vehicles equipped with manual transmissions will shift at less than 3 MPH with the clutch disengaged. Transfer case shifting is done by an electric motor which drives a rotary helical

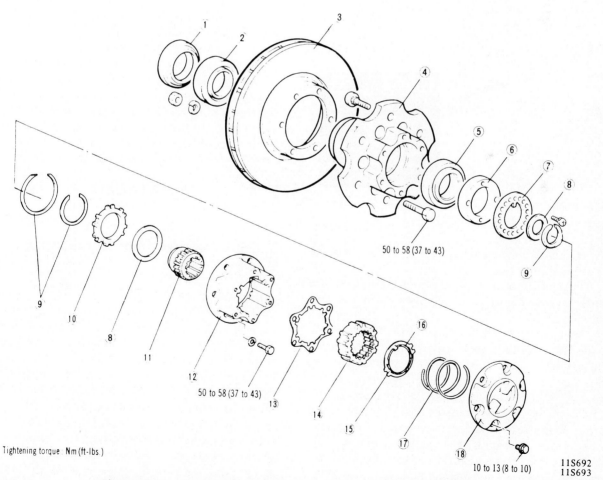

Tightening torque: Nm (ft-lbs.)

11S692
11S693

Figure 22-12. Freewheeling Front Hub. *(Courtesy of Chrysler Canada)*

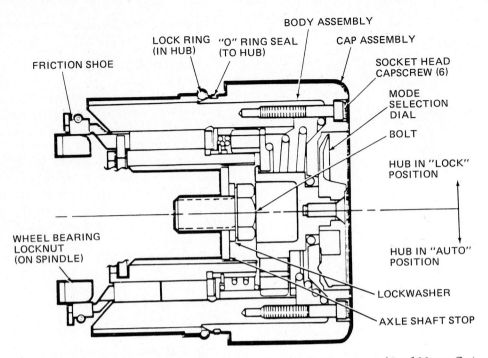

Figure 22-13. Automatic Locking Front Drive Axle Hub. *(Courtesy of Ford Motor Co.)*

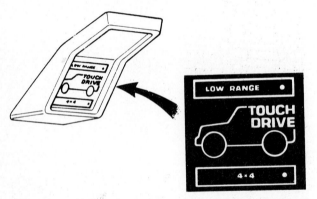

Figure 22-14. Touch Control for Electronic Shifter Mechanism. *(Courtesy of Ford Motor Co.)*

cam at the 2W–4W mode shift fork and the 4H–4L reduction shift fork.

The shift motor is shown removed from the transfer case in Figure 22-15 and installed on the case in Figure 22-16.

A magnetic clutch is located in the transfer case beside the 2W–4W mode shift collar. This clutch also enables the entire front drive system to spin up from zero to vehicle speed in milliseconds. When this occurs, the front drive axle system engages instantaneously. As the transfer case front and rear output shafts reach synchronous speed, the spring-loaded mode shift collar mechanically engages the mainshaft hub to the chain drive sprocket, and the magnetic clutch is then deactivated.

The magnetic clutch is shown in Figure 22-17.

Electronic Control System

The shift motor and the magnetic clutch are operated by the electronic control module. When the roof console buttons are touched, a signal is sent to the electronic control module, which operates the shift motor and the magnetic clutch to perform the requested command. A transfer case speed sensor sends a speed signal to the electronic control module.

The electronic shift control system is shown in Figure 22-18.

Vacuum-Operated Front Wheel Lockup System

Some 4W drive vehicles use a vacuum-operated lockup system on one front drive axle in place of locking hubs. This system is illustrated in Figure 22-2. When the vehicle is operating in 2W drive, the shift fork in the front drive axle positions a differential carrier connector so that the right front drive axle is disconnected from the right differential output shaft. Therefore, freewheeling is provided.

If the transfer case is shifted to 4W drive, the transfer case vacuum switch applies vacuum to the vacuum actuator, which operates the shift cable and moves the right front drive axle shift fork. This movement shifts the differential carrier connector

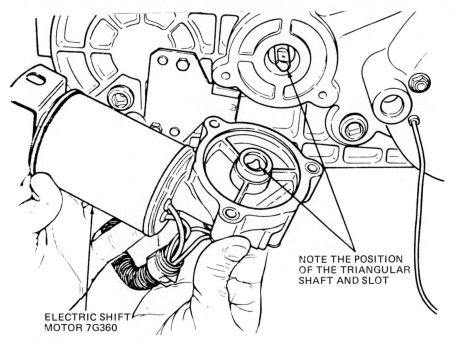

NOTE THE POSITION
OF THE TRIANGULAR
SHAFT AND SLOT

ELECTRIC SHIFT
MOTOR 7G360

Figure 22-15.   Shift Motor Removed from Transfer Case. *(Courtesy of Ford Motor Co.)*

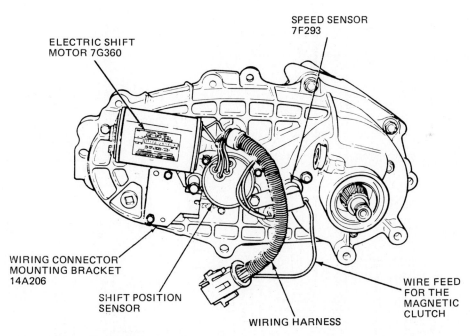

SPEED SENSOR
7F293

ELECTRIC SHIFT
MOTOR 7G360

WIRING CONNECTOR
MOUNTING BRACKET
14A206

SHIFT POSITION
SENSOR

WIRING HARNESS

WIRE FEED
FOR THE
MAGNETIC
CLUTCH

Figure 22-16.   Shift Motor Installed on Transfer Case. *(Courtesy of Ford Motor Co.)*

so that the differential output shaft is connected to the drive axle to provide front wheel lockup. The vacuum actuator will only move the shift fork under light-throttle, high-vacuum conditions. This type of 4W drive system has front drive axles and hubs sim- ilar to those used in front-wheel-drive cars. Flanges on the inner drive axle housing are bolted to match- ing flanges on the differential output shafts. (Refer to Chapter 18 in *Automotive Principles: Repair and Service*, Volume II, for 4W drive service.)

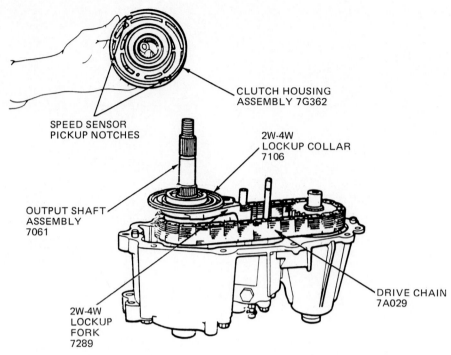

Figure 22-17.   Transfer Case Magnetic Clutch. *(Courtesy of Ford Motor Co.)*

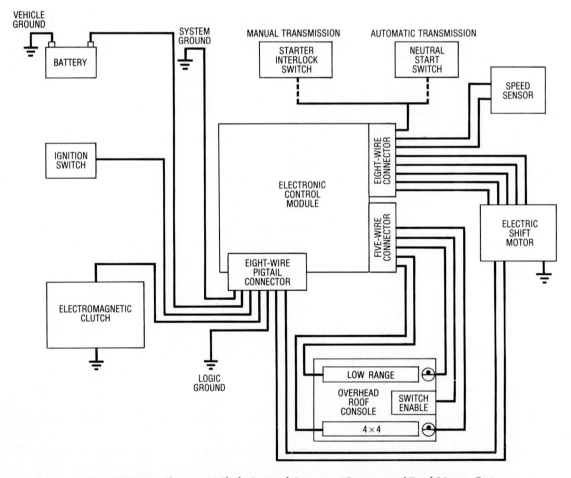

Figure 22-18.   Electronic Shift Control System. *(Courtesy of Ford Motor Co.)*

Test Questions

1. When the transfer case is operating in 4L, the sun gear is driving the:

    a) planet carrier.

    b) annulus gear.

    c) both the planet carrier and the annulus gear.

2. If the transfer case lockup clutch is engaged, the transfer case is in 4W drive.   T F

3. An automatic-locking front drive axle hub may be rotated to the "lock" position to provide continuous hub lockup.   T F

4. In an electronic shift control system, the magnetic clutch is operated by the:

    a) shift motor.

    b) speed sensor.

    c) electronic control module.

5. In an electronic shift control system with the automatic transmission in neutral, a shift to the 4L range can be done with the vehicle speed below:

    a) 3 MPH.

    b) 11 MPH.

    c) 20 MPH.

6. In a vacuum-operated front wheel lockup system, the vacuum actuator will shift the front axle to the lockup position when the engine is operating at _____ _____.

23

Suspension Systems and Wheel Alignment Theory

Chapter Completion Objectives

1. Understand various types of front suspension systems and explain the purpose of each system component.
2. Demonstrate a knowledge of different types of rear suspension systems and height control systems.
3. Indicate a knowledge of tire design and problems.
4. Explain these steering angles:

a) Steering axis inclination.

b) Scrub radius.

c) Caster.

d) Camber.

e) Toe.

f) Toe-out on turns.

g) Setback.

h) Thrust line.

Front Suspension

MacPherson-Type Suspension

Many front-wheel-drive vehicles have a Mac-Pherson-type front suspension. In this type of suspension, the upper end of the shock absorbing strut is attached to the upper fender reinforcement, and the lower end of the strut is bolted to the steering knuckle. The lower control arms are attached inboard to a crossmember and outboard to the steering knuckle through a ball joint to provide lower steering knuckle position. A pivot bearing at the upper end of the strut allows the strut and steering knuckle to turn as an assembly when the wheels are turned.

The components in the front suspension are illustrated in Figure 23-1.

Coil springs are located in an offset position around the strut. These springs are mounted between the strut lower spring seat and the upper strut mount. The top of each strut assembly is bolted to the upper fender reinforcement through rubber-isolated mounts. Two bolts are used to attach the lower end of the strut to the steering knuckle. One of these bolts may have an eccentric cam which provides camber adjustment.

Each steering knuckle is a single casting which has legs that are machined for attachment to the strut, steering arm, brake adaptor, and lower control arm ball joint. The knuckle also contains the front drive hub bearing.

The lower control arm is a stamping with an extended rear leg. A stub strut is riveted to this leg and attached to the crossmember through rubber bushings. The forward inner pivot is bolted to the cross-

1. FRONT SUSPENSION CROSSMEMBER
2. FRONT PIVOT BOLT
3. LOWER CONTROL ARM
4. SWAY ELIMINATOR SHAFT ASSEMBLY
5. LOWER ARM BALL JOINT ASSEMBLY
6. STEERING GEAR
7. TIE ROD ASSEMBLY
8. DRIVESHAFT
9. STEERING KNUCKLE
10. STRUT DAMPER ASSEMBLY
11. COIL SPRING
12. UPPER SPRING SEAT
13. REBOUND STOP
14. UPPER MOUNT ASSEMBLY
15. JOUNCE BUMPER
16. DUST SHIELD

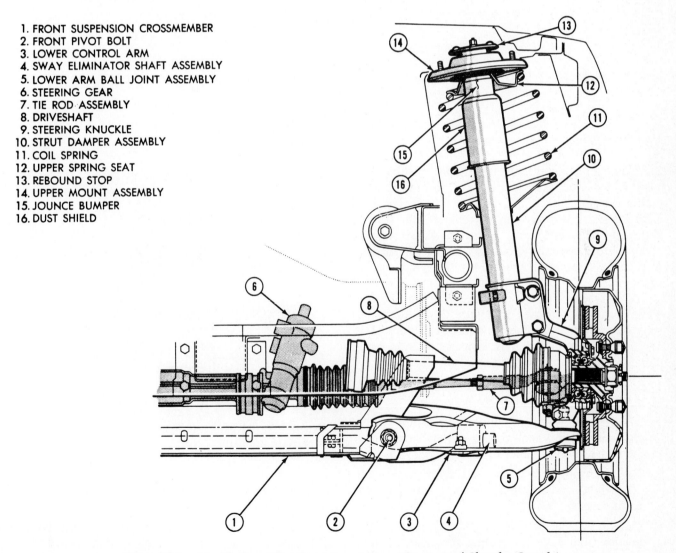

Figure 23-1. MacPherson Strut Front Suspension. (*Courtesy of Chrysler Canada*)

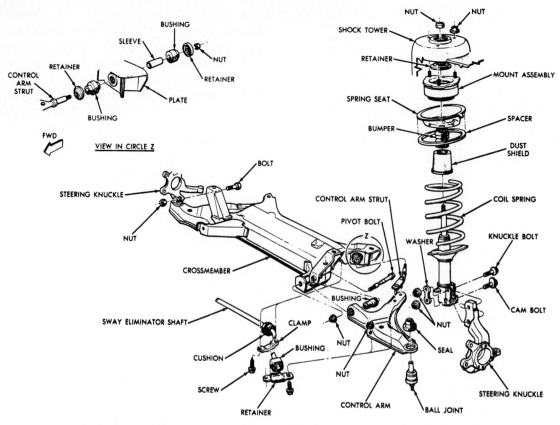

Figure 23-2. Front Suspension Disassembled. (*Courtesy of Chrysler Canada*)

member and isolated through rubber bushings. A non-tapered stud extends from the ball joint. This stud has a notch for clamp bolt clearance. The ball joint is pressed into the control arm, and the stud is clamped and locked into the steering knuckle with a clamp bolt. A rubber-isolated sway bar is used to interconnect the lower control arms on each side of the vehicle.

A disassembled view of the front suspension components is provided in Figure 23-2. An upper strut mount and bearing is illustrated in Figure 23-3.

The purpose of the main front suspension components may be summarized as follows:

1. *Lower control arms*—control lateral (side-to-side) movement of each front wheel.

2. *Stabilizer bar*—controls longitudinal movement (fore and aft) of wheels to reduce harshness when the wheels contact road surface irregularities.

3. *Coil springs*—allow proper setting of suspension ride heights and control suspension travel during driving maneuvers.

4. *Shock absorber struts*—provide necessary suspension damping and limit downward wheel movement with an internal rebound stop, and

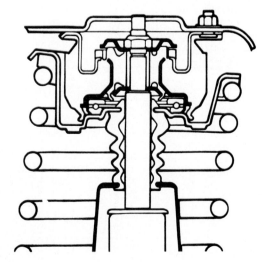

Figure 23-3. Upper Strut Mount and Bearing. (*Courtesy of Chrysler Canada*)

upward wheel movement with an external jounce bouncer.

5. *Strut upper mount*—insulates the strut and spring from the body and provides a bearing pivot for the strut and spring assembly.

6. *Ball joint*—connects the outer end of the lower control arm to the steering knuckle and acts as a pivot for the strut, spring, and knuckle assembly.

All suspension mounting points must be rubber-isolated to reduce the transfer of road noise and vibration from the suspension to the body and vehicle interior.

Torsion Bar Suspension

Some rear-wheel-drive cars have a front suspension system with transverse torsion bars which react on the outer ends of the lower control arms. Each torsion bar is anchored to the front crossmember on the opposite side of the vehicle from the lower control arm to which it is attached. A pivot cushion bushing is mounted around the torsion bar, and this bushing is bolted to the crossmember opposite to the torsion bar anchor. An isolating bushing is positioned on the end of the torsion bar where it is connected to the lower control arm.

Vehicle height is controlled by the torsion bar anchor adjusting bolts in the crossmember. Front suspension heights must be within specifications for correct wheel alignment, satisfactory tire wear, comfortable ride, and accurate bumper heights.

A conventional sway bar is connected between the lower control arms and the crossmember. Ball joints are located in the upper and lower control arms, and both ball joints are bolted into the steering knuckle. The shock absorbers are connected between the lower control arms and the crossmember support, as illustrated in Figure 23-4, and the inner ends of the lower control arms are bolted to the crossmember and pivot through a bushing.

Coil-Spring Suspension Systems

The front suspension systems on some rear-wheel-drive cars have coil springs positioned between the lower control arm and the spring housing on the frame. Spring seats are located in the lower control arm and the spring housing. The lower control arm is bolted to the frame through press-in bushings. A cross shaft is connected to the inner ends of the upper control arm through rubber isolating bushings and bolted to frame brackets. Ball joints are attached to the upper and lower control arms and bolted to the steering knuckle.

The shock absorbers are mounted inside the coil springs and connected from the lower control arms to the upper frame bracket. Rubber isolating bushings are located on each end of the shock absorber. Side roll of the front suspension is controlled by a steel stabilizer bar, which is mounted to the lower control arms and the frame with rubber bushings as shown in Figure 23-5.

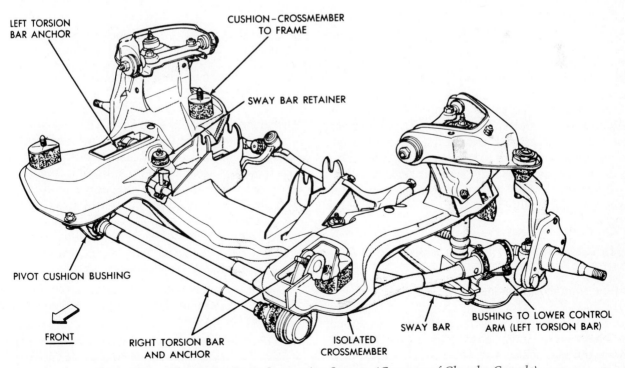

Figure 23-4. Torsion Bar Front Suspension System. (*Courtesy of Chrysler Canada*)

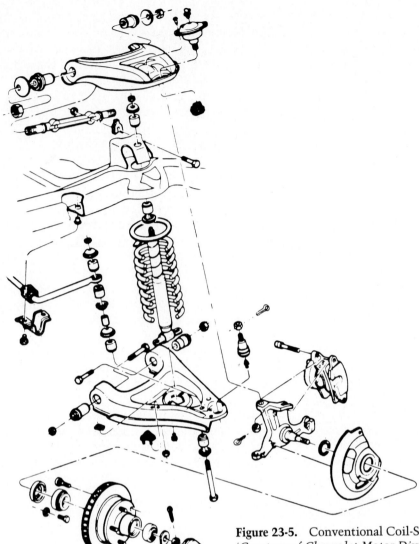

Figure 23-5. Conventional Coil-Spring Front Suspension System. *(Courtesy of Chevrolet Motor Division, General Motors Corporation)*

Modified MacPherson Strut Suspension

A modified MacPherson strut front suspension is used on some vehicles. This type of suspension has MacPherson struts with coil springs positioned between the lower control arms and the frame. The struts in these systems may be gas-filled or oil-filled.

A modified MacPherson strut front suspension system is pictured in Figure 23-6.

Rear Suspension

Independent Rear Suspension

Some front-wheel-drive vehicles have a modified MacPherson-type independent rear suspension. Each side of the rear suspension has a shock strut, lower control arm, tie rod, forged spindle, and a coil spring

mounted between the lower control arm and crossmember side rail.

A modified MacPherson-type independent rear suspension is pictured in Figure 23-7.

The shock strut has a rubber-isolated top mount with a one-piece jounce bouncer dust shield. This top mount is attached to the body side panel with a nut, and the lower end of the strut is bolted to the spindle. The stamped lower control arms are bolted to the crossmember and the spindle. A tie rod is connected from the spindle to the underbody.

The purpose of each rear suspension component may be summarized as follows:

1. *Stamped lower control arm*—controls the lateral (side-to-side) wheel movement, and contains the lower spring seat.

2. *Tie rod*—controls fore-and-aft wheel movement and positions the spindle to provide the rear suspension toe setting.

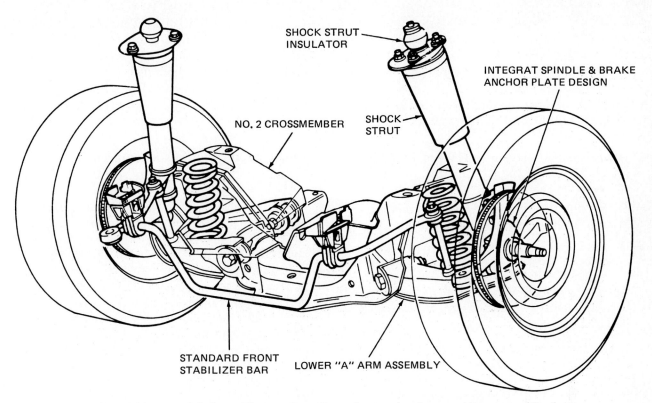

SHOCK STRUT
INSULATOR

INTEGRAT SPINDLE & BRAKE
ANCHOR PLATE DESIGN

NO. 2 CROSSMEMBER

SHOCK
STRUT

STANDARD FRONT
STABILIZER BAR

LOWER "A" ARM ASSEMBLY

Figure 23-6.   Modified MacPherson Strut Front Suspension System. (*Courtesy of Ford Motor Co.*)

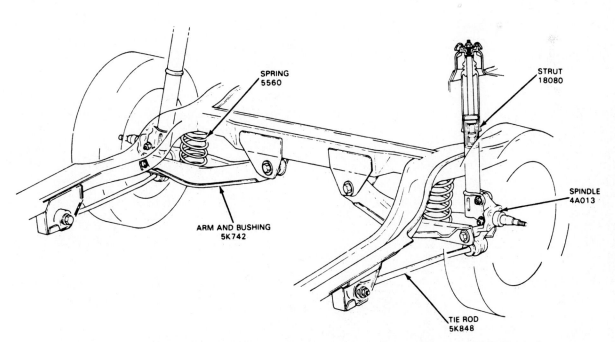

SPRING
5560

STRUT
18080

SPINDLE
4A013

ARM AND BUSHING
5K742

TIE ROD
5K848

Figure 23-7.   Modified MacPherson-Type Independent Rear Suspension. (*Courtesy of Ford Motor Co.*)

3. *Shock absorber strut*—reacts to braking forces and provides suspension damping. A strut internal rebound stop provides rebound control, and an external jounce bouncer supplies jounce control.

4. *Coil spring*—controls suspension travel, provides ride height control, and acts as a metal-to-metal jounce stop.

5. *Forged spindle*—supports the wheel bearings, and attaches to the lower control arms, tie rod, brake assembly and strut.

6. *Suspension bushings*—isolate road noise and vibration from the chassis and passenger compartment.

7. *Suspension fasteners*—connect components such as the spindle and strut. These fasteners must always be replaced with equivalent-quality parts, and each fastener must be tightened to the specified torque.

Some rear suspension systems have the coil springs mounted directly on the struts. A semi-independent rear suspension with this type of coil spring mounting is illustrated in Figure 23-8.

Some cars, such as Ford Taurus and Mercury Sable, have a MacPherson strut independent rear suspension with two parallel control arms on each side. A tension strut is connected between the spindle and knuckle assembly and the frame support, as shown in Figure 23-9.

Independent Rear Suspension with Transverse Fiberglass Leaf Spring

Some front-wheel-drive cars have an independent rear suspension system with a transverse fiberglass spring which provides a combination of ride spring and roll stabilizer. This type of spring is compact, lightweight, and corrosion-free. Struts are mounted between the lower control arms and the frame supports as shown in Figure 23-10.

An automatic level control may be used with this rear suspension system. A 12V electric motor positioned on the rear suspension support drives a small air compressor. Air lines are connected from the compressor to the rear struts as shown in Figure 23-11.

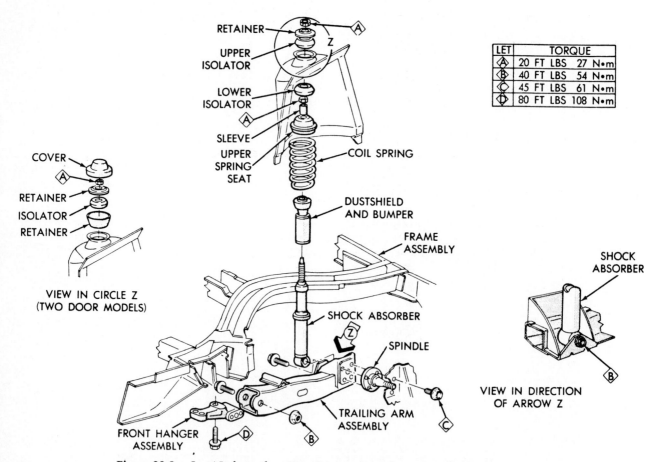

LET	TORQUE	
Ⓐ	20 FT LBS	27 N•m
Ⓑ	40 FT LBS	54 N•m
Ⓒ	45 FT LBS	61 N•m
Ⓓ	80 FT LBS	108 N•m

Figure 23-8. Semi-Independent Rear Suspension. (*Courtesy of Chrysler Canada*)

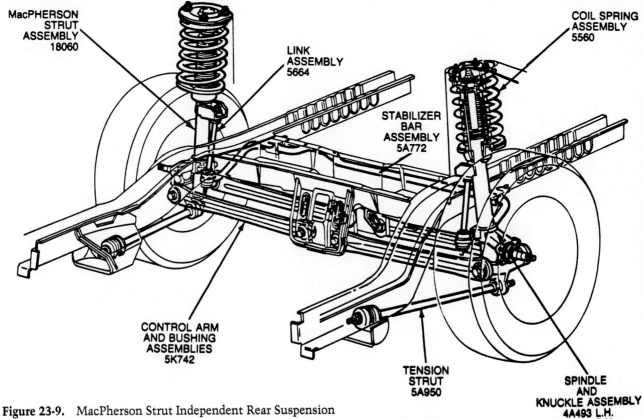

Figure 23-9. MacPherson Strut Independent Rear Suspension with Parallel Control Arms. (*Courtesy of Ford Motor Co.*)

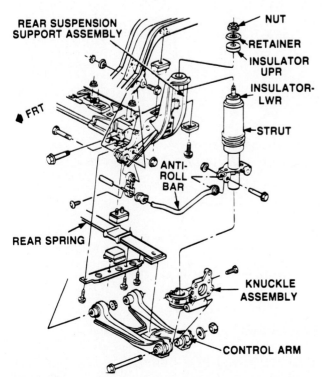

Figure 23-10. Independent Rear Suspension with Transverse Fiberglass Leaf Spring. (*Courtesy of General Motors Corporation*)

The electric motor is controlled by a height-sensor assembly mounted on the rear suspension support. A sensor control arm is connected to the lower control arm. If additional weight is placed in the trunk, the change in vehicle height operates the height-sensor switch and starts the motor and compressor. The compressor action increases the air pressure in the rear struts and restores the specified rear suspension height.

The height sensor is illustrated in Figure 23-12.

Leaf Spring Rear Suspension

A leaf spring is used on each side of the rear suspension on some rear-wheel-drive cars. These relatively flat springs provide excellent lateral stability and reduce side sway, which contributes to a well controlled ride and good handling. The springs are semielliptical, with steel leaves and zinc interleaves to reduce corrosion and improve spring life. A large rubber bushing is installed in the front eye of the main spring leaf, and a bolt retains the bushing to the front spring hanger. The rear spring shackle is bolted to a rubber bushing in the rear main leaf eye.

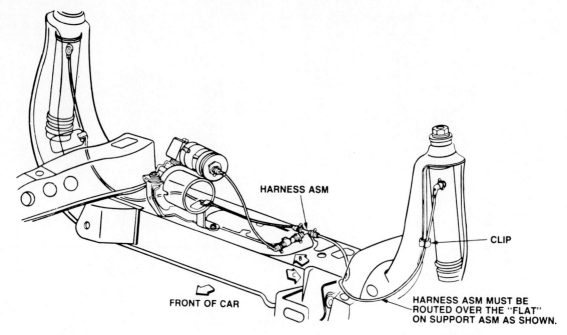

Figure 23-11. Automatic Level-Control Rear Suspension. (*Courtesy of General Motors Corporation*)

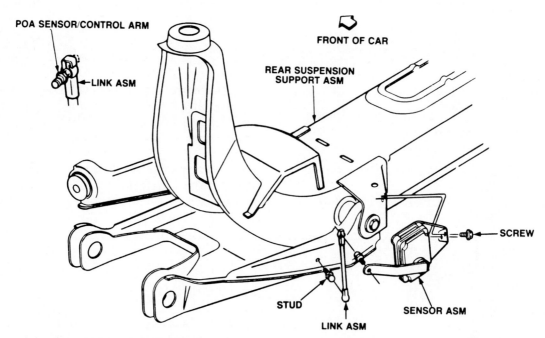

Figure 23-12. Rear Suspension Height Sensor. (*Courtesy of General Motors Corporation*)

The upper shackle bolt extends through a similar rubber bushing in the rear spring hanger. A spring plate with an isolating clamp and "U" bolts retain the springs to the rear axle housing. The shock absorbers are mounted between the spring plates and the frame as illustrated in Figure 23-13.

Conventional Coil Spring Suspension

Some rear-wheel-drive cars have a coil spring rear suspension. Upper and lower suspension arms with isolating bushings are connected between the differential housing and the frame. These arms control dif-

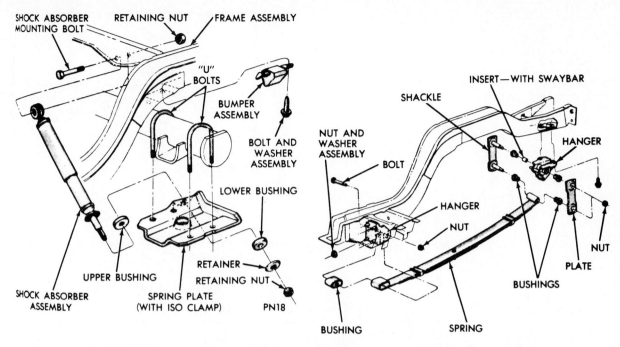

Figure 23-13.   Rear Suspension with Leaf Springs. (*Courtesy of Chrysler Canada*)

ferential torque and lateral movement. The coil springs are mounted between the lower suspension arms and the frame, and the shock absorbers are mounted between the back of the suspension arms and the frame. This type of rear suspension is illustrated in Figure 23-14.

Trailing-Arm Rear Suspension

Many front-wheel-drive vehicles have a trailing-arm rear suspension with a solid axle connected between the rear wheels. This axle is fabricated from a transverse inverted "U" section channel which has an in-

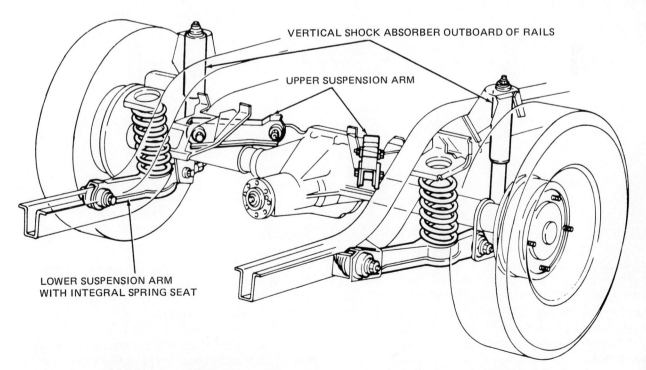

Figure 23-14.   Conventional Coil Spring Rear Suspension. (*Courtesy of Ford Motor Co.*)

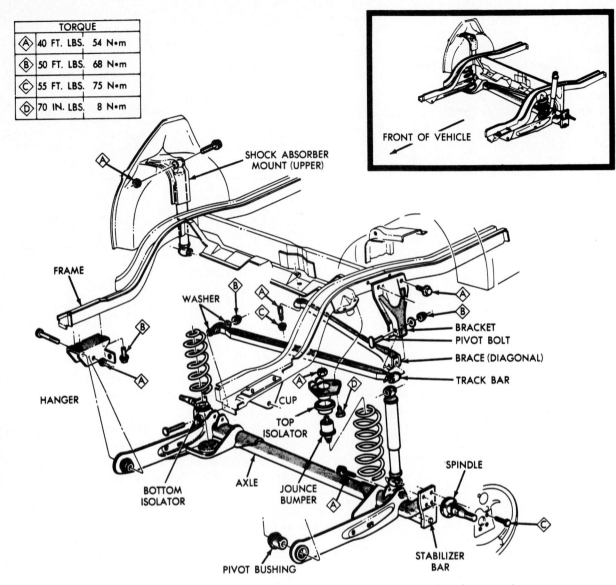

TORQUE		
Ⓐ	40 FT. LBS.	54 N•m
Ⓑ	50 FT. LBS.	68 N•m
Ⓒ	55 FT. LBS.	75 N•m
Ⓓ	70 IN. LBS.	8 N•m

FRONT OF VEHICLE

SHOCK ABSORBER MOUNT (UPPER)

FRAME

WASHER

HANGER

BRACKET
PIVOT BOLT
BRACE (DIAGONAL)
TRACK BAR

CUP

TOP ISOLATOR

SPINDLE

BOTTOM ISOLATOR

AXLE

JOUNCE BUMPER

PIVOT BUSHING

STABILIZER BAR

Figure 23-15.   Trailing-Arm Rear Suspension. (*Courtesy of Chrysler Canada*)

tegral tubular stabilizer bar inside the "U" section. This bar is attached to spindle mounting plates at each end of the axle. The trailing arms and coil spring seats are welded directly to the channel. Rubber bushings are mounted in the front of the trailing arms and attached to the body mounts. Lateral movement is controlled by a track bar. Conventional vertically mounted shock absorbers and coil springs are used in this type of suspension. All the suspension mounting points are rubber-isolated.

A trailing-arm rear suspension is shown in Figure 23-15.

Tires

Design

The most commonly used tire designs are bias-ply, bias-belted, and radial belted. In a bias-ply or bias-belted tire, the body plies crisscross each other at an angle of 30 to 38 degrees, whereas a radial tire has the body plies running at right angles to the beads. Bias-belted tires usually have fiberglass belts, while radial tires may have fiberglass or steel belts. Body plies may vary from one to four, and two to four belt layers may be used.

Many passenger cars and light-duty trucks use steel-belted radial tires. Radial tires provide less rolling resistance, improved steering, and longer tread life compared to bias-ply tires.

Three different tire designs are pictured in Figure 23-16.

Driving habits determine tire life to a large extent. Severe brake applications, high-speed driving, turning at high speeds, rapid acceleration and deceleration, and striking curbs are just a few driving habits that shorten tire life.

Most car manufacturers recommend tire rotation at specified intervals to obtain maximum tire life. The tire rotation procedure for bias-ply and radial tires is outlined in Figure 23-17.

Tire pressures are also very important to tire life. The car manufacturer's specified tire pressure should always be maintained.

Many tire manufacturers provide tire sizes in metric measurements, as illustrated in Figure 23-18. The letters "A", "B", "C", or "D" are used to indicate the tire load rating. A tire with a "D" load has a higher load carrying capacity than a tire with a "C" rating. Replacement tires should always be the same size and have the same load rating as the original tires.

Radial tires must not be mixed with other types of tires on the same vehicle, or steering characteristics will be adversely affected.

Tire Problems

Radial and Lateral Runout   Ideally, a tire and wheel assembly should be perfectly round. However, this condition is rarely achieved. A tire and wheel assembly that is out of round is said to have radial runout. If the radial runout exceeds manufacturer's specifications, vibration can occur, because the radial runout causes the spindle to move up and down. To measure radial runout, a dial indicator gauge may be positioned against the tire tread as the tire is rotated slowly. If this measurement exceeds manufacturer's specifications, the runout of the rim should be measured with a dial indicator positioned against the lip of the rim while the rim is rotated. If the wheel and the tire both have a certain amount of runout, this condition may be corrected by changing the position of the tire on the wheel. When the wheel or tire has excessive radial runout, replacement is necessary.

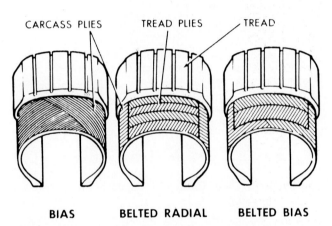

Figure 23-16.   Tire Designs. (*Courtesy of Chevrolet Motor Division, General Motors Corporation*)

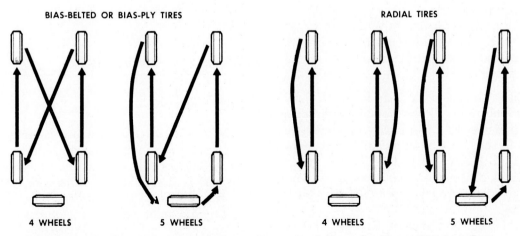

Figure 23-17.   Tire Rotation Procedure. (*Courtesy of Chevrolet Motor Division, General Motors Corporation*)

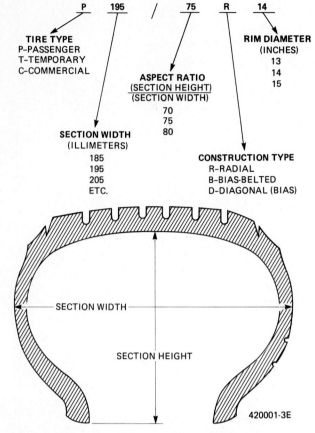

Figure 23-18. Tire Size Identification. (*Courtesy of Pontiac Motor Division, General Motors Corporation*)

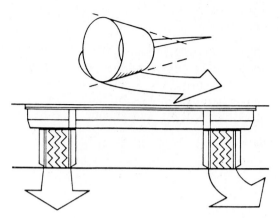

Figure 23-19. Tire Conicity. (*Courtesy of Chrysler Canada*)

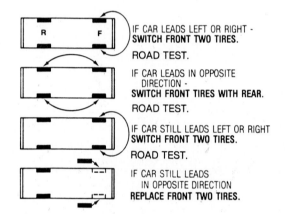

Figure 23-20. Tire Conicity Diagnosis. (*Courtesy of Chrysler Canada*)

Lateral tire runout may be measured with a dial indicator located against the sidewall of the tire. Excessive lateral runout causes the tire to wobble as it turns, and vibration due to this wobbling may be transmitted to the passenger compartment. Measure the lateral runout of the wheel with a dial indicator positioned against the edge of the wheel as the wheel is rotated. Wheels with excessive lateral runout should be straightened in a wheel-straightening machine or replaced. Tires with excessive lateral runout should be replaced.

Tire Conicity   Sometimes a manufacturing defect occurs in which the belts are wound off-center on the tire. This is referred to as conicity. A cone-shaped object rolls in the direction of its smaller diameter. Hence, a tire with conicity tends to lead, or pull, to one side, which causes the vehicle to follow the action of the tire. Tire conicity is illustrated in Figure 23-19.

Since tire conicity cannot be diagnosed by a visual inspection, it must be diagnosed by switching the two front tires and reversing the front and rear tires. Wheel alignment defects will also cause the

vehicle to pull to one side. (Wheel alignment angles are explained later in this chapter.)

The tire-switching procedure for tire conicity diagnosis is illustrated in Figure 23-20.

Wheel Alignment Theory

Road Variables

Vehicles are subjected to many variables in road surfaces and other conditions which affect wheel alignment. These variables must be counteracted by the suspension design and alignment, or steering would be very difficult. Some of the variables that affect wheel alignment and suspension design are the following:

1. Road crown, the curvature of the road surface.
2. Bumps and holes.

3. Natural crosswinds or crosswinds created by other vehicles.

4. Heavy loads or unequal weight distribution.

5. Road surface friction and conditions such as ice, snow, and water.

6. Tire traction and pressure.

7. Side forces while cornering.

8. Relationship of suspension parts as wheels turn and move with road bumps and holes.

9. Drive axle forces (in front-wheel-drive vehicles).

Wheel Alignment Purpose

Automotive engineers design suspension and steering systems that provide satisfactory vehicle control with acceptable driver effort and road feel. (Refer to Chapter 24 for an explanation of road feel.) The vehicle should have a tendency to go straight ahead without being steered, which is referred to as directional stability. A vehicle must have predictable directional control, which means the steering must provide a feeling that the vehicle will turn in the direction steered. The wheels must be reasonably easy to turn, and tire wear should be minimized.

One method to reduce tire wear would be to have the tire perfectly vertical so that is always is flat on the road. However, if the tire and wheel were perfectly vertical, when the driver entered the car, turned a corner, or added weight to the luggage compartment, the tire would move from its true vertical position, and tire wear and steering operation would be adversely affected. Therefore, the suspension and steering are designed with steering angles which provide directional stability, predictable directional control, and minimum tire wear despite road variables. Steering angles and alignment also control the track of the vehicle, which is the straightness of the back wheels in relation to the front wheels.

Definition Wheel alignment may be defined as a refitting of suspension parts to original specifications to ensure design performance.

Wheel Alignment Angles

Body Height Body height is the distance from the chassis to the road surface. This measurement is determined by the springs and suspension arms. When the vehicle load is within the manufacturer's recommended capacity, the springs distribute weight and maintain suspension arm angles and body height at specified limits. The correct body height provides the baseline for all other wheel alignment angles.

Steering Axis Inclination Steering axis inclination (SAI) refers to the angle of an imaginary line through the top center of the strut and the center of the ball joint, in relation to an imaginary vertical line through the center of the tire viewed from the front. When the SAI angle is tilted toward the center of the vehicle and the wheels are straight ahead, the height of the spindle is raised so that it is closer to the chassis. With this SAI angle, the height of the vehicle is lowered because of gravity.

If the wheels are turned, the spindle moves through an arc and tries to force the tire into the ground. Since this reaction cannot take place, the chassis lifts when the wheels are turned. When the steering wheel is released after a turn, the vehicle has a tendency to settle to its lowest point of gravity. Hence, SAI helps to return the wheels to the straight-ahead position after a turn, and also tends to maintain the wheels in the straight-ahead position. However, SAI does increase steering effort, because the chassis has to lift slightly on turns.

The SAI angle is illustrated in Figure 23-21.

Scrub Radius Scrub radius affects steering quality related to stability and returnability. However, scrub radius is not an alignment angle, and it cannot be measured on conventional alignment equipment. Scrub radius is the distance from the point at which the imaginary vertical line through the center of the tire contacts the road, and the point at which the imaginary line through the top center of the strut and the center of the ball joint meets the road surface. If the line through the strut and ball joint centers meets the road surface inside the vertical line through the tire, the scrub radius is positive. When the line through the strut and ball joint centers meets the road surface outside the line through the tire, the scrub radius is negative. Positive and negative radius are illustrated in Figure 23-22.

Conventional front suspension systems which have two ball joints with upper and lower control arms usually have a positive scrub radius. Many front-wheel-drive vehicles have a negative scrub radius.

When a negative scrub radius is used in front-wheel-drive cars, straight-line braking is ensured and directional stability is maintained. As the vehicle moves forward, the negative scrub radius tends to turn the front wheels inward. This action causes unequal forces applied to the steering to act inboard of the steering axis and pull the vehicle from any induced swerve.

In a front-wheel-drive vehicle, a swerve to one side can be caused by one front wheel contacting an ice patch while the other front wheel is on dry pave-

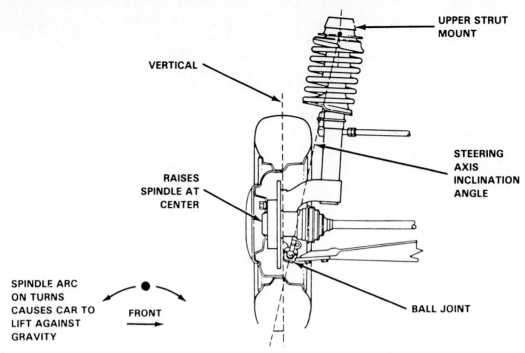

Figure 23-21.   Steering Axis Inclination Angle. *(Courtesy of Chrysler Canada)*

PROJECTED PIVOT LINE CONTACTS ROAD OUTSIDE CENTERLINE OF TIRE CONTACT

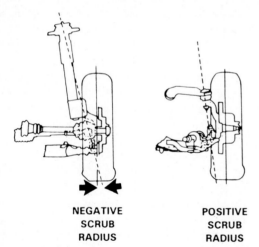

Figure 23-22.   Scrub Radius. *(Courtesy of Chrysler Canada)*

ment. Failure of half of the diagonal brake system, a sudden blowout of one front tire, or a grabbing brake on one front wheel also can cause a vehicle to swerve.

If a vehicle has a positive scrub radius and the right front brake grabs, the grabbing brake and the positive scrub radius both tend to turn the right front wheel outward, the vehicle pivots around the right front wheel. This action induces a swerve to the right. In a vehicle with a negative scrub radius, when a right front brake grabs the right front wheel turns outward and the vehicle tends to pivot around the right front wheel. However, the negative scrub radius tends to turn the right front wheel inward. The two forces on the right front wheel will cancel one another to maintain directional stability.

Caster   Caster refers to the tilt of an imaginary line intersecting the center of the ball joint and the top center of the strut, in relation to an imaginary vertical line through the center of the wheel and spindle as viewed from the side. When the strut and ball joint center line is tilted backward toward the rear of the vehicle in relation to the vertical line through the wheel, this is referred to as positive caster, as shown in Figure 23-23.

Negative caster means that the strut and ball joint center line is tilted ahead toward the front of the vehicle in relation to the vertical line through the center of the wheel.

Positive caster projects the vehicle weight ahead of the wheel center, whereas negative caster projects the vehicle weight behind the wheel center. Since positive caster causes a larger area of road contact behind the caster pivot point, this large contact area will tend to follow the pivot point. This action tends to return the wheels to a straight-ahead position after a turn, and also helps to maintain the straight-ahead

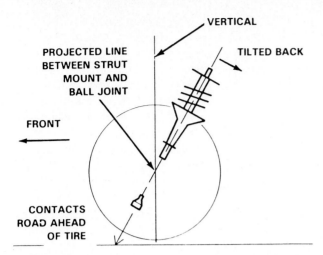

Figure 23-23. Positive Caster. (*Courtesy of Chrysler Canada*)

position. Positive caster increases steering effort, because the tendency of the tires to remain in the straight-ahead position must be overcome during a turn. The returning force to the straight-ahead position is proportional to the amount of positive caster.

Negative caster moves the strut and ball joint center line behind the center line of the wheel at the road surface. If this condition is present, the friction of the tire causes the tire to pivot around the point where the strut and ball joint center line meet the road surface. When this occurs, the wheel is pulled

away from the straight-ahead position, which decreases directional stability. Negative caster reduces steering effort.

Positive caster is used on most front-wheel-drive vehicles. If one front wheel has more positive caster than the other front wheel, the vehicle tends to pull toward the side that has the least positive caster.

Many highways are higher at the center, or crown, than at the shoulders, which causes vehicles to drift to the right. To offset this effect, some car manufacturers recommend less positive caster on the left front wheel than on the right front wheel.

Camber   Camber refers to the tilt of the wheel inward or outward in relation to the vertical line in the center of the tire as viewed from the front. Positive camber means that the top of the wheel is tilted outward away from the wheel center line; negative camber means the top of the wheel tilts inward. Passenger load and road forces tend to move the chassis downward or the wheel upward, which moves the wheel toward a negative camber position. Therefore, many vehicles have a slightly positive camber on the front wheels.

The camber setting may be adjusted on some vehicles by rotating an eccentric cam on a bolt that holds the strut into the steering knuckle, as shown in Figure 23-24.

A wheel that is tilted tends to steer in the direction it is tilted. For example, a bicycle rider tilts the

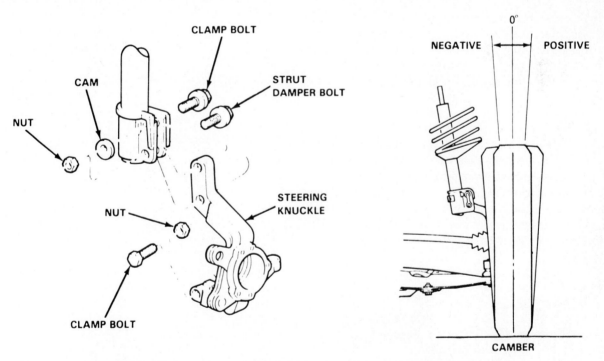

Figure 23-24.   Camber and Camber Adjustment. (*Courtesy of Chrysler Canada*)

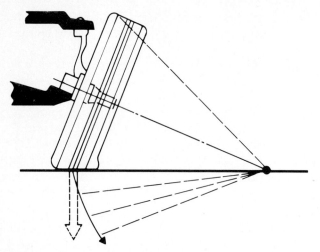

Figure 23-25. A Tilted Wheel Turns in the Direction of the Tilt.

bicycle in the direction he or she wishes to turn, which makes the turning process easier. This principle is illustrated in Figure 23-25.

When camber angles are equal on both front wheels, the camber steering forces are equal, and the vehicle tends to maintain a straight-line position. If the camber on the front wheels is significantly unequal, the vehicle will drift to the side that has the greatest degree of positive camber.

Crowned highway design prevents water buildup on the driving surface. When a vehicle is driven on a crowned road, it is actually driven on a slight slope, which causes the vehicle to pull to the right. Some car manufacturers use the pulling effect of camber to offset this effect. In these vehicles, the left front wheels may have $\frac{1}{4}°$ to $\frac{1}{2}°$ more positive camber than the right front wheel. The effect of a crowned road surface is pictured in Figure 23-26.

Incorrect camber concentrates vehicle weight on a narrow area of the tire, which results in rapid tire wear on one side. Excessive positive camber causes wear on the outside edge of the tire, whereas too much negative camber results in rapid wear on the inside tire edge. Therefore, correct camber adjustment is essential for normal tire life. The included angle on a front suspension is the SAI angle and the camber angle added together.

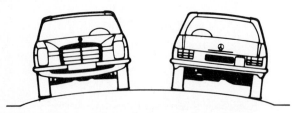

Figure 23-26. Effect of a Crowned Road Surface.

Toe The front of the tire is referred to as the toe. If both front wheels are turned outward from the straight-ahead position, this is referred to as toe-out. Toe-in is the term used when both front wheels are turned inward from the straight-ahead position.

On a front-wheel-drive car, drive axle forces and negative scrub radius tend to turn the wheels inward toward a toe-in position. Positive camber tends to make the front wheels turn outward toward a toe-out position. A slight toe-out setting of $\frac{1}{16}$ in. (1.58 mm) is used on many front-wheel-drive vehicles. When the vehicle is driven on the road, the effects of camber, axle forces, and road resistance on the tire balance each other and straighten the front wheels to a zero toe position.

If the toe is not set correctly, tire treads will become scuffed and feathered as if they were dragged sideways on the road surface. The toe setting on front wheels and the method of toe adjustment are illustrated in Figure 23-27.

Toe-Out on Turns Because of the vehicle width, when a vehicle is completing a turn, the outer wheel must travel farther in a wide circular arc than the inner wheel. The steering arms are angled inward to provide the two different front wheel paths during a turn. This steering arm angle causes the inner wheel to turn outward when the wheels are turned. Since the front of the tire is called the toe, this angle is referred to as toe-out on turns.

There is no adjustment for toe-out on turns be-

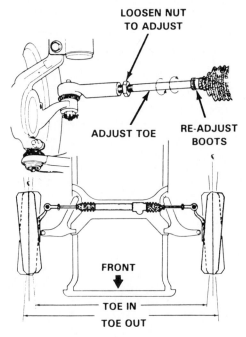

Figure 23-27. Front-Wheel Toe and Toe Adjustment (*Courtesy of Chrysler Canada*)

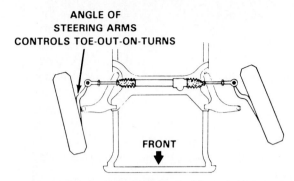

**LEFT TURN: INNER WHEEL TOES OUT —
TURNS MORE SHARPLY THAN OUTER WHEEL**

Figure 23-28. Toe-out on Turns. (*Courtesy of Chrysler Canada*)

cause it is controlled by the angle of the steering arms, as indicated in Figure 23-28.

Setback   Setback is the distance that one front strut is moved rearward in relation to the other front strut. If any appreciable amount of setback is present, it is usually caused by severe collision damage or incorrect manufacturing procedures. Car manufactures do not provide setback specifications, because they do not build a specific amount of setback into their vehicles. Some later model computer-type wheel aligners will measure setback.

Rear Wheel Alignment

Camber   Many front-wheel-drive vehicles have a slightly negative rear wheel camber, which provides improved cornering stability. Rear-wheel camber is basically the same as front-wheel camber, as indicated in Figure 23-29.

Toe   On a front-wheel-drive vehicle, driving forces tend to push back the rear wheel spindles. Therefore, these rear wheels are designed with zero toe-in, or a slight toe-in, depending on the vehicle. A correct

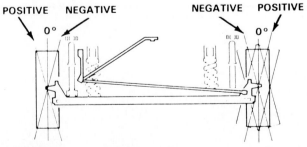

Figure 23-29. Rear-Wheel Camber. (*Courtesy of Chrysler Canada*)

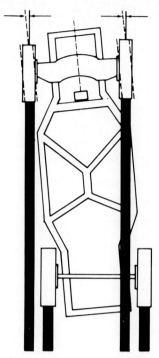

Figure 23-30. Effects of Incorrect Wheel Thrust or Tracking.

rear wheel toe setting is important to obtain normal tire life.

Thrust   The thrust line refers to the tracking of the rear wheels in relation to the front wheels. Rear wheels should track directly behind the front wheels within the manufacturer's specified limits.

Many front-wheel-drive vehicles have a unitized body construction, meaning there is not a separate frame for the chassis. After a severe collision, this type of body construction can become bent so that the rear wheels no longer track behind the front wheels. If this occurs, the rear tire wear will be excessive and the steering will pull to one side when the vehicle is driven straight ahead, as indicated in Figure 23-30.

(An explanation of wheel alignment procedure and wheel balancing is provided in Chapter 19 of *Automotive Principles: Repair and Service*, Volume II.)

Test Questions

1. Negative scrub radius on a front wheel tends to :
   a) turn the wheel outward.
   b) turn the wheel inward.
   c) maintain the wheel in a straight-ahead position.

2. If the left front wheel has 1° positive caster and the right front wheel has 3° positive caster, the vehicle will tend to:

   a) maintain directional stability.

   b) drift to the right.

   c) drift to the left.

3. If the right front wheel has a 2° negative camber setting, the right front tire will have:

   a) wear on the inside edge.

   b) wear on the outside edge.

   c) normal tread wear.

4. Many front-wheel-drive cars have a front toe setting with a:

   a) slight toe-in.

   b) slight toe-out.

   c) zero.

5. To offset the effects of road crown, the left front wheel may be set with:

   a) less positive camber than the right wheel.

   b) more positive caster than the right wheel.

   c) less positive caster than the right wheel.

6. If the turning angle, or toe-out on turns, is not correct, the _____ may be bent.

7. A bent chassis on a unitized body could result in an incorrect thrust line reading.   T F

24

Steering Systems

Chapter Completion Objectives

1. Understand basic hydraulic principles related to power steering systems.

2. Indicate a knowledge of power steering pumps.

3. Demonstrate a knowledge of rack-and-pinion steering gears.

4. Understand manual and power recirculating ball steering gears and related steering linkages.

Gases and Liquids

Compressibility

Liquids and gases may be classified as fluids because they are both substances that flow. When a container is filled with a gas, more and more gas can be forced into the container as the gas is compressed. If an automotive tire is flat, it is filled with air at atmospheric pressure. As the tire is inflated, more air is compressed into the tire, and the tire pressure is increased.

Once a container is filled with a liquid, no more liquid can be added. If more pressure is applied to the liquid, the pressure increases everywhere in the container, but the liquid is not increased. This fact is one of the basic principles of hydraulic systems.

Liquids and gases contain small particles called molecules. (Molecules were explained in Chapter 9.) In a gas, the molecules have plenty of space between

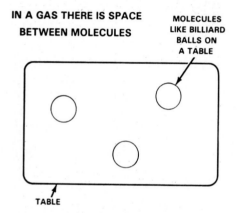

IN A GAS THERE IS SPACE BETWEEN MOLECULES

MOLECULES LIKE BILLIARD BALLS ON A TABLE

TABLE

BALLS ARE STILL FREE TO MOVE AND BOUNCE BUT WITH LESS SPACE AND MORE ACTIVITY

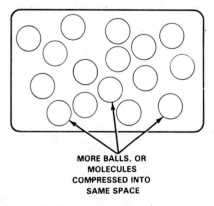

MORE BALLS, OR MOLECULES COMPRESSED INTO SAME SPACE

Figure 24-1. Gas Compressibility Illustrated by Billiard Balls. (*Courtesy of Chrysler Canada*)

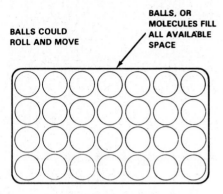

SIMILAR TO A LIQUID, MOLECULES OCCUPY ALL SPACE. THERE IS SPACE BETWEEN BUT NOT ENOUGH FOR ANY MORE FULL MOLECULES.

BALLS COULD ROLL AND MOVE

BALLS, OR MOLECULES FILL ALL AVAILABLE SPACE

Figure 24-2. Noncompressibility of Liquids Illustrated by Billiard Balls. (*Courtesy of Chrysler Canada*)

them. As illustrated in Figure 24-1, molecules in a gas can be compared to a few balls on a billiard table. More balls can be placed on the table, just as additional gas can be compressed into a container. As molecules are added the molecules are not able to move as freely, but more molecules fit easily.

The molecules in a liquid are very close to each other, similar to a billiard table that is completely filled with balls. The balls can roll around, but extra balls cannot be added to the table because balls cannot be compressed. As illustrated in Figure 24-2, molecules in a liquid, like balls on a billiard table, are noncompressible.

Liquid Flow in a Tube

The flow of liquids in a tube can be illustrated by the movement of billiard balls packed in a tube. As shown in Figure 24-3, when the outlet is open, more

BALLS CAN ROLL IN AND OUT AS LONG AS OUTLET IS CLEAR

TUBE

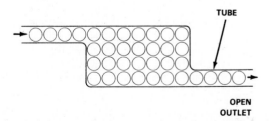

OPEN OUTLET

Figure 24-3. Liquid Flow in a Tube Illustrated by Billiard Ball Movement. (*Courtesy of Chrysler Canada*)

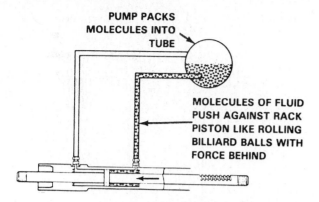

Figure 24-4. Fluid Molecules Transfer Pressure from Pump to Rack Piston. (*Courtesy of Chrysler Canada*)

balls can be added at the inlet to maintain the flow. If the outlet is closed, more balls cannot be squeezed into the tube.

The billiard balls can be compared to molecules of power steering fluid in the high-pressure line to the steering gear. The outlet is in the hydraulic chamber of the rack piston. Since noncompressible fluid fills the tube and chamber, the force developed by the pump is transferred through the lines to the chamber. This force pushes against the surface of the rack piston and causes it to move, as illustrated in Figure 24-4.

Liquids as a Flexible Machine

Hydraulic fluid under pressure has the same benefit as a mechanical lever, because the fluid multiplies the effort exerted, enabling more work than normal to be done. To illustrate, if a fulcrum is placed at the center of a lever, 10 pounds (lbs) (4.5 kg) of effort is required on the lever end to lift a 10 lb (4.5 kg) weight on the other end. When a lever is divided into five equal spaces and the fulcrum is placed at the end of the first space, the level will have a 4 to 1 mechanical advantage. Under this condition, $2\frac{1}{2}$ lbs (1.1 kg) of effort will lift 10 lbs (4.5 kg) on the short end of the lever, as pictured in Figure 24-5.

Fluid under pressure applies force to every square inch of the rack piston shown in Figure 24-6. As illustrated in the figure, if the power steering pump pressure is 1,000 psi (7,000 kPa), the fluid can push on every square inch of the rack piston with a force of 1,000 lbs (7,000 kPa).

The rack in the rack-and-pinion steering gear pushes the steering arms, which offer the mechanical advantage of levers. Therefore, the explanation for power steering assistance lies in the mechanical advantage of the hydraulic fluid pressure applied to the rack piston and the lever action of the steering arms.

A rack-and-pinion steering gear with steering arms is illustrated in Figure 24-7.

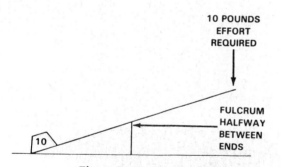

Figure 24-5. Mechanical Advantage of a Lever. (*Courtesy of Chrysler Canada*)

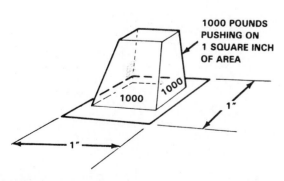

Figure 24-6. Force per Square Inch. (*Courtesy of Chrysler Canada*)

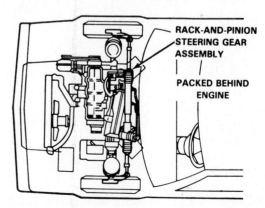

Figure 24-7. Rack-and-Pinion Steering Gear with Steering Arms. (*Courtesy of Chrysler Canada*)

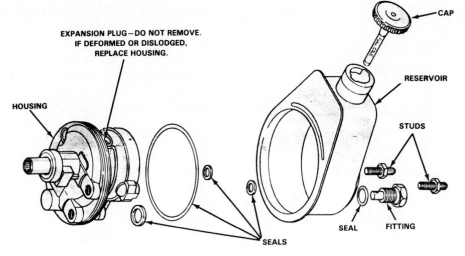

Figure 24-8. Power Steering Pump Housing and Reservoir. (*Courtesy of Chrysler Canada*)

Power Steering Pumps

Design

A balanced pulley is pressed on the steering pump drive shaft, and this pulley and shaft are belt-driven by the engine. The oblong pump reservoir is made from steel or plastic. Prying on the reservoir must be avoided, because it could easily puncture. A large "O" ring seals the front of the reservoir to the pump housing, as shown in Figure 24-8.

Smaller "O" rings seal the bolt fittings on the back of the reservoir. The combination cap and dipstick keeps the fluid reserve in the pump and vents the reservoir to the atmosphere.

The pump housing assembly is illustrated in Figure 24-9, and the drive shaft with the rotor and vanes is pictured in Figure 24-10.

The flow control valve is mounted in the bottom of the housing. This is a precision-fit valve controlled by spring pressure and fluid pressure. Any dirt or roughness on the valve results in erratic pump pressure. The flow control valve contains a pressure relief valve, as indicated in Figure 24-11.

High-pressure fluid is forced past the control valve to the outlet fitting. A high-pressure hose connects the outlet fitting to the inlet fitting on the steering gear, and a low-pressure hose returns the fluid from the steering gear to the inlet fitting in the pump reservoir.

Operation

As the belt rotates the rotor and vanes inside the cam ring, centrifugal force causes the vanes to slide

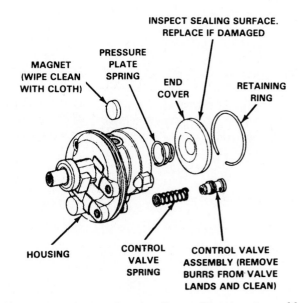

Figure 24-9. Power Steering Pump Housing Assembly. (*Courtesy of Chrysler Canada*)

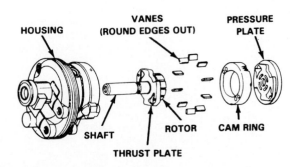

Figure 24-10. Power Steering Pump Drive Shaft, Rotor, and Vanes. (*Courtesy of Chrysler Canada*)

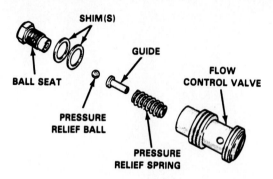

Figure 24-11. Flow Control Valve. (*Courtesy of Chrysler Canada*)

out of the rotor slots. The vanes follow the lobed surface of the cam. When the area between the vanes expands, a low-pressure area occurs between the vanes, and fluid flows from the reservoir into the space between the vanes. As the vanes approach the higher portion of the cam, the area between the vanes shrinks and the fluid is compressed, as shown in Figure 24-12.

High-pressure fluid is forced into two passages on the thrust plate. These passages reverse the fluid direction, and fluid is discharged through the cam crossover passages and pressure plate openings to the flow control valve. The fluid is discharged from the flow control valve through the outlet fitting, as illustrated in Figure 24-13.

While most of the fluid is discharged from the

pump, some fluid returns to the bottom of the vanes through the center holes in the pressure plate. This high-pressure fluid forces the vanes against the cam ring and increases the pump pressure. Therefore, when pump pressure becomes higher, pressure behind the vanes also increases.

A machined venturi orifice is located in the outlet fitting. A fluid passage applies pressure from the venturi area to the spring side of the flow control valve, as pictured in Figure 24-14.

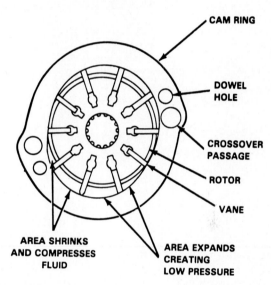

Figure 24-12. Vane and Cam Action. (*Courtesy of Chrysler Canada*)

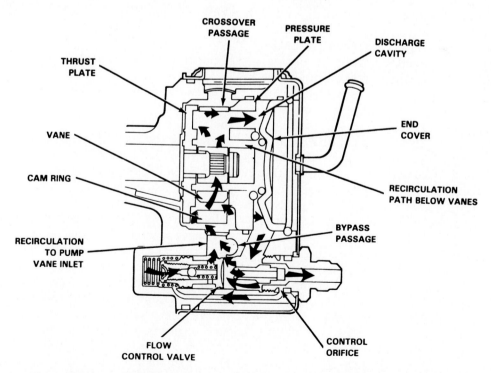

Figure 24-13. Power Steering Pump Fluid Flow. (*Courtesy of Chrysler Canada*)

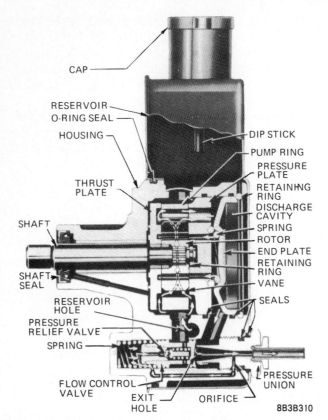

Figure 24-14. Power Steering Pump Flow Control Valve Operation. *(Courtesy of Buick Motor Division, General Motors Corporation)*

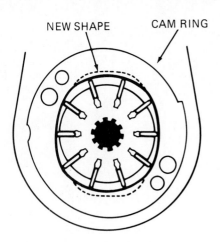

Figure 24-15. Cold-Prime Cam Ring. *(Courtesy of Chrysler Canada)*

Some later model power steering pumps have a cam ring that provides improved cold-prime operation. This type of pump will prime in 12 seconds at 700 rpm at 0°F to −40°F (−18° to −40°C). The shape of the cold-prime cam ring is shown in Figure 24-15.

Rack-and-Pinion Steering Gears

Fundamentals

A basic rack-and-pinion steering gear is illustrated in Figure 24-16. The steering gear functions also are provided in the figure.

Steering Characteristics

In a rack-and-pinion steering gear, a pinion is attached to the steering shaft. This pinion meshes with the rack, and linkages are connected directly from the rack to the steering arms on the front wheels. A rack-and-pinion steering gear is compared to a recirculating-ball steering gear in Figure 24-17.

In the recirculating-ball steering gear, a steering wheel and shaft rotate a wormshaft which rolls inside a set of ball bearings. The movement of the bearings causes a ball nut to move, because the balls run in spiral grooves inside the ball nut. Gear teeth on the outside of the ball nut are in mesh with gear teeth on the sector shaft. Therefore, ball nut movement results in sector shaft rotation.

Since the pinion is in direct contact with the rack in the rack-and-pinion steering gear, this type of steering gear is more responsive than the recirculating-ball steering gear. Most front-wheel-drive vehicles have rack-and-pinion steering gears.

When fluid flow in the venturi increases, the pressure in this area decreases. (This venturi principle was explained in Chapter 16.) At low-volume fluid flow, pressure in the orifice is higher. This high-pressure assists the flow control valve spring in closing the flow control valve, which restricts fluid flow past the flow control valve to the vane inlet. When this occurs, pressure on the vanes is decreased, which also reduces pump pressure.

When the front wheels are turned, fluid rushes from the pump into the steering gear chamber. Therefore, fluid flow is increased and pressure in the venturi area is decreased. The pressure reduction is sensed at the spring side of the flow control valve. The pump discharge pressure forces the flow control valve open, which results in additional fluid flow past the flow control valve to the vane inlet. Under this condition the increased fluid pressure on the vanes creates a corresponding increase in pump pressure. Since the entire power-assist system is filled with fluid, a large volume of flow is not required. The opening of the flow control valve allows high-pressure output force on the rack piston in the steering gear. A pressure relief valve in the flow control valve limits the pump pressure.

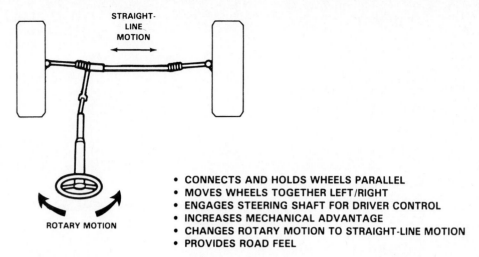

Figure 24-16.   Rack-and-Pinion Steering Gear Functions. (*Courtesy of Chrysler Canada*)

Power Rack-and-Pinion Steering Gear

Design and Operation

In the power-assisted rack-and-pinion steering gear, hydraulic fluid pressure from the power steering pump is used to reduce steering effort. A rack piston is integral with the rack and located in a sealed chamber in the steering gear housing. Hydraulic fluid lines are connected to each end of the chamber, and rack seals are positioned in the housing at ends of the chamber. A seal is also located on the rack piston, as pictured in Figure 24-18.

(Refer to Figure 24-7 for steering gear location.)

When a right turn is made, fluid is pumped into the right side of the fluid chamber, and fluid flows out of the left end of the chamber. Thus hydraulic pressure is exerted on the right side of the rack pis-

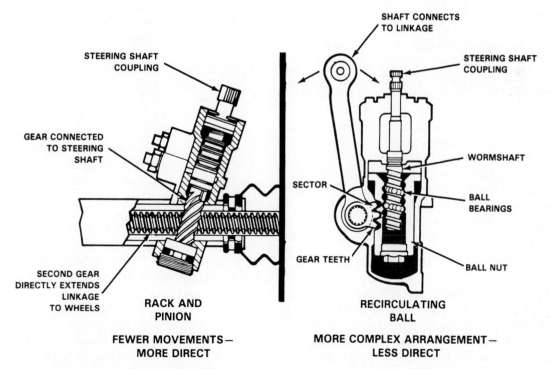

Figure 24-17.   Comparison Between Rack-and-Pinion and Recirculating-Ball Steering Gears. (*Courtesy of Chrysler Canada*)

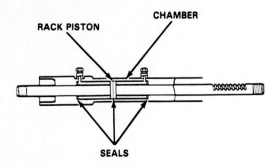

Figure 24-18. Hydraulic Chamber in Rack-and-Pinion Steering Gear. (*Courtesy of Chrysler Canada*)

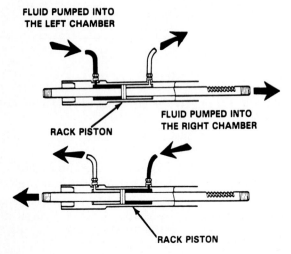

Figure 24-19. Rack Movement During Right and Left Turns. (*Courtesy of Chrysler Canada*)

ton which assists the pinion gear in moving the rack to the left.

When a left turn is completed, fluid is pumped into the left side of the fluid chamber and exhausted from the right chamber area. This hydraulic pressure on the left side of rack piston helps the pinion to move the rack to the right, as shown in Figure 24-19.

Since the steering gear is mounted behind the front wheels, rack movement to the left (from the driver's seat) is necessary for a right turn, while rack movement to the right causes a left turn.

Rotary Valve and Spool Valve Operation

Fluid direction is controlled by a rotary valve attached to the pinion assembly. A stub shaft on the pinion assembly is connected to the steering shaft and wheel. The pinion is connected to the stub shaft through a torsion bar that twists when the steering wheel is rotated and springs back to the center position when the wheel is released. A rotary valve body

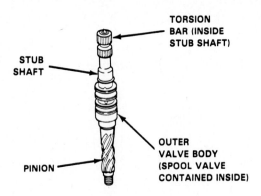

Figure 24-20. Pinion Assembly. (*Courtesy of Chrysler Canada*)

contains an inner spool valve that is mounted over the torsion bar on the pinion assembly. The complete pinion assembly is shown in Figure 24-20.

When the front wheels are in the straight-ahead position, fluid flows from the pump through the high-pressure hose to the center rotary valve body passage. Fluid is then routed through the valve body to the low-pressure return hose and the pump reservoir.

The rack-and-pinion steering gear with connecting hoses and lines is illustrated in Figure 24-21.

Telfon rings, or "O" rings, seal the rotary valve ring lands to the steering gear housing. Because of the vehicle weight on the front wheels, a great deal of force is required to turn the pinion and move the rack. When the driver turns the wheel, the stub shaft is forced to turn. However, the pinion resists turning, because it is in mesh with the rack that is connected to the front wheels. This resistance of the pinion to rotation results in twisting of the torsion bar, which moves the spool valve inside the rotary valve. If the driver makes a left turn, the spool valve movement aligns the inlet center rotary valve passage with the outlet passage to the left side of the rack piston. Therefore, hydraulic fluid pressure applied to the left side of the rack piston helps move the rack to the right.

When a right turn is made, twisting of the torsion bar moves the spool valve and aligns the center rotary valve passage with the outlet passage to the right side the rack piston. Under this condition hydraulic fluid pressure applied to the rack piston helps move the rack to the left. The action of the torsion bar provides a feel of the road to the driver.

The spool valve movement inside the rotary valve is illustrated in Figure 24-22.

When the steering wheel is released after a turn, the torsion bar centers the spool valve and power assist stops.

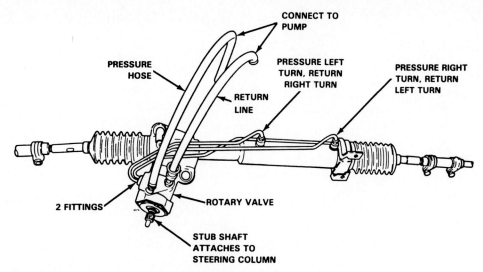

Figure 24-21. Rack-and-Pinion Steering Gear with Connecting Hoses and Lines. (*Courtesy of Chrysler Canada*)

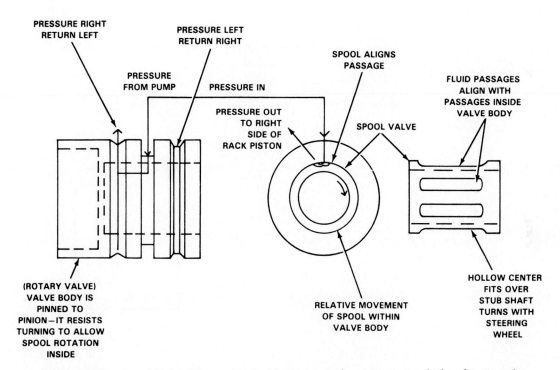

Figure 24-22. Spool Valve Movement Inside Rotary Valve. (*Courtesy of Chrysler Canada*)

If hydraulic fluid pressure is not available from the pump, the power steering system will operate like a manual system, but greater steering effort will be required. When the torsion bar is twisted to a designed limit, tangs on the stub shaft engage with drive tabs on the pinion. This action mechanically transfers motion from the steering wheel to the rack and front wheels. Since hydraulic pressure is not available on the rack piston, more steering effort is required. If a front wheel raises going over a bump or drops into a hole, the tie rod pivots along with the wheel. However, the rack and tie rod still maintain the left-to-right wheel direction.

The rack boots are clamped to the housing and the rack. Since the boots are sealed and air cannot be moved through the housing, a breather tube is

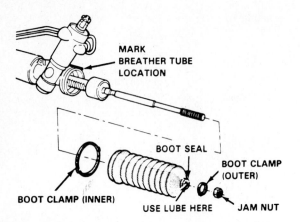

Figure 24-23. Breather Tube and Boot. (*Courtesy of Chrysler Canada*)

necessary to move air from one boot to the other when the steering wheel is turned. The breather tube and boot are shown in Figure 24-23.

Types of Rack-and-Pinion Steering Gears

Saginaw Steering Gears

Many vehicles have a rack-and-pinion steering gear manufactured by Saginaw. The components in this type of steering gear are illustrated in Figure 24-24.

TRW Steering Gears

Some vehicles are equipped with a TRW rack-and-pinion steering gear. This type of steering gear is similar to the Saginaw gear, except for these differences:

1. Method of tie rod attachment.
2. Bulkhead oil seal and retainer.
3. Pinion upper and lower bearing hardware.

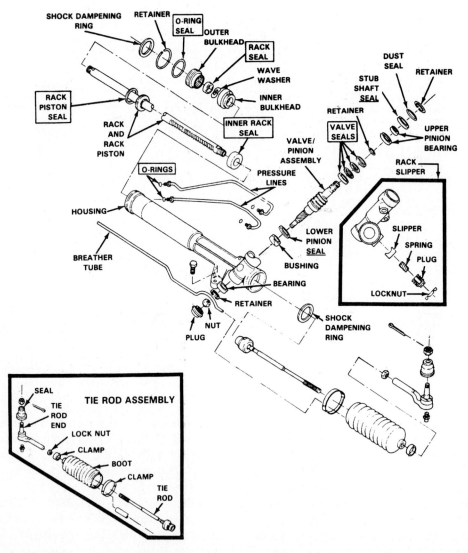

Figure 24-24.   Saginaw Rack-and-Pinion Steering Gear. (*Courtesy of Chrysler Canada*)

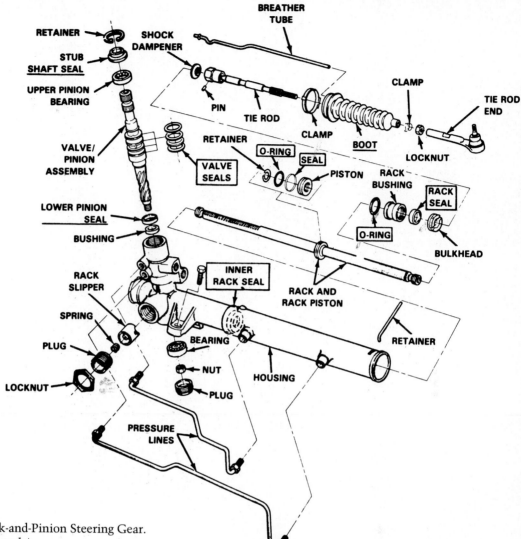

Figure 24-25. TRW Rack-and-Pinion Steering Gear. (*Courtesy of Chrysler Canada*)

The components in a TRW steering gear are shown in Figure 24-25.

Recirculating-Ball Steering Gears

Operation

In a recirculating-ball steering gear, the steering wheel and steering shaft are connected to the worm shaft. A ball nut is mounted over the worm shaft and ball bearings run in grooves in the ball nut and worm shaft. When the worm shaft is rotated by the steering wheel, the ball nut is moved up or down. The gear teeth on the ball nut are meshed with matching gear teeth on the pitman shaft sector. Therefore, movement of the ball nut causes rotation of the pitman shaft sector. Since the pitman shaft sector is connected through the pitman arm and steering linkage to the front wheels, the front wheels are turned by the pitman shaft sector.

A recirculating-ball steering gear is illustrated in Figure 24-26, and the complete steering linkage, with

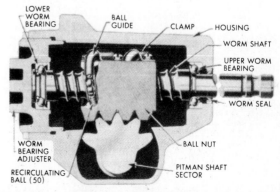

Figure 24-26. Recirculating-Ball Steering Gear. (*Courtesy of Buick Motor Division, General Motors Corporation*)

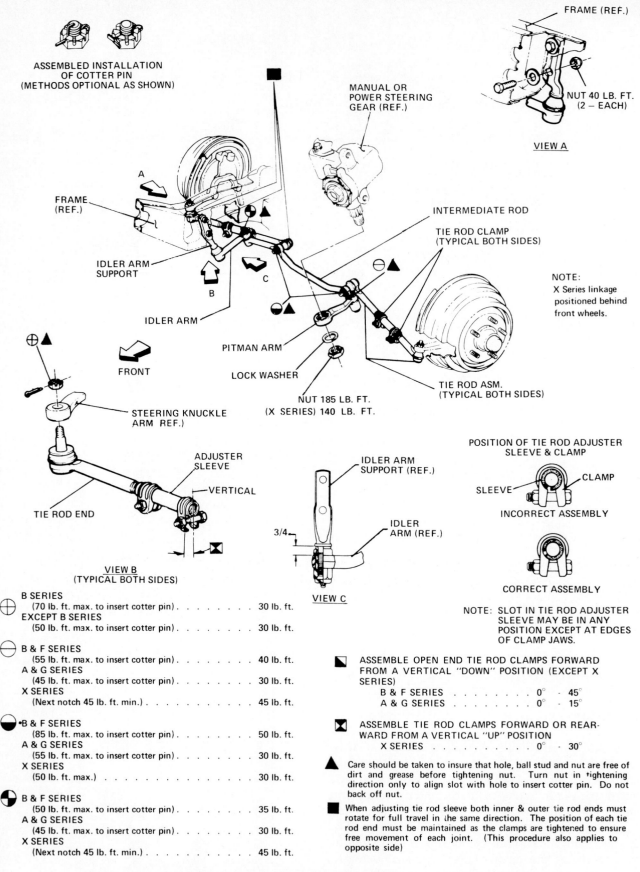

ASSEMBLED INSTALLATION
OF COTTER PIN
(METHODS OPTIONAL AS SHOWN)

FRAME (REF.)

NUT 40 LB. FT.
(2 – EACH)

VIEW A

MANUAL OR
POWER STEERING
GEAR (REF.)

FRAME
(REF.)

INTERMEDIATE ROD

TIE ROD CLAMP
(TYPICAL BOTH SIDES)

IDLER ARM
SUPPORT

NOTE:
X Series linkage
positioned behind
front wheels.

IDLER ARM

PITMAN ARM

LOCK WASHER

NUT 185 LB. FT.
(X SERIES) 140 LB. FT.

TIE ROD ASM.
(TYPICAL BOTH SIDES)

FRONT

STEERING KNUCKLE
ARM REF.)

ADJUSTER
SLEEVE

VERTICAL

TIE ROD END

IDLER ARM
SUPPORT (REF.)

IDLER
ARM (REF.)

3/4

VIEW C

POSITION OF TIE ROD ADJUSTER
SLEEVE & CLAMP

CLAMP

SLEEVE

INCORRECT ASSEMBLY

CORRECT ASSEMBLY

NOTE: SLOT IN TIE ROD ADJUSTER
SLEEVE MAY BE IN ANY
POSITION EXCEPT AT EDGES
OF CLAMP JAWS.

VIEW B
(TYPICAL BOTH SIDES)

B SERIES
(70 lb. ft. max. to insert cotter pin) . . . . 30 lb. ft.
EXCEPT B SERIES
(50 lb. ft. max. to insert cotter pin) . . . . 30 lb. ft.

B & F SERIES
(55 lb. ft. max. to insert cotter pin) . . . . 40 lb. ft.
A & G SERIES
(45 lb. ft. max. to insert cotter pin) . . . . 30 lb. ft.
X SERIES
(Next notch 45 lb. ft. min.) . . . . 45 lb. ft.

B & F SERIES
(85 lb. ft. max. to insert cotter pin) . . . . 50 lb. ft.
A & G SERIES
(55 lb. ft. max. to insert cotter pin) . . . . 30 lb. ft.
X SERIES
(50 lb. ft. max.) . . . . 30 lb. ft.

B & F SERIES
(50 lb. ft. max. to insert cotter pin) . . . . 35 lb. ft.
A & G SERIES
(45 lb. ft. max. to insert cotter pin) . . . . 30 lb. ft.
X SERIES
(Next notch 45 lb. ft. min.) . . . . 45 lb. ft.

ASSEMBLE OPEN END TIE ROD CLAMPS FORWARD
FROM A VERTICAL "DOWN" POSITION (EXCEPT X
SERIES)
B & F SERIES . . . . 0° - 45°
A & G SERIES . . . . 0° - 15°

ASSEMBLE TIE ROD CLAMPS FORWARD OR REAR-
WARD FROM A VERTICAL "UP" POSITION
X SERIES . . . . 0° - 30°

Care should be taken to insure that hole, ball stud and nut are free of
dirt and grease before tightening nut. Turn nut in tightening
direction only to align slot with hole to insert cotter pin. Do not
back off nut.

When adjusting tie rod sleeve both inner & outer tie rod ends must
rotate for full travel in the same direction. The position of each tie
rod end must be maintained as the clamps are tightened to ensure
free movement of each joint. (This procedure also applies to
opposite side)

Figure 24-27. Complete Steering Linkage, Rear-Wheel-Drive Car. (*Courtesy of Pontiac
Motor Division, General Motors Corporation*)

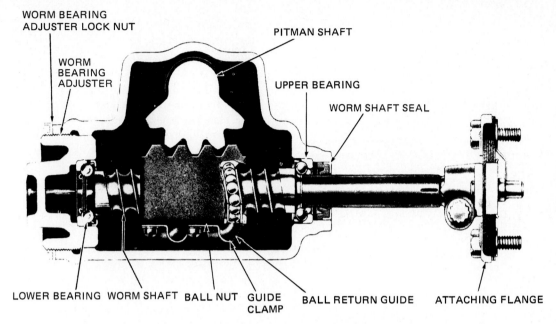

Figure 24-28.   Recirculating-Ball Steering Gear with Attaching Flange and Coupling. (*Courtesy of Buick Motor Division, General Motors Corporation*)

service precautions and torque specifications, is shown in Figure 24-27.

A worm bearing adjuster may be turned to adjust the preloading of the upper and lower worm shaft bearings. The worm shaft is connected to the steering shaft with a flange and flexible coupling, as pictured in Figure 24-28.

The pitman shaft sector is supported on a bushing in the gear housing. When the front wheels are straight ahead, a tighter fit exists between the ball nut teeth and the pitman shaft sector teeth. An adjusting nut on top of the pitman shaft sector provides proper gear engagement, as shown in Figure 24-29.

Recirculating-Ball Power Steering Gears

Operation

The ball nut and pitman shaft sector are similar in both manual and power recirculating-ball steering gears. In the power steering gear, a torsion bar is connected between the steering shaft and the worm shaft. Since the front wheels resting on the road surface resist turning, the parts attached to the worm shaft also resist turning. This turning resistance causes torsion bar deflection when the wheels are turned. The extent of deflection is limited to a predetermined amount.

The worm shaft is connected to the rotary valve

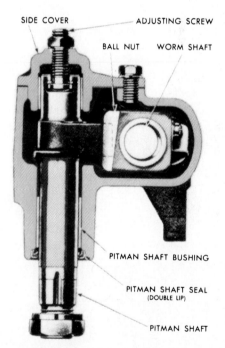

Figure 24-29.   Pitman Shaft Sector Adjusting Nut. (*Courtesy of Pontiac Motor Division, General Motors Corporation*)

body, and the torsion bar pin also connects the torsion bar to the worm shaft. The upper end of the torsion bar is attached to the steering shaft and wheel. A stub shaft is mounted inside the rotary valve and a pin connects the outer end of this shaft to the torsion bar. The pin on the inner end of the

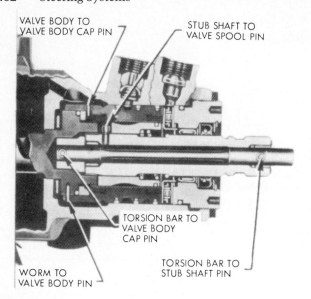

VALVE BODY TO
VALVE BODY CAP PIN

STUB SHAFT TO
VALVE SPOOL PIN

TORSION BAR TO
VALVE BODY
CAP PIN

TORSION BAR TO
STUB SHAFT PIN

WORM TO
VALVE BODY PIN

Figure 24-30. Torsion Bar and Stub Shaft. (*Courtesy of Buick Motor Division, General Motors Corporation*)

stub shaft is connected to the spool valve in the center of the rotary valve.

The torsion bar and stub shaft are illustrated in Figure 24-30.

When the car is driven with the front wheels straight ahead, oil flows from the power steering pump through the spool valve and rotary valve body, as illustrated in Figure 24-31.

When the driver makes a left turn, deflection of the torsion bar moves the valve spool inside the rotary valve body so that oil flow is directed through the rotary valve to the upper side of the recirculating ball piston. This hydraulic pressure on the piston assists the driver in turning the wheels to the left.

The oil flow through the steering gear is illustrated in Figure 24-32, and an expanded view of the spool valve and valve body is provided in Figure 24-33.

When the driver makes a right turn, deflection of the torsion bar moves the spool valve so that oil flows through the steering gear as pictured in Figure 24-34.

During a right turn, hydraulic pressure applied to the lower end of the recirculating-ball piston helps the driver to turn the wheels.

When a turn is being made and a front wheel strikes a bump which drives the wheel in the direction opposite to the turning direction, the recirculating-ball piston tends to move against the hydraulic pressure and force oil back out the pressure inlet port. This action would tend to create "kickback" on the steering wheel, but a poppet valve in the pressure inlet fitting closes and prevents kickback.

In the straight-ahead steering gear position, oil pressure is equal on both sides of the recirculating-ball piston. The oil acts as a cushion which prevents road shocks from reaching the steering wheel.

Many recirculating-ball power steering gears have a variable ratio which provides faster steering

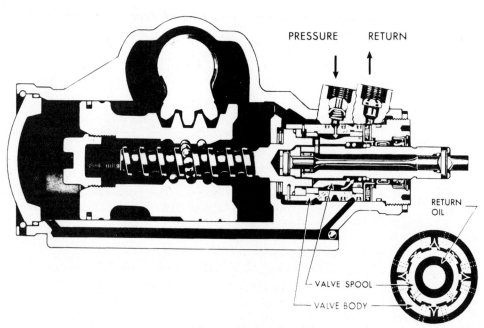

PRESSURE   RETURN

RETURN
OIL

VALVE SPOOL

VALVE BODY

Figure 24-31. Power Steering Gear Oil Flow with Wheels Straight Ahead. (*Courtesy of Buick Motor Division, General Motors Corporation*)

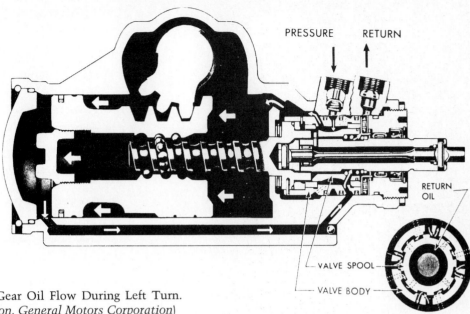

Figure 24-32. Power Steering Gear Oil Flow During Left Turn.
(*Courtesy of Buick Motor Division, General Motors Corporation*)

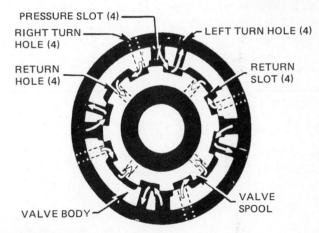

Figure 24-33. Spool Valve Position During Left Turn.
(*Courtesy of Buick Motor Division, General Motors Corporation*)

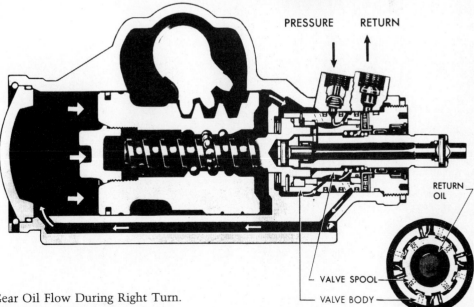

Figure 24-34. Power Steering Gear Oil Flow During Right Turn.
(*Courtesy of Buick Motor Division, General Motors Corporation*)

484   Steering Systems

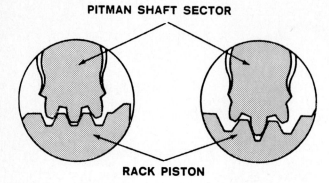

PITMAN SHAFT SECTOR

RACK PISTON

CONSTANT RATIO   VARIABLE RATIO

Figure 24-35. Constant-Ratio and Variable-Ratio Steering Gears. (*Courtesy of Pontiac Motor Division, General Motors Corporation*)

with fewer steering wheel turns. Constant-ratio and variable-ratio steering gears are compared in Figure 24-35.

(Steering gear service is explained in Chapter 20 of *Automotive Principles: Repair and Service*, Volume II.)

Test Questions

1. Liquids may be compressed.   T F

2. When the power steering pump flow increases, the pressure in the outlet fitting venturi:
   a) remains the same.
   b) decreases.
   c) increases.

3. When a right turn is made, hydraulic fluid is pumped into the chamber on the _____ side of the rack piston.

4. Twisting of the torsion bar rotates the:
   a) spool valve inside the rotary valve.
   b) rotary valve ahead of the spool valve.
   c) rack bearing.

5. In a power rack-and-pinion steering gear, feel of the road is provided by:
   a) rack bearing adjusting nut torque.
   b) torsion bar action.
   c) pinion lock nut torque.

6. A breather tube is required on a power-assisted rack-and-pinion steering gear.   T F

25

Brake Systems

Chapter Completion Objectives

1. Understand basic hydraulic principles related to brake system operation.
2. Indicate a knowledge of brake fluid requirements and classifications.

3. Demonstrate an understanding of master cylinders, wheel cylinders and calipers, brake shoes and pads, warning light switches, metering valves, proportioning valves, power brake boosters, parking brakes, and anti-lock brake systems.
4. Comprehend complete diagonally split and front-to-rear split brake systems and their applications.

Hydraulic Principles

Principles Related to Master Cylinder and Wheel Cylinder Size

One of the basic hydraulic principles is that liquids are not compressible. (Refer to Chapter 24 for hydraulic principles related to power steering systems.) Because they are not compressible, liquids can transmit force. The French scientist Blaise Pascal discovered the principle that: "pressure on a confined fluid is transmitted equally in all directions and acts with equal force on equal areas."

If 10 pounds (lbs) (4.5 kg) of force is applied to the brake pedal and the master cylinder piston area is 1 sq in. (6.4 cm^2), the force exerted by the fluid in the master cylinder is 10 lb (4.5 kg) force divided by 1 sq in. (6.4 cm^2) or 10 pounds (4.5 kg) per square in. (psi). When the wheel cylinders also have an area of 1 sq in. (6.4 cm^2), the 10 psi (4.5 kg) from the master cylinder exerts a pressure of 10 psi (4.5 kg) in each wheel cylinder. This application of Pascal's Law is illustrated in Figure 25-1.

The following hydraulic principles relate to master cylinder and wheel cylinder size:

1. When the master cylinder piston and bore size is decreased, the pressure exerted by the master cylinder will increase for a given pressure on the brake pedal.
2. As the master cylinder piston and bore size is increased, the pressure exerted by the master cylinder will decrease for a given brake pedal force.
3. A smaller diameter master cylinder requires more piston travel to displace the same amount of fluid as a larger piston.
4. The force on the brake pedal and the diameter of

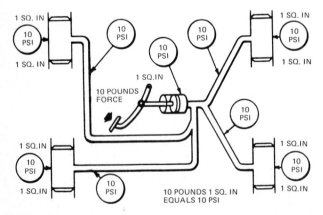

Figure 25-1. Pascal's Law Applied to the Master Cylinder and the Wheel Cylinders. (*Courtesy of Chrysler Canada*)

the master cylinder piston determine the pressure in the brake system.

5. The diameter of the wheel cylinders determines the force against the brake shoes. A larger diameter wheel cylinder or caliper piston exerts more force on the brake shoes, or pads, than a smaller piston. When smaller diameter wheel cylinder pistons are used, the force that pushes against the brake shoes is reduced.

If 10 lbs (4.5 kg) of force is applied to the brake pedal, and the master cylinder piston has an area of 2 sq in., the pressure developed by the master cylinder is 5 psi (34 kPa), as indicated in Figure 25-2.

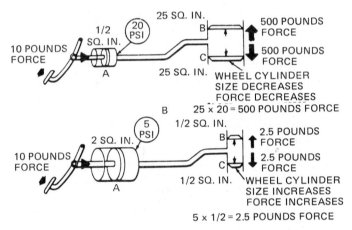

Figure 25-2. Hydraulic Principles. (*Courtesy of Chrysler Canada*)

When the master cylinder piston area is $\frac{1}{2}$ sq in. (3.2 cm^2), and the force on the brake pedal is 10 lb (4.5 kg), the master cylinder pressure is 20 psi (140 kPa), as shown in Figure 25-2. If 20 psi (140 kPa) is supplied from the master cylinder to a wheel cylinder with an area of 25 sq in. (161 cm^2), the wheel cylinder exerts a force of 500 lbs (226.8 kg) against the brake shoes. If a master cylinder pressure of 5 psi (34.4 kPa) is supplied to a wheel cylinder with an area of $\frac{1}{2}$ sq in. (3.2 cm^2), the wheel cylinder force is 2.5 lbs (1.1 kg). These hydraulic principles are illustrated in Figure 25-2.

Complete Brake System

Design

Many vehicles have drum-type rear brakes and disc-type front brakes. On rear-wheel-drive vehicles, one half of the dual master cylinder supplies pressure to the front brakes, and the other half supplies pressure to the rear brakes. On front-wheel-drive vehicles, the hydraulic brake system is a diagonally split system in which one half of the master cylinder supplies pressure to the left front and the right rear brakes, and the other half of the master cylinder supplies pressure to the right front and left rear brakes. This diagonally split system prevents spin-out on turns should half the brake system fail.

A metering valve, proportioning valve, and a brake warning light switch are connected in the brake system on a rear-wheel-drive car, as shown in Figure 25-3. A diagonally split brake system on a front-wheel-drive vehicle is pictured in Figure 25-4.

Brake Tubing

Double-wall steel tubing must be used in hydraulic brake systems. Copper tubing must not be used in brake systems because it can corrode or burst. Brake tubing must be routed so that it is not in contact with sharp edges, moving components, or excessive heat. All brake tubing must be properly attached to the vehicle chassis with recommended retaining clips. Brake tubing ends must be double flared. (Refer to Chapter 1 in *Automotive Principles: Repair and Service*, Volume II, for the double flaring procedure.) When brake tubing is routed on the vehicle, it must not be kinked.

Brake Fluid

Brake fluid quality is extremely important to obtain proper brake system operation. The requirements for brake fluid are the following:

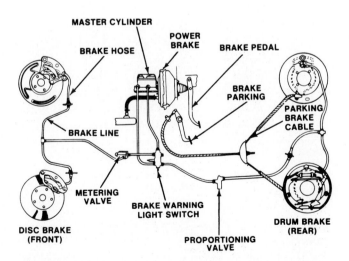

Figure 25-3. Complete Brake System on a Rear-Wheel-Drive Car. (*Courtesy of Chrysler Canada*)

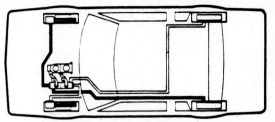

The crisscross hydraulic brake systems work independently for greater safety.

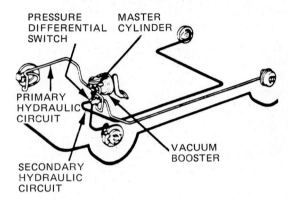

Brake line routing of the diagonally split brake system.

Figure 25-4. Diagonally Split Brake System on a Front-Wheel-Drive Vehicle. (*Courtesy of Chrysler Canada*)

1. *Operation at temperature extremes.* Brake fluid must operate at temperatures up to 500°F (260°C), and at temperatures as low as −104°F (−75.5°C).

2. *Lubricating ability.* Smooth operation of many brake system components depends on the lubricating quality of the brake fluid.

3. *Anti-corrosion and anti-rust properties.* The brake fluid must combat rust and corrosion in the brake lines and other components.

4. *Resistance to evaporation.* Brake fluid must resist evaporation even at high temperatures.

5. *Compatibility with rubber.* To avoid damage to wheel cylinder and master cylinder cups, or to caliper piston seals, the brake fluid must be compatible with rubber.

6. *Controlled amount of swell.* Brake fluids must provide a controlled amount of swell in cups and seals to provide adequate sealing. If swelling of these components is excessive, brake drag and poor brake response result.

7. *Adherence to classification standards.* Each brake fluid container has identification letters from the Society of Automotive Engineers (SAE) and the Department of Transportation (DOT). In 1945 SAE compiled basic specifications for brake

fluid to ensure quality, safety, and performance. These standards were adopted by DOT in 1963, and an updating of brake fluid standards was completed in 1972. Three basic brake fluid classifications used at the present time are the following.

DOT 3   This brake fluid has a minimum dry equilibrium boiling point (ERBP) of 401°F (205°C) and a minimum wet ERBP of 284°F (140°C).

DOT 4   This brake fluid has a minimum dry ERBP of 446°F (230°C) and a minimum wet ERBP of 356°F (180°C).

DOT 5   This type of brake fluid is a silicone-based fluid with a minimum dry ERBP of 500°F (260°C) and a minimum wet ERBP of 356°F (180°C).

The brake fluid recommended by the vehicle manufacturer must always be used.

Master Cylinders

Design

The master cylinder forces pressurized brake fluid through the brake lines to the wheel cylinders. This fluid pressure is caused by the brake pedal rod pushing the primary and secondary pistons against the brake fluid. Prior to 1967, master cylinders had a single piston which forced brake fluid to the four wheel cylinders. In this type of system, if a leak occurred that allowed the master cylinder fluid to escape, the entire brake system would fail.

Since 1967, master cylinders have dual pistons. On front-wheel-drive cars, one piston supplies fluid pressure to the left front and right rear wheels, and the other piston forces brake fluid to the right front and left rear wheels. If a leak occurs and drains the fluid at the right front wheel, the other master cylinder piston will continue to supply fluid to the left front and right rear wheels. Hence, the dual master cylinder prevents complete failure of the brake system when a leak occurs at one wheel.

The primary and secondary pistons are mounted in the master cylinder bore. Piston cups are used to seal the pistons to the bore. Each piston has a return spring which holds the pistons in the released position. The brake lines are connected to the fluid outlets. On rear-wheel-drive vehicles, the primary piston outlet is connected to the front brakes, and the secondary piston outlet supplies fluid to the rear brakes, as indicated in Figure 25-5.

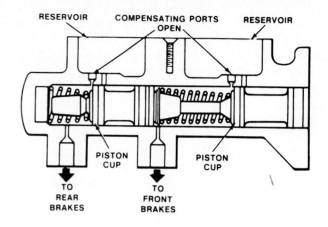

Figure 25-5. Master Cylinder Pistons. (*Courtesy of Chrysler Canada*)

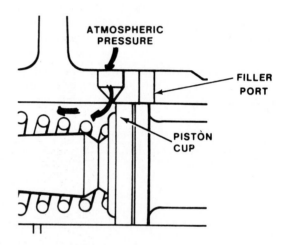

Figure 26-6. Master Cylinder Filler Ports. (*Courtesy of Chrysler Canada*)

Compensating ports are connected between the fluid reservoirs and the piston bores. Filler ports are located near the compensating ports, as illustrated in Figure 25-6.

Dual master cylinders are made from cast iron or aluminum. The reservoirs may be integral with the master cylinder casting, or a plastic reservoir assembly may be attached to the cylinder casting. A cover bail is used to retain the cover and gasket on top of the reservoirs, as shown in Figure 25-7.

Operation

When the brake pedal is depressed slightly, the primary piston moves down the master cylinder bore and the primary cup seal covers the compensating port. This movement creates pressure in the primary piston cylinder, which forces fluid from the primary

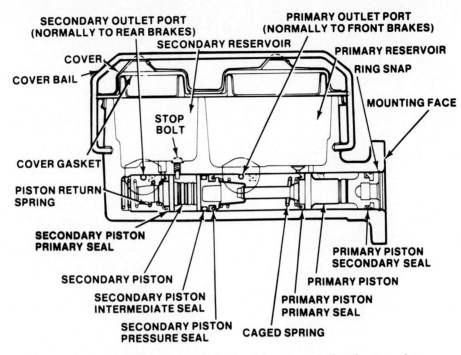

Figure 25-7. Complete Master Cylinder. (*Courtesy of Chrysler Canada*)

outlet port. Pressure in the primary piston bore moves the secondary piston down its bore, and the secondary cup seal covers the secondary compensating port. When this occurs, pressurized brake fluid is forced from the secondary outlet to the wheel cylinders or calipers. When fluid is forced from both piston outlets, the brakes are applied, as indicated in Figure 25-8.

When the brakes are used repeatedly, such as in congested traffic, the brake linings or pads and wheel cylinders or calipers become very hot. This additional heat causes the brake fluid to expand. When this occurs, brake fluid can flow through the compensating ports back into the reservoirs when the brakes are released. Therefore, the compensating ports prevent excessive pressure buildup in the brake system.

When brake shoe adjustment is not correct, or when air enters the brake system, excessive brake pedal movement will be required to apply the brakes. Under this condition the driver may pump the brake pedal rapidly to apply the brakes. This action causes a pressure drop in the master cylinder because the fluid cannot flow back from the wheel cylinders into the master cylinder as quickly as the master cylinder pistons can move when the brakes are released. If pressure drops in the master cylinder bores, atmospheric pressure on top of the fluid in the reservoirs forces brake fluid through the filler ports past the cup seals and through holes in the ends of the pistons into the piston bores.

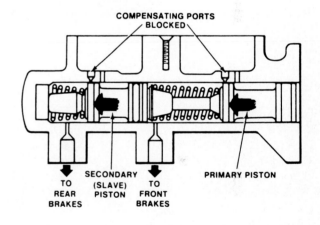

Figure 25-8. Master Cylinder in the Applied Position. (*Courtesy of Chrysler Canada*)

The cover gasket provides a tight seal on top of the reservoirs to prevent moisture from entering the system, which could break down the lubricating qualities of the brake fluid and cause corrosion in the system. Atmospheric vents are located between the cover and the gasket.

Most cover gaskets have a bellows design. If the brake fluid level goes down in the reservoirs, the bellows expand into the reservoirs, and air flows through the vents into the space between the cover and the gasket. When the brakes are released and fluid returns to the reservoirs, the bellows move upward and some of the air above the gasket is forced out the vents.

Residual Pressure

Dual master cylinders used with drum brakes prior to 1974 had residual check valves installed in the primary and secondary outlets. These valves maintained a low residual pressure in the brake system, which kept the wheel cylinder cups expanded outward to provide better cup sealing and eliminate the possibility of air entering the system.

Many vehicles now have front disc brakes and rear drum brakes. Master cylinders on some of these vehicles have a residual valve in the secondary outlet to the rear brakes. After 1974 wheel cylinders have cup expanders which hold the cups against the wheel cylinder bores. This eliminates the need for residual pressure in the system, so that residual valves are no longer required.

Quick Take-up Master Cylinders

Since disc brakes calipers have a greater fluid volume requirement than wheel cylinders used with drum brakes, a quick take-up master cylinder may be used with these systems. The quick take-up valve provides a larger volume of fluid to the calipers at low pressure with initial brake application. The location of the quick take-up valve is shown in the master cylinder in Figure 25-9.

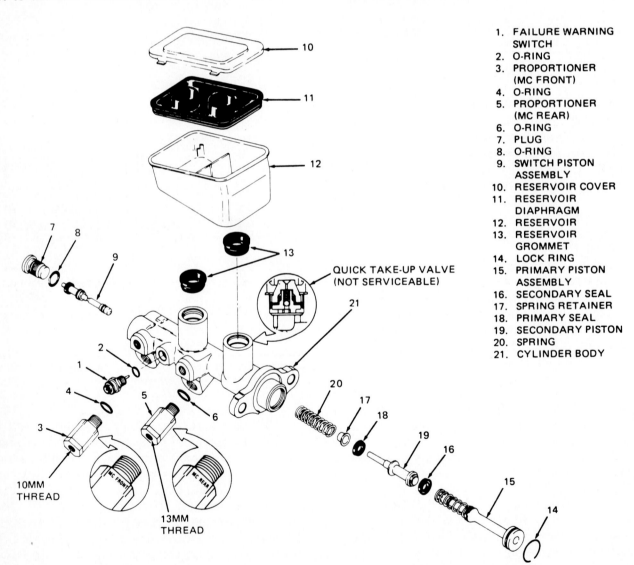

1. FAILURE WARNING SWITCH
2. O-RING
3. PROPORTIONER (MC FRONT)
4. O-RING
5. PROPORTIONER (MC REAR)
6. O-RING
7. PLUG
8. O-RING
9. SWITCH PISTON ASSEMBLY
10. RESERVOIR COVER
11. RESERVOIR DIAPHRAGM
12. RESERVOIR
13. RESERVOIR GROMMET
14. LOCK RING
15. PRIMARY PISTON ASSEMBLY
16. SECONDARY SEAL
17. SPRING RETAINER
18. PRIMARY SEAL
19. SECONDARY PISTON
20. SPRING
21. CYLINDER BODY

QUICK TAKE-UP VALVE (NOT SERVICEABLE)

10MM THREAD

13MM THREAD

Figure 25-9.   Quick Take-Up Master Cylinder. (*Courtesy of Pontiac Motor Division, General Motors Corporation*)

Drum Brakes

Wheel Cylinders

Wheel cylinders change hydraulic pressure into force at the brake shoes. Most wheel cylinders are the double-piston type which have two rubber cups, two cup expanders, a coil spring, and two rubber dust boots with push rods. The wheel cylinders are bolted to the brake backing plate, and a bleeder screw extends from the cylinder through the backing plate opening.

When the brakes are not applied, the coil spring holds the cups firmly against the pistons. If the brakes are applied, the cup lips are designed to press tightly against the wheel cylinder bores as the fluid pressure increases. The cup expanders prevent air from entering the system when the cups are in motion, and this eliminates the need for residual master cylinder valves. When the brakes are applied, the push rods transmit the piston motion to the brake shoes. The dust boots keep dirt and water from entering the cylinder. If the brake pedal is depressed, hydraulic pressure from the master cylinder forces the wheel cylinder piston outward, and the push rods move the brake shoes outward against the brake drums.

A typical wheel cylinder is pictured in Figure 25-10.

Brake Shoes and Linings

Drum brake shoes are made from stamped steel with brake linings bonded, or riveted, to their outer surfaces. The brake shoes and linings are curved to match the contour of the brake drum inner surface. Brake linings are made from asbestos mixed with special compounds. Some linings have woven asbes-

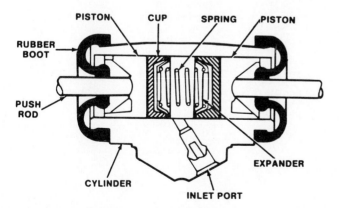

Figure 25-10. Wheel Cylinder Design. (*Courtesy of Chrysler Canada*)

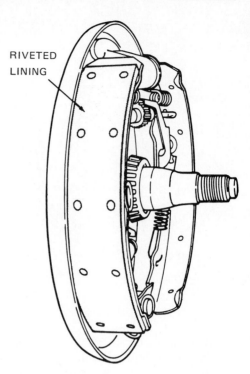

Figure 25-11. Riveted Brake Lining. (*Courtesy of Chrysler Canada*)

tos threads combined with very fine copper wire. Metallic-type linings are used on some heavy-duty applications. Brake shoes with riveted linings are shown in Figure 25-11.

When the brakes are applied, the brake shoes and linings are forced outward against the brake drums by wheel cylinder action. The rubbing of the brake shoes against the drums creates friction, which results in braking action.

Kinetic energy developed from the weight and speed of the vehicle in motion is converted into heat energy by the friction of the brake linings against the drums. After this energy is converted into heat, it is dissipated into the surrounding air.

The relationship between the force created by the weight and motion of the vehicle divided by the pressure required to force the brake shoes outward and stop the vehicle is referred to as the coefficient of friction. (Refer to Chapter 3 for a further explanation of the coefficient of friction.) Materials such as zinc, brass, copper, graphite, and ceramic may be added to the asbestos brake linings to give the linings more gripping action and improve the coefficient of friction. These additives also provide improved heat resistance. Many brake shoes can withstand temperatures up to 600°F (316°C). When a vehicle is stopped from 60 MPH (96.5 KPH), brake lining temperature could reach 450°F (232°C). Brake

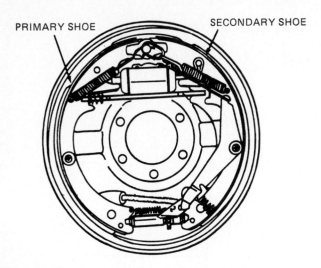

Figure 25-12. Primary and Secondary Brake Shoes. (*Courtesy of Chrysler Canada*)

linings wear faster at higher temperatures. Metallic-type brake linings have improved heat resistance.

The primary brake shoe is positioned toward the front of the vehicle, and the secondary shoe faces the rear of the vehicle. In a duo-servo brake, the secondary lining does about 75 percent of the braking. Therefore, this lining is longer than the primary lining, which results in even wear on the two shoes. The secondary lining may contain different material than the primary lining. Primary and secondary brake shoes are illustrated in Figure 25-12.

Complete Drum Brake Assembly

The top ends of the brake shoes contact an anchor pin. A star wheel adjuster is connected between the lower ends of the brake shoes. Return springs hold the shoes against the anchor pin when the brakes are released. Shoe retainers hold the shoes lightly against the backing plate.

A self-adjusting mechanism is attached to the secondary shoe. This mechanism rotates the star adjuster when the brake shoes move outward a specific distance. Therefore, the brake shoes are adjusted automatically to compensate for the lining wear. This self-adjusting action occurs when the brakes are applied while the car is moving in reverse on many brake systems.

The parking brake lever is attached to the secondary shoe on rear wheel brakes, and a strut is connected from this lever to the primary shoe.

A complete drum brake assembly is illustrated in Figure 25-13.

When the brakes are applied, the primary shoe moves outward against the rotating brake drum and tries to rotate with the drum. This action forces the star adjuster against the secondary shoe, which assists the hydraulic pressure to force the secondary shoe against the brake drum. Servo action is the term applied to this type of drum brake.

If the brakes are applied while the vehicle is moving in reverse, force is transferred from the sec-

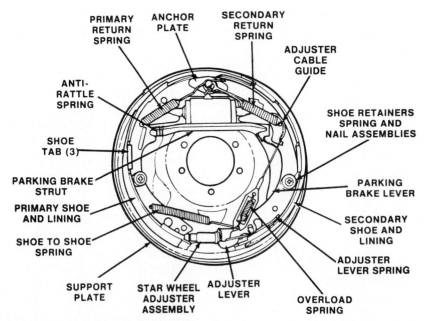

Figure 25-13. Complete Drum Brake Assembly. (*Courtesy of Chrysler Canada*)

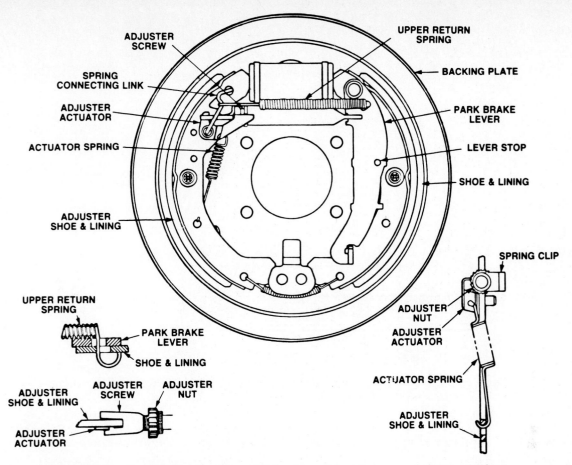

Figure 25-14. Leading/Trailing Drum Brake Assembly. (*Courtesy of GM Product Service Training, General Motors Corporation*)

ondary shoe through the star adjuster to the primary shoe. Since the servo action occurs while the vehicle is moving forward or backward, the term duo-servo is used for this type of brake mechanism.

Brake Drums

The brake drum is bolted between the wheel and the hub. Therefore, when the wheels turn, the drum must rotate around the stationary brake shoes. A small clearance exists between the drum and the backing plate so that water and dirt cannot enter the brake mechanism easily. The braking area of the drum must be smooth, round, and parallel to the shoe surface.

Leading/Trailing Drum Brakes

Design

Some 1986 General Motors front-wheel-drive cars have leading/trailing drum brakes on the rear wheels. In this type of brake, both primary and secondary shoes are positioned against an anchor at the lower

end. Therefore, servo action is eliminated in this type of brake, so that the possibility of rear wheel lockup is reduced during a hard brake application.

A leading/trailing brake assembly is illustrated in Figure 25-14.

The self-adjusting mechanism is positioned near the upper ends of the brake shoes. A thermal spring clip is mounted between the adjuster nut and the adjuster socket to prevent the self-adjusting mechanism from operating when the brakes are extremely hot. After several panic stops, the brake drums expand because of excessive heat. If the self-adjusting mechanism were to adjust the shoes to fit the expanded drums, the brakes would be too tight when the drums cooled.

A thermal spring clip is shown with the adjuster mechanism in Figure 25-15.

Disc Brakes

Linings

Disc brakes are used on the front wheels of many vehicles. The lining on disc brake pads must be made from very hard material to withstand the higher

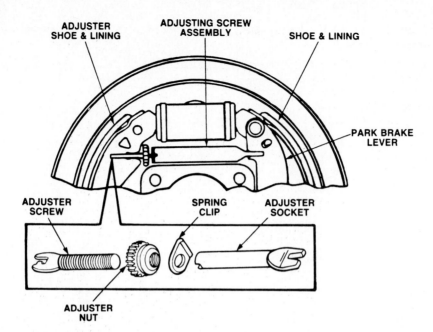

Figure 25-15. Thermal Clip and Self-Adjuster Mechanism. *(Courtesy of GM Product Service Training, General Motors Corporation)*

forces and higher temperatures that are encountered in this type of brake mechanism.

Disc brake pad linings are made from organic material. Some linings have metal particles blended with the organic material. The linings may be riveted, or bonded, to the steel disc plates. Disc brake pad linings are usually thicker than drum brake linings.

Disc brake pads with riveted linings are shown in Figure 25-16.

Wear-sensing indicators are used in some brake pads. These indicators are electrical rivets which contact the rotor when the lining becomes worn. When this contact occurs, a circuit is completed to the monitor system in the instrument panel, and the

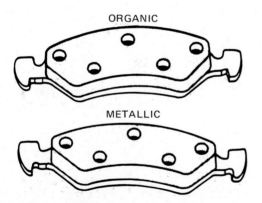

Figure 25-16. Disc Brake Pads with Riveted Linings. *(Courtesy of Chrysler Canada)*

monitor system informs the driver that the brake linings are worn. (Refer to Chapter 15 for an explanation of monitor systems.)

Metal lugs on the brake pads position the pads in the calipers. Some brake pads have clips which hold them into the caliper. Tabs are used as wear sensing devices on some brake pads. These tabs contact the rotor and create a rubbing noise when the linings are worn.

Calipers and Disc

The cast iron braking disc, or rotor, is part of the wheel hub. Flat-ground friction surfaces are positioned on each side of the disc. When the brakes are applied, the pad linings contact these friction surfaces. Most brake discs have ventilating louvers between the two friction surfaces which act as a fan to dissipate heat during brake applications.

The caliper and brake pads are positioned over the brake disc, and most calipers are bolted to the steering knuckle. Some early-model calipers contained four pistons, two behind each brake pad.

Since disc brakes do not have any servo action, the brake pads must be applied with higher pressure. Therefore, caliper pistons are larger than wheel cylinder pistons used with duo-servo drum brakes. Each piston has a seal which seals the brake fluid behind the piston, and a dust boot to keep dirt out of the piston area.

When the brakes are applied, hydraulic pressure forces the piston against the brake pads. This action forces the linings against the disc friction surfaces to provide braking action. The brake action occurs very quickly, because there is very small clearance between the brake linings and the disc surfaces. When two pistons are used in each side of the caliper, the application force is equal on each brake pad.

A brake caliper with four pistons is shown in Figure 25-17, and a caliper with the brake disc and steering knuckle is illustrated in Figure 25-18.

Many later model vehicles are equipped with single-piston floating calipers. When the brakes are applied with these calipers, the caliper piston movement forces the inner brake pad lining against the disc surface. Hydraulic pressure is applied equally to the piston and the bottom of the piston bore. Since the caliper is free to move laterally, the hydraulic force on the piston bore moves the caliper inward, which forces the outer brake pad lining against the outer disc surface. The force on each brake pad is equal.

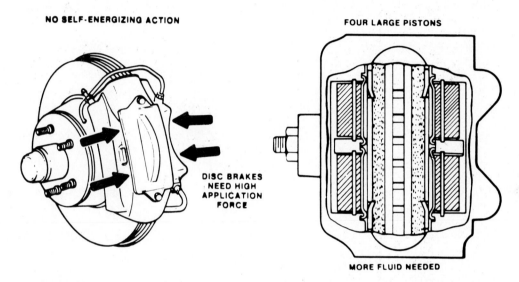

Figure 25-17.   Early-Model Brake Caliper with Four Pistons. (*Courtesy of Chrysler Canada*)

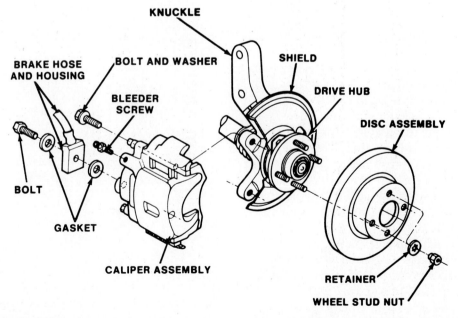

Figure 25-18.   Brake Caliper with Disc and Steering Knuckle. (*Courtesy of Chrysler Canada*)

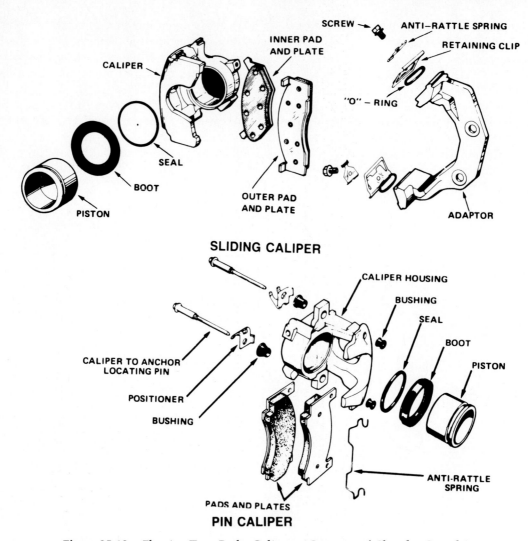

SLIDING CALIPER

PIN CALIPER

Figure 25-19. Floating-Type Brake Calipers. (*Courtesy of Chrysler Canada*)

Floating-type calipers may be sliding-type or pin-type, as indicated in Figure 25-19.

Sliding calipers are positioned and aligned by two abutments on the adapter. Two clips retain the caliper in a guideway on the adapter. The caliper can move laterally on the adapter guideway.

Pin calipers move through four rubber bushings located on two steel guide pins that are threaded into the adapter. Two rubber bushings are positioned in each side of the caliper.

Many piston seals are designed to twist when the piston moves outward during a brake application. When the brakes are released, the seal returns to its original shape, which pulls the piston back slightly and provides a very small clearance between the lining and the disc to prevent brake lining drag on the disc. The piston seal action is shown in Figure 25-20.

Caliper pistons are made from chrome-plated steel, aluminum, or a phenolic material. Phenolic pistons resist corrosion and remain stable in size

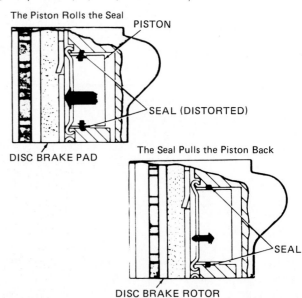

Figure 25-20. Piston Seal Action. (*Courtesy of Chrysler Canada*)

even at high temperatures. Phenolic pistons are lighter in weight and also transfer less heat to the brake fluid.

The front wheels must provide 60 percent to 85 percent of the total stopping force, because the vehicle's weight balance is shifted forward in proportion to the braking forces during a brake application. On front-wheel-drive cars, the percentage of stopping force on the front wheels is higher compared to rear-wheel-drive cars, because of the additional weight on the front wheels.

Since disc brakes have no servo action and provide less lining area than drum brakes, higher force must be used to apply the brake pads. This higher force is obtained with the use of larger caliper pistons as compared to wheel cylinder pistons. Brake calipers have greater fluid requirements than wheel cylinders. The hydraulic principles in disc brakes are basically the same as the principles in drum brakes.

Repeated hard braking with drum brakes causes extreme heat, which expands the brake drum. When this occurs, increased brake shoe and pedal movement are required to apply the brakes. This increased pedal movement is referred to as brake fade. Brake fade cannot take place with disc brakes, because the disc friction surfaces move closer to the pad linings if the disc expands because of extreme heat. Disc brakes do not require adjustment, and the linings and discs are self-cleaning.

Brake System Valves and Switches

Brake Warning Light Switch

Most switches and valves in the brake system are safety devices. In a dual master cylinder system, if the brake fluid leaks out of one half of the system, the other half of the system still provides braking action on two wheels. Although brake pedal travel and effort are increased when only half of the brake system is operating, the driver may not be aware that a defect exists in the system.

Hydraulic pressure from each half of the brake system is applied to opposite ends of the piston in the brake warning light switch. An electrical contact is mounted in a recessed area in the center of the piston. This contact is connected to a brake warning light in the instrument panel. When both halves of brake system are working normally, the pressure is equal on each end of the piston. Under this condition the piston remains centered in the switch and does not touch the electrical contact. If fluid leaks out of one half of the brake system, the

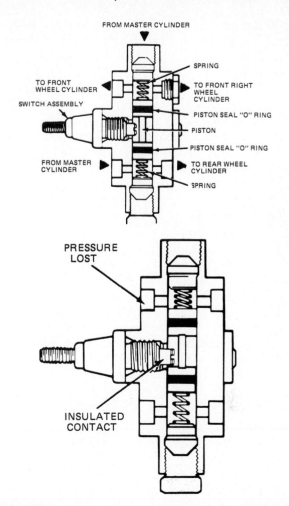

Figure 25-21. Brake Warning Light Switch. (*Courtesy of Chrysler Canada*)

pressure from the other half of the system forces the piston over until it grounds the electrical contact. This illuminates the brake warning light on the instrument panel.

The brake warning light switch connections and operation are illustrated in Figure 25-21.

When the ignition switch is turned on, voltage is supplied to the brake warning light bulb. The circuit from this bulb may be connected to ground through the brake warning light switch, or through a switch on the parking brake mechanism which closes when the parking brake is applied. Therefore, the brake warning light is also illuminated when the parking brake is applied.

Metering Valves

When the brake pedal is applied, the braking response of the front disc brakes is immediate and directly proportional to the effort applied to the pedal.

In the rear drum brakes, braking response is delayed slightly as the wheel cylinder pistons move the brake shoes outward against their return springs. The servo action of the rear brake shoes tends to multiply the pedal effort.

Full hydraulic pressure to the front disc brakes is momentarily held off by the metering valve until the rear brake shoes contact the drums. This action provides simultaneous braking on front and rear wheels, which prevents premature wheel locking and provides an important anti-skid feature when the brakes are applied lightly on slippery roads. The metering valve does not interfere with front brake pressure during hard stops.

Hydraulic pressure to the front brakes is supplied through the metering valve. If the brakes are released, fluid can flow freely through the metering valve. When pressure from the master cylinder reaches 3 to 30 psi (20.5 to 207 kPa) during initial brake application, the metering valve rod moves to the left, which allows the check valve to close. This movement holds fluid pressure to the front disc brakes at 3 to 30 psi (20.6 to 207 kPa).

If the master cylinder pressure increases to a predetermined hold-off level, the metering valve rod moves further to the left against the spring tension. When this occurs, the valve plate and check valve became unseated, which allows fluid pressure to the front brakes. The hold-off function of the metering valve delays the higher fluid pressure to the front disc brakes so that the front disc brakes and rear drum brakes are applied simultaneously. When the brakes are released, the brake fluid flows back through the valve plate and check valve to the metering valve inlet.

A metering valve is pictured in Figure 25-22.

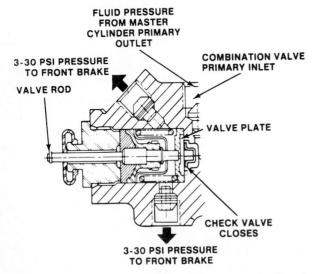

Figure 25-22. Metering Valve. (*Courtesy of Chrysler Canada*)

Proportioning Valve

Rapid deceleration and hard braking shift a substantial percentage of the vehicle's rear weight to the front wheels. Therefore, compensation for the loss of weight on the rear wheels is necessary to avoid rear wheel skids. The proportioning valve reduces pressure to the rear brake system and delays rear wheel skidding. On some station wagons, the distribution of weight and rear-to-front weight transfer is such that a proportioning valve is not required.

The proportioning valve does not operate during normal braking, when low master cylinder pressures are insufficient to operate the proportioning valve. Under this condition, brake fluid is forced through the insert and angular hole to the proportioning valve. Brake fluid continues to flow past the open valve to the proportioning valve outlet. The proportioner plunger is spring-loaded to keep the valve open until a predetermined split-point pressure is exceeded.

A proportioning valve is illustrated in the open position in Figure 25-23.

When the driver applies more force to the brake pedal, higher fluid pressure from the master cylinder moves the proportioning valve upward and closes the valve. This maintains fluid pressure to the rear brakes at a relatively low split-point pressure, which prevents rear wheel skidding when some of the vehicle's rear weight is shifted forward to the front wheels.

If additional force is applied to the brake pedal, the increased master cylinder pressure and the plunger spring pressure cause the proportioning valve to open. When this occurs, the fluid pressure at the rear brakes continues to increase at a ratio determined by the cross-sectional area of the angular space and the area of the exposed valve plate. If the brake pedal is released, the proportioning valve becomes unseated by spring pressure, so that brake fluid can flow back through the valve to the master cylinder.

Some later model vehicles have a combination valve which includes the metering valve, proportioning valve, and the brake warning light switch. The location of the combination valve was shown in Figure 25-4, and the separate metering valve, proportioning valve, and brake warning light switch were illustrated in Figure 25-3. A typical combination valve is pictured in Figure 25-24.

Load-Sensing Proportioning Valve

A load-sensing proportioning valve may be used on some light-duty trucks or vans. On these units, the load in the vehicle can affect the rear-to-front weight

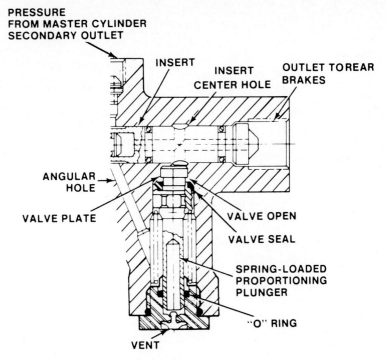

Figure 25-23.   Proportioning Valve. (*Courtesy of Chrysler Canada*)

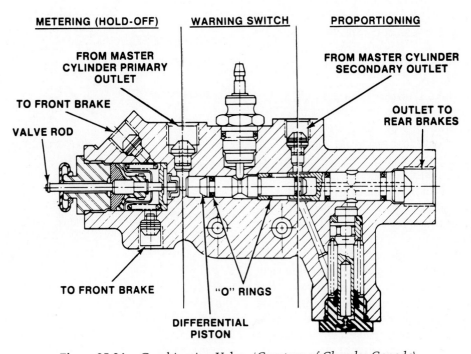

Figure 25-24.   Combination Valve. (*Courtesy of Chrysler Canada*)

transfer during a brake application. A bracket is connected to the axle and the proportioning valve is mounted on the frame. A spring is attached from the bracket to the proportioning valve lever. As the vehicle load increases, the distance between the frame and the axle decreases. This movement causes the

spring to pull the proportioning valve lever and move the valve to a preset split point. Fluid pressure to the rear brakes is then adjusted in relation to vehicle load and frame height.

A load-sensing proportioning valve is shown in Figure 25-25.

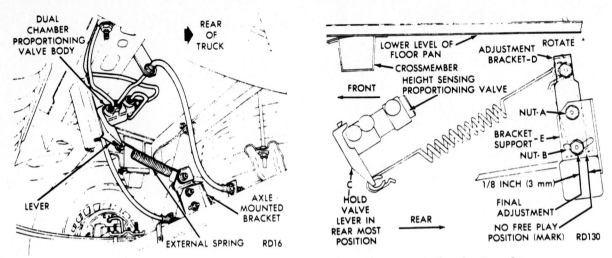

Figure 25-25. Load-Sensing Proportioning Valve. (*Courtesy of Chrysler Canada*)

Power Brakes

Basic Principles

Power brake boosters are used on many vehicles to reduce effort during brake pedal applications. Vacuum-operated power brake boosters which operate mechanically are most commonly used. These power brake boosters maintain a positive feel of braking on the brake pedal.

Some power brake boosters are operated by hydraulic pressure from the power steering pump. This type of brake booster may be used with diesel engines, which have a very low manifold vacuum.

The vacuum-operated power brake booster is attached to the cowl panel under the hood, and the master cylinder is bolted to the brake booster. A linkage is connected from the brake pedal to the booster, and a push rod extends from the booster to the master cylinder.

Manifold vacuum is supplied through a hose to the brake booster. When the brake pedal is released, an atmospheric valve closes off atmospheric pressure to the booster. Under this condition, manifold vacuum is supplied to both sides of the booster diaphragm if the engine is running. Since the vacuum is equal on both sides of the diaphragm, the diaphragm remains stationary, as indicated in Figure 25-26.

When the brake pedal is depressed with the engine running, the brake pedal rod opens the atmospheric valve in the booster and closes the vacuum valve. This action seals the manifold vacuum in the master cylinder side of the diaphragm and opens the other side of the diaphragm to the atmosphere. The

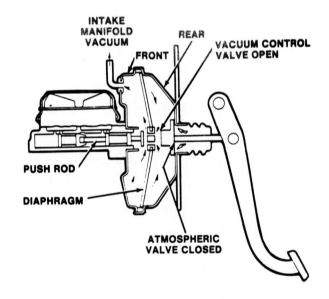

Figure 25-26. Power Brake Booster, Released Position. (*Courtesy of Chrysler Canada*)

pressure difference in each side of the diaphragm moves the diaphragm toward the master cylinder, and the brake booster rod exerts a force on the master cylinder piston. Therefore, the brake booster force and the driver's force on the pedal work together to apply the brakes.

A brake booster in the applied position is pictured in Figure 25-27.

Single-Diaphragm Brake Booster

A return spring is used to hold the power piston and diaphragm in the released position. When the engine

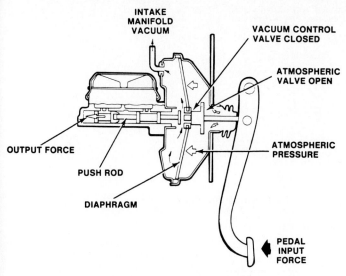

Figure 25-27. Brake Booster, Applied Position. (*Courtesy of Chrysler Canada*)

is running, manifold vacuum is supplied through the open vacuum control port in the booster to both sides of the diaphragm. Therefore, equal pressure exists on each side of the diaphragm and the diaphragm remains stationary. Under this condition, the atmosphere control port is closed, as shown in Figure 25-28.

When the brake pedal is depressed, the vacuum control port is closed and the atmosphere control port is opened by the brake pedal rod movement. When this occurs, the manifold vacuum is sealed off from the brake pedal side of the diaphragm, and at-

mospheric pressure is allowed to enter this area. Under this condition, manifold vacuum is maintained on the master cylinder side of the diaphragm. The pressure difference on each side of the diaphragm forces the booster rod against the master cylinder piston, which assists the driver to apply the brakes. This process is illustrated in Figure 25-29.

The brake fluid pressure applies a reaction force to the booster push rod and the rubber reaction disc. A portion of this reaction force acts directly on the power piston. The remainder of the reaction force causes the reaction disc to extrude into the space to the left of the valve plunger. This force is then transmitted through the brake pedal rod to the pedal, which provides the driver with a feel of the braking effort. During a moderate brake application, this reaction force moves the valve plunger to the right and closes the atmosphere control port and the vacuum control port. This maintains the pressure differential on each side of the diaphragm and keeps the brakes in the partly applied position until the brake pedal is released or applied harder.

During a normal brake application, the reaction force on the power piston and the return spring tension are overcome by the pressure differential across the diaphragm and the force on the brake pedal. The total force on the master cylinder piston is the sum of the brake pedal force and booster diaphragm and power piston force. Therefore, part of the braking force is supplied by the driver, and the greater part of the force is supplied by the booster.

The amount of brake pedal effort determines the

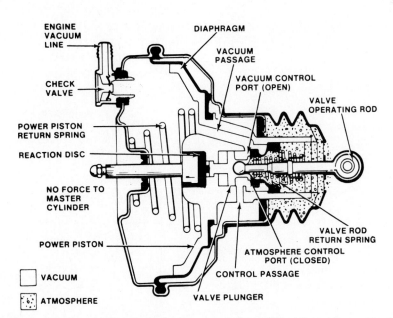

Figure 25-28. Single-Diaphragm Brake Booster, Released Position. (*Courtesy of Chrysler Canada*)

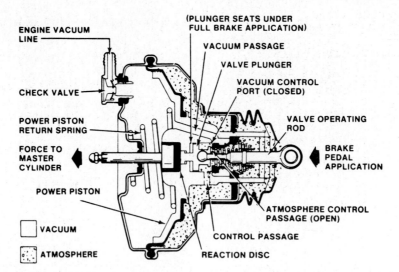

Figure 25-29. Single-Diaphragm Brake Booster, Applied Position. (*Courtesy of Chrysler Canada*)

opening of the atmosphere control port and the amount of atmospheric pressure supplied to the right side of the diaphragm. During a hard brake application, the atmosphere control port opens sufficiently to allow full atmospheric pressure on the right side of the diaphragm. Under this condition, there is maximum pressure differential across the diaphragm and power piston. This is referred to as the "vacuum run-out" point of the booster. When this point is reached, the valve plunger seats on the power piston, and directly transmits the valve opening force from the brake pedal. During the vacuum run-out mode, greater braking effort must be supplied by increased pedal pressure.

Some brake boosters have a bridge and reaction levers to transmit reaction force from the brake fluid to the power piston and the brake pedal, as illustrated in Figure 25-30.

Tandem-Diaphragm Brake Boosters

Some brake boosters contain two diaphragms rather than a single diaphragm. The operating principles of the tandem-diaphragm, or dual-diaphragm, brake boosters are the same as the single-diaphragm boosters. A tandem-diaphragm brake booster is shown in Figure 25-31.

Hydraulic Power Brake Boosters

Hydraulically operated power brake systems have a hydro-booster bolted to the engine side of the cowl panel. An operating rod from the brake pedal is connected to one end of the hydro-booster and the master cylinder is bolted to the other end. The power steering pump supplies pressurized fluid through an

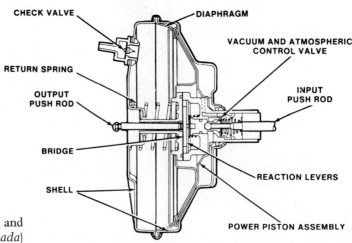

Figure 25-30. Brake Booster with Bridge and Reaction Levers. (*Courtesy of Chrysler Canada*)

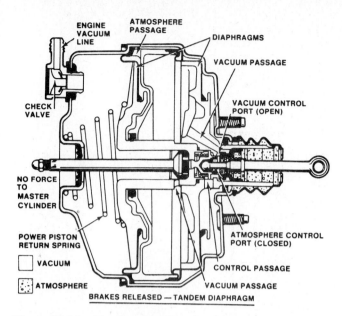

Figure 25-31. Tandem-Diaphragm Brake Booster. (*Courtesy of Chrysler Canada*)

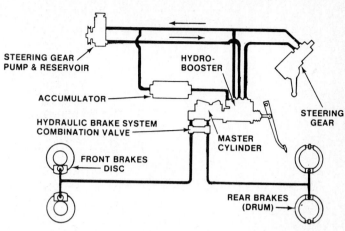

Figure 25-32. Hydraulically Operated Power Brake System. (*Courtesy of Chrysler Canada*)

open center valve in the hydro-booster to the center valve in the power steering gear. Fluid returns from the power steering gear to the pump reservoir. (Refer to Chapter 24 for an explanation of power steering systems.)

A diagram of the hydraulically operated power brake system is provided in Figure 25-32.

When the brakes are applied, the brake pedal rod moves a small hydraulic cylinder in the hydro-booster. This movement provides hydraulic pressure from the hydro-booster to the master cylinder rod, which assists the driver to apply the brakes.

Parking Brakes

Design and Operation

The parking brake system operates the rear brake shoes mechanically to apply the rear brakes. A parking brake pedal is mounted under the dash panel. When this pedal is depressed, the pedal mechanism pulls the front cable. This pulling movement is transmitted through an intermediate cable and rear cable to the rear brakes. A ratchet in the pedal mechanism holds the cables in the applied position, and a brake-release lever handle must be pulled to release the ratchet and cable tension.

The pedal mechanism is shown in Figure 25-33, and the cable routing is illustrated in Figure 25-34.

Some parking brakes have a vacuum diaphragm which releases the brake mechanism. The gear se-

lector operates a switch on the steering column. When the gear selector is placed in reverse or drive, the switch supplies manifold vacuum to the diaphragm, which releases the parking brake.

An adjusting bolt is connected to the right rear cable adjustment, and an equalizer in the cable supplies equal cable movement and tension at both rear wheels. When the parking brake is applied, the cables pull the levers connected to the rear secondary brake shoes. A strut is connected from the lever to the primary brake shoe. Therefore, lever and strut movement force the primary shoe against the drum.

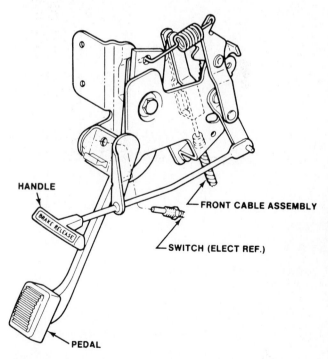

Figure 25-33. Parking Brake Pedal Mechanism. (*Courtesy of Chrysler Canada*)

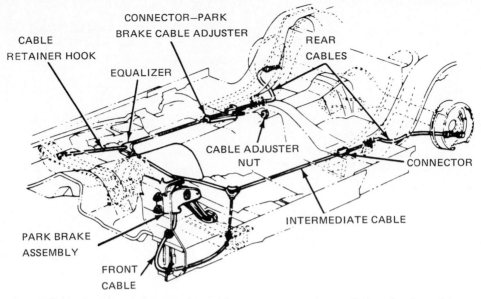

Figure 25-34. Parking Brake Cable Routing. (*Courtesy of Chrysler Canada*)

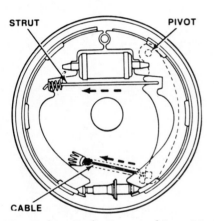

Figure 25-35. Parking Brake Lever and Strut Mechanism. (*Courtesy of Chrysler Canada*)

Once this occurs, additional lever movement forces the lever pivot outward to apply the secondary brake shoe.

The parking brake lever and strut mechanism are pictured in Figure 25-35.

Four-Wheel Disc Brakes

Rear Caliper Design

A few vehicles are equipped with four-wheel disc brakes. The rear calipers operate the same as the front calipers that were described previously. The parking brake cables are connected to levers on the rear calipers. When the parking brake is applied, these levers rotate an actuator screw in the calipers which moves the piston and forces the brake pads against the rotor surfaces.

Parking brake cable connections to the rear calipers are pictured in Figure 25-36, and the actuator screws are shown in Figure 25-37.

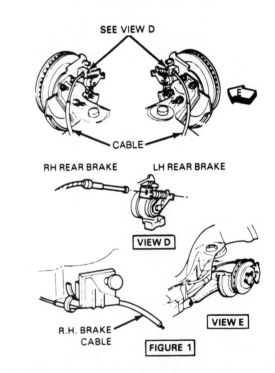

Figure 25-36. Parking Brake Cable Connections to Rear Calipers. (*Courtesy of Cadillac Motor Car Division, General Motors Corporation*)

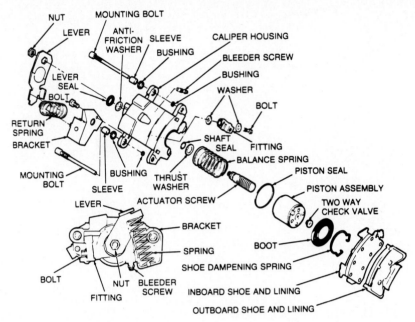

Figure 25-37. Rear Calipers with Actuator Screws. (*Courtesy of Cadillac Motor Car Division, General Motors Corporation*)

Anti-Lock Brake Systems

Components

Master Cylinder and Hydraulic Brake Booster The master cylinder contains a hydraulic pump motor which supplies pressure to a booster piston and provides power assist during a brake application. A fluid reservoir on the master cylinder has two main chambers which are connected through hoses to the master cylinder and the pump motor. Integral fluid-level switches are located in the reservoir cover. A solenoid valve body that is mounted on the master cylinder contains three pairs of electrically operated solenoid valves. One pair of solenoid valves is connected to each front wheel and the other pair is connected to the rear wheels.

A master cylinder used in the anti-lock brake system is illustrated in Figure 25-38.

The accumulator is a gas-filled pressure chamber that is mounted on the pump and motor assembly in the master cylinder, as indicated in Figure 25-39.

Electronic Controller The electronic controller is located in the luggage compartment underneath the

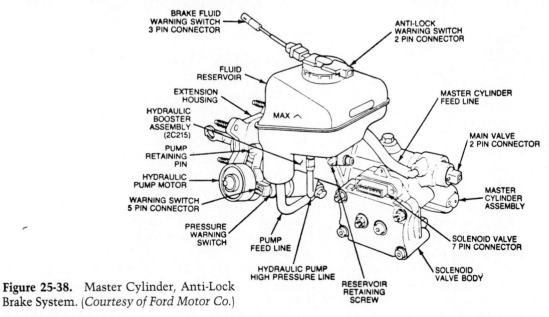

Figure 25-38. Master Cylinder, Anti-Lock Brake System. (*Courtesy of Ford Motor Co.*)

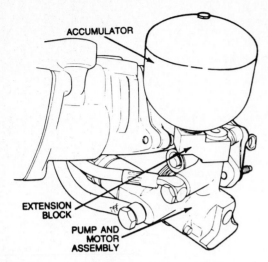

Figure 25-39. Accumulator on Pump and Motor Assembly. (*Courtesy of Ford Motor Co.*)

package tray. This controller contains two microprocessors that monitor the brake system during normal driving conditions, and also while the system is providing an anti-lock function. When the controller receives input signals from the wheel sensors that indicate the beginning of wheel lockup conditions, the controller operates the master cylinder solenoid valves to control master cylinder pressure and prevent wheel lockup. If a defect causes the electronic system to be inoperative, normal power-assist braking will be maintained.

The electronic controller is illustrated in Figure 25-40.

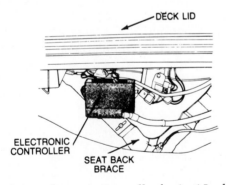

Figure 25-40. Electronic Controller for Anti-Lock Brakes. (*Courtesy of Ford Motor Co.*)

Wheel Sensors   Wheel sensors at each wheel are mounted directly above a toothed sensor ring. These sensors provide input signals to the electronic controller. During a hard brake application, the wheels may lock up and begin to skid, which could cause the vehicle to spin out of control. When the wheel sensor signals indicate a wheel lockup condition, the controller immediately operates the solenoid valves to control master cylinder pressure.

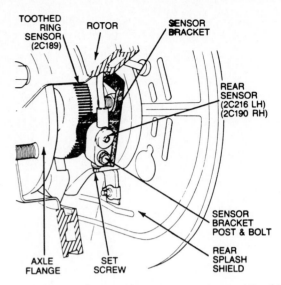

Figure 25-41.   Rear Wheel Sensor. (*Courtesy of Ford Motor Co.*)

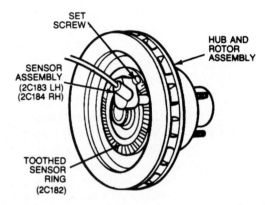

Figure 25-42.   Front Wheel Sensor. (*Courtesy of Ford Motor Co.*)

A rear wheel sensor is pictured in Figure 25-41, and a front wheel sensor is shown in Figure 25-42.

Master Cylinder Operation

The hydraulic pump maintains a pressure of 2,030 to 2,610 psi (14,000 to 18,000 kPa) in the accumulator. This pressure is also supplied to a control valve that is controlled by brake pedal movement. If the brakes are applied, the scissor lever mechanism activates the control valve, which allows pressure from the hydraulic pump to enter the boost chamber. This pressure will be proportional to brake pedal travel. Pressure to the boost chamber is also supplied through the normally open solenoid valve, and the proportioning valve, to the rear brakes. The boost chamber pressure and the brake pedal force move the master cylinder pistons, which supplies fluid pressure through the normally open solenoid valves to the front brakes. Therefore, the hydraulic pump

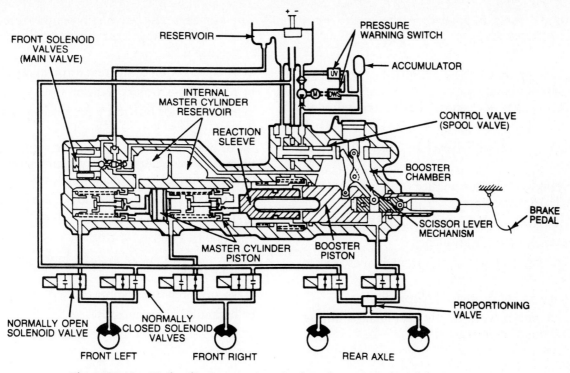

Figure 25-43. Hydraulic System, Anti-Lock Brakes. (*Courtesy of Ford Motor Co.*)

pressure assists the driver to apply the brakes, which reduces brake pedal effort.

The electronic controller closes the normally open solenoid valves and opens the normally closed solenoid valves to reduce the master cylinder pressure and prevent wheel lockup. When the normally closed solenoid valves are opened, fluid returns from the calipers, or wheel cylinders, to the reservoir.

During normal braking, the brake pedal application feels the same as with a normal power brake system. In the anti-lock mode, slight pulsations are felt on the brake pedal and a small change in pedal height is experienced.

The anti-lock brake hydraulic system is shown in Figure 25-43.

Service and Diagnosis of Anti-Lock Brake System

Anti-Lock Brake Warning Light   An anti-lock brake warning light is located in the roof console, and the conventional brake warning light is positioned in the instrument panel. When the ignition switch is turned on, the electronic controller performs a check of all the anti-lock brake system components. This check requires three to four seconds, and during this time the anti-lock brake light is illuminated. If either, or both, warning lights are illuminated after this interval, a defect exists in the brake system.

The anti-lock brake warning light in the roof console is illustrated in Figure 25-44.

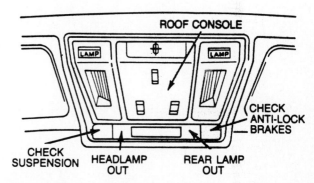

Figure 25-44. Check Anti-Lock Brake Warning Light. (*Courtesy of Ford Motor Co.*)

(Brake system service is explained in Chapter 21 of *Automotive Principles: Repair and Service*, Volume II.)

Test Questions

1. When the master cylinder piston size is reduced, the master cylinder output pressure for a given brake pedal force:

   a) increases.

   b) decreases.

   c) remains the same.

2. Additional force is applied to the brake shoes when a larger diameter wheel cylinder is used.
   T F

3. In a brake system used on a front-wheel-drive car, the right front and right rear brakes are connected to the primary section of the master cylinder.
   T F

4. A brake fluid classified as DOT 5 has a _____ base.

5. Disc brake linings are applied with greater force than drum brake linings.   T F

6. The metering valve allows simultaneous front and rear brake application by:

   a) reducing pressure to the front brakes during light brake applications.

   b) increasing pressure to the front brakes.

   c) reducing pressure to the rear brakes during hard brake applications.

7. The proportioning valve reduces pressure to the rear brakes during light brake applications to compensate for:

   a) delayed action of the rear drum brakes.

   b) rear-to-front weight transfer.

   c) increased application force on the front calipers.

8. In an anti-lock brake system, the normal fluid pressure supplied from the hydraulic pump in the master cylinder to the accumulator would be:

   a) 1,000 to 1,200 psi (6,895 to 8,274 kPa)

   b) 1,500 to 1,600 psi (10,342 to 11,032 kPa)

   c) 2,000 to 2,600 psi (13,790 to 17,927 kPa)

9. In the anti-lock brake system, brake pedal assist is provided by:

   a) vacuum booster diaphragm.

   b) hydraulic pump pressure.

   c) power steering pump pressure.

26

Heating and Air Conditioning Systems

Chapter Completion Objectives

1. Understand heater systems.
2. Demonstrate a knowledge of basic air conditioning principles.

3. Display an understanding of manually operated and semi-automatic air conditioning systems.
4. Indicate a knowledge of computer-controlled air conditioning systems.

Heating System

Design and Operation

The heater core, blower motor, and operating doors are contained in a heater case located under the instrument panel. A heater control panel is located in the instrument panel. Cables are connected from the control panel levers to the operating doors. An intake duct supplies air from a cowl opening below the windshield to the heater case. Heater hoses are connected from the cooling system to the heater core, as pictured in Figure 26-1.

The temperature-blend door directs airflow through the heater core or past the heater core, depending on the door position. This door may be positioned to direct some air through the heater core, while the remainder of the airflow is allowed to bypass the core. Movement of the temperature-blend door is controlled by a cable from the temperature lever in the heater control panel.

When the temperature lever is in the "cool" position and the function lever is off, the temperature-blend door allows air to bypass the heater core and the air-outlet door prevents airflow through any of the heater outlets.

When the function lever is moved to the "panel" position, the air-outlet door rotates to direct air through the instrument panel outlets. When the temperature lever is in the "warm" position, the temperature-blend door directs all the intake air through the heater core, as indicated in Figure 26-2.

If the function lever is moved to the "floor" position, the air-control door will direct airflow from the heater core to the floor ducts. When the temperature control is in the "cool" position, the temperature-blend door shuts off airflow through the heater core and allows all the air to bypass the core, as pictured in Figure 26-2. In the "defrost" function lever position, the air outlet door directs airflow from the heater case to the defroster outlets.

A plenum is connected from the heater case to the various outlets. This plenum is tightly sealed to the heater case.

The floor and defrost outlets are shown in Figure 26-3, and the instrument panel outlets are illustrated in Figure 26-4.

Blower Motor Electrical Circuit

Voltage is supplied through a fuse and a thermal limiter to one blower motor brush. The thermal limiter and three resistors are located in a resistor assembly mounted in the heater case. A wire is connected from the other blower motor brush to the resistor assembly, and a wiring harness is connected between the resistor assembly and the blower switch in the heater control panel.

In the high-speed position, the blower switch directly grounds the blower motor brush. When the

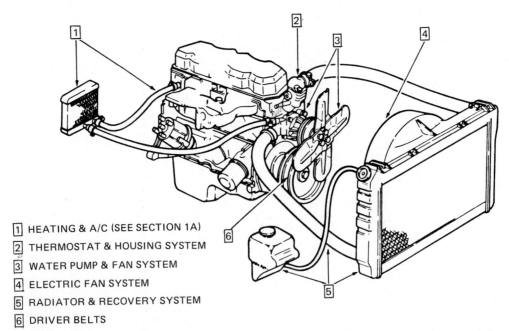

1 HEATING & A/C (SEE SECTION 1A)
2 THERMOSTAT & HOUSING SYSTEM
3 WATER PUMP & FAN SYSTEM
4 ELECTRIC FAN SYSTEM
5 RADIATOR & RECOVERY SYSTEM
6 DRIVER BELTS

Figure 26-1. Heater Hose Connections. (*Courtesy of Pontiac Motor Division, General Motors Corporation*)

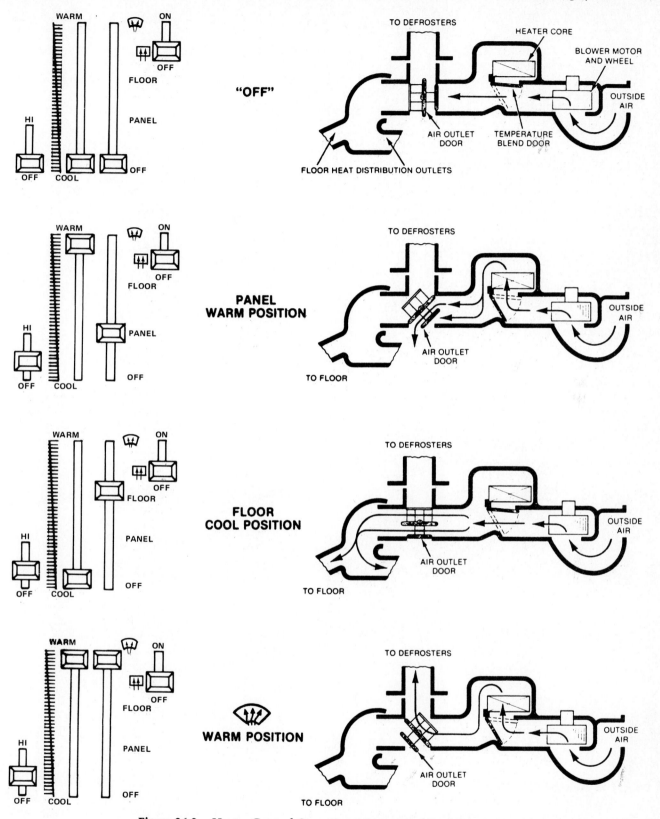

Figure 26-2. Heater Control Operation. *(Courtesy of Ford Motor Co.)*

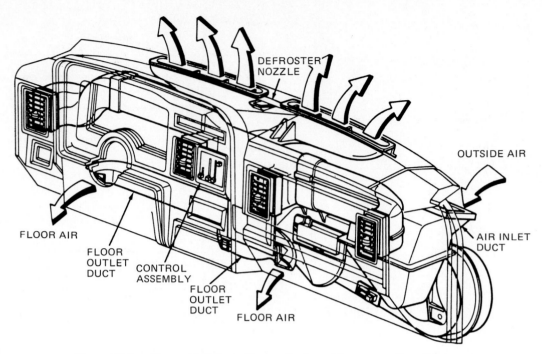

Figure 26-3.   Floor and Defrost Heater Outlets. (*Courtesy of Ford Motor Co.*)

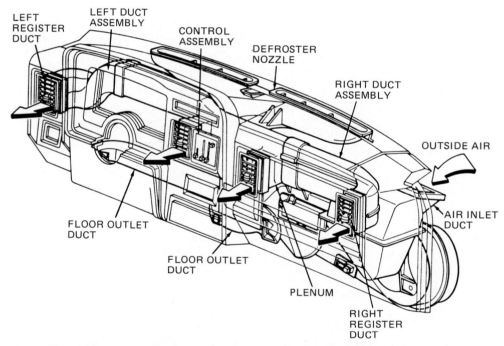

Figure 26-4.   Instrument Panel Air Outlets. (*Courtesy of Ford Motor Co.*)

blower switch is positioned in one of the other positions, one or more of the resistors in the resistor assembly is connected in series with the switch contact. Heater blower speed is reduced when more resistors are connected in series with the blower switch. When the blower switch is moved to the off position, the circuit from the resistor assembly to ground is open.

The thermal limiter opens the circuit to the blower motor if the temperature exceeds 212°F (100°C). If the thermal limiter opens the circuit, replacement of the resistor assembly is necessary.

The heater blower circuit is pictured in Figure 26-5, and the resistor assembly is shown in Figure 26-6.

Some blower motor switches are designed so the

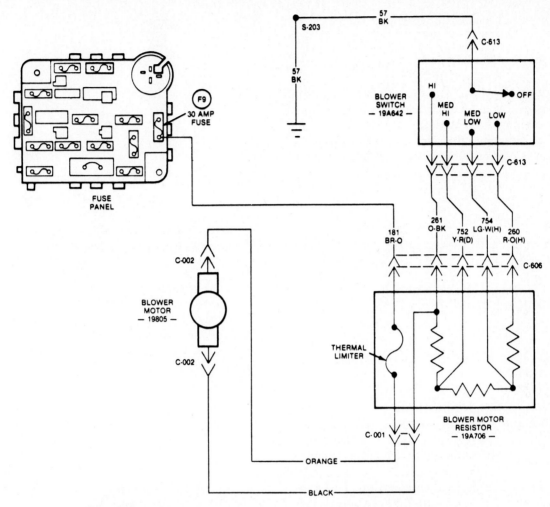

Figure 26-5.   Blower Motor Electrical Circuit. (*Courtesy of Ford Motor Co.*)

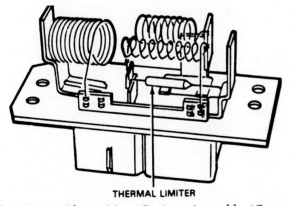

Figure 26-6.   Blower Motor Resistor Assembly. (*Courtesy of Ford Motor Co.*)

blower motor operates at a very low speed with the blower motor switch in the off position and the ignition switch on. This blower motor mode provides air movement through the vehicle for ventilation purposes.

Some vehicles have body exhaust valves in the body pillars which open when air pressure increases slightly in the vehicle interior. These exhaust valves allow increased airflow through the vehicle interior, as indicated in Figure 26-7.

The body pillar exhaust valves are one-way valves that do not allow dust to enter the passenger compartment.

1   FRONT INLET GRILLE

2   BODY LOCK PILLAR EXHAUST VALVE

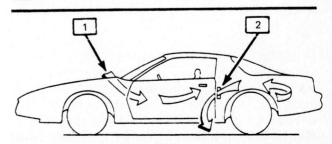

Figure 26-7.   Body Pillar Exhaust Valves. (*Courtesy of Pontiac Motor Division, General Motors Corporation*)

Principles of Air Conditioning

Heat Energy

Heat energy can be converted to another form, but it cannot be destroyed. Heat is transferred by conduction, convection, and radiation. As an illustration of conduction, consider a pan placed on a hot stove. As burner heat is applied to the bottom of the pan, heat travels by conduction to the handle of the pan until the handle becomes very hot, as indicated in Figure 26-8.

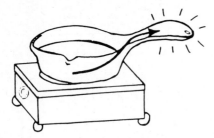

Figure 26-8. Heat Transfer by Conduction. (*Courtesy of Chrysler Canada*)

Convection can be illustrated by a container filled with liquid placed on a hot stove burner. Heat applied to the bottom of the container convects to the water that is in contact with the container bottom. The heated water expands and rises to the top, and the colder water moves to the bottom. This convection method of heating a liquid is shown in Figure 26-9.

Figure 26-9. Heat Transfer by Convection. (*Courtesy of Chrysler Canada*)

A heat lamp is a good example of heat transfer by radiation. When we sit in front of a heat lamp, radiant heat waves from the lamp have a warming effect on our body, as indicated in Figure 26-10. Radiant heat will travel through the atmosphere or through a vacuum and then be absorbed by a solid, such as a car or a person. The sun gives off radiant heat.

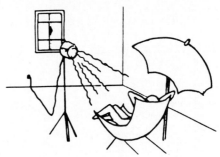

Figure 26-10. Heat Transfer by Radiation. (*Courtesy of Chrysler Canada*)

An automotive air conditioning system uses all of these principles of heat transfer.

Removal of Heat Energy

Automotive air conditioners operate on the principle that evaporation cools. During the air conditioning process, heat is removed in the form of energy from the passenger compartment and is transferred to the outside air, as illustrated in Figure 26-11.

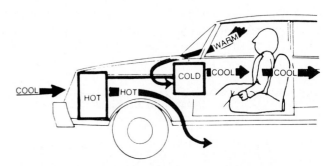

Figure 26-11. Heat Energy Removed from Passenger Compartment and Transferred to Outside Air. (*Courtesy of Chrysler Canada*)

The following basic principles are used in an air conditioning system:

1. Heat flows from hot to cold, i.e., from a region of high temperature to a region of low temperature. For example, if a warm container is placed in ice, the ice melts and the container is cooler.
2. Heat is absorbed when a liquid changes to a gas.
3. Heat is given off when a gas is changed to a liquid.
4. For a given temperature of a material, there is a corresponding pressure.
5. The boiling point of a liquid varies in relation to its pressure.

Refrigerant

Characteristics

The refrigerant used in automotive air conditioning systems is dichlorodifluoromethane (CCl_2F_2), a colorless, almost odorless chemical referred to as R12. The boiling point of R12 is $-21.6°F$ ($-29.7°C$). The substance is heavier than air.

Variations in pressure change the boiling point of a liquid. For example, at sea level water boils at 212°F (100°C). However, at the top of a mountain, the atmospheric pressure is less so water boils at a lower temperature. Gasoline boils at 85° to 437°F (30° to 225°C) under normal atmospheric pressure. However, when the pressure is reduced, such as in an intake manifold, the boiling point of gasoline is greatly reduced. (This principle is explained in Chapter 16.) Therefore, an increase in pressure raises the boiling point of a liquid, and a decrease in pressure lowers its boiling point.

Since R12 boils at $-21.6°F$ ($-29.7°C$) at 14.7 psi (101 kPa) pressure experienced at sea level, pressure must be greatly increased to keep R12 in liquid form. When the liquid refrigerant is released from pressure, it immediately flashes into a vapor and absorbs a vast amount of heat. This ability to absorb large amounts of heat even at low temperatures makes R12 a very suitable refrigerant for automotive air conditioning systems.

The temperature-pressure relationship for R12 refrigerant is provided in Table 26-1.

Air Conditioning System Components

Compressor

The compressor is belt-driven from the crankshaft. An electric clutch engages and disengages the compressor pulley from the shaft. The compressor receives R12 in gaseous form at the inlet and pressurizes the refrigerant to a high pressure. This pressure from the compressor causes the R12 to move through the air conditioning (A/C) system.

Many compressors have pistons that are mounted in axial cylinders around the compressor shaft. An axial plate on the shaft moves the pistons back and forth as the shaft rotates, and the movement of the pistons compresses the R12. Valve plates and reed valves control the movement of R12 in and out of the cylinders. The compressor shaft is supported on needle bearings and vertical needle bearings absorb end thrust on the shaft. Refrigerant leaks are prevented by a front shaft seal, and cylinder "O" rings.

A diagram of a compressor is provided in Figure 26-12.

Many compressor clutch electrical circuits have a cycling switch to cycle the compressor on and off. The cycling switch and compressor switch clutch circuits are described later in this chapter.

Some late-model compressors have an infinitely variable displacement that matches air conditioning system demand under all conditions without cycling. This type of compressor has a variable-angle axial plate that is controlled by a balance of force on the five pistons. A pivot pin on the axial plate is used to change the plate angle. The balance of force on the pistons is varied by changing the compressor crankcase-suction pressure by use of a bellows-type control valve in the rear compressor head.

When the A/C capacity demand is low, suction pressure at the inlet is below the control point. Under this condition the control valve bleeds discharge pressure into the crankcase and simultaneously closes a passage from the crankcase to the suction plenum. This valve action increases crankcase-suction pressure differential, which creates a force on the pistons that results in axial plate movement

TABLE 26.1.   R12 Refrigerant Temperature-Pressure Relationship.
(Courtesy of Pontiac Motor Division, General Motors Corporation)

The table below indicates the pressure of Refrigerant — 12 at various temperatures. For instance, a drum of Refrigerant at a temperature of 80°F (26.6°C) will have a pressure of 84.1 PSI (579.9 kPa). If it is heated to 125°F (51.6°C), the pressure will increase to 167.5 PSI (1154.9 kPa). It also can be used conversely to determine the temperature at which Refrigerant — 12 boils under various pressures. For example, at a pressure of 30.1 PSI (207.5 kPa), Refrigerant — 12 boils at 32°F (0°C).

(°F)(°C)		(PSIG)(kPa)		(°F)(°C)		(PSIG)(kPa)	
-21.7	-29.8C	0(ATMOSPHERIC PRESSURE)	0(kPa)	55	12.7C	52.0	358.5
				60	15.5C	57.7	397.8
-20	-28.8C	2.4	16.5	65	18.3C	63.7	439.2
-10	-23.3C	4.5	31.0	70	21.1C	70.1	482.7
-5	-20.5C	6.8	46.9	75	23.8C	76.9	530.2
0	-17.7C	9.2	63.4	80	26.6C	84.1	579.9
5	-15.0C	11.8	81.4	85	29.4C	91.7	632.3
10	-12.2C	14.7	101.4	90	32.2C	99.6	686.7
15	-9.4C	17.7	122.0	95	35.0C	108.1	745.3
20	-6.6C	21.1	145.5	100	37.7C	116.9	806.0
25	-3.8C	24.6	169.6	105	40.5C	126.2	870.2
30	-1.1C	28.5	196.5	110	43.3C	136.0	937.7
32	0C	30.1	207.5	115	46.1C	146.5	1010.1
35	1.6C	32.6	224.8	120	48.8C	157.1	1083.2
40	4.4C	37.0	255.1	125	51.6C	167.5	1154.9
45	7.2C	41.7	287.5	130	54.4C	179.0	1234.2
50	10.0C	46.7	322.0	140	60.0C	204.5	1410.0

420005-1B

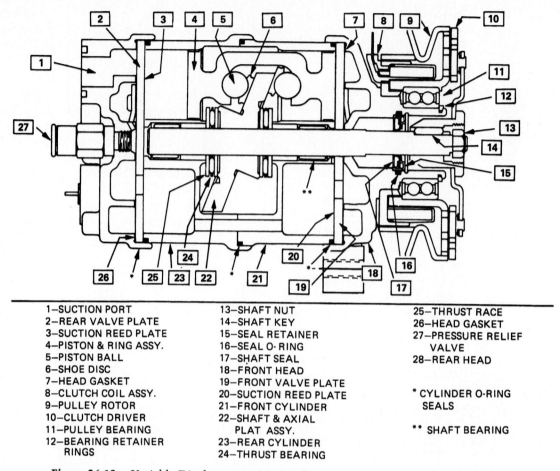

Figure 26-13.   Variable-Displacement Air Conditioning Compressor. (*Courtesy of GM Product Service Training, General Motors Corporation*)

1—SUCTION PORT	13—SHAFT NUT	25—THRUST RACE
2—REAR VALVE PLATE	14—SHAFT KEY	26—HEAD GASKET
3—SUCTION REED PLATE	15—SEAL RETAINER	27—PRESSURE RELIEF
4—PISTON & RING ASSY.	16—SEAL O-RING	VALVE
5—PISTON BALL	17—SHAFT SEAL	28—REAR HEAD
6—SHOE DISC	18—FRONT HEAD	
7—HEAD GASKET	19—FRONT VALVE PLATE	
8—CLUTCH COIL ASSY.	20—SUCTION REED PLATE	* CYLINDER O-RING
9—PULLEY ROTOR	21—FRONT CYLINDER	SEALS
10—CLUTCH DRIVER	22—SHAFT & AXIAL	
11—PULLEY BEARING	PLAT ASSY.	** SHAFT BEARING
12—BEARING RETAINER	23—REAR CYLINDER	
RINGS	24—THRUST BEARING	

about the pivot pin to reduce plate angle, piston movement, and compressor displacement.

When the A/C system demand is high, the suction pressure is above the control point, and the control valve maintains a bleed from crankcase to suction at the inlet. This reduces the crankcase-suction pressure differential, and the change in force on the pistons causes the axial plate to move on the pivot pin to provide maximum piston movement and compressor displacement.

The variable-displacement compressor provides smooth, continuous compressor operation and minimizes the fuel economy penalty for A/C. A variable-displacement A/C compressor is illustrated in Figure 26-13.

Condenser Core

The condenser core is usually located in front of the radiator. On some vehicles the condenser is located beside the radiator, and a separate electrically driven fan moves air through the condenser. This con-denser cooling fan is activated when the A/C clutch is energized. Hot refrigerant flows at high pressure from the compressor through a hose to the condenser. The purpose of the condenser is to cool this hot, high-pressure gas so that it changes to a liquid.

On some refrigeration systems, a muffler is located in the high-pressure hose between the compressor and the condenser to reduce compressor noise and high-pressure line vibrations.

A condenser core is shown beside the radiator in Figure 26-14.

Filter/Drier

One hose is connected from the condenser to the filter/drier, and another is connected from the filter/drier to the expansion valve and evaporator. The filter/drier removes foreign particles and moisture from the refrigerant. This unit also provides a storage space for refrigerant if the system is not demanding a full supply.

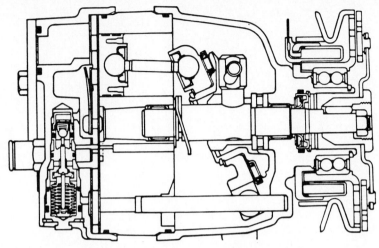

Figure 26-13.   Variable-Displacement Air Conditioning Compressor. (*Courtesy of GM Product Service Training, General Motors Corporation*)

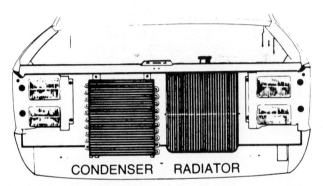

Figure 26-14.   Condenser Core. (*Courtesy of Chrysler Canada*)

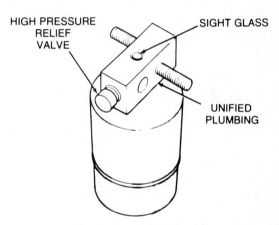

Figure 26-15.   Filter/Drier with Sight Glass. (*Courtesy of Chrysler Canada*)

A pressure relief valve is located in the filter/drier to protect the refrigerant system from excessive pressure. This relief valve discharges refrigerant if the system pressure reaches 450 to 500 psi (3,100 to 3,790 kPa). If the relief valve discharges, the cause of the high pressure must be corrected. High system pressure could result from an overcharge of refrigerant, or a restricted airflow through the condenser.

Most filter/driers are replaced as a unit, and some of these units contain a sight glass for diagnostic purposes, as indicated in Figure 26-15.

Cycling Clutch Switch and Expansion Valve Assembly

The expansion ("H") valve contains an orifice that meters liquid refrigerant to the evaporator. When the refrigerant flows through the "H" valve orifice, the pressure is reduced and the refrigerant boils and changes to a vapor. When this vaporizing occurs, a

large amount of heat is absorbed from the air flowing through the evaporator, so that the air entering the passenger compartment is cool.

The clutch cycling switch and "H" valve assembly are located in the engine compartment where the refrigerant sealing plate is connected to the evaporator at the firewall. A capillary tube connected to the clutch cycling switch extends into a well in the compressor suction line. The well is filled with a special grease that is essential for correct temperature sensing.

When a predetermined low temperature is reached in the evaporator and suction line, the capillary tube signal causes the cycling clutch switch to open the compressor clutch electrical circuit and stop the compressor. This action causes the refrigerant to stop flowing, and the evaporator temperature increases gradually. At a specific evaporator temperature, the capillary tube signals the cycling clutch

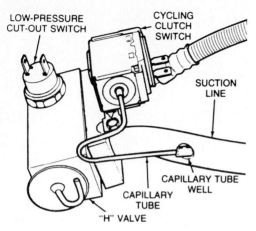

Figure 26-16. Cycling Clutch Switch and Expansion ("H") Valve Assembly. (*Courtesy of Chrysler Canada*)

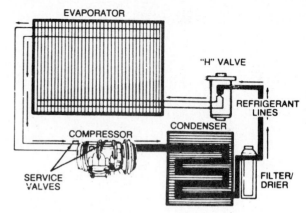

Figure 26-17. Refrigeration System. (*Courtesy of Chrysler Canada*)

switch to close the circuit to the compressor clutch, which restores the normal refrigerant flow through the system. The compressor cycling action prevents evaporator freeze-up.

A low-pressure cut-out switch is mounted in the cycling clutch switch and "H" valve assembly. This low-pressure cut-out switch opens the electrical circuit to the compressor clutch if the system runs out of refrigerant and system pressure becomes very low. This switch also opens the compressor clutch circuit to stop the compressor when the atmospheric temperature drops below 32° F (0° C) and the engine idles for an extended period.

A cycling clutch switch and "H" valve assembly is illustrated in Figure 26-16.

Evaporator Core

The evaporator is located in the evaporator-heater assembly. This assembly is mounted in the passenger compartment under the dash on some vehicles. Other cars have the evaporator-heater housing assembly mounted on the firewall under the hood.

Refrigerant enters the evaporator from the "H" valve. When the refrigerant flows through the "H" valve restriction, the pressure is reduced and the liquid refrigerant changes to a vapor in the evaporator. This vaporizing action absorbs heat from the air entering the passenger compartment through the air passages in the evaporator core. The air is also dehumidified as it flows through the evaporator core. Refrigerant enters the evaporator as a pressurized liquid and leaves the evaporator as a low-pressure gas that returns through the suction hose to the compressor inlet.

The refrigeration system is shown in Figure 26-17.

Air Distribution Ducts

Air distribution ducts are located under the instrument panel to route the air from the evaporator-heater housing to the various air outlets in the passenger compartment. Heat outlets discharge warm air on the vehicle floor under the instrument panel, and defrost outlets direct heat from the instrument panel outlets to the windshield.

The A/C outlets are located in the front of the instrument panel. These outlets have horizontal and vertical deflectors to direct the flow of cool air. It is possible to close the A/C outlets completely by facing the deflector vanes fully upward. Some A/C outlets have a valve with an operating lever near the outlets which is used to close the outlet.

The airflow from the instrument panel outlets is shown in the various modes in Figure 26-18.

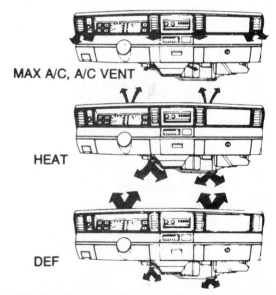

Figure 26-18. Heating and Air Conditioning Air Outlets. (*Courtesy of Chrysler Canada*)

Manual Air Conditioning Systems

Controls

Temperature Lever   Many A/C systems operate on the blend-air reheat principle. In these systems, all the air entering the system passes through the evaporator, and a selected portion of the air passes through the heater core, depending on the position of the blend-air door, as indicated in Figure 26-19.

A cable is connected from the temperature lever to the blend-air door so that the position of the door is controlled by the temperature lever. All air temperature outputs, except maximum A/C, are controlled by the temperature lever.

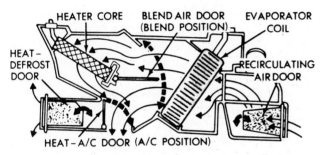

Figure 26-19.   Air Conditioning Control Doors. (*Courtesy of Chrysler Canada*)

Blower Switch   The blower switch is used to operate the blower at four different speeds, which are provided by a resistor block in the blower motor circuit. This resistor block located in the evaporator-heater case is similar to the resistor block in a conventional heater system, which was explained previously.

Push Button Selector   Six push buttons are used to select various modes of heating or air conditioning. These modes include off, max A/C, A/C norm, bi-level, heat, and defrost. Vacuum and electric switches are operated by the push buttons. The vacuum portion of the switches controls the water shutoff valve and all the doors in the system except the blend-air door. Electrical contacts in the switches control the compressor clutch and the blower.

The heater and A/C control panel is pictured in Figure 26-20.

Modes

Off   When the "off" button is depressed, the inlet-air door is closed to outside air and open to recirculating air from inside the passenger compartment. The heat-A/C door is in the "A/C" position and the

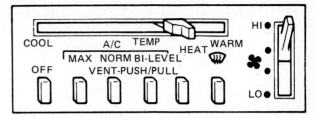

Figure 26-20.   Air Conditioning and Heater Control Panel. (*Courtesy of Chrysler Canada*)

heat-defrost door is in the "heat" position. Coolant flow through the heater core is shut off by the water valve, and there is no airflow through the system. The blower motor and compressor clutch are inoperative because both of these circuits are open.

Max A/C   In the "max A/C" mode, all the doors remain in the same position as in the "off" mode. The "max A/C" mode closes the electrical circuits to the compressor clutch and the blower motor. This mode is recommended for initial fast cool-down, extreme outside humidity, or very high atmospheric temperature. The temperature lever must be in the "cool" position to obtain maximum cooling.

A/C Norm   In the "A/C norm" mode, the vacuum is applied to the outside-air actuator so the outside-air door opens and the recirculating-air door closes. Vacuum is also shut off from the water valve actuator diaphragm, which allows the valve to open. All other door positions remain the same as in the "max A/C" mode. The blower motor and the compressor are on.

When the "A/C norm" button is pulled outward, the compressor clutch is disengaged on some models, which provides normal venting of outside air through the system in this mode. Other models have a vent button that must be depressed to obtain the vent mode.

Bi-Level   In the bi-level mode, the inlet-air door is positioned for outside air entry, and the heat-A/C door is set at bi-level, which allows airflow from the instrument panel outlets, and a lesser portion of air from the floor and defroster outlets. The heat-defrost door is in the "heat" position and the water valve is open. Electrical circuits are completed to the compressor clutch and the blower motor.

On some models, a vent mode is obtained if the bi-level button is pulled outward to disengage the compressor clutch.

Heat   In the heat mode, the outside-air door is open and the vacuum actuator diaphragm moves the heat-A/C door so that it directs airflow out the heater ducts and shuts off airflow to the air conditioning outlets. The heat-defrost door is in the "heat" position, but a small amount of air bleeds past this door to the defrost outlets.

Defrost   When the "defrost" mode button is depressed, the vacuum is shut off to the heat-defrost door actuator diaphragm, and the heat-defrost door moves to the "defrost" position, because it is spring-loaded in this position. All other door positions remain the same as in the heat mode. In the defrost mode, the heat-defrost door is positioned so that 70 percent of the airflow is directed through the defrost outlets, while the remaining 30 percent continues to flow through the heat outlets. The compressor clutch is engaged in the defrost mode.

Vacuum diagrams in the various modes are provided in Figure 26-21.

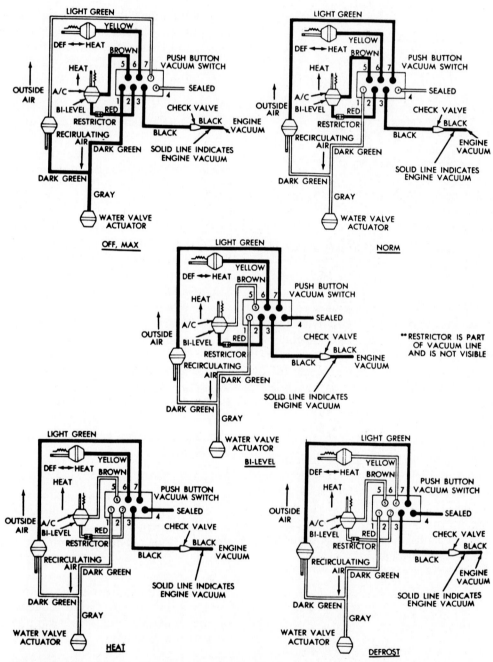

Figure 26-21.   Vacuum Diagrams for Air Conditioning Operating Modes. (*Courtesy of Chrysler Canada*)

Compressor Clutch Electric Circuits

Many compressor clutch circuits are protected by a conventional fuse and a thermal fuse, or a fusible link. Some compressor clutch circuits have a wide-open throttle switch with a time-delay relay. The wide-open throttle switch is operated by the throttle shaft. This switch opens the compressor clutch circuit and stops the compressor to maximize engine power when the throttle is 10° from the wide-open position. The time-delay relay in the switch prevents A/C clutch reengagement for four to eight seconds after a wide-open throttle is released.

The wide-open throttle switch is shown in the compressor clutch circuit in Figure 26-22.

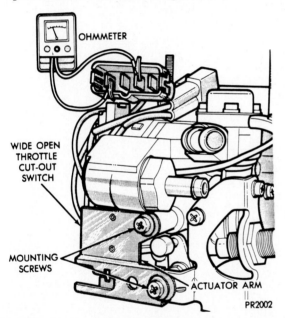

Figure 26-22. Compressor Clutch Wide-Open Throttle Switch. (*Courtesy of Chrysler Canada*)

A computer-controlled compressor clutch circuit is explained later in this chapter. (Refer to Chapter 18 for other computer-controlled compressor clutch circuits.)

Semi-Automatic Temperature Control Systems

Design and Operation

In the semi-automatic temperature control (SATC) systems, the temperature control lever operates a variable resistor. A servomotor rotates the blend-air door, and an electronic module is contained in the servomotor assembly. An in-car air sensor is mounted in the instrument panel, and an ambient, or outside, air sensor is located in the rear surface of the evaporator-heater assembly. Outside air flows past the ambient sensor. When the temperature of these sensors decreases, the sensor resistance increases. If the temperature lever is moved to a higher temperature, the resistance of the variable resistor increases. Pressurized air from the blower motor housing is fed through an air drive tube to the aspirator and the evaporator-heater housing. This airflow creates a slight vacuum in the aspirator, which draws air from the passenger compartment past the in-car air sensor assembly.

The in-car air sensor, aspirator, and electronic servomotor are pictured in Figure 26-23.

The variable resistor on the temperature control lever and the sensors send input signals to the electronic module. On the basis of these input signals, the module operates the servomotor to obtain the precise blend-air door position that provides the temperature selected by the driver. A temperature

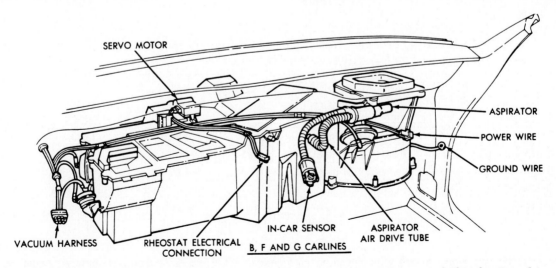

Figure 26-23. Semi-Automatic Temperature Control Components. (*Courtesy of Chrysler Canada*)

scale is provided under the temperature lever on the (SATC) dash control, as pictured in Figure 26-24.

The operation of the SATC system is summarized in Figure 26-25, and the mode door operation is provided in Table 26-2.

Electronic Climate Control Systems

Body Computer Module

The body computer module (BCM) is the control center for the electronic climate control (ECC) system. A microprocessor is located in the BCM and supported by random-access memories (RAMs), read-

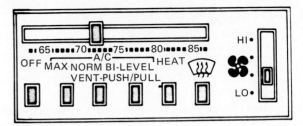

Figure 26-24. Semi-Automatic Temperature Control Dash Control. (*Courtesy of Chrysler Canada*)

only memories (ROMs), and programmable read-only memories (PROMs). The microprocessor also contains stored programs and input/output interfaces. (A complete description of additional BCM functions is provided in Chapter 18.)

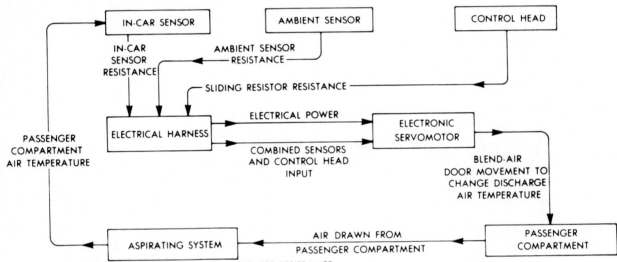

Figure 26-25. Semi-Automatic Temperature Control Operation. (*Courtesy of Chrysler Canada*)

TABLE 26-2.   Semi-Automatic Temperature Control Mode Door Operation.
(*Courtesy of Chrysler Canada*)

CONTROL CHART

PUSH BUTTON	OFF	A/C MAX	A/C NORM	A/C BI-LEVEL	HEAT	DEFROST
Inlet Air Door (Open to)	Inside	Inside	Outside	Outside	Outside	Outside
Heat-Defrost Door (Open to)	Heat	Heat	Heat	Heat	Heat	Defrost
Upper Bi-Lev Door (Open to)	Bi-Lev-A/C	Bi-Lev-A/C	Bi-Lev-A/C	Bi-Lev-A/C	Heat	Heat
Lower Bi-Lev Door (Open to)	A/C	A/C	A/C	Bi-Lev/Heat	Bi-Lev/Heat	Bi-Lev/Heat
Compressor Clutch	Off	On	On*	On*	Off	On**
Blower	Off	On	On	On	On	On
Water Valve	Off	Off	On	On	On	On

* Pulling out NORM button provides VENT mode with refrigeration off. BI-LEVEL button pull-out works same way.
** Pulling out DEF button provides DEFROST mode with refrigeration off.

Sources of Input and Output Control Functions

The BCM receives input signals from these sources:

1. ECM data.
2. ECC setting.
3. Outside temperature.
4. In-car temperature.
5. Sunload temperature.
6. Vehicle speed.
7. Low refrigerant pressure switch.
8. A/C high-side temperature.
9. A/C low-side temperature.

The BCM controls the output functions illustrated in Figure 26-26.

The BCM displays information for the driver on the climate control panel (CCP), or on a diesel data center (DDC) if the car has a diesel engine. When the driver wants a specific ECC mode, he or she depresses the appropriate button on the CCP, which signals the BCM to perform the necessary output function.

Data links are connected between the BCM and the electronic control module (ECM). The ECM is a computer that controls such functions as air-fuel ratio and spark advance. (Refer to Chapter 18 for a description of the ECM and data links.) Data links transfer data from the BCM to the ECM and also from the ECM to the BCM. The bidirectional data links between the ECM and the BCM are identified as the 800 circuit.

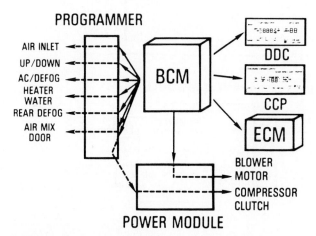

Figure 26-26. BCM Output Control Functions. (*Courtesy of GM Product Service Training, General Motors Corporation*)

Compressor Clutch Control

The BCM and the ECC power module operate the air conditioning compressor clutch. If any of the following conditions are present, and compressor clutch will remain off:

1. The outside air temperature is below 45° F (10° C).
2. The engine coolant or compressor output temperatures are too high.
3. Refrigerant pressure or charge is too low.
4. The throttle is wide open.

When all the BCM inputs are within calibrated values, the BCM signals the ECM to engage the air conditioning compressor clutch. The ECM then transmits a voltage signal to the power module, which grounds the compressor clutch relay winding so that the relay points close and voltage is supplied to the compressor clutch. If the air conditioning compressor clutch is on, any of the following conditions will signal the BCM to disengage the clutch:

1. A/C low pressure switch open.
2. A/C low-side temperature below 30° F (−1° C).
3. A/C high-side temperature above 199° F (93° C).
4. Coolant temperature above 259° F (126° C).
5. Open or shorted A/C low-side sensor circuit.

These conditions will force the ECM to disengage the compressor clutch:

1. Wide-open throttle signal from throttle position sensor (TPS).
2. System over voltage.
3. System under voltage.
4. Power steering cutout switch open.

The compressor clutch circuit is shown in Figure 26-27.

Blower Speed Control

For every electronic climate control (ECC) setting and program number, the BCM has a calculated blower voltage signal which is sent through the A/C programmer to the power module. This module amplifies the signal and sends it to the blower motor to supply the desired blower speed. Feedback information is sent from the blower motor back to the programmer.

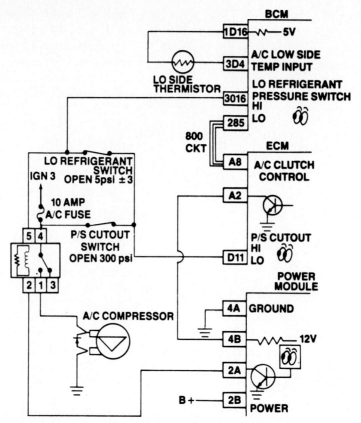

Figure 26-27. Air Conditioning Compressor Clutch Circuit. (*Courtesy of GM Product Service Training, General Motors Corporation*)

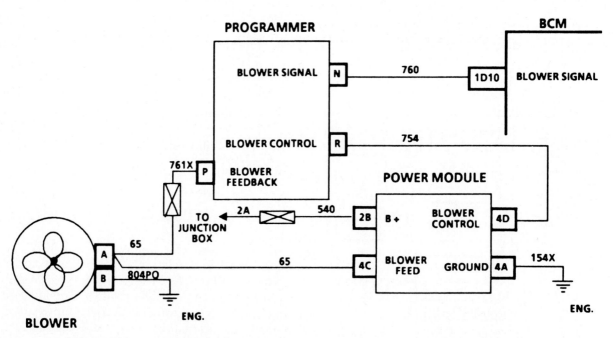

Figure 26-28. Blower Motor Circuit. (*Courtesy of GM Product Service Training, General Motors Corporation*)

The blower motor circuit is shown in Figure 26-28, and the electronic climate control panel is illustrated in Figure 26-29.

Mode Door Control

The BCM operates a group of solenoids in the programmer which turn the vacuum on and off at the mode door actuator diaphragms. When the BCM energizes a solenoid, vacuum is supplied to an actuator diaphragm, which moves the appropriate door. The programmer vacuum system, actuator diaphragms, and mode doors are illustrated in Figure 26-30.

If vacuum is shut off to the air-inlet door actuator, this door provides 100 percent outside air to the ECC system. When vacuum is supplied to the air-inlet door actuator diaphragm, the door is moved to provide 80 percent inside air and 20 percent outside air to the ECC system.

A vacuum supply to the up/down door actuator diaphragm results in door movement that provides airflow to the A/C-defog door, with an air bleed to the heater outlets. When the programmer shuts off the vacuum to the up/down door actuator, this door directs airflow to the heater outlets, with an air bleed to the A/C-defog door.

If vacuum is supplied to the A/C-defog door actuator diaphragm, this door directs air to the A/C outlets. The A/C-defog door supplies airflow to the defog outlets if the vacuum supply to the actuator diaphragm is shut off.

When vacuum is supplied to the heater water valve, this valve blocks coolant flow through the heater core, whereas a zero vacuum at the valve actuator causes the valve to open.

Air-Mix Door Operation

An air-mix door motor in the programmer is linked to the air-mix door. The BCM sends a signal to the programmer which informs the programmer to drive the motor and provide the exact air-mix door position to obtain the condition requested by the driver. A potentiometer connected to the air-mix door sends a feedback signal to the BCM, which provides precise information regarding air-mix door position. The BCM checks this feedback signal before it commands the air-mix door to move.

A diagram of the air-mix door control system is provided in Figure 26-31, and the temperature sensor circuits connected to the BCM are illustrated in Figure 26-32.

Rear Defog Control

When the driver presses the "rear defog" button on the CCP, a signal is sent from the CCP to the BCM. Once this signal is received, the BCM informs the ECC programmer to ground the rear defog relay winding, which closes the relay contacts and energizes the rear defog. The rear defog circuit is pictured in Figure 26-33.

The BCM is capable of diagnosing the air conditioning system and many other functions. (This complete diagnosis is explained in Chapter 13 of *Automotive Principles: Repair and Service*, Volume II.)

Test Questions

1. A variable-displacement air conditioning compressor has a cycling switch in the compressor clutch circuit. T F

2. The cycling action of the compressor clutch prevents:
   a) premature compressor failure.
   b) excessive pressure at the compressor outlet.
   c) evaporator freeze-up.

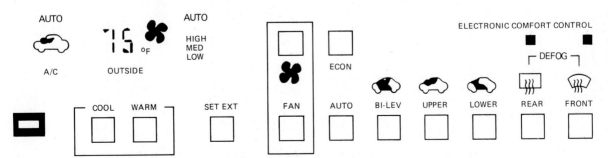

Figure 26-29. Electronic Climate Control Panel. (*Courtesy of GM Product Service Training, General Motors Corporation*)

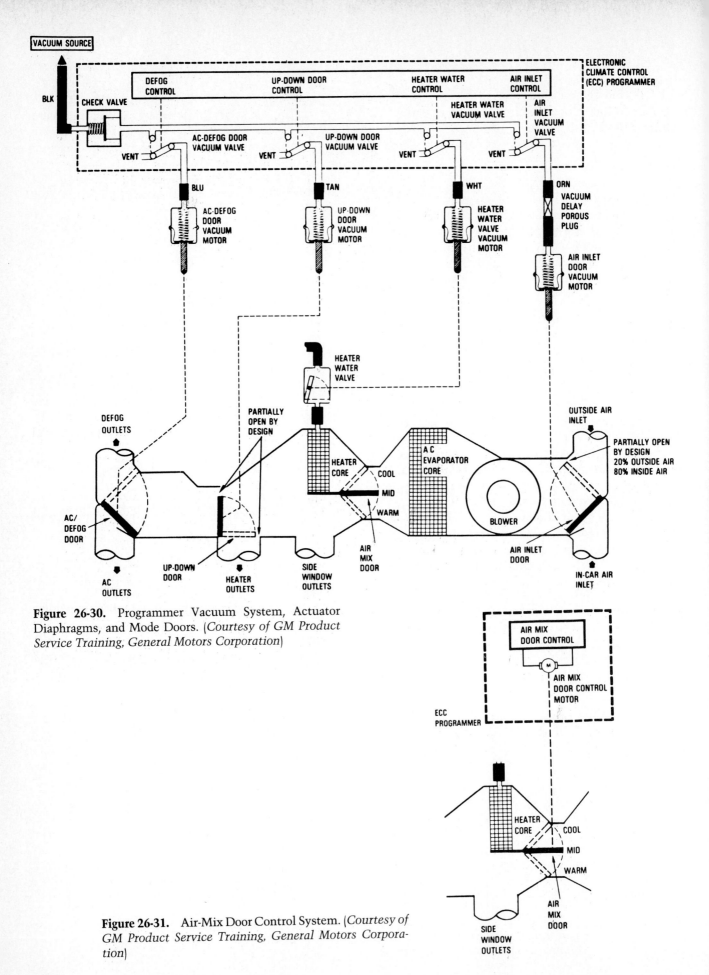

Figure 26-30. Programmer Vacuum System, Actuator Diaphragms, and Mode Doors. (*Courtesy of GM Product Service Training, General Motors Corporation*)

Figure 26-31. Air-Mix Door Control System. (*Courtesy of GM Product Service Training, General Motors Corporation*)

526

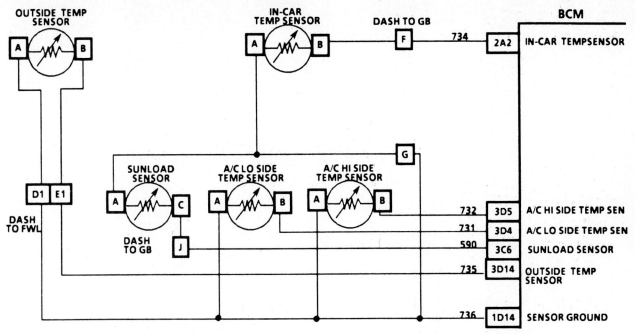

Figure 26-32. Temperature Sensor Circuits. (*Courtesy of GM Product Service Training, General Motors Corporation*)

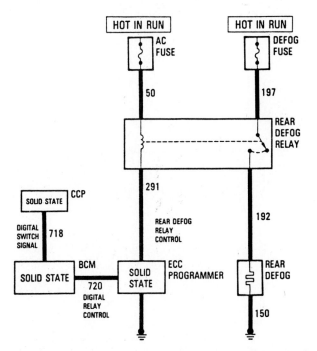

Figure 26-33. Rear Defog Control. (*Courtesy of GM Product Service Training, General Motors Corporation*)

3. The refrigerant changes from a liquid to a gas in the:

   a) evaporator.

   b) condenser.

   c) filter/drier.

4. In a semi-automatic temperature control system, the blend-air door is rotated by the:

   a) maximum A/C push button.

   b) temperature lever.

   c) servomotor.

5. Refrigerant R12 boils at:

   a) 32° F.

   b) −10° F.

   c) −21.6° F.

6. When the pressure on a liquid is decreased, the boiling point of a liquid is reduced.   T F

Index

Voice-alert systems, 246–50
Voice synthesizers, 153, 154
Voltage regulators
    electronic, 175–81
    point-type, 173–75
Voltmeter, 138, 139

W

Wheel alignment
    angles, 463–67
    theory, 462, 463

Wheel bearings, 401–403
Wheel cylinders, 491
Windshield washers, 231–33
Windshield wiper motors
    depressed park, 228, 229
    permanent magnet, 229, 230
    pulse type, 230, 231
    shunt field, 226–28
Wire gauge size, 143

Z

Zener diode, 147